The Union Assaults at Vicksburg

MODERN WAR STUDIES

William Thomas Allison
General Editor

Raymond Callahan
Jacob W. Kipp
Allan R. Millett
Carol Reardon
Dennis Showalter
David R. Stone
James H. Willbanks
Series Editors

Theodore A. Wilson
General Editor Emeritus

THE UNION ASSAULTS AT VICKSBURG

Grant Attacks Pemberton, May 17–22, 1863

TIMOTHY B. SMITH

University Press of Kansas

© 2020 by the University Press of Kansas
All rights reserved
Paperback edition 2025

Published by the University Press of Kansas (Lawrence, Kansas 66045), which was organized by the Kansas Board of Regents and is operated and funded by Emporia State University, Fort Hays State University, Kansas State University, Pittsburg State University, the University of Kansas, and Wichita State University.

Library of Congress Cataloging-in-Publication Data
Names: Smith, Timothy B., 1974- author.
Title: The Union assaults at Vicksburg : Grant attacks Pemberton, May 17–22, 1863 / Timothy B. Smith.
Description: Lawrence, Kansas : University Press of Kansas, [2020] | Series: Modern war studies | Includes bibliographical references and index.
Identifiers: LCCN 2019025715 | ISBN 9780700629060 (cloth) | ISBN 9780700629077 (epub) | ISBN 9780700640799 (paperback)
Subjects: LCSH: Vicksburg (Miss.)—History—Siege, 1863. | Vicksburg (Miss.)—History—Civil War, 1861–1865. | United States—History—Civil War, 1861–1865—Campaigns. | Pemberton, John C. (John Clifford), 1814–1881 | Grant, Ulysses S. (Ulysses Simpson), 1822–1885—Military leadership.
Classi ication: LCC E475.27 .S695 2020 | DDC 973.7/344—dc23
LC record available at https://lccn.loc.gov/2019025715.

British Library Cataloguing-in-Publication Data is available.
EU Authorised Representative Details: Easy Access System Europe
Mustamäe tee 50, 10621 Tallinn, Estonia | gpsr.requests@easproject.com

In memory of my mother

CONTENTS

List of Maps *viii*
Preface *ix*
Prologue *xiii*
1. "I Will Fortify Vicksburg and Prevent Its Capture" *1*
2. "The Accomplishment of This One Object" *26*
3. "Tumbling Back into Vicksburg in Utter Confusion" *50*
4. "Within Musket-Range of the Defenses of Vicksburg" *76*
5. "My Whole Division Dashed Forward" *102*
6. "The Enemy Are Evidently Preparing for an Assault" *128*
7. "Each Column Will Attack by the Watch" *152*
8. "There Was Not a Twig between Us and the Fort" *180*
9. "They Seemed to Be Springing from the Bowels of the Earth" *234*
10. "I Could Not Disregard His Reiterated Statements" *270*
11. "The Assault Was Feeble Compared with the Fierce Onslaughts Earlier in the Day" *297*
12. "It Is Absolutely Necessary That They Be Dislodged" *320*
13. "Five Days of Peril, Hardship, and Privation" *342*
Epilogue *369*
Appendix A: Union Order of Battle at Vicksburg, May 17–22, 1863 *373*
Appendix B: Confederate Order of Battle at Vicksburg, May 17–22, 1863 *383*
Notes *387*
Bibliography *443*
Index *469*

Photo gallery follows page 205.

MAPS

1. Vicksburg Area *xv*
2. Civil War Western Theater *7*
3. Vicksburg Fortifications *20*
4. Grant's Attempts *29*
5. Inland Campaign *37*
6. March to Vicksburg *60*
7. Vicksburg Advances *88*
8. Blair's Assaults *107*
9. Union Supply Routes *142*
10. Sherman's Assaults *164*
11. McPherson's Assaults *187*
12. McClernand's Assaults *242*
13. Sherman's Assaults *277*
14. McPherson's Assaults *301*
15. McClernand's Assaults *327*

PREFACE

The second week in May 1863 was one of the busiest of the war. The titanic battle at Chancellorsville had just ended days before, with repercussions extending in many cases for lifetimes, but certainly into the next week. One of the major results of the fighting occurred on May 10, when Stonewall Jackson, mortally wounded a few days earlier, died from the complications resulting from the amputation of his left arm. The funeral in Richmond took place on May 12, with thousands of mourners filing by and looking for one last time into the face of the hero. Although Chancellorsville was a huge Confederate victory, it came at the cost of losing thousands, Jackson foremost among them; General Robert E. Lee summed it up best when he noted, "he has lost his left arm; but I have lost my right."[1]

Chancellorsville and its ramifications were certainly not all that occurred in that second week in May. In Tennessee, Major General William S. Rosecrans was marshaling a large Federal army to push southward through Middle Tennessee and onward toward Chattanooga. In Mississippi, Major General Ulysses S. Grant was moving north from the Port Gibson area after crossing the Mississippi River. By the start of the next week, he would have routed the Confederates five times and was approaching the very gates of Vicksburg. It was not all military in value, either; Grant by then had also taken Jackson, the political capital of Mississippi, and destroyed it as an economic and logistical hub.[2]

Perhaps the most important event of this week, however, did not occur in a state capital or on the battlefield amid the horrific sights and sounds of death, screams, fright, and destruction. In fact, as similarly described by C. S. Lewis in *The Screwtape Letters*, one of the most important decisions of the war occurred in the calm atmosphere of a presidential office amid finely dressed statesmen speaking in soft tones and with calm demeanors. In Richmond, Virginia, capital of the Confederate States of America, President Jefferson Davis huddled to discuss with his cabinet and his preeminent general, Robert E.

Lee, how to handle the evolving and deteriorating situation facing their brand-new nation.[3]

Uppermost in all minds was what to do about Vicksburg; War Department clerk John B. Jones noted that there was "a dark cloud over the hopes of patriots, for Vicksburg is seriously endangered." The odds were obvious, and all knew the monumental differences between the east and the west at this point. Lee had just beaten the huge Army of the Potomac at Chancellorsville, while out in Mississippi Lieutenant General John C. Pemberton—emerging as no genius among rebel commanders—had been or would be defeated five times in seventeen days. Virginia seemed to be stable if still heavily threatened, but Mississippi was endangered.[4]

Obviously, something had to be done, and an ill Jefferson Davis quarantined himself in Richmond with his cabinet and Lee to work out an answer. Davis was frail and sick, and upon his return to the office on May 15 Jones noted: "But [he] is not fully himself yet." Still, there were big decisions to make. On the surface, it seemed best to send some of those hearty troops and commanders from Virginia to the crisis zone in Mississippi. Secretary of War James A. Seddon had even broached with Lee the subject of sending Major General George E. Pickett's idle division to the Mississippi Valley. The idea also emerged to send part of Lee's army to Middle Tennessee to force pressure there, thus relieving some of the stress in Mississippi.[5]

Lee was an eastern-centric Virginian, and he floated a very different plan during the closed-door session on May 15 with Davis and Seddon at the War Department, as well as with the full cabinet on May 16 at Davis's house. He had earlier argued by dispatch that the question was likely one of losing either Mississippi or Virginia, but he conceded that he would send Pickett if necessary. Now in person in Richmond, Lee used his full persuasive skills to argue for a plan where, instead of sending troops to Tennessee or even the more remote Mississippi River, Lee would again take the offensive into Northern territory. He had desired to make a real invasion of the North ever since the debacle of the Antietam campaign the previous year, and this provided the perfect opportunity to do so now that his army had won several victories in a row. The invasion would act as a giant raid, acquiring goods and supplies in the North while Virginia's farmers would be able to relax. If a decisive battle could be fought and won on Northern soil, it would do much toward convincing wavering Northerners that the war was unwinnable; it might even produce some good results in the diplomatic arena as well. Most concerning—and really the major factor in this analysis—if Lee could invade the North, then he might pull some of Grant's pressure away from the Mississippi Valley and thereby aid Vicksburg.[6]

The cabinet debated this idea, and the Mississippian Davis, not as western-centric as Lee was eastern-centric, soon warmed to the plan. At the least, Pickett's possible transfer west was nixed, and Richmond citizens soon saw the division marching northward to rejoin Lee's army near Fredericksburg. The cabinet came around as well, due in most part to the firm but gentle persuasion of Lee, whom Postmaster General John H. Reagan remembered "was not a man of many words and when he spoke it was in the fullness of conviction." Almost all at the meeting came away with a firm commitment to the eastern invasion strategy to relieve the pressure on Vicksburg. Only Reagan demurred, likely because the Texan had more at stake than most if Vicksburg fell and the trans-Mississippi was cut off.[7]

It was the beginning of the Gettysburg campaign, though it would take a month for Lee to prepare and move northward. Still, it might have been avoided if events in Mississippi erased the need for an invasion of the North in the first place. If Grant somehow took Vicksburg during the next few days, perhaps there would be no need to relieve pressure there. If Grant took Vicksburg within the week—which was what he planned—would Davis still allow Lee to make such a gamble when the Confederacy could ill afford another defeat?[8]

The world watched as Grant moved westward to the ramparts of Vicksburg, intending to take the prize that would allow Federal control over the entire length of the Mississippi River as quickly as possible. Although he did not know about the plan being designed in Richmond or the titanic struggle it would set up, Grant did know that the quicker he neutralized Vicksburg the better it would be for the Union effort and his own future as a commander. As such, even as he approached Vicksburg, his mind was focused on a single objective: a speedy assault that would make quick work of the city and its defenders.[9]

The stage was thus set for Grant's dramatic and strategically important assaults against Vicksburg; they started on May 19, followed by action on a larger scale on May 22. Yet, for all their importance, the initial assaults against this strategically vital river city have garnered little attention in the literature. Such an oversight is odd in itself because the battlefield is preserved as the Vicksburg National Military Park. In fact, most histories of the war gloss over these events as unimportant, and even the more detailed military histories of the Vicksburg campaign sometimes assign less time to these events than is warranted. And there has never been a comprehensive book dedicated solely to what was, in terms of numbers engaged, the largest battle of the Vicksburg campaign. Rather, the larger, more complex, and more impressive land campaign from Port Gibson to Champion Hill to Big

Black River Bridge most often takes the limelight, as does the lengthy siege that came afterward. Sandwiched between those two events, the Vicksburg assaults are often viewed as minor and unimportant. But such was not the case. Huge ramifications hinged on quick victory or defeat—including, much farther east, Lee's proposed invasion of the North, which would lead to the largest and most iconic battle of the Civil War.[10]

Many people have aided me in writing this book. I am extremely appreciative to all the archivists and staff at the various repositories throughout the nation that assisted my research, whether in person or otherwise. Particular thanks must go to Sara Strickland and Jenny Leasor at the Vicksburg National Military Park, who made my trips there enjoyable and my investigations profitable.

As always, I am also indebted to my mentor and friend John F. Marszalek for his support and encouragement on this volume, especially his detailed editing of the manuscript. My friend Terry Winschel also read the manuscript and provided many valuable insights. Working with the University Press of Kansas has also, as always, been a delight. This book covered a time of change at the press. Mike Briggs contracted it before his retirement, and Joyce Harrison saw it to fruition. Both are consummate professionals. Kelly Chrisman Jacques shepherded it through the publication process with her usual grace and care, and Mike Kehoe covered the marketing front well. Copy editor Jon Howard did a wonderful job on polishing the final version for publication.

My family, as always, is my passion, including the love of my life Kelly and our two beautiful and sweet daughters, Mary Kate and Leah Grace. My dad continues to be a firm foundation in my life, and I dedicate this book to the memory of my sweet mother. I am joyful that she has reached her Heavenly home and that I have the assurance that I will see her again there one day.

—Timothy B. Smith
Adamsville, Tennessee
September 2019

Prologue

Vicksburg, Mississippi, is synonymous with Civil War history. Most average Americans certainly know of Gettysburg, and Vicksburg runs close behind in name recognition. But among learned buffs and trained historians, many argue that even though Gettysburg has stolen all the popular acclaim, Vicksburg was vastly more important. No less an authority than Bruce Catton once wrote, "The real pull of fate was at Vicksburg. Lee took the eye but the pivot of the war was down here by the great river."[1]

For all its importance, Vicksburg at the start of the war was a relatively new city in western Mississippi. It had none of the long history of Natchez or other frontier towns that had actually been under Spanish control in the past. Rather, the Vicksburg area had long been part of Indian territory, closed to settlers until the early nineteenth century. As the eventual progress of American civilization raced westward, however, it ultimately came to affect the area that would become Vicksburg.[2]

The city's namesake was Reverend Newit Vick, who with his wife settled in Mississippi in 1812. Vick was a Methodist minister who staked a claim to an area northeast of the present-day site of Vicksburg. He named his plantation "Open Woods," because the natives in the area had previously cleared the area, a convenient development for him as he moved in and began to till the land and preach the gospel. Vick and his wife, Elizabeth, took the scriptural command to be fruitful and multiply very literally and raised thirteen children on their new homestead. Other friends and relatives soon migrated to the area as well, and Vick emerged as the patriarch of a developing clan.[3]

Amid all his other endeavors, Vick soon became interested in a certain nearby plot of land and by the mid-1810s had acquired several hundred acres to his southwest, on the high bluffs overlooking the Mississippi River. There, Vick marked off streets and avenues and developed one of the most important cities in America. Mississippi's admission to the Union as a state in 1817 aided Vick in his enterprise, but sadly he and Elizabeth both died in August

1819 of yellow fever, within hours of each other. Vick's dream did not die with him, however; he left in his will instructions for family members to continue his work, and his son-in-law John Lane, also a minister, soon laid out a new town in lots and named it after the developer of the idea, Newit Vick.[4]

Elected lawmakers in the newly admitted state incorporated Vicksburg in January 1825, and over the course of the next decade lateral migrants from the Carolinas as well as settlers from Vick's original home state of Virginia flooded the small town. By 1835, Vicksburg had nearly three thousand residents; by 1860, at the threshold of the war, it would total 4,591 people of all colors, 3,158 of them being white. On the Mississippi River near plantation country, many big planters called Vicksburg home, most living in the city while owning and visiting their outlying plantations in the Mississippi Delta to the north or in the fertile plantation country to the east nearer to the developing state capital at Jackson. By the start of the Civil War, many stately families with names that resound in Mississippi history—Yerger, Smede, Prentiss, Sharkey—called Vicksburg home, and certain of its residents were also gaining national fame. Two presidential cabinet officers were from the Vicksburg area: Joseph Holt, who was James Buchanan's Postmaster General and secretary of war and later the army's judge advocate general, as well as Jefferson Davis, recently United States senator and secretary of war. In addition to many other landholdings, Jefferson and his brother Joseph shared a large bend in the Mississippi River just south of Vicksburg, where Jefferson lived on his plantation "Brierfield."[5]

Very quickly, Vicksburg grew to be a bustling city on a hill; newspapers, churches, businesses, and hotels soon appeared. But with the development also came trouble, including ruffians who flocked to take advantage of nefarious river activities. Others simply looking for business also came, many floating southward on the river before the age of steam or plying both ways once steam travel became possible. In fact, the steamboat revolutionized Vicksburg's place in the American economy and society. At one time, Vicksburg became the largest and most important inland port in the state. Ironically, one traveler who viewed the city on the high bluffs was none other than an Illinoisan named Abraham Lincoln, who made two trips southward to New Orleans in 1828 and 1831.[6]

With prosperity also came responsibility, and with the gloom settling over the nation in 1860 and 1861, Vicksburg was certain to play a central role in the coming conflict. Despite its delegates to the Mississippi Secession Convention opposing disunion until the final vote, the city itself and its parent Warren County ultimately contributed as many as twenty-four military companies to the Confederate cause. Yet recruiting and war fever were not

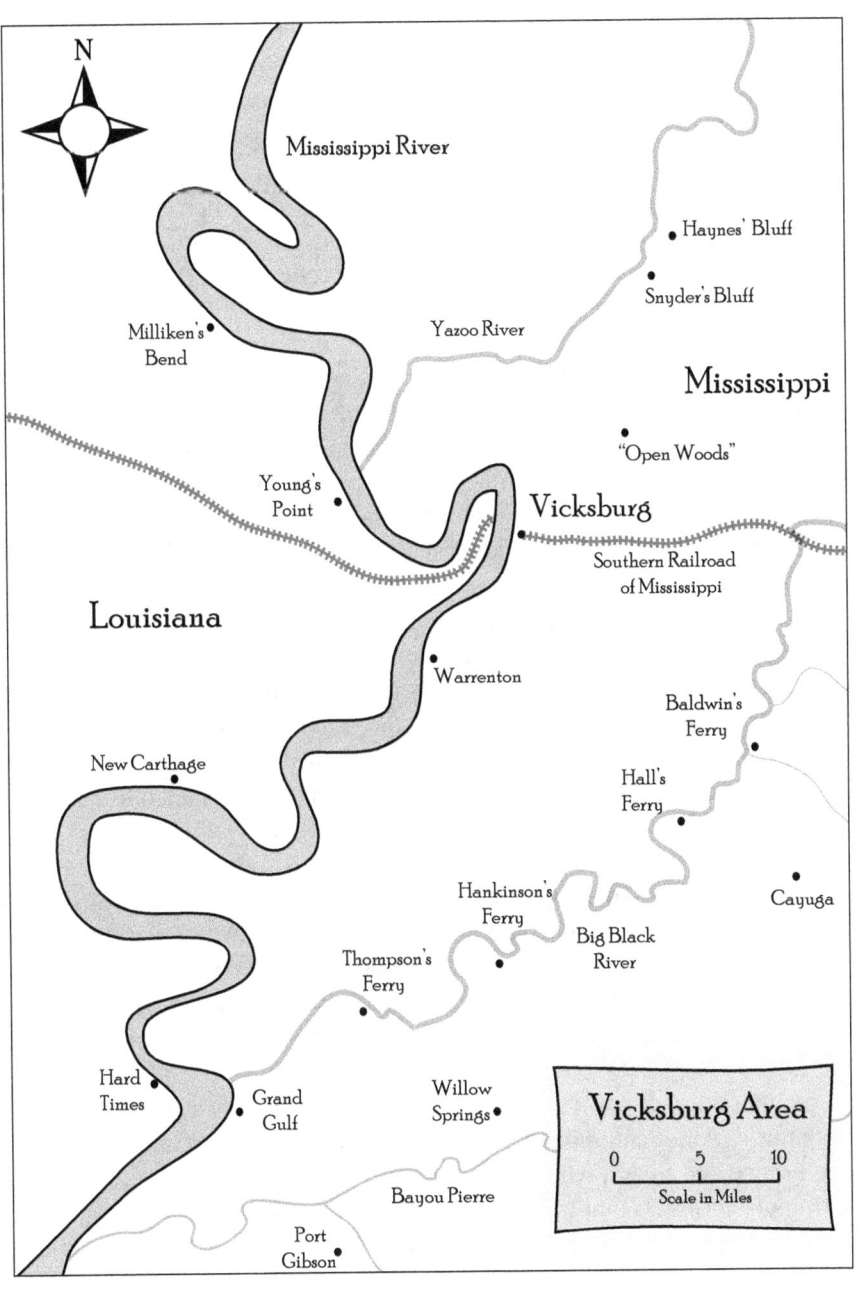

Vicksburg's sole contribution to the war. It would soon become one of the single-most important bastions in the Confederacy.[7]

The obvious reason Vicksburg became so well known in Civil War history was its major lifeline to the outside world, the Mississippi River. Vicksburg, although containing nothing to make it any more special than other places in the state, sat at a more important position than any other, right atop bluffs overlooking the Mississippi River. Added to its vital location, Vicksburg was the only locality in the state that lay at the connection of the Mississippi River with a railroad.[8]

The great river flowed from Mississippi's northern border with Tennessee southward for nearly three hundred airline miles (410 river miles today because of the winding watercourse) to the state's southern border with Louisiana. The massive river was, and still is, a major geographical obstacle, not then crossable except by boat anywhere south of St. Louis. In fact, today there are only four places within the state that the river can be crossed by bridge: across from Helena, Arkansas, and at Greenville, Vicksburg, and Natchez, Mississippi. And no one can cross it without being in awe of the majesty. Books, songs, and poems have all been written to try to honor its mystique, but few have been able to match the sheer power of simply observing it.[9]

The river has played just as critical a role in the history of the nation. Draining two-thirds of the United States through its numerous tributaries and tributaries of tributaries, the Mississippi, especially before the age of aviation and automobiles, affected most Americans in some way. Much of the nation's population that spilled over the Appalachian Mountains was tied to it or the rivers draining into it, including the Missouri, Ohio, Tennessee, Cumberland, Red, and on and on. In a day when steamboats were the mainstay of lengthy travel, the rivers feeding into the Father of Waters allowed for transnational movement and also opened the interior to international travel. Goods shipped by boat along the river to New Orleans and through intercontinental trade to its north were major factors in a blossoming economy based in the United States.[10]

The international politics affecting the Mississippi River were just as important after American independence. Early on, the United States worked to keep France and Spain, which bordered it at one time or another to the west, on friendly terms so that travel up and down the great river was not halted; certainly, New Orleans was kept close to facilitate trade out of that mammoth port. One of the truly decisive events in American history came when President Thomas Jefferson consummated the Louisiana Purchase, buying much of the continent west of the river, ensuring that the river and its tributaries, as well as the port at New Orleans, would all be under one government forevermore—or so he thought. An equally important event came when Andrew Jackson defended the river and its Gulf port in 1815, keeping the region sovereign for the United States. The victor of New Orleans became a national hero in the process and would later be elected president.[11]

By 1861, the thought of losing control of the Mississippi River was unacceptable to the Union and the Confederacy, mainly because it had occupied such a special place in American hearts. Those west of the Appalachians always looked at the Mississippi as theirs: not just one region's and certainly not just for the benefit of the one or two states that straddled it, not even the state that bore its name. That is why such an uproar occurred as Mississippi and Louisiana, and later Arkansas and Tennessee, threatened and then performed the act of secession, dividing the artery's ownership once again. But this time it was even worse: Before, the tenuous diplomacy had been between owners that sat on either bank of the great river; now, an entire corridor of territory was wrenched from the United States, fully encapsulating not only the lower river and its valley but also New Orleans.[12]

To no one's surprise, Northerners, who could be deprived of commercial access and navigation, rose in opposition. Despite overtures from both the Mississippi and Louisiana secession conventions promising "the right of the free navigation of the Mississippi River," many states, including Wisconsin, Ohio, and Minnesota, which had a direct stake in keeping the Mississippi open to commerce, passed denunciations through their legislatures decrying secession. As an example, Minnesota's "Joint Resolutions on the State of the Union" declared the South "in open rebellion against the Government" and that "the Government of the United States is supreme." Minnesota "hereby pledges and tenders to the General Government all its military power and industrial resources," and "concessions and compromise are not to be entertained or offered to traitors."[13]

Mississippi, following rather rashly its governor, the fire-eater John J. Pettus, did not help itself in this matter. On January 11, 1861, just two days after the state seceded, the Cincinnati-based steamer *A. O. Tyler* approached Vicksburg, the United States flag clearly fluttering in the breeze. Governor Pettus had already sent militia to defend Vicksburg and the state's most important asset: the Mississippi River. This "trigger-happy ragtag force," as historian Michael B. Ballard described it, opened fire, but the *Tyler* escaped and soon landed at Vicksburg. The Vicksburg *Evening Citizen* reported: "Had it not been for another boat the 'City of Louisiana' coming in between her and the shore, she would no doubt have been fired into." The next day another vessel,

Silver Wave, arrived safely despite wild rumors that she was carrying invading United States troops. Nothing of the sort was true, but the population was whipped into a frenzy nonetheless.[14]

It was a wonder that neither boat was blown out of the water, and their escapes were probably attributable to the rawness of the state's militia at the time. Nevertheless, it was a clear signal that Mississippi was defiant, that it intended to defend itself, and that it would use force if necessary. The episode also exhibited the frayed emotions that possession of the Mississippi River passages could evoke, and it underscored just how important Vicksburg would become in the years ahead. Most important, the Mississippians who fired on the undefended steamboats foreshadowed the coming chaos of war, just around the corner. In that sense, Mississippians at Vicksburg fired the first shot in a war that had not even been declared.

Many quickly understood the river's importance amid this growing crisis. Confederate general Braxton Bragg early on quipped that the river was "of more importance to us than all the country together." More to the point, the robust Union commander William T. Sherman later voiced what many Northerners felt about secession and the threat to free navigation of the Mississippi River: "To secure the safety of the navigation of the Mississippi River I would slay millions. On that point I am not only insane, but mad. Fortunately, the great West is with me there."[15]

And they were, as would be seen in the numerous battles and skirmishes that Sherman and others fought in order to control the river and its great valley. Famous battles of American history with captivating names such as Shiloh and Champion Hill ring with mystique, but it was perhaps the Vicksburg attacks and the city's defenses that most determined how lengthy this obsession with opening the Mississippi River would actually be.

The Union Assaults at Vicksburg

1

"I Will Fortify Vicksburg and Prevent Its Capture"

"See what a lot of land these fellows hold," President Abraham Lincoln declared while pointing to a map of his broken United States. The president was worried to say the least, having called his top military commanders and advisers together in November 1861 to hash out how to deal with the war situation that was not going terribly well at that point. Union arms had suffered reverses in the summer and early fall at Manassas, Wilson's Creek, and elsewhere, and little had been done to carve off any of that massive territory still held by the enemy now seven months into a war that almost all had thought would last only two or three.[1]

With Lincoln at the meeting was the army general in chief Major General George B. McClellan as well as navy brass, including the secretary himself, Gideon Welles, and his undersecretary Gustavus Fox, along with other naval officers. The future admiral David Dixon Porter was also there and left a vivid account of Lincoln's concerns, particularly in the west where resided most of that land "these fellows" controlled. Of particular interest to the president was the area west of the Mississippi River, which was abundant with supplies that could underpin Confederate armies and operations for years to come. "Here is Red River, which will supply the Confederates with cattle and corn to feed their armies. There are the Arkansas and White Rivers, which can supply cattle and hogs by the thousand. . . . It means hog and hominy without limit, fresh troops from all the States of the far South, and a cotton country where they can raise the staple without interference."[2]

Although lacking any formal military education, the extremely perceptive president was able to quickly see a solution to at least some of the issues. "Vicksburg is the key," he declared, elaborating that "from Vicksburg these supplies can be distributed by rail all over the Confederacy. Then there is that great depot of supplies on the Yazoo. Let us get Vicksburg and all that country is ours." He then added in his homespun manner, "I am acquainted with that region and know what I am talking about, and, valuable as New Orleans will be to us, Vicksburg will be more so. We may take all the northern ports of the Confederacy, and they can still defy us from Vicksburg."[3]

Lincoln was so convinced of Vicksburg's importance that he flatly declared after labeling the river city as the key to success: "The war can never be brought to a close until that key is in our pocket."[4]

Lincoln could declare all he wanted from the relatively safe confines of Washington, but actually placing that key into the nation's pocket was a much more difficult task. Even with the Union aim squarely focused on Vicksburg, Federal officials soon learned just how much of a problem they were facing. Significantly, Vicksburg's central location on the Mississippi River positioned it to play a vital role in the Civil War. Geography perhaps played an even greater role in Vicksburg's defense, making it an extremely difficult bastion to get to, much less attack. Therein lay the dual problem that many commanders as well as historians have conflated: just getting into a position to attack Vicksburg was harder than almost anyone realized, and then the actual attack had to be made on the fortress city, which likewise was an extremely difficult proposition. Ulysses S. Grant later wrote in the midst of trying to find success in just the first of the dual problems: "I am . . . much perplexed. Heretofore I have had nothing to do but fight the enemy. This time I have to overcome obstacles to reach him."[5]

The problem for the Union high command was not so much that Vicksburg itself was so defensible, which it was; rather, before any plans could be made to attack the city itself, the major problem was just getting to its vicinity so it could be attacked or placed under siege. A perfect storm of factors combined to make just getting to what one Federal described as "the burg" one of the most difficult undertakings of the war.[6]

The fact that Vicksburg sat on three-hundred-foot-high bluffs overlooking the Mississippi River was one of the major factors in making it defensible. Those bluffs, even if undefended, made a direct amphibious assault from the river virtually impossible. If such a ludicrous attempt was even contemplated, it would have to be accompanied by a prior naval bombardment, and that brought additional geographical factors into play. The Federal navy would need to be in position both above and below Vicksburg for a direct assault, and getting gunboats below Vicksburg meant passing the heavy guns along the city's waterfront, an extremely hazardous proposition. Although heavy batteries could be passed, and would be at various places during the war,

Vicksburg carried even more significant geographical complexities. The Mississippi River made a sharp bend just before passing the city, actually a hairpin turn from a northerly flow to a southerly direction. Any vessels passing or even attacking frontally at Vicksburg would have to negotiate this bend and its currents in order to support any infantry landing and assault. The geographical factors of the bluffs and the bend, coupled with a hearty Confederate defense along the river, simply precluded any chance of direct attack from the west.[7]

With the western approach completely out of the question, secondary approaches became more important. The next most logical direction from which to attack the city was from the north, conveniently the direction the Federals would approach if the main invasion took place from the United States itself. But that area also included major geographical problems and would ultimately preclude any major, army-wide attempt to reach the city from the north. Namely, the major geographic oddity that was the Mississippi Delta stood in the way.[8]

Extending from the Tennessee border at Memphis southward to Vicksburg in the central part of the state, the flat Delta region in Mississippi extended inland for some sixty or seventy miles at its widest. A maze of rivers, creeks, and bayous filled with alligators, snakes, and any number of other vicious animals such as bobcat or bear covered the area and was extremely confusing in normal circumstances and almost impassable in high water. As at Vicksburg itself, Confederate defenses on the high ground overlooking the Delta could easily stop any advance from that direction. As a result, although logic said that the Federals could move up the Yazoo River and deposit forces on the southern bank preparatory to moving up the bluffs, the geography of the area would not allow it. Grant certainly realized as much later on after taking a personal look at the bluffs along the flooded Yazoo River north of Vicksburg, writing, "the extent of ground upon which troops could land at Haynes' Bluff is so limited that the place is impregnable." He also wrote, "I am satisfied that an attack upon Haynes' Bluff would be attended with immense sacrifice of life, if not with defeat." Consequently, approaching Vicksburg from the north was a severely difficult proposition as well.[9]

If reaching the city, much less attacking it, from the north and west was all but impossible, that left the southern and eastern approaches as the only real possibilities. The southern approach had just as many difficulties. To move on Vicksburg from the south meant getting an army south of the city, and the easiest ways to do that would obviously be to bring it up from the Gulf of Mexico or move it downriver on the western side of the Mississippi and then cross it over. The former entailed a voyage of thousands of miles by water around the tip of Florida. Opting for the latter approach again meant the need for the navy south of Vicksburg, including passing any Confederate defenses. Then, any army would have the same trouble landing on dry ground east of the Mississippi River as anywhere else; the Confederates could counter the landing at the river bank itself or could position men and guns on the bluffs inland for a stronger defense. Either way, the Federals would be limited as to what they could do because the Confederates could possibly catch them astride the river, part on one side and part on the other. That, of course, was a recipe for disaster.[10]

If by some miraculous design a landing occurred without a hitch south of Vicksburg, the southern approach, once inland, also entailed significant concerns. Depending on where the Federals landed, they would have to cross many easily defensible large creeks or rivers, including Bayou Pierre and the Big Black River, in order to reach Vicksburg. Once across the major threshold of the Big Black, any Federal army would be caught in a triangle-shaped area of land between the Mississippi and Big Black Rivers, which would severely limit mobility and maneuver. Confederate defenders would have a good chance of stopping a Union advance in this area, especially with their base firmly in their rear at Vicksburg. "The broken nature of the ground would have enabled him to hold a strong defensible line from the river south of the city to the Big Black," Grant later wrote of this possibility, "retaining possession of the railroad back to that point."[11]

If the western, northern, and southern approaches to Vicksburg all had their major difficulties, then the only direction to easily approach Vicksburg was from the east. But again, how to get to that area was the real question, as it was firmly in the center of hostile central Mississippi, an area that would be difficult to enter while covering exposed flanks. The fact that several Confederate railroads ran through the region and congregated at the state capital of Jackson, just forty miles east of Vicksburg, also meant that the Confederates could quickly bring troops from every direction of the compass to defend the area and hit those exposed Federal flanks. Still, the eastern approach seemed to be the only real viable direction of attack.[12]

It must also be remembered, however, that Vicksburg's geographical setting provided headaches not only for the Federals; it also made planning difficult for any defending Confederates. The same isolation that made Vicksburg so difficult for the Federals to reach meant that it could easily be cut off from the larger Confederacy. Gunboats positioned north and south of Vicksburg could effectively cut off all river transportation, which had of course been Vicksburg's main axis of trade and transportation prior to the war. Gunboats could effectively halt any transportation across the river as well, where a ferry connected the two railroads that met on opposite sides of the river at Vicksburg. That meant that the only secure land connection to the larger Confederacy, and as a result the only lifeline for supplies and communication, was eastward, where the Southern Railroad of Mississippi ran from Vicksburg to Jackson and thence on to Meridian, where it connected with lines that allowed access to the rest of the Confederacy. Significantly, any Union army that reached the city from the east would not only be using the best available approach route, but it would also simultaneously cut the only lifeline for the river city itself.[13]

There was a larger problem as well for any Confederate garrison at Vicksburg. As defensible as the bastion was, it was still susceptible to the thorn in the flesh of every stationary, fixed garrison: the turning movement. Fixed fortifications, on which the Confederacy had to depend simply because it lacked the resources to counter the mobile brown-water naval threat of the Federals, were notoriously vulnerable to being reduced no matter how strong their local defenses were. Any enemy could march around a fixed position blocking a river and render it useless simply by cutting access. It had been done numerous times in history before the Civil War and would be done numerous times thereafter. Perhaps the most notable example of this strategy was the Allies' successful island-hopping campaign in the Central Pacific during World War II.[14]

Consequently, while the geography of Vicksburg's region precluded any easy access to approaching the citadel, it also formed a cauldron of potential disaster for Confederate defenders who could not maneuver with a fixed fortification. Yet Federal officials seemed to conflate just getting to Vicksburg with taking it, which were two extremely different activities. Grant himself later wrote that the area east of Vicksburg was "the ground I so much desire," but he wrongly declared that "foot once upon dry land on the other side of the river I think the balance would be of but short duration."[15]

That would certainly be the case if the Confederates did not fortify Vicksburg. But they did.

As the war unfolded into a much more lengthy operation than almost anyone expected, dual Union thrusts began to move along the Mississippi River. Obviously, the river had played a major role in American history, and military planners, General Winfield Scott foremost among them early in the war, realized this fact. Scott's famous Anaconda Plan had as one of its major tenets the opening of the Mississippi River and division of the Confederacy, something Lincoln agreed with, perhaps having learned it from his general in the first place. Planners accordingly began to promote operations to gather the river's full length into Union hands. Two movements consequently developed, one from the north moving southward along the river from Missouri and Illinois and another from the Gulf moving northward. At the time, Vicksburg seemed to factor less in the strategy for most planners except perhaps Lincoln, simply because there was so much of the river to be conquered on either end before Federal forces reached the middle section, where Vicksburg was situated.[16]

Consequently, in all the excitement of mobilization and early conflict, Vicksburg in particular and Mississippi as a whole fared rather well, actually for more than two years into the war. Most of the chaos and movement in Mississippi in the first half of the fighting came on the positive side as the state mobilized for war. The secession convention itself began to lay the groundwork for the conflict, setting in motion plans to take care of almost every area of concern for the state, including political, economic, social, logistical, and military efforts. Once the convention adjourned for good, the governor and state legislature took the reins and continued to build up Mississippi's military might.[17]

That safety began to erode by the spring of 1862 as Federal forces started to operate on both the northern and southern extremities of the Confederate-held portions of the river. The major thrust came from the north, where Union forces under General Ulysses S. Grant soon won smashing victories at Forts Henry and Donelson and then took Nashville, Tennessee, and Columbus, Kentucky. Worse for the Confederates, the Federals pushed southward on the rivers, with a small force on the Mississippi itself but the main thrust moving along the parallel Tennessee River in West Tennessee. There, by March 1862, the Federals concentrated around one of the many landings on that river, Pittsburg Landing, which had a good road inland to the Federals' next major objective: Corinth, Mississippi. There, one Federal general declared that the Union army would have to "drag them out as we draw a badger out of his hole." Thus the war came to Mississippi's doorstep.[18]

The Union operations against Corinth were ultimately successful, but not before much heartache and fighting. The Confederate western commander, General Albert Sidney Johnston, concentrated his forces in the west to defend Corinth, or in actuality the railroads that crossed there, and he decided the best way to do that was by going on the offensive and attacking the enemy before any more Federals arrived at their concentration point. "I would fight them if they were a million," he declared, but it was obviously better to fight as few as he could at any one time. The result was Shiloh in April, which failed to halt the Federals, and a renewed Union advance on Corinth in May. Marking the first major invasion of Mississippi at that time, the Federals soon

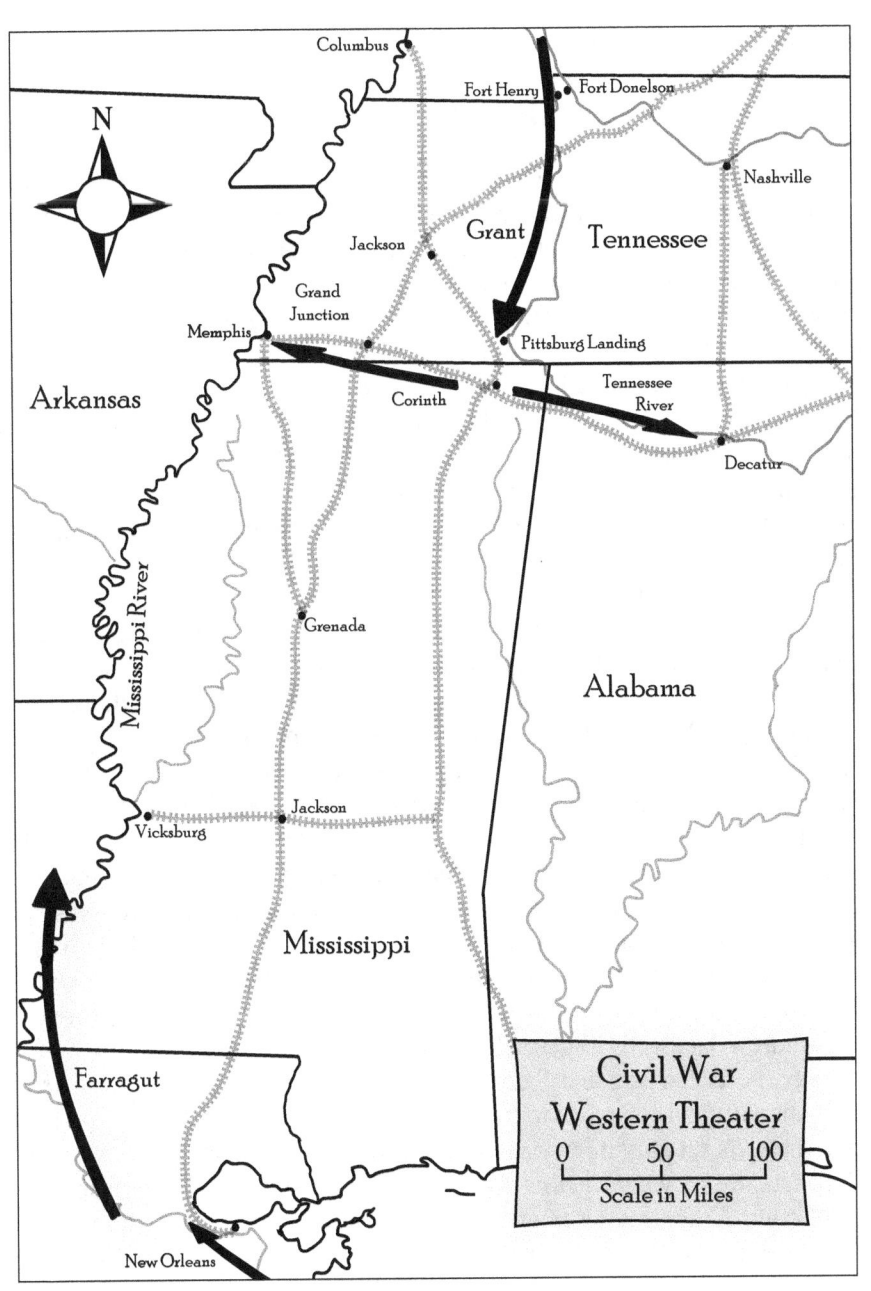

took the town without much of a fight. But there the invasion ended, because the overall Federal commander at the time, Major General Henry W. Halleck, chose to consolidate his gains rather than push on any farther into the state. Halleck sent components of his army eastward and westward, taking Memphis and putting Chattanooga in the crosshairs of Federal intentions as well.[19]

There matters stood for the remainder of the summer and into the fall. A few Federal incursions went forward down the Mississippi River itself, but nothing even remotely close to an invasion of the state took place. The net result was that by October 1862, nearly two years after secession, the vast majority of Mississippi still lay safely protected from the enemy. While roving gunboats on the Mississippi River kept a threat to Mississippi looming from the west, the only actual Union occupation was in the very northeast county of the state, Tishomingo. There, the Federals were content to remain at Corinth and defend their gains, which they had to do in one of the larger battles in the state in early October at Corinth, when the Confederates unsuccessfully tried to retake the town.[20]

While Confederates fought the northern Union advance down the Mississippi Valley with almost everything they had, the southern Federal advance, up the Mississippi from the Gulf of Mexico, was actually the thrust that first threatened Vicksburg and forced the Confederates to begin to think about defending the bastion. The blue-water navy in the Gulf of Mexico, under Flag Officer David G. Farragut, began to ascend the Mississippi River in early 1862, accompanied by army forces under the politician-soldier Major General Benjamin F. Butler. The Federals found their going much more difficult than had the British in 1814 and 1815. The presence of Fort Jackson, a major post–War of 1812 fortification far down the river protecting against advances toward New Orleans (an earlier version of Fort Saint Philip was already in existence), proved to be difficult. Whereas the British had been able to move northward almost the entire way to New Orleans in 1814 before they met Andrew Jackson's forces near Chalmette just four miles from the French Quarter, Forts Jackson and Saint Philip now sat on a large bend in the river more than fifty airline miles to the southeast, and even more by river miles. In fact, the forts sat only thirty or so miles upriver from the mouth of the Father of Waters, thereby interdicting river traffic far outside of New Orleans.[21]

Of course, the usual problem with fixed fortifications was that they could be turned, and Union commanders explored ways to do so. But the United States and later the Confederates had fortified additional approaches to New Orleans from the Gulf, ironically making the best conceivable route northward to the Confederacy's queen city by the fortified river itself. Thus, the

Federal navy, both its oceangoing vessels under Farragut and a fleet of mortar boats under David Dixon Porter, pummeled the river forts in mid-April, just after Grant had won the major but close-run victory at Shiloh in the northern thrust. Seeing that the forts would not bow to mere bombardment, Farragut chose to run the batteries "with my little fleet," he wrote, a tricky proposition because the Federal vessels would be going against the mighty current, slowing the ships and making them much easier targets. He did it nevertheless on the night of April 23, effectively turning the fortifications, which surrendered quickly on April 28. "I witnessed this daring exploit," Benjamin Butler wrote, "from a point about 800 yards from Fort Jackson and unwittingly under its fire, and the sublimity of the scene can never be exceeded." More important than the sublime scene, of course, was that fact that there was nothing else to stop the Federal advance on New Orleans.[22]

Farragut and Butler plied ahead quickly and soon reached New Orleans. Major General Mansfield Lovell, the Confederate general commanding the city, was adamant that New Orleans could not be held, describing "the perfect absurdity of confronting more than 100 guns afloat of the largest caliber, well manned and served, and looking down upon the city." While he would not surrender, and told a Union captain who demanded such a course as much on April 25, Lovell fully realized he should try to mitigate any damage to the city and its people and thus proposed that he evacuate. "To this demand [surrender]," Lovell wrote, "I returned an unqualified refusal, declaring that I would not surrender the city or any portion of my command, but added that, feeling unwilling to subject the city to bombardment, and recognizing the utter impossibility of removing the women and children, I should withdraw my troops and turn it over to the civil authorities." In taking such an action, Lovell reminded his superiors that because of the concentration of troops that had led to Shiloh, "every Confederate soldier in New Orleans, with the exception of one company, had been ordered to Corinth, to join General [P. G. T.] Beauregard in March, and the city was only garrisoned by about 3,000 ninety-day troops, called out by the governor at my request, of whom about 1,200 had muskets and the remainder shot-guns of an indifferent description." Lovell thus evacuated and the mayor surrendered New Orleans on April 25. And so, the Federals not only took control of the South's largest city, but they also took the financial and trade capital of the Confederacy, as well as a symbolic venue of immense proportions. Also acquired was the fresh grave of Albert Sidney Johnston, who had perished instead of conquered just nineteen days earlier on the plains of Shiloh. Johnston's remains would rest in an occupied city for the remainder of the war.[23]

While much of the Confederacy's attention had been focused to the north on the critical and newsworthy Battles of Forts Henry and Donelson, Shiloh, and Corinth, Farragut's activities farther to the south were not, at first, deemed as critical or newsworthy. Perhaps that was because events in Kentucky and Tennessee gained far more attention in the newspapers, including the humiliating raid by Federal naval gunboats up the Tennessee River immediately after Fort Henry that showed just what a hollow shell the Confederacy actually was. Papers all across the Confederacy tracked the flotilla's progress as the gunboats penetrated all the way into Mississippi and Alabama. Perhaps also, the confidence in masonry fortifications was so immense that most thought that Forts Jackson and Saint Philip would easily hold at bay the Federal navy to the south, just as the Americans had done against the British at Fort McHenry in 1814.[24]

Then Farragut broke through and New Orleans fell, undefended as it mostly was. After that, the river was also open all the way northward into Mississippi, another hollow shell. All saw that something had to be done, that some intermediary defense had to be established within the inner bowels of the Confederacy to stop Union progress along the river. Eventually, all saw that the place was Vicksburg, one Confederate writing long after the war that "the occupation of Vicksburg was the immediate result of the fall of New Orleans." Given the recent events, including the halt of farther advance into Mississippi by Halleck and the subsequent arrival of Union troops and naval vessels from the south near Vicksburg, the actual impetus for the development of Vicksburg as a fully fortified bastion came from the south.[25]

Regardless of which direction the initial threat came from, a flurry of activity soon emerged to make Vicksburg the point at which river traffic stopped. But this burst of activity quickly illustrated the quirky geographical puzzle that Vicksburg was and the need to defend it more than just along the riverfront. Indeed, three major sets of Confederate fortifications soon emerged to fully defend Vicksburg. One was a series of heavy artillery batteries established along the river itself to hopefully block any movement by water past Vicksburg. The second was a line of earthworks and batteries extending northeastward from Vicksburg along the Walnut Hills up to Snyder's and Haynes' Bluffs, covering the lower stretches of the Yazoo River and thus access to the all-important high ground east of Vicksburg. The third was a line of earthen fortifications in the rear of Vicksburg, or on the land side, protecting it from any land army that sought to turn the position.[26]

Although Mississippi erected batteries on the Vicksburg bluffs as early as mid-January 1861, the first mention of fortifying Vicksburg in any important way emerged only in December 1861, a full eleven months after those first shots at the *A. O. Tyler*. A Mississippi ordnance officer in Jackson, Lieutenant Colonel Edward Fontaine, recommended beefing up the defenses leading to New Orleans. Obviously, Mississippi would be threatened if the defenses in Louisiana at the time were not secured, but few listened. Fontaine was a mere lieutenant colonel at that point, and a state militia officer at that. Still, all would have done well to have listened to him. In the same mid-December letter to Louisiana governor Thomas O. Moore, Fontaine described how the Federals would not try to move down the Mississippi River past Columbus, Kentucky, but would rather make the line of the Tennessee and Cumberland Rivers their axis of advance. That is exactly what the Federals did in February. Fontaine also determined where the New Orleans defenses were weak, and of course the concurring Federals used those to advantage as well.[27]

Fontaine fully realized that Mississippi lay in jeopardy and thus informed Governor John J. Pettus that "I shall go to Vicksburg tomorrow, to lay out fortifications and to make an estimate of the number of Negroes it will take to finish them." Yet just arming the river defense would not be enough, he noted. "I will fortify Vicksburg and prevent its capture," he added, "but I cannot prevent the enemy from burning it and passing it. I can keep them from entering the corporation, but they can shell it from the river and from the Louisiana side."[28]

Few took Fontaine's prophesies to heart, and apparently no one remembered his words later the next spring when the Federals did exactly as he had predicted. Unfortunately, no one acted then on his latest recommendations either. Mansfield Lovell came to a different conclusion altogether and would not give Fontaine so much as the time of day. Fontaine even found it necessary to write Governor Moore more than once, although the governor did forward Fontaine's December 18 letter on to Lovell. Lovell was still not in any mood to help the Mississippian, writing that although "I do not disapprove of fortifying Vicksburg," he said that he did not have engineers, guns, or time to aid the effort. "If they wish to build it, however, let them do so, although I must adhere to my previous opinion, that it is better to concentrate the forts and obstructions at the point where the batteries already exist." Lovell added, "I can give them no competent officer, no guns, and no powder."[29]

It is not known if Lovell recalled Fontaine's correspondence in April 1862 as he fell back from a now-captured New Orleans toward Vicksburg, but even if he did it did not matter, as little work had progressed at Vicksburg. He was a believer now, though, and even before New Orleans fell, he notified the new department commander General P. G. T. Beauregard (he having taken over for Albert Sidney Johnston when the latter was killed at Shiloh) and even

General Samuel Cooper in Richmond that he would fall back into Mississippi and make his next line of defense at Vicksburg and Jackson along the Southern Railroad of Mississippi. In fact, Lovell asked for an engineer from Beauregard and, knowing what was coming, began plans to fortify Vicksburg even before New Orleans fell.[30]

Lovell specifically told Beauregard, then defending Corinth just days after the defeat at Shiloh, that he wanted to fortify Vicksburg "for the double purpose of protecting the river and giving you a *point-d'appui* for the left of your line in case you are compelled to occupy a position in rear of your present one." He also renewed the request for the engineer, as the only one he had at the time was Brigadier General Martin L. Smith, who was then busy at New Orleans. "There is no engineer officer here to be sent on that duty," Lovell somewhat disingenuously wrote, "or I should have fortified Vicksburg long since. Have you any one in your army who, with the help of a few thousand Negroes, could put up the works . . . ?" He added (a little late), "The subject of fortifying Vicksburg strikes me as of pressing importance, and if you agree with me I will endeavor to push it as much as possible."[31]

As matters deteriorated south of New Orleans and it looked like the city would easily fall, Lovell became more concerned about Vicksburg and actually sent Smith with a brigade of troops to take command there. Once New Orleans fell, Lovell also sent ten or twelve of the heavy guns he had saved northward to Vicksburg, although he stopped what meager infantry force he had at Camp Moore near Tangiapahoa, Louisiana. He could only do so much, especially with Beauregard actually calling on him to send more troops to Corinth. Lovell responded that he had sent all he could and had a mere fraction of his force at Vicksburg while trying to hold out farther to the south to delay the enemy as much as possible. He could only hope that the Federals would be delayed and that the hindrance might allow for some fortification at Vicksburg, which would have to suffice for the time being. "If at all fortified," Lovell informed Beauregard, "[Vicksburg] will be able (with the troops I shall send there), to hold its own against any force they will be likely to send for some time to come."[32]

The threat that loomed against New Orleans and thus the rest of the river northward because of the attack on Forts Jackson and Saint Philip also moved Beauregard to action. He had shown some concern earlier, but he had not put any firm action in place. Being "extremely anxious," in his own words, while in west Tennessee before Shiloh, Beauregard proposed a river-long analysis with potential bastions at Port Hudson, Louisiana, and Helena, Arkansas. Beauregard, at the time at Columbus, Kentucky, was convinced that the next fortifications to his south such as Island No. 10 and Fort Pillow were "but temporary barriers to the enemy's gunboats and great resources." He recommended to Johnston that the west's chief engineer, Lieutenant Colonel Jeremy F. Gilmer, be sent to this duty, but Johnston would not spare his engineer. Beauregard then sent another, Captain Andrew B. Gray, but he was killed at Fort Pillow.[33]

The loss of New Orleans shook Beauregard, now in full command, out of his lethargy, perhaps because it was his hometown. Although heavily involved in reorganizing his army after the major defeat at Shiloh, ushering in Major General Earl Van Dorn's troops from the trans-Mississippi, and working to confront the expected advance of Halleck's legions toward Corinth in late April, Beauregard also took time to see to other components of his shattered department, including a new line to fall back on perhaps both from the north and the south. He "at once" responded to Lovell's most recent letter, on April 21 in fact, by sending an engineer and getting the work started at Vicksburg. "Understanding that there are no points sufficiently high on the river between Memphis and Vicksburg which could be fortified for the defense of the Mississippi, I have concluded to construct some defensive works on the bluffs at or about Vicksburg," Beauregard informed the engineer he was sending southward, Captain David B. Harris, then at Fort Pillow.[34]

Beauregard wanted Harris to make a "careful reconnaissance of the locality," he told him, adding that although he did not know the area himself, he had been told of the general lay of the land: "From what I am told, I should think the bluffs immediately above that city not far from where a small stream empties into the river, would be a proper point for said works, provided it is not commanded by surrounded heights within 2 miles." Beauregard also cautioned that the large bend in the river made the area "susceptible of being canalled across from the river above to the river below," and he accordingly recommended works south of Vicksburg to shut off the river there as well. Beauregard also added that "there should be ample space in those works for magazines, traverses in every direction, field bomb-proofs, a store house, and cisterns." To aid Harris, Beauregard also sent other officers, one pair being a father and son whom "I am well acquainted with" and "are very reliable, practical men, and will be of much assistance to you." Finally, Beauregard also notified Harris that he was ordering a thousand slaves to be sent to Vicksburg to perform the manual labor and that he had called on the state of Mississippi and its commander then on the scene, Lieutenant Colonel James L. Autry, to provide food and supplies. Beauregard continued to correspond with Harris in the ensuing days, giving him instructions on the fortification of the hill city.[35]

The Federal threat also sparked rapid movement from the new commander at Vicksburg, Martin L. Smith, who arrived and took command on May 12. Smith "proceeded at once to prepare for the approach of the enemy, then known to have passed Baton Rouge with a formidable fleet, having in view to open the river." Smith found preparations woefully lacking, mainly because Engineer Harris had only recently arrived and begun work. Laborers were also scant. Only three batteries were in working order, Smith describing them as "mostly completed," with a fourth having been begun. Only a few troops were on site, mostly troops from his own brigade (the 27th Louisiana and 8th Louisiana Battalion) that Smith had sent on ahead of him. Later arriving units such as the 20th and 28th Louisiana and still later the 4th and 5th Louisiana as well as assorted battalions of other regiments and artillery batteries also helped in the defense. The troops, Smith noted, were mainly "disposed for disputing inch by inch the approach by land."[36]

Smith went to work with a will, keeping Colonel Autry as well as Engineer Harris on duty and working through them. He reported the two had been "pushing the works forward vigorously," but Smith wanted more effort, and in the next six days he "pushed forward night and day with all possible vigor." It was a good thing, because the Federals were soon approaching. By May 18, when Farragut first appeared below Vicksburg, some six batteries had been completed and four more soon would be. The work, Smith noted with an obvious lack of confidence, put "us in a condition to dispute with a fair prospect of success a farther advance."[37]

The Federals had indeed not stopped at New Orleans, choosing rather to take advantage of the lack of Confederate defenses in depth along the river. In that sense, the Confederacy was definitely very much an empty shell with only a minimal outer crust of defense. Grant had found as much when he broke through this initial crust at Forts Henry and Donelson in February; once through, there were no Confederate defenses to slow a Union advance for another hundred miles. From the south, there was nothing to confront the Federal advance up the river for more than two hundred miles past Forts Jackson and Saint Philip, except where the water was shallow, prompting Farragut to surmise that "the large ships, I fear, will not be able to go higher than Baton Rouge." But he added, even while reporting on his success at New Orleans on May 6, "I have sent the smaller vessels, under Commander [S. Phillips] Lee, as high as Vicksburg, in the rear of Jackson, to cut off their supplies from the west." Surprisingly, the river was high enough for all to proceed, and Farragut soon easily took possession of numerous Confederate cities such as

Baton Rouge, the capital of Louisiana, and Natchez, Mississippi, even while approaching Vicksburg itself.[38]

It was not until the Federal vessels reached the Vicksburg vicinity that they came to a stop, although Vicksburg at the time was much less defended than it would later be. In fact, Farragut was easily able to run what defenses there were at the time and place his navy north of the city by June 28. Yet because of the natural defensibility of Vicksburg, an accompanying infantry force under Brigadier General Thomas Williams was unwilling to attempt an attack at this point. As Farragut put it, "The forts can be passed and we have done it, and can do it again as often as may be required of us. It will not, however, be an easy matter for us to do more than silence the batteries for a time, as long as the enemy has a large force behind the hills to prevent our landing and holding the place." The Federals instead spent most of their time trying to dig a canal across the narrow point of land on the De Soto Peninsula to divert the river's course, as Beauregard predicted, thereby bypassing Vicksburg and its high ground altogether and rendering it a nonissue from then on. Unfortunately for this summer 1862 expedition, the river did not change course (until 1876), and an attempt to bluff the Confederate defenders into surrendering went just about as well. One Confederate commander at Vicksburg, Mississippi State Troops lieutenant colonel James L. Autry, boldly told the Federals that "Mississippians don't know, and refuse to learn, how to surrender to an enemy." He added that "if Commodore [David] Farragut or Brigadier General [Benjamin] Butler can teach them, let them come and try."[39]

The Federals on the river soon found they could do little but bombard the city, which they did mercilessly. Still, one Confederate described the result as "nearly harmless.... Vertical fire is never very destructive of life." Another soldier noted that "the Yankees still keep up their Bombarding us from the lower fleets. Throw from fifty to one hundred shells per day and have done so for the last three or four weeks, though they are doing themselves more damage than anyone else. It is true they knock a hole in a house in Vicksburg occasionally but we don't care for that for the rascals are selling us goods so high that I don't care if the Plaugued town was torn down and a few deaths with it." The people of Vicksburg were certainly not so uncaring or used to the explosions and damage, and even some of the military men never became comfortable with them. One Confederate, a Frenchman, willingly admitted, "I no like ze bomb; I cannot fight him back!"[40]

Yet, bombard was about all the Federals could do, and they soon realized that was futile. With no other recourse, with the river level falling, with the Confederate ram *Arkansas* on the loose, and with Vicksburg still holding out high atop its bluffs, Farragut had no other choice by July but to fall back down the river to Baton Rouge and await developments from the north. In fact, he recommended that he and his ships be sent back to the Gulf of Mexico, especially since Flag Officer Charles H. Davis had reached the Vicksburg vicinity after the last high ground north of the city fell on June 6 at Memphis: "The services of my squadron would be much more essential to the interests of the country on the coast than in this river." Indeed, for now the Federals had unlimited access to the river, except for "fortified points on the river . . . , which is now reduced to the town of Vicksburg. . . . The river is open from one end to the other except this town of Vicksburg." But Farragut saw clearly what was needed to fully open the river: "These towns are regularly reduced by the army getting in the rear, whereby they are able to hold them when once taken." It was plain that Farragut and the navy could do no more, and he actually admitted that "I can do nothing here but blockade the port until the army arrives, which can be done as well by Flag-Officer Davis as by both." Secretary of the Navy Gideon Welles agreed and just four days later allowed Farragut to steam back southward. Still, the Federals had penetrated all the way to Vicksburg itself, though briefly, and that was enough to get the Confederate high command's full attention. The next time the enemy returned, they would find Vicksburg much more prepared.[41]

The scare that was the Federal approach and passage of the batteries at Vicksburg seemed to shake the Confederate high command to the core. Soon, more troops arrived to defend the important position on the river, including multiple brigades of Major General John C. Breckinridge's command. Also sent was a new department commander to take over from the humiliated Lovell. Earl Van Dorn, recently transferred from the trans-Mississippi, was left in Mississippi to defend his home state when Braxton Bragg took what would become the Army of Tennessee into that state and beyond. Van Dorn took over on June 28, right in the middle of the Vicksburg crisis.[42]

Also sent to Vicksburg was the engineer who would become synonymous with its defenses: Captain Samuel H. Lockett. A native of Alabama, he was still a young man but had made a name for himself, primarily by graduating second in his class at West Point in 1859. Once Alabama seceded, Lockett resigned his position in the regular army and cast his lot with the new Confederacy, obtaining a commission as a captain and soon serving on high-ranking generals' staffs. Most recently, Lockett had served on Bragg's staff, and at Shiloh he alerted Albert Sidney Johnston of a major threat to his right and thus caused a rethinking of the battle. Bragg detached Lockett from his staff on June 20 and sent him to Vicksburg to report to Martin L. Smith. For his part, Smith was glad to get Lockett, proclaiming him as "the accomplished engineer officer of my staff." He went on to remark: "I have to speak in terms of unqualified praise, both as regards skill in his profession and qualities as a soldier. The services of such an officer are so important and indispensable as to have all the effect of a positive increase of force in determining the issue of a contest." Lockett soon arrived and immediately fell in love with the place: "No point on the river," he wrote his wife, "is more picturesque than Vicksburg."[43]

Although Lockett's initial work was simply laying out camps for regiments, about which he complained ("I reckon any body can do what I am entrusted with just as well as I"), he soon gained the responsibility of fortifying Vicksburg over and above the river batteries, which were strengthened themselves during the next several months. He fortunately arrived during a lull period and found that "at the time of my arrival no enemy was near, but the work of preparation was going on vigorously." Lockett soon laid out more batteries and began to make a detailed map of the area. By the time several fall inspections took place, Lockett had already overseen a complex and powerful system of defenses along the river, mostly dug into the banks rather than atop the bluffs. The defenses ultimately included five major sites north of Vicksburg and six below, complete with magazines and other fixtures. Others were then in process, making a total of fourteen different battery sites planned, all armed with large cannons such as 18-, 32-, and 42-pound rifles, as well as various assortments of Columbiads, Dahlgrens, and one Blakely rifle. There was also a mortar.[44]

But the defenses were certainly not complete, even by the turn of the year. After a personal inspection that winter, Jefferson Davis himself pushed for more firepower and ammunition for Vicksburg, writing his secretary of war that "very much depends upon prompt supply." Moreover, the biggest needs once the river batteries were in a good state were land defenses, and Lockett soon turned his attention to the second and third levels of fortifications at Vicksburg.[45]

A second level of fortifications consisted of outlying earthworks to the north and south of the city, as well as up the Yazoo River. Obviously, with the river batteries interdicting traffic, any enemy could land troops to the left or right and take those batteries and the city in the rear. Thus, Lockett began to lay out fortifications northward along the Walnut Hills, including earthworks with abatis at the bases of the bluffs near Chickasaw Bayou and the main road north out of Vicksburg all the way to the high ground at Snyder's and Haynes' Bluffs. "Our works there," Lockett notified his wife in mid-September, "and elsewhere [are] all going on steadily and slowly." The hope was that those fortifications would stop river traffic on the Yazoo and block any Federal land force from landing and getting in rear of the Vicksburg river batteries from the north. At the same time, Lockett also extended fortifications southward toward Warrenton for the same reason, and Grand Gulf was not too far southward as well. Yet in all the bustle and planning, these outer works received less attention and were thus in a less ready state. One inspector at Snyder's Bluff commented that "this battery does not bear the least evidence of care."[46]

Obviously, the Confederates could extend their fortifications out from Vicksburg as far as they wanted, only to be potentially outflanked by an even wider turning movement. Facetiously, Lockett could build earthworks all the way to the Gulf of Mexico only to be turned by a Federal land movement through Central America and Mexico. That fact ushered in the need for a third level of fortifications at Vicksburg, earthworks ringing the city itself from the river north of town to the river south of it. That would allow the city to be defended by an army even if the enemy somehow managed to break through the outer works and reach the high ground east of the city. Confederate leaders who had seen the lessons of Columbus, Kentucky, Island No. 10, Fort Donelson, and countless other fixed sites being turned by land armies deemed this third layer of vast importance. If Vicksburg's batteries blocking the river were to be able to hold out, they would have to have rearward fortifications that could hold long enough to allow a relief from the outside to raise any siege laid against them.[47]

Lockett noted dolefully that "it became my duty to plan, locate, and lay out that line of defense." It would be no easy task, Lockett later testifying that "a month was spent in reconnoitering, surveying, and studying the complicated and irregular site to be fortified." In fact, Lockett surmised that "no greater topographical puzzle was ever presented to an engineer," and another observant soldier agreed, writing home that "why it is just one hill piled up against another." The work was especially difficult in wet weather, one Louisianan describing how "the ground becomes so slippery that one can scarcely walk up and down these wretched steep hills." Lockett also found the initial surveying and exploration slowed by the fact that virgin timber still stood on many of the ridge tops, including large stands of magnolias and extremely dense thickets of cane. The weariness could still be heard in Lockett's voice many years later when he explained, "At first it seemed impossible to find anything like a general line of commanding ground surrounding the city; but careful study gradually worked out the problem."[48]

Perhaps because of the tedious work, Lockett also enjoyed his free time, although he terribly missed his ailing wife in Alabama. He wrote her of grand parties in Vicksburg and even noted how "I have gotten acquainted with some right nice young ladies here since my return and with your permission I will visit them occasionally to keep myself in the ways of civilized life." He perhaps unwisely continued, "There are lots of very pretty girls here and they swarm the streets every evening about sundown giving quite an animated appearance to the town." He also remarked of others clogging the city's streets as a result of Vicksburg being an exchange point under the Dix-Hill Cartel: "The town is pretty well filled with Yankee prisoners waiting to be exchanged." He also mentioned going to church regularly "and try[ing] to be good for your sake."[49]

Over time, Lockett found his line of defense and began to first clear it and then erect fortifications. The major work of building the defenses did not begin until later in the fall, after his comprehensive plan had been submitted to new department commander John C. Pemberton, it taking that long for Lockett to get his bearings, strengthen the river batteries that were under fire until late July, and scout out where he wanted the defensive line. Once begun, the work went quickly, Pemberton desiring that the effort be "carried out with the utmost dispatch." The actual work was "generally done by fatigue parties detailed from each command to work within the limits of its own line." Also helping were large numbers of slaves brought in from the surrounding counties.[50]

Lockett proposed fortifications some eight miles long extending from the Mississippi River above Vicksburg around to the Mississippi River below the city, that being in Pemberton's words "the shortest defensible line of which the topography of the country admitted." Pemberton also described how "the line of defense around the city of Vicksburg consisted . . . of a system of detached works (redans, lunettes, and redoubts) on the prominent and commanding points, with the usual profile of raised field-works, connected, in most cases, by rifle-pits." Most of the major works would be on the highest points of land, which also, not by coincidence in that day, sat on the major roadways in and out of Vicksburg. Early settlers almost always utilized the high ground of ridges when they could in building roads, obviously to keep out of marshy and muddy lowlands as much as possible. This factor aided Lockett in that he could both man the highest ground and cover the major roads with the same bastions. To the flanks of the major forts would sit lesser field works, and simple rifle pits would connect the various complexes in the intervening areas.[51]

Six major roads and one railroad fanned out from Vicksburg, almost as spokes on a half-wheel, and Lockett obviously had to make sure these were well covered. Running due north out of the city was the Valley Road, which

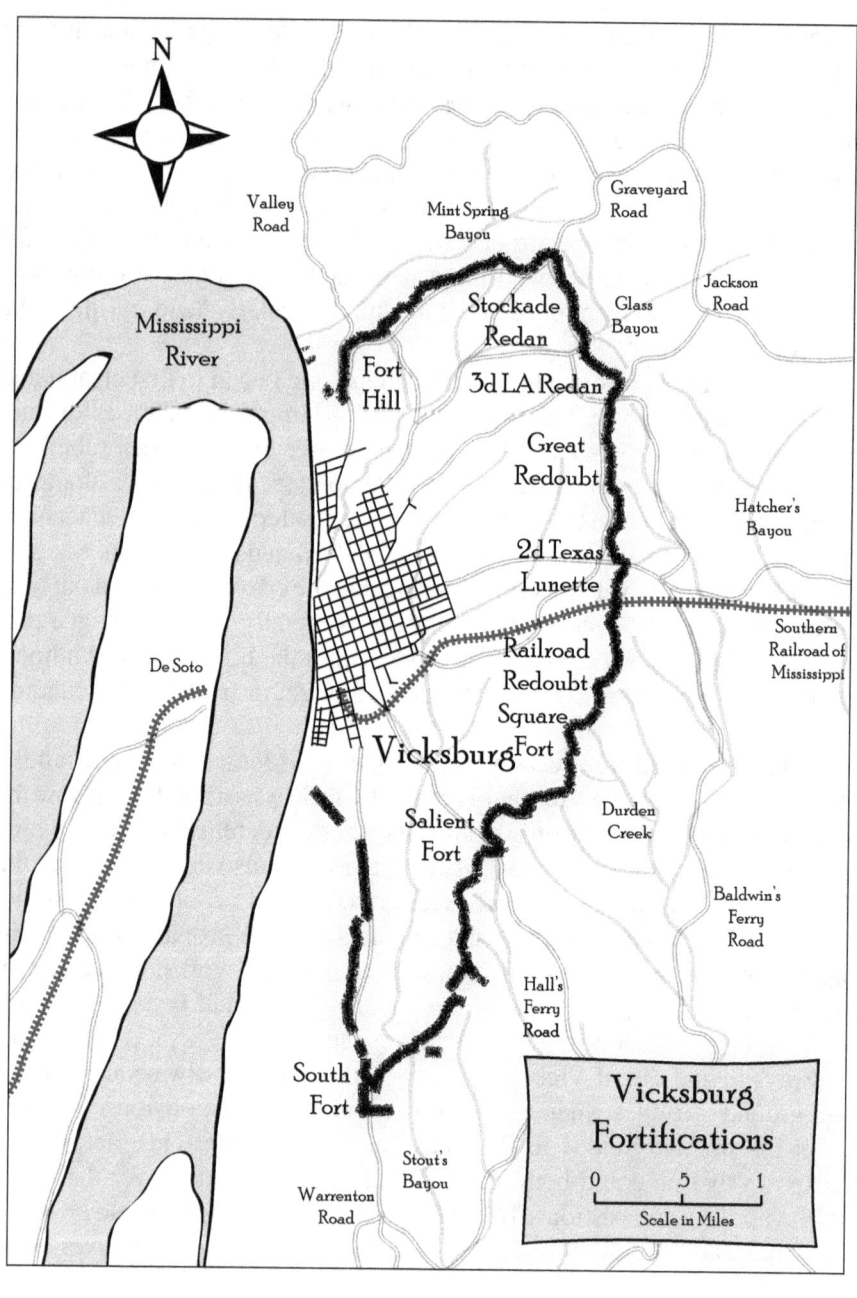

paralleled the river until the watercourse bent westward in the hairpin turn. From there the road continued on below the bluffs to the Chickasaw Bayou area and thence on up the Yazoo River watershed. Running to the northeast was the Graveyard Road, it gaining its name because it passed by the city cemetery a mile and a half out of town where originally "a number of gamblers and misdoers were taken to the suburbs and hanged, and buried at a cut in the ridge that surrounded the town." Running due east was the main road into town, the Jackson Road. South of the main road were two others running more or less southeastward, both toward major ferries on the Big Black River. The Baldwin's Ferry Road ran just south of the Jackson Road, while the Hall's Ferry Road was much farther south. Finally, the Warrenton Road ran due south, parallel with the river, toward that locale south of Vicksburg. The only other major transportation route to enter the city was the Southern Railroad of Mississippi, which wove across the route of the Baldwin's Ferry Road in various places. To secure these major transportation avenues, Lockett ordered nine major fortifications, eight of the nine sitting astride or athwart the roads and railroad.[52]

Lockett struggled to locate a series of ridges covering these roads that could be interconnected by fortifications on most of the line. Fortunately, the area directly north of Vicksburg posed no such problems. The large watershed of Mint Spring Bayou flowed directly westward from high ground two miles or so inland. The bayou itself was not that much of a barrier, but the deep valley created by the water caused a steep and precipitous ridge directly to the south that rose some one hundred and fifty feet. Principal tributaries flowed into the bayou from the north, chopping up the ridge north of the bayou, but the southern wall was almost devoid of large tributaries and thus formed what the geographer Warren Grabau later described as "an unbroken rampart more than 150 feet high along its entire length." As a result, Lockett laid out a line of works on the crest, and these would prove to be the strongest fortifications at Vicksburg. It was logical and obvious to place the Confederate defensive line on this high ridge, taking advantage of its height as well as slope, although Lockett also built earthworks on the northern ridge that was much more "ragged and discontinuous." In all, the line ran nearly a mile and a half due eastward from the bluff overlooking the Mississippi River, below which the Valley Road ran, to where the high ground met another defile that could shield the line as it turned southward.[53]

On this Mint Spring Bayou line, Fort Hill anchored the extreme left of the Confederate defenses high atop the bluffs overlooking both the Mississippi River to the west and Mint Spring Bayou to the north. In that position, it effectively controlled entrance and exit along the Valley Road, although it was far too high to be made into one of the major river-controlling batteries.[54]

The defiles that ended the fortification line running eastward consisted of the upper reaches of Glass Bayou, which ran parallel with Mint Spring Bayou just a mile or so to its south. In fact, the lowlands of Glass Bayou and its feeder branches formed the southern boundaries of the ridge on which Lockett's initial line ran along Mint Spring Bayou. The ridge that ran eastward between Mint Spring and Glass Bayous came to a halt a mile and a half inland because of a tributary of Glass Bayou that branched off the east-west watershed and ran north and south. The uppermost reaches of this tributary began on a narrow ridge that separated it from Mint Spring Bayou to the north, and it was along this ridge separating the Mint Spring and Glass Bayou watersheds that the Graveyard Road ran.[55]

At this point the ridge narrowed precipitously, actually only about the width of the Graveyard Road itself. There, Lockett located a major system of fortifications collectively known as the Stockade Redan. The redan itself, a V-shaped work with the apex pointed eastward along the road toward any enemy that might approach, was a formidable work itself, but it also had flanking fortifications protecting such a salient in the line. Because the Confederate works made basically a ninety-degree turn to the south at this point, it would be easily enfiladed and needed more elaborate aid on the flanks. Thus, Lockett positioned a lunette, or a crescent-shaped fortification, to the west of the main redan, across the Graveyard Road. To the south, on the redan's right flank, Lockett placed another smaller redan. It was hoped that these side works, major fortifications in and of themselves, would deflect any major activity on the Stockade Redan itself. The main redan, and consequently the entire complex itself, became known as the Stockade Redan because of a seven- or eight-foot-high stockade wall positioned across the roadway between the main redan and the lunette to the west. Workers had dug a trench and placed tree trunks side by side for some 100 yards.[56]

Because of the north-south shield provided by this tributary of Glass Bayou, Lockett turned the fortifications here and began to run the line due south. It followed just west of the tributary of Glass Bayou but had to cross that major watershed at some point. Once across, the line followed other smaller north-south tributaries south of Glass Bayou, actually all the way southward toward their beginning points on another tall ridge separating the Glass Bayou watershed from a much larger system of adjoining creeks to the south. It was on this high ridge separating the Glass Bayou and Durden Creek watersheds that the Jackson Road ran into Vicksburg.[57]

Lockett positioned two major works along this ridge, one on either side of the Jackson Road, obviously indicating its importance as an avenue into the city. On the northern side of the road on the highest ground in the county, Lockett constructed a redan (eventually to be known by its defending regiment, the 3rd Louisiana Redan although Federals referred to it mostly as Fort Hill) to command the roadway. On the south side of the road he fashioned a redoubt, or a multisided fortification with an open rear. Because of its immense size, actually containing three different works connected together and so being the largest work on the Confederate line, it gained the name Great Redoubt.[58]

Once south of the Jackson Road, Lockett found placing a continuous line much more difficult. Hennessey's Bayou dominated the area to the south, although its tributaries of Stout's and Hatcher's Bayous and Durden Creek actually created the topographical ridges that could be fortified. In fact, Hatcher's Bayou curved far to the south and east of the fortifications, but the upper reaches of one of its tributaries actually provided a shielding effect for the Confederate line just south of the Jackson Road. The more important creek system was Durden Creek farther south, which flowed in many branches southward toward their combination into one channel and thence into Hatcher's Bayou. No less that five branches of Durden Creek began on a high ridge running northeast to southwest from the Jackson Road high ground south of Glass Bayou. Although the branches of Durden Creek did not run necessarily parallel with the ridge, instead affording high ground that branched off the main ridge like fingers from a hand, the series of five branches effectively provided a maze of hills and valleys that any approaching army would find problematic. In that case, Durden Creek effectively shielded much of the Confederate line from the Jackson Road ridge down across another major road, the Baldwin's Ferry Road, as well as the railroad, to another high ridge that separated the Durden Creek watershed from the next major system to the southwest, the main channel of Hennessey's Bayou. It was on this ridge between Durden Creek and Hennessey's Bayou that the Hall's Ferry Road ran southeastward, and Brigadier General Stephen D. Lee later correctly explained to a Federal, "We had the only line of continuous hills from the river above to the river below; we had fortified it with the greatest military skill; while to you were left the spurs and the hollows."[59]

Several important bastions rose in the expanse between the Jackson Road and Hall's Ferry Road, all of the line fronting more or less Durden Creek's feeder branches. From the major complexes on the Jackson Road, the fortification line continued southward nearly another mile to the Baldwin's Ferry Road, where Lockett fashioned a lunette (also eventually known by its defenders, the 2nd Texas Lunette) to block that roadway. In the intervening area, the line fronted the declivities of numerous headwaters of branches of Durden Creek, most of them flowing away from the line but affording undulating ground that would cause hardships to any attacking force. Just a short distance south of the lunette on the Baldwin's Ferry Road was the railroad, and Lockett positioned another redoubt (logically known as the Railroad Redoubt) to cover that thoroughfare. The large, elongated redoubt sat on the south side of the railroad atop a high bank fronting one of the branches of Durden Creek.[60]

A little over three thousand feet to the southwest sat the enclosed Square Fort, the only major fortification not on a transportation thoroughfare. It sat on another salient of the line, essentially where the Confederate works turned from a southerly to a southwesterly direction. Thus, as at the Stockade Redan, a major work was needed to hold that vulnerable position. Nearly a mile southwest of Square Fort was the Hall's Ferry Road atop the ridge running between the Durden Creek watershed and the upper reaches of Hennessey's Bayou. There, Lockett placed another elongated redoubt, this time stuck out from the line to cover a slight depression in the fortification line. Situated primarily on the north side of the roadway, this "Salient Work" covered the major concern area in the south.[61]

From the Hall's Ferry Road ridge, the ground again dropped off into Hennessey's Bayou feeder branches, one of which effectively shielded the Confederate line as it turned more southwestward. Soon, the line topped another high ridge separating Hennessey's and Stout's Bayous, Stout's being one of the major problem areas. The bayou ran due southward into Hennessey's Bayou, and it crossed the Confederate line at more of a perpendicular angle rather than shielding it in parallel fashion, as Lockett was able to do in the other areas. But the bayou had to be crossed, the bayou and valley then forming the rear slope of the ridge on which the fortifications sat. From there, the fortifications ascended the high ridge separating Stout's Bayou and the Mississippi River, on which the Warrenton Road ran. There was no good way to cross Stout's Bayou, so Lockett simply ran the line perpendicular across it, reaching eventually to the bluff overlooking the river south of Vicksburg. There, Lockett positioned the final fortification, South Fort, a redoubt that sat on the bluff and commanded the Warrenton Road a little to its east. It was there that, a little over seven miles in length, the major Confederate fortifications ringing Vicksburg ended. If the works added from South Fort northward along the bluffs of the river were added, the length of the line managed some eight miles in total.[62]

One Federal later noted that "Vicksburg is one continued pile of hills, and on every hill a fort." Each of the major bastions was a large, thick, and powerful fortification, complete with embrasures for cannon and steps for infantry. The walls were two or three feet thick, with large ditches some ten or so feet deep and wide in front of each except the redan north of the Jackson Road. Lockett also interspersed other smaller batteries capable of holding artillery between the major works, covering swells and other dangerous points of attack. Simple rifle pits of several feet in depth with steps for the infantry covered most of the rest of the line, although these were the least priority and often lagged behind the other more formidable works. These defenses atop steep ridges and ravines ("so steep," one soldier described, "that their ascent was difficult to a footman unless he aided himself with his hands") made the task of attacking the city, even if Federals could get to it, even more difficult. In addition to what one soldier described as the "intricate net-work of ravines and ridges, the latter everywhere sharp, and the former only having level bottoms when their streams become some size," workers also cut down trees along the lines to open fields of fire, and at many points abatis loomed in front as well. "The heavy timber is being cut down half mile wide," one Louisianan wrote, "[to] barricade the Yankees and entrenchments with breast works, batteries, &c, fast making for our protection, and security of Vicksburg." The wily Confederates also strung telegraph wire to trip up any attacking Federals, causing one observer to note that such artificial barriers "under fire were absolutely impassable." A different engineer described the combined effect as "rather an intrenched camp than a fortified place, owing much of its strength to the difficult ground, obstructed by fallen trees in its front, which rendered rapidity of movement and *ensemble* in an instant impossible."[63]

Vicksburg was an entrenched camp to be sure. As the work continued on through October and November 1862, mostly by slaves, the troops who were subjected to more drilling than work began to move inside the line of fortifications to build winter quarters, mostly wood huts. "The works of defense are progressing here very rapidly for the past month," one Louisianan wrote in his diary in mid-November. "With the advantages that nature gives us, this place can certainly be made very strong."[64]

It was indeed a formidable line, and the Confederates intended to fight, one Louisianan declaring, "I think our Generals wood see these hills running down with blood before they will give it up." But it had to be. Despite one Alabamian declaring in mid-April that "it is very probable that we will go to Tennessee soon. The yanks have left here," the Federals under one of their most determined generals would soon test their strength, although just getting to the point where they could attack these Vicksburg defenses would prove every bit as troublesome as the defenses themselves.[65]

2

"The Accomplishment of This One Object"

If there is a name synonymous with Vicksburg, it is not Jefferson Davis, Joseph E. Johnston, or even John C. Pemberton. Rather, it is Ulysses S. Grant. What he did there was nothing short of remarkable, and it placed the general in the pantheon of all-time great commanders. His dogged determination won for him Fort Donelson and Shiloh, his calm demeanor won for him Chattanooga, and his grand strategy won for him the Overland Campaign and the war. But if there was a campaign that compares with some of the greatest in all of history it is Vicksburg. Henry Halleck—no fan of Grant but certainly a student of military history—perhaps said it best when he congratulated Grant on the operation at its conclusion: "In boldness of plan, rapidity of execution, and brilliancy of results, these operations will compare most favorably with those of Napoleon about Ulm."[1]

But Grant had to learn patience before he could make such a bold statement on history's canvas. In fact, just getting to a command level to make his own decisions was problematic in the early days of the war. Had it been up to Grant, he would have continued the movement southward upon the capture of Corinth in May 1862. Grant was not in command, of course, Henry Halleck was, and he believed in a Jominian policy of consolidating gains rather than boldly pushing onward on all fronts. Accordingly, Halleck dispersed his armies east and west to hold the newly acquired territory rather than diving off down into Mississippi to conquer once and for all the final stretch of the Mississippi Valley. For Grant's part, he almost did not survive this period, seriously contemplating going home in disgust.[2]

Fortunately for his military (and political) career as well as for the United States as a whole, Grant stuck it out and remained with the army. Still, he was not able to make decisions on strategy for quite a while. The chance for elevation could have come when Lincoln called Halleck to Washington in July. Grant was the second-ranking general in the west and should by all rights have inherited Halleck's command of the entire western theater. But Halleck still did not trust Grant to oversee such a large command, evidently thinking only he himself was so capable. Consequently, Halleck split up the department into subdistricts and gave Grant, Major General Don Carlos Buell, and others equal areas within the former large whole. Halleck planned to coordinate all of his subordinates' moves from Washington, and thus no one was in total charge and there was no unity of command. "When General Halleck left to assume the duties of general-in-chief," Grant later wrote, "I remained in command of the district of West Tennessee. Practically I became a department commander, but no one was assigned to that position over me and I made my reports direct to the general-in-chief; but I was not assigned to the position of department commander."[3]

The Confederates' fall invasions across an eight-hundred-mile front from Maryland to Kentucky to West Tennessee showed the lack of wisdom in Halleck's command structure. With so much going on, Halleck soon realized he could not see to it all and finally, grudgingly, gave the permission for Grant to take semiautonomous control of his department, to command as he saw fit with only larger strategic oversight from Washington. "In compliance with General Orders, No. 159, Adjutant General's Office, War Department," Grant wrote on October 25, "the undersigned hereby assumes command of the Department of the Tennessee." It was a major decision that produced major ramifications. "This was a great relief," Grant later wrote, "after the two and a half months of continued defense over a large district of country, and where nearly every citizen was an enemy ready to give information of our every move." In fact, after taking full command, Grant took all of one day to order an advance southward toward Vicksburg.[4]

Ordering an advance was the easy part, and Grant soon found just how difficult it was to even approach the place. For the next six long months, Grant tried his best to find a way to solve the riddle that was Vicksburg. Attempt after attempt went forward only to meet unfavorable terrain, Confederate defenses, or both. And that was just to get to Vicksburg; most of Grant's first six and a half months of operations were pointed simply at just getting to a place where he could approach Vicksburg. Then, of course, the attack on Vicksburg's actual defenses had to be made. By the time that occurred, Grant had encircled Vicksburg with outlying operations to the north, south, east, and west. At one time or another, he had portions of his army at all compass points from Vicksburg, but was no closer to actually attacking the city than before.[5]

In the six months after major operations against an extremely defensible Vicksburg began, Grant tried six major attempts to reach the city between October 1862 and April 1863. All ended in failure as a result of geographical restrictions and Confederate resistance. The main impediment was the huge Delta that stretched far inland from the Mississippi River between Vicksburg and Memphis. It was a natural barrier to any approach to Vicksburg from the north, and Grant soon found just what an obstacle it was. In fact, its presence was why Grant first attempted to reach the Vicksburg vicinity by traversing the hilly area east of the Delta in central Mississippi, the same area where the railroad companies, for obvious reasons, had built their rail lines.[6]

Grant moved southward along the Mississippi Central Railroad in November and reached Oxford by early December with advance elements as far south as Coffeeville, nearer to the Yalobusha River and the main Confederate defensive line then at Grenada. He had high hopes of moving through central Mississippi toward Jackson, where he would reach the area east of Vicksburg that was the best avenue of approach toward the city. Importantly, this plan had logistical support as required by the chief military thinkers of the day, mainly through the Mississippi Central Railroad. "I go forward with the advance; will push on to Grenada if possible, opening railroad and telegraph as we advance," Grant wrote at the outset. He indeed had the rail line rebuilt as he moved ever so slowly southward through the wet winter weather in northern Mississippi.[7]

Unfortunately for the Federals, a couple of cavalry raids in their rear completely disrupted this advance and caused Grant to withdraw back to West Tennessee. Earl Van Dorn led a cavalry raid northward from Grenada and captured Grant's supply depot at Holly Springs on December 20, completely destroying the huge Federal stockpile of food and ammunition. Meanwhile, another raid under Brigadier General Nathan Bedford Forrest crossed the Tennessee River from Middle Tennessee and moved westward toward the critical railroads supplying Grant's army. Forrest destroyed the important Mobile and Ohio Railroad bridges over the Obion River forks in late December and then sped away, although he was almost caught at Parker's Crossroads later on. He escaped, but the dual blow to Grant's communications and supply line caused him to recall his forces and move back northward, living off the land for what the troops needed in foodstuffs. It was not all disaster, however, as Grant learned an army could live off the land in many ways: "Our loss of supplies was great at Holly Springs, but it was more than compensated for by those taken from the country and by the lesson taught." He would put that lesson to good use in the future.[8]

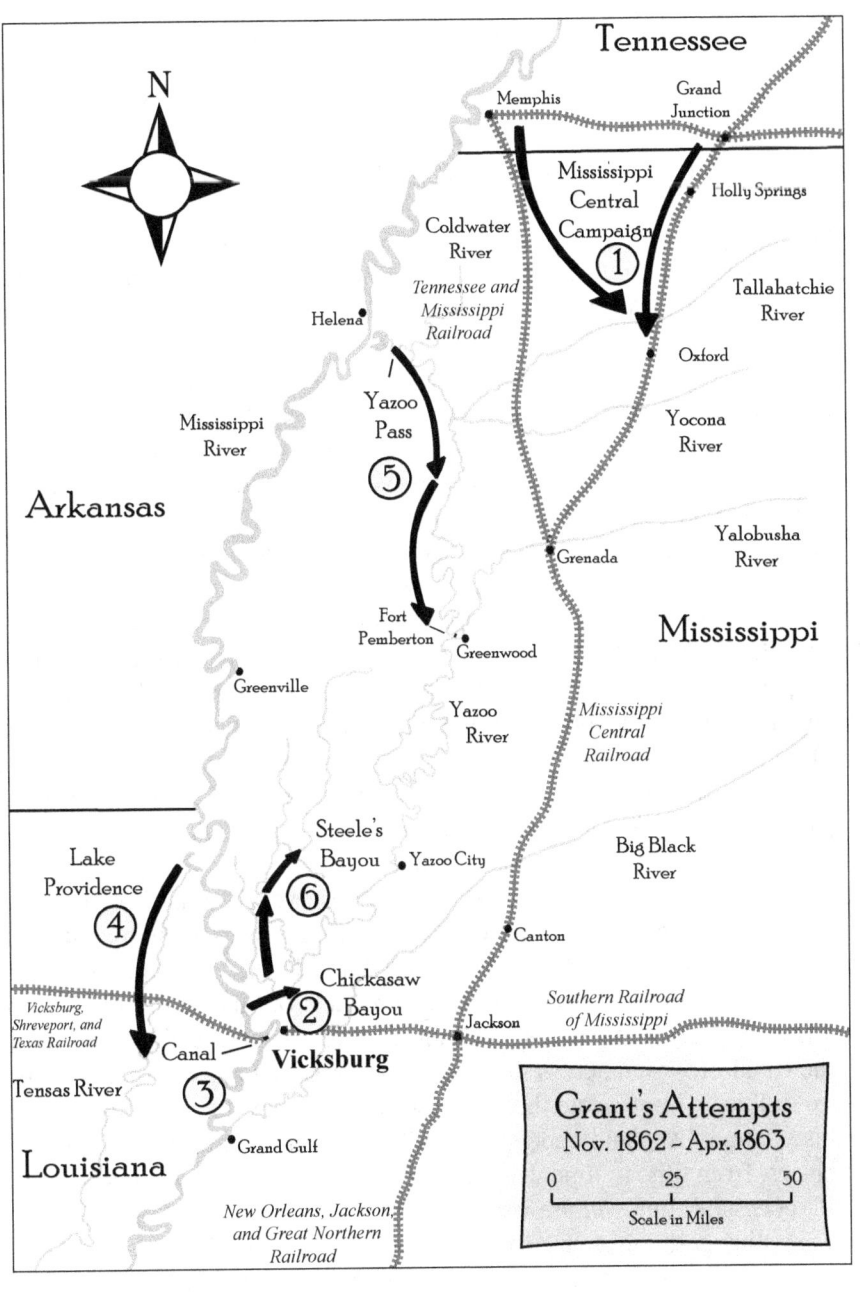

While raiders attacking supply routes turned back Grant's thrust through the hills east of the Delta, another prong of the advance saw more death and destruction. Grant had split his advance in December, sending his favored subordinate Major General William T. Sherman down the Mississippi River itself with four divisions of infantry to attack Vicksburg. As almost anyone would, Sherman divined that the best way to approach the city and its almost impregnable western bluffs was by moving up the Yazoo River north of Vicksburg and gaining the high ground to its northeast. Sherman landed his troops in late December and then on December 29 attacked toward the steep hills Lockett had fortified, only to find out personally just how difficult getting to Vicksburg really was. "I reached Vicksburg at the time appointed, landed, assaulted, and failed. Re-embarked my command unopposed," he tersely reported. His troops suffered severe casualties in the process, adding to the bloody winter the Federal armies were enduring as a result of Fredericksburg and Stones River.[9]

After deciding, for political reasons as much as anything else, to make his advance to Vicksburg a one-avenue approach along the Mississippi River in January, Grant came down himself and established headquarters at Milliken's Bend, on the Louisiana side of the river just north of the city. There, he dispersed his corps in more attempts to either bypass Vicksburg or reach the high ground north and east of the city that Sherman had failed to capture in December. One of Grant's first attempts was to change the course of the river at Vicksburg by renewing work on the canal across the base of the loop, bypassing the city and allowing river traffic to pass without having to run through the gauntlet of Confederate batteries. It was certainly a possibility, as the river itself had changed courses many times over thousands of years, the many oxbow lakes surrounding it testament to the ever-changing nature of the river's winding path.ABraham Lincoln himself was especially interested in this effort, as he had witnessed such products of change during his trips on the river. Halleck telegraphed Grant to "direct your attention particularly to the canal proposed across the point. The President attaches much importance to this." Grant wrote that "Mr. Lincoln had navigated the Mississippi in his younger days and understood well its tendency to change its channel, in places, from time to time. He set much store accordingly by this canal."[10]

If successful, this venture would offer Grant a clear way to get gunboats and supplies past Vicksburg for other operations. While it was not an end-all prospect, it was a start, and why would the river not change course with massive human nudging when it had done the same thing so many times on its own accord? Grant wanted the effort "prosecuted day and night until its completion," he ordered. "I am pushing everything to gain a passage, avoiding Vicksburg," he wrote Halleck.[11]

It was not to be. In the high water of January and February 1863, Grant's soldiers could not keep water out of the canal long enough to continue digging. Dams holding the water back broke, causing the workers to toil in mud and water while digging and cutting stumps. The corps commander working on the project, Major General John A. McClernand, reported that "the water flows 3 feet deep in the canal, but gives no evidence of diverting the channel of the river." Sherman was more to the point: "Our canal here don't amount to much. It is full of water, but manifests no disposition to change the channel. It is a very small affair, and we can hardly work a barge through it for stumps." Engineers brought in heavy numbers of former slaves, known as contrabands, as well as heavy machinery in the form of steam dredges, but the task proved too difficult. Grant soon decided that "the task was much more Herculean than it at first appeared, and was made much more so by the almost continuous rains that fell during the whole of the time this work was prosecuted. The river, too, continued to rise and made a large expenditure of labor necessary to keep the water out of our camps and the canal."[12]

While the canal faltered—this third attempt being swamped literally by the rising river—Grant decided to use the mounting waters to his advantage and began work on another roundabout project west of the river. "By inquiry I learn that Lake Providence, which connects with Red River through Tensas Bayou, Washita and Black Rivers, is a wide and navigable way through," Grant wrote. "As some advantage may be gained by opening this [waterway], I have ordered a brigade of troops to be detailed for the purpose, and to be embarked as soon as possible."[13]

This Lake Providence route far west of Vicksburg was likewise not an end-all solution, but it could potentially afford Grant the opportunity to get steamboats and perhaps light gunboats past Vicksburg without having to run the vicious batteries. It might also allow for supplies to be taken safely through the area in case he chose to operate the army south of Vicksburg. "With this open," Grant wrote, "a vast foraging district would be opened, and our gunboats of light draft would be enabled to cut off the enemy's commerce with the west bank of the river. I have determined to make the experiment, at all events." Reports from Sherman buoyed his determination, Sherman telling him, "I have hastily read the reports of the Lake Providence scheme. It is admirable and most worthy a determined prosecution. Cover up the design all you can, and it will fulfill all the conditions of the great problem."[14]

Grant had high hopes for this project too, writing "this bids fair to be the most practicable route for turning Vicksburg," and adding, "by a little digging, less than one-quarter that had been done across the point before Vicksburg, will connect the Mississippi and lake, and in all probability will wash a channel in a short time." Yet this experiment too was destined for failure. The river began to fall after a couple of months of work, which also made the water level in the various bayous and creeks on the Lake Providence route fall. Soon, only small steamers could get through, and Grant had pitiful few of them. "I let the work go on," Grant nevertheless wrote, "believing employment was better than idleness for the men."[15]

Grant was ultimately fine with leaving his pet project through Lake Providence, his fourth attempt, because he was soon consumed with two more ideas, this time both east of the Mississippi River. With all the high water early on, Grant attempted to move through the Delta's many bayous and rivers to reach high ground north and east of Vicksburg. East of the Mississippi River, Grant's subordinates tried to bypass the Confederate fortifications at Snyder's and Haynes' Bluffs near the mouth of the Yazoo River by reaching the headwaters of that river far to the north, which would, Grant wrote, "enable us to get high ground above Haynes' Bluff, and would turn all the enemy's river batteries." Consequently, in what became known as the Yazoo Pass Expedition, transports cut across Moon Lake and Yazoo Pass and reached the major rivers of the Delta. An infantry division moved down the Coldwater River to the Tallahatchie, and thence down that river toward the Yalobusha, where both rivers formed the Yazoo at Greenwood.[16]

The Confederates knew that the upper reaches of the Yazoo had to be defended; this route, after all, had long been used, before the erection of levees along the Mississippi River, by Delta planters to get their cotton to market without making the long, circuitous trip down to the mouth of the Yazoo. The Confederates accordingly built a fort using cotton bales on the Tallahatchie River near Greenwood, and the Federals were stopped when they reached this point. Water let into the Delta to fill Yazoo Pass and the other streams also filled the bottomland, and only Fort Pemberton, as it was called, stuck out of the water on a bit of high ground. The Federals had no place to land troops as a result, and the navy's ironclads accompanying the expedition could not silence the fort's guns. "They were at Greenwood," Grant informed a comrade glumly of the last he had heard of the expedition, "on the Yazoo, a fortified place, and had abandoned all idea of getting past until they could receive additional ordnance stores." Another attempt was a failure, but Grant was not giving up.[17]

A sixth effort was by this time also going forward. Known as the Steele's Bayou operation, Federal forces steamed up Steele's Bayou near the mouth of the Yazoo River but below the defending Confederate guns. From there, they moved through a series of bayous and creeks such as Black Bayou, Deer Creek, and Rolling Fork, and hoped to exit into the Yazoo River above the Confederate defenses via the Sunflower River. Admiral Porter explored the possibilities and recommended Grant try it out; he did so "with a view of effecting a landing with troops on high ground on the east bank of the Yazoo, from which to act against Haynes' Bluff." Grant was extremely excited at the possibility "to get all our forces in one place, and . . . [a] firm foothold . . . secured on the side with the enemy."[18]

The Union forces continually moved forward, the narrow streams causing all sorts of problems. Grant wrote that the ironclads "ploughed their way through without other damage than to their appearance. The transports did not fare so well." More trouble emerged as the Federals moved onward, and as in all the other attempts, Grant's forces met defeat and this time almost disaster. The maze of interconnecting rivers, bayous, and creeks became painfully narrow as the Union navy plodded along and the slower Federal infantry followed behind. The wily Confederates cut trees in front of the Union boats and then began to do the same behind them, very nearly trapping the Federal gunboats in the narrow streams. Only with Herculean efforts did the infantry save the navy, soldiers running throughout the night to reach the flotilla, which was manned as if to repel a pirate attack. Admiral Porter was able to back his boats out but did not recommend any more such roundabout routes for Grant's consideration.[19]

Six attempts and six months into the Vicksburg Campaign, Grant was no closer to approaching, much less taking, Vicksburg than when he started. The outermost portions of Lockett's fortifications, ably aided by fortuitous terrain, had kept Vicksburg safe and sound. And the inner line had not even been so much as sighted by the Federals.

Perhaps because of the close call on the Steele's Bayou operation, Grant decided he would make no more such attempts. Obviously, as in the case of Steele's Bayou, they could produce more negative results than a simple failure to reach Vicksburg. Yet in reality, most of the six attempts had been fairly conservative and safe efforts to get to Vicksburg, the near debacle of Steele's Bayou notwithstanding. Grant had prodded and poked around with small numbers; none of the efforts ever put a large command, much less the entire army, in grave danger. The result was that none of them worked, either.

Accordingly, Grant began to see that heavier lifting was needed and, perhaps, a greater willingness to gamble with the army. Obviously, none of the small efforts had netted anything, and Grant was running out of options. In a moment of gravity, he even decided that the only possible recourse was to assault again against Lockett's outer works along the steep bluffs on the Yazoo River that Sherman had found so difficult back in December. He went to see the lay of the land again, but instead of choosing where to launch the assault, he made up his mind that it was just not possible. "After the reconnaissance of yesterday," he wrote, "I am satisfied that an attack upon Haynes' Bluff would be attended with immense sacrifice of life, if not with defeat."[20]

Grant reverted back to his original ideas, which he had craftily kept to himself all along. The general later said that he had been thinking of a southward move throughout "the whole winter," adding that because it "could not be undertaken until the waters receded[,] . . . I did not therefore communicate this plan, even to an officer of my staff, until it was necessary to make preparations for the start." Thinking that gaining the high ground east of Vicksburg could actually be done easiest from the south, Grant began to prepare for a truly risky campaign: throwing his entire army on a march southward west of the Mississippi River, crossing that river south of Lockett's outlying fortifications, and maneuvering northward to reach the hills east of Vicksburg. It was a gamble, to be sure. It included the march southward through Louisiana; the navy running the Vicksburg batteries because no other way southward on the river could be found; crossing the army in the face of the enemy; and finally moving northward with a tenuous (at best) supply line that extended back to the river south of Vicksburg, across it, and along the western side to Milliken's Bend. In these plans, Grant was breaking every rule of warfare in the book.[21]

Consequently, without any other recourse and under immense pressure politically not to withdraw from Vicksburg, Grant made one of the truly major decisions of the conflict, what Bruce Catton described as "one of the two or three important decisions of the Civil War." Grant took his army southward through Louisiana west of Vicksburg, then to the Mississippi River at Hard Times Landing south of the city. He asked Admiral Porter to move south past Vicksburg's batteries on April 16 and again with additional vessels on April 22. Partially manned by infantry volunteers, Porter's boats passed Lockett's river defenses with only minimal damage and then attacked Grand Gulf, where Grant intended to cross, on April 29. Porter found the Confederate guns there too strong to carry, and Grant sent the army and the flotilla farther southward to Disharoon's Plantation for a landing even farther south. By April 30, he was ready, with Federal troops crammed onboard the transports ready to cross to Bruinsburg at first light. Significantly, this was well south of Lockett's outer fortifications, which extended only as far as the Warrenton area.[22]

If Grant was going to make it through this gamble of gambles, he had to have a little help. If the Confederates were watching and ready, they would be there to meet those first Federals as they stepped off the steamboats at Bruinsburg, likely turning them back. Grant would be facing a major problem then, with the army spread out and the navy condemned to operations south of Vicksburg. But if the enemy was not vigilant and watchful and had no defenders at Bruinsburg, and even better yet where the road to Port Gibson rose out of the river valley and up onto the high ground, then Grant's gamble would likely be successful, at least in making an initial lodgment in Mississippi. It all depended on what Grant found when dawn on April 30 came and the first Federals approached the Mississippi shore. As Providence would have it, Abraham Lincoln had declared months before that this very day was to be "a day of national humiliation, fasting, and prayer."[23]

To keep the Confederates from being vigilant and watchful, and hopefully to keep them from having troops on site, Grant needed their attention turned elsewhere. This could only be achieved through the use of feints and diversions at other points, most opportunely north and east of Vicksburg, exactly in the opposite direction from his ongoing operations south and west of the city. Thus, at the very moment he peered across the river, he had several diversions either just concluded or still in process, including a major raid by Colonel Benjamin H. Grierson. And it all worked perfectly. Confederate commander John C. Pemberton was totally fixated for some five days on Grierson's trek through Mississippi at the exact time Grant was preparing and crossing the river.[24]

A big part of the gamble had succeeded, but Grant was still miles from Vicksburg and would likely have to fight his way inland to even approach the city. And then, Lockett's strong defenses themselves still loomed ahead.

Ulysses S. Grant crossed his Army of the Tennessee thirty-five airline miles (many more in winding river miles) south of Vicksburg. One of his soldiers commented at the time that they were "way down here in 'Dixie.'" Handily outflanking even Lockett's outlying defenses as far south as Warrenton and even the detached and earlier-constructed works at Grand Gulf, Grant faced no opposition as he crossed five divisions on April 30 and May 1. "The move by Bruinsburg undoubtedly took the enemy much by surprise," Grant later crowed. He was also easily able to march inland to the high ground above the

Mississippi Valley floodplain: "I deemed it a matter of vast importance that the highlands should be reached without resistance." It was the high ground that he had desired for so long, but not exactly where he had first envisioned beginning the movement against Vicksburg. Even if he was many miles from his original landing point, at least he was there now. "Once landed on the other side of the river I expect but little trouble," he had written earlier, even going so far as to state that "I feel that the battle is now more than half won." He elaborated on his feelings many years later in his memoirs: "When this [maneuver] was effected I felt a degree of relief scarcely ever equaled since. Vicksburg was not yet taken it is true, nor were its defenders demoralized by any of our previous moves. I was now in the enemy's country, with a vast river and the stronghold of Vicksburg between me and my base of supplies. But I was on dry ground on the same side of the river with the enemy. All the campaigns, labors, hardships and exposures from the month of December previous to this time that had been made and endured, were for the accomplishment of this one object."[25]

Success often breeds additional decisions, and the main question Grant faced once he landed was what to do now? The first order of business, over and above defeating any Confederates who opposed him, was to get across the formidable Bayou Pierre. Because of the change of plan from a landing at Grand Gulf to one at Bruinsburg, that placed him south of the bayou as well as Grand Gulf itself. Grant had to get across the barrier and hopefully take Grand Gulf, where supplies could begin to roll in much more easily than if carried south of Bayou Pierre. Yet doing so was more troublesome than he wanted, as the Confederates soon appeared and the terrain was anything but hospitable; it was, Grant later stated, "the most broken country I ever saw. The whole country is a series of irregular ridges, divided by deep and impassable ravines, grown up with heavy timber, undergrowth, and cane."[26]

The first resistance to Grant's inland move developed during the night of April 30 around the A. K. Shaifer house southwest of Port Gibson, still well south of Bayou Pierre. As the morning came, McClernand moved forward, only to face stiffer resistance. McClernand deployed three divisions on the main road to Port Gibson while sending another along a farm road toward another major road to the north nearer Bayou Pierre. Confederate forces appeared on both roads but were pushed back as Grant brought up more divisions, including soldiers from the next corps to cross, Major General James B. McPherson's. Throughout the day on May 1, McClernand pushed Confederates under Brigadier General John S. Bowen back toward the town until they finally broke and fled across Bayou Pierre, one Ohioan writing home that they gave the Confederates "a good thrashing." Grant took the town and

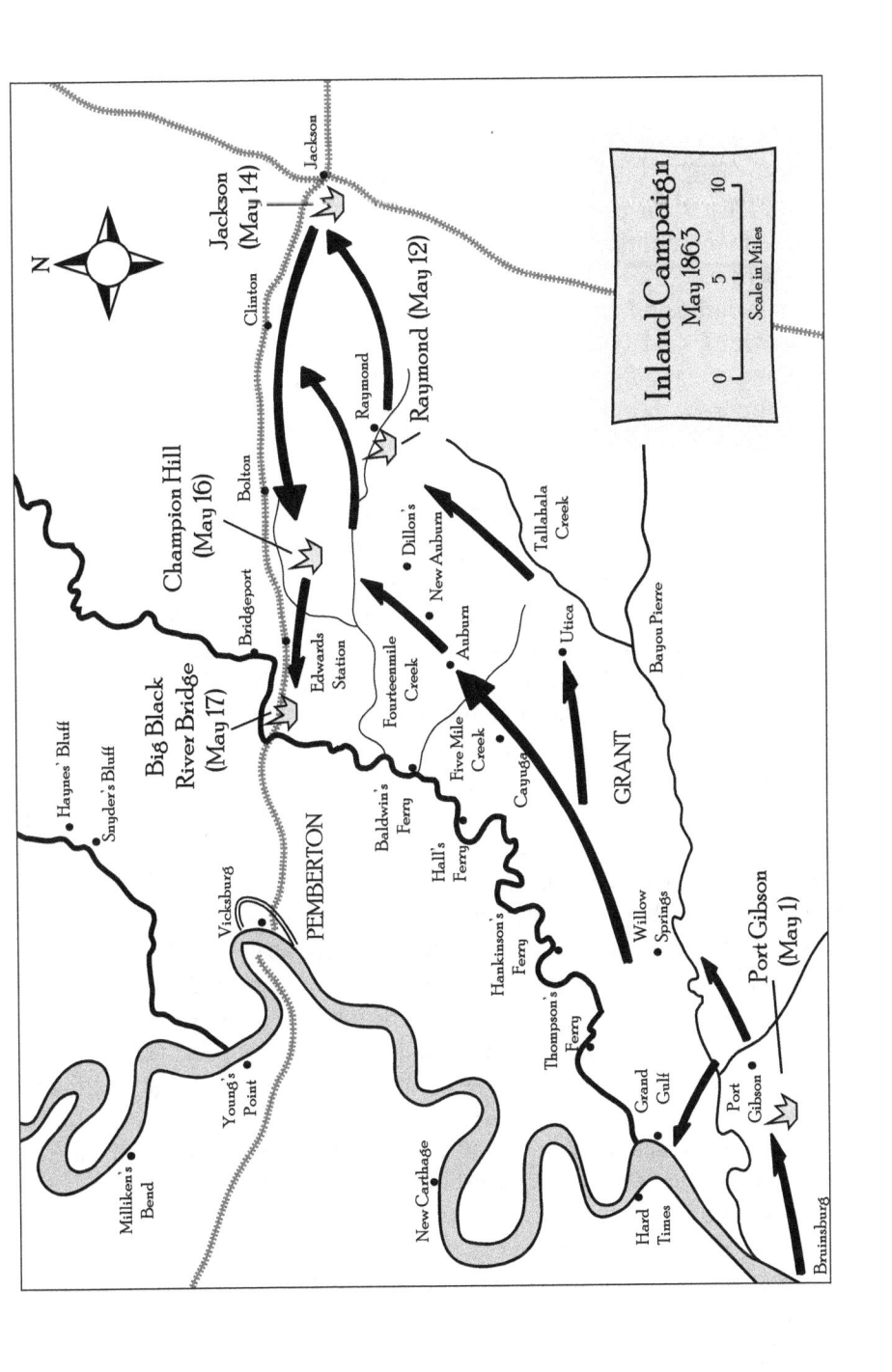

more importantly several crossing points on the bayous, which by that point had split into big and little branches.²⁷

Grant was elated but not satisfied. In the next several days, he crossed the army over Bayou Pierre but stopped forward progress while he went after bigger game. In this case it was Grand Gulf itself, which the Confederates had evacuated once Grant had it outflanked. Grant himself soon rode to the place and met Admiral Porter there. Supplies then began to flow much better than before. "Possession of Grand Gulf too I look upon as virtual possession of Vicksburg and Port Hudson and the entire Mississippi River," he argued. Now with Grand Gulf in his hands and his army spread eastward toward Willow Springs, Grant continued the halt to allow rearward units to catch up. Other troops of McPherson's corps soon crossed, as did divisions of William T. Sherman's corps following along. Some of that corps had served as a diversion north of Vicksburg, the troops landing at the same place where they had been defeated back in December. This attempt to confront Lockett's works near Chickasaw Bayou was merely a feint, however, the main movement going on south of Bayou Pierre where no defenses stood.²⁸

By May 7, Grant was ready to resume his advance, but it was fraught with danger. He was supposed to stop once across the river and fortify, sending troops southward to support Major General Nathaniel Banks and his operations against Port Hudson before trying to tackle Vicksburg by himself. Having experienced the success he had, however, he saw no way to stop: "Meeting the enemy . . . as I did south of Port Gibson, I followed him to the Big Black, and could not afford to retrace my steps." He knew he would take criticism if he judged wrong, but he was willing to take that chance. "I knew well that Halleck's caution would lead him to disapprove of this course," Grant thought, "but it was the only one that gave any chance of success." He also added that "the time it would take to communicate with Washington and get a reply would be so great that I could not be interfered with until it was demonstrated whether my plan was practicable." He continued, "I remember how anxiously I counted the time I had to spare before that response could come," and he came to the conclusion that "you can do a great deal in eight days."²⁹

Deciding to seek forgiveness rather than permission, Grant so informed his superiors and set out, writing Washington: "I shall not bring my troops into this place [Grand Gulf], but [will] immediately follow the enemy, and, if all promises as favorable hereafter as it does now, not stop until Vicksburg is in our possession." He also alerted his army: "A few days continuance of the same zeal and constancy will secure to this army the crowning victory over the rebellion. More difficulties and privations are before us. Let us endure them manfully. Other battles are to be fought. Let us fight them bravely. A grateful country will rejoice at our success, and history will record it with immortal honor."[30]

Once again success bred the need for more critical decisions. The next major barrier between Grant and Vicksburg was the Big Black River, which angled northeastward from its mouth south of Vicksburg. Grant had options at this point, but he still had to make the right decisions in the attempt to just reach the city so he could then concentrate on capturing it. One option was to dive right across the Big Black River at Hankinson's Ferry or Hall's Ferry, but that option seemed fraught with problems. Grant would sacrifice the ability to maneuver if he did that, as he would be caught in the narrow triangle of land between the Big Black and Mississippi Rivers. That triangle would expand as he moved northward toward Warrenton and eventually Vicksburg, as the Big Black River gradually angled away from the Mississippi River. Still, he would nevertheless be hemmed in with the Confederate defenders of Vicksburg squarely atop the inverted triangle even if they chose to come out of their vast fortifications ringing Vicksburg. "The broken nature of the ground would have enabled him to hold a strong defensible line from the river south of the city to the Big Black," Grant explained, "retaining possession of the railroad back to that point."[31]

A better option was to move northeastward on the east side of the Big Black River, allowing it to shield Grant's left flank from the Confederate army defending Vicksburg. Such an option would let Grant move in relative safety, unless Pemberton chose to come out of Lockett's works and meet him in battle east of the Big Black. Whether he did so was irrelevant to the other positive ramification that would come from such a move, namely getting astride the Southern Railroad of Mississippi, the one and only outside link Vicksburg had with the rest of the Confederacy. If Grant could move northeastward east of the Big Black and cut the railroad between Vicksburg and Jackson, he would have Vicksburg isolated. He only had to watch and make sure no threat came from the Jackson area to the east, but it was assumed that the Confederates would put most of their combat potential into securing Vicksburg itself. Sherman picked right up on the logical decision, writing just after he crossed the river that "the enemy has escaped across Big Black River, and Grant will now probably strike in the direction of the Jackson Railroad."[32]

Grant chose the second option as he moved forward along what McPherson described as "the divide between Big Black and north fork of Bayou Pierre." One of his soldiers wrote home that "after them we went full clip." Grant noted that "it was my intention here to hug the Big Black River as closely as possible," but he soon found even that plan was not as safe as he had thought.

For one thing, the farther he moved from Grand Gulf, the more delicate his supply line became. He had cut away from a traditional line of supply, instead relying on wagon trains guarded by large numbers of troops moving to the front. He planned to "disregard his base and depend on the country for meat and even for bread. Beef-cattle and corn are both abundant everywhere." Grant had learned this could be done in north Mississippi and later admitted: "Had I known [in north Mississippi] the demoralized condition of the enemy, or the fact that central Mississippi abounded so in all army supplies, I would have been in pursuit of Pemberton while his cavalry was destroying the roads in my rear." He later bragged that "we started from Bruinsburg with an average of about two days' rations, and received no more from our own supplies for some days. Abundance was found in the mean time. Some corn meal, bacon, and vegetables were found, and an abundance of beef and mutton."[33]

Grant also expected resistance soon, writing that "many days cannot elapse before the battle will begin which is to decide the fate of Vicksburg." He expected resistance as early as the first major creek he came to, Fivemile Creek, but none emerged. Such was not the case upon nearing the next major creek, Fourteenmile Creek. There, again expecting resistance from the enemy whom he now understood to have come out of their fortifications and moved east of the Big Black River, Grant thought the fight would come on the left, closer to Vicksburg. Rather, the major confrontation came on the other end of the line at Raymond on May 12, where McPherson's corps had trudged forward through the hot, dusty terrain devoid of ample water. "McPherson is undoubtedly in Raymond and has had, from the amount of firing heard, a hard fight," Grant wrote that afternoon. A Confederate brigade fought McPherson nearly to a standstill at Raymond before retreating northeastward toward Jackson. The small fight alerted Grant not only that the enemy would combat him but also that there were apparently large units to his right as well as to his left.[34]

The ever-adaptable Grant thus put another change in motion, realizing that he had to take care of any threat from the east before fully committing to operations going west toward what all assumed would be heavy fighting at the works surrounding Vicksburg. "I therefore determined to make sure of that place [Jackson] and leave no enemy in my rear," he noted, and thence to "work from there westward." Accordingly, Grant swiveled from his northward trek to a much more northeastward advance aimed at Jackson, the state capital. He would still cut the railroad, but before heading west for Vicksburg he would move east to neutralize Jackson and any troops there.[35]

The logic was unarguable, but there were problems. For one, Grant was willingly placing himself between two enemy forces. He had been alerted that "General Joe Johnston is in Jackson, and it is reported they have 20,000 men. I do not think there is that many, though they have collected considerable of a force. They have fortified on the different roads on this side of town, and are forming abatis." Second, his rear would be open to attack by what he knew was a formidable force under Pemberton now east of the Big Black River. McClernand, in fact, had alerted him that rumors "report[ed] the enemy to be concentrating between the bluffs on the east side of Big Black and Bolton. Edwards Station is about the center of this line on the east side of the Big Black." Accordingly, Grant put into motion a complex plan by which McClernand's corps would shield the rear as McPherson and Sherman took Jackson. That occurred with little resistance on May 14, although "the rain fell in torrents all the night before and continued until about noon of that day, making the roads at first slippery and then miry." The fight soon took place nevertheless, one Federal remarking that "it was a rush between our Brigade and [another] . . . to see which would get over the enemys works first." Grant now possessed the state capital, with rumors flying that Governor John J. Pettus was also taken, and he ordered Sherman to hurriedly destroy Jackson as a production and transportation center that could support a Confederate concentration and movement on his new rear once he turned west. Sherman did, one Federal writing that they left Jackson "in ashes." Meanwhile, Grant quickly turned McClernand and McPherson westward toward Vicksburg: "It is evidently the design of the enemy to get north of us, and cross the [Big] Black River and beat us into Vicksburg. We must not allow them to do this. Turn all your forces toward Bolton Station, and make all dispatch in getting there. Move troops by the most direct road from wherever they may be on receipt of this order."[36]

Grant knew the Confederate army defending Vicksburg was near, east of the Big Black River, and he expected a fight soon. "Two days more, or Tuesday next," he wrote his wife, Julia, "must bring on the fight which will settle the fate of Vicksburg. No Army ever felt better than this one does nor more confidant of success. Before they are beaten they will be very badly beaten." Hopefully, the big fight would take place out in the open where the army could maneuver rather than against the formidable ramparts of Vicksburg. In that, it seemed Pemberton was playing right into Grant's hands. Accordingly, the big fight did erupt away from Vicksburg as the armies slowly moved toward a confrontation along the Jackson Road.[37]

"Move your command early to-morrow toward Edwards Depot," Grant ordered McClernand on May 15, "marching so as to feel the force of the enemy, should you encounter him, and without bringing on an engagement, unless you feel entirely able to contend with him." The Army of the Tennessee was thus greatly prepared for what would turn out to be the most significant battle of the Vicksburg Campaign, one that would in actuality decide the fate of the city. Fortunately for him, Grant had his army well in hand. Multiple divisions marched along the three major roads leading toward two crossings of Baker's Creek, which flowed in a bend eventually southward into Fourteenmile Creek. Three divisions and Grant himself marched along the Jackson Road to the north, two divisions on the Middle Road that joined the Jackson Road at a crossroads, and two more divisions on the Raymond Road farther south. Perhaps as important, Grant's troops were well rested, having gone into camp early the night before after fairly short marches.[38]

The condition of the Confederate army was altogether different. Having left two of his five divisions around Vicksburg itself, Pemberton had marched eastward out of Lockett's defenses and then out of the additional defensible area west of the Big Black River, where more defenses existed to protect the railroad bridge. Now, Pemberton's army was on open ground east of the Big Black River with no defenses available. Worse, the entire army that marched out of Vicksburg was already exhausted from long marches with early mornings and late nights. The weary Confederate army was likewise plagued by questionable command structures wherein Pemberton set the example of disobeying orders from his superior, which his subordinate officers quickly assumed as their response to him. The Confederate army that met Grant on May 16 was consequently not in good shape, especially to fight the climactic battle of the Vicksburg Campaign.[39]

Battle came whether Pemberton wanted it or not, and Grant soon began driving the enemy away from their initial lines on top of Champion Hill and its emanating ridges, as well as from the crucial crossroads to its south. "Go down to [Major General John A.] Logan and tell him he is making history today," a jubilant Grant ordered. Then a stunning counterattack by John Bowen's Confederate division brought up from the Raymond Road sector to the south achieved much success, driving the Federals back and regaining all lost territory. Conversely, new Federal reinforcements still arriving on the field once again turned the seesaw battle in Grant's favor for good as the counterattack was broken and the masses of disillusioned Confederates began to flee toward any crossing of Baker's Creek they could find. The northern crossing was soon in Federal hands, forcing all Confederates to muddle toward the southern crossing, where many were cut off and had to leave the road and any chance of rejoining Pemberton's army.[40]

By its end, the Battle of Champion Hill had broken the back of Confederate resistance out in the field, one amazed Federal writing that "the dead rebs lay scattered over the ground." Pemberton quickly realized that he would have to fall back into Lockett's defenses so his combat potential could be multiplied by the fortifications. Plus, he had two fresh divisions near town. Unfortunately for him, in the process of being defeated and falling back, Pemberton lost most of another entire division that was cut off, as well as massive casualties for the numbers engaged and much of his artillery. It was a banner day for Ulysses S. Grant. "I am of the opinion that the battle of Vicksburg has been fought," he wrote Sherman that night.[41]

Grant's good fortune was not over, however, in large part because he did not let up. Included in his jubilant message to Sherman was the addendum that "we must be prepared however for whatever turns up." Pemberton unwisely halted much of his army at the Big Black River waiting on the wayward division that would never come. He did not know that it had marched away in a different direction, and so he ordered the defenses at the Big Black River manned. While the Confederate division never came, Grant's Federals did the next day, and they had fight on their minds once more.[42]

Pemberton's problems were compounded by the fact that the defenses at the river were on the low ground east of the railroad bridge rather than on the high ground on the west side of the river. They had been put in place back in April when Grierson's famous raid had moved uncomfortably close; Pemberton ordered fortifications established east of the river to defend the critical railroad bridge from Grierson's cavalry, who if they came would approach from that direction. Now, much of what was left of Pemberton's shocked army from Champion Hill manned those breastworks that were in the wrong position for the task at hand. They had been perfectly placed to defend the bridge in April, but now the railroad was a nonfactor; the bridge was useless now that Grant was astride the line. The Confederates, if defeated again, would face a bottleneck during any retreat across the river.[43]

That is exactly what happened. Grant's divisions deployed and attacked on the morning of May 17, led by the large Brigadier General Michael K. Lawler on the extreme right. Years later Grant remembered hearing "great cheering to the right of our line and, looking in that direction, saw Lawler in his shirt sleeves leading a charge upon the enemy." The Confederate line quickly broke, and the fleeing Southerners who were not captured, killed, or drowned trying to cross the river barely made it across the paltry bridges to safety. One Confederate described how "we only had a small bridge to cross on and that was set on fire before near all our men got across to prevent the enemy crossing after us." The Battle of Big Black River Bridge was another disgrace for Pemberton, wherein he lost more of his army and precious artillery despite what one Federal artilleryman described as a "splendid line of cotton breastworks."[44]

Perhaps more notable was that the Confederates would stage no more stands until the armies reached Vicksburg itself. Grant now had the Big Black River in hand and had only to cross it uncontested and move on toward Vicksburg, although as one Ohioan described it, "we got the railroad bridge but the buggers put fire to it and burned it after they got across so as to cut us off." Still, Grant was finally where he had pictured himself for nearly seven months, on the dry, high ground east of Vicksburg. He had finally managed to put his army in a position to begin the process of taking the city, one of his soldiers writing home that "the secret of our success has been in our quick movements." Even Sherman admitted as much, writing his wife, "Grant's movement was the most hazardous, but thus far the most successful of the war. He is entitled to all the credit, for I warned . . . him against it."[45]

Yet the final taking of the city would be an altogether different process, a seeming restart of entirely new operations. Most notably, Grant would now have to confront the fortifications he had yet to even view. While he had been operating around, against, and over Lockett's outlying defenses for months now, this was the first time he had even come close to approaching the inner line and the actual city of Vicksburg itself.

The defenses ringing Vicksburg were never far from John C. Pemberton's mind as he continually watched Grant's growing army maneuver and approach closer and closer in May 1863. He told one of his division commanders flatly to "withdraw to intrenchments if they advance in heavy force." But Pemberton, who awoke on April 30 to a brand-new world because of Federals on the east side of the Mississippi River, was not the sole decision-maker. His two superiors, Joseph E. Johnston and Jefferson Davis, were not much help, and neither were his subordinates. At one point amid the crisis, Pemberton's adjutant general had to send a scathing note to one of his generals: "The lieutenant-general commanding directs me to say to you that he finds great difficulty in having his views comprehended, and wishes to see you at once personally."[46]

Pemberton awoke on the morning of April 30 in Jackson, Mississippi, where he had kept his headquarters throughout most of the six-month-long campaign to date. It was from there in the past few days that he had kept a tight focus on the most tangible threat in Mississippi, where actual Federals were located east of the Mississippi River in the form of Benjamin Grierson's horse soldiers rampaging through the length of the state. Once they hit Vicksburg's and Pemberton's only outside connection with the rest of the Confederacy, the Southern Railroad of Mississippi, at Newton Station on April 24, Pemberton focused intently on catching the raiders for the next five days. It was, unfortunately for him, at the expense of not focusing on the less tangible threat of a possible invasion by the Federal army maneuvering southward on the Louisiana side of the river. He had been warned of the possibility time and time again and even spoke of "the report of a heavy movement to the southward on the Louisiana shore," but his emphasis was on stopping Grierson.[47]

Obviously as reports filed in on April 30 that a major crossing of the Mississippi River was under way, Grierson's nine hundred troopers suddenly became irrelevant compared to the multiple infantry divisions Grant was putting ashore at Bruinsburg. Knocked off his balance quickly, Pemberton never recovered. "On April 30, I received the first information of the landing of the enemy on the east bank of the Mississippi River," he noted, adding that news indicated "that they were still landing at Bruinsburg."[48]

Part of the problem was Johnston, Pemberton's theater commander, who over the course of the next fifteen days would come to Mississippi and council leaving Vicksburg to the enemy, escaping with the army intact. It was good advice, as Confederate commanders often had a problem with losing the army defending a place while in the process of losing the place. A classic example was Fort Donelson, with lesser episodes such as Island No. 10 and Arkansas Post also showing a pattern. That said, there were some notable times when Confederate commanders realized fixed fortifications could not be held when outflanked, and the commanders chose to save the defenders while losing the fortifications. Brigadier General Lloyd Tilghman at Fort Henry was a minor example, although Tilghman himself stayed and was captured. A better example was P. G. T. Beauregard at Corinth in May 1862. Corinth was going into Federal hands one way or another, and Beauregard was smart enough to save the army to fight another day. Joseph E. Johnston was smart as well and counseled over the next few days that Pemberton leave the trap that Vicksburg was becoming.[49]

That choice might look logical a hundred and fifty years later, and might have seemed so then, but Pemberton's other superior, and actually Johnston's too, further complicated matters. President Jefferson Davis, to whom Pemberton wrote that "I think the enemy has landed nearly his whole force on this side," was from the Vicksburg area, owning multiple plantations, most notably Brierfield on a great bend of the river just south of Vicksburg. Whether personal affairs entered into Davis's mind or not, he ordered Pemberton to hold Vicksburg: "To hold both Vicksburg and Port Hudson is necessary to a connection with Trans-Mississippi." Yet Davis was never really that sound on strategic matters in the first place. His defense of nearly every inch of Southern soil at the beginning of the war caused more problems than it cured, and his dependence on King Cotton Diplomacy never worked either. Of course there are always two sides to every situation, and Davis had the whole states' rights issue to contend with in defending many portions of the Confederacy whether confronted by the enemy or not. Still, his adamancy to hold on to Vicksburg over the course of the next few weeks was in direct opposition to Johnston's idea of getting out of the trap. John Pemberton was caught in the middle, and his natural indecisive disposition was further fuel for a major disaster. The fact that the Confederates faced the Union's best general did not help either.[50]

One of Pemberton's first decisions, besides shuffling troops southward to confront Grant, was to move his headquarters to Vicksburg itself. He was there by May 1, indicating which of his superiors he was more inclined to agree with. In fact, he later wrote of his decision-making process: "I believe that I fully estimated the importance of preventing an advance upon Jackson, if it could be done without sacrificing Vicksburg; but if the latter was lost, the former was comparatively of little value. Vicksburg might still be held with Jackson in possession of the enemy." Over the course of the next two weeks, Pemberton shifted his troops around the Vicksburg area from his headquarters there, trying to figure out Grant's intention and to come up with some way to stop it. Always in the back of his mind, though, loomed Lockett's fortifications. He could always depend on them as a last resort if it came to that.[51]

Pemberton first began by concentrating as many forces as he could in the city's defense. He realized "I should as rapidly as possible concentrate my whole force for the defense of Vicksburg from an attack in the rear by Grant's army, which was hourly swelling its numbers." He now realized that Grierson and Sherman and all the other feints for which he had fallen were nothing compared to the real move by Grant, the one that could end his career in defeat. He therefore called in all troops he could from the east and north, including those from the Meridian area under Major General William W. Loring, who had been trying to trap Grierson: "Bring all your force immediately to Vicksburg. Use all possible haste." Also called in were troops from the north as far away as Fort Pemberton at Greenwood. Lesser areas just had to be sacrificed to turn back what was a significant movement by the enemy.[52]

Pemberton sent Loring and the gathering troops to aid Bowen near Grand Gulf while the other three divisions under Major Generals Carter L. Stevenson, John H. Forney, and Martin L. Smith still guarded the line from Warrenton through Vicksburg to Snyder's Bluff. Loring and Bowen were given vast authority, but they soon concluded—and rightly so—that they could not hold Grand Gulf "with so small a force" and accordingly fell back northward far enough to get across the Big Black River and into the shield it provided. Pemberton waited anxiously to hear their news, writing, "my anxiety to hear is very great, and I hope you will keep me constantly and regularly informed of your position and current events." Thereafter, while Grant marched northeastward east of the Big Black River, Pemberton shadowed him on the west side, keeping between Grant and Vicksburg. He also watched and waited to see whether the Union goal was the railroad or the capital at Jackson, or both. In reality, it mattered little, because Pemberton had made a major decision by then: to defend Vicksburg at all costs. He actually told Bowen, "You must endeavor to cross Big Black, abandoning Grand Gulf," and ordered ordnance officials to send everything in Jackson to Vicksburg. He also determined to cling to Port Hudson, informing Major General Franklin Gardner to hold that place: "President says both places must be held." Accordingly, a growing force at Jackson would have to tend to itself, as Pemberton was committed to the defense of Vicksburg on his side of the Federal advance. He informed Governor Pettus that "I think it would be well to remove the State archives from Jackson," along with other military items and Mississippi State Troops.[53]

Then the indecisive Pemberton waffled under pressure from Johnston. Pemberton first thought Grant would cross the Big Black River and approach Warrenton, but then he began to realize Grant would head for the railroad and perhaps Jackson. As Grant did just that, Pemberton began inching farther outside Lockett's protective fortifications at Vicksburg, first making his headquarters at Bovina, east of the city. Then, he marched three divisions outside the protective shield of the Big Black River to try to do something—anything—that might turn the tide. He even notified a portion of the small command he left at Jackson to hit Grant's flank as he moved northward toward the railroad; the result, of course, was the fight at Raymond on May 12. Pemberton ultimately decided on the course proposed by several of his officers at a council of war (which is never a good option for an indecisive general) with which he did not agree, to march southeastward and disrupt Grant's supply line, hoping that would turn Grant back. One problem, of course, was that Grant did not have a traditional line of supply that could be broken. A larger issue was Pemberton's lack of leadership, he actually writing in his report: "My own views were strongly expressed as unfavorable to any advance which would separate me farther from Vicksburg, which was my base. I did not, however, see fit to put my own judgment and opinions so far in opposition as to prevent a movement altogether."[54]

It mattered little, as Grant finally caught Pemberton and pounced on his army at Champion Hill on May 16, where Pemberton himself directed the debacle. There, his indecisiveness caught up with him, as did his habit of disobeying direct orders, which he had been doing all along with Johnston. Now, two of his division commanders, Bowen and Loring, chose to disregard

Pemberton's orders, perhaps an action they learned from observing him. Pemberton laid the blame for the defeat squarely on their shoulders, writing that "had the movement in support of the left been promptly made when first ordered, it is not improbable that I might have maintained my position, and it is possible the enemy might have been driven back."[55]

Debacle fostered more debacles as Pemberton then ordered much of the army into the Big Black River trenches to await Loring's cut-off division, which never came. Pemberton later stated that he halted and "awaited in vain intelligence of the approach of General Loring" and that "I then determined not to abandon so strong a front while there was yet a hope of his arrival." Another severe defeat was the result the next day at Big Black River, Pemberton describing the line that was "shamefully abandoned almost without resistance," while a staff officer echoed that "our troops shamefully abandon[ed] the trenches." One Missourian admitted they ran "in regular Bull Run style." By the afternoon of May 17, Pemberton was headed back westward toward Vicksburg, his crumbling army all around him. James L. Power scratched in his diary that "the retreat of our army may be properly denominated a rout." One Federal similarly recognized the significance: "They fired the bridge and this cut off the retreat of a division of their own troops."[56]

The rout almost became even more costly. Many of those who tried to swim the river drowned. One of Pemberton's best generals, Stephen D. Lee, almost became a casualty as well. He had seen action in the east under Robert E. Lee and would rise to be the youngest lieutenant general in the Confederacy, but he was almost captured or killed on this day. As he was falling back toward Vicksburg, Lee came upon Union cavalrymen and shouted "Who are you?" to which the mounted men replied "Who are you?" The Confederate admitted, "I am Gen. Lee," whereupon the Federals retorted "All right General come on." Lee quickly became wise to the ruse, especially since the enemy had their pistols out. He waved his hand and wheeled his horse, yelling "No you don't." The Federals fired at him but he was able to escape to continue helping defend Vicksburg.[57]

It was all an unmitigated disaster for Pemberton and everyone knew it, one Missourian only mustering enough patriotism to write of "the several fights we have had of late in this state." Obviously, the Federals saw it differently, one Union artilleryman boasting in his diary that the fight at the bridge was "a glorious ending to the most glorious week of the war. Now for the great prize." Another wrote home that "the rebs found themselves badly thrashed and started for their intrenchments at Vicksburg on double quick."[58]

But there was some consolation for Pemberton. He had done what his commander in chief had desired: he was defending Vicksburg to the last man.

Another bright spot was that he also had two fresh divisions with which to defend Vicksburg. Perhaps foremost in Pemberton's mind, however, was that he had on his side possibly the main defensive factor in any Federal attempt to take Vicksburg: Lockett's fortifications. The past seventeen days had been a disaster, but hopefully that would change with the admission of this new factor into the equation. Yet morale was at its lowest even with the idea of fortifications being available to aid the army. One Texan seemed less than thrilled with "the whole army that night being promiscuously scattered around the city in trenches."[59]

Pemberton obviously had quite a task in front of him.

3

"Tumbling Back into Vicksburg in Utter Confusion"

Ulysses S. Grant was ecstatic. He had tried long and hard to get to this point, nearly seven months of tortuous campaigning and thousands dead through disease and fighting; in fact, many of his wounded still lay in numerous towns through which the army had passed. But now he was on the brink of what he considered victory as he peered across the Big Black River immediately after his victory there on the morning of May 17. He had managed to defeat the enemy five times in the last two and a half weeks, causing even one Confederate general to admit that "by his bold and rapid movements after crossing the river [he] outwitted his antagonist." The Big Black River was now the last natural impediment to him reaching Vicksburg, and he was already planning how to get across and move on the great hill city. One of his soldiers exemplified his attitude: the army was "on the road to Vicksburg, resolved to capture the city or get badly whipped. We have not known defeat since we left Fort Donelson, and we propose to keep our good record up. We have seen some hard times on some hotly contested fields, but mean to have nothing but victory, if possible, on our banner."[1]

As had been the case numerous times before, however, Grant was getting a little ahead of himself. If historians blame him for many personal problems such as his drinking or being a butcher, both of which have been far overplayed in many accounts, his chief drawback as a general, at least early in the war, was overconfidence. He had believed himself the master of the field at Belmont and could not fathom anything happening unless he directed it—that is, until the Confederates did not cooperate and counterattacked with reinforcements, nearly trapping the small army as well as Grant himself. At Fort Donelson, Grant was again trapped in his overconfidence, thinking he alone could be the instigator of affairs. Absent from the army when the Confederate breakout attempt occurred on February 15, he admitted, "visit[ing]

Flag-officer Foote I had no idea that there would be any engagement on land unless I brought it on myself." Of course, Shiloh ranks as the height of Grant's overconfidence. A swift and surprising Confederate attack quickly made him realize that the enemy did not always do as he wanted. Grant was certainly not the only one in the high command to think in such a way, but he was the commander.[2]

Such overconfidence continued to plague Grant as he entered the Vicksburg operations, he often telling his wife, Julia, over the long winter months that he hoped to be in Vicksburg in a matter of days. In one letter, dated February 15, he optimistically wrote that "a few weeks more I hope will settle the business here favorably." The swiftness and tediousness of the inland campaign in May had not given Grant much time to be overconfident, although he continually thought the hard part would be getting across the Mississippi River itself; five battles in seventeen days proved otherwise. Now, Grant began to get ahead of himself once more, but he can perhaps be excused for his feelings. After all, he had routed the main enemy army twice in the past two days, taking thousands of prisoners and artillery pieces. The flower of the Confederate army defending Vicksburg, along with its commander, was fleeing westward in rout toward the city. Perhaps all Grant had to do, he surmised, was to follow up and reap the rewards.[3]

Still, Grant's earlier campaigns had taught him that things may not be as easy as they appeared. He accordingly placed his emphasis on two major strategic points, one an intermediate and highly likely target (Haynes' Bluff) and the other actually the main goal of the entire campaign (Vicksburg). Grant believed he might be able to go on and take Vicksburg itself if he hurried and pushed hard enough. That would certainly be welcome, but there were still Confederates ready to defend the hill city, and they were behind Captain Samuel Lockett's extensive fortifications. If taking Vicksburg immediately turned out not to be feasible, he could certainly take the high ground overlooking the Yazoo River at Snyder's and Haynes' Bluffs. Then the Union navy, now unencumbered along the Yazoo River, could open a safe and secure line of supply for Grant's army confronting Vicksburg. "My first anxiety was to secure a base of supplies on the Yazoo River above Vicksburg," he later wrote. Then, he would be in perfect position to move against Vicksburg itself.[4]

Grant's correspondence showed as much. Even Sherman, no supporter of this advance, began to think in grandiose terms upon receiving orders to move across the Big Black toward Vicksburg. Grant had sent him northward to Bridgeport to outflank the Confederates at the railroad bridge as well as to block any movement in that direction. The historian Michael Ballard observed that "clearly Grant thought Pemberton might turn north," which was in fact what Joseph E. Johnston had ordered Pemberton to do. Sherman was in position to block the move but wanted more, asking his commander: "Shall I push into the city, or secure a point on the ridge?" Grant responded that he should push across the Big Black River and "secure a commanding position on the west bank of Black River as soon as you can." Then, he added, "if the information you gain after crossing warrants you in believing you can go immediately into the city, do so. [But] if there is any doubt in this matter, throw out troops to the left, after advancing on a line with the railroad bridge, to open communications with the troops here. We will then move in three columns, if roads can be found to move on."[5]

Consequently, Grant did not rule out anything, writing that he would "either have Vicksburg or Haynes' Bluff to-morrow night." The Haynes' Bluff idea was possible and much more feasible than taking Vicksburg quickly. There was no overconfidence in that part of the plan, because Pemberton would certainly call in all his outlying troops now that they were outflanked and in danger of being cut off. But the idea of taking Vicksburg and ending this campaign immediately was also tossed about, even if it was, unknown to Grant, unrealistic at this point. The enormous effort to reach Vicksburg had been achieved, but now the lofty goal of taking the city loomed large.[6]

The main reason: between Grant and Vicksburg lay Lockett's major line of fortifications, even now being filled to the brim with Confederate troops and artillery.

Even with those fortifications in the back of his mind, John Pemberton was every bit as distraught as Grant was thrilled on May 17. In fact, as he fled westward from the disaster area at the Big Black River bridge, Pemberton could see his world crashing down around him. His army was in shambles; much of it had already been shattered at Champion Hill, and now apparently his best division under John Bowen had been treated just as harshly at the river. Then there was the matter of General Loring. Where he was, whether the division had escaped, and whether it would somehow make its way to Vicksburg were all in question.[7]

Pemberton's concerns were also of a personal manner. As he rode westward toward Bovina, leaving the details of the retreat to division commander Carter Stevenson, he seemed to reflect on what it all meant. Pemberton knew he was losing control of the army; that very day, Mississippian James L. Power noted in his diary that "confidence appears to be lost in our Department Commander." Samuel Lockett was the only staff officer with Pemberton, and he simply let him alone until the general, after some time, quietly spoke: "Just thirty years ago I began my military career by receiving my appointment to a cadetship at the U.S. Military Academy, and to-day—the same date—that career is ended in disaster and disgrace." Taken aback, Lockett did not know what to say, but he tried his best to cheer up Pemberton, telling him there was still a lot of hope. The fortifications were ready, Lockett pointed out, and there were "two excellent divisions" that were fresh and ready to man them. In fact, Lockett proposed that these two could be centered on the most important area, with the shocked remnants of Bowen's and Stevenson's divisions "in the less exposed parts of the line, or in reserve, until they had steadied themselves." Warming to his logic, Lockett insisted that Vicksburg was strong and that it "could not be carried by assault," at the same time reminding Pemberton that Davis had promised relief when he had ordered him to hold Vicksburg. A still distraught Pemberton would have none of it, simply telling Lockett that "my youth and hopes were the parents of my judgment." Lockett added that "he himself did not believe our troops would stand the first shock of the attack."[8]

Indeed, there were bright spots, even if Pemberton could not see them. Lockett's fortifications were undeniably substantial if somewhat eroded by now. One Missourian admitted as much, writing that "we are now inside the fortifications of Vicksburg expecting an attack at any moment." But he chided that "the fortifications of Vicksburg are not as good as we expected to find them, though are confident we can hold the place. The natural fortifications are very strong, but our engineers have not improved them as much as they should have done." Likewise, there were two fresh divisions of troops now inside Vicksburg, those of Martin L. Smith and John H. Forney. Perhaps the combination of those two—fresh troops stationed behind substantial fortifications that could quickly be brought back up to strength—would at the least allow time and maybe even blunt the Federal advance all knew was coming.[9]

Yet there was still in the back of Pemberton's mind a foreboding feeling about the larger situation, even causing him to send his cavalry out of Vicksburg. In question was what would happen once his defeated army reached Vicksburg, fresh troops beside the point. Even those fresh troops would be inside a trap, as all saw it now was. Certainly, Johnston had warned Pemberton as much, and Pemberton knew it himself. So, the lift in spirits that came from the knowledge that there were two divisions of fresh troops to man the works was somewhat mitigated because that only meant there were more mouths to feed inside this trap that was Vicksburg. And the question was on more minds than Pemberton's. As one of his soldiers wrote home: "Don't know whether we will be surrendered or cut our way out." Another jotted in his diary, "I recon we would keep on [retreating], but we are as far as we can go for the Miss River."[10]

As the afternoon of May 17 wore on, however, the situation eased somewhat. Whether Pemberton began to see it or not, those under his command started to work with a will to redeem as much of the situation as possible, Lockett among them. As he and Pemberton reached Bovina, Lockett insisted that Pemberton give him an order to return to Vicksburg immediately to get the fortifications in order. He also requested that the order state that all commanders "of whatsoever rank" obey his commands to provide whatever was needed. Fortunately, there was no fuss over rank or command as all saw the crisis that was at hand. Stevenson and Bowen were likely too shocked and exhausted to resist, and Lockett later wrote that Smith and Forney "responded heartily." And so the revitalization of Vicksburg began, just in the nick of time.[11]

In actuality, Pemberton had already started thinking about the process of defending the city before the disaster at Big Black River occurred. He later reported that he saw plainly the problems facing him: "It had become painfully apparent to me that the morale of my army was not such as to justify an attempt to hold the line of the Big Black River." Having been trained in Jominian Napoleonic warfare at West Point, he realized the critical situation he faced in terms of turning movements, which in fact Grant had already started by sending Sherman to Bridgeport. At the time he thought the fortifications at the railroad bridge over the Big Black River would hold and thus worried more about his flanks. "So strong was the position, that my greatest, almost only apprehension was a flank movement by Bridgeport or Baldwin's Ferry, which would have endangered my communications with Vicksburg," Pemberton wrote. Of course, Pemberton now faced an even greater crisis because the strong position at the river had not held.[12]

Fortunately, Smith and Forney were even then moving inside Vicksburg. These two divisions, left under Forney's command while Pemberton was east of the Big Black River, had guarded the city and its flanks up the Yazoo River and down the Mississippi River. One of Forney's brigades manned the fortifications from the Mississippi River northeastward to Haynes' Bluff while the other manned the Mississippi River front south of Vicksburg around Warrenton. In Smith's division, one of the brigades held the city itself, including the waterfront, while the two remaining brigades as well as some cavalry and state troops manned the fortifications area on the approaches to Vicksburg. All heard the heavy artillery fire on May 17 but did not know what it meant. "Our minds were in deep suspense as to the results," admitted William L. Foster of the 35th Mississippi. Then a large plume of smoke appeared, and he realized that the railroad bridge was burning. "Then for the first time," he admitted, "the dark suspicion crossed our minds that we were defeated and compelled to fall back."[13]

With the distant possibility of Pemberton's line at the Big Black River being outflanked and then having it actually bowled over on the morning of May 17, orders had gone to the commanders to leave their outlying positions and make their way into the city. Pemberton feared that "the enemy . . . might reach Vicksburg almost simultaneously with myself, or perhaps interpose a heavy force between me and that city. Under these circumstances nothing remained but to retire the army within the defenses of Vicksburg, and to endeavor as speedily as possible to reorganize the depressed and discomfited troops." Forney relinquished command when Pemberton returned to the vicinity, retaking command of his division alone. He recalled Louis Hébert's troops from their positions north of Vicksburg, where on May 16 and 17, one member of the 36th Mississippi related, they had listened intently to "heavy cannonading away to the South." He also called in Brigadier General John C. Moore's troops from Warrenton. At the same time, Martin Smith recalled all three of his brigades including Brigadier Generals Francis Shoup's, William Baldwin's, and John C. Vaughn's Tennesseans, who had participated in the debacle at the Big Black River.[14]

The movement of so many troops inside Vicksburg was a telltale sign that war was coming to the city. Moore's troops from Forney's division simply marched northward and took a position in the trenches straddling the Baldwin's Ferry Road, which all assumed would be a line of advance for the enemy. Getting Hébert's troops into position was a much bigger problem, not so much because of the troops themselves but because of distance and all the equipment and stores located at Haynes' and Snyder's Bluffs. In addition, some of the troops refused to go to Vicksburg, a member of the 38th Mississippi declaring that they "bundled up their clothes and took a French furlough." Forney sent wagons to aid the evacuation and destruction of what could not be withdrawn, which took all day and most of the night. Hébert's troops simply marched (by "easy stages," one Mississippian remembered) into their positions astride the Jackson Road and all the way up to the Stockade Redan around daylight on May 18. The brigade entered Vicksburg "just at daybreak," and George Clarke of the 36th Mississippi was enthused that he had finally caught a "glimpse of the mighty 'Father of Waters.'" Hébert had also managed to bring much of the ordnance and stores with him, including all his field artillery and some larger pieces, including a Whitworth cannon. He also brought a herd of cattle and anything else that could be gained on the trek inside the fortifications while also sending a lot northward up the Yazoo

River. Only a few companies were left at Snyder's Bluff to "keep up a show of occupation" and to destroy anything that was left. Yet what Forney's troops found at the defensive line at Vicksburg was not promising, Hébert writing that "in spite of the previously vaunted report that Vicksburg had been surrounded by fortifications that were impregnable, we found a very feeble line, with gaps at intervals, and very weakly thrown up, with little redoubts here and there." He nevertheless "informed the men that they held the key to the city, on the most exposed portion of the line."[15]

Likewise, Martin L. Smith gathered his troops and placed them in line north of Vicksburg, covering the position from the Mississippi River to the Stockade Redan, although these troops also found the earthworks much lacking. Colonel Claudius W. Sears of the 46th Mississippi noted that he "found the works very slight—not two feet high." Even worse, some on his line were constructed in such an illogical manner that one company commander decided that "the field marks of the Engineer had been moved or obliterated before the trench was dug." And even though they were fresh and had not taken part in the debacles of the previous days, the rumors of defeat still swirled around these troops. Although one rumor that "the Northern soldiers were said to have crossed the Big Black River and marched unhindered into Vicksburg" was obviously untrue, sadly most of the others were terrifyingly valid. And some soldiers even in these fresh divisions were already predicting defeat. Chaplain William L. Foster described to his wife how one lieutenant commented on the brigade as it marched toward Vicksburg that "it makes me feel sad to look upon that army. . . . Those men will soon be disarmed and on their way to some Northern prison." The chaplain countered, "No sir, they will soon be shouting victory, victory, while pressing the routed foe."[16]

The other two divisions not surprisingly caused much more concern, Francis Shoup describing them as "tumbling back into Vicksburg in utter confusion." Carter Stevenson's four brigades had been allowed to lead the way westward even while Bowen was holding the line at the Big Black River, and so they were in somewhat better shape due to the unhurried march. Still, they were exhausted, bloody, and beaten, but even so they constituted the largest division in the army and thus had to take a section of the line. As Lockett advised, they could be placed in a less threatened area because all expected the Union advance to come from the Baldwin's Ferry Road northward. After what he described as a "leisurely and orderly" retreat, during which one of his brigades guarding the wagon train rejoined him, Stevenson positioned his troops south of that road midafternoon on May 17. Only one regiment of Lee's brigade, the 23rd Alabama, mistook the orders and remained to combat the Federal crossing of the Big Black River until that night, Stevenson reporting that they "only withdrew upon the receipt of a peremptory order."[17]

Similarly, Bowen's troops, hailed as the best in the army but now probably the roughest handled of all the divisions, made their way inside the city as well. At least according to Francis Shoup, Bowen himself was dejected and believed "every thing was lost," which was quite understandable given what he and his division had been through the past couple days. On top of everything else, many troops of his had lost their camp equipage at the Big Black. "We fell back to Vicksburg that night all tired and worn out and hungry," remembered George Bradley of the 5th Missouri. Another dejected Confederate tramping in from the Big Black River simply noted that "we fell back to Vicksburg or to our ditches in front of Vicksburg." Pemberton found Bowen's troops to be so shot up and dazed that he decided to hold them in reserve to plug any gap made by the inevitable Union advance and attack.[18]

The appearance of these two divisions was in stark contrast to Forney's and Smith's commands. Pemberton himself described "the large number of stragglers, who, having abandoned their commands, were already making their way into Vicksburg," and he later described the need to "arm all men who had either unavoidably lost or who had thrown away their arms on the retreat." Staff officer John C. Taylor described the army as "shockingly demoralized." One of Hébert's Mississippians commented that "entering the city from the north, we met the retreating columns of Pemberton's Army," and he described them as in "shattered condition."[19]

Vicksburg's residents could hardly believe their eyes either, when the downtrodden and beaten remnant of Bowen's and Stevenson's divisions began to file through the opening of the works along the major roads into the city. One of Bowen's Arkansans commented that "when we reached Vicksburg, I was surprised to find a great number of ladies on the streets." Numerous diarists and civilians left their impressions of the condition of the army. Most famously, Emma Balfour admitted that "I hope never to witness again such a scene as the return of our routed army." She continued: "From twelve o'clock until late in the night the streets and roads were *jammed* with wagons, cannons, horses, men, mules, stock, sheep, everything you can imagine that appertains to an army—being brought hurriedly within the intrenchment. Nothing like order prevailed, of course, as divisions, brigades, and regiments were broken and separated." She could only wail over these "poor fellows, it made my heart ache to see them." It was so bad that "centers at which they could assemble" had to be set up.[20]

The morale of the entire army seemed to be just as bad. One army doctor,

Joseph Dill Alison, wrote, "I never saw men more dispirited. A rumor is circulated that Gen. Pemberton has sold Vicksburg and many believe it. If an attack is made tomorrow, we are lost. Things looks very gloomy. I have never been low spirited before, but things look too dark for even me to be hopeful." Another surgeon in Bowen's division labeled Pemberton a traitor, arguing that "such incompetency has never been witnessed; it looks like design." A Louisianan described how "our Wagon trains that were not captured are coming in[,] Stragglers are passing, and everything denotes a defeat. . . . The news gets worse our army is said to be completely demoralized—have thrown away their arms and all is confusion and dismay." Colonel Winchester Hall of the 26th Louisiana described how "there would be a squad of infantry, a horseman . . . a gun . . . a few more infantry, and so on; with no more order than travelers on a highway." An amazed Louis Hébert, commanding one of Forney's brigades, simply described the whipped Confederates from Big Black River bridge as "rather demoralized by recent defeats," and another Louisianan admitted "everybody looking blue."[21]

Matters were so bad, in fact, that John Bowen took the extraordinary step of giving Pemberton some unsolicited advice as the situation seemed to be spiraling out of control. "Since my return to camp," Bowen wrote, "I find that the wildest and most absurd rumors of surrender are in existence, not only among the men, but the officers of the command." These rumors hinged on the tale that "Grant and yourself had an understanding, and that they would have this place on the 20th instance." Bowen asserted that the rumors were "general throughout the army," and he advised that an order be sent out quickly to quash them, even stating that a council of general officers was supportive of Pemberton's "determination not to evacuate or surrender, but to hold the place to the bitter end." Bowen apologized for being so bold, but the situation demanded it. Pemberton simply did not seem to have full control of the situation. It was a growing nightmare, and one Louisianan described the worst of it: the stragglers were loudly proclaiming that "Yankees are coming."[22]

U lysses S. Grant was not about to let up his pressure on Pemberton, especially with much of the Confederate army streaming westward in total rout and to what one Federal described as "the last ditch." The signs were unmistakable, given the detritus of battle the Federals were finding as they moved westward: guns, artillery, and all sorts of equipment, mostly destroyed. Pockets of Confederates themselves also emerged, waiting for someone to capture them. One such amazing scene occurred when the newspaper correspondent Sylvanus Cadwallader rode up on a group of beaten Confederates. "What are you doing here boys?" Cadwallader asked in a nervous tone. His fears quickly subsided when the Irish spokesman answered, "Well sir, we've been waiting for you to come along." Cadwallader asked if they wanted to be captured, the Irishman admitting, "Well, that's about it sir." The Federals were also finding other refugees from the fighting, mostly slaves. One 83rd Indiana soldier in Sherman's division described how they would cajole: "Sambo, fall in here, we are going to take Vicksburg; help us." The slaves would respond, "No, Massa, Ise 'fraid. Da has big guns and da's looking this way. Wait 'till you all take Vicksburg, then we all come."[23]

Grant quickly pointed his corps commanders westward and told them to move on, keeping in supporting distance. His sights were set first on Haynes' Bluff and even Vicksburg itself if possible: "The enemy have been so terribly beaten yesterday and to-day that I cannot believe that a stand will be made unless the troops are relying on Johnston's arriving with large re-enforcements, nor that Johnston would attempt to re-enforce with anything at his command if he was at all aware of the present condition of things." The result was an army-wide movement westward, one Iowan declaring in his diary: "On the war-path for Vicksburg."[24]

The main barrier was of course the Big Black River, and some opposition from the west bank greeted McClernand's troops as they moved on to where the still smoldering railroad bridge halted their crossing. Brigadier General Peter Osterhaus declared that the Confederates "gained more than twelve hours' time over us by burning the railroad bridge." There was also some initial defense on the west bank of the river, although McClernand was easily able to squash it, reporting that "the enemy made a feeble stand to cover his trains and retreat upon Vicksburg, but several hours before sunset was dislodged by my forces, leaving tents, a considerable quantity of clothing and other stores, together with a large number of small-arms, a smoking ruin." There was also opposition on the west side of the river at Sherman's position farther north at Bridgeport. Sherman explained that the enemy defense evaporated quickly once Captain Peter Wood's Chicago Light Artillery came up: "The enemy had a small picket on the west bank in a rifle-pit commanding the crossing, but, on exploding a few shells over the pit, they came out and surrendered—a lieutenant and 10 men." One member of the battery scribbled in his diary that "they volunteered to help fix the bridge."[25]

With the opposition dwindling, Grant was able to push his troops across the river that night and the next morning. The only delay came in fashioning bridges over which the army could cross, and it could not be done quickly enough for Grant. Ultimately, no fewer than four different bridges took form over the Big Black River along a stretch of five or six miles. The river flowed

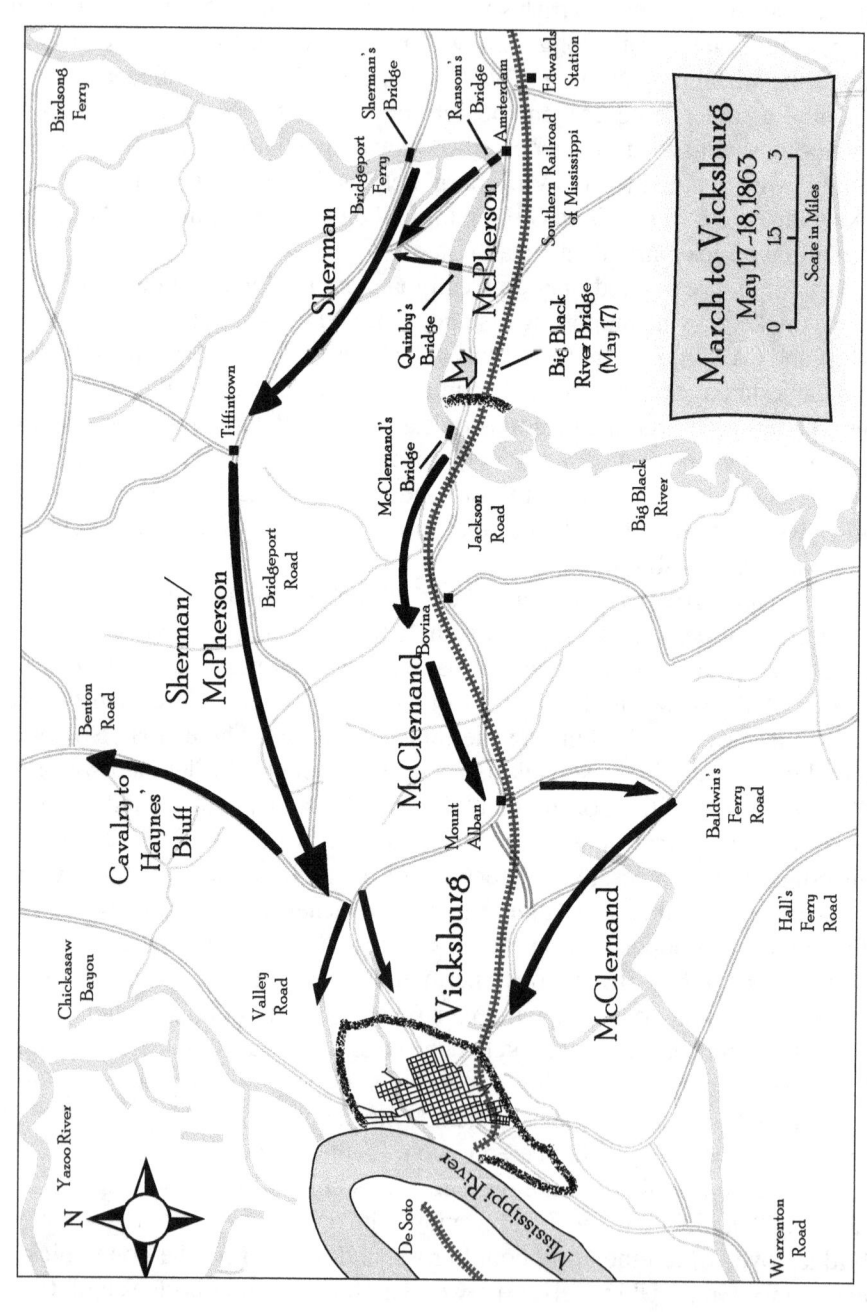

from northeast to southwest toward its mouth at Grand Gulf, but near the battlefield it flowed due south for a time before turning at more than a ninety-degree angle to a northwesterly flow. Just north of where the battle had been fought on May 17 at the railroad bridge, the river then turned ninety degrees to the south and meandered on toward the Mississippi River. Thus, McClernand's corps at the railroad bridge was several miles from Sherman's position at Bridgeport and much farther west, with McPherson in the middle.[26]

The first bridge to go up was on Sherman's front at Bridgeport. Sherman himself arrived there about noon on May 17, not yet knowing of the major events to his south. In fact, Grant intended to use Sherman as his fulcrum to wedge the Confederates out of their defenses to the south along the railroad bridge corridor. "I will endeavor to hold the enemy where he is," Grant informed Sherman, "to give you time to cross the river, if it can be effected." He added that "the moment the enemy begins to give way, I will endeavor to follow him so closely that he will not be able to destroy the bridge." Of course, neither happened: McClernand did not need Sherman to turn the Confederate position because McClernand was able to break through himself. And despite the Union breakthrough, the Confederates still managed to burn the bridge.[27]

Sherman determined to quickly cross this last barrier, which one of his artillerymen described as "a yellow, deep, narrow stream with very steep banks and a swift current." He was afforded that opportunity when he arrived at Bridgeport. In actuality, Major General Frank Blair's division, part of Sherman's own corps, actually beat him there by an hour, Blair having come from Grand Gulf directly to the army. Once Grant moved on westward after Champion Hill, he sent Blair northward to Bridgeport to act as the lever with the rest of Sherman's divisions, which marched directly to the river crossing.[28]

Making the crossing easier, Blair had with him "the only pontoon train with the expedition." Although most might take this as a reference to wooden boats such as those used so famously at Fredericksburg in December 1862, these pontoon boats were actually "India-rubber boats" and were inflatable. They consisted of "three rubber tubes all connected with loops for handles and also some to tie a sort of sleeper to each tube. These were inflated with bellows." When Blair and Sherman arrived, and the opposing Confederates were dispersed, engineer Captain Henry C. Freeman quickly assembled the bridge and Sherman's troops began crossing that night. Grant himself rode northward to check on the progress and see his friend Sherman, who described how that night "we sat on a log, looking at the passage of the troops by the light of those fires; the bridge swayed to and fro under the passing feet, and made a fine war picture." Soon, Blair's division was across and bivouacked in a cornfield two miles west of the river, as did Major General Frederick

Steele's troops that night as well as Brigadier General James Tuttle's early the next morning.[29]

McPherson's work, a little over a mile to the south, did not go as quickly despite the fact that he was an army engineer by trade. He had much less material to work with than did Sherman with his ready-made boats. McPherson's commanders soon remedied the situation, however, after they approached the river near Amsterdam, which was a mile or more south of Bridgeport but around the great bend back to the northwest. There, McPherson's troops fashioned two separate bridges.[30]

The lead brigade of McPherson's corps, moving on a connecting road that branched off the Jackson Road at Amsterdam and entered the Bridgeport Road on which Sherman was moving, was that of Brigadier General Thomas E. G. Ransom of Brigadier General John McArthur's division. Much like Blair's division of Sherman's corps, Ransom's troops had recently arrived after guarding one of the last wagon trains to reach the army from Grand Gulf. Although they missed out on the fight at Champion Hill, the brigade was now with the army and leading the corps, despite their being the only brigade from the division then present. Following were the divisions of John A. Logan and Brigadier General Isaac F. Quinby, who had actually just arrived and taken command of the division from the ill Brigadier General Marcellus M. Crocker. Ransom quickly went to work and let his ingenuity shine. While most of the men were "busily killing beeves [and] sheep," he ordered a detail to cut down large trees from either side of the river so that their branches interlocked and their trunks, "still fast to the stump," nearly met. With such a stable platform, the men then laid planks repurposed from a nearby cotton gin along the trunks so that a walkway was soon fashioned. Engineer McPherson was impressed, calling it a "solid raft bridge of timber." It may have been solid, but those crossing, especially in the artillery, became frightened. One watching infantryman marveled that "as the artillery came across . . . the water raised a few inches over the boards."[31]

With orders to build a different bridge so that his own division could cross while Ransom's and Logan's troops used the tree bridge, Quinby determined to foster a different design using "cotton bales and boards." Under orders of the XVII Corps engineer Captain Andrew Hickenlooper and Logan's engineer Captain Stewart R. Tresilian, the men gathered cotton bales, which floated, from the surrounding fields and a nearby gin and threw them into the river within a "framework of timber." In all, some forty-seven cotton bales were used, with boards taken from the nearby cotton gin used as the flooring. Using the cotton bales much like the wooden boats at Fredericksburg or Sherman's rubber boats at Bridgeport, the men fastened them together and planked over the tops to make another crossing. McPherson stated this bridge was "built of timber and cotton bales," and it was impressive, spanning 102 feet in water thirty feet deep. Engineer Tresilian was duly impressed with his own efforts, writing, "I am of the opinion that the cotton bridge is equal, if not superior, to the pontoon, being much steadier and easily constructed." As evidence, he added, "I witnessed the crossing of the division, and found that the 20-pounder Parrott sunk the structure only 14 inches, leaving an excess of buoyancy of 16 inches." Others were impressed as well, Edward Wood of the 48th Indiana writing his wife of "building a bridge of cotton bales (!)."[32]

By 8:00 A.M. on May 18, both bridges were complete and ready for traffic. The corps then began to cross at the two sites, Logan and Ransom on one and Quinby on the other. Left behind temporarily was Colonel John B. Sanborn's brigade of Quinby's division to guard the bridges until more units appeared. Once across, the corps marched northwestward on what McPherson termed a "plantation road" until it met the Bridgeport Road on which Sherman was advancing. There, McPherson's troops stopped, brigade commander Brigadier General John E. Smith noting that his troops were "detained by General Sherman's command, which was in advance."[33]

The fourth bridge took shape near the original railroad bridge some three or four more miles to the southwest, in McClernand's sector. There, Captain William F. Patterson of the Kentucky "pioneer corps" crafted a bridge that allowed McClernand to move his troops across. Sighted a few hundred yards north of the railroad bridge, the Federals of Osterhaus's division stripped the burning railroad bridge as well as local houses and cotton gins to fashion a "floating bridge" two hundred feet long. It was completed by the early hours of May 18, and McClernand moved across three of his divisions—Smith's, Osterhaus's, and Brigadier General Eugene A. Carr's in that order—leaving Brigadier General Alvin P. Hovey's, still back at Champion Hill, to bury the dead and police the field.[34]

The mood was jubilant as the Army of the Tennessee crossed the last natural barrier between them and Vicksburg. One Ohioan remembered there was a band on the west side of the river playing "national airs." He also remembered in his diary how enthusiastic the troops were:

Every man felt the combined Confederate army could not keep us out of Vicksburg. It was a grand sight, the long lines of infantry moving over the pontoons, and winding their way up the bluffs, with flags flying in the breeze, and the morning sun glancing upon the guns as they lay across the shoulders of the boys. Cheer after cheer went up in welcome and triumph from the thousands who had already crossed and stood in waiting lines upon the bluff above. This is supposed to be the last halting place before we knock for admittance at our goal—the boasted Gibraltar of the west.[35]

Accordingly, by early May 18, Grant had leaped the last natural barrier between him and Vicksburg, and had his three corps on three different roads moving westward toward Vicksburg. One Federal gratefully acknowledged the right of way: "bright and early we were on the road, which the rebels had kindly left unobstructed." But it was not totally clear; the scene betrayed an obviously chaotic situation for the enemy. Osterhaus reported that "every step forward showed the utter confusion of his retreat; the road was literally strewn with the *debris* of the dissolved army."[36]

Yet while no more natural barriers loomed ahead, one very concerning man-made obstruction did, courtesy of Samuel Lockett.

Swirling rumors engulfed the Federals as they trudged westward on the morning of May 18. One Illinoisan in Brigadier General John D. Stevenson's brigade of Logan division jotted in his diary that "many think the city evacuated, but the way we are being pushed through I don't think so." He hedged his bets by noting that "they have either made their escape towards Yazoo Haines Bluff, or gone into their works at Vicksburg. We shall know tomorrow."[37]

Grant established his headquarters around 9:00 A.M. at the Evans plantation, where a mulatto informed staff officer Lieutenant Colonel James H. Wilson that "all the troops of the Rebels have been called into Vicksburg." The slave estimated Pemberton's force at about sixty thousand but intimated that "they will surrender after a show of fight." Other pieces of information made the picture clearer as well, including captured Confederate communications. Also at Evans's, Grant tried to issue orders that would make the approach to Vicksburg a concerted and coordinated effort, but he was terribly unaware of the road network that would play against him. At times, Grant still had to give such inconclusive orders as "we will then move in three columns, if roads can be found to move on." He sent staff officers out to locate the various roads, and in the process they found that there were few defenses short of the actual Vicksburg fortifications. Grant gave orders to McClernand to find parallel roads for his and McPherson's corps, but it was unfeasible. In fact, the major problems would not come with a joining of McClernand's and McPherson's corps but of McPherson's and Sherman's.[38]

What was on those roads was also a nightmare. Prisoners were numerous the closer the Federals came to Vicksburg: "We are picking them up all along the road," one Federal wrote. The dust was also oppressive. Edward Wood of the 48th Indiana described the choking filth: "And oh! such a 20 mile march it was. Most intolerably hot, with not a breath of air stirring, and the dust six inches deep, rolling up in thick volumes from the slightest tread of man or horse encircling & enveloping you filling your mouth, nose eyes & ears and permeating every pore of the skin until you felt like one great sandbag."[39]

Sherman led the way westward in these terrible conditions, as his was the first corps to cross the Big Black River. He marched on the Bridgeport Road, which, if followed, led through Tiffentown and would bring him in contact with the Confederate works northeast of Vicksburg, near where the Bridgeport, Jackson, and Graveyard Roads all converged. The road on which McPherson was moving led into the Bridgeport Road a few miles west of the river crossing. Accordingly, two corps utilized the same road until they drew closer to the Confederate fortifications.[40]

The progress was even slower because Sherman did not go directly to Vicksburg without stopping first. After his lead division under Blair passed the opening of the road on which McPherson's troops were, they continued to another road opening within three or four miles of the city, which was the entrance of the Benton Road that led northeastward, parallel with the Yazoo River. Knowing he was so near to Haynes' and Snyder's Bluffs and that Grant wanted them taken as quickly as possible, Sherman halted at the forks, forcing McPherson to do the same in the rear. Thus, all forward movement stopped for the two corps operating on the Bridgeport Road.[41]

It was worth it, however, because Sherman was after one of Grant's two major prizes: Haynes' Bluff. "My first anxiety was to secure a base of supplies on the Yazoo River above Vicksburg," Grant later wrote, and Sherman had succeeded in "interposing a superior force between the enemy at Vicksburg and his forts on the Yazoo." Sherman called a halt to the march until Grant could come up, but he quickly sent the 4th Iowa Cavalry northeastward to "secure the place." Grant later sent a message to Admiral Porter: "Please send a boat up to Haynes' Bluff, which I think is evacuated. Our cavalry have gone up to see." He did so, and the cavalry eventually opened communication with the ironclad *Baron De Kalb* on the Yazoo River.[42]

The bluff was indeed evacuated, the Iowa cavalry capturing several guns as well as a hospital with around fifty patients and all camp equipage. Grant did have Haynes' Bluff by the next night, just as he had hoped, and now he could see a clear path to ample provisions for his army. "I have sent for forage and supplies to be sent to Lake's Landing at the mouth of Chickasaw Bayou," he wrote the next day. One jubilant Federal who realized the significance of this development simply wrote in his diary: "This is all we wanted; now we are all right." Still, the soldier took umbrage at Porter and the navy taking the credit for capturing the place and all its heavy artillery. "Porter landed with his paint pot again as at Grand Gulf," he wrote, "and labeled all the artillery with the familiar words 'Captured by Rear Admiral Porter at Haines Bluff!'" He likened it to the old saying that it "may be modern modesty, but damn me if it ain't very like old-fashioned impudence."[43]

Others were just as impressed as the full knowledge of just how important this development was came over the next few hours and into the next day. Correspondent Cadwallader wrote his wife, "I think it brilliant. All his [Grant's] plans have worked to a charm." Sherman was most impressed, Grant writing that eventually "Sherman had the pleasure of looking down from the spot coveted so much by him the December before on the ground where his command had lain so helpless for offensive action." Another Federal arriving a few days later agreed, writing that "it is not to be wondered at that Sherman met a bitter repulse here last winter." For his part, Sherman was finally able to admit that Grant had been right all along. He had never been a supporter of this roundabout movement, preferring instead after all the failures of the spring to head back to Memphis and restart an overland campaign. Grant had not listened, and Sherman was finally able to breath a sigh of relief: "He turned to me," Grant later remembered, "saying that up to this minute he had felt no positive assurance of success. This, however, he said was the end of one of the greatest campaigns in history and I ought to make a report of it at once. Vicksburg was not yet captured, and there was no telling what might happen before it was taken; but whether captured or not, this was a complete and successful campaign." Lower-level Federals realized the same thing. Don Pardee wrote to his wife, "As we have possession of the Chickasaw Bluffs for which we fought so hard last winter, our right rests on the Yazoo River, and our line of communication is much shortened." Isaac Williams of the 30th Ohio wrote his brother, "General U. S. Grant our commander has been trying for a long time to occupy the position we now hold."[44]

The other and more important goal—Vicksburg itself—still lay farther to the west, and Grant of course pushed on. He had Sherman continue to move along the Bridgeport Road until he approached the Confederate defenses. There, he was to deploy and test to see how strong they were. Sherman accordingly moved on with Blair's division in the lead, but they soon reached another fork in the road that led to different entrances through the Confederate works. There, about dark on May 18, Sherman halted to await Grant and the overall plan of how he desired to approach the enemy. One of Sherman's Iowans was proud of the day's work nevertheless, writing in his diary, "It was intended that Gen. McClernand should reach the city first, but Gen. Sherman was too fast for them."⁴⁵

Because of Sherman's activities in the lead, McPherson's corps was relegated to simply follow along while Sherman reconnoitered Haynes' Bluff and then restarted his advance. As a result, McPherson's troops made less progress than Sherman's simply because of the road network. By dark, Ransom's brigade was closed up nearer Sherman's troops just east of the Confederate lines, but Logan and Quinby stretched farther to the rear, bivouacking on the road where they found good water. Deployment would have to wait until the next morning's light, as well as the light Grant would shed on what to do next.⁴⁶

McClernand's command has no such roadway worries, it operating solely on the Baldwin's Ferry Road. His orders from Grant were to press ahead to Mount Alban, where he was to find multiple roads on which to approach Vicksburg. Being somewhat confused, McClernand wrote Grant: "You say take a parallel road if I find one; I suppose you mean to divide my forces on two roads, if I can. If I am mistaken, please correct me." McClernand nevertheless moved on, aided by the locals who gave him information; brigade commander Brigadier General Stephen G. Burbridge recalled that "we soon learned from Negroes there was no enemy between us and Mount Alban." The corps moved on, one Ohioan describing how "we passed the beautiful little convent of St. Albans." Burbridge then reported that "about half a mile beyond Mount Alban we found a bridge so burned and broken as to be impassable. Examination showed it would cause considerable delay to repair it so that artillery could pass over it in safety. We therefore made a considerable detour to the left, taking a route through the country which in the course of a couple of miles struck the Baldwin's Ferry road, which was the route we were seeking." As the corps moved on, it increasingly came upon Confederates still making their way toward Vicksburg as well as wagons with supplies; all were captured. Once on the Baldwin's Ferry Road, McClernand's three divisions moved forward to a range of hills several miles outside the Confederate works. There McClernand halted at about sunset, having, due to the heat, dust, distance, lack of water, and rapidity of march, concluded "among the hardest marches we had endured," as a 67th Indiana soldier remembered. Without further orders, McClernand stopped until he could also get a clear indication from Grant what to do next.⁴⁷

By nightfall on May 18, then, Grant had his three corps in close proximity to Vicksburg, one Federal writing to his wife that "on the 18th we pushed on to this place running all the rebels in behind the rifle-pits and forts where we are keeping them pretty close." Just like Grant, the troops were thrilled at the idea that they had finally reached their goal, especially after marching so far for so many days. One 4th West Virginia surgeon described the elation: "We congratulated each other upon the fact that our marching was over for the present. Since the 12th, we had marched about eighty miles in an irregular circle around Vicksburg." An Indianan wrote home, "Didn't we have a glorious succession of victories, until we drove the enemy into a box?" True, Grant's main goal was not accomplished as he had desired the day before, but the secondary act of obtaining Haynes' Bluff had been, and that in and of itself meant Vicksburg was near. And this presented Grant with options. Now that an open line of supply was available, despite the fact that it would take time to start the improvement processes at the landing itself and then to offload supplies and get them to the troops, the process had begun. It was just a matter of time before Grant's underfed troops would have all the best the supply officers could obtain. The future was clearly in Grant's hands, and all he had to do was to decide what course to pursue. He therefore had many questions to answer as he stopped that night, his headquarters at the Cook plantation just a few miles east of Vicksburg. But they were all good options, as Vicksburg seemed to now be well within his grasp even if the key was not quite yet fully in Lincoln's pocket.[48]

Despite the approaching Federals, the mood inside Vicksburg became better with the dawn on May 18. The fact that the enemy had not yet arrived only added to the relief. One Mississippian even waxed eloquent in his diary of the beauty of the day:

> The morning of May 18th 1863 dawned clear and beautiful. Not a cloud obscured the sky; the air was soft, balmy and redolent of wild flowers; and as the sun arose, the dew drops on the grass sparkled in his rays like myriads of diamonds. The mocking birds were filling the air with melody, and the little wrens, tem-tits and thrushes were tittering with gladness, as they built their nests or sought their food, all unconscious of the terrible tragedy impending. It was a typical May morning, cool and pleasant, bright and lovely; all nature seemed restful and glad, and man alone was out of harmony with the peaceful scene.

Certainly, Pemberton was out of harmony, but he was now revived and doing all he could to remedy the situation.[49]

In fact, by the morning of May 18 when he was able to make a survey of his fortifications, Pemberton, perhaps because of rest (he later wrote that "during the night of the 17th, nothing of importance occurred"), had regained some of his edge and was ready to formally deploy his troops for the defense of Vicksburg. Others were feeling better as well. The normally optimistic but now downhearted Dr. Alison was a similar case in point, writing the day after he declared everything was nearly lost that "many of our troops who were supposed to have been cut off, have come in, and all is not as bad as appeared yesterday, but still far from bright." Yet Pemberton did not gloss over the major predicament he was in. He later recounted all that faced him at the time: "The prospect of a protracted siege, and the uncertainty as to how many assaults we might have to repel, and in view of the possibility of having to march out from our intrenchments to meet and co-operate with an assisting army expected under General Johnston, rendered it a matter of vital importance that every charge of ammunition on hand should be hoarded with the most jealous care." Pemberton also displayed his regained nerve in an update to President Jefferson Davis: "We are occupying the trenches around Vicksburg. The enemy is investing it, and will probably attempt an assault. Our men have considerably recovered their morale, but unless a large force is sent at once to relieve it, Vicksburg before long must fall. I have used every effort to prevent all this, but in vain."[50]

Morale was indeed rebuilding among the Confederate defenders. The same Mississippian of Hébert's brigade who had described Bowen's and Stevenson's troops as in "shattered condition" went on to say that "they were not demoralized, but were still ready for a fight." He added that "as we met them that morning of the 18th of May their demeanor said louder than words, 'we will defend the city of Hill' to the last." Word also leaked that Pemberton believed that he could hold out militarily as long as provisions remained, and the "commissaries say they can feed the army six weeks."[51]

Orders went out for the troops to assume the basic positions they were already in but also delineated certain zones for the brigades and divisions. Knowing the area east and northeast of Vicksburg was critical, Pemberton placed his two freshest divisions there, Smith's and Forney's. Smith's line began on the river along the Valley Road and ran eastward south of Mint Spring Bayou, although some of the troops also occupied the line of works on the ridge north of the bayou, which were quickly abandoned during the night of May 18. Pemberton chalked the confusion up to "General Smith . . . misapprehending my instructions given him immediately after my return from the Big Black." The bayou became less of a defensive factor the farther east it was, so Smith's best troops were placed there on the left of the Graveyard Road and running westward. Francis Shoup's brigade and then William Baldwin's held the line as it ran toward the Mississippi River and the deeper confines of Mint Spring Bayou, which close to the river were well-nigh unassailable. It was for that reason that Smith placed his weakest troops in this area, where no attack was expected. John C. Vaughn's conscripted Tennesseans, who had broken so quickly at Big Black River, took position here, as did a couple of equally questionable Mississippi State Troops regiments under Brigadier General Jeptha Harris. The line had to be manned at all points, but Pemberton and Smith wisely chose to put the least dependable troops in the most defensible locations. Also attached to Smith's division was a small contingent of Loring's division that had managed to break away from its parent division at Champion Hill and follow the army into the Vicksburg defenses.[52]

Division commander Smith described the fortifications in his sector, writing:

> The works occupied by me, and which may be termed my front, were along a narrow ridge, and consisted of a line of rifle-trenches, with points prepared for field artillery. This point was rather strong, although parallel with it, and some 600 yards distant, ran another ridge of the same elevation, and in every respect similar, which was occupied by the enemy, and afforded excellent positions for their batteries as well as sharpshooters, and, when prepared with field-works looking in our direction, became itself as difficult to assail as our own line. Many advantages would have resulted from occupying this parallel ridge, and it was included in the system of defense; but, increasing as it did the length of the entire line of defense, was abandoned for want of sufficient force to occupy it.[53]

Such was not the case as the line ran close to the Graveyard Road and thence southward. Smith's right connected with Forney's left at the Stockade Redan, which could have caused problems. Some of the weakest points in military lines were where two differing units joined. It had to be done somewhere, and inside the massive and strong Stockade Redan was the best place. Accordingly, Forney's division ran southward from the Graveyard Road, Hébert's troops fresh from Haynes' Bluff holding the position between the Stockade Redan and the fortifications on the Jackson Road, where Brigadier General John C. Moore's regiments picked up the line and carried it southward to the Baldwin's Ferry Road and the railroad. In all, Forney's line, covered by two brigades, was more than two miles long.[54]

In another example of placing the most tired and dejected troops on less problematic sections of the line, Pemberton ordered Carter Stevenson to man the fortifications south of the railroad down to the South Fort and thence along the bluff back toward Vicksburg, including the river front where Colonel Edward Higgins's heavy artillerymen manned the river batteries. In all, Stevenson's lines were some five miles in length, but he had four brigades with which to cover that distance. Brigadier General Seth Barton's troops manned the city front and line along the river, while Colonel Alexander W. Reynolds's came next, all the way to the Hall's Ferry Road. From there, Brigadier General Alfred Cumming's Georgians held the line as it moved northward, and Stephen D. Lee's hard-fighting Alabama troops, the best in the division, took position south of the railroad and around the Square Fort. To aid in his defense, Stevenson also gave Lee Colonel Thomas N. Waul's Texas Legion: more troops that had not been mauled in the previous fighting.[55]

Pemberton kept his remaining division as a grand reserve. Despite the thrashing Bowen's two brigades had taken at both Champion Hill and Big Black River, and at Port Gibson even earlier, he still looked on them as some of his best troops, especially after a little rest and time brought in stragglers and wounded. "It was absolutely necessary to keep a reserve always ready to re-enforce any point heavily threatened," he explained, noting "it was also necessary that the reserve should be composed of troops among the best and most reliable." Bowen's division was that and formed the ready reserve, with Colonel Francis M. Cockrell's troops to the north where the line turned ninety degrees at the Stockade Redan, and Brigadier General Martin Green's farther south along the Baldwin's Ferry Road.[56]

Obviously, Pemberton wanted his freshest and best troops in the critical area from just left of the Graveyard Road down to just south of the railroad. That would appear to be the best routes of advance for the Federals, containing as they did the entrances of the Graveyard, Jackson, and Baldwin's Ferry Roads, not to mention the railroad. Pemberton knew most of the Federal army was on the Jackson Road or northward and so surmised that this would be the critical area. For the Federals to move northward and mass along the Valley Road would be problematic, and to get down as far as the Hall's Ferry Road and mass for an attack there would be far too distant from the enemy's new supply base on the Yazoo River. Consequently, Pemberton wanted his two freshest divisions and his reserve drawn up in this critical expanse of less than three miles where the enemy would logically deploy. There, he presumed, the fate of Vicksburg would be decided. And that fate was on everyone's minds, many a soldier whispering to his comrade, "'Will they come,' 'when will they be here?'"[57]

The troops were quick to man these fortifications but found them less than satisfactory. Lockett himself admitted that they were not in the best shape on the evening of May 17 and morning of May 18 when the troops manned them, prompting his desire to return forthwith to Vicksburg and begin work. He explained, "Not having been occupied they [the major earthworks] were now much washed and weakened by the winter's rains. The rifle pits connecting the main works had suffered in the same way, while on many parts of the line these pits had never been finished." A Mississippian described his section of the works as "a very inferior ditch about four feet wide and as many deep."[58]

As soon as he arrived, Lockett restarted work at a furious pace, dividing the line into three sections under subordinate engineers: Stevenson's line under Captain J. J. Conway, Forney's and Smith's lines under Captain David Wintter, and the riverfront under First Lieutenant William O. Flynn. Each man had a number of other engineers under them doled out to the various brigades while Lockett himself kept a larger party of miners, mechanics, and "hired negroes," many of whom were sick, to work in special places with mules and oxen. He noted that "before nightfall [on May 17] work was under way all along the lines of defense." As more troops appeared during the night and the next day, each regiment and brigade went to work on their sections of the line. "Fatigue parties were set to work making these repairs and connections," Lockett noted, "at the same time all field artillery, Parrott guns, and siege pieces on the river front were moved to the rear line, platforms and embrasures were prepared for them, and ammunition was placed in convenient and protected places." As the troops marched in, they also placed any field guns that survived Champion Hill and Big Black River Bridge, making a total of 102 cannons on the line in a matter of hours, although the placement of the artillery was haphazard at best. Carter Stevenson reported that "several sections and companies of artillery not properly belonging to my division were posted on my line." To disrupt the avenues of advance, the Confederates also placed additional abatis on some sections, as well as more "entanglements of telegraph wire."[59]

Although manpower and zeal were not missing, the commodities most in need were tools to perform the work. Lockett estimated there were only about five hundred total picks and shovels inside Vicksburg, which he doled out to the brigades "according to the amount of work required." Logically, the idea was to continually transfer the scattered tools to the points of greatest need, but officers were loath to let go of precious tools that might be needed in the future. Lockett described how the shovels and picks "being much scattered along our lines were considered so precious by both men and officers that when not in actual use they were hidden for fear that they would be stolen by other troops, or ordered to some other part of the line by the chief engineer." Lockett described the paltry number as "entirely inadequate for the work" and how the troops soon fashioned shovels of wood, using their bayonets as picks.[60]

Despite the lack of resources, the fortifications grew only stronger over the course of May 18 and the following night, Pemberton himself inspecting them with Lockett by his side. It was a good thing, as advance Federals began to appear all along the line by noon on May 18, especially in the critical area Pemberton had correctly determined was the point they would appear, that is, between the railroad and the Graveyard Road. But it seemed to take the Federals a long time to bring up their divisions and encircle Vicksburg. Of course, as the Federals slowly coiled around the city, its defenders were using every precious hour to further strengthen the fortifications defending it, hoping for enough time to make them more formidable.[61]

Yet it was clear that time was running out as the Federals began their approach all along the line. Even before Pemberton had his troops fully in the trenches, riders gave warning that the enemy was nearing. Apparently, the slow Federal advance still caught Pemberton somewhat off guard, one staff officer, James C. Wiggs, relating how he was positioning a Louisiana regiment when firing erupted up ahead and a bullet sang close to him. "I thought it was some of our boys so I raised up in my Stirrups and hollered out 'what the Hell are you shooting at." The response was a volley: "It seemed to me a whole platoon." Wiggs placed the regiment barely in time and returned to Pemberton as fast as he could to report the enemy advance. Pemberton did not believe him, stating that his reports indicated the enemy was just then crossing the Big Black River. Wiggs told him to listen: "You ought to have seen him hustle," Wiggs remembered. It was a close call, and several reflected that had Sherman continued on the Federals could have "force[d] their way into Vicksburg that evening without much difficulty." In a similar account, a civilian on a foaming horse rode up to Francis Shoup on the Graveyard Road and told him the Federals were right behind him. Shoup immediately formed a regiment and sent it forward, where sure enough they ran into Federals. Shoup also sent the rider to Pemberton.[62]

Pemberton first reported "constant and heavy skirmishing along the left of our center on the Graveyard Road, accompanied with brisk artillery fire." One Mississippian, in fact, marveled at watching "their artillery approaching at a gallop to take position." Much of the fire fell on Smith's right and Forney's left at the Stockade Redan. Smith reported the enemy advancing early on the afternoon of May 18, with some of the regiments of Shoup's and Baldwin's brigades meeting them in front of the works and then falling back into the main fortifications during the night. William Pitt Chambers of the 46th Mississippi described how "while deploying we suddenly encountered a Federal Reg't executing a similar maneuver," and another member of the regiment added that "if we had been a half hour later, the Federals could have walked into our works unopposed."[63]

Not all the Confederates endured this initial baptism of fire well, illustrating the lingering morale problems among some of the defenders. Simeon

Martin of the 46th Mississippi described how a regiment to his right, also out in front of the works, broke at the initial skirmishing: "Some of our troops on the immediate right of our Regiment were in bad shape on the evening; they did not like to face the rifle fire of the enemy, and when he brought up some cannon and began to throw grape and canister, they broke and ran down the hill. The officers got them back with some difficulty, but their heart was not in the work and they seemed more anxious to protect themselves from danger than to fight." Then a curious episode occurred when the Confederates hit a Federal skirmisher and he "raised the most awful yell I ever heard in my life." Martin went on to describe how "this seemed to put them in good humor, they began to laugh and crack jokes, their line was reformed and their fire became steady." Martin wondered at the "important effect a slight circumstance may sometimes have on the morale of troops in action."[64]

As if the Federal advance was not enough to worry about, Joseph E. Johnston was also peppering Pemberton with messages ranging from demanding evacuation and retreat to something so small as "can you get rid of your teams? It would be better to kill them than feed them." Another message from Pemberton's superior, however, created an end-all decision on the future. As Pemberton rode the lines with his generals and Lockett, a courier rode up and handed him a note from Johnston. It contained wise advice, the same that Ulysses S. Grant knew, that "if Haynes' Bluff is untenable, Vicksburg is of no value and cannot be held." Johnston prophesied surrender in the future and starkly wrote: "Under such circumstances, instead of losing both troops and place, we must, if possible, save the troops. If it is not too late, evacuate Vicksburg and its dependencies, and march to the northeast."[65]

Pemberton was aghast at the thought, not to mention disobeying a direct order from the president to hold the place. But being the indecisive soul he was, and perhaps looking for cover if he disobeyed, Pemberton called a council of war with his generals and laid out the situation, asking only for their opinions as to the "question of practicability." Unanimously, they agreed that "it was impossible to withdraw the army from this position with such morale and material as to be of further service to the Confederacy." Pemberton accordingly wrote Johnston his final decision: "I have decided to hold Vicksburg as long as is possible. . . . I still conceive it to be the most important point in the Confederacy." A Louisianan agreed, writing in his diary that "with the fall of this place and this army the Confederacy will totter if not fall." Others disagreed. One Mississippian huddled in the trenches defending Vicksburg later remembered that this was "the great mistake of his [Pemberton's] life."[66]

So Pemberton decided to hold, even though he believed he had only a little more than eighteen thousand troops to man the lines. He placed all his hope in quick relief from Johnston. In fact, Pemberton sent word out to the troops to "hold the place for only twelve hours longer," one Mississippian remembered. Yet even as Pemberton met with his officers, more Federal artillery opened up, indicating the enemy was drawing ever closer, not Johnston, and that they were preparing for an all-out assault. Another Mississippian, in fact, related that "Anaconda like, the Federals at once began to tighten their coils around us, and this artillery firing was designed to cover their movements." Pemberton had made his decision, but how long "as is possible" lay heavy on everyone's minds throughout the long night of May 18. He and the army may not have twelve more hours left.[67]

All accordingly came to the realization that the next day, May 19, would be an important one. One Louisianan admitted, "Every thing pointed to the morrow as the great day of battle," and a Federal in the 72nd Illinois voiced similar sentiments in his diary across the way. He had reached Vicksburg, "the goal of our hopes for months past, the object of so many hard marches, the Rebel stronghold in the West." Then he added, "We knew there would be bloody work for the morrow, as we would have to assault their works to get into Vicksburg."[68]

4

"Within Musket-Range of the Defenses of Vicksburg"

Colonel Winchester Hall of the 26th Louisiana had a perfect welcome planned for the Federals when daylight appeared on May 19. Although he was more than ready to give the enemy shot and shell, with an ample dose of small arms fire as well, he thought it would be more polite to greet them that morning initially with a good old Confederate tune. "I had ordered out the band," he wrote, "and intended to give our opponents 'Dixie' at daylight." Hall's brigade commander, Francis Shoup, nixed the idea, however, Hall relating that he "considered it untimely to make overtures to the enemy." The Louisianans' bullets would have to suffice.[1]

More than just Colonel Hall knew something was afoot, one Louisianan writing early that morning in his diary that "the day promises to be a bloody one—decisive can I not say? Of the fate of this nation and having an important bearing on the destinies of the World." A Mississippian described the fright the coming day held, writing:

> That night was a solemn night for the soldier. None but those who have had the experience can tell the feeling of the soldier's heart on the night before the approaching battle; when upon the wings of fond imagination his soul visits the loved ones at home—and while he thinks of a lonely and loving wife whose face he may never look upon again and who may never see his form any more on earth, his heart bleeds and dark forebodings fill his mind.[2]

Others were having different problems across the lines. Although most on the Union side had also come to the same conclusion that this was to be a horrible day, most Federals awoke with no certain knowledge of the day's schedule. Captain John J. Kellogg of the 113th Illinois recalled how "every man of my company proceeded, by the aid of twigs and dry leaves, to make just fire enough on the protected slope of the hill, to boil his tin cup of coffee and broil a slice of diaphram um et swinum for the morning meal." He went on to describe how the orders soon came down the line; not having gotten a good look at the Confederate fortifications the day before, he snuck forward to observe his chances. Now, "in the first, feint light of the morning," he saw fort after fort with entrenchments and stockades in between. "It required but a brief inspection to satisfy me that more than likely we wouldn't go into town that day," he confessed. Others thought so as well and began to give their possessions to the sick and those who would stay behind. Kellogg had the inclination to do the same, until he "happened to recollect I had no valuables."[3]

Songs and valuables aside, Grant had other issues on his mind. The major decision he had to make that morning was what to do now. Obviously, he could take the cautious and conservative approach and lay siege to the city. That, of course, would take time, and Grant was well aware that the sooner he wrapped up this Vicksburg business the better for all involved—except the Confederates. Politically, Grant was still being questioned by both the president and some in Congress. Militarily, he was still receiving orders to join Nathaniel Banks, which he ignored. If he now became entrapped in a months-long siege, it would potentially cause a final fit of exasperation among those who could doom Grant's career. As much personally as anything, he needed a quick victory.[4]

The military situation dictated haste as well and was obviously more important than Grant's personal situation. Grant's army would likely not conduct siege operations with a will if they thought some quicker method would work; Chief Engineer Frederick Prime noted that "our own troops, buoyant with success, were eager for an assault, and would not work well if the slow process of a siege was undertaken." Grant himself said as much later in his memoirs, believing that "the troops themselves were impatient to possess Vicksburg, and would not have worked in the trenches with the same zeal, believing it unnecessary." Likewise, if it boiled down to a lengthy siege, Grant would require reinforcements, which would obviously be better utilized some place else if Vicksburg was already in Federal hands. Conversely, the longer Grant dallied in front of Vicksburg, the more chances there were that Johnston, lurking to the east, would become stronger and be more of a factor. If Vicksburg were quickly reduced, Grant could then turn on Johnston and acquire much of Mississippi, even "all territory west of the Tombigbee, and this before the season was too far advanced for campaigning in this latitude." Lastly, and perhaps most important, Grant believed a quick assault would succeed. He knew he had the Confederates on the run and that they were probably more than demoralized. He surmised that the Confederates "would not make much effort to hold Vicksburg."[5]

Consequently, Grant decided that the best way to capture Vicksburg was simply to storm the city's ramparts and take the place by force. Although that would entail casualties, he deemed it necessary and ordered an attack on May 19.[6]

Getting the various corps into position would prove more difficult than Grant thought. While all three corps made good progress, it took time to position thousands of troops along a lengthy line that ran along broken and undulating ground that had never before been examined or even seen by the Federals. And it all had to be done close enough to the Confederate line to launch an assault, which was certainly within range of the Confederate guns inside the defenses of Vicksburg. Those fortifications made a strong initial impression on the Federals, one Ohioan writing that "as the column climbed up out of the ravine it turned a curve in the road near a large white house.... Rounding this curve, the great line of defenses was suddenly disclosed. For three miles to the right and left, along the whole front, the sharp cut crest of the Rebel fortifications formed the horizon line. Instinctively the men wheeling into view of the scene, began to cheer." One Federal division commander, Peter Osterhaus, also gave a vivid report on the approach to Vicksburg, writing that "we [soon] came within sight of its extensive fortifications. Numerous flags floating over the works proved that the persisting leaders of the enemy would try a last attempt to rally their men to fight again, and to save, if possible, the stronghold of rebeldom on the Mississippi River."[7]

Sherman made the most progress toward an assault, as he was farther along than the other two corps. He had stopped the evening before well back from Vicksburg at another fork in the road, the right one the Graveyard Road and the left the main Jackson Road. Only his leading skirmishers made any contact with outlying Confederates on the evening of May 18. Fortunately, what little daylight had been left at that time allowed Sherman to do some reconnoitering by sending the 8th Missouri along the left fork toward the enemy lines and the 13th United States Infantry Regulars along the right, at the same time posting a battery at the fork itself. With word from Grant, who was present at the crossroads to direct Sherman to deploy on the right while McPherson took the center and McClernand the left, Sherman deployed his leading division, Blair's, close in and kept Tuttle's troops behind in rear. He also sent Steele's division along what he termed a "blind road to the right" to hopefully reach the bluffs overlooking the Mississippi River.[8]

Throughout the night and especially the next morning, Sherman's divisions continued their work, eventually reaching "within musket-range of the defenses of Vicksburg," prompting one Indianan to remark on the irony that they were now back within sight of their old campsites at Young's Point. One Iowan declared that "we have traveled to get here 175 miles and it is about 12 miles from where we started." Steele continually moved westward toward the bluffs "till he reached the Mississippi," Sherman noted, in the process taking control of the critical Valley Road running north out of Vicksburg. As Steele's brigades under Colonels Francis H. Manter and Charles R. Woods and Brigadier General John M. Thayer went into line on the bold ridge north of Mint Spring Bayou, they found a line of Confederate earthworks that had been abandoned the night before for a better position south of the bayou; any attack would be better defended by making the Federals trudge through the "deep and broken valley intervening," brigade commander Charles Woods wrote. One Confederate Mississippian in the new works south of the bayou wrote of the joke they had: "A few volleys of musketry were heard near the position we held there over-night, then a cannon shot or two, and then *a charge*. The enemy had assaulted and doubtless carried our deserted works." Samuel Lockett was also amused at the Union charge "with shout and cheer," noting that they continued on "apparently with perfect confidence that there would be another 'walk over.'" Indeed, one 25th Iowa soldier in Woods's brigade noted that they "drove the enemy back out of their rifle pits for at least 1 ½ miles, without losing scarcely any men." But there was some actual success. Company K of the 30th Missouri was sent out initially to sweep the camps of stragglers, one member writing that "we captured more officers and men than there were in Co. K." An Iowan in Woods's brigade also boasted of the "plenty of corn meal molasses meat honey &C and you believe we had a good breakfast." At another point, Steele himself sent a company out to clear the Martha Edwards House between the lines, it being used by Confederate sharpshooters.[9]

By the mid- to late morning hours on May 19, Steele was in position, Sherman declaring that "we had compassed the enemy to the north of Vicksburg, our right resting on the Mississippi River, with a plain view of our fleets at the mouth of the Yazoo and Young's Point, Vicksburg in plain sight." But even one quick view of the terrain to the front showed that an assault here would be virtually impossible. Sherman pointed out that "nothing separated us from the enemy but a space of about 400 yards of very difficult ground, cut up by almost impracticable ravines, and his line of intrenchments." It was obvious the attack would have to come farther inland from the river.[10]

In order to gain as much ground as he could without assaulting on this easily defensible far right flank, Sherman asked the cooperation of the navy in the river. He asked Porter: "Can't you send a couple of gunboats down?

They can easily see and distinguish our men.... You will have no trouble in distinguishing our flank." Realizing he had perhaps broken protocol in this semi-emergency, Sherman added, "I would get General Grant to make this request, but he is far on the left flank and it would take hours to find him."[11]

There was nevertheless some resistance as Steele deployed, a slave telling the troops there were 40,000 Confederates defending Vicksburg. Some of the minor skirmishing resulted from the short Confederate occupation of the line of earthworks north of Mint Spring Bayou. Parts of Baldwin's and Shoup's brigades of Smith's division as well as Cockrell's of Bowen's initially held the line north of Mint Spring Bayou and the Graveyard Road the night before, Cockrell being slightly wounded in the initial skirmishing. This resistance caused a slowdown in Union deployment and offered dangerous areas on top of that. As Grant, still on the right at this point, and Sherman watched Steele deploy on the far right, Sherman remembered that "a man was killed by the side of General Grant and myself, as we sat by the road-side looking at Steele's division passing to the right." On another occasion, one of Sherman's staff officers, Captain Julius Pitzman, received "a dangerous wound in the hip" while following up the regulars as they approached the Confederate lines. Steele's brigades likewise found it dangerous on the front line. Charles Woods described "the enemy strongly posted, with from twelve to seventeen siege guns in position, covered by strong earthworks, and commanding our position." Woods went into slight skirmishing that soon turned heated, deploying the 25th Iowa and then a battery of artillery on the reverse slope of a ridge. Unfortunately, a lieutenant in the 9th Iowa of Thayer's brigade was shot by his own pickets.[12]

The Confederates south of Mint Spring Bayou also suffered, finding it difficult to man batteries and fortifications under the increasing small arms and particularly artillery fire that the deploying Union army threw out. The withdrawal to the inner line of works south of Mint Spring Bayou also caused confusion, but the troops went to work "strengthening the defenses on all the unprotected intervals," Baldwin noted. In the confusion, some of the troops earlier deployed north of the bayou were even forgotten, a company of Mississippians being left in the bustle north of Mint Spring Bayou to confront the entirety of the Federal force: "I saw myself and company at the mercy of Grant's army," the captain wrote, and he quickly gave positive orders to "move down the hill, and by way of the lowest ground into the works." Their new fortifications provided only slightly better relief, substandard at least according to Francis Shoup, who described them as "poorly run and poorly constructed." Still, he admitted that "there was no point of the whole line which could not have been carried by simple assault without ladders or any sort of machines." Casualties on the Confederate side also began to mount in the skirmishing; William Baldwin's chief of artillery, Major Joseph W. Anderson, was "mortally wounded while passing around a parapet to select a position for the guns."[13]

Farther inland from Steele's position was Blair's division of Sherman's corps, which proceeded late on the evening of May 18 toward Vicksburg from the forks in the road along the Graveyard Road. There, they met the first defending Confederates in the form of Colonel Leon D. Marks's 27th Louisiana, which had been sent forward for foraging. Brigade commander Francis Shoup was with them and upon reaching the line of fortifications was given word that the Federals "were upon us" on that very road. Shoup quickly deployed skirmishers to the front "to check his advance and to allow us time to occupy the trenches." The skirmishers found the enemy less than three hundred yards out, which gave very little time. Still, Shoup deployed the Louisianans, although he could not cover the entire open area. He sent word to Louis Hébert to his right to see if that brigade could extend their line a bit toward the Graveyard Road "to close the interval," which they did. Fortunately, other troops also appeared and took station on the left, although some regiments found absolutely no fortifications in their front. The tired soldiers quickly began remedying that.[14]

Despite the vigorous work needed on the Confederate lines, Sherman could already tell that the enemy works "were . . . strong and well manned." He probed for any opening he could find, and the best he could locate was along the Graveyard Road. While the terrain was still cut up abruptly in Blair's area, it nevertheless offered a much better chance of a successful attack than farther to the right on Steele's front. As a result, Blair began to deploy his three brigades under Colonels Giles A. Smith and Thomas Kilby Smith and Brigadier General Hugh Ewing. Yet Blair's troops were no more thrilled with their terrain assessment than Steele's had been, especially when they saw the deep and cavernous ravines on either side of the road itself and the woods between them and the open spaces in front of the Confederate works. Kilby Smith noted that he sent out skirmishers because of "the woods in front being filled with the enemy."[15]

The most promising ground was along the road itself, where a narrow ridge split the headwaters of Mint Spring Bayou to the north and Glass Bayou to the south, with even a road cut looming along part of the highest ground. Sherman, who soon arrived in person, quickly saw this was perhaps the best area to attack, although he correctly guessed that almost every Confederate cannon and rifle would be trained on that very ground, thinking the enemy attack would be funneled through the best approach. And from the initial look of things, it seemed there was indeed a lot of firepower across the way inside the formidable looking Stockade Redan. Blair deployed behind the opposite ridge from the Confederate works nevertheless and prepared as best he could for an assault. Meanwhile, Tuttle's division of three brigades under Brigadier Generals Ralph P. Buckland, Joseph A. Mower, and Charles L. Matthies were still on the road back toward Bridgeport and, once they arrived, would be held in reserve, not taking a position on the front line for the time being.[16]

Farther south, McPherson had a tougher time getting his troops in an attack position, causing some concern in Sherman's corps that the Confederates, who were evidently burning something in Vicksburg, "may try to escape by way of ridge road," one Missourian confided. In fact, the only brigade of McPherson's corps to actually take a position by midday on May 19 was Ransom's of McArthur's division, which was actually the only brigade in the division with the larger army at this time. Brigadier General Hugh T. Reid's small brigade was still across the river and would stay there for the duration. McArthur himself and Colonel William Hall's brigade were still manning the Grand Gulf area. Ransom was thus on his own, and once Sherman turned to the right off the Jackson Road, Ransom's troops "had the Road to themselves" and deployed around the Shirley House on the Jackson Road. Once more troops came up, Ransom took a position on the left of Blair's troops.[17]

The following divisions under John Logan (three brigades under Brigadier Generals John E. Smith, Mortimer D. Leggett, and John D. Stevenson) and Isaac F. Quinby (three brigades under Colonels John B. Sanborn, Samuel A. Holmes, and George B. Boomer) were still making their way forward from bivouac sites farther back on the Bridgeport Road, Holmes's brigade having been left even farther back at the Champion Hill battlefield. All three of Logan's brigades eventually made their way along the left fork of the road, which joined the Jackson Road, and the division began to locate positions from which it could combat the enemy and, if possible, launch an attack from a line formed on the left of Ransom's new position; two brigades manned the front at first nearer to Ransom's position across Glass Bayou but eventually moved back down near the "white house." In all the jockeying for position, the Confederate skirmishers were continually driven back, John E. Smith noting that "our skirmishers [were] still driving the enemy, who finally retired behind their intrenchments." The artillery also deployed and moved forward, Captain Samuel De Golyer placing a gun within a hundred and fifty yards of the Confederate line by "daring and intrepidity." Quinby's troops eventually took a position even farther to the left, on Logan's flank, with Holmes's brigade, arriving later, forming a reserve behind the line. Only Boomer's troops of Quinby's division arrived in the vicinity in time to take a position during the day, however, the rest still marching in, Sanborn's enduring a hike of "17 miles with a most intense heat and suffocating dust all day."[18]

McPherson's troops met the Confederates along the Jackson Road, more of Hébert's Mississippians and Louisianans as well as John C. Moore's mixed brigade to the south. Colonel Ashbel Smith of the 2nd Texas declared: "Soon clouds of the enemy's skirmishers were seen emerging through the woods on the hills some 2 miles distant, and deploying to the right and left." Skirmishers fought them throughout the day but gradually fell back, one Mississippian asserting that the fighting reached great enough proportions that the "bullets had now begun to whistle, reminding one of angry bees, seeking some object upon which to vent their wrath." Brigade commander Louis Hébert similarly noted that the enemy "made his appearance in front of my line . . . , as if intending to assault." Most appeared on Hébert's left on the Graveyard Road, forcing him to move the 36th Mississippi and the 7th Mississippi Battalion from his right to his left upon Martin L. Smith's call for help. Hébert described how "the enemy opened artillery . . . , but no attempt at a charge was made, as had been anticipated. . . . Our skirmishers (by direction of the lieutenant general commanding) were drawn into our lines, pickets alone being put out." More Federals continually arrived, and both the Graveyard Road and Jackson Road sectors were heavily under fire by midday on May 19, the Confederates unable to respond due to orders to save ammunition until it was actually needed. "So far as my front was concerned," Hébert reported, "he may be said to have completed his investment."[19]

John C. Moore had different problems south of the Jackson Road and extending all the way down to the railroad. While most of Quinby's full division would be late in arriving, the Mississippians, Alabamians, and Texans in this sector found inferior fortifications, including the lunette along the Baldwin's Ferry Road. "We found the trenches and redoubts in a very imperfect state," Moore complained, "the trenches being too narrow and shallow." Plenty of labor was on hand, and Moore explained how "by working at night with the small number of tools in our possession, we soon greatly improved them; also constructed approaches which seem to have been overlooked or deemed unnecessary." The troops also worked on the fields of fire, Colonel Smith of the 2nd Texas noting that "houses were burned, trees were cut down, and other obstructions were removed, and dispositions made to receive the enemy." The diarist Emma Balfour gave more detail about the houses, writing that the night before "the darkness was lit up by burning houses all along our lines. These were burnt that our firing would not be obstructed. It was sad to see.

CHAPTER FOUR

Many of them we knew to be handsome residences put up in the last few years as country residences—two of them very large and handsome houses." She realized the situation nonetheless and added, "but the stern necessity of war has caused their destruction." It was a good thing; by the morning of May 19, Federals had appeared in front of this section of the line as well, but Forney directed that little resistance be made in the form of skirmishing "in order to husband ammunition."[20]

McClernand's corps had the most difficulty getting into position, not even counting the heat and dust. One soldier noted in his diary "considerable difficulty in getting water among the briers and bushes." The corps had halted at dark the night before on the Baldwin's Ferry Road several miles out of Vicksburg, and early the next morning McClernand himself and his staff moved forward to get their first look at the ground they would have to traverse. He did not like what he saw. The general moved forward some two miles to the ridge overlooking the valley of Durden Creek, within two miles of the city and within range of the enemy's skirmishers; one of the Confederates almost killed Colonel John J. Mudd. From their vantage point, the Union officers could see "the Rebel fortifications and crowds of men on top of the works." McClernand surmised that the "hill runs north and south, and conforms very much to the line of Vicksburg's defenses, in plain view in a similar range a mile west." McClernand also correctly noted that "the intervening space between these two ranges [the valley of Durden Creek] consisted of a series of deep hollows separated by narrow ridges, both rising near the enemy's works, and running at angles from them until they are terminated by the narrow valley of . . . [the] Creek." He went on to describe how "the heads of the hollows were entirely open. Nearer their termination they were covered with a thicket of trees and underbrush" in which Confederate pickets were located. Despite the danger, McClernand could also see the Confederate fortifications: "The enemy's defenses consist of an extended line of rifle-pits occupied by infantry, covered by a multitude of strong works occupied by artillery, so arranged as to command not only the approaches by the ravines and ridges in front, but each other."[21]

It was obviously not an ideal situation, and McClernand certainly had second thoughts as he returned from his "personal reconnaissance." He nevertheless ordered his divisions forward around 6:30 A.M., they having been held in formation to "commence the investment of the city" for two and a half hours while McClernand made his inspection. The orders came down the chain of command where they had their effect, one Illinoisan in Brigadier General

William P. Benton's brigade describing his "Colonel very cross, swearing like a good fellow." The same Illinoisan was in no better mood, being in the midst of frying his breakfast when the orders to fall in arrived; he had to dump it in the dust. Later, after some soldiers detailed to cook dinner brought it forward, another order to advance came and the same men had to turn away from that meal as well: "We turn away dinnerless, as we did breakfastless, because military law just now interferes with nature's promptings." To make it worse, the result was not even an all-out assault. McClernand was not sure about making an attack, so he only ordered his divisions forward to occupy the reverse slope of the ridge east of Durden Creek. That would provide shelter while more decisions were made.[22]

Accordingly, Brigadier General Andrew Jackson Smith in the lead moved forward during the morning hours of May 19 and took a position on the right of the Baldwin's Ferry Road, his two brigades under Colonel William J. Landram and Brigadier General Stephen G. Burbridge fanning out behind the ridge for protection. To the left of the road deployed Peter J. Osterhaus's two brigades under Colonel Daniel W. Lindsey and Brigadier General Albert L. Lee, Osterhaus having returned from his slight wound two days earlier at the Battle of Big Black River Bridge. McClernand held Eugene Carr's division in reserve in the valley behind the hill, Brigadier Generals William P. Benton and Michael K. Lawler's brigades providing fresh support if necessary. Colonel Marcus Spiegel of the 120th Ohio in Osterhaus's division wrote his wife that "we have Vicksburg already surrounded and it must fall. From our position we can see the Church steeples but they have a heavy line of fortifications clear around."[23]

Throughout the morning, McClernand continually moved his troops forward despite constant skirmishing, raising a cloud of dust discernable to all watching, even the Federals of McPherson's corps farther to the right. The Confederates were watching as well, one Texan declaring that "we could already see the Northerners marching." McClernand kept Grant well informed and later reported that "skirmishers were thrown forward, who engaged the enemy's skirmishers, and artillery was opened from the most commanding positions upon the enemy's works." Smith and Osterhaus eventually crossed Durden Creek and took a position nearer the slopes of the ridge on which the Confederate lines sat. The corps continued to inch its way forward so that by midafternoon it was no more than eight hundred yards from the Confederate lines. An amazed Illinoisan jotted in his diary that "the fortifications in front of us look really formidable, fort after fort can be seen, bristling with cannon, with rifle pits stretching in almost every direction. The rebel flag can be plainly seen flaunting in the breeze." A nearby Iowan echoed, "In front of the

Union lines were the Confederate fortifications. No towering specters, but real frowning battlements. Spades were trumps."[24]

The same minor skirmishing that had occurred elsewhere thus ensued on McClernand's front as well. Confederate division commander Carter Stevenson reported that as early as the evening of May 18 "the enemy made his appearance in front of our lines, and immediately began to push forward his sharpshooters." More concerning was the artillery that began to bombard the Confederates. Stevenson indicated that it did severe damage almost immediately: "The number of guns, superiority of range and metal, and exhaustless supply of ammunition, enabled them in very short time to plant many batteries is such commanding positions as to damage our works materially, and inflict a very considerable loss among the men." With Federals this far down it certainly seemed they were laying siege. One Mississippian put it simply: "The impudent foe is indeed encircling us."[25]

"By this disposition," Grant wrote, "the three army corps covered all the ground their strength would admit of, and by the morning of the 19th the investment of Vicksburg was made as complete as could be by the forces at my command." Still, he had nowhere near the numbers needed to fully bottle up Vicksburg, and so he opted to cover the northern and eastern faces, that being where the main roads entered and exited and the direction where his supply base at Haynes' Bluff was emerging. Furthermore, the left of the line was not covered because, if the Confederates retreated in that direction, they would be boxed in by the Big Black River.[26]

Yet, McClernand's corps was still much too far away to launch at attack, and one of its divisions, Alvin Hovey's, was still to the rear. McPherson had done little better, and he was missing a good portion of his corps as well. Sherman's troops had progressed the farthest, but the terrain precluded an attack across a broad front north of Mint Spring Bayou. Matters were accordingly looking difficult as midday on May 19 approached. But Grant would not halt. The enemy was certainly demoralized and would hopefully give in: "During the day there was continuous skirmishing, and I was not without hope of carrying the enemy's works . . . relying upon the demoralization of the enemy, in consequence of repeated defeats outside of Vicksburg." He similarly wrote to Admiral Porter that any naval shelling would "demoralize [further] an already badly beaten enemy. . . . We beat them badly on the 16th, near Edwards Station, and on the 17th, at Black River Bridge, taking about 6,000 prisoners, besides a large number killed and wounded." Grant was confident of success. When he issued his final orders for the attack that morning, he added: "When the works are carried, guards will be placed by all division commanders, to prevent their men from straggling from their companies." Grant intended to end the campaign that day, May 19, 1863.[27]

If the campaign were to end this day, matters would have to go better for Grant than they had thus far. The old military adage, traced to the Prussian Helmuth von Moltke, is that "no plan survives first contact with the enemy." That was certainly the case for Ulysses S. Grant as he approached Vicksburg. He had dreamed about a coordinated assault by all three of his corps, with a presumed breakthrough, and he even had ideas about what to do once the Confederate lines broke and the Federals swept on into Vicksburg. Grant described his thinking years later in his memoirs: "The enemy had been much demoralized by his defeats at Champion's Hill and the Big Black, and I believed he would not make much effort to hold Vicksburg." Unfortunately for Grant, those plans would be terribly shattered, and not just once contact was made with the enemy. In fact, Grant's plans began to disintegrate even before major contact came and certainly before an actual assault took place; namely, only one of the corps was able to get into position to even launch an attack, and that one corps did so with only one division. It was not the start Grant had hoped for. Nevertheless, as one Indianan described it, the "greate Battle began at Vicksburg."[28]

Despite dense smoke rising from Vicksburg on the morning of May 19 and the rumor that the Confederates were evacuating, Grant issued his final orders at a late 11:16 A.M., and they quickly trickled down the chains of command. The orders simply told his commanders to "push forward carefully, and gain as close position as possible to the enemy's works, until 2 P.M.; at that hour they will fire three volleys of artillery from all the pieces in position. This will be the signal for a general charge of all the army corps along the whole line." Grant sounded confident, seeing no reason why the corps commanders could not accomplish his desires. He continued that "when the works are carried. . . ." The impact was not lost on the common soldier, one Iowan in Sherman's corps writing in his diary that morning: "It is a beautiful morning. We expect to see hard fighting before night."[29]

If Grant could see no reason why the assault would fail, his corps commanders did not agree; Grant spent much of the day on the left with McClernand, worried he might not be as forceful as necessary. Evidently, all three corps commanders focused on the word "carefully" rather than "charge," and as a result only one division of the three army corps was in a position to launch an assault. And that division had not had time to fashion any ladders or

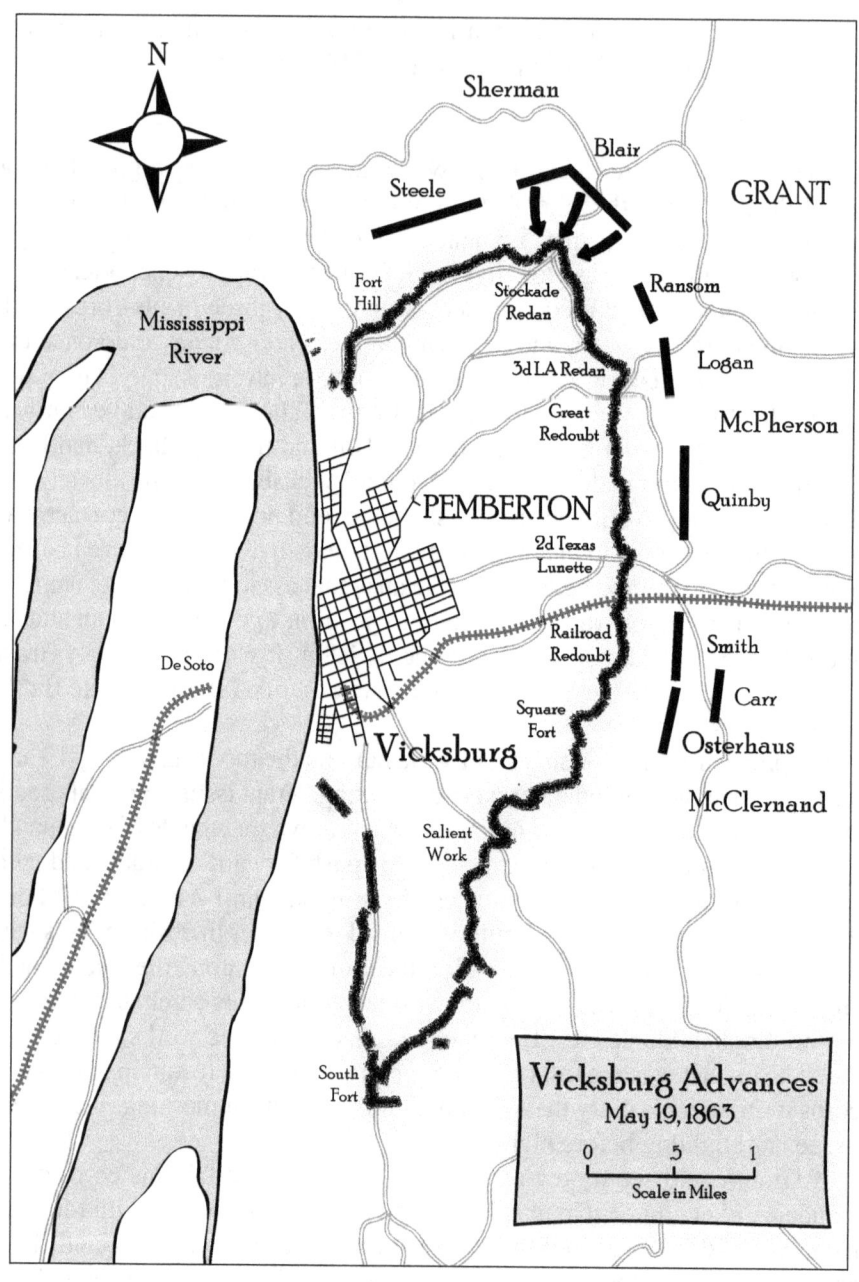

bridging material to get across the wide ditches that normally fronted earthworks of this nature. There was plenty of blame to go around, but this had certainly been a rushed process, with little time for preparation.[30]

Throughout the hours prior to the 2:00 P.M. deadline, McClernand on the far left pushed forward through the valleys of Durden Creek and its tributaries, battling the terrain as much as anything. One geographer has labeled this area "a nightmare of vicious little ravines." Yet the Confederate works dominated thought, one Federal in the 99th Illinois writing home: "On 19th May catch our first sight of Vicksburg. I remember the clay-like bank—a fort—that I first saw." As the day progressed, the "scorching rays of the sun," as the German Jewish colonel Marcus Spiegel of the 120th Ohio described them, also became a factor. Even worse for the Ohioans who were marching in from keeping prisoners at Raymond, they endured "a continuous march of 33 miles with little rest and scanty rations," remembered Ohioan James B. Taylor. The terrain was also difficult and unexplored, McClernand writing that "the ground in front was unexplored and commanded by the enemy's works." Still, McClernand pushed forward with Smith's division on the right and the wounded but now mounted Osterhaus on the left, with Carr's division in reserve. It was a narrow front now exclusively south of the railroad, between the redoubt defending that line and the Square Fort to the south, most of it defended by Stephen D. Lee's Alabamians, one of whom described their tactics: "My pickets fire & fall back as the enemy advances." The going was tough and slow, Colonel Spiegel remarking that "I never saw shot, shell, crape, and Bullets fly thicker in my life. . . . [But] my men stood and kept their line as on dress parade while on the charge and during the hottest [fighting]." Still, by the 2:00 P.M. deadline the corps had not made enough progress to launch an outright assault. "By 2 o'clock, with great difficulty, my line had gained a half mile, and was within 800 yards of the enemy's works," McClernand explained.[31]

Eight hundred yards was still too far to assault across at the double-quick, so McClernand did the best he could. "At the appointed signal," he wrote, "my infantry went forward under such cover as my artillery could afford, and bravely continued a wasting conflict until they had approached within 500 yards of the enemy's lines." Even that was difficult going, Osterhaus describing the enemy guns "which commanded (mostly by cross-fire) every hill, every ravine, gully, and gorge leading to the fortifications." By the time the troops made much headway, the day was well spent, and the soldiers were bordering on exhaustion. The up and down nature of the ridges and ravines along Durden Creek, what one officer described as "a country very much broken in character and difficult for the passage of troops," had been a major deterrent to a rapid advance, most of McClernand's troops not being able to utilize any roads on which to advance and then deploy close to the enemy.[32]

Command problems also arose. Brigadier General Albert L. Lee had just taken over one of Osterhaus's brigades that morning, Theophilus Garrard having been promoted and transferred to duty at Helena, Arkansas. Finding Colonel James Keigwin, the ranking officer, and introducing himself, Lee requested Keigwin to call the other regimental commanders. They soon arrived, meeting their new brigade commander. Once Lee had made his introductions, Keigwin remembered, "he read the order from Gen'l Grant directing him to charge and take the works in front." As the brigade advanced, Lee complimented Colonel Spiegel of the 120th Ohio: "Spiegel . . . you are a man after my own heart; you are doing bully and your men are the bravest I ever saw." After crossing one bald ridge, the brigade halted and Lee and Keigwin climbed the next hill to scout their advance. Lee did not like the looks of things, telling Keigwin, "We can't make it Col." He sent Keigwin and his 49th Indiana off to the right to flank the Square Fort while the rest of the brigade moved toward it from the southeast. Keigwin's Indianans did so, reaching a point of cover in the valley in front of the fort, but not long afterward Lee took a nasty and potentially fatal wound to the face, although he was able to write the next day of "the ball entering my right cheek and passing out at the back of my neck." As he was being taken to the rear he shouted to the 120th Ohio "stick it to them boys" and later told Spiegel, "By George, Col. You did well." Spiegel was also wounded, though less seriously; a piece of shrapnel simply "knocked the skin off" his left knee. While Spiegel remained in action, Lee obviously could not. Although he could write, he was in no shape to command the brigade, and it then went back to Colonel Keigwin's command.[33]

Others were having a similarly bad time. Colonel Theodore E. Buehler of the 67th Indiana described his troops' problems: "All at once found itself saluted by a shell and volley of musketry from the breastworks just when the left wing of the regiment was separated from the right by a burning building, set on fire by the rebels early in the morning. A few steps more and my regiment must have been exposed to the enfilading fire of four different forts." Buehler ordered his men to "lie down behind the brow of the hill which we had been ascending." James Leeper of the 49th Indiana had a closer call when a shell fragment hit his watch and his groin area. Leeper explained to his wife, "It is said by all the surgeons had not been for my watch I would have certainly been killed."[34]

McClernand accordingly called a halt near dark, admitting that "an advance had been made . . . , and the ground gained firmly held, but the enemy's works were not carried." Yet, McClernand had done some fighting against Lee's Alabamians, sustaining seven killed and ninety-three wounded in the entire corps, all in Smith's and Osterhaus's divisions. Plus, the Confederates fronting him were greatly annoyed all day, one Texan in reserve describing how

> the Yankees came in great numbers to us. Firing was stronger so that we had to lie flat on the earth and could not raise our heads without anxiety. Six of our men were wounded in spite of the caution we used. The Northern sharpshooters shot without ceasing and in such a mass that we were lacking in courage. In between the cannon balls and bombs hissed. Most of them went rather high over us. Several fell short distances from us and hurled the dust high.

The danger was not just to man either; the same Texan described going to the wagon camp in rear and that "several of our mules were hit."[35]

McPherson's corps to McClernand's right was likewise not able to launch a coordinated or even comprehensive attack, despite one soldier in John D. Stevenson's brigade writing that there was skirmishing and movement and "McPherson, Logan and Stevenson are in the thickest of it." Many of the brigades faced such rough terrain that one Illinoisan in Logan's division described it as "nothing but hills and vales of the deepest kind." As McPherson took a position on either side of the Jackson Road, that thoroughfare allowed him a better opportunity to march swiftly and deploy closer, but McPherson did not show much aggressiveness and by the 2:00 P.M. deadline was not ready to launch an assault either. Logan's division straddled the Jackson Road, and Quinby's eventually nestled in to the left, all fronting the right of Hébert's brigade at what was becoming known as the 3rd Louisiana Redan (because of its defenders) north of the road and Moore's brigade to the south of the Great Redoubt. Illustrating the lack of any attempt to fight and the extended use of cover along the Jackson Road, Logan reported no casualties whatsoever and Quinby suffered only two killed and three wounded, although one of his Illinois soldiers wrote that they "were immediately, upon arrival at this place, thrown into line of battle and advanced under the range of the rebel cannon. And for four hours they shelled us most terrifically." Only John Logan and the artillery seemed to fight with a will, one Iowan noting that Logan "was in full uniform, his long black hair swept his shoulders, his eyes flashed fire, he seemed the incarnation of the reckless, fearless soldier. He must have thought cannonballs would not hurt him. For five minutes, perhaps, I stood in a little dip in the ground, comparatively protected, while he rode up and down under a storm of cannonballs, calling at the top of his warrior's voice." The artillery did not stop either. Major Charles J. Stolbrand, one of the division artillery chiefs in the XVII Corps, reported that "the batteries opened fire, and soon thereafter the rebel artillery in their works modified and materially slackened fire." But it did not stop, as a couple of members of the 81st Illinois of Logan's division found out all too well. Edmund Newsome noted that, while lying down supporting a battery, "one shell went into the ground under the man next to me, but he scratched it up and rolled it down the hill before it exploded."[36]

One singularly sad event occurred as the batteries supporting the infantry fired away at the Confederates. A premature discharge on one of the guns of the 6th Wisconsin Artillery mangled the gunner ramming the piece. One Illinoisan described how it "blowed left hand and forearm off and the right hand off. Oh it was pitable sight the cords & sinews hanging. . . . Burned the side of his face and set his shirt on fire which he cried to have cut off. Poor man he is taken to the rear & his comrades still keeps the guns going."[37]

The lethargy shown on the Jackson Road was not the case for McPherson's other unit in the area. North of the road as well as Glass Bayou, between it and the Graveyard Road, was the only brigade of McArthur's division on the field, Thomas E. G. Ransom's. McArthur was with another of the division's brigades at the time, so Ransom was primarily on his own and by this time had taken over a spot of ground initially held by one of Sherman's regiments, the 93rd Indiana. Sherman's troops had by that time moved to the right, and Ransom sent out Major Joseph Stockton to "see if I could not find a way to join the brigade to Sherman's left without cutting through the cane brakes, which were as thick as they could grow." Stockton dove in but found the terrain extremely difficult: "I never had such work in all my life, climbing up and down ravines, my horse at one time getting so tangled that I was afraid I would have to leave him—through cane, over and under fallen trees." Eventually, Stockton popped out near the Chicago Light Artillery of Sherman's corps and managed to find a road on which the brigade could form. Ransom quickly took the position.[38]

Although having no military experience of his own except being educated at a Vermont military school, Ransom was the son of a United States regular colonel who had been killed storming the ramparts at Chapultepec in the Mexican War. He quickly displayed his ability early in the war as an officer in the 11th Illinois, during which he was wounded several times, including at Fort Donelson and Shiloh. His brigade at Vicksburg contained three Illinois (11th, 72nd, and 95th) and two Wisconsin (14th and 17th) regiments, some of them veterans of Shiloh. Charles Dana[39] contended that "no young man in all this army has more future than he," and as early as around 11:30 A.M., Ransom, itching for a fight, passed along the written orders from McPherson to launch the attack at 2:00 P.M. Added was the direction to "secure a position previous to that hour (2 P.M.) as near to the enemy as possible without unnecessarily exposing my command," remembered Colonel Thomas W. Humphrey of the 95th Illinois. Idolized by his men, one writing home that "*he is the man:* we want no other," Colonel Humphrey immediately set out to reconnoiter the ground in his front and did so "as much as time and circumstances would permit" amid what one historian has described as "an incredible tangle of ravines." He soon led his Illinoisans forward: "I gained without loss a position in rear of the second ridge in front of the enemy's works." The other regiments in the brigade did the same.[40]

Ahead of the advance was a company of skirmishers from the 17th Wisconsin. Regimental adjutant John Crane sent out Company K, "nine-tenths of whom were Indians from the Green Bay Region of Wisconsin. These Indians were Christians," Crane went on, "descendents of the Christians that were baptized by the early French Missionaries. Probably nine-tenths of them were full blooded Indians and almost one-tenth half breeds. Very few of them spoke more than a few words of English. Some of them spoke French fairly well." But they knew their job. Crane noted, "I will say for them that a better lot of fighters I never saw and especially when it came to skirmishing." They proved their mettle later when the brigade advanced, taking out a battery to the left.[41]

By the time the natives were skirmishing, the rest of the brigade was moving forward into position, although the movement forward to their assault locations was harrowing in itself. George Carrington of the 11th Illinois remembered crossing a peach orchard and cornfield, the corn about knee-high, and taking heavy fire from a gun in the 3rd Louisiana Redan off to the left: "The Officers cautioned every one to be silent and quiet as we were right under the guns of Fort Hill [3rd Louisiana Redan]." In fact, the lay of the land was such that at one point in the march across the field, the gun played especially heavily on the column, one cannonball passing over their heads but plowing under an entire row of soldiers in a regiment parallel with them and producing a huge cloud of smoke. Carrington marveled that all four in the rank went down but then "all escaped unhurt, jumping up laughing and moving on with their Regt."[42]

Ransom was aggressive while others were passive, and as 2:00 P.M. neared he sneaked his brigade forward some five or six hundred yards across the ridges east of the tributary of Glass Bayou. The aggressive Ransom sent his troops forward in two lines but reported "a terrific fire of musketry in my front and an enfilading artillery fire on my left flank." This fire came from the 37th and 38th Mississippi of Louis Hébert's brigade to the front and artillery fire from the flank. That fire, as well as the tangled ravines, caused some confusion in the brigade, as did an intervening ravine they did not know was there: "To our surprise the rebs were not where we expected," wrote one Illinoisan, "and we were obliged to go down a hill and up another." Timing disrupted the effort as well. Lieutenant Colonel Thomas McMahon of the 17th Wisconsin apparently had a fast watch, because he ordered the charge of his regiment ahead of the others. Colonel Humphrey, next in line with his 95th Illinois, was dumfounded, noting that "the Seventeenth Wisconsin . . . on my right, started on the charge before the Fourteenth Wisconsin, Eleventh and Seventy-second Illinois came in sight." Humphrey explained that "although, according to my time, the appointed hour had not arrived by seventeen minutes, yet the firing was so continuous as to render the signal of the volleys uncertain, and as the Seventeenth Wisconsin had started on what Lieutenant-Colonel McMahon deemed was correct time, I deemed it my duty to support him." The Illinoisans moved forward on the left of a huge ravine, the left company of the trailing 72nd Illinois, which had been cut off from the regiment due to the odd terrain, following along.[43]

It cost the Illinoisans. Humphrey described how "we charged across the first ravine, over an almost impassable abatis of felled timber, exposed to a direct and concentrated fire of musketry and a murderous enfilading fire from the enemy's batteries of the redan on our right front, and the heavy works on the Jackson road . . . on our left." The rest of the brigade not appearing, Humphrey noted, "I deemed it rashness to proceed farther." He had only reached within a hundred yards of the Confederate lines, but Ransom, after receiving a report of his activities, sent him a note soon thereafter to hold his position and that he held the next ridge back with the majority of the brigade. He added, "You have done well, nobly." Interestingly, one of the soldiers in the 95th Illinois down in those tortured ravines was Albert Cashier (actually a female named Jennie Hodgers).[44]

Back with the main portion of the brigade, Ransom was doing no better. As men began to go down, particularly in the front ranks, Ransom pushed on to the ravine in front of the Confederate works and there found out why other commanders had shied away from blindly launching their assaults. "After advancing 200 yards, with severe loss, to the first line," Ransom admitted, "I found the ravine in my front, which I had not had time to reconnoiter, impassable for troops." He also complained of little to no support on his flanks, where Logan to his left was not advancing and where a gap existed between his right and Federals of Sherman's corps to the north. Thus, the isolated Ransom called a halt on the best ground he could find for cover, the 95th Illinois locating an area farther on ahead near a ridgetop where they could fire on the enemy line. One 11th Illinoisan admitted that "we could hear the boys [95th Illinois] cheer but could not see them." The Illinoisans' beloved Colonel Humphrey was wounded in the foot for his loyal efforts but refused to yield. Not surprisingly, Ransom declined to send them onward again, satisfied, isolated as he was, with the ground gained without making an all-out assault.[45]

With the frontline Federals stopped, the rest of the brigade took what cover they could and also harassed the Confederates to the front on their high hill. One 72nd Illinois soldier found an especially good spot between the split of a giant white oak tree. He was covered from Confederate fire and peppered the enemy until he ran out of ammunition. His position was so good that he would not give it up, and nearby members of his regiment who were huddling in much worse cover soon began throwing cartridges to him so he could keep up the fire. Still, Ransom was stalled and suffered more casualties than the rest of his corps combined, with McClernand's thrown in for good measure. In the partial advance, Ransom lost fourteen killed and 110 wounded, most in the 95th Illinois that had come to the aid of their anxious comrades.[46]

McClernand and McPherson therefore had done little to assault the lines, Grant writing simply in his memoirs that the majority of the troops' advance that day "resulted in securing more advanced positions for all our troops where they were fully covered from the fire of the enemy." It certainly was not what he had in mind for McClernand and McPherson when he issued the 2:00 P.M. assault orders, but the fighting was not so timid on every front. Sherman had led the army westward on May 17 and 18 and was accordingly the first to arrive and deploy, having gotten Steele's entire division in line north of Mint Spring Bayou and Blair's along the Graveyard Road close enough to attack. Another, Tuttle's, lay just to the rear if needed. And Sherman's troops were the freshest, having seen no fighting since the small affair at Jackson five days ago and little else besides that.[47]

Sherman would take advantage of his forward position as he managed the only actual assaults on this May 19. Yet even in the XV Corps, most of the brigades simply skirmished with few casualties, one Iowan in Woods's brigade of Steele's division describing how the regiments took position on a ridge where "we can now plainly see the rebels. They are fortified on a good ridge, there is a wide valley between them and us, I should think 300 yards across as near as I can judge. We can see them load their cannons plainly and as our guns will carry a thousand yards, when we elevate the sight we commence firing on them." The Federals fired some twenty rounds each throughout the afternoon.[48]

One particularly sad case occurred as the brigades continually skirmished.

In one of Woods's Iowa regiments, W. J. Jones lost his bayonet while on the skirmish line. When replaced by the 76th Ohio, the soldier climbed to high ground to see if he could see it. "He ought to let the old bayonet go some would say," a colleague remarked, adding that "there is more guns and bayonets here than we need." He wanted it, though, and was hit in the hip and stomach because of it, dying the next day. Some of the skirmishing became quite heavy. One of Sherman's brigades, John M. Thayer's of Steele's division, maneuvered heavily on his front to the west of the Stockade Redan but never really assaulted (he still lost seven killed and forty-three wounded); you could not tell that to one 9th Iowa soldier who wrote in his diary: "[We] were in a hot place all the afternoon, especially when our regiment charged over a hill and ran 30 or 40 yards in full view of the enemy." He added, "Only our regiment went over."[49]

Others of Steele's division farther to the west saw the folly of trying to cross the formidable Mint Spring Bayou so far down its watershed, but one effort was successful. As Charles Woods's brigade continually slid westward on the ridge north of Mint Spring Bayou, he eventually came to the Mississippi River and planted a battery on a nearby Indian mound. There, Captain Clemens Landgraeber's ("Old Leather Breeches," he was called) Company F, 2nd Missouri Artillery took a position after a worrisome gallop across bald ridges while under fire, earning the label "Flying Dutchmen." There, on the mound, the battery commanded both the river as well as the Confederate "Water Battery," which was quickly evacuated. Perhaps most important, the battery also commanded the Valley Road, one of the avenues of escape John Pemberton could have used to move northward toward Joseph E. Johnston.[50]

Grant had no idea of letting Pemberton escape, if indeed Pemberton even considered it, which he did not. While there was clearly a difference between cutting off an escape route and assaulting, there was one division in line along the Graveyard Road and the Stockade Redan that was not so dismayed by the terrain. And it was there that the sole major attempt of Grant's confident effort to break Vicksburg's fortifications on May 19 took place.

As it turned out, the only point of attack Grant's forces could manage by 2:00 P.M. on May 19 came at one of the most heavily defended positions along the Confederate lines. The entire area was strong and well defended, becoming even more so with every passing hour. Yet there was a foreboding feeling in those Confederate works. Many a Southerner was aghast as the sun finally came up to see "they [the Federals] had during the night erected a solid line of entrenchments, which were now full of men, who very soon began to pop at us with the rifles. They had also during the night brought up all their remaining field batteries and had them well protected by earth works." The Confederates could only strengthen their own lines in what little time they had, one Louisianan lamenting that "this work was not done long ago." Making the tension greater, messages also ran among the Confederate high command: "A large force of the enemy are moving down the Baldwin's Ferry Road"; "a column of infantry coming down Baldwin's Ferry Road is now moving down toward our right. . . . Another column of dust is seen on the Baldwin Road"; "I now see dust on the Hall's Ferry Road"; and "a column of dust has been seen to our front and left of Jackson Road since about 9 o'clock. Can't tell which way it is moving."[51]

Certainly, there were isolated locales that may have offered steeper ground or deeper fronting creeks, and the entire extreme left wing of the Confederate fortifications fronting the deepest valley of Mint Spring Bayou was all but unassailable. But for the majority of the line that Grant's forces confronted, he could not have chosen a stronger position to assault with a small portion of his army than the Stockade Redan. If there was any consolation, it was in the fact that the area on either side of the Graveyard Road was "a very decided salient," as brigade commander Francis Shoup termed it, that bent the line in a ninety-degree angle. Normally, salients are more dangerous in that they can be assaulted in isolation and bombarded mercilessly along the lengths of their lines. In situations such as these, if the Federals could find the exact location of the works and plant artillery to pour down the lines in parallel fashion rather than firing only perpendicular, they could perhaps achieve a greater degree of softening the assault area than was otherwise normal. Yet in the haste to launch the assault, Sherman took little time to find the exact points of enfilade. Most thought Vicksburg would fall easily and there was no need to take such lengthy measures.[52]

In reality, and in opposition to the thinking on that morning, the Stockade Redan area was terribly strong. In fact, for just such a reason as enfilading artillery, the fortifications contained more than only one major earthwork; it actually consisted of three such redans linked together with rifle pits and stockades. And it was manned to the teeth with fresh Confederate infantry of Forney's and Smith's divisions, not those trampled at Champion Hill and at the Big Black River bridge. Thus, the attempt would certainly not be the pushover that Grant and his officers expected.[53]

The general defense of the Stockade Redan area fell to the Mississippians of Hébert's brigade on the eastern face and the Louisianans of Shoup's brigade on the northern front, both part of divisions that "were not in the least demoralized," Samuel Lockett noted. He added that "these men stood to their arms like true soldiers, and helped to restore the *morale* of our army." The fact that the two brigades joined right in the Stockade Redan itself was less concerning than if they joined elsewhere, but the connection of the brigades also meant the connection of their parent divisions as well, which only added another layer of command to the area. For instance, if one or the other experienced trouble and needed aid from nearby units, they might be under not only a different brigade commander but also an entirely different division commander. Added in was yet another layer of command in that Cockrell's brigade of Bowen's division was drawn up as a reserve just to the rear of the redan, acting as the reserve that would plug gaps or counterattack if needed. Pemberton told Bowen that "your discretion is relied upon to move where the assault is most heavy near you, and within aid of you. Look well to this, and make such disposition as an emergency requires. I am on the line looking to our general interests. Do you so, too." As a result—and this was certainly the case elsewhere along the line as well but most importantly here at the Stockade Redan where the Union attack was about to hit—Hébert, Shoup, Forney, Smith, Cockrell, and perhaps even Bowen, from his headquarters "about midway between the railroad and the Jackson road, in the valley between Mr. Youst's and Mrs. Hughes' houses," would all have to work together well and keep up good communication. Even if all except one isolated area were in good shape, that compromised area could spell doom for the entire defense and potentially Vicksburg itself.[54]

As Mint Spring Bayou grew generally less deep the farther east up the watershed the lines ran, Shoup's brigade fronted a lesser but still strong position on the northern flank of the Stockade Redan. Connecting with Baldwin's brigade farther to the west, Shoup's two Louisiana regiments (the 29th Louisiana having been detached) manned a curving section of the line. It was here that the original outer line that ran along the ridge north of Mint Spring Bayou and abandoned by Smith's division the night before joined the main line. More important, it was also here that the main line made a deep indentation atop the ridge to skirt a slight feeder branch of Mint Spring Bayou. Several slight feeder branches and their ravines existed along the southern side of Mint Spring Bayou, but this one ran farther than most, causing the high ridge south of the bayou to dive farther southward than at other places, thus causing the Confederate line, which ran along the ridgetop, to skirt the ravine as well in a bowl.[55]

The 26th and 27th Louisiana on this front had been in service for more than a year but had not fought in any large battle as yet, they having been held in reserve in the defense of New Orleans and thence in the Vicksburg area; the

26th Louisiana had participated in repelling the December attack at Chickasaw Bayou, but that was the extent of their combat. Nevertheless, Colonel Winchester Hall's 26th Louisiana eventually manned the left of the brigade, to the right of the 17th Louisiana of Baldwin's brigade and the Green Riddle House to their front; they held the western half of the bowl-shaped indentation, although when they arrived they found very little in the way of earthworks to protect them. The Louisianans went to work and, Shoup proudly reported, "few tools could be had, but in a surprisingly short time a very tolerable cover was constructed." Colonel Leon D. Marks's 27th Louisiana picked up the line on the eastern half of the bowl and continued it on to the stockade on the Graveyard Road. Accordingly, Marks's Louisianans manned the leftmost of the three major fortifications in the complex, the one north of the Graveyard Road and west of the stockade itself. The crescent-shaped fort quickly became known as the 27th Louisiana Lunette, and it contained a single 12-pound howitzer of Captain Francis McNally's Arkansas Battery.[56]

Hébert's line joined Shoup's in the Stockade Redan itself, which sat immediately south of the Graveyard Road and commanded that avenue and the high ground on which it ran. Manning the line from the stockade southward on the east face were the Mississippians of Hébert's brigade, the Louisianans in the brigade taking a position farther south. The 36th, 37th, and 38th Mississippi and the 7th Mississippi Battalion had all been engaged prior to this day, including at Iuka and Corinth and in the campaigning of the earlier Vicksburg efforts. Colonel William W. Witherspoon's 36th Mississippi held the Stockade Redan itself with one 12-pound howitzer of the Appeal Arkansas Battery. The Mississippians extended southward from the main fortification to the third of the three major earthworks that would later become known as Green's Redan, although Martin Green's troops would only occupy that section of the line later. Now, the Mississippians held the line, and Witherspoon's Mississippians connected with the 7th Mississippi Battalion and then Colonel Orlando S. Holland's 37th Mississippi, which in turn connected with the 38th Mississippi. Finishing out Hébert's line was the 43rd Mississippi, at the crossing of Glass Bayou, and the 21st and 3rd Louisiana, the latter of which lent its name to the redan it defended on the Jackson Road. It was the more left-middle portion of the brigade that Ransom's advance fronted, although no official assault took place.[57]

Studding this section of the line were multiple pieces of artillery, including guns of the 2nd Alabama Artillery Battalion and the Appeal Arkansas Battery in the Stockade Redan itself. On Shoup's front, McNally's Arkansas Battery defended the line. Near the stockade itself was a 2.71-inch Whitworth rifle of

Wall's Texas Artillery. Behind, as well, were regiments of the famed Missouri Brigade under Francis M. Cockrell; the 1st, 2nd, 3rd, 5th, and 6th Missouri regiments were poised to aid in any way they could.[58]

Obviously, the strength of the Confederate position was not just with the dense Confederate regiments that were packed into the fortifications: five regiments and a battalion of infantry on the main line, not to mention the artillery and Cockrell's regiments in reserve. The terrain that the Confederate line faced was also an important factor, mainly because of the geographical limitations fronting any attacking force. To the north, Mint Spring Bayou was still a substantial and deep ravine even this far out from its mouth on the Mississippi River. Although not nearly as substantial as it was farther to the west were the conscripted Tennesseans and Mississippi State Troops held the line, the bayou and its cavernous valley still created an enormous obstacle for any Federals attacking directly south toward Shoup's lines.[59]

The same phenomenon occurred to the south of the redan, only this time it was because of a feeder branch that ran north and south until it reached the east-west Glass Bayou farther south. Although not as large or wide as Mint Spring Bayou, this ravine was actually more of a hindrance because its sides were steeper due to the compacted nature of the watershed. It also had another feeder branch that ran into the main tributary, which ran parallel and closer to the ridge on which the Confederate line lay, causing another deep ravine paralleling the main one and confounding Ransom's troops regarding where the Confederate line actually was. Any Federals attacking due west against Hébert's position would have to cross the steeper ravine and, conceivably, another one with a steep ridge between along at least a certain portion of the Confederate line.[60]

Because of the proximity of the headwaters of Glass Bayou and Mint Spring Bayou, the only level, high ground in the vicinity of the Stockade Redan was the slender ridge separating the two bayous. It was on this high ground that the Graveyard Road ran, a narrow corridor or approach that was well defended by the Stockade Redan, the road itself blocked by the stockade across the avenue. The deep ravines feeding into both bayous offered cavernous chasms for any attacker to cross, all cleared whether by the farmers in the area who worked the ridgetops or the army workers who cut the timber in the bottoms.[61]

The Confederates were well aware of this limited approach path, and they hoped to use it to full advantage. Despite the lack of much time between their own arrival in the early hours of May 18 and the Federals' appearance just a few hours later, Shoup's and Hébert's troops did their best to implement some kind of abatis in the deep valleys so that an enemy assault would be constricted to the well-defended high ground. If the enemy chose to come across the low ground and up the steep sides, so be it. The abatis and Confederate fire could likely withstand such an approach. If the Federals chose to constrict their attack along the high ground on the road, even better, and the concentrated volleys of both infantry and artillery could blunt any attack on such a narrow front more easily.

Even if the Federals managed to traverse the ravines or the bullet-swept high ground, the Stockade Redan itself and its outlying and supporting fortifications all had deep and well-constructed ditches and parapets to further hinder any chance of the enemy breaching the line. The ditch in front of the Stockade Redan itself was as much as ten feet wide and that deep, certainly more than mere men could bound by themselves or even in coordination with others. Likely, debris and scaling ladders would be needed to top the earthworks, that is, if the Federal approach even made it that far. Carrying such items only added yet another level of difficulty for the attackers; trying to lug ladders or debris across the ravines or even along the ridge on the road would certainly be tiring at the least and likely more problematic than could be overcome.[62]

More than just the frontline Confederates defending the Stockade Redan were preparing, however. One chaplain described how "the surgeons select places for the wounded in the hollows just behind their respective regiments." They detailed litter-bearers to carry the wounded, but litters were few and far between, so "they begin to construct some out of bark and poles." Chaplain Foster decided to stay in the rear for now, "since I regarded it my duty to be with the wounded and dying." Yet he remained nervous amid the already flying projectiles, commenting that the rear "was by no means secure from danger. This valley was about the right distance to catch the spent minnies and shell. They would come whizzing too near our ears to be pleasant; and the spent bullets, coming with sufficient force to kill, would strike so near us that we would reach out our hands and pick them up without moving from our position."[63]

Still, the watching Confederates could only wait as they endured the heavy artillery barrage that was already building that morning. George Clarke of the 36th Mississippi remembered how "the Federals opened a furious cannonade on our works, from their batteries, which they had rolled up within a quarter of a mile of our line. It seemed that they would sweep everything from the hill on which our line of works was located."[64]

Yet, Lockett's fortifications, particularly the Stockade Redan, could handle it. It was a massive fortification that was enormously strong. And it just happened to be where the main Union assault came on May 19.

5

"My Whole Division Dashed Forward"

The unfortunate task of attacking the formidable Confederate Stockade Redan fell to Missourian Frank Blair and his three brigades. They had led Sherman's advance westward from Bridgeport, which meant they led Grant's entire army. Consequently they were the first Union troops to confront the Confederate fortifications. Blair's was also the only division in place by the 2:00 P.M. deadline for the attack. His Federals were primarily on their own.[1]

Blair was a force within himself—not even counting the troops in his division—but his power, as only one man, was less militarily oriented than politically. Blair hailed from a longstanding political family of Missourians who were confidants to presidents and power brokers within their own rights. His father, Frank Blair Sr., had been a confidant of Andrew Jackson, serving in his "kitchen cabinet" and as the administration's spokesman through an affiliated newspaper. Frank, Jr.'s brother, Montgomery, was even then a major power broker in Washington, appointed by Abraham Lincoln as Postmaster General. Having a father as a well-known confidant of President Jackson and a brother in the Lincoln cabinet certainly helped Frank, Jr.,'s political ambitions back in Missouri, which he parlayed into a seat in Congress and then a commission as a general officer. On the battlefield he was brave, if a little sloppy, and seemed to be better suited to the halls of Congress. Charles Dana, the civilian reporting to the War Department on events at Vicksburg, thought Frank, Jr., would soon "leave the army, and . . . prefers his seat in Congress to his commission."[2]

Blair was no slouch, however, even when compared to his father and brother. He had served in the Mexican War, as attorney general for the New Mexico Territory, in the state legislature in Missouri, and finally as a representative in Congress in the late 1850s and even earlier during the war itself. Despite no formalized military training, he always had an eye for battle, serving as chairman of the House Committee on Military Affairs. The call to fight was so great that he soon left Congress to become colonel of a regiment, although he quickly worked his way up the chain of command and now commanded the division under Grant that was about to make the first attack on Vicksburg.[3]

Even though Blair was a prominent figure, his political ties did not help him in the Union army commanded by professional military officers. In fact, there was great angst when he entered the service and was sent to Grant. Never at a loss for words or opinions, Sherman declared that "Frank Blair is a 'disturbing element.' I wish he was in Congress or a Bar Room, anywhere but our Army." Grant likewise had his concerns with now having yet another politician in his army (McClernand was causing all sorts of problems), but he was more nuanced in his response. It was a good thing, as Blair turned out to be a better than adequate officer. In fact, Grant later admitted:

> I dreaded his coming; I knew from experience that it was more difficult to command two generals desiring to be leaders than it was to command one army officered intelligently and with subordination. It affords me the greatest pleasure to record now my agreeable disappointment in respect to his character. There was no man braver than he, nor was there any who obeyed all orders of his superior in rank with more unquestioning alacrity. He was one man as a soldier, another as a politician.[4]

Blair had three brigades under his command, mostly veterans units that had seen action before, although probably nothing like what they now faced. Brigadier General Hugh Ewing and Colonels Giles A. Smith and Thomas Kilby Smith commanded the brigades, and they had eased forward late in the day on May 18, inching as close as they could toward the Confederate lines in order to make their eventual sprint forward that much easier. Blair had led the corps on the march, stopping at the intersection of the Jackson and Benton Roads while the remainder of the corps closed up, and then approached the Confederate lines late on May 18. The lead brigade under Giles Smith soon stopped to send out skirmishers, which they did during the night. Some of the few regular army troops with Grant were in this brigade, and Smith sent Captain Edward C. Washington and his battalion of the 13th United States Infantry forward as skirmishers. The regulars pressed forward continually, eventually taking a position within a hundred yards of the Confederate line on the Graveyard Road. The Confederate skirmishers had scampered back into the earthworks.[5]

With the skirmishers taking the enemy's attention, Blair deployed his entire division in a crescent around the Confederate salient. On the north face, across Mint Spring Bayou, he positioned Hugh Ewing's troops, which had just arrived around midnight on a march from Grand Gulf, they being some of the last of the army to arrive from the Mississippi River crossing points to the south. This brigade had marched eighty-five miles in three days, so it was not exactly fresh. It nevertheless took a position on the high ridge north of Mint Spring Bayou, facing the northern front of the Confederate works, most importantly the 27th Louisiana Lunette. Fortunately for its safety, the brigade joined (by skirmishers) with another unit down the line to the west, John Thayer's brigade of Iowans, which was the leftmost brigade in Frederick Steele's division of Sherman's corps.[6]

On a northern spur of the ridge on which the Graveyard Road ran, Blair deployed Giles Smith's troops next, on Ewing's left and in what would become the center of the division. By daylight on May 19, Smith recalled the regulars from their isolated position to a safer area some two hundred yards farther to the rear. There, artillery from the division deployed as well, within easy range of the Confederates in the fortifications but also shielded somewhat by the lay of the land. Facing Giles Smith's troops, however, was a deep and wide ravine created by yet another of the feeder branches leading into Mint Spring Bayou. On the other side of that steep ravine sat the Stockade Redan itself, manned by the 36th Mississippi and 27th Louisiana.[7]

Blair deployed his last brigade under Kilby Smith to the south, on Giles Smith's left. The right of the brigade was atop the high ground on which the road ran, but the left extended down along the ridge east of the tributary of Glass Bayou. This brigade accordingly also faced a deep and wide ravine, more precipitous than what the others fronted, and they could also count on stiff Confederate resistance from the southernmost redan in the Stockade Redan area, now manned by Mississippians of Hébert's brigade. Making the situation worse, and unlike Ewing's troops to the right, Kilby Smith had no such force immediately on his left. The next troops in line were several hundred yards to the south, Thomas Ransom's brigade, which was all McPherson had been able to get into position by that time. Kilby Smith was so concerned that he sent a regiment and part of another "far to my left, with a view of connecting with General Ransom's picket."[8]

"During the morning of the 19th," Blair reported, "the entire line of skirmishers of my division was pushed forward, with a view of obtaining a closer position and of reconnoitering the ground." Artillery also opened up, Sherman reporting that it was "disposed on the right and left to cover the point where the road enters the enemy's intrenchments," causing Confederate brigade commander Shoup to describe the hail of projectiles as "very heavy." He also noted, "We made little reply, waiting for further development." Still, the information gained by the Union skirmishers and artillery was demoralizing, and even one not trained in military affairs could see it. The skirmishers obviously found the deep ravines filled with abatis and other entrapments, as well as a solid fire from the Confederate works, but Blair's position had other problems as well. He effectively ringed the Stockade Redan with a crescent-shaped line. As a result, he was operating on exterior lines of communication, where he would have to travel great distances on an arc to personally command his troops and, more important, to support any position with fresh troops. Meanwhile, the Confederates had the advantage of interior lines of communication, whereby they could easily position troops within the bubble and send them quickly to any needed area. To aid in this issue, Sherman positioned Ralph Buckland's brigade of Tuttle's division in line to the rear of Blair's deployed division with the other two brigades on the road behind it. But it was looking more and more like Blair was own his own. Indeed he was.[9]

Grant's orders to sound the attack at 2:00 P.M. came right on time. Sherman himself took a position near the front lines so that he could see the entire division's advance, and Grant was also on site by this time to watch the assault. Suddenly, the artillery unleashed the three volleys, right on time. It was the first attack against Vicksburg itself, and it had taken most of seven months just to get to this point. Hopefully, Grant thought, it would end today. Others were excited as well, Blair writing that "at 2 P.M. the signal was given for an assault, and my whole division dashed forward." But Sherman saw immediate troubles as soon as the brigades lurched ahead: "At the appointed signal the line advanced, but the ground to the right and left of the road was so impracticable, cut up in deep chasms, filled with standing and fallen timber, that the line was slow and irregular in reaching the trenches."[10]

The watching Confederates marveled at the pageantry, whispers of "A charge! A charge!" running along the silent lines. One Mississippian described how "the firing ceased and the Federals advanced in two lines of battle, halting about 300 yards from our position to reform their lines." He went on to describe how "numbers of battle flags could be seen just behind the hill, waving in the ... breeze." Most concerning, he added, "we could plainly hear when the order was given to advance; the flags were seen mounting up the hill, and soon the long, glittering line of bayonets came in sight, as with martial tread this tremendous war machine marched to the attack."[11]

On the far right of Blair's line was Hugh Ewing's brigade. Like Blair, Ewing himself was no stranger to high-level connections either; his father was

Thomas Ewing, a United States senator. Hugh also had two other brothers who were generals in the army, as well as one spectacular other relationship that also mattered much. William T. Sherman had been taken into the Ewing household as a child and was thus considered, although never formally adopted, as a foster brother. Perhaps Sherman's legitimacy in the Ewing family was solidified when he married one of Ewing's sisters. In a twist of irony, Ewing had been to Vicksburg before while traveling downriver and was thus somewhat acquainted with the environs he was now attacking.[12]

Ewing had not necessarily used his family connections as his path to success; he was a bold fighter in and of himself. He had attended West Point (just barely failing to graduate) and had served in the eastern theater at such battles as South Mountain and Antietam before heading out west as colonel of the 30th Ohio. He served in his foster brother/brother-in-law's corps until the appointment to brigadier general came and Sherman gave him his own brigade under another politics-oriented officer, Frank Blair. Ironically, Ewing's father, Thomas, had been staunchly anti-Jackson while Blair's father, Frank, had been a major supporter. Whether the political differences of their fathers was an issue or even discussed is not known.[13]

Ewing commanded a brigade of mostly Ohio units, with one Virginia regiment added in for good measure. On the right of the line was the all-German 37th Ohio under the command of Lieutenant Colonel Louis von Blessingh, down three companies on skirmish duty farther to the right toward Thayer's brigade. To the Ohioan's left and in the center was Colonel James H. Dayton's 4th West Virginia, whose name was somewhat of an anomaly as the state of West Virginia would not officially join the Union until a month and a day later, on June 20, 1863. More ironic, most of the troops in the regiment were from Ohio, seven full companies' worth. Colonel Augustus C. Parry's 47th Ohio was on the left of the brigade, with Ewing's old regiment, the 30th Ohio, now under Colonel Theodore Jones, holding a position in reserve. It was a good thing for them, the 30th Ohio having made a thirty-one-mile march the day before, much of it without water. As fate would have it, when they arrived there was water, but as Edward Schweitzer described it, "There was green scum on it 1 in. thick and the water a green color." Only a few of the regiment made the entire march, most falling out, but they trickled in this day as Ewing prepared to send them toward the ramparts of Vicksburg.[14]

All the regiments had been together for most of the war, although not in the Mississippi Valley campaigns. In fact, the mostly Ohio regiments had been sent southward into the western Virginia area around the Kanawha Valley until January 1863, when they were sent westward. They wore eastern kepis rather than the wide-brimmed slouch hats more prevalent in the west. Across

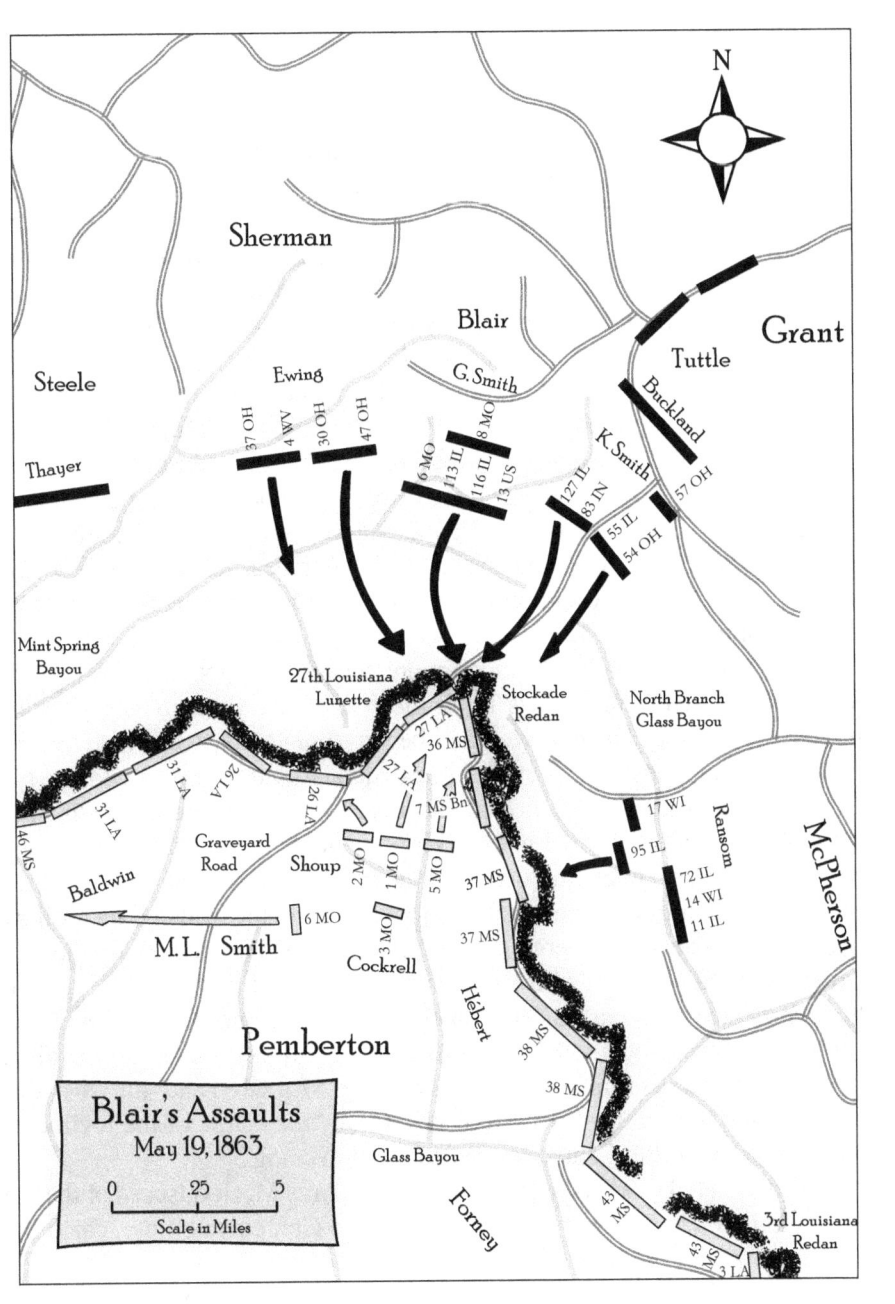

the deep valley of Mint Spring Bayou lay their target, the 27th Louisiana Lunette, which they termed the "Cemetery Fort." Most thought it would be quick work, one Ohioan remembering Ewing himself telling his troops that "it would be a short job, and that we would be inside of the works, in less than ten minutes after receiving the order to move."[15]

As soon as the three volleys of artillery sounded, Ewing led his eastern troopers southward into some of the most foreboding country of Mississippi, but they were not fazed, as they had previously campaigned in the rough terrain of western Virginia. In fact, they were out to show what "the strange brigade from the eastern army" could do. Nevertheless, the right of the brigade found the terrain impossible to move through, and Lieutenant Colonel von Blessingh's 37th Ohio, along with the reserve 30th Ohio, found they could not go any farther, one soldier writing his wife that they "lost so many men [they] had to fall back." Ewing himself noted that the right, "on account of obstacles, was unable to cross the ravine but covered the left in its advanced position by a heavy fire." Still, the Ohioans were heartened when they saw von Blessingh himself walking up and down his line, "perfectly indifferent to rebel bullets."[16]

The left of the brigade had much more success, the abatis and other impediments evidently being less thick there than elsewhere. The regiments moved across Mint Spring Bayou and began to scale the steep slope toward the Louisianans' position. Some of the Federals used a small building, the Adam Lynd House, as protection in this area. Colonel Parry of the 47th Ohio and Colonel Dayton of the 4th West Virginia were able to lead their men up the slope under the withering fire from the Louisianans and actually reached the base of the entrenchments, with Colonel Parry in the lead yelling "follow me." One Ohioan remembered that "when we gained the foot of the hill we sprang up its sides with a wild Yankee yell." Up the hill they went: "Forward the men rushed with enthusiastic cheers," wrote another Ohioan, "over and through the brushwood and fallen timber up the hillsides, and into the ditch they poured in a determined mass." There, the 47th Ohio and 4th West Virginia planted their flags, Ewing remarking that "the colors of the regiments waved near them [the Confederate lines] until evening."[17]

Unfortunately killed in the attack was Major Arza M. Goodspeed of the 4th West Virginia. He fell near the log cabin at the Confederate line, which the Louisianans later realized was an obstruction to their fire and an aid to any advancing Federals. Several Confederates scurried out of the works and set fire to the Lynd house and surrounding ground cover, and the West Virginians later found their major's body, charred from the fire, as well as "some articles which belonged to him." Others of the 47th Ohio were also killed and charred, although Colonel Parry endured a different ordeal. One Ohioan declared that "Col. Parry was caught and suspended on the point of a bayonet while in the ditch, which wound left a triangular scar on one of his ribs."[18]

Yet Ewing's troops could go no farther. Shoup's Louisianans had opened up a heavy fire from their works, with Shoup himself declaring that "the enemy debouched in force from a gorge in front of the center of my position. We opened on him." The Confederate artillery also did grim work, the howitzer in the lunette serving the entire time; the Whitworth rifle had burst during the fighting. The slope of the ravine was also daunting, almost straight up, but that was nothing compared to the thickness and almost vertical slope of the lunette itself, in front of which was a deep ditch and tall rampart. The 27th Louisiana thus opened up on the almost trapped Federals using the burning Lynd House for cover, while the 26th Louisiana to the left opened up as well, the unit's record book declaring there was a "galling flank fire from our regiment." Ewing's Federals who made it that far had to halt and began to take cover as best they could from the Louisianans' fire, soon augmented by one of Cockrell's Missouri regiments brought forward from its reserve position. The 1st Missouri under Colonel Amos C. Riley moved into the works between the Louisianans and the 36th Mississippi of Hébert's brigade to the right. Given the concentration of Confederate fire, it was almost miraculous that the Federals had made it that far, but that was as far as they could go—unless something changed drastically.[19]

While Cockrell's Missourians gave aid on the front line, an assortment of ironic hilarity played out behind the lines. Engineer James T. Hogane was riding north up the Graveyard Road when he spied a cannon stuck in the ditch beside the route. He was unable to get it out even though it was hitched to several mules, the engineer blaming a "want of concert between Major, mules, drivers, and drink, that all hands seemed to be filled up with." Hogane offered to help, and in his words the major "met me half-way by offering the bunghole of his little keg of whiskey." Hogane countered and "proposed to lubricate the mules by giving the drivers a drink." It worked, and Hogane gave orders that the drivers not stop "until the gun landed in the rear of the works." He insultingly remembered that "one old white-haired darkey, whose temples sported a silk plug hat, . . . allowed 'he'd go with that dar gun to them folks fighting sure.'" Unfortunately, the mules responded with too much gusto and the gun overturned at the top, where the Federal fire was sweeping the area. Hogane admitted that all involved then "ceased putting on any heroic airs."[20]

Despite such theatrics, most of Ewing's Federals simply sought cover, one of Shoup's staff officers yelling, "See, General, they are running!" At that exact moment, a bullet killed the staffer, and Shoup's adjutant was killed by a shot in the neck and two other staff officers were less seriously wounded. A Louisianan described how the "enemy seem to be fond of flaunting their miserable old flag close to our works. An adventurous Yankee has planted one within 100 yards of our line & has dug him a *trench* from which to shoot." Not satisfied, Ewing had to think quickly and could see only one way to restart his advance. He had two full regiments to his right with no hope of being able to advance, so he recalled them and moved them to the left, where they took a position on the tall ridge north of Mint Spring Bayou. Ewing intended to send them forward "over the track of the preceding portion of the brigade" but also wanted to coordinate his renewed assaults with Colonel Giles Smith to his left. He did so, working out a combined plan for the renewal of the assault, and he even worked out artillery support to aid the advance. Ewing told the artillerymen to open up when the line reached the bottom of the ravine and "began to ascend the opposite hill."[21]

Ewing now only had to wait for the signal from Giles Smith to restart his assault. Unfortunately, the artillery did not cooperate and began to fire before the 30th and 37th Ohio moved forward. With instructions to open only when the Ohioans started to go up the opposite slope, the artillery fired early. Compounding the confusion, Colonels Dayton's and Parry's troops, stuck on the forward slope under the guns of the Louisianans, were looking for any opportunity to get out of their predicament and took the artillery barrage, without seeing any supporting troops coming to their aid, as a covering fire for them to retreat. Thus, portions of the 47th Ohio and 4th West Virginia began to stream back northward under the cover of the artillery barrage, across Mint Spring Bayou and to safety. Shoup declared that the enemy "broke and fled to the cover of the hills."[22]

Left behind was the flag of the 47th Ohio, the bearer having been shot in the hand, causing it to go down. When the wounded bearer returned without the flag, he told an incredulous Colonel Parry that he could not get it out "because of the dead men lying on it." Parry, already irritated because of the bayonet-shaped puncture in his chest, would have none of it and, according to one Ohioan, "cursed him, called him a coward, and threatened to cut his head off with his sword."[23]

By this time, Giles Smith was having his own troubles to the east. He was slightly wounded, so the prearranged signal was never given and, as Ewing reported, "the charge was not renewed." Accordingly, there was pitifully little aid to those who remained huddling in the ditch in front of the 27th Louisiana Lunette. Clearly fluttering in the breeze were some of the colors of the two regiments, planted on the Confederate earthworks but obviously not inside them. One Ohioan recalled, "But vainly they strove time and again to climb the parapet. What a scathing fire swept its crest. It could not be stood, and from each effort the brave men recoiled into the ditch; but they maintained the struggle therein."[24]

Soon it was evident that nothing more could be done. Confederate division commander Martin L. Smith noted that "the first effort was directed against the center of Shoup's brigade; but being exposed to a heavy and well-directed fire, the enemy broke and fled." Cockrell echoed him, writing that "this brigade, with General Shoup's brave Louisianans, had the honor of receiving the first assault of the enemy and repulsing them—suffering, too, the dangers incident to such clash of arms, losing 8 killed and 62 wounded in this engagement." Ewing's assault had indeed failed due to lack of power and coordination as well as the hideous terrain. If the Stockade Redan was to be breached, it would have to be by a different brigade.[25]

Just a little after Ewing's assault to the west, Giles A. Smith led his brigade forward toward the stockade wall itself between the apex of the Stockade Redan and the 27th Louisiana Lunette. Smith placed his advance at 3:00 P.M., an hour after Ewing's and an hour after the set time of attack, but differing watches were perhaps to blame for most of the discrepancy. Nevertheless, Smith led his regiments forward slightly after Ewing's attack, in conjunction with the prearranged effort with Ewing's proposed second advance that turned into a rout. Despite what was occurring to the west in Ewing's brigade, Smith led his troops forward for their own attack.[26]

Giles Smith was no stranger to battle. The younger brother of Brigadier General Morgan L. Smith, one of Sherman's division commanders wounded terribly at Chickasaw Bayou and now recovering at home, the younger Smith brother had seen his own share of fighting. Having joined his brother's 8th Missouri, he saw heavy action at Fort Donelson and Shiloh, later taking command of the regiment when his brother was promoted to general. Smith likewise saw action with the regiment in the Vicksburg Campaign, including at Chickasaw Bayou and Arkansas Post, although few of Sherman's troops engaged in any of the inland battles in May 1863. Now was their chance.[27]

Smith had five units under his command, including his own 8th Missouri, now under Lieutenant Colonel David C. Coleman. As deployed in preparation for the attack, Lieutenant Colonel Ira Boutell's 6th Missouri held the right of the brigade near Ewing's regiments, with the first battalion of the 13th United States Infantry under Captain Edward C. Washington, a grandnephew of George Washington himself, on the far left. Between the two veteran units were the two newest regiments, Colonel George B. Hoge's 113th Illinois on the right-center, and Colonel Nathan W. Tupper's 116th Illinois on the left-center. Much like Ewing holding his former regiment in the rear, Smith kept his old regiment, Lieutenant Colonel Coleman's 8th Missouri, in rear as a reserve.[28]

With his brigade so aligned, Smith made ready to attack and moved forward soon after the three-volley signal from the nearby Chicago Light Artillery. But what Smith saw up ahead concerned him. His own regulars had been within a hundred yards of the Confederate lines, and they reported the difficulties the brigade would face. Smith by now could also see them plainly, remarking that "the ground over which I had to move to reach the enemy's intrenchments was a succession of deep ravines and precipitous hills." Indeed, this feeder branch of Mint Spring Bayou was deep and rugged.[29]

Smith decided to add as much supporting fire as he could. In addition to the artillery, he utilized his own 8th Missouri on the high ridge east of the branch. He told Lieutenant Colonel Coleman to "open a heavy fire from the crest of the hill next to the enemy's works, while the other regiments were crossing the ravine in his front." Coleman did so, but he could not lure the total attention of the defending Confederates. Colonel Mark's Louisianans in their lunette and the left of the 36th Mississippi watched and waited for the opportune time to open their vicious fire. It soon came.[30]

Smith's regiments had as hard a time getting across the ravines as had Ewing's. Smith himself noted that "my line then advanced under a heavy fire over almost impassable ground." In particular, the right of the brigade found the going especially difficult, and the 6th Missouri and 113th Illinois soon bogged down in the gorge, hit as they were by Confederate fire while trying to negotiate the tangle of thickets, abatis, and other obstacles. Smith noted that many became "entangled in the brush and fallen timber, [and] took such shelter as the ridges, stumps, and logs afforded." One Illinoisan put it more bluntly, writing to his mother that "we made a charge on the rebel fort and our brigade got cut up pretty bad," although he informed her that he and his friends all "come out rite side up." Not all did. Captain John J. Kellogg described seeing a lieutenant in the neighboring regiment "in his shirt sleeves and [wearing] a white shirt; he and I went side by side several steps, when he lunged forward upon the ground, and in the quick glance I gave him I saw a circle of red forming on his shirt back." In fact, the two right regiments of Missourians and Illinoisans would not even make it up the slope toward the 27th Louisiana Lunette, Confederate defender Francis Shoup writing that "our fire staggered him." Most of the men "had to pick his own way forward as best he could," Kellogg remembered.[31]

Smith had more success on his left, where his regulars and Illinoisans made some progress despite the mortal wounding of Captain Edward Washington.

As he led the regulars, he was hit twice while crossing a rail fence near the bottom of the ravine. Despite the heavy abatis and telegraph wire strung through the downed trees and a rail fence, the regulars made it through the ravine and up the hill, their two flags carried by a succession of bearers, most of whom were hit, one of the color guard almost immediately "just after passing the crest." Captain Charles Ewing, brother of Hugh (and another of Sherman's step/brothers-in-law), was one of them. He took command and grabbed the flag, taking it all the way to the parapet despite being wounded himself in the hand after three other color-bearers went down. Perhaps because the ground was not quite as deep where it rose toward the ridge on which the Graveyard Road ran, or because the Federals fronted the apex of the Stockade Redan itself and thus were shielded from some of the most vicious fire, the regulars managed to pick their way forward, ultimately to the base of the redan itself, where Ewing planted their flag and thereby gained the sobriquet "First at Vicksburg." To their right the 116th Illinois also managed to ascend the ravine to the ditch of the redan but, like the others, could go no farther. Smith noted that many in these regiments succeeded in "pushing themselves up under the parapets of the enemy's works." Confederate brigade commander Shoup noted as much, writing that despite the heavy fire of his Louisianans "fragments of several regiments succeeded in gaining the cover of a ridge in front of the redan." Given the angle of the works, they were comparatively safe from Confederate fire and hugged the ground for safety. Shoup noted that the Federals just on the other side of the parapet were "almost wholly free from our fire."[32]

Still, the Confederate fire was withering, especially now that the Louisianans on the northern face of the Stockade Redan complex were able to give their full attention to Smith's troops, Ewing having by this time fallen back because of the confusion of orders. One Mississippian described how "a thousand deadly guns are aimed and the whole lines are lighted up with a continuous flash of firearms and even the hill seems to be a burning smoking volcano." Confederate division commander Martin L. Smith, now facing another Smith across the way, similarly described how "a second advance [Ewing's probably being construed as the first] was attempted against my extreme right, and a bold effort made to rush over and into the works." Smith was amazed at the attack, writing that as many as six or seven Union regiments came forward, mistaking Ewing's two reserve regiments as part of this second wave: "After coming into view, it moved confidently and determinedly forward." Shoup also described a renewed second effort: "He finally made a rush, with the intention of carrying our line, but was met by a terrific fire in front and flank, and fled in utter confusion, leaving many dead."[33]

Martin Smith was thus able to parry the assault with the vicious volleys of the 27th Louisiana and a now unengaged 26th Louisiana farther to the left. He also brought up more of Cockrell's reserve regiments, the Missourian marveling at the "most furious and determined assault" taking place. The 1st and 2nd Missouri had already moved into position after a grueling mile march on the double-quick, the former taking a position behind the works at the stockade and the 2nd Missouri reinforcing the 26th Louisiana to the left. Colonel Marks of the 27th Louisiana balked at allowing the Missourians to enter the works, yelling that "it was his fight." Smith also asked for and sent another regiment of Cockrell's brigade, the 6th Missouri, down the line to the left to support John C. Vaughn's shaky brigade, he having reported that "the enemy were massing troops opposite his position and desiring reinforcements." Together, Smith declared, the Louisianans and Missourians "received the charge with a withering fire, and after the second volley the enemy fled in confusion, leaving five colors on the field, and the ground strewn with the dead and wounded." The Confederates also suffered, however, Shoup admitting that "our loss was heavy." Among the wounded was Lieutenant Pierre N. Ternier of the 26th Louisiana, shot through the heart, his last words being, "I am gone, I am gone." Colonel Hall of the 26th Louisiana was also wounded in the leg below the knee, as was Sergeant William F. Luckett, an aide at Cockrell's side. Two guns also burst along the line during the fighting, including a 30-pounder Parrott and the Whitworth.[34]

Attempts to rally Giles Smith's brigade were unsuccessful. Martin L. Smith declared that "one or two feeble attempts to rally were easily repulsed." The Federals of Giles Smith's brigade who could thus fled back across the deep gorge toward the safety of the ridge they had just left, their friends of the 8th Missouri still providing some cover as they now recrossed the ravine. Perhaps part of the reason no rally was made was that Giles Smith himself had been shot, if only a minor wound in the right hip. Left to the front on the parapet of the Stockade Redan were the remnants of the 13th US regulars and the 116th Illinois who could not get away safely; they nonetheless kept up "a terrific fire until dark," according to Confederate brigade commander Shoup. Also there were the colors of the regiments, still waving proudly but, like those to the west on Ewing's front, clearly indicating that the Confederate fortifications had not been breached.[35]

Colonel Thomas Kilby Smith was no stranger to military action either, and judging from the problems both Hugh Ewing and Giles Smith were having to his right, he would need all the experience he had to overcome the obstacles in front of him. Although not a trained military man, Smith nevertheless became lieutenant colonel of the 54th Ohio and soon its colonel. He led the Zouave regiment exceptionally well at Shiloh, holding, along with the 55th Illinois, the critical extreme left flank that Confederate general Albert Sidney Johnston was so intent to turn. Smith participated in later actions as well, including the siege of Corinth and at Chickasaw Bayou. The brigade would need that previous experience as they now moved forward. Another wave of Federals now confounded the watching Confederates, one of whom remarked, "They think of their late successes and on they rush with flying banners and glittering arms."[36]

Smith's brigade contained a total of five regiments, a far cry from the paltry numbers with which he had defended those ridges at Shiloh. But there were problems too as Smith led the brigade forward, including what he described as "brigadier-generals here, with bright, new stars upon their shoulders, but without command, who are doubtless eagerly seeking my place." Another, more pressing problem was the terrain, one factor of which was the Graveyard Road "leading to what was supposed to be a sally-port in the fortifications," Smith wrote. His brigade straddled the roadway and more importantly the ridge on which it ran. Compounding the problems, the closer the brigade moved toward the Confederate lines, the steeper became the ravines on either side of the narrow ridge, creating a situation in which Smith could not at any one time see the portions of his brigade on either side of the ridge without standing atop the roadway. This, of course, would have been suicide. He therefore decided to turn command of the right of the brigade over to a trusted colonel while he commanded the left in person.[37]

The right of the brigade, in the same but upper reaches of the ravine that Giles Smith was trying so desperately to slog through north of the Graveyard Road, contained two late-mustering regiments, Colonel Hamilton N. Eldridge's 127th Illinois on the right, and Colonel Benjamin J. Spooner's 83rd Indiana on the left next to the road. Smith gave Colonel Spooner command of these two regiments not only because he was the senior officer on that side of the ridge but also because Smith described him "in whose ability and dauntless courage I repose fullest confidence." Smith ordered Spooner to "press forward as rapidly as possible, and in such order as he could best get over the ground."[38]

Spooner took his demi-brigade command to heart and gave his troops a speech, especially the Indianans. Knowing Jefferson Davis had slighted Indiana troops during the Mexican War at Buena Vista, calling them cowards, Spooner reminded his soldiers that this was the day to show Jeff Davis just how well they could fight. "This is the day of all days you are expected to show your valor," one Indianan described Spooner's speech, "and to show Jeff Davis that Indiana soldiers are not cowards." More ominously, the Indianan also remembered Spooner telling them that "if anyone should fall in battle or get wounded we were not even to turn him over or give him a drink of water until the battle was over."[39]

With the right of the brigade in Spooner's capable hands, Smith made his way to the left, where he took charge of the three regiments south of the road and its high ridge. There, he placed Colonel Oscar Malmborg's 55th Illinois, which had been with him on that flank at Shiloh and which the Swede Malmborg had taken through several evolutions of square formation right in the midst of battle. The Illinoisans took position on the right nearer the road while Smith's own 54th Ohio, now under Lieutenant Colonel Cyrus W. Fisher, formed on the left. The last regiment was also a Shiloh veteran unit, although they had not fared as well as Smith's and Malmborg's regiments; Colonel Americus V. Rice's 57th Ohio had taken quite a shock near Shiloh Church and had all but disintegrated early in the battle. Now, they formed a second line behind the Ohioans and Illinoisans, although Smith was careful to note that they were "in the rear but not in reserve."[40]

If the Graveyard Road was a problem, effectively splitting the brigade, the terrain on either side of the path was even more of an issue. Smith saw immediately that it would be difficult to cross the ravines:

> A reconnaissance of the ground over which I should pass had developed the fact that it would be impossible to advance my whole brigade in line of battle, the hills and knobs being exceedingly precipitous, intersected by ravines in three directions, the bottom treacherous, filled with sink holes, concealed by dried grass and cane; the whole covered by abatis of fallen timber from a dense forest cut six months or more ago, affording spikes and *cheveaux de frise* most difficult to surmount.

If that was not enough, Smith also spied the Confederate earthworks, which he described at the point they touched the Graveyard Road as "an embankment some 18 feet high." One wonders if Smith had already made his mind up that success was not possible even before the attack began.[41]

Even if Smith did, the watching Confederates did not realize it. One member of the defending 36th Mississippi recalled how "on reaching the top of the hill and coming into plain view, they gave a prolonged yell, and broke into a double quick towards our lines." It is funny how the mind works, and years later he added: "I noticed that they were carrying their guns at a 'right shoulder shift.'" The Mississippian nevertheless knew what was happening even in the fog of war and noted how, "in grim silence, with guns ready for instant use, we awaited the shock."[42]

Because of the lay of the land, essentially two attacks developed as Smith pushed his regiments forward. One was Smith's south of the road and the ridge, and the other was Spooner's north of it, the Indianan giving the simple order, "Boys, remember your state. Forward." In actuality, Smith's advance south of the Graveyard Road never had the force of Ewing's or Giles Smith's, indicating he looked at the situation at the beginning and decided he would do just enough to participate but would not murder his men in front of the massed volleys of the 36th Mississippi and the deep tones of the howitzer in the redan itself. Although he reported that the regiments "advanced gallantly and without hesitation," Smith immediately added that "it was almost vain to essay a line, owing to the nature of the ground." In fact, the order to move forward came as a surprise to some, Lieutenant Colonel Cyrus Fisher of the 54th Ohio writing: "I had no previous notice of the forward movement, or an idea that the regiment was the front of an assaulting column, which was to charge through fallen timber, over at least four ravines, very steep and difficult to pass over under the most auspicious circumstances." As the Ohioans and Illinoisans moved forward together through the deep and steep ravine leading southward to Glass Bayou, Smith halted them not once, not twice, but a grand total of three different times to "dress upon their colors." All the while, they were taking fire from the Mississippians, but Smith nevertheless continued on some four hundred yards "under a most galling and destructive fire." After nearing the Confederate line, Smith realized the men were "thoroughly exhausted" (one commander called his men "breathless"), and he called a temporary halt at a convenient ridge that, in Smith's words, was "comparatively sheltered from the small-arms of the enemy."[43]

That Confederate fire was indeed heavy, the 36th Mississippi unleashing volley after volley into the oncoming Illinoisans and Ohioans. George Clarke recalled how "at the proper time our batteries opened on them with grape, canister, and shrapnel shells, which told fearfully upon their crowded ranks." But the Federals kept on coming, the Mississippian then describing how "when they had reached within fifty yards of our lines we opened upon them with musketry, using the 'buck and ball' cartridge with murderous effect." He explained that "this cartridge was made with a round ounce ball, to which three large buckshot were fastened, so that when fired from the musket they scattered, giving a man four chances to hit every time he fired."[44]

The Mississippians fired so fast, in fact, that they soon began to run out of ammunition. Henry J. Reynolds queried his comrades and found they were down to about an average of five rounds per man. He ran to Colonel William W. Witherspoon, commanding the 36th Mississippi, who told Reynolds to run down the ravine in rear to the ordnance trains and bring more ammunition forward. Reynolds did so but found the ravine swept with artillery fire from the Union lines: "It seemed that they all swept down the hollow." Reynolds made it but then found a different obstacle when he located the ordnance sergeant: "Our brigadier general [Hébert] . . . had ordered him to stay there and he wouldn't go." Explaining the situation, Reynolds finally worked out a compromise in which the sergeant loaned him his horse to carry a box of ammunition forward. Reynolds found he could not carry a bulky box, and so the two procured a sack in which they poured the cartridges once they broke the box open. Now with a hundred-pound sack of cartridges, Reynolds charged the horse "back up the hollow where the shells were as thick as ever." He got the sack to the ditch in the rear of the line and called for help; he and another soldier sprinted with the sack to the breastworks, calling the Mississippians "to come up and draw their rations."[45]

It was a good thing, because Smith's Federals renewed their assault about that time, and the ammunition was desperately needed. So was courage. Reynolds found a young Mississippian who wanted badly not to have to shoot anymore. He told Reynolds he could not shoot over the parapet, and Reynolds told him he had to. The boy then worked out a plan by which Reynolds would fire both their muskets while the young lad loaded them. A happy Reynolds declared that although the boy "was too nervous to do fast work at first, . . . [he] soon got more composed and so I did almost twice as much shooting as the other boys." He also described another scene in which a lone Federal dashed over the ridge fronting them, trying to catch up with his brigade that had already passed. "He made a target too conspicuous for me to resist," Reynolds admitted, and "I took careful aim and fired." Reynolds watched as the Federal tumbled to the ground, when he excitedly yelled, "Boys . . . did you see that fellow come running over the hill alone just now?" Several responded that they had, and Reynolds boasted, "Well, I believe I killed him. . . . I shot at him and he fell." Then Reynolds was brought back to reality when "'so did I shoot at him,' was the reply from every man within shouting distance." Reynolds dejectedly confessed, "I was immediately robbed of the belief that I had been the cause of there being one less [Federal] to contend with. It seemed that he had made a target of himself for the whole regiment."[46]

Down the line to the right, the 37th Mississippi was also getting its fair share of attention. James Carlisle noted how "their [Federals] appearance at a distance resembled the assemblage of myriads of black birds." Then they came closer, and Carlisle described how "soon their well drilled squadrons filed in sight." But the Mississippians' fire was telling. Carlisle noted that they "came boldly up to our works; their ranks swept down by the awful hail of lead.... Our first shots would cause many to right about face, others to throw up their hands falling on their backs in death, others still to fall to the earth for protection, whilst some straggled in broken groups up to the ditches we occupied."[47]

Making the output of deadly fire than much greater, more reinforcements from Cockrell's brigade soon joined the Mississippians. While two regiments had reinforced Shoup's line, with another being sent farther to the west to support Vaughn's command, the 5th Missouri went into position with the Mississippians on the east face of the redan and poured a withering fire into the charging Federals. Even the drummers took station on the line. Cockrell himself noted how "the enemy in large masses, without any regular lines, pressed forward very close to our works, but were soon severely repulsed and driven back in disorder; and every subsequent effort was likewise repulsed." And there was more if needed; Cockrell also held the 3rd Missouri in the rear "in readiness to re-enforce any point," but even there the regiment sustained several casualties.[48]

Even with a renewed surge, Smith's Federals had little chance of success given the terrain, heavy Confederate defense, and their seemingly uninterested brigade commander. The depiction of the advance by the 55th Illinois well described the problems south of the Graveyard Road. "The waiting battle-line rushed cheering to the charge," wrote one Illinoisan, "a human wave that seemed irresistible when it began surging onward towards the rebel lines." Yet the farther they went, the less of them there were. "As it dashed over stumps and tangled limbs of fallen trees," one Illinoisan recalled, the regiment "struggled through deep gullies bristling with brush and cane, and climbed the steep slopes opposite in the face of a roaring, whistling storm of lead and iron rain, men dropped by tens, stopped behind some sheltering log or bank, slackened speed for sheer want of breath, until all the momentum of the start had worn itself out." A few soldiers managed to push ahead, "a thin line of panting, staggering humanity pressed on and on until a few of the pluckiest and strongest perhaps straggled nerveless into the ditch, attempted to climb the abrupt scarp, and were there either slain, desperately wounded or captured."[49]

Here Smith evidently decided he had done enough. "I have been in a slaughter pen," he wrote his mother. "Talk of Balaklava—it sinks into significance. And they went on horseback, while we had to work in on foot, over tangled abatis, up precipitous hills, and against ramparts bristling with cannon and rifle." Looking to the left, he saw no supporting infantry from McPherson's corps (Ransom was out of sight), but his regiments were taking a galling fire from Confederate artillery stationed near the Jackson Road, in particular a 20-pound Parrott and a 3-inch Ordinance Rifle. "I determined to halt my command, report, and wait for further orders," Smith admitted. One member of the 55th Illinois corroborated his report, writing that the regiment took a position near the crest of a hill, "within fifty paces of the east curtain of the bastion at the Graveyard Road," and that "our colors waved for hours within pistol shot of the line of defense and were riddled with bullets."[50]

To give the best information in his report, Smith also made his way back and across the road ridge to check on Spooner, whom he saw far to the front. Thinking he could do no better for them, Smith simply returned to his left wing and sent a message to Blair that he had been stalled and requested further orders. These were forwarded not from Blair but from Sherman himself, who ordered Smith to "get my men as close to the parapet as possible and be ready to jump in when they began to yield." He also assured Smith that McPherson was attacking to the left and that Grant himself was on site. Probably not impressed, Smith ordered his men to fix bayonets and await the opportunity to surge over the Confederate works. That chance never came, partly because Smith further convinced himself that any more forward movement was impossible. "Upon closer view," he later wrote, "I discovered the works too steep and high to scale without proper appliances; a few men could have been got over by the aid of a ladder of bayonets or digging holes in the embankment, but these would have gone to destruction." Smith decided enough was enough; "therefore I determined to maintain the position and await developments."[51]

The effect was not lost on the defending Mississippians and Missourians. George Clarke of the 36th Mississippi wrote that "they were brave men and did not falter, though hundreds were falling all around them, until within a few feet of us. Then they wavered, rallied once, but finally gave way and retreated." Nevertheless, some of the foremost Federals who had reached the ditch remained, within feet of their enemies but separated by the thick wall of dirt that defended Vicksburg. Smith lamented, "Men could not scale a perpendicular wall of fifteen feet. Men could not have gone up without guns in their hands and with no enemy in front. We did [what] all mortal men could do—but such slaughter!" There was also loss in the Confederates ranks, of course, one cannonball so shredding a private in the 5th Missouri that body parts lay all over the trenches.[52]

Making the Federal situation worse, the front line of Union troops soon expended most of its ammunition while waiting for a renewal of the assaults. At times, officers even exchanged companies on the front line. Some ran out of ammunition because of the earlier skirmishing; sharpshooters had moved forward "with carte blanche to select the best cover." Kilby Smith recorded that "a most deadly fire was kept up, and none of the enemy ventured his head above the wall who failed to pay the penalty." In one instance, the entire 54th Ohio, which had shot away nearly its entire allotment of ammunition in the skirmishing of the previous days, had to be replaced by the 57th Ohio. Once ammunition did arrive, it was found to be the wrong caliber, although the boxes clearly indicated the correct size. Lieutenant Colonel Cyrus Fisher of the 54th Ohio ordered his men to "reserve one round in the piece, fix bayonet, and lie down until ammunition could be sent, or we should be relieved."[53]

Anyone who could soon began to ferry ammunition forward. In some cases, entire companies of rear regiments from Tuttle's division were detailed to carry it forward, such as Company C of the 12th Iowa. On other occasions, it was more dramatic, including one of the singular famous episodes of the Vicksburg assaults on the 55th Illinois's front. Two young brothers, pets of their regiment and termed the "infant drummers," were musicians, the youngest, Orion P. Howe, volunteering to take cartridges to the front from his position in the rear. He did so several times, one brigade member describing how they watched him scamper across the bullet-swept ravines in rear on several occasions: "We could see him nearly the whole way as he ran through what seemed like a hailstorm of canister and musket-balls, so thickly did these fall about him, each throwing up its little puff of dust where it struck the dry hillside." Many feared he was wounded, especially when he went down: "Often he stumbled, he often fell prostrate, but was quickly up again, and finally disappeared from us." What the troops did not know was that he was actually wounded in the leg and Sherman himself sent him to the rear, but not before issuing his call for ammunition and, as he went to the rear, yelling back to the general "Calibre 54!" Sherman wrote a commendation to the War Department a couple of months later: "What arrested my attention there was, and what renews my memory of the fact now is, that one so young, carrying a musket-ball wound through his leg, should have found his way to me on that fatal spot, and delivered his message, not forgetting the very important part even of the calibre of the musket, 54, which you know is an unusual [one]." The general recommended Howe for a position at the United States Naval Academy, Sherman deeming him "too young for West Point."[54]

While Kilby Smith struggled south of the Graveyard Road, more progress had been made north of it, where Colonel Spooner led the Indianans and Illinoisans toward the apex of the redan at the sound of the bugle. The going was difficult from the start here too, with one Illinoisan writing: "The

Order was given forward boys forward and away we went over the hills on over logs helter skelter the balls coming thick and fast men falling wounded and killed on every side, but we pressed on loading and firing as fast as we could." Colonel Hamilton Eldridge of the 127th Illinois described how his men were hit as soon as they passed over the covering ridge they had formed behind: "In crossing the brow of the hill, just beyond the point from which we started, we received a murderous fire from the enemy, which killed and wounded many of my men. The unevenness of the ground, added to the fact that it was thickly covered with brush and fallen trees, soon broke our lines and scattered to a considerable extent the men." One of the captains in the unit, Thomas Sewell, echoed that "most of these [trees] had been cut down so that it would have been no ordinary undertaking for a person to have taken his way down one side, cross the ravine, and then ascend the opposite side." Yet, they kept going.[55]

Unlike Smith's effort to the south, Spooner was able to reach the parapet with many of his men, just as others in Ewing's and Giles Smith's brigades had done. Colonel Eldridge noted that "the most of them, however, worked their way up close under the enemy's works, where the regiment's colors were planted." Both the 83rd Indiana, despite losing several captains killed and wounded, and the 127th Illinois planted their colors on the face of the redan just to the left of the regulars' position, the Confederates reaching and touching the flag with their bayonets. Many described the advance as "the most desperate [charge] of the war." Kilby Smith, in fact, related that when he moved to his right wing, "hid from my view by the embankment of the road," he "perceived their colors advanced to the very base of the parapet." Smith had left his wing under Colonel Americus Rice, the ranking colonel, Oscar Malmborg of the 55th Illinois, having been wounded in the eye. Smith further credited the right wing with courageous work, reporting that "their loss had been fearful, falling upon their best line and non-commissioned officers. Captain after captain had been shot dead; field officers were falling; still there was no flinching."[56]

There also existed some interbrigade rivalry. One Indianan with Spooner's column described how his regiment "passed the Thirteenth Regulars in good shape," adding that "we often received that order when the enemy's fire was too hot." He actually termed the regulars as "Sherman's body-guard," which explains much of the resentment. Yet, he added that "the next regiment we passed was the Sixth Missouri, one of the best regiments in Sherman's army." Even the Indianans slowed under the withering fire, however, the same soldier admitting that the regiment "got somewhat demoralized," mainly because the two color-bearers split apart with the regiment not knowing which way to go. Most soldiers followed the regimental colors while a few went with the United States flag.[57]

The national colors, held aloft by the color-bearer John Castens, was entirely unsupported on a small ridge nearly sixty yards from the redan, but Spooner himself quickly arrived and told the small group to plant the colors on the ridge while he reformed the regiment. They doubted audibly whether he could but promised him "we would place the colors on the breastworks, if he would like to have them there." In the chaos of battle Spooner simply yelled "plant the colors," and the small group did so.[58]

Not among the small group who moved on was John Roberts, who noted that he had gone as far as he could when two bullets hit him in the breast. "I saw the gun, which the bullets came out of," he amazingly reported. He went back to a stump that his small group had used to hold the flag earlier and there met Spooner again, telling him "I thought I had received my death wound." Spooner replied that he hoped not, and a captain also came up and gave him water and whiskey, telling him upon examination that he was not terribly hurt. Roberts nevertheless felt the blood flowing freely and that he was becoming weaker. He had read in a newspaper that gunpowder would stop the blood flow, so he "tore open a cartridge and gave the wound an application by emptying it into the wound, using my fingers as a swab, until I could see the flow becoming less." Roberts eventually went rearward and lay beside his dead captain, remarking that "it then seemed to me a happy thought to die by my captain and doing my duty." He lay down and went unconscious, not caring what happened to him as "I wasn't afraid to die," he insisted. In fact, he later related that his thoughts turned toward home and those who had gone on before him. Then he heard someone call his name: "I hardly knew if it were in this world or the next. I thought if from earth I would be permitted to see my wife and children, if from heaven I could see my dear mother and those gone before. I cared little which way the hand turned." The voice was indeed from earth, and a couple of friends helped him to the rear.[59]

Whether there was immense bravery or not, the story on the north side of the road was the same as on the south: Spooner's regiments had been stopped, mainly by the huge earthworks, one Illinoisan saying that "when we got to the fort we could not climb it the fort is 15 feet high and a big ditch on this side 5 feet deep & 7 wide." The Confederates nevertheless gave some grudging respect, with brigade commander Hébert writing that the Federals "several times pressed on to the assault, but were as often repulsed, notwithstanding the effort of the officers. Before long he fell back discomfited, having suffered severely." In that sense, Kilby Smith's attack was no different from Giles Smith's or Ewing's. All had made it to the parapet of the

Confederate fortifications, but there they had been halted. As late afternoon came, it seemed that Grant's attempt to crack Vicksburg's defenses had failed miserably, although these Federals of Blair's division were all that had really tried.[60]

It did not take long after the attack had stalled for almost all of Blair's Federals to realize that they had failed. The ravines were deeper than expected, the ridges higher, and the obstructions in between more problematic than anyone had guessed. Worse, the Confederate fortifications were more mammoth than anyone had dared to imagine. If a successful attempt at storming the works was going to be made, it would require much more planning and forethought than this rushed effort. Ladders would be needed in abundance to allow the troops to pour over the works in large numbers. Material to bridge or to fill in the ditches in front of the works would be required to allow the men to utilize the ladders. And enough men would be needed at the front to make the storming of the works a success, not just a temporary breach. This had been a hurried attempt, and all saw that much more planning was needed to succeed. Grant had thought the Confederate defenders would crumble; it had been worth a shot, and now he knew.[61]

There were also additional problems that did not exist before the attempt had been made. Blair had scores, perhaps hundreds, of troops trapped in no man's land. They could not go forward over the works, and as long as the sun was still up they could not go back without running the gantlet a second time, allowing the Confederates to concentrate their fire on the few men leaving the ramparts. The colors of at least six regiments were also planted on the works and could not be gotten out without drawing massive attention to them and their carriers. They certainly could not just be left there, so the Federals trapped on the ramparts of Vicksburg could only hold on. Blair reported that "they held their positions . . . with the utmost tenacity until night."[62]

Blair soon gave orders to his brigade commanders, including to Kilby Smith in person as he had wandered to the rear looking for "report and explanation," to reform the brigades and "occupy the last ground from which they moved to the assault to-day" as well as to press skirmishers forward "as near as possible to the enemy's works, for the purpose of occupying his attention." Blair also added that the troops should "be prepared to assault at daybreak in the morning."[63]

The result was a miserable few hours for the men caught on the ramparts and for their officers who were worried about them, one Missourian describing them as "checkmated at every point." Most could not fight back, looking up as they were. A few were able to keep up some fire, one of the regulars describing how he baited one Confederate by throwing a stick at his musket. The Confederate raised up, and the ready Federal shot him, the man throwing "up both his hands falling backwards." The wounded were worse off, one captain in the 127th Illinois remembering that "during the time I lay on the field, it seemed to me that no living mortal could escape. The wounded, dead and dying lay in many directions, and the zip, zip of the 'minies' were as thick." Fortunately, those regiments stationed behind under whatever cover they could find kept up a brisk fire to aid their counterparts trapped at the front. Confederate general Forney certainly thought so, declaring that his men could not capture the enemy colors on the parapets "on account of the very severe fire of the enemy's sharpshooters." Martin Smith likewise reported that the enemy artillery and sharpshooters kept "up a continuous and heavy fire."[64]

The Federal artillery knocked out numerous Confederate guns during the afternoon, but the relieved and now revived Confederates had a few tricks left themselves. Louis Hébert, who had beat back the assaults, told one of his cannon crews on a Parrott gun to wait until the Federals hit near the gun and it sent up a large cloud of dust to remove the cannon and keep it safe. Sure enough, a round soon came and created the diversion, whereupon the gun was safely removed and the artillery fire moved elsewhere. The Federals cheered again, as they did when they knocked out a piece, but one Confederate thought "the laugh was turned on them."[65]

Mercifully, the sun eventually began to sink to the west behind the Confederate lines, and the Federals huddling on the ramparts could not watch it go down fast enough. They knew they were condemned to their positions until dark afforded them a chance to escape under cover. But even that had pitfalls. It was bad enough traversing the harsh terrain in the daylight, but negotiating it at night could be even worse, although without heavy Confederate fire. They could only hope that the Union regiments that had not made it all the way in would not mistake them for Confederates and fire on them on the way out. Making an escape even harder, Confederates set fire to several structures behind the lines to illuminate the surroundings and offer them a better idea of what was occurring. Kilby Smith noted that "the whole scene was brilliantly lighted by the flames" but that "this purpose had been anticipated by Colonel Spooner, who, with skill and good judgment, withdrew from the ditch beneath the parapet to shelter. A few moments later, and hand-grenades and the grave would have been supper and bed for his men." An Illinoisan conversely declared that "this proved more dangerous to them than to us." Also dangerous was the plight of one Mississippian who came to Henry Reynolds of the 36th Mississippi with a jammed musket. The ball was lodged half way down and could not be rammed home, so Reynolds simply held the weapon over the parapet and fired it, where it would hurt Federals if it exploded. It did not, and Reynolds was grieved that "after I shot that choked gun I had to do the same with about a half dozen more."[66]

Ultimately, most Federals made it out of the incredibly taxing situation and the firing—audible as far south as Grand Gulf during the day—died down. Union regimental commanders began to withdraw their men as the darkness settled in, but in many cases it took hours. Heroically, they brought most of the flags back with them. Ultimately, orders arrived from Blair for the brigade commanders to withdraw all the troops, even from the forward positions, and form a line on the ridges to the west and north, either across Mint Spring Bayou or the tributary of Glass Bayou. There, they could hold the line until someone figured out what to do next. Curiously, after his nonimpressive showing during the day, Thomas Kilby Smith had the gall to question the orders, arguing that they were in direct contrast to what Sherman had told him earlier and that "I had won by severe loss the best position to fortify in our whole front. Already I had made arrangements to plant batteries upon the hill I occupied." He went back to Blair's headquarters to argue his case in person but was given peremptory orders to retire, which he did. All Federals who could move were back to the main line by 3:00 A.M. on the morning of May 20.[67]

Yet the cost was staggering, one Louisianan describing the ground as "blue with the Yankee dead and wounded." This rushed attack claimed 613 total casualties (120 killed, 485 wounded, and eight missing) out of Blair's division alone. Army wide, the skirmishing and fighting made for a total of 942 (157 killed, 777 wounded, and eight missing). Sherman could only admit that "the rebel parapets were strongly manned, and the enemy fought hard and well," but he realized the cost. While wading among the regulars he formerly commanded, he tenderly asked "Is that all that was left of the 13th? Are either of the color Sergeants saved?" When told one had somehow survived and actually brought his flag out, Sherman responded "well, we can give him something better" and made him a quartermaster, out of harm's way.[68]

The wounded were particularly miserable. Mississippi chaplain Foster, behind the Confederate lines, described the arrival of a captain in his regiment. "Presently the litter bearers came with their mournful burden. There the Captain lies, mangled and bleeding and groaning. His leg is most awfully mangled—a twelve pound rifle shell struck him on the left thigh, inflicting a most severe flesh wound, and then passed down on the same leg, tearing off the entire calf. The same fatal shell had struck a private, removing almost entirely one hip." Foster could do little while the surgeons worked on the captain's leg: "The doctors worked and dressed these awful wounds while I endeavored to remove the dust from their hands and faces—for they were covered with dirt."[69]

Everyone tried to make sense of what had just happened. The Union army was stunned after so many seemingly easy victories in the previous weeks. One Illinoisan jotted in his journal that "we have received a very severe check, and everybody is badly discouraged." Still, they pressed on; one Ohioan remembered hearing the strains of "The Union forever, hurrah boys! Hurrah!" A Confederate Tennessean knew a victory when he saw one, commenting that the attack came on "some fresh Louisianans who were not in the fight the day before." Chaplain Foster simply wrote his wife, "Thanks be to the Great Ruler of the Universe, Vicksburg is still safe."[70]

The failed assault also produced some interarmy rivalry between the Union corps, over and above that which had been building all campaign long. Although McPherson had not pushed his advances vigorously, he was a Grant and Sherman insider and would likely come under little if any blame. Not so McClernand, Sherman later confiding that "I never make a practice of speaking or writing of others, but during our assault of the 19th several of my brigade commanders were under the impression that McClernand's corps did not even attempt an assault." One of Sherman's men in Blair's division noted in his diary that "Gen. McClernand failed to obey orders and the consequence was that the 15 A. C. [army corps] did all the fighting."[71]

Perhaps most important, the quick attempt at the assault, which proved short of overwhelming, only added to Confederate confidence. Much like the initial Union ironclad advances at Fort Donelson on February 12 and 13 before the major attack on February 14, in which the limited and minor advances interpreted as defeats by the dejected Confederate gunners built up morale for the big day, this small-scale attempt proved to bolster Confederate morale and show all involved that the lines could hold. It was an enormous boost of confidence for the entire garrison, which would no doubt face a much more determined and widespread assault in the future, maybe even the next morning. But with this victory, Confederate confidence soared and with it the strength of the Confederate defenses for whatever Grant attempted next.[72]

"The resistance offered was quite unexpected," recalled one Federal. Grant himself was disappointed at the result as well and would clearly have to make some hard decisions in the future. He had been sure the Confederates would crack under the slightest pressure, but he had underestimated both the strength of the Confederate works and the soldiers who manned them. What now?[73]

Ulysses S. Grant was already working on that.

6

"The Enemy Are Evidently Preparing for an Assault"

John C. Pemberton was perhaps as surprised as anyone as nightfall descended on the Vicksburg battlefield on May 19. Certainly, Ulysses S. Grant, William T. Sherman, and a whole host of Federals who believed the Confederates would fold quickly when pushed were terribly mistaken, but Pemberton was most astonished at the stiff defense his troops had put up that day. Heartening reports had come in throughout the fighting, and by nightfall it was evident Vicksburg would hold at least for another day. Suddenly, the man who just two days ago had declared that he "did not believe our troops would stand the first shock of the attack" now saw some glimmer of hope for the future.[1]

Others were also more optimistic. Mississippian William Drennan admitted to his wife, "I am still in good health and better spirits than yesterday." The pessimistic Dr. Alison wrote in his diary about the heavy fighting on May 19, declaring that "the enemy attacked our lines at 8 o'clock this morning, and have made several desperate attempts to storm our trenches, but were repulsed with heavy loss." Then he added significantly: "Fighting steady all day but we still hold our own. The sprit of the men is improving. Things begin to look better." A Missourian who had helped defend the "Fort with Palisades" the day before similarly confided to his diary that "the result of the engagement on yesterday has caused a general glow of satisfaction to pervade our entire army; as it demonstrated our ability to cope successfully with [the enemy]."[2]

Pemberton's hope especially grew with the messages he received throughout the fighting during the afternoon of May 19. John H. Forney, whose division had partially borne the brunt of the attacks, kept Pemberton regularly informed. Although the future still looked bleak, the news from May 19 was encouraging. Forney reported after the sun set that three regiments and one battalion of General Hebert's brigade repelled the attack of the enemy to-day, commencing at 2:30 P.M., advancing in three lines. They succeeded in getting immediately under the parapet of the battery, in position on the Graveyard road. Two colors were left within 10 feet of the works, but were not taken, on account of the very severe fire of the enemy's sharpshooters, and were either destroyed or taken away after dark.[3]

Hope grew as well because of the ability to shift reserves. For example, Waul's Texas Legion had not been engaged on May 19, even though it had been sent to the crisis area far to the north. Albert C. Lenert remembered in his diary how "a courier came in full speed bringing orders for the Legion to reinforce some Regiment (to the left) where they were fearful the enemy would over-power them." Lenert continued that "we all formed the companies as quick as possible and the Colonel came charging up on his horse as the men were in the act of loading their guns and before some could get ready, ordered us by the left flank DOUBLE QUICK MARCH!" Lenert reported that the column had advanced only a couple of hundred yards before the orders were countermanded "as the enemy assault had been repulsed."[4]

Yet Forney did not mince words and informed his commander of all that still confronted the Vicksburg defenders. Most thought new assaults would come, probably even the next morning. Forney said that "their pickets tonight are advancing to the right of the Jackson road, and within 200 yards of our lines, and a line of battle was discovered late this evening in rear of these skirmishers. Our pickets, concealed, heard them say, 'They would be in our lines in five hours.'" Some back-and-forth evidently took place all along the lines as well, Captain W. L. Faulk of the 38th Mississippi noting in his diary "spirited conversation between the pickets along the line." Others took exception to such an adventure. George Durfee wrote that "the pickets were talking and black guarding one another until one of our guns opened on them which brought the conversation to a close."[5]

The idea of taking Vicksburg that night may have been only a hope, as night action was extremely rare in the Civil War, and few actors were terribly concerned about anything happening while it was dark. What concerned Forney and many others the most was Federal artillery, even then being positioned closer to the Confederate lines and behind strong earthworks of their own. All knew what that portended for the next morning, as the Federal artillery had heavily damaged the Confederate fortifications already. Forney reported that his works were damaged, guns were dismounted, and casualties were numerous. "Six batteries of theirs are now bearing immediately on the work on the Jackson road," he informed Pemberton, "and others on the Baldwin's Ferry road. . . . I think they are moving artillery between the two roads. These batteries have kept up a continuous fire all day upon the works between the roads."[6]

Perhaps worse than the field artillery to the Confederates was the bombardment throughout the next several days of the naval guns from the Mississippi River, both the gunboats and mortar boats. One Federal wrote how "the mortar fleet was at work all night, we could see the shell rise, descend, and some of them explode." A Union Missourian described how "mortar boats have floated down the opposite side of the peninsula fronting Vicksburg and about 20 huge mortars engaged in shelling the City." Not all the Union soldiers were as thrilled, one noting in his diary that "many of the boys complain of the noise of the gunboats which kept up firing most of the night." Confederates seemed to take it all in stride. One Tennessee cavalryman acting as a courier for Pemberton described how the troopers dug holes for protection in the city, "and when things became too warm for us, we would crawl in our holes and pull the holes in after us." A Texan was no more impressed, jotting in his diary how "the last I heard before I went to sleep was still the roar of cannonading from their Fleet below the city."[7]

There was optimism nevertheless inside Confederate Vicksburg. After all, those who thought the Southerners would not put up much of a fight had been proved wrong by the determined stand the troops had made that day. In fact, portions of two Confederate brigades, only two regiments in one and three and a battalion in the other, had held off an entire Union division of three full brigades through hours of assaults and attempts to breach the Confederate lines. And while the Federals were no doubt jockeying for better positions, the Confederates were doing the same. "Our men are at work throwing up traverses, &c.," Forney reported, "making themselves more secure." He also added that "my men are in excellent spirits, and will behave as they should."[8]

The long night helped, when much work went on and some fighting as well. One Mississippian detailed at the Stockade Redan to repair the works described how the Federals discovered them and "at once began to throw shells from their batteries." Most shells went over their heads, but they nevertheless made "a most frightful noise, and the burning fuses throwing out long tails of lurid fire." One eventually hit "in the midst of the fatigue party," ending the work despite few casualties. A nearby Louisianan took a walk during the night over the ground and could only comment that "the stench of the dead was awful!"[9]

Still, Pemberton knew the Federals were not going anywhere, and he expected a continuation of the assault the next morning. He sent a bevy of orders on the evening of May 19 alerting his division commanders that he had "reason to believe that there will be a heavy assault on the left of the lines tomorrow morning." That was Martin Smith's position, Pemberton narrowing the focus for Smith even more to indicate his left was the major place of concern, perhaps because of Sherman's movement in that area and coordination with the gunboats. Pemberton also warned Bowen and other reserve troops such as Waul's Texas Legion to be prepared to reinforce any danger zone. Even Carter Stevenson all the way over on the right was tasked with sending reserves if necessary, although Stevenson countered that there was heavy movement on his front and that he had few if any men to spare. Pemberton acquiesced, writing that "if you are certainly threatened, the movement of your reserve regiments will not be made, nor will they be concentrated." He nevertheless informed Stevenson of "the complete failure of the enemy in his various assaults on our works to-day" and implored him that "your command will emulate the glorious example of their comrades."[10]

Pemberton knew Grant had a bulldog mentality; he would be back, perhaps as soon as early the next morning.

As daylight broke over the Vicksburg battleground early on May 20, everyone expected a continuation of the assaults from the day before and probably on a much grander scale. "Tomorrow," Indianan Louis Knobe wrote in his diary, "we expect some heavy work." There was much trepidation, one Missourian confiding his innermost thoughts to his diary that "this is hard work to take this position by storm. I don't think it can be done by such weak lines. By a more concentrated movement and with great loss of life we may be able to take them by charge." John Pemberton certainly thought a renewal was coming and went so far as to order "all soldiers confined for trivial offenses returned to their commands."[11]

William T. Sherman thought the same. He penned a note to his wife, Ellen, after Blair's advance and admitted that "we assaulted yesterday but it is very strong. . . . We had a heavy fight . . . [and] suffered much." He added that "we reached the very rampart but did not enter the works." Perhaps part of Sherman's growing caution came because of his family and friends. He informed Ellen of Captain Washington's death, as well as her brother Charley being wounded in the hand while "he saved the colors." He also noted that "Hugh [Ewing] is also under fire [and] had a hard time." Problems were already emerging once again in the high command as well. Sherman remarked that McClernand "did *not* press his attack as he should." He also admitted that "this is a death struggle and will be terrible." With that cheery note, Sherman informed his wife that "I must again go to the front amid the shot and shell which follow me but somehow thus far have spared me."[12]

At the same time, however, Sherman was upbeat about eventual success, knowing that he had sent only one division of the army against the Confederates. "We are all in good health & spirits at this moment & having reached & secured the Yazoo will soon have plenty to eat." He knew more attacks would come and he welcomed them: "They are fortified and we must attack. Quicker the better."[13]

Surprisingly, the exact opposite occurred, as there were no attacks on May 20. Nor were there any on May 21, with an astonished Pemberton staff officer, John C. Taylor, writing briefly in his diary "no assaults." The Federals, to Pemberton's delight, did not assault on either day, although there was much talk of it and even some preparation. Pemberton notified Johnston of the developments: "The enemy assaulted our intrenched lines yesterday at two points, center and left, and was repulsed with heavy loss. Our loss small." He also reported that "at this hour, 8.30 A.M., he is briskly cannonading with long-range guns." A nervous Pemberton, who followed his May 20 notes with four more on May 21, explained that he had ordered his troops not to return fire to save ammunition, and he asked Johnston to send "musket caps," they being "our present main necessity." In fact, Pemberton gave orders to fire only when necessary because of the lack of caps, one Confederate remarking that "nothing is more painful; nothing is more demoralizing than to lie under a fire without the power of replying." Another found time to observe and marveled at the heavy barrage, writing that some of the Union cannon fire "go entirely across our lines and some fall into the river."[14]

Still, Pemberton prepared for the inevitable assault, once again moving Bowen's brigades and Waul's Texas Legion to be ready to go to the crisis point. Not surprising, with so many phantom Federals being reported everywhere, such movement grew tiresome quickly. By May 21, Bowen complained that his troops were being exhausted and wrote to "suggest the propriety of assigning to my division some portion of the intrenchments, and allowing each division to have its own reserves at call." He explained that "at present my men do double duty, some being always in the trenches, and those in reserve suffering more loss actually than the others. Besides, their efficiency will be very greatly impaired by having to march long distances at a double-quick before getting to the scene of action." As proof, Bowen forwarded a message from Francis Cockrell, describing how some of his regiments were even then in the trenches supporting "Colonel Witherspoon's brigade," so that if he moved as ordered he would leave entire sections "wholly without any troops in the trenches." Cockrell described the Stockade Redan as "one of the most assailable in our lines," but requested Shoup and Witherspoon [Hébert] to see to its defense by themselves.[15]

Of course, the fear was that the Federals might not allow time for such a compromise. All through the day on May 20, Forney reported that "there appears to be a column of dust this side of Ferguson's, but from my position on top of this house can't locate it." Stephen D. Lee farther south reported that "the enemy are evidently preparing for an assault." Forney even detected that "the enemy has commenced signaling from the top of Ferguson's house." So went the long day of May 20, but with no assaults taking place. Again, a nervous Pemberton sent out warnings of another possible night attack.[16]

There were, in fact, desires among the Federals to go ahead and make the grand attack. Envious of any information they could gather, the Federal signal corps even drove pegs into holes in a large oak tree to allow them to climb it and look across Confederate lines. McClernand specifically wanted to make the attack. He informed Grant on May 20, "I propose to assault the enemy's works in the morning," and he detailed A. J. Smith's division to move closer, although there is debate whether an actual assault was ordered. It did not happen either way, one of McClernand's staff officers griping that Smith "fooled around all day and finally didn't do it at all." One of McClernand's Illinoisans, writing on that May 20, noted that they "were drawn up in line of battle to make a charge on the fort, but for some reason or other we did not do it and I was glad of it."[17]

There was a chance McClernand may have acted on his own if he had been able to get all his troops in line, but there had been a major mix-up earlier involving Hovey's division that caused him to wait and seek more information from Grant. When leaving the Big Black River for Vicksburg, McClernand had ordered Hovey to march with the corps, although Grant had told Hovey to leave one brigade at the river. The fault was indeed Grant's for sending direct orders to division commanders without notifying the corps commander, and a confused Hovey wrote Grant, once he received McClernand's order to move both of his brigades: "I am bound to presume that this is in accordance with your orders." He added, "This leaves the bridges entirely unguarded." Finding out the mix-up, McClernand wrote Grant that "my order to him was written in ignorance to him to remain at Big Black." But in planning his assault, McClernand asked: "Cannot his division, or a part of it, be permitted to take part in the assault to-morrow?" Further exhibiting the attitudes within the army's high command, Hovey also disregarded an order from McClernand to march on to Vicksburg, Hovey telling him "my command is too much fatigued to move to-night. . . . Should the troops march to-night they will be worthless for service to-morrow."[18]

By this point on May 20 McClernand was getting on Grant's nerves in other ways as well. It had been growing for months now, McClernand thinking he would be a better choice to lead the army, and McClernand seemed to take pleasure in reporting on and complaining of what he perceived as a lack of effort of the other corps. "I have suffered considerable loss," he wrote at one point, "but am pressing for a sharp engagement up to the enemy's works. I hear nothing on the right or center." Later, he informed Grant that A. J. Smith was within a hundred yards of the enemy line: "He says McPherson should advance on his right." Of course, McClernand's sniping did not have the desired effect on Grant, with whom both McPherson and Sherman on the right and center were much more friendly. And it filtered down into the army as well, one rumor going around on May 20 that "General McClernand is under arrest."[19]

There was nevertheless some gain from McClernand's efforts in that he found a great deal about the enemy's defenses in the continual repositioning of May 20 and 21. He informed Grant that "in my front we have met a formidable line of earthworks, chiefly square redoubts or lunettes, connected together by a line of rifle-pits, and the whole line in a very commanding position." He also understood that there were "another two inner lines in addition." One Illinoisan described as much to his sister: "In this manner we advanced over hill and dale through a shower of deadly missiles to within six hundred yards of their Batteries, where we laid, under cover of the hill, firing at them, the balance of the day, when we were ordered forward on to the next hill one hundred yards nearer." Taking together all the information he had gained, McClernand could not resist adding his own thoughts. He lectured Grant: "I do not think the position can be carried with our present extended lines. In my opinion a change of the plan of attack and the concentration of our forces on some particular point or points would give better assurance of success. Otherwise, perhaps, a siege becomes the only alternative."[20]

Consequently, all that came of the next two days was massive amounts of work and skirmishing. The Federals took the opportunity between the May 19 assaults and whenever the next ones would come to build and strengthen their own works, to gain better positions, and to prepare for the inevitable next offensive attack. The records are replete with explanations of all that occurred. Frank Blair wrote that his troops were "employed in skirmishing with the enemy, reconnoitering the ground, and improving our position." One of his brigade commanders, Giles Smith, elaborated on the process, especially "throwing forward sharpshooters, with instructions to intrench themselves as they gained ground." John D. Stevenson's brigade worked to drive "the enemy within their lines, and had gained positions for our batteries" and "strengthened our positions, and steadily advanced our skirmish lines until they were within 100 yards of the works of the enemy." George Durfee of the 8th Illinois wrote that "our men keep up such a fire that they hardly dare show their heads."[21]

The artillery was also used to keep the Confederates' heads down and therefore make them unable to work within their own entrenchments or to hamper the enemy troops as they toiled at Union positions. Samuel Barrett, commanding one of the Chicago Light Artillery batteries, reported that "firing was kept up at intervals during the day, mostly directed at the enemy's fort opposite us." One of Sherman's artilleryman at the Stockade Redan noted that his battery concentrated on the stockade itself as well as embrasures where the Confederates "were working like beavers strengthening the work." He marveled that they worked all night too, writing on the morning of May 21 that "the Bastion looks as good as new this morning, our friends having evidently been improving [during] the night as well as ourselves." One Confederate attested to the heavy Union fire, an aggravated Alabamian on Lee's line writing in his diary of the Federal sharpshooters: "I'l tell you a gnat cant live for 'em. They shoot at ever hat they see stick above the ditch."[22]

One humorous event occurred as Battery E, 1st Illinois Artillery pummeled the Confederate lines. As each shot landed, the Federals would hear one smart-aleck Confederate yell "a little more to the right." The next would produce the yell "a little more to the left." The Illinoisans kept firing away despite dwindling ammunition, and the taunting soon stopped, making the Federals think they had gotten the culprit. They had not, because soon the yell came back: "Cease firing." One infantryman watching the episode determined that "he [the smart-aleck] had evidently had a close call."[23]

Not everything was so entertaining, of course, one Illinoisan writing that during these interim days "dead and wounded are being constantly brought in." Such was the case with the 8th Indiana skirmishers. Nicholas Miller described the sad fate of Richard Lamb, who was skirmishing beside him when the Confederates sent "a few shots neer to whare we were lying." The shots came from a tree to the front, and Lamb responded, "d____ if he would take that." Miller cautioned him not to be foolish or to expose himself, but Lamb's blood was up and he stood to fire, "but he would not listen to me." The Confederate shot Lamb through the "bowles." Miller ran to him, but it was too late. Several others then carted Lamb off for medical aid, but he died in two hours. "In all my life I never saw a man suffer so," Miller remembered, adding, "to the last begging me to cut his throat and kill him as quick as possible."[24]

There was also some relocation of lines, as in the case of Frederick Steele's troops of Sherman's corps. John Thayer's brigade had maneuvered near the Stockade Redan while Francis Manter's and Charles Woods's brigades held the position to the river bluffs. In this interim, the 76th Ohio of Woods's brigade nearest the river built rifle pits on the ridge, they "having procured a few spades and shovels." Some positions were just naturally exposed, however, as was the case of the 3rd Missouri of Woods's brigade, which John T. Buegel described as "a bad position. The enemy had a fort near the river and could bombard the hill when [where] we were located. So we were not safe for a single minute from his batteries." Eventually, he noted, "in order to protect ourselves somewhat from the enemy fire we dug holes in the side of the hill." Buegel described how "as soon as the batteries began to shell us, each one slipped into his hole like mice." The 12th Missouri also moved to the right all the way down the bluffs to the Mississippi River, capturing some of the outlying Confederate batteries. Frank Blair likewise redeployed his division around the Stockade Redan, utilizing some of James Tuttle's reserve troops as well.[25]

Confederates inside Vicksburg were well aware of what the enemy was doing and worked feverishly to strengthen their lines any way they could and to repair the damage continually being done by the Federal artillery. Pemberton reported to Johnston on May 21 that "their artillery fire was very heavy, and plowed up our works considerably and dismounted two guns on the center [at the 2nd Texas Lunette]. The works were repaired and the guns replaced last night." Martin L. Smith reported that the two days were "spent by the enemy in erecting new batteries and keeping up from daylight till dark the heaviest possible firing, both of musketry and artillery." One of Smith's brigade commanders, William E. Baldwin, agreed: "The enemy was busy erecting batteries and placing guns in position in front of our line, keeping up an incessant fire of sharpshooters." Down the line to the south, the same was occurring on Louis Hébert's front, he describing how the enemy "rapidly pushed on his works in intrenching, sapping, constructing batteries, &c., under cover of heavy sharpshooting and cannonading." The accompanying yells of the Federals "whenever they make a good shot which they done very often" was perhaps just as aggravating. A Texan described how "the Yankees yelled again" when an artillery round set on fire a nearby house, evidently containing gunpowder.[26]

Smith and Forney had their troops working hard anyway. One Confederate lamented the way the trenches had been dug for temporary use to repel an attack rather than as living quarters: "We found them uncomfortable and very dangerous to go in or out during the day, and as we had to have water and food it was the first difficulty to solve." The first couple of days were spent in jumping on the rear bank and making a run for it, but the soldiers soon dug trenches to the rear ravines for protection. Indeed, Forney related that the intent was to work and not fight, because "by this time my entire division front was completely and closely invested. My skirmishers were withdrawn, and skirmishing prohibited (by order), in order to husband ammunition." On his right, Forney sent John C. Moore thirty bales of cotton, "which he thinks you can use to advantage by placing them in such positions as to shield your gunners from the enemy's Sharpshooters." Dead mules and horses were also ordered skinned so that their hides could cover the cotton bales and parapet. Elsewhere along the line, Confederate soldiers who were obviously proficient at wielding the musket now showed just as much adeptness with the few shovels and picks that were available. Baldwin reported that "our trenches were rapidly completed and strengthened, and traverses erected as positions subject to an enfilading fire were developed." Francis Shoup reported the same thing, but with a dire warning attached: "We improve every moment to strengthen our line and protect ourselves from the incessant fire. Our artillery is almost useless, since we have no properly constructed protection. Being almost without intrenching tools, we can do little to repair the evil."[27]

Some of the skirmishing over the next two days, even with no formal assaults and more working than fighting, almost reached battle proportions, Colonel Marcus Spiegel of the 120th Ohio writing that he continually changed "companies when out of ammunition and their guns too hot to handle." Even those regiments that had been heavily involved in the past couple of days were sent in again, Charles Smith of the 83rd Ohio writing in his diary on May 21: "This morning as we were congratulating ourselves on the prospect of a day of rest, Genl. McClernand rode by and seeing us idle, the consequence was the regiment was ordered back to its old position in advance." And the growing Federal host, as could be viewed from the Confederate works, was not lost on the Southerners. Colonel Ashbel Smith of the 2nd Texas noted the increasing Union numbers, writing that "all this day (the 19th), 20th, and 21st, heavy black columns of the enemy, or clouds of dust marking their movements, were seen pouring through the timber over the hills, taking positions where they were concealed by the irregularities of the ground." The artillery and skirmishing "increased hour by hour with their augmenting numbers, until the uproar and rattle was almost incessant and very grand." Some tried to respond, but the ravines covered the enemy "as effectually as we were sheltered by our breastworks."[28]

Across from the Texans, Colonel Theodore E. Buehler of the 67th Indiana described how his men kept up that severe fire, "sending balls wherever a head would show itself above the breastworks." The Indianans took cover behind a few burned-out buildings until "at one time a chimney was tumbled over them by a solid shot from a rebel battery." An impressed Buehler noted that "nothing daunted, though almost buried in its ruins, they crawled to the next one, and again commenced their firing." Forney noted that enemy sharpshooters were "annoying us very much," but the same was happening on the Federal side. One Ohioan described how they had "the pleasure of jerking our necks almost out of joint dodging their balls."[29]

There was also much fraternizing among Federal and Confederate troops even amid the skirmishing, especially at night despite warning from Union headquarters that there were signs of an imminent Confederate breakout attempt under the cover of darkness. Louisianan William Tunnard told of a case where a member of his 3rd Louisiana "found some acquaintances, and was invited into the enemy's lines, with the assurance that he would be allowed to return." He went over, "trusted himself to the honor of the foe," and was given "a feast, accompanied with a sociable chat and several drinks." The impressed Confederate was then allowed to return, which he amazingly did, carrying word of the affair. That induced more Confederates to seek friendships, and many found acquaintants, two brothers in the Louisiana regiment finding a third brother in a Federal unit nearby. On the Union side, members of the 47th Ohio, out in the field looking for their dead to bury after the May 19 assault, were captured and were "marched around inside of their fortifications for a few hours to find a competent officer to judge of our case. We were then again sent back to our lines, after we had explained our business in a straightforward manner."[30]

But it was all done, on both sides, with a constant fear of more assaults in the near future. Few if any Federals were satisfied with just one division's attempt to break an isolated portion of the Confederate works, and few if any Confederates thought that the Federals would give up and go away any time soon. If any did, they had no understanding of the enemy commander's mindset; after all, Grant had spent much of the last seven months just trying to get to Vicksburg. He was not about to give up when he was this close to the goal.[31]

Contrary to what almost everyone expected, the first step for Grant was to take a couple days to get his affairs in order so that he could do the next assault more effectively. The main item needing to be organized was his supply system, one Ohioan writing on May 19 in his diary that "most of the boys entirely out of rations and suffering much from lack of food." Another noted that he offered a soldier five dollars for a piece of cornbread but it was not accepted, the man responding that "bread was worth more to him than money."

The maneuver campaign just ended had not only provided five victories out of five confrontations and hemmed the Confederates inside Vicksburg; it had also uncovered what were probably the keys to the whole campaign: Haynes' and Snyder's bluffs along the Yazoo River. It was the ground that Grant had been trying to occupy for months now, and he rightly divined that taking that area would all but secure Vicksburg eventually. Now that they were secure, Grant detailed some of his troops, including the 5th Ohio Battery, to defend the area.[32]

Grant certainly needed to open his supply line—and soon. The troops had suffered from the lack of normal rations for the previous three weeks. The plantations along the march provided some foodstuffs, and the wilderness allowed for picking ripe fruit such as blackberries and other produce. "Plums are very plenty both white and red," wrote an Illinoisan in his diary. Yet the farther the Federals went, the less food they had, one Illinoisan declaring that "our men then marched or rather fought & starved their way up." Grant realized as much, writing that "they were cheerful, and did their duty well, although a great portion of the time they were without rations, and had to live on meat alone, as a considerable portion of the hard bread issued on the road proved to be moldy and unfit to eat."[33]

One Iowan, Calvin Ainsworth of the 25th Iowa, elaborated on his hunger on May 18, writing in his diary: "We go into camp at last, our long hard march is ended. For three days we have had nothing to eat. I have seen the boys offer a dollar for a hard tack, but no one had any to sell. I have had nothing myself for three days, still I am not so very hungry. I picked a few blackberries once or twice when there was a halt." Ainsworth and his comrades were nevertheless confident in the future, even if that confidence was misplaced. He declared there was food in the wagon trains: "We know we will get all we want tomorrow. Our division commanded by General Steel guarded the provision train through and did not steal a cracker, though deprived of food for three days." There were no crackers to steal, but the overall sentiment was correct: Grant had taken Haynes' Bluff, and the supply lines would be opening any day now. Fortunately, the water in the area was good, one Illinoisan writing home that it was "better than any place I bin in Dixie Land."[34]

Cheerfulness lasted only so long, however, as the Federal troops became hungrier and hungrier, the heavy dust continually roiling up and making it even worse. Grant commiserated with them: "Most of the troops had been marching and fighting battles for twenty days, on an average of about five days' rations drawn from the commissary department." He continued: "Though they had not suffered from short rations up to this time, the want of bread to accompany the other rations was beginning to be much felt."

Sherman agreed, his men generally being the rear of the column after Jackson and thus moving through swept-over territory. He described how "our men had literally lived upon the country, having left Grand Gulf May 8 with three days' rations in their haversacks, and received little or nothing till after our arrival here." One Ohioan was so excited he told his diary on May 18: "Captured a goose skinned and roasted it for supper."[35]

One Ohioan indicated how the hunger was not just confined to the lower ranks. Osborn Oldroyd of the 20th Ohio told how "General Leggett walked into our camp, and in his usual happy way inquired, 'Well, boys, have you had your supper?'" The troops responded with, "No, General, we have not had any," to which Leggett shot back, "Well, boys, I have not had any either, and we shall probably have to fight for our breakfast." That satisfied the men: "Very well, General; guess we can stand it as well as you."[36]

Some soldiers took their grievances directly to Grant. As he rode through his troops after the failed May 19 assault—some claimed it was the 83rd Ohio—Grant heard a solitary soldier call out in a low voice: "Hard Tack." Then, he marveled, "in a moment the cry was taken up all along the line, 'Hard Tack! Hard tack!'" While many today look upon hardtack as perhaps the least desirable commodity in a Civil War soldier's fare, bread was essential to their diet. The quick-thinking Grant immediately spoke to the growing chorus, informing them that "we had been engaged ever since the arrival of the troops in building a road over which to supply them with everything they needed." He was amazed that "the cry was instantly changed to cheers." George Carrington of the 11th Illinois related this excitement in his diary, writing on May 20 of news that Haynes' Bluff was theirs and that "bread is coming that way," although he admitted he had nothing to eat that day itself. Another noted as late as May 20 that "our grub [is] rather scarce, but we should not complain."[37]

The overwhelming evidence indicates that between May 16 and 19, Grant's Army of the Tennessee was entering a crisis period in terms of sustenance. It was also, significantly, a time of heavy marching and fighting. Food had run out, and what had earlier been brought forward in wagon trains from Grand Gulf had been consumed by that time and no more trains were on the way. Isolated soldiers may have found food to live on, but the army as a whole was entering a period of hunger that, if effectively utilized by Pemberton, if he had known it, could have possibly changed the campaign. Put simply, if Pemberton had somehow been able to delay Grant a few days longer, not even requiring a victory but just delay, Grant's troops could have possibly entered a time when their bodies began to truly suffer due to the lack of food—and their fighting ability as well. The most logical place for Pemberton to delay was either at the Baker's Creek or Big Black River crossings, but Pemberton met the enemy east of the crossings in each case rather than defend the western side of each stream.

Fortunately for the famished Union army, Grant could make the promise that food was coming now that Haynes' Bluff was in his possession. He had immediately started the flow of supplies to that point, although it would take a few days for them to reach the soldiers surrounding Vicksburg. "I have instructed my quartermaster and commissary to send up boats to Lake's Landing with forage and provisions; will you please send a convoy?" Grant wrote to Admiral Porter on May 19. Lower-level officers were also asking for immediate aid, Frederick Steele similarly writing to Porter: "We are short of rations, and want rations sent up the Yazoo to Snyder's, if the Chickasaw Bayou is not navigable."[38]

Those supplies soon began to arrive, Grant reporting that "the 20th and 21st were spent in perfecting communications with our supplies." Much of the work was done by the navy itself in getting the goods first to the mouth of Chickasaw Bayou and then later to Haynes' Bluff; rockets fired from the vessels answered by Federals on the shore assured the supply boats that the landings were in Union hands. Just getting supplies to Chickasaw Bayou and Haynes' Bluff was only part of the solution, however, and the easy part of it too. The Yazoo River had always been open to commerce except for the Confederate guns blocking its path, and that was no longer an issue. Thus, Porter could easily send the supplies up to Haynes' and Snyder's Bluffs, and even to Chickasaw Bayou at Lake's Landing, which was even closer to the army.[39]

Getting the supplies and ammunition inland to the troops was the real problem, and it fell to the army to open the necessary avenues. Grant set the engineers and pioneers to building roads from the various landings inland so that each corps could be supplied quickly. He elaborated on the process in his memoirs years later, writing that "in the interval between the assaults . . . , roads had been completed from the Yazoo River and Chickasaw Bayou, around the rear of the army, to enable us to bring up supplies of food and ammunition." XV Corps engineers and pioneers did much of the work, they being the corps on the north and northeast of Vicksburg, the direction from which the supplies emanated. While others were positioning batteries on the main line, a few engineers saw to what Sherman described as the effort to build "bridges and roads . . . to bring up ammunition and provisions from the mouth of Chickasaw, to which point supply boats had been ordered by General Grant." Captain William L. B. Jenney of the XV Corps did much of the work, making a reconnaissance on May 19 "for a road to communicate with the Johnston Place Landing, on the Yazoo River." He also forwarded

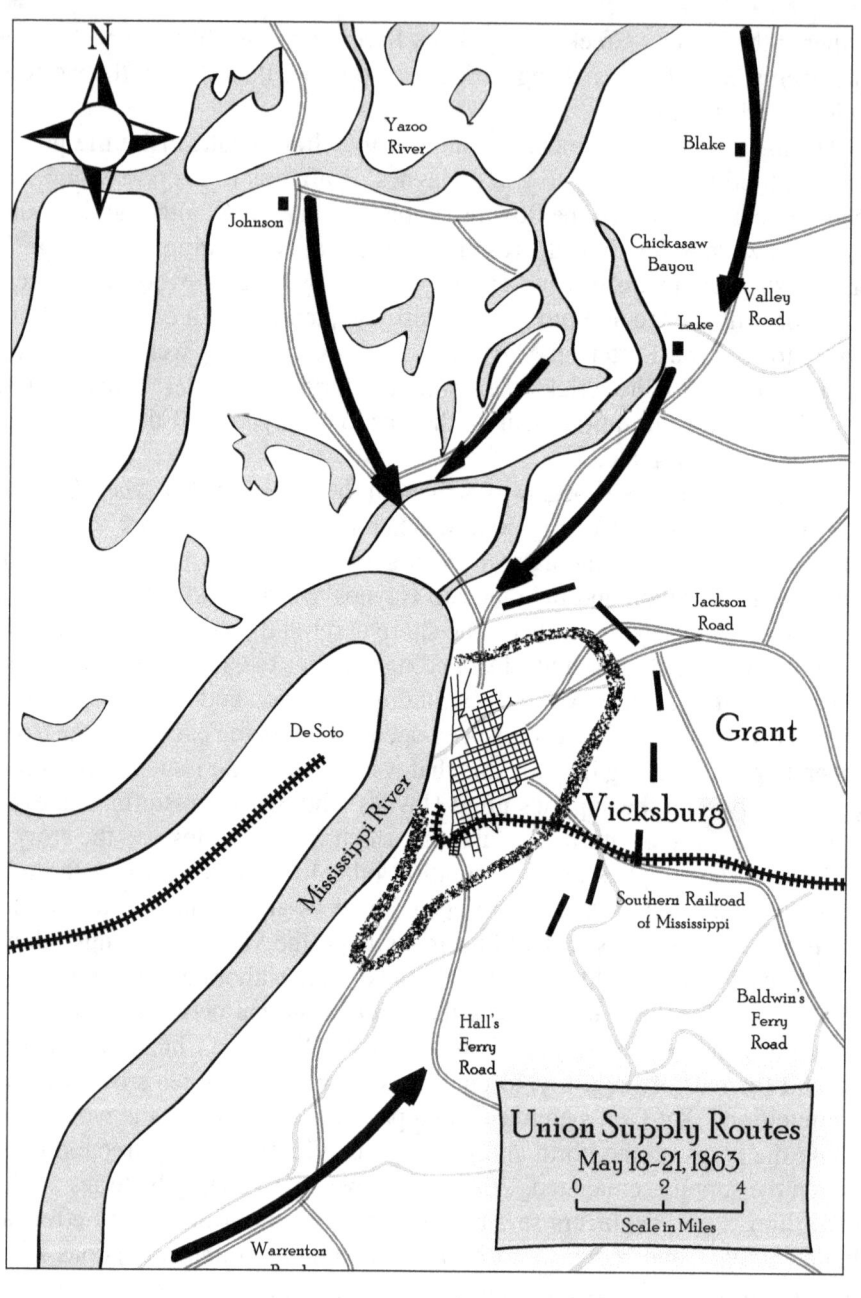

the pontoon train to Chickasaw Bayou, which would ease transportation, although a span of some three hundred feet was needed. Eventually, having the use of infantry troops at his disposal, Jenney had this "main road" open by May 22.[40]

Captain Herman Klosterman, head of one of the pioneer companies, was also reconnoitering the best areas for roadways, determining that the old Confederate road along Chickasaw Bayou was not useable as it "crossed several small bayous, and was obstructed by fallen trees." Obviously, the Confederates had damaged it all they could when they evacuated. Instead, Klosterman located another route that was "of far easier construction," and he soon had his pioneer company as well as the 83rd Indiana of Kilby Smith's brigade of Blair's division at work clearing the path. The road was open by 11:00 A.M. on May 20, and the first supply train from Chickasaw Bayou arrived at the front lines by 6:00 P.M. Grant ordered the corps commanders to fully supply their commands, organizing their own trains, although one of McClernand's staff who was back at the river notified his commander it would be much easier to supply the XIII Corps from Warrenton than Chickasaw Bayou.[41]

Some of the troops were taken out of line after the assaults and tasked with opening roads, the 83rd Indiana history noting that unit "turned out to be pretty fair road builders." One of the Indianans, James H. St. John, added that on May 20 "this morning the 83 starts for the yazoo Rver with the trane to make a Rode." Others in Sherman's corps were also tapped with guarding the thoroughfares, the 26th Iowa in particular, and most regiments were required to ferry their own goods once they were available. One 124th Illinois soldier marveled that from his regiment "20 teams went to Yazoo to get rations."[42]

Most important, a bridge had to be constructed over Chickasaw Bayou to forward the rations. Engineer William L. B. Jenney gained the task of constructing the pontoon bridge. He had a regiment detailed for the work, but famished as they were, the colonel let his men bivouac for the night early and then hunt for food the next morning. "A flock of sheep had been discovered," Jenney wrote, "and soldiers were chasing sheep in every direction. Soon mutton chops were broiling at a hundred fires made from fence rails." Jenney continued, "I protested against the long delay, but the colonel insisted, stating that his men had not had a square meal since they crossed the Mississippi. At length, the last bone was picked, and the march was resumed." The regiment soon had the bridge completed and supplies started flowing, too much so for the commissary in fact. Lieutenant Colonel Robert McFeeley attempted to ride across the bridge while it contained a wagon train going the opposite way. The guard tried to stop him, yelling, "The orders are to pass but one way at a time." McFeeley thought he outranked such orders and attempted to cross, but in the middle his horse spooked and both horse and rider went headlong into "the middle of the muddy bayou." Both went fully under but soon came back up and made it to the bank.[43]

Most Federals were overjoyed at the arriving rations, but a few were not satisfied even with that. William E. Lewis of the 26th Missouri was already sick and having problems with the doctor, who would not send him to the hospital because he could walk. The surgeon argued that "they will send him back for they will not Keep any one their that Can walk. So you see that in the survis A man has to be in A manner Dead before the will take him in to the hospital so they Can Kill him off the quicker." Lewis remonstrated about what could be done, and the surgeon told him "Dyetting well" is the key. Lewis continued: "Well here is the Diet hard Crackers sow belley shugar & Coffe, all of which is the worst Diet to Digest in the known world and at the same time, he says you must not use any Coffe or tea that leaves me Crackers & sowbelly to Diet on."[44]

All the while, a system of camping and security had to be worked out as well. Grant described how "ground had been selected and cleared on which the troops were to be encamped, and tents and cooking utensils were brought up. The troops had been without these from the time of crossing the Mississippi up to this time." Even if the coming assaults worked, whenever they would be tried again, Grant's army was destined to remain in the area at least for a few days. Accordingly, the troops were "withdrawn and bivouacked in the valleys and along little streams of water in them, carefully hiding their camp-fires," one Federal wrote.[45]

It all worked, and rather quickly. By the night of May 21, Grant was able to proclaim that "all the troops had full rations issued to them. The bread and coffee were highly appreciated." The men in the ranks were indeed grateful, John P. Jones of the 45th Illinois confidently writing his wife that "we have a perfect line of communication . . . , so that we can get a plenty of supplies with little trouble and as long as our communications are straight, I think we can stand it as long as Pemberton." The same Iowan who noted he had not had a bite in three days, Calvin Ainsworth, wrote, "We have now plenty of rations, never did hard tack and salt pork taste as well as it did tonight, washed down with a cup of good black coffee." Of course, other items were also welcomed, such as tents and cooking utensils. The lines of communication worked the opposite way as well, as Grant now had an outlet for the thousands of prisoners he had accumulated over the past two weeks. One Ohioan marveled at "the reb prisoners (7000) . . . are passing on their way north." There was also now an outlet for the many wounded Grant had left behind.[46]

The abundance in the Federal ranks was, of course, in stark contrast to the

Confederate defenders inside Vicksburg. Although not nearly as dire as the situation would become, Vicksburg was still not terribly well endowed at this point, and one Missourian bemoaned his fare of "sweet potatoes, cow peas, and corn dodger." It was even worse knowing "the boys in blue [were] luxuriating on ham fat, hard-tack, and coffee."[47]

Yet food, as essential as it was, was not foremost in Grant's mind. Most coveted was ammunition, which would be needed in bulk because Grant was all the while continuing his plans for another major assault, this time hopefully to result in the final capture of Vicksburg.

The wheels in Grant's mind were already turning even while he was allowing the army to catch its breath and resupply from the now free-flowing line of communication. Unfortunately for him, allowing his army to refit and rest up also allowed the enemy the same luxury. Every minute that Grant delayed his major assault gave Pemberton and his Confederates that much more time to strengthen their defenses, recover their morale, and rest up for the hard fighting to come. It also gave Joseph E. Johnston's relief effort more time to organize as well. "While we were at work to advance our lines," observed division commander Peter Osterhaus, "the enemy did not lose any chance to strengthen and enlarge his works and repair damages. Guns either disabled or withdrawn from the forts one day reappeared on the next morning, either on their old or new fortifications." Perhaps it would have been better to keep pounding away, this time with the entire army, at daylight on May 20 just as the Confederates suspected and feared. Grant chose to slow the timeline down and do it right, however. If he still retained one advantage, it was that only his side knew when the next assault would come. Conversely, the Confederates had to keep on the lookout continually, both tiring their bodies and wearing their nerves. Still, Grant wanted to attack as soon as possible. "My arrangements for drawing supplies of every description being complete," Grant reported, "I determined to make another effort to carry Vicksburg by assault."[48]

Grant had been thinking of this plan all along, and he set the time for the next assault for May 22. He gathered all three corps commanders on May 20 and went over the idea with them, although he already had his mind made up. "We compared notes," Sherman remembered. "It was not a council of war, but a mere consultation, resulting in orders from General Grant for us to make all possible preparations for a renewed assault on the 22d, simultaneously, at 10 A.M." Thereafter, Grant met with his corps commanders—Sherman, McPherson, and McClernand—again to go over the specifics of the operation. Grant wanted the attack to be simultaneous, to keep the enemy from shifting reserves across their front to support any weak area. Indeed, the Confederates had the luxury of interior lines inside the Vicksburg fortifications and could be counted on to use them to full advantage. "All the corps commanders set their time by mine, that there should be no difference between them in movement of assault," Grant remembered.[49]

Despite the realization that Grant had his mind made up, McClernand could not resist giving his opinion again. He renewed his argument for "concentration of our forces against one or two points, and not the dispersion of them into a multitude of columns." He thus took umbrage with Grant's plan to assault on a three-corps front. For his part, Grant paid little attention to McClernand, although the discussion continued with the talkative and opinionated Sherman also adding that in reality it was simply "a question of how many men he [Grant] was willing to lose."[50]

To make the advance as wide-ranging as possible, in direct opposition to McClernand's desire for smaller pinprick attacks, Grant also alerted the non–corps affiliated assets he had. He kept Admiral Porter well informed. Grant also had a brigade and division headquarters south of Vicksburg that had been garrisoning Grand Gulf. John McArthur's division, containing only one brigade physically with him at that point, took a position on the Warrenton Road south of Vicksburg. Grant alerted him, "I want you to move with your entire force on the Vicksburg Road, toward the city. Move cautiously, and be prepared to receive an attack at any moment. Penetrate as far into the city as you can." Because McArthur was separated from his parent corps (McPherson's), Grant sent him direct orders: "Your command being detached, will necessarily have to act independently."[51]

Written orders embodying what had occurred in the discussions went out on the evening of May 21: "A simultaneous attack will be made to morrow at 10 A.M. by all the corps of this army." The orders instructed corps commanders to "have examined all practicable roads over which troops can possibly pass." An artillery bombardment would proceed the attack "at an early hour." Perhaps in the vein of McClernand's desire, Grant stipulated that the assault would be by "columns of platoons, or by a flank if the ground over which they may have to pass will not admit of a greater front." Thus, corps commanders could launch their attacks on the one or two isolated and reinforced positions they so chose. Still, the troops were to move forward "at quick time, with bayonets fixed, and march immediately upon the enemy without firing a gun until the outer works are carried. The troops will go light, carrying with them only their ammunition, canteens, and one day's rations."[52]

McClernand was still not happy with the plan. He issued the orders as he got them on the afternoon of May 21, whereupon, at least according to his account, several of his commanders argued that the plan was "unfortunate and likely to bring disaster upon us rather than the enemy." McClernand responded that "it was an order, and, if possible, must be executed." The officers retorted that "if we fail it shall not be our fault." Clearly, McClernand's mentality was not good going into the biggest assault of the Vicksburg campaign.[53]

Grant was confident, however. He added: "If prosecuted with vigor, it is confidently believed this course will carry Vicksburg in a very short time, and with much less loss than would be sustained by delay. Every day's delay enables the enemy to strengthen his defenses and increases his chance for receiving aid from outside." It was time to fully test the Vicksburg defenses once and for all, and Grant hoped—and earnestly believed—that May 22 would tell the tale.[54]

A slight rain came in on the early afternoon of May 21, one soldier writing in his diary that "we were blessed with a delightful heavy shower about one o'clock, which effectually laid the dust which had got to be almost insufferable." Not everyone enjoyed the break, however. Henry Seaman of Steele's division on the far Union right noted that "the enemy took advantage by sending a shower of shell and shrapnel at us during the rain storm. Our battery boys wanted to suspend operations till the rain was over but they couldn't be idle and allow the secesh to play a one-sided game. They were soon silenced when our men commenced replying to their shots." Others were refreshed by visiting with old friends, even those on the opposite side. One Mississippian described how the Missourians of Cockrell's brigade soon located Missourians of Sherman's corps opposite the Stockade Redan. "They discovered this in some way," he wrote, "and until late at night we could hear the Confederates calling to their old neighbors and asking of the loved ones in their faraway homes."[55]

Yet thoughts of the looming assaults hung heavy over the Federals. As the target time came closer, many dealt with the prospects in different ways. Grant later claimed that all his troops supported another attack and would not have worked in a siege had they not been convinced that assault would not have worked better. Most of the soldiers told no such tale, one historian labeling the memoirs' claim as "misleading hogwash." The freshness of the rain could not take away the foreboding thoughts as orders trickled down the chains of command. The Confederates had no idea of the specifics, but once orders went out on the evening of May 21 and they filtered down the commands to the individual regiments, a feeling of seriousness settled over the Union Army of the Tennessee. One Iowan simply lamented what it was all about: "The enemy seem determined in their defense of this place. Their courage, constancy and devotion are worth a better cause than the one they base their hopes upon." Most Federals nevertheless went about their business preparing for the assault. Artillery batteries were told to stock up on ammunition so they would have enough to support the infantry attacks. Many also looked over the ground to be crossed in the attack. Lieutenant Peter C. Hains, chief engineer of the XIII Corps, related that during the interim "every effort was made to determine by reconnaissances the weakest points of the enemy's line, and to obtain as accurate information of the ground as possible."[56]

For those who would actually make the attack, the experience was different. Illinoisan George Carrington described how the opposing skirmishers talked with one another all night. It seemed "strange to talk this way apparently friendly and then shoot at each other." An artilleryman noted that "the works themselves appear insignificant, but perched on high ridges, steep and sometimes precipitous, across difficult ravines which may be rendered almost impassable by cutting down the timber, the task of carrying them by assault is going to be no child's play." George Durfee of the skirmishing 8th Illinois marveled at how "the boys are as cool and unconcerned as though they were in camp," but thoughts of the assault loomed large. "I expect that we will be called on to charge the works soon," he wrote, adding the next morning to his letter, "I expect we will have to storm the works some time today. The Boys do not like the idea, but will go if ordered but hope they will not be ordered." Gould Molineaux, also of the 8th Illinois in front of the Great Redoubt, described building scaling ladders "as this fort is on a very steep bank," adding that "it is and will be a hazardous job but *I go* if my Regt does. . . . The Lord Almighty protect me. I put my trust in him alone now." Henry Schmidt of Blair's division wrote his wife that "all night [I] prepared for my last day on earth," and an Illinoisan later declared most "felt little hope of a successful issue."[57]

Some were clearly depressed. "Our brigade and regimental officers look sad," one wrote, "and my heart is much depressed when meditating upon our duty for the morrow." One Iowan in Steele's division, Thomas H. Johnson, wrote his wife about the miserable conditions: "A soldier that gets killed in battle is lucky to the sick one that goes to the Hospital. I think the Hospital one of the most miserable places this side of hell." He thought his chances of recuperating if sick or wounded were slim, writing that discharges were impossible and living through the hospital treatment equally so. "General Steel says it is much easier to dig a hole in the sand than to write a discharge," he noted. Thus, his hopes of living through this assault were diminished: "I have all along until now lived in hopes of seeing you again but I have now given all hopes up. I think it will be an accident if I ever see home again." Another simply wrote, "I think if we ever undertake to storm their Batterys it will be done at the sacrifise of thousands of lives."[58]

Some soldiers admitted that they were scared, and such an admission sometimes brought some humor to the situation. In the 20th Ohio, Colonel Manning Force gave the troops a good speech, ending with "boys, I expect we shall be ordered to charge the fort. I shall run right at it, and I hope every man will follow me." At that exact moment, a lieutenant ran a cowering soldier out from behind a tree root, and his only retort was: "Lieutenant, I do not believe I am able to make such a charge." Others in the regiment were more concerned with their dirty uniforms, with the thought they might be moving into Vicksburg tomorrow: "If we were to enter Vicksburg to-morrow, some of our nice young fellows would feel ashamed to march before the young ladies there." Others were more concerned with the Vicksburg courthouse and the Confederate flag they could see. Osborn Oldroyd admitted, "What fun it will be to take that down, and hoist in its stead the old stars and stripes."[59]

Many of the soldiers prepared rather than worried. Captain Seth M. Barber of the 42nd Ohio tried to reconnoiter the front of Osterhaus's division the night before but was turned back by Confederate pickets. He tried again the next morning, only to receive a ball in the leg that shattered the bones. Colonel William M. Stone of Michael Lawler's brigade in Carr's division noted that he received word of the assault only on the evening of May 21. At that time, his brigade commander Lawler came to him and said "that I would have the advance, and that I could approach any point of the enemy's works I considered the most salient, and in any form I thought proper." It was quite a responsibility for a lowly colonel, but Stone went forward from his lines "between sundown and dark" and looked over the ground, at times only fifty yards in front of the Confederate works. "My observations satisfied me," Stone wrote, "that the fort next to the railroad could be carried more easily and with less sacrifice than any other point on our front, and I determined to direct my regiment against it." In the 72nd Illinois, Major Joseph Stockton similarly "climbed a tall tree and could see over their works," he noted, adding that "they have formidable abattis in front and we will have to charge under every disadvantage."[60]

When word trickled down to the regiments, the response was predictable. "When the regiment had been dismissed," recalled Samuel D. Pryce of the 22nd Iowa, "the men stood around in anxious groups under the big trees, talking in low whispers and churchyard voices." Little changed as the hours moved on. "The men sat around in groups under the big trees in the steep ravine south of the Jackson Railroad and waited patiently in the darkness.... The men talked of home and friends and confidences were exchanged upon that solemn night under the stars, and heart-to-heart pledges made that were never known to others." Many gave valuables such as money or watches to cooks and other noncombatants to send home in the event of their deaths.[61]

Higher-ranking officers also prepared. Lawler himself went forward and looked over the ground with his colonels, directing a two-pronged effort: two regiments under Colonel Stone of the 22nd Iowa against the Railroad Redoubt, and two regiments to his left under Colonel Charles L. Harris of the 11th Wisconsin against the rifle pits south of the fort. In the XVII Corps, Colonel George Boomer was up late. Two of his soldiers had already bedded down when near midnight they heard talking and realized it was Boomer "giving to his men with him an outline of what was to be done the next day." They also heard him say at the end, "I can carry any fort on the line with my brigade. Now I will lie down and take a little rest." One of the soldiers punched the other and asked, "Did you hear that?" The other affirmed he did but took Boomer's lead and added, "Well, we are in for it, but lets take a little more sleep if we can."[62]

McClernand himself was also up much of the night, writing Grant through his staff officers at 1:30 A.M. that "he has adopted his lines—taken his positions—and is prepared." He also mentioned a feint on the left, as well as an annoying Confederate battery on his right that required McPherson's attention "early this morning." McClernand also informed his division commanders of other corps actions and warned them of a possible night attack. If so, he told Osterhaus to "push into the city and fall upon the rear of the enemy."[63]

Sherman also held a meeting with his commanders on the evening of May 21. "There was a general desire for the privilege of the lead," Hugh Ewing wrote, "but Sherman settled the question promptly by stating that Ewing had his brigade under the best control and that his troops, therefore, should have first place." Ewing was also the senior brigade commander in Blair's division. The discussion then turned to how to cross the wide ditch in front of the Stockade Redan, Ewing arguing that the immense amount of cane in the area could be used to make fascines that would then be used to fill in the ditch as well as to protect the lead soldiers. Others wanted the men to carry planks to create a foot bridge, and Ewing "protested against the bridge, as being impracticable." "However, I was out-voted, and the bridge was decided on." Where to obtain the planks was the next question, and an odd location was soon found. Ewing described how "upon information that the flooring of the cottage occupied by General Grant, to the rear of our position, was suitable for the purpose, a request was sent to him for the planks." Ewing noted that "he was aroused from his sleep, and readily vacated the cottage to provide us with the desired flooring."[64]

Other Federals turned introspective. Colonel Marcus Spiegel of the 120th Ohio thought of home. He wrote his wife that "the greatest consolation I have during the last two weeks of continual fighting, marching and hardship, is that lovely picture of you and the dear children. I sent one of my men 34 miles to the Rear for it where I had left it in my trunk. I am looking at it about 5 times an hour and I fear that some times I am talking to it." An Illinoisan was just as reflective; he wrote the next morning at 8:00 A.M. that the charge would be made at ten o'clock: "It is a solemn time, these two hours, for well we know it is the last some of us will have to live."[65]

Colonel Theodore E. Buehler of the 67th Indiana in Burbridge's brigade also wrote of his innermost feelings: "For the first time since I had the honor of serving my country, I felt the heavy responsibility resting on my shoulders as a commander; that the lives of hundreds, perhaps, hung on my order then and there to be given. I knew my duty and was determined to execute it at the risk of my own life; but how about others?"[66]

It was a feeling not unlike most, although not all ("everybody was sanguine of success," wrote one Ohioan), of those nervously preparing amid the Federal camps that night as they readied to assault fortress Vicksburg the next morning, May 22.[67]

7

"Each Column Will Attack by the Watch"

William T. Sherman had hardly been a strong proponent of Ulysses S. Grant's latest effort to reach Vicksburg. Now that it had been successful and Grant was knocking at the city's door, Sherman was big enough to admit that Grant's ideas had been sound. The major factor in Sherman's participation was that even though he had been against this latest roundabout effort south of Vicksburg, and had railed against it, Sherman had totally supported his chief and friend even when his heart may not have been in it. "I confess I don't like this roundabout project," Sherman wrote to one of his generals, "but we must support Grant in whatever he undertakes." In fact, he did so to the point of even executing a feint in late April at the same place where he had endured such a stinging defeat back in December, at Chickasaw Bayou. In combination with other diversions such as Grierson's Raid, Sherman helped to turn Confederate attention away from Grant's critical crossing of the Mississippi River south of Vicksburg, even if it meant what the public might construe as another unsuccessful attempt to get to Vicksburg on his record.[1]

Whether it was because of Sherman's change of heart as exemplified personally to Grant at Haynes' Bluff or simply because his had been the first corps to reach Vicksburg, it had been Sherman's troops that carried the weight in the attack on May 19. Because of the haste involved, it is hard to read anything into Sherman's important position there, but Grant certainly had big plans for Sherman and his men on May 22. That said, it was certainly not to be solely a Sherman show, as the other two corps were to assault as well. Still, one wonders if Grant had higher hopes for Sherman than the rest. At any rate, he was impatient to find out exactly what the XV Corps could do at the appointed time for attack.[2]

As soon as Grant gave overall direction for the assault, his orders were read at the head of Sherman's regiments. And these orders included changes in the style of attack from May 19. Grant had been pondering the best way to assault the Confederate fortifications around the Stockade Redan and the other forts along the line since the line-abreast formation and attack that Blair had utilized three days ago had not worked. Several regiments had reached the parapet of the Confederate works, but only in fairly small numbers and certainly without enough punch to break through and sustain a lodgment inside the fortifications. If this attack was going to be more successful, Grant would have to come up with a better plan.[3]

Grant laid no blame at Sherman's feet for the failed attack on May 19 or for the widely dispersed tactics used. In fact, Sherman later stated that at the meeting of the corps commanders on May 20 they all agreed that "the assault of the day before had failed, by reason of the natural strength of the position, and because we were forced by the nature of the ground to limit our attacks to the strongest parts of the enemy's line, viz., where the three principal roads entered the city." This time, Grant made sure certain parameters were in place to cause Sherman and the others to attack in a different way, with needle pinpricks in columns or flank formations rather than spread-out linear lines.[4]

Grant's stipulated use of columns and attacks by the flank was certainly not new to warfare, even in American infantry tactical manuals. But Grant's ideas at Vicksburg predated some of the more famous episodes such as Emory Upton's narrow but weighty attack at Spotsylvania the following year. Certainly, the terrain factored into when and how to use these formations, with Shiloh being a classic example of when not to use columns, as the Confederates did during the initial attack. Here on the open expanses at Vicksburg, where many of the approaches were through deep ravines clogged with natural and man-made impediments (as Blair's brigades had found on May 19), perhaps columns or attacking by the flank was the best option. Of course, that was perhaps also exactly what the Confederates desired and was one reason for those impediments: to funnel the attacks into narrowly defended corridors that were well covered with small arms and artillery fire.[5]

Still, almost anything would be better than what Blair had done on May 19, so Grant went with the column approach in advising his generals how to proceed in this new attack. A few hours more would show whether that was the correct decision.

Sherman wrote that Grant ordered the attack "to be rapid by the heads of columns," but in doing so Sherman had a major disadvantage on his front that the other two corps commanders did not. His entire corps's area of operations fronted two major watersheds. The east-west valley of Mint Spring

Bayou and the north-south tributary of Glass Bayou effectively shielded the Confederate lines on all of Sherman's front except for the ridge that loomed between the two. The same narrow ridge on which the Graveyard Road ran was the only high and level ground that Sherman could utilize to approach the enemy lines, and it had caused problems on May 19 for the brigade trying to negotiate it and the ravines on either side. McPherson and McClernand had no such restrictions.[6]

The Confederates realized the situation on Sherman's front and worked to funnel any attack into a narrow corridor that could be easily defended, but Sherman did not take the bait back on May 19. He had attacked with Blair's brigades abreast and fanned out in linear formation across a wide expanse, shying away from the very high ground the enemy intended for the Federals to use. It had still worked out for the Confederates under Shoup and Hébert, because trying to make a mass attack across such terrible ground was all but impossible.[7]

To determine the best way to assault within the parameters set by Grant, Sherman "reconnoitered my front thoroughly in person, from right to left." Yet there was no doubt that this change in tactics necessitated using the very high ground his troops had dodged three days earlier. No one had wanted to be caught out in that open, level field of fire on May 19, for the very reasons the Confederates wanted to funnel the attacks there. Kilby Smith's brigade had split as a result. But now, the Union high command was dictating that the divisions use that killing ground during their next attack.[8]

Sherman soon sent out his orders for the divisions to use the Graveyard Road in the primary attack, with other advances either supporting the main effort or assaulting elsewhere. On the right, Steele's division, which had seen little to no action on May 19, was to form as a mass and advance on the front occupied originally by Thayer's brigade, "about half a mile to the right," Sherman noted. Thayer had maneuvered a little on May 19, even crossing Mint Spring Bayou, but had not advanced up the southern ridge let alone attacked. Now, the brigade would be tasked with leading an actual assault, but supporting them would be the regiments of both Francis Manter's brigade as well as Charles Woods's, which held the line all the way to the Mississippi River. Repositioning would take some time, and it would be necessary to leave some of the troops on the original lines to the right of Thayer's position. Still, the division would advance in columns of brigades and hopefully break the Confederate line west of the Stockade Redan. Unfortunately, casualties occurred even before the movement; John Buegel of the 3rd Missouri in Wood's brigade noted that, before leaving their lines on the morning of May 22, "the head of our ensign (an Irishman) was shot off while he was reading a paper in his hole." Those left behind wondered at the noise and chaos, one Iowan declaring "by the frequent discharge of musketry and artillery there must be something in the wind. I know the Brig. Left here some 2 hours ago headed in that direction."[9]

While Steele advanced to the right, Blair's division was to make the main assault, targeting the Stockade Redan itself. This would be a very different attack than the one that took place three days ago, however. "Generals Blair's and Tuttle's divisions will assault along the main road," Sherman's orders read, "by the flank." Blair was not to fan his brigades out but rather stack them up in line on the Graveyard Road, that is, behind the ridge for cover. Then, the brigades—Ewing's in the lead, Giles Smith's next, and Kilby Smith's in the rear—covered by the division's artillery on the ridges to the rear, would plunge ahead in a very narrow column, the regiments marching by the flank on the road itself. "The road lies on the crown of an inferior ridge," Sherman said, "rises over comparatively smooth ground along the edge of the ditch on the right face of the enemy's bastion, and enters the parapet at the shoulder of the bastion." This part of the assault was to be the equivalent of a narrow needle's prick rather than a wide blow by a sledgehammer.[10]

The plan was to assault in a narrow column and overwhelm the enemy in only one or two specific areas, thereby allowing the Federals to penetrate and then build on that rupture with a mass of following troops, who could then spread out left and right once inside the Confederate defenses. Logically, more damage could be done by regiments flanking the enemy than by outright assaulting them, and it would only take one break that could be built upon to allow the Federals a permanent lodgment inside Vicksburg and, perhaps, to end this campaign.[11]

The trick was to make the penetration, which would not be easy given the stout Confederate fortifications and defense. If May 19 proved anything, it was a warning not to underestimate Confederate ability or morale, which Grant had continuously done. Restricting the assault to a very narrow corridor would allow the Confederates to strengthen their defense and fire on that narrow corridor. Although few Confederates showed their faces, especially after Sherman ordered "a line of select sharpshooters . . . to keep them down," they were still ready to respond in force at a moment's notice. In fact, Sherman said that "the skirmishers along our whole front will, during the night, advance within 100 yards of the enemy's works, and will, with the spade or ax, prepare pits, or fallen trees, so as to give them cover from which to kill artillerists who attempt to load the guns, also to keep down the fire of the enemy's infantry in the rifle-pits during the assault."[12]

There were positive aspects to this new tactical effort, however. Any lessons the Confederates had learned on May 19 would likely be muted by this completely different second attack. The Confederates certainly blunted a widespread assault on May 19 and likely sought lessons on how to do it better in the future. This pinprick style of advance had not been tried before, however, so no lessons had been learned about how to defend against it. More important, the Graveyard Road led to the direct apex of the Stockade Redan, which was a salient in the line that actually stuck out partially from the fortifications left and right. Accordingly, the attack would come at an area where only limited defensive fire could hit an advancing party. Because the Confederates were operating on interior lines of communication, their lengthy defenses would be hard-pressed to train all their weaponry on a singular point of attack. Moreover, the Federals would have to overpower only the isolated defenders of the Stockade Redan itself rather than all the brigades defending the larger sectors.[13]

Whether it was a pinprick or a wide sledgehammer blow, the main obstacle besides the fire put out by the enemy defenders was the stout fortifications themselves. And whether the attack was on a broad front or a narrow corridor, it still would have to overcome the lengthy advance under fire, then the wide ditch fronting the bastion, and finally the high parapet. That would not be easy in normal circumstances; doing it under fire added a great deal of additional difficulty. Sherman thus saw clearly the need for an advance storming party.[14]

Sherman desired this initial storming party, which "might be called a forlorn hope," he explained, to lead the way: "The head of the column preceded by a selected, or volunteer, storming party of about 150 men." He called for fifty volunteers and two officers from each brigade, making a party of a little more than one hundred and fifty soldiers who would lead the advance along the winding road, through the cut in the forward ridge, and then to the ditch fronting the redan. These volunteers would carry with them "boards and poles to cross the ditch," items that could be used to fill in or bridge the ditch in front of the redan and then allow the soldiers following to mount the parapet. Behind them would follow, like a snake slithering along the road, the regiments of Ewing's brigade, marching by the flank. The only brigadier commanding the brigades, Ewing had the privilege of going first "by right of rank," Kilby Smith noted. Hopefully, his troops would be able to utilize the tools the "forlorn hope" had carried to the parapet and make their way inside Vicksburg's fortifications. The two Smiths (Kilby and Giles) would follow in like fashion. "The troops were grouped so that the movement could be connected and rapid," Sherman explained.[15]

Other items in the orders dealt with peripheral aspects. The artillery was to bombard the enemy lines heavily. "The artillery will collect all the ammunition they can, close at hand," Sherman dictated, "and will begin at daylight to fire on the enemy's sally port, the bastions, and batteries, that have a fire on the ground over which the column must pass, firing with great care and precision." He also stipulated that "no wagons of any kind will attend the assaulting columns." He even demanded that officers should advance on foot and dictated that "each column will attack by the watch, and not depend on signals."[16]

Sherman exhibited great confidence in his orders. In detailing what would happen after a breakthrough, he advised that "as soon as the enemy gives way, he must be pushed to the very heart of the city, where he must surrender." He also stated that "there is another valley, or bayou, on the other side of the one now separating us from the enemy. If the enemy retreats across that bayou, our troops must follow at their heels, and not permit them to rally in an interior work." He also gave explicit detail on what to do after the victory had been won. For example, he ordered that "as soon as the head of the column is seen to enter the works, these skirmishers will hastily scale the works and fire upon the enemy and drive him as far as possible." Elsewhere, he ordered that the artillery hold enough ammunition "for service after passing the parapet," that officers could have their horses brought forward "by their servants, as soon as the troops have passed in," and that artillery and ammunition wagons and ambulances could move forward "as soon as the infantry has passed inside." Only after "we are in full possession of Vicksburg," he said, may baggage wagons move forward. Finally, Sherman gave his division commanders some leeway to operate in the changing surroundings of battle: "Division commanders near may take advantage of any opening toward a lodgment inside the enemy's works."[17]

The preparations began as soon as the orders went out, and most importantly, Sherman soon had his men for the forlorn hope. "Volunteers of 50 were called from each brigade," Kilby Smith explained, "and promptly furnished *pro rata* of regiments." Colonel Hamilton N. Eldridge of the 127th Illinois noted that "it would have been an easy matter to have raised quadruple the number called for, so anxious were the men to distinguish themselves and be of service to their country." One enlisted soldier of the 127th Illinois gave details about the volunteer process, he being an orderly sergeant in charge of acquiring the necessary men. When told by an officer that he would have to detail the men from the regiment if not enough volunteered, he responded, "I wouldn't detail any man on such an expedition as was proposed, but that I would volunteer." He also noted the proposed duty: "As far as we subordinates understood them, [we] were to scale the walls at a certain portion of the fort, get a lodgment and keep the gunners inside from firing at short range and pouring grape and canister into the troops that were to follow us." These men certainly knew what they were getting into, with Theodore Hyatt of the 127th Illinois writing that "it was an awful expedition, as well we knew." It did not help that Blair, the division commander himself, when questioned why the men could only take ammunition and a canteen and no haversack, replied, "No, . . . you can go without your dinners; you'll be inside the walls of Vicksburg or in hell for supper." Hyatt recalled later, "I detested Blair to the day of his death for that remark, but it served to indicate then the peril of our undertaking."[18]

Another Illinoisan gave a slightly different rendition of the volunteer process. Andrew McCormack wrote that "they wanted 11 out of our Regt to Volunteer to go ahead of the regiment, when they started to carry rails boards and ladders so the troops could climb the works." When volunteers were called for, "the boys was all silent not a word spoke for a few minutes it was a Solem thing and almost sure death but none of the Boys would go." McCormack then stepped forward, stating "I would go as far as I could and if I was killed I knew the Lord would be with me." As he strapped on his equipment, the boys gathered round and wished him safety: "As I left to join the crowd there was many a wishful eye on me."[19]

Others were also preparing themselves and their men. John O'Dea remembered the process in the 8th Missouri, writing that "when Colonel [Lieutenant Colonel David C.] Coleman addressed the regiment everyone cheered." Then he called for the volunteers to step forward two steps, and O'Dea admitted that "I felt an uncontrollable emotion weighing me to the spot," although he added that "my will rebuked me and I managed to step out of the line two spaces. Somebody had to go, I thought, so I volunteered." The members of the forlorn hope then marched to Blair's headquarters, where he gave a "clear, brief and a most gruff [speech], but thoroughly characteristic of the old fellow. He told us just what he wished us to do, and with as much seeming unconcern as a boss ordering hands in detail to do some easy, practicable job." He did joke, however, that they should not "eat and drink all the good things we found."[20]

Hugh Ewing, who was in charge of the advance, brought out a brand-new flag for the occasion, his headquarters banner, "a new flag of my brigade," he recounted. He entrusted it to Private Howell Trogden, "a mere boy" of the 8th Missouri. He told Trogden to place it on the ramparts of Vicksburg, and Trogden responded heartily "that this he would do or die." Kilby Smith also got into the action, addressing the volunteers with General Sherman by his side. The two officers promised a sixty-day furlough if the small group captured the Confederate bastion.[21]

Sherman also added to his orders that "all must presume that others are doing their best, and do their full share.... The general now looks to his corps to give the world the signal example of steady courage and its results—success. We must have Vicksburg, and most truly have we earned it by former sacrifices and labors." Then, he noted, "I took a position within two hundred yards of the rebel parapet, on the off slope of a spur of ground, where by advancing two or three steps I could see everything."[22]

While the forlorn hope assembled, Blair marshaled his brigades in a low area south of the Graveyard Road but behind the covering ridge. Hoping to follow up the anticipated breach with massive numbers of troops, Sherman also positioned his reserve division under James Tuttle on the road behind Blair's waiting troops. If the forlorn hope was able to bridge the gap and Ewing's brigade entered the works, Blair and Tuttle would flush brigade after brigade right through the puncture, where they could turn left and right and take the rest of the Confederate defenses in the flank. That would cause quite a stir among the Confederate defenders, especially with Steele's assault to the right and McPherson's and McClernand's to the left. One small puncture could doom the Confederate defense of Vicksburg, and Sherman hoped to make that pinprick at the Stockade Redan.[23]

What Sherman's troops would find behind the ramparts of the Stockade Redan this time was anybody's guess, simply because few if any Confederates showed themselves. If the resistance from May 19 was any indication, however, the area would be well defended, although few if any Confederates had been seen during the last two days. "No men could be seen in the enemy's works," Sherman explained, "except occasionally a sharpshooter would show his head and quickly discharge his piece." But they were there, all knew, Sherman reporting that "the men were partially sheltered until it was necessary to take the crown of the ridge and expose themselves to the full view of the enemy, known to be lying concealed behind his well-planned parapet."[24]

They were indeed there—and in greater numbers than on May 19. All had expected another and bigger assault in the last three days, and Forney and Smith had made sure they had a deeper defense this time despite the fairly easy repulse they gave the enemy on May 19. Most of the resulting reinforcement came from Cockrell's reserve brigade, despite Bowen's plea for better duty, and several of the Missouri regiments took a position on the first line. In fact, the 5th Missouri went into the main line on the right of the 36th Mississippi holding the eastern face of the Stockade Redan and the small redan to its south. On the Mississippians' left went the 3rd Missouri, manning the section of the stockade itself and the northern faces of the earthen redan. Farther to the left, five companies of the 2nd Missouri went into line on the 3rd Missouri's left, between them and the 27th Louisiana in their redan, this time the wounded Colonel Marks being grateful for the support; the other five companies were held in the rear as a reserve. To further strengthen the 36th Mississippi on the critical eastern face of the main redan, six companies of the 1st Missouri took position among the Mississippians, with another company going into the small redan to the right. Three other companies of the regiment were also held as a reserve, while the final regiment of Cockrell's brigade—the 6th Missouri that had reinforced the far left on May 19—moved, after many had to be awakened from their sleep on the reverse slope of the hill, southward to support Forney's other brigade under John C. Moore. In addition to Cockrell's Missourians, two Louisiana regiments of Smith's division were drawn up in reserve behind Forney's division as well, and the burst Whitworth rifle had been replaced with a 3-inch rifle of Company C, 1st Mississippi Artillery. And all were swelled with pride at the victory of three days ago, Samuel Lockett writing that all "were now thoroughly restored to their old-time confidence and aroused to an enthusiastic determination to hold their lines."[25]

As a result, the Confederate line at the Stockade Redan was significantly heavier than it had been on May 19, with the area from the 27th Louisiana Lunette around to the redan on the right of the 36th Mississippi, originally held by two regiments on May 19 with some of Cockrell's forces appearing during the fight, now containing a total of six regiments, or three times as many troops. Obviously, Forney, Smith, and Bowen thought this would be a central area in any future Union assaults, and they packed as many Confederates in the three bastions and their attending rifles pits as possible.[26]

They mainly kept out of sight, however. The Confederates of Shoup's, Cockrell's, and Hébert's brigades awoke on May 22 to a massive barrage of artillery fire from Sherman's guns across the ravines, Francis Shoup describing it as "fire from the enemy before dawn; keep it up with extreme vigor." Francis Cockrell likewise described the bombardment: "A most furious fire from the enemy's numerous batteries, of shell, grape, and canister. The air was literally burdened with hissing missiles of death." Forney added that "the sharpshooters and artillery of the enemy opened on my entire front early in the morning, and kept up an incessant fire during the whole day." Twelve-year-old Fred Grant, accompanying his father on the campaign, simply regarded it as "a sight that will probably never again be witnessed in this country." Wounds were numerous, some logically enough from flying splinters at the wood stockade just northeast of the Stockade Redan.[27]

The view from the rank and file was a little more awestruck, one describing the "pent-up expectancy." James H. Jones of the 38th Mississippi south of the Stockade Redan noted that "it was the grandest and most awe-inspiring scene I ever witnessed." He went on to describe more of the bombardment, especially the predawn aspects: "The air was ablaze with burning and bursting shells, darting like fiery serpents across the sky, and the earth shook with the thunderous roar. . . . I do not hesitate to assert that coarse print could have been read by the light of these blazing missiles." He decided "the scene recalled descriptions of the meteoric shower of 1833, only these meteors were too close and too solid for pleasant contemplation."[28]

Little damage was done, however, at least according to Mississippian Jones. He asserted that "a ditch is almost a perfect protection against a shell fired across it, provided one sits against the side next to the battery. Its momentum carries even the fragments of an exploded shell forward, and there is little danger from it. It is only when the messengers of death are dropped from above, or when they enfilade a line of breastworks that they get in their deadly work."[29]

More troubling signs appeared around midmorning, however, as Union infantry began to stir on the ridges to the east. By 10:00 A.M., George Clarke of the 36th Mississippi remembered that "we could plainly see that another attack would be made on our works." The bombardment had obviously been for a special purpose, and now, around 10:00 A.M., that purpose became very evident as the guns slacked off. An eerie silence soon enveloped the battlefield, Clarke describing it as "for the space of perhaps a half hour there was complete silence all along both lines. Not a shot was heard, not a man was seen in our front during the short space and the experienced soldier knew that it was the calm that precedes the storm."[30]

Nervous glances slipped among the Union troops massed in line along the Graveyard Road as the clock ticked closer to 10:00 A.M. "The breathless suspense made seconds seem minutes and minutes seem hours," John O'Dea admitted as he waited amid the ranks of the forlorn hope. One commissary asked O'Dea if he wanted some whiskey before they pushed off, and O'Dea declined, telling him "I had nine chances of going into eternity to one for escape, and did not care to knock at St. Peter's gate with thick tounge or tangled feet." Nervous commanders continually glanced at their watches to make sure they were precisely on time, this supposedly being the first time a coordinated attack was used in such an assault. Perhaps worse than the fire they would soon be receiving was the thought of being late for the assault; it could end a career or, at the least, bring a harsh scolding from their political general or from Sherman himself. Even worse, of course, was the thought of letting down comrades who might be depending on them.[31]

There was no need to worry about timing, as Blair had his troops ready to go. He took a position at the head of the ravine near the Confederate line to watch. "I massed my division in the ravine to the left of the Graveyard road," he explained, "where it debouches upon that road as it passed across the valley immediately in front of the bastion." At the head of the column was Captain John H. Groce and Lieutenant George O'Neal of the 30th Ohio. With them was Private Howell G. Trogden of the 8th Missouri, who bore Ewing's flag. The rest of the one hundred and fifty–man storming party filed in behind them.[32]

The timing went well, at least on Sherman's front, and that was all that mattered for these troops because they were not in any way dependent on the other corps' advances. James B. McPherson later argued that "the difference in time was not great enough to allow of any changing or massing of the enemy from one part of the line to the other." If McClernand was a few minutes late in launching his attack miles to the south, for example, it would not hinder operations on the Graveyard Road. The major concern was thus timing within the corps; if Ewing was late in supporting the forlorn hope, that could be disastrous. Fortunately, it was all on time, Sherman writing that "at the very minute named in General Grant's orders, the storming party dashed up the road at the double-quick, followed by Ewing's brigade, the Thirtieth Ohio leading." Sherman's brother-in-law, Hugh Ewing, disagreed slightly: "At 10.04 A.M. of the 22d, a storming party, composed of 50 volunteers from each brigade of the division, bearing the colors of my headquarters, and followed by my troops in column, charged down a narrow, deep-cut road upon a bastion of the enemy's works."[33]

"Fall in, right face, forward, double quick March, and away we went down the road for the fort as fast as our legs could carry us," one member of the forlorn hope recalled. Time seemed to stand still as the troops began the mad dash forward toward the Stockade Redan: "We ran as fast as we could," wrote Sergeant James W. Larrabee of the 55th Illinois, actually remembering that he gained on the flag Trogden was carrying at the front. Ready to follow was the 30th Ohio, Edward Schweitzer admitting that even on May 22 they were still "entirely worn out, stiff and stupid from the hard march" from Grand Gulf. Next came the 37th Ohio, and then the rest of Ewing's brigade, followed by the other brigades of the division. "When all was ready they moved forward," remembered a member of the 30th Ohio, "and we followed in silence." Watching from the Confederate works, Louis Hébert knew exactly what it meant: "He again advanced to the assault, and apparently with serious and strong determination." One of Hébert's Mississippians saw what was coming, writing that "soon blue columns were seen advancing four lines deep. . . . We knew from all indications that this was going to be a desperate assault, and we nerved ourselves for the shock." Even more telling: "A large number of men came in front bearing rails on their shoulders." The Mississippians knew what that meant.[34]

The Federals quietly made their way to the covering ridge along the Graveyard Road, watched carefully by the Confederates. The calm was heartrending, George Clarke in the attentive 36th Mississippi noting that "everything was as still as death, except the wild tumultuous beating of thousands of hearts, as with mingled feelings of dread and awe, we await the shock of the coming conflict fingers on the triggers of our muskets, ready to send the hurtling messengers of death into the devoted band." The waiting Mississippians could easily hear noises from the Union lines, including shouts of orders: "We heard an officer, with the voice of a Stentor, giving the word 'forward.' Their scurried ranks came pouring over the hill and rushed right on our works." Still to a man, the Confederates held all fire.[35]

The quiet soon ceased, as the artillery of Blair's Union division was by this time firing rapidly again, they and the sharpshooters having been softening up the redan and its defenders for some time now, actually since dawn. Sherman reported that "Wood's, Barrett's, Waterhouse's, Spoor's, and Hart's batteries kept a concentric fire on the bastion, which was doubtless constructed to command this very approach." Sherman placed some of the artillery (Barrett's Chicago Light Artillery) forward to within four hundred yards of the Confederate works, where Samuel Barrett noted "we intrenched ourselves as well as possible, and during the day were engaged in action for a large portion of the time." At one point, the division's artillery chief, Ezra Taylor, sent some guns even farther forward. He ordered First Lieutenant J. R. Reed of the 2nd Iowa Battery to send a section farther forward by hand, which was done with help from the nearby 114th Illinois after the cannoneers became exhausted because of the rough terrain. As soon as Reed took his new position, however, he saw it had to be abandoned: "Soon discovering that the position was very much exposed, and that I could accomplish nothing by holding it, I asked and obtained permission to withdraw my guns." The artillery fire, as well as that of the special skirmish line put in place for just that purpose, nevertheless kept the enemy pinned down while much of the forlorn hope moved forward.[36]

Problems emerged in the artillery, however. With the Union batteries having been firing for days, ammunition was running low and, though resupply

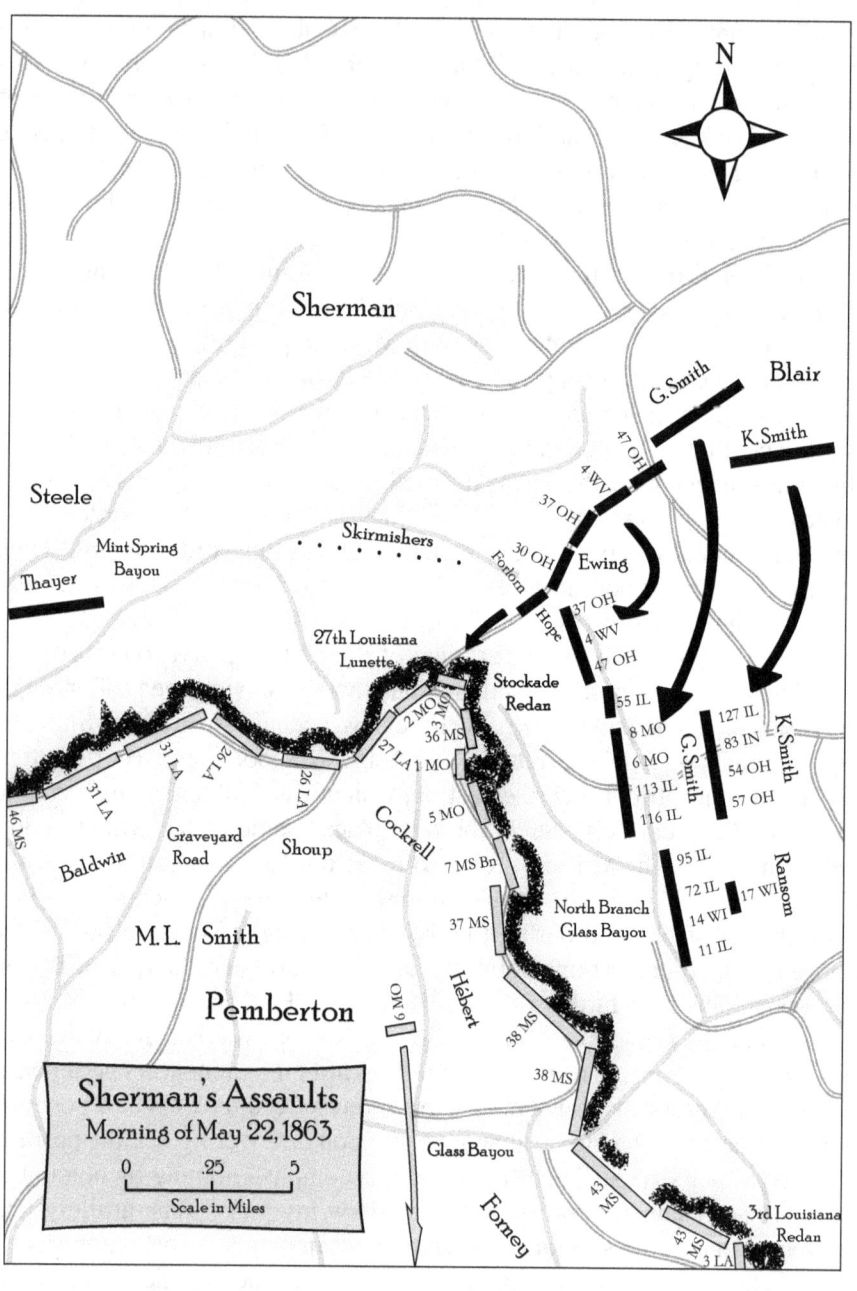

was expected every day, was replenished only on the afternoon of May 22. Casualties also began to mount, Charles Affeld of the Chicago Light Artillery describing one cannoneer who was "shot through the heart, while thumbing the vent." He went on to describe the agony: "He was shot through the left breast, the shot penetrating the upper end of the heart and passing through his body. He fell on his back, never spoke a word but breathed for five or ten minutes. The blood meanwhile streaming out in strong jets, which was increased with every throb of his heart." The cannoneers toiled on nevertheless, although they could not help but watch the pageant in front of them: "We saw the whole charge, . . . we watched the party until we saw the flag planted on this side of the fort."[37]

And then it happened: just as the head of the column emerged from the slight road cut mere yards from the Stockade Redan, the waiting Confederate infantry rose and fired a massive volley into the oncoming Federals. Confederate brigade commander Louis Hébert remarked that the enemy came on "apparently with serious and strong determination." Forney described the enemy moving forward "in three or more lines of battle. The first advanced as sharpshooters. This line kept up a constant fire over the parapets, under cover of which the second and third lines advanced." Perhaps Sherman best described what happened. All morning, he noted, "the rebel line, concealed by the parapet, showed no sign of unusual activity." The ring of sheer awe could be heard in his description of what occurred when the Union troops headed forward out of the cut: "The storming party reached the salient of the bastion and passed toward the sally port, when rose, from every part commanding it, a double rank of the enemy, that poured on the head of the column a terrific fire." Scores went down with that first volley. The forlorn hope, caught out in the open, quickly learned the truth behind their name.[38]

Theodore Hyatt of the 127th Illinois detailed the excruciating few seconds when the forlorn hope dashed toward the Confederate lines. "For a distance of about eighty rods," he wrote, "there was nothing to protect us, and as we were the only Union troops moving at the time we got all the fire." He described the road being "swept by a perfect hurricane of shot and shell. There was a constant whiz of bullets, and it didn't seem as if a man of us could reach that fort without being shot full of holes. And not many of us did." Hyatt was carrying two muskets, his own and one for a friend who was carrying an eight-inch plank to help get across the ditch. That plank, it turned out later, had twenty-two bullet holes. Hyatt was amazed that he was not hit: "I saw comrades dropping all around me . . . , and although I was not wounded, several bullets passed through my clothing. . . . It didn't seem that a man could hold up a finger without having it shot off, so thick the balls were flying."[39]

John O'Dea described the same experience from his vantage point. "The hot flames of death leaped in fury from thousands of guns," he wrote, "so close that we could feel their seething breath." He went on to describe how "it is frightful to see your comrades torn to pieces and falling around you, while the earth is shaking under you. It made me feel that hell was escaping through one great vent and we were rushing into that opening."[40]

It was "a most desperate and protracted effort to carry our lines by assault," Francis Cockrell remembered, but the concentrated fire of the 36th Mississippi and the adjoining Missourians of Cockrell's brigade, along with the two Arkansas howitzers and the Mississippi 3-inch rifle, completely stopped the forlorn hope. "A withering fire of musketry, grape, canister and shells greeted them as they came in sight," one Mississippians declared, "and men fell like grass before the reaper." Another Mississippian described the rush of Confederate Missourians to the front lines, writing that "their officers could not hold them back, but they came rushing without orders to our assistance." Thus reinforced, the Confederates were able to blunt the forlorn hope itself, one Confederate writing that "it seemed that the pitiless storm swept away half of their ranks at the first fire. But others would gather up and bear them on, only to share the same fate." He also noted that "their battle flags were often seen to go down, but in a moment was soon seen fluttering in the breeze, as other hands bore them on toward the flaming crest of the hill in their front."[41]

"It halted," Sherman noted of the forlorn hope, "wavered, and sought cover." Although there was some safety to the rear at the road cut, the road in that direction was soon blocked by the column of following Union regiments. The steep ravines to either side afforded no protection, as these very Federals had found just three days ago. The only cover, it seemed, was up ahead, and although the spear point of the forlorn hope was blunted and shattered, there was still a native desire to rush for the nearest available cover—and that was on the Confederate parapets. In small groups, pairs, or individually, the members of the forlorn hope moved on, one Confederate admitting that "the rail bearers reached the ditch in front of the Fort, bridged it, crossed over to the Fort and planted their colors on our breastworks in several places." A marveling Sherman explained how "the head of the column crossed the ditch on the left face of the bastion, and climbed upon the exterior slope." He continued that the men "burrowed in the earth to shield themselves from the flank fire."[42]

Miraculously, in the mad rush for safety, much of the forlorn hope had achieved their goal: they had reached the parapet of the Stockade Redan, many with their poles and boards to cover the ditch. They had been instructed to "bear to the left, and cross the curtain if the ditch at the salient could not be bridged," but they made a "foot-path at the salient" and moved on to the parapet. Captain Groce and Lieutenant O'Neal, along with Private Trogden, managed to climb "half way up the exterior slope" and place Ewing's headquarters flag on the slope, alerting all who came behind that a lodgment had been made on the works and that all that was needed were reinforcements. As he placed the flag, Trogden yelled, "You sons of bitches surrender this fort," but almost immediately the flag "was shot all into strings." Others below helped push forward those at the front, Sergeant Larrabee pushing Trogden up by the leg. Groce and O'Neal were both wounded for their trouble, as were other officers, leaving Lieutenant William C. Porter in command on the slopes at the Stockade Redan.[43]

Sergeant Hyatt was just as amazed that he was alive once he reached the fortifications—which in itself was a miracle. "How any of us ever reached that fort I can't tell, but some of us did." Once there, a lieutenant ordered him to help lift up others so they could go over the parapet or at least get a shot inside the fort. "The first man I lifted went up too high," he sadly noted. "He was shot through the brain the instant he showed his head above the walls, and fell back dead in my arms. The rest, though, went up more cautiously, and inside of fifteen minutes we were all on top and had planted our flag."[44]

The Confederates were firing as best they could over the parapet or out the embrasures while simultaneously trying to keep from being picked off by one of the sharpshooters Sherman had specifically positioned for that purpose. "Nobly did the officers and soldiers of this brigade greet every assault of the enemy with defiant shouts and a deliberately aimed fire," Francis Cockrell wrote, "and hurled them back in disorder." Even the 27th Louisiana down the line past the stockade was able to dial in a flanking fire, several of the boys loading while "a little Frenchman in our company who was one of the most deadly marksmen I ever saw" fired as fast as his comrades could hand him a loaded weapon. That said, at least one Confederate officer later admitted that it took all their efforts to keep the men in line, "the greatest difficulty in preventing a stampede of his men." The amazed Confederates also later asked a Federal if they had been given gunpowder and whiskey, stating that "he could not conceive how men could have been put over that ground in their sane condition, for that they had especially prepared the ground for us, and felt sure that they could annihilate us."[45]

A safer way for the defending Confederates to hurt the invaders was to throw ordnance over the parapet by hand. The 36th Mississippi's soldiers as well as those Missourians behind the walls of the Stockade Redan soon began throwing cannonballs and other explosives over the top. "Hand-grenades were used at each point with good effect," General Forney remembered, and Cockrell elaborated on the process on one portion of his line: "Colonel [William

R.] Gause, of the Third Missouri Infantry, procured some fuse-shell, and, using them as hand-grenades, threw them into the ditch, where they exploded, killing and wounding some 22 of the enemy." Lieutenant Porter recorded how the Confederates threw "12-pounder shells, burning the fuse and then rolling them into the ditch." The Federals turned the trick back on the Confederates at times, however: "We succeeded in throwing back three [grenades] with our bayonets, which burst on the inside, causing the same effect they intended for us." Sergeant Hyatt recalled that "it was an awful position" just laying there keeping as low as they could, but they soon learned to "knock them back with the butts of our guns, and then they exploded inside the fort." A few shells did burst in the Federals' midst, however, one killing a soldier and wounding four others. Hyatt described another explosion that "blew the head of the second man from me clean off his shoulders."[46]

With Groce, O'Neal, and other officers wounded, Lieutenant Porter of the 55th Illinois took command and reported that the storming party had moved quickly, "occupying but three minutes from the ravine to the bastion." That was a hard three minutes, George Clarke of the 36th Mississippi declaring that "their dead and wounded covered the ground over which they had so gallantly moved to attack." A watching Missourian added that the artillery "belched forth charge after charge of grape into the masses ... scattering death and disorder." Porter realized that "all I could then do was to prevent the rebels from carrying them [the colors] in (which they tried), and wait for support." He was incredulous that none was forthcoming, at least immediately: "Some men of Ewing's brigade came up, but not sufficient to warrant my thrusting them over the ramparts, to be either slaughtered or taken prisoners."[47]

It is true that those following the forlorn hope were not immediately on site, but they were not far behind. After a short interval, the 30th Ohio followed the forlorn hope down the road, through the cut, and out toward the withering Confederate fire. One Ohioan described how Blair was with them at the road cut, hat in hand, as well as Ewing "in his shirt sleeves, with his revolver at his side and sword in his hand." Blair halted the Ohioans for about three minutes to give the forlorn hope time to set their poles and planks, then sent them onward with the simple command "forward." Lieutenant Colonel George A. Hildt repeated the order, and the Ohioans moved forward at the double-quick. "Away we went," remembered an Ohioan, adding that "the enemy instantly opened upon us with artillery and small arms." The forlorn hope had shattered in such a way that the concentrated Confederate fire now registered on the Ohioans. "Our way led us down and through a cut in the road about three or four feet deep," Lieutenant Colonel Hildt remembered. He added, "This cut on account of the severe fire of the enemy soon became impassable—choked with dead and wounded, preventing our further advance in force." Adding to the chaos and confusion, one of the Ohioans described "the cloud of smoke arising from the enemies Fort, and the shells bursting over us made the atmosphere so dense that the eye could not penetrate it 10 feet." Sherman reported the same effect: "The rear pressed on, but the fire was so terrific that very soon all sought cover." Brigade commander Ewing told how the Ohioans "moved close upon the storming party, until their progress was arrested by a front and double flank fire, and the dead and wounded which blocked the defile. The second company forced its way over the remains of the first, and a third over those of the proceeding, but their perseverance served only further to encumber the impassable way." Many of the 30th Ohio filed off to the left into the deep ravine while pressing on. They reached the works but in a scattered and haphazard manner because even there they were under the heavy Mississippi and Missouri fire.[48]

Although the Confederate counterfire had blunted the Union advance and scattered it mainly to the south of the Graveyard Road, the net result had been that many Federals of both the forlorn hope and the 30th Ohio had been able to make it up to the face of the redan. One Ohioan, Robert McRory, thought that "the regiment and also the whole brigade was close up behind him. He never stopped but went right over in." Others were not so fortunate. Captain Thomas Hayes of the 30th Ohio perished in the ditch, as did several color-bearers who planted the flag. Others guarded the unit flags with their fire, one Federal writing that "our colors were on the Fort all day and could not be reached by either friend or foe. We killed every Johnnie that laid a hand on that flag."[49]

In one sense, despite the carnage, all was going according to plan. It was probably not expected that the first two waves of troops would break the line, as so many were massed behind for that job. As a result, the plan was technically still proceeding as the following regiments of Ewing's brigade moved up the same narrow road toward the Stockade Redan. Then the plan went totally awry. As the 30th Ohio ground to a stop, one of the members later wrote that "all was confusion to the front, and the whole regiment came to a halt." Then the other regiments began to stack up. The 37th Ohio was next in line, Ewing noting "its left breaking the column where the road first debouched, upon a deadly fire." The Ohioans, minus three companies out on skirmish and fatigue duty at the time, became pinned down on the road itself before reaching the ditch in front of the redan. A few managed to slip by "but were mostly shot," Ewing explained. Lieutenant Colonel von Blessingh as well as Ewing himself waded in among the Ohioans to try to get them to go, but the Ohioans would not budge.[50]

Henry Schmidt wrote home that the regiment marched out, "our Bayonets fixed in four ranks." There was no going forward, as "the CS [Confederates] fired so hard on us with muskets & canons that we had to fall behind a hill for we could not get up their breastworks on the above account." Major Charles Hipp of the 37th Ohio ascribed the problems to the three companies in the lead, which stalled under the pressure: "The progress was soon retarded by some of our men of the first three companies blocking up the way with some men of the previously advanced regiment." Hipp simply stated that the rearward companies "forced their way over them," but it apparently was not that easy.[51]

In fact, while brigade commander Ewing spared the Ohioans of much blame, division commander Blair did not. Obviously agitated, Blair described a perfect storm wherein the Ohioans "faltered and gave way under the fire of the enemy, which was far from being severe on this regiment, and was, in fact, directed upon the head of the column." He described how the men "lay down in the road and behind every inequality of ground which afforded them shelter." Ewing and von Blessingh were still trying in vain to urge the men onward: "Both these officers exposed themselves very much in the effort to encourage this regiment, and they were seconded in their efforts by the officers of the regiment." Others tried as well, including one of Ewing's aides, Lieutenant Archie C. Fisk. He pointed forward to comrades "who could be seen already upon the very intrenchments of the enemy," but no one would press on. Even the regiment's sergeant major, Louis Sebastian, "went along the whole line of the regiment, exposing himself to the heaviest fire of the enemy, exhorting and remonstrating with the men and urging them forward." Blair noted simply: "But it was all in vain."[52]

The forward movement consequently ended as the Ohioans blocked the roadway. An obviously incensed Blair explained that "they refused to move, and remained in the road, blocking the way to the other regiments behind." It seemed that General Grant's desire for a pinprick attack with columns by the flank was no better suited to attack the Confederate defenses than was a widespread linear attack. In reality, Blair had walked right into what the Confederates had hoped the attackers would do: funnel troops into a killing zone that could be easily blocked. A joyous Martin L. Smith simply noted that the attack "was immediately driven back."[53]

All eyes were on the assault, including those of the forlorn hope who had reached the ditches before any others. "We turned to see the coming of the division which was to follow us," John O'Dea wrote. "Some regiment started, but the rain of death hurled them back," he added dejectedly. Watching from the rear, Blair knew this attempt at assault by the flank had failed, but he still had time to rectify the situation. But how?[54]

Obviously, Blair's assault had faltered, and he was told as much by one member of the 30th Ohio who went back and informed the politician-general that the Confederate fort could not be taken. Blair apparently gave him bluster: "The way he talked I guess he thought your humble servant was scared." But Blair knew what had happened, and he knew he had to do something quickly for those stranded in the roadway and especially to support the few who had made it all the way to the parapet. He hurriedly ordered the regiments in the rear—all of them stalled behind the recalcitrant 37th Ohio—to change course immediately: "I was finally compelled to order the Forty-seventh Ohio and Fourth West Virginia forward by another route, to the left of the road."[55]

Those regiments had been following behind at a run, Colonel Parry of the 47th Ohio yelling, "Every man of the 47th follow me." He also gave explicit orders that there be no shirking: "If you see any officer behind a tree or a stump, shoot him on the spot." Turnabout was fair play when he added to the officers, "If you see any privates behind trees or stumps, shoot them on the spot." It was all for naught in the long run, as the 47th Ohio did not make it into the fight on the Graveyard Road. They plowed into the rear of the 37th Ohio and became entangled.[56]

Ironically, in so reforming his line, Blair reverted to the same plan that had not worked three days ago, the one that had prompted Grant to utilize this "by the flank" assault formation. Returning to the old system was much more pragmatic in this case, and it was an easy decision for Blair. Sending his brigades into line rather than column would allow them to operate as they were trained to do. At the same time, he utilized the horizontal folds in the terrain for protection while the vertical deployment exposed troops along the entire length of the approach. In fact, the 30th Ohio had been right behind the forlorn hope and was "so long unsupported," Blair noted, that it had already decided on its own to morph back to this style of tactics and formation. The regiment had been "compelled to recoil and shelter themselves," Blair explained, from its exposed position to the front while their fellow Ohioans were bottling up the roadway in the rear and depriving the regiment of much needed support. Most of the 30th Ohio had fallen back because of the furious Mississippi musketry. It was now on a slight ridge south of the Graveyard Road, some one hundred yards from the Confederate bastion. There, Ewing himself reformed their line and tried to unclog the mess to the right.

Their new position did not ensure fewer casualties, however. Even Lieutenant Colonel von Blessingh of the 37th Ohio went down with a nasty wound after which Major Hipp took command.[57]

Another Ohioan met a similar fate. George Clark of the 36th Mississippi told of an Ohio soldier who was "shot on our works and fell over into the trench within a few feet of where I was." The Mississippians cared for the man who "with the most pathetic language lamented his sad lot." He apparently knew his wound was mortal and thus admitted that "if he could just have been at home then he would never again take up arms in the same cause." Clarke admitted a tinge of regret: "I could not help feeling sorry for the poor fellow. . . . He spoke of home, of his mother and sisters, saying that he had seen them for the last time." The Confederates removed him to a hospital, but he soon died.[58]

Meanwhile, Blair was trying his best to further unclog the road, on which casualties were rising. Because it was impossible to move along the path any longer, Blair ordered his other brigades to the left as well, down into the valley of the tributary of Glass Bayou that the left wing of Kilby Smith's brigade had traversed on May 19. There, these brigades also fanned out in linear formation, completing the transformation back to the older style of tactics Grant had tried to avert.[59]

Leading the way were Hugh Ewing's other two regiments, the 4th West Virginia and 47th Ohio. "These regiments advanced with commendable spirit and alacrity," Blair noted, which was easy to understand given the fire they were under. They quickly filed to the left amid the heavy fire, which one soldier reported "sounded like the clanking of great chains." They were off the road—"a better route," Ewing attested. The Ohioans tumbled down the ravine, forming a line parallel to the Confederate works to the front less than a hundred yards away, ultimately taking a position on the slight ridge on which the 30th Ohio had stabilized their line. "Here we protected our advanced men and wounded until they were gradually withdrawn, and, with a heavy and well directed and sustained fire, covered" the further movements of Federals toward the Confederate lines.[60]

The western Virginians did the same. Colonel James H. Dayton led the 4th West Virginia well, but the lieutenant colonel was a different matter. One West Virginian wrote home that "[John L.] Vance has disgraced himself by his drunkeness on the field of battle." Apparently Vance "was so drunk that he was staggering round in everyone's way." Vance even "mistook the 113th Illinois Regiment for ours and commenced cursing them but the officers of that Regiment drew their revolvers and made him crawfish on the double quick." Vance later resigned: "The man of many wounds," one soldier noted, "has sent in his resignation after receiving a very pressing invitation to do so from his Col. backed by every officer in the Regiment (cause—drunkenness on duty and off duty and in fact all the time.)"[61]

Unfortunately for the Ohioans and West Virginians, friendly fire now began to pepper their ranks from the rear as well, as both artillery and small-arms fire was sent over their heads into the Confederate ranks. Colonel Parry quickly detailed a man to return to Ewing to report the situation, but he went down en route. He sent another soldier, who also went down. Then a third fell as well. Finally, Parry was able to get a fourth runner through the two-hundred-yard expanse. "It was literally running a gauntlet of fire through a hail storm of leaden bullets," one Ohioan recalled. Fortunately, the fire from the rear soon slackened.[62]

Next in Blair's line was Giles Smith's brigade, minus the decimated 13th US Regulars. Blair likewise ordered Smith to the left and down into the valley. The Illinoisans and Missourians moved across the rear of Ewing's troops, farther down the tributary until they reached a point on Ewing's left. There, they went into line and moved forward toward a position from which they both received and delivered fire on the Confederates above them and to the front. It was tough going, given the abatis and other impediments. Blair simply told Smith to "go forward as rapidly as the nature of the ground would admit, and to assault whenever he found it practicable to do so."[63]

Fortunately, Giles Smith was not alone in the valley. As he moved leftward, Smith detected other Federals farther to his left: Ransom's brigade of McPherson's corps. They had been there all along, even during the May 19 assault when Kilby Smith was operating in this area. Giles Smith was now farther down the tributary's watershed toward Glass Bayou than Kilby Smith had been on May 19 and thus reached as far as Ransom's Federals. Giles Smith and Ransom met behind their lines and talked over what to do next. In actuality, because of the nature of the terrain, Ransom had been able to press ahead slightly farther than Smith, allowing him to get closer to the Mississippians to the front and in a better-protected area as well. Smith's troops could only get on top of a small ridge about a hundred yards from the Confederate line, still intent, as he described his orders, to "try the strength of their works at that point."[64]

Finishing out Blair's new deployment was the last brigade in line, Kilby Smith's. As the third brigade in line, he had waited while the others moved forward, hearing the distinct roll of musketry and knowing full well that many of his comrades were dying in front of the Stockade Redan. Ewing's brigade had moved out promptly at 10:00 A.M., followed by Giles Smith's a little later. Eventually, Kilby Smith formed his brigade and maneuvered it in behind Giles Smith's troops as they advanced, although still behind the covering ridge and on the "winding and covered roadway, constructed through the ravines near my line the night previous."[65]

The plan Kilby Smith was anticipating was not in place by the time he and his brigade popped over the ridge in full view of the Confederate works. "As we emerged upon the high ground from the cover of the woods and hills," Smith related, "I discovered that the programme had been changed. Instead of a dense column marching by the flank down the road, as I had expected, the ground I had passed over in the first assault on the 19th instant was covered by scattered masses. The flag of General Ewing was flying from the hill from which I had been withdrawn."[66]

Obviously, something had gone wrong. Smith rode over to Blair's command post, where he found the division commander in the throes of changing his plan in the midst of the crisis. By this point, Blair had already decided to send the brigades off to the left down into the ravines, and he promptly ordered Kilby Smith to follow and support Giles Smith, who, Smith noted in his orders, "was endeavoring to make a position somewhere between General Ewing and General Ransom." Kilby Smith was incredulous: "This movement I could not have anticipated," he wrote. "Knowing the ground well," he wrote, "I threw the brigade in column of regiments, and, by regiments, moved rapidly over the brow of the hill."[67]

The Confederate fire was heavy even this far back, causing casualties all along the line. In fact, George Clarke of the 36th Mississippi "chanced to glance along the lines to my right, and it appeared to be one solid sheet of fire and smoke." One casualty of note was Colonel Americus Rice of the 57th Ohio, who was in a "half sitting position" for cover. The bullet went through his leg below the knee and then through once more above the knee before lodging in his stomach; Lieutenant Colonel Samuel R. Mott took command of the regiment. Smith pushed the column of regiments forward, "massing them as best I could under cover from the enemy's musketry and a Whitworth gun, waspish in its annoyance." The regiments rushed forward with what Smith declared as "promptitude and gallantry," and miraculously the heavy fire such a target drew passed completely over the heads of each regiment as it went over, although one cannon ball went through the flag of the 83rd Indiana, which had just at midnight returned from its road-building duty in the rear and had had no sleep whatsoever. One member of the regiment declared the ball took "out some of 'the stars.'" Once in position, Smith motioned his regiments to the left and they "defil[ed] down a long ravine that skirts the main chain of bluffs." As soon as all the regiments made it into the ravines, Smith formed them again in columns of regiments behind Giles Smith's brigade, particularly in support of the 8th Missouri. Kilby Smith even added some of his own weight to the front line by sending the 55th Illinois forward to hold a position on the flank of the Missourians. Meanwhile, Kilby Smith personally found Giles Smith, and the two officers discussed their next moves. Kilby Smith's formal orders were simply to "support any movement Col. Giles A. Smith should make," and so his regiments waited amid what Kilby Smith described as "horrible heat in the ravines and hillsides."[68]

The situation was just like three days ago. Blair was finding out the troubles in these ravines yet again, describing how his brigades were now again struggling with the impediments: "But this route, while it was better covered from the fire of the enemy, led through ravines made almost impassable with abatis of fallen timber, and did not admit of anything like a charge."[69]

With Blair's division in its new deployment (two brigades on the front and one in reserve), Sherman now had a solid line from the Graveyard Road southward to McPherson's corps. Nothing but skirmishers held the line north of the road, but Sherman was little worried that the enemy would come out of their fortifications and counterattack. In fact, there was little major force for a half-mile to the right, until the line of another of Sherman's divisions, under Frederick Steele, began. Nevertheless, Blair was preparing for an assault, Giles Smith and Ewing up front and Kilby Smith "on the off slope of one of the spurs." All three, Sherman reported, "kept up a constant fire against any object that presented itself above the parapet."[70]

The Confederates were duly impressed. John Forney, on whose left brigade most of the action at the Stockade Redan fell, marveled that the attacks "were made by larger bodies and apparently with greater determination than those of May 19." Still, the Mississippians and Missourians had held easily. Although several Federals had made it to the ditches in front of the works, none had penetrated. Casualties were accumulating, however, especially in the 3rd Missouri at the stockade itself, whose member I. V. Smith marveled that there was "one attack after another." There, the Missourians were caught in an enfilading fire from Sherman's artillery east of the redan, and the numbers eventually showed; the 3rd Missouri regiment suffered more than half of the entire brigade's casualties. Cockrell described how they were "exposed during the assault to an enfilading and rear fire in the redan, against which there was then no protection or defense." Still, the Missourians caught a breath between assaults, allowing them to "watch the battle at other points of the line."[71]

Of course, Sherman did have another option. James Tuttle's entire division of three brigades was still massed on the roadway east of the Stockade Redan and offered plenty of fresh troops to renew the assault. Tuttle pushed his troops forward slightly to the last position of cover before exposing themselves, and there they awaited clarification on what to do next.[72]

Sherman himself sought the same thing.

Sherman was evidently concerned, watching the failed assault and remarking that it was "more deadly than the assault on the Bridge at Lodi." But he still had one whole division, in addition to Tuttle's, to his right that had not attacked. Frederick Steele's three brigades were supposed to advance at the moment Blair went forward, but Sherman, over on the Graveyard Road, heard and saw no evidence of an attack being made down the line to the west. It was for good reason: Steele had run into some major problems getting into position.[73]

The effort to get the three brigades of Steele's division together for the attack of columns or by the flank that Grant desired was more problematic for Steele than it was for Blair or Tuttle. Both of those divisions were concentrated along the Graveyard Road, whereas Steele's three brigades were fanned out in a lengthy line nearly a mile and a quarter long, extending all the way from the Mississippi River to the Stockade Redan area. This was also some of the roughest terrain on the battlefield as well. Certainly, it precluded any assault across Mint Spring Bayou down the watershed near the Mississippi River, but it also affected the timing for concentrating the division for an attack nearer to the Stockade Redan.[74]

Making the timing more difficult, Sherman suggested that the division's planned attack be made on John Thayer's front, which was on the extreme left of the division's line. That position was the logical one, however, it being farther up the Mint Spring Bayou watershed and thus allowing better terrain to traverse. It was also the position on the division's front nearest to the attacks being made along the Graveyard Road. Sherman obviously wanted the attacks as close together as he could get them for supportive purposes. Of course, concentrating everything on one end of the division's line meant that the other brigades had farther to travel than if the concentration had been done in the center.[75]

Steele began moving his brigades early. However, he soon found that the terrain and the Confederate fire on exposed areas of the route of march hampered his efforts to be in position in time for the 10:00 A.M. assault. In fact, it was well after noon before Steele was able to get most of his division concentrated, leaving only a small number of Federals behind to hold their original lines in the unlikely case of a Confederate counterattack.[76]

John Thayer's brigade of Iowans consequently held their position all morning as the ruckus erupted to their left. They took what cover they could find while nervously awaiting the other brigades and their turn at the dreadful advance up the steep and precipitous hill to their front. The next brigade down the line was Francis Manter's, which had a fairly short distance to traverse to take a position in rear of Thayer's men. Still, it was after noon before it came into formation. Charles Woods's Missouri, Ohio, and Iowa brigade, however, had much farther to move over difficult and hostile terrain, and they were even later in arriving, causing the entire timetable to be completely thrown off in Steele's area of operations.[77]

Part of the problem included the ravines and gullies that had to be crossed: "Owing to the difficulty of moving my brigade so as to prevent the enemy from seeing our movements," Charles Woods explained, "several hours were consumed in reaching our position." More problematic was Confederate fire. The Confederates of William Baldwin's and Francis Shoup's brigades watched as the Federals sidled eastward, trying to keep out of sight. Such was not possible in all places, as several bald ridges had to be crossed to get into the correct position for the assault. Confederate small arms were useless at that range, but the artillery in the fortifications on the high ridge south of Mint Spring Bayou was not. Confederate cannoneers raked any target that presented itself, doing a great deal of damage to the Federals who had yet to even begin their assault. One Louisianan described a single-file Union advance, writing in his diary that "a large number of the enemy passed by one at a time to the bottom of the hill. We in the meantime keeping up a brisk fire on them." Woods explained that "it was necessary to press over several pieces of open ground within close range of the enemy's rifle-pits, part of the road being swept by artillery." Fortunately, the lead regiment, the 25th Iowa, was able to get into a position under some cover and deploy skirmishers, which cut down on the Confederate fire. Yet the regiment, as well as the 12th Missouri that followed a little too closely, suffered heavily in the process. In fact, some fifty or sixty men of Woods's brigade went down merely getting into correct position.[78]

Henry Seaman described just how slow the process of getting into attack position was:

We had to pass through a narrow contracted ravine under a most galling fire from eight pieces of the enemy's artillery. The distance we had to go through this ravine before we could again seek shelter was about twenty rods and to get through with little loss of life as possible we were ordered to take a single company through at a time and run rapidly through on single file. Thus company after company passed through until the entire regiment was all over the perilous position with the loss of only two men, one killed instantly by a shell and the other mortally wounded.

An Iowan in Woods's brigade told a similar tale: "We had to run two or three places where the secesh could see us run the Blockade the boys call it. One place was awful hard to pass running down a steap hill." The first three companies of the regiment made it fine, but the later ones were not so fortunate. "After we got down to the other hill," he recalled, "we was safe and it was hard to look back [and] see many of our soldiers shot down while they were running down the other hill." Obviously, such deployment took a great deal of time.[79]

Calvin Ainsworth of the 25th Iowa in Woods's brigade gave an even more vivid picture of the ordeal: "We marched around to the center," he wrote in his diary, "it is very hot and a good many think we are going to charge; there is a certain class that give out." The brigade had to cross three distinct ridges, all "exposed to the enemy's fire while on top of the ridges, also while we run down the hills." Ainsworth and his comrades made it over the first hill without loss in his company, although he was running so fast "the first thing I know one leg is mired in the mud but I manage[d] to draw it out mighty quick for the balls are plowing the mud all around me." The second hill was similarly passed, but the third posed the major problem as both small-arms fire and canister, which Ainsworth declared "the soldiers feared . . . more than large solid shot or shells," were getting very close. The captain, James D. Spearman, had been ordered to halt at the top and send the men down "singly or Indian file." Spearman froze when he reached the top and huddled with his lieutenant, who was also his brother-in-law, behind a tree. The men were exposed, and Ainsworth shouted, "'Why don't you take this company down,' and I used two or three very emphatic words, for I was mad." The captain did not respond, so Ainsworth took it upon himself to get out of the fix, running clear around the entire company. When he reached safety at the bottom, he was surprised that several others had come along with him, but the captain and lieutenant were still behind their tree and the majority of the company was still exposed on top of the ridge. Finally, after several minutes, the captain came down at a run, stumbling near the bottom, and "commenced to roll very rapidly the rest of the way. He rolled clear to the bottom." Ainsworth found the captain had been hit in the back and was soon carried off the field, Ainsworth and others wondering if the unpopular officer had been shot by one of his own men. Ainsworth finally came to conclusion that no one would have done that and that the captain was not a coward, but it was simply a case where "that was a mighty hard place to stay and a mighty hard place to leave." The rest of the company came down single-file, although one suddenly turned and went back up the hill after his canteen, which he had dropped. Once he reached it, the Iowan found a bullet hole in it: "When I picked it up I saw the hole in the middle of it and knew it wasn't good for anything so threw it away." An amused Ainsworth thought, "For my part, I would want 10,000 dollars a second to stop in a place like that."[80]

Most of the concentration was done in full view of the Confederates, who knew what it meant and responded with a heavy fire. Francis Shoup recorded almost in real time that "a force on my extreme left begins to assemble. Taking advantage of the gorge in front, they gain the cover of the steep declivity at the foot of ridge running down from our line into the gorge. Several regiments are finally assembled." One of his Louisianans also described how the Federals "were running under the hill to make a charge on our regiment."[81]

Frederick Steele was ultimately able to get his brigades aligned and in order during the morning and early afternoon hours. Three of Thayer's Iowa regiments were in line in the front (the 30th, 9th, and 26th Iowa left-to-right) while the 4th Iowa guarded a nearby battery. Behind was Woods's troops drawn up in column of regiments as best they could due to the terrain. Manter's brigade constituted the reserve farther to the rear. The division had obviously missed the 10:00 A.M. launch by a long shot, but they no doubt knew that Blair's troops had met the starting time because at that moment a ferocious pitch of noise emerged to their east, indicating that the attack was on. They could only hurry to get in place so they too could take their part.[82]

Whether they would get that chance was the question. By this point Sherman—watching Blair's failure a second time even with greater numbers—was convinced that none of these assaults could work. He related how "our men had been fairly beaten back from off the parapet, and had got cover behind the spurs of ground close up to the rebel works."[83]

It was a disaster in the making, and Sherman wanted no part of continuing the horror.

8

"There Was Not a Twig between Us and the Fort"

Time certainly changes things. Just a little more than two years prior, most members of the Union high command of the Army of the Tennessee were civilians. Ulysses S. Grant was a clerk in his father's dry goods store in Galena, Illinois. William T. Sherman was an educator in Louisiana. John A. McClernand was a congressman. How different their lives were now, just two short years later.[1]

Although coming from varying and different backgrounds, these officers, now in charge of the best army the United States fielded in the Civil War, had risen to high command early and along similar trajectories. They were all general officers within months of the war's beginning. One year in, at Shiloh, Grant was commanding the Army of the Tennessee as a major general of volunteers, and both Sherman and McClernand were division commanders with stars on their shoulders.[2]

However, one general took an altogether different approach compared to Grant, Sherman, and McClernand. James B. McPherson was seemingly everything they were not. Whereas not one of the other three was a regular army officer at the beginning of the war, McPherson was a highly touted army engineer on duty at various engineering jobsites throughout the nation. He was brilliant, as evidenced by his graduating West Point at the top of his class and his subsequent commissioning into the vaunted Corps of Engineers.[3]

Yet the engineering field was not one in which fast promotions came, and as a result while Grant, Sherman, McClernand, and a host of others were fast rising in the general officer ranks, McPherson languished in his lower staff officer status. In fact, at Shiloh, when Grant and the others were making names for themselves in the biggest battle in American history to that time, McPherson was still a comparatively lowly lieutenant colonel engaged in staff work. He was actually assigned to the department commander Henry

Halleck's staff but was on loan to Grant; as such, he witnessed the horrors of Shiloh.[4]

Yet even as Grant and his other corps commanders steadily rose in rank, McPherson's rise became meteoric. Soon after Shiloh he became a colonel, then a brigadier general. By the fall of 1862—just six months after being named a lieutenant colonel—McPherson found himself with two stars on his shoulders as a major general. His sudden rise confounded many, including McPherson himself. When told of his promotion to major general, he responded, "I don't know what for."[5]

It has long been argued that Grant and Sherman had a lot to do with McPherson's advancement. Grant certainly thought a lot of the young man six years his junior. He once wrote Julia that McPherson was "one of the nicest gentlemen you ever saw." McPherson in fact became so close to Grant that Julia actually sewed on his brigadier general's shoulder straps when his first promotion to general officer came. She gushed with enthusiasm as well: he "brought in to me his first general's shoulder straps and, kneeling on one knee before me, asked me to fasten them on his shoulder. I did so with pleasure. . . . I firmly fastened McPherson's first stars for him on his brave, broad, handsome shoulders." Grant's favoritism since then had been obvious, and many used the word "protégé" in reference to the Grant-McPherson relationship. Historian Edwin C. Bearss takes a slightly different view: "If Grant turned a corner, McPherson would break his nose."[6]

Although sometimes a poor judge of character, whether it be in staff officers or later in his cabinet, Grant realized McPherson was inexperienced and needed to be guided at times. In all the operations heretofore in the Vicksburg Campaign, Grant had given McPherson the safest duties and positions, most often squarely between Sherman and McClernand and rarely holding flanks or other more dangerous positions. Such was the case with the movement southward through Louisiana, crossing the Mississippi River, and on the roundabout march to Vicksburg. When McPherson was at one point forced on the flank out of necessity, Grant thinking it was entirely safe, he was somewhat surprised at Raymond just ten days before. Many historians have not given McPherson great credit for his conduct there that day.[7]

True to form, as these assaults began on the morning of May 22, McPherson's XVII Corps held the center of the line squarely between McClernand and Sherman, and Grant was right there with McPherson as the troops went forward, much as he was six days previously at Champion Hill. Perhaps Grant's positioning was because of McPherson's inexperience, perhaps it was because it was the obvious position to see down the lines in both directions, or perhaps it was both.[8]

CHAPTER EIGHT

Grant's presence with McPherson was perhaps also because his XVII Corps was the most disordered of the three. The corps had been having some problems throughout the campaign, and it was still not in the best shape as the assaults began to move forward on May 22. One of McPherson's three divisions was not even there. John McArthur's three brigades were widely separated, one still across the Mississippi River and one way to the south around Warrenton, where the commander, McArthur, physically was. That left only one of the three brigades in this division actually on McPherson's lines. Even more, Thomas E. G. Ransom's brigade was detached from the rest of the corps by the deep valley of Glass Bayou. Ransom actually operated with Sherman's brigades more than with McPherson's.[9]

The other two divisions were also having problems. One was under a new leader who had just taken command five days previously. Although Isaac F. Quinby had been in command of the same troops before, he had been replaced due to sickness by Marcellus Crocker, who in turn had become sick and was replaced when Quinby came back to the army. Quinby was a veteran, but the change in command, especially in the midst of the fighting campaign and near the eve of the assaults, was not good. Moreover, at least according to War Department liaison Charles Dana, Quinby was not that good even when well: "A good commander of a division he is not, though he is a most excellent and estimable man, and seemed to be regarded by the soldiers with much affection." A classmate of Grant at West Point, Quinby also seemed to be in the commander's favor.[10]

The third division was perhaps the most solid, but in some eyes there was a problem there as well in that a politician-general much like McClernand and Blair, John A. Logan, led it. Although Logan had made a name for himself and had shown ability during several fights, most notably at Champion Hill, he was quirky, and thoughts of competency seemingly always existed in the back of the minds of doubters about non–West Point officers. For instance, Dana described him as "heroic and brilliant, [although] he is sometimes unsteady" and that he was "a man of instinct and not of reflection, his judgments are often absurd."[11]

There was also jealousy among some of the divisions. The argument over the lead on the march to Raymond had caused some hard feelings between Logan and Crocker and presumably their troops. Crocker was no longer in command, but that animosity still lingered.[12]

McPherson had nevertheless positioned the present portions of his corps astride the Jackson Road back on May 18, and the relative positions had not changed even though more of the brigades had marched in. The corps took little part in the May 19 assaults, but by the morning of May 22 it was in position with the rest of the army. Now centered on the all-important Jackson Road was John Logan's division, having moved to the left to "occupy the grounds around the white house in front of Fort Hill," with John E. Smith's Illinoisans and Indianans on the right of the road and John D. Stevenson's Illinoisans, Ohioans, and Missourians on the left. In reserve was the third brigade of the division under Mortimer D. Leggett, the 20th and 78th Ohio supporting Smith and the 68th Ohio and 30th Illinois behind Stevenson.[13]

Isaac F. Quinby's division of three brigades held a position on Logan's left, with John B. Sanborn's Indianans, Minnesotans, and Wisconsin troops on the right and George B. Boomer's Iowans, Illinoisans, and Missourians on the left. Samuel A. Holmes's brigade, like Leggett's to their right, was held in reserve, but because of the lay of the land that division was at an unfortunate angle with the Confederate line. The left was much farther back from the right, causing historian Bearss to describe the situation as "an eccentric angle." Of course, the only brigade of McArthur's division present, Thomas E. G. Ransom's, was entirely detached, it being the only brigade of the corps operating north of Glass Bayou.[14]

Still, McPherson held perhaps the critical point in the line, the area where Confederate commanders had placed their best and freshest brigades to defend where they thought the main attack would come. McPherson straddled the all-important main route into Vicksburg, the Jackson Road, and his lines also extended far down toward the similarly important Baldwin's Ferry Road. McPherson's corps held an extremely important section of the line and was thus tasked with assaulting some of the major Confederates fortifications defending Vicksburg.

Those Confederate works defending McPherson's front were indeed important. And strong. Although a portion of McPherson's troops deployed north of Glass Bayou, there were no major Confederate works on that stream, and none until the high ground south of it. There, a narrow ridge existed much like that on which the Graveyard Road ran, dividing the tributaries of Glass Bayou to the north from the upper reaches of Hatcher's Bayou to the south. The result was a ridge connecting the positions of the Union and Confederate lines. It was on this ridge that the Jackson Road ran into Vicksburg and through the Confederate defenses. A similar but lower area of high ground a mile to the south contained the Baldwin's Ferry Road entrance into the city, and the Southern Railroad of Mississippi ran directly below that thoroughfare. McPherson's corps extended toward the railroad, and the corresponding Confederate troops holding these two major roads and the railroad consisted of the right half of Hébert's brigade and the entirety of John C. Moore's brigade. Both made up John H. Forney's division, who remarked that his "entire division front was completely and closely invested."[15]

Forney's Confederates fortunately had ample and strong fortifications all along this mile-and-a-half-long front, made up of heavy rifle pits with abatis and natural ravines and steep hills in front. There were also three major fortifications on this section of the line, not surprisingly guarding the two major roads into Vicksburg. Because the Jackson Road—the principal entrance into the city—was of such importance, Samuel Lockett had established two large bastions to guard it, one on either side.[16]

As the Confederate line rose out of the marshes of Glass Bayou and ran toward the highest elevation along the defenses, a major V-shaped bastion loomed on the north side of the Jackson Road. It commanded all the surrounding area, including the ravines of the tributaries of Glass Bayou to the north as well as the feeder branches of Hatcher's Bayou to the southeast. More important, it commanded the Jackson Road itself and the approaches to the Confederate line.[17]

Just south of the major redan on the roadway itself, actually on the south side of the road but extending much farther than the simple redan north of the road, was a series of fortifications together known as the Great Redoubt. It was by far the strongest Confederate work on the lines, and such heavy works exemplified the need to hold at all cost the Jackson Road sector and deprive the enemy of any chance to enter Vicksburg by that route.[18]

That was not all. A mile to the south was the Baldwin's Ferry Road, and it too had a major bastion to control it. A lunette, or a crescent-shaped fort, loomed on the south side of the road itself, between it and the railroad, and provided some cover, mostly against anyone trying to enter Vicksburg by that roadway.[19]

Although the left of Hébert's brigade had already been in heavy action at the Stockade Redan, his right had also seen plenty of fighting. The line continued southward from the Stockade Redan and its defenders, the 36th Mississippi, to the 7th Mississippi Battalion, the 37th Mississippi, and 38th Mississippi, all of which had been involved in stopping Blair's and Ransom's brigades for two days now. The line continued on southward across Glass Bayou, which was defended by two companies of the 43rd Mississippi, with that regiment extending down toward the redan on the Jackson Road. There, the two Louisiana regiments picked up the line. Unfortunately, given the terrain and the length of the line, there were sections such as in the 38th Mississippi farther north where there were no intrenchments at all, and in some areas on the 43rd Mississippi's line there were lengths without any troops. Yet the line grew stronger as it approached the Jackson Road. The 3rd Louisiana manned the redan itself, and it became known to history as the 3rd Louisiana Redan. The fortification also contained a 3-inch rifle of the Appeal Arkansas Battery; a 12-pound howitzer of Company A, 1st Mississippi Light Artillery astride the Jackson Road; and a 3-inch rifle of the Appeal Arkansas Battery and a 20-pound Parrott rifle of Waddell's Alabama Battery inside the redan itself. The 21st Louisiana continued the line southward at the Great Redoubt, where four cannons manned the defenses: three 3-inch rifles of the Pointe Coupee Artillery and a 12-pound howitzer of the Appeal Arkansas Battery, one of which was knocked out by Union artillery fire prior to the assault.[20]

Hébert's brigade was solid and veteran, the 3rd Louisiana having been at Wilson's Creek and Pea Ridge before crossing the Mississippi River. Hébert was their first colonel and had a soft spot for his troops, although the others had seen plenty of action as well. Only the 21st Louisiana was not as veteran, although one of its early colonels was Martin L. Smith, now one of Pemberton's division commanders. The other brigade of Forney's division was also veteran. As colonel of the 2nd Texas, John C. Moore had seen his share of fighting, including at Shiloh, even commanding a brigade at times. Thereafter he had commanded a brigade at Iuka and later Corinth, where his unit was nearly destroyed. In the action there and at Davis Bridge, his brigade sustained huge casualties.[21]

Moore's own 2nd Texas formed the core of the brigade and held the lunette on the Baldwin's Ferry Road itself. Obviously, Moore had the most confidence in his old regiment and wanted it to hold the most critical position; he referred to it as "that veteran and gallant regiment, the Second Texas." The regiment's colonel, Ashbel Smith, certainly thought so, writing that "this was the assailable point of our lines; the place of danger; the post of honor; the key of this portion of our works and defense." In fact, the 42nd Alabama had originally occupied the fort, but Moore switched them out and the fortification, like that held by the Louisianans on the Jackson Road, took the name of its defenders and became in history the 2nd Texas Lunette. Colonel Smith noted that "the other similar point was where the Jackson road crossed our lines to enter the city, and this position, for a similar reason, appears to have been manned by the Third Louisiana Infantry, a most gallant corps."[22]

The Texas regiment was elite by this point in the war, but the Alabama regiments that flanked the lunette (the 42nd Alabama to the right and the 37th Alabama to the left) were excellent too. In line to the north of the Texans and Alabamians, defending the lunette itself, were the other three regiments of the brigade. The 40th Alabama was in line next to the 37th Alabama; the two Mississippi regiments, next to the north and connecting with Herbert's brigade, contained notable political figures as well. Commanding the 35th

Mississippi was none other that Colonel William S. Barry, who had been president of the Mississippi Secession Convention. The colonel of the 40th Mississippi, Bruce Colbert, was a delegate to the convention.[23]

There were reserves for this line as well, including Waul's Texas Legion drawn up behind and assigned to Moore for the coming assaults. Also close by were the brave but weakened regiments of Martin Green's brigade of Bowen's division; the other brigade, Francis Cockrell's, stood behind Hébert's troops to the north. Also sent southward to act as a reserve were two Louisiana regiments from Smith's division.[24]

Like the defenses to the north, it was a fairly small band of defenders along a stretch of a mile and a half along McPherson's front. A mere ten regiments—just a brigade and a half and twenty-seven pieces of artillery—had the task of holding off an entire Union corps of three divisions made up of nine full brigades. Although there were only seven Union brigades present at this point on May 22, McPherson still had the numerical advantage, more than tripling the force Forney had on McPherson's front. But the Confederates had a dual advantage: extremely strong fortifications that fronted heavily broken and difficult terrain. The Federals would need every advantage of manpower to overcome the natural and artificial barriers.[25]

For all the concern about McPherson's inexperience and the condition of his corps, he actually did as well as Sherman and perhaps better in some respects. While Sherman's division commanders had trouble getting ready and then launching the assault at 10:00 A.M., the net result was that only one undermanned brigade of the nine actually assaulted the Stockade Redan in the morning, and that with only one regiment and the advance guard. While Steele's brigades worked to get into position north of Glass Bayou and Tuttle's brigades were held in reserve, only Blair's division made an assault, and of its three brigades only Hugh Ewing's approached the Confederate fortifications and planted flags on the slopes. With the majority of the brigade stalled, the other two brigades of Blair's division fanned out to the left and sought a position from which they could continue the assaults. In contrast, while McPherson had almost as much trouble as Sherman, he actually had two brigades make the assault at 10:00 A.M., doubling Sherman's total.[26]

That being said, assaulting with only two brigades out of seven—although better than the one out of nine that Sherman had managed—was not a good percentage. Many factors had to be taken into consideration, however, including the area of ground available and the number of troops there. Grant himself explained that "each corps had many more men than could possibly be used

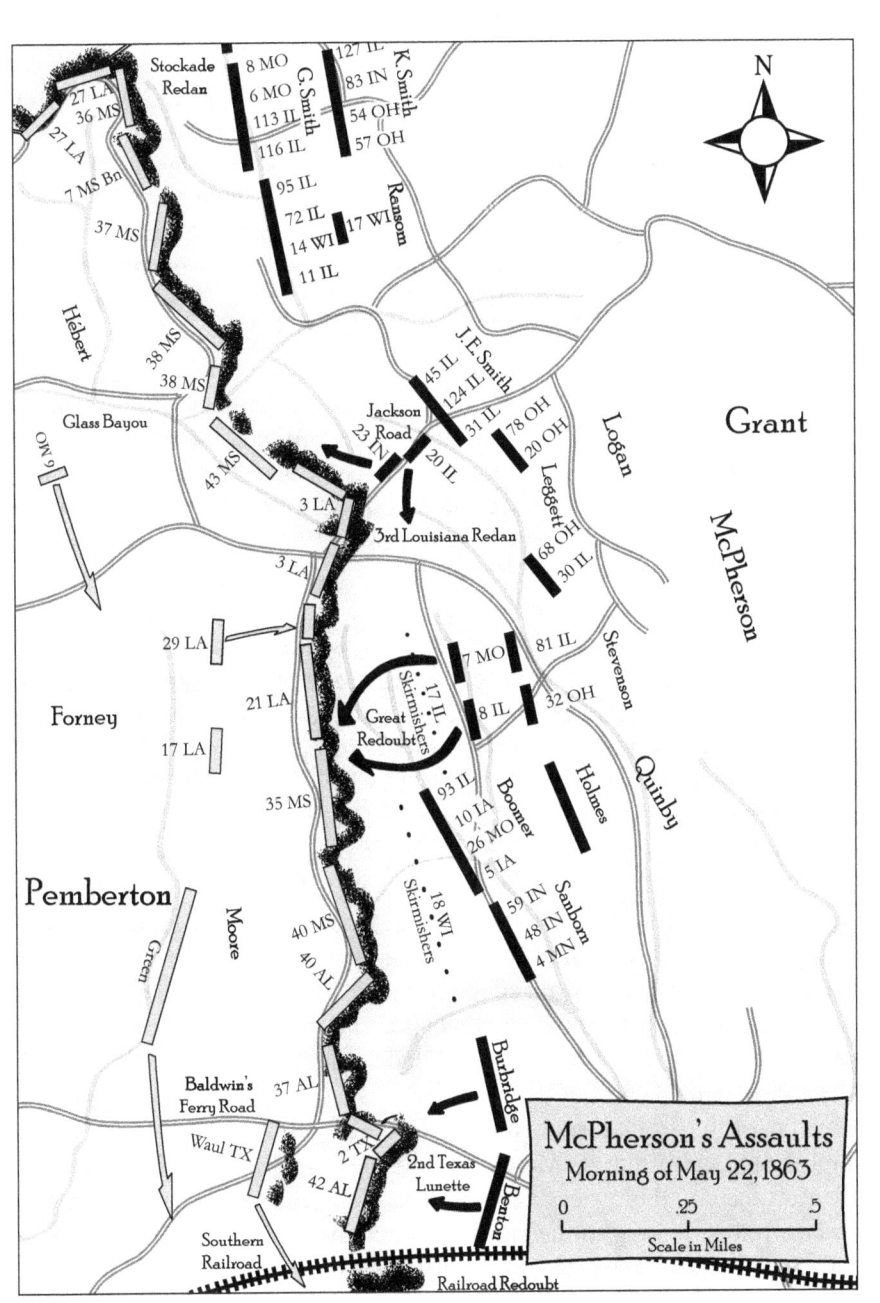

in the assault over such ground as intervened between them and the enemy." Still, of the frontline brigades preparing to assault the Confederate positions they confronted, only two of five did so at 10:00 A.M.[27]

Surprisingly, one unit that did not manage an attack that morning was under the command of Thomas Ransom, one of the boldest brigade commanders in the corps. On the far right flank of the corps, across Glass Bayou, Ransom's brigade had a hard time getting into position for its assault. Logically, Ransom was more interested in what was happening on his right with Blair's brigades than on his left, across the wide and formidable valley of Glass Bayou. In fact, his left was much more protected than his right, even though it was disconnected from his own corps, simply by the presence of the watershed. Because of the way Blair had positioned his brigades for the assault by the flank along the Graveyard Road, there was initially nothing on Ransom's right to support him. He was truly, at first, isolated and alone.[28]

Ransom nevertheless prepared his troops and moved them forward in an effort to do all he could at 10:00 A.M.; he wanted nothing more than to be in the thick of the "simultaneous assault." A report from Major Joseph Stockton of the 72nd Illinois, high in his tree, that there was only one line of Confederate works whetted his appetite even more. Yet the hours passed slowly that morning. Ransom and his officers sat in the rear and joked about the upcoming fight. Ransom kidded Lieutenant Colonel Joseph C. Wright of the 72nd Illinois, who "had a splendid field glass": "Colonel, if you are killed I want you to leave that glass to me." Wright assented, until Major Stockton reminded him, "Stop, Colonel, you forget you left that to your boy when you made your will at Memphis." "That is so," echoed Wright. The morbid jocularity aside, Ransom moved forward at 9:00 A.M. to get into position to assault, quickly finding, despite his operations here three days ago, that the ground was more troublesome than he had realized. He previously sent skirmishers ahead and moved the regiments by the flank down into the valley of the branch of Glass Bayou, "through a network of ravines filled with fallen timber and canebreaks to a point within 60 yards of the enemy's works, massing my troops as well as the nature of the ground would admit." George Carrington of the 11th Illinois simply noted in his diary: "Marched out through the ravines and hollows."[29]

Unfortunately, the cover was not total. The brigade took heavy fire as it maneuvered and clung to the sides of the ravine in the valley of the branch looking upward at the massive heights it had to scale. One soldier in the 95th Illinois wrote his parents that "truly the fortifications may be called walls." The fire from them was already heavy as well. Ransom wrote that "the enemy had in the mean time massed troops behind their works in our front, and poured into my ranks one continuous blaze of musketry, while the artillery on my left threw enfilading shot and shell into my columns with deadly effect." The colonels formed their regiments as best they could to keep them covered, Colonel Humphrey of the 95th Illinois forming his companies in "column by divisions closed in mass." Eventually a line of four regiments formed, the 11th Illinois on the left, with the 95th Illinois, 14th Wisconsin, and 72nd Illinois filling the line to the right. The 17th Wisconsin, which had advanced early on May 19, was held in reserve. Isolated as they were, however, Ransom's troops could do little and became trapped down in the ravine. George Carrington remembered the Illinoisans "chewing canes that were growing at our feet, to keep our minds from what we knew was coming."[30]

The wait seemed almost surreal. At one point a woodpecker, one Federal remembered, "lit on an old dead snag sounding a tattoo with his bill then flew away with a 'chirp.' (Happy woodpecker)." More ominously, another Illinoisan seemed to break under the strain. George Carrington noticed that one unarmed Federal with only a knapsack slung over his shoulder started to calmly ascend the hill under which they lay. "He reached nearly the top when a musket bullet struck him in the shoulder and sent him whirling." He tumbled down the hill and landed on a brush heap, "'kerslap' there he sat looking so foolish." Carrington admitted that he "had to laugh in spite of the deadly surroundings, I never knew who he was or what became of him or what he was trying to do there."[31]

While waiting in the ravines, the Illinoisans and Wisconsin troops could hear the awful ruckus growing around them. To their left was Logan's division, which had, judging from the noise, evidently pushed off on time and assaulted along the Jackson Road. They were of course little help to Ransom, as they were too far away and across the foreboding valley of Glass Bayou. That was not the case on the right, however. The same unearthly sounds and more came from the Stockade Redan to the north as Blair's troops moved forward, but then something else occurred to lighten the load on Ransom's isolated troops. The assault on the Graveyard Road had apparently faltered or been redirected, because Blair's brigades began to flood down into this same valley that Ransom's troops held. Ewing's unit was nearer the redan and Kilby Smith's was farther to the rear, but closest to Ransom appeared Giles Smith's Illinoisans and Missourians. Ransom soon walked over and met Smith, and the two quickly agreed to support one another in the assault that had been scheduled for 10:00 A.M. but that neither had yet begun.[32]

The same story played out farther to the south past Logan's division where Quinby's brigades held the line. Isaac Quinby had been in command of the division for only six days, but he had a veteran division that had seen a lot of action in the past. On Quinby's right was the mixed brigade under

George B. Boomer. The left brigade was under John B. Sanborn, Charles Dana describing him as "a steady, mediocre sort of man." With Holmes's brigade in reserve, these units were at Shiloh, Iuka, and Corinth as well as Port Gibson twenty-one days ago and Champion Hill seven days ago and thus made up one of the most veteran divisions in the Army of the Tennessee.[33]

The brigade commanders, despite all being colonels, had also been in their roles for a while now; they knew what to do and what not to do. In fact, Sanborn and Boomer took the opportunity the night before to reconnoiter the ground in front of them under the cover of darkness: "I spent the night of the 21st," Sanborn wrote, "in connection with . . . Colonel Boomer, commanding the Third Brigade, reconnoitering for the best approaches for infantry to the enemy's works in our front." He went on to relate that "it was ascertained that we could approach to within about 80 yards under cover of the hills and form without great exposure to the men." The next morning the men were in line and moving forward to their assault positions as early as 8:00 A.M.[34]

George Boomer led his troops forward that morning nearly a quarter of a mile and formed in line, the regiments being in columns of companies, the 93rd Illinois on the right near Logan's troops and the 10th Iowa, 26th Missouri, and 5th Iowa, some of whom had no shoes, filling the line to the left. Boomer had positioned his brigade in "the hollow, slightly protected from the fire of the enemy," but that did not provide aid from what Lieutenant Colonel Ezekiel S. Sampson of the 5th Iowa described as "a burning sun." Another Iowan declared that "the heat was so great that our suffering became almost intolerable. Several men were sunstruck and carried off." Nevertheless, at the 10:00 A.M. signal, Boomer led his troops forward up the hill, but at the crest the regiments were greeted by a devastating fire. Colonel Holden Putnam of the 93rd Illinois wrote that they were "met by a terrible storm of grape, canister, and musketry." H. M. Trimble of the same regiment jotted in his diary that the men "moved as soon as we had orders to the brow of the last hill between us and the rebel works. As we went up the rebels showered bullets among us like hail." It was worse for two companies of the 5th Iowa that mistakenly went too far over the hill and had to tumble back. Boomer could now see in daylight the exact ground he had to cover. It was "almost impassable from gullies, covered by a heavy abatis of fallen trees, underbrush, vines, &c., the whole position enfiladed by the guns of the enemy." Boomer did not like what he saw and ordered his men to hit the ground.[35]

While most of the brigade lay still under the burning sun, some in the rear were having their own problems. Samuel Byers was tasked with providing ammunition for his 5th Iowa, and the colonel ordered him to strap two ammunition boxes on a mule and follow the front line. Byers led the ornery creature forward while another swatted him with a bush on the back side to make him move forward. When the mule came under fire crossing a ridge, several bullets hit the boxes on his back. He dug in and refused to move on: "He braced himself, held his ears back, and stood stock still." The men tried to push, pull, and beat the mule but nothing worked until the bridle came loose and the two Iowans decided they had better head for cover. Byers went down into the ravine in front, to which the mule now raced, "right where he was wanted." Byers could not help but "laugh . . . to see the antics of that animal's ears as the bullets whizzed past him."[36]

Similarly, Lyman Baker of the 93rd Illinois was put in the rear of his regiment as it marched toward the assault in columns of fours. The regiment moved across the bullet-swept ridge and into the protection of the valley, where it formed a line of battle. Only one man was missing, and Colonel Putnam sent Baker back to the rear to find him. "Baker, bring him back or kill him," the colonel yelled. Baker went to the rear and searched the camp and hospital but could never find the missing man. When he returned, he could not find his regiment either, which had moved forward. Under fire, he took position behind a giant stump, where he felt alone in the world: "I never felt so bad in my life as I did behind that stump," he recalled. "I might be killed or wounded away from my regiment or perhaps I could not find my regiment. Disgrace and dishonor looked me in the face." Fortunately, he soon saw another regiment on the move and recognized it. Following it, he eventually caught up with his own unit and took position under the broiling sun, at one point waking up to find his friend pouring water on his face. That act "saved me from a heatstroke," Baker recalled.[37]

At the same time, Sanborn led his troops forward on Boomer's left, the 59th Indiana at times supporting and operating with Boomer's troops. Sanborn also took advantage of the cover of the ground and positioned the troops within a hundred yards of the Confederate line. Then the plan hit a snag. Sanborn related that "Colonel Boomer had some doubts as to his ability to carry the works in his front," as evidenced by the brigade being halted and put under as much cover as possible. This put Sanborn in a quandary. He could not go on alone: "As the works left in my front could not be held, if carried, while those on my right were in possession of the enemy," Sanborn went to Boomer to decide what to do.[38]

Evidently, Boomer did not think he had enough power to take the works, so Sanborn offered to aid his brigade. He sent out the 18th Wisconsin as skirmishers "along our whole front" and likewise sent the 59th Indiana to Boomer to increase his potential for carrying the works. That act evidently did not satisfy Boomer. Sanborn wrote that after they agreed on the plan to renew the attack he went back to his brigade and issued orders for the regimental commanders to "advance upon the works immediately upon the movement commencing on our right." Whether Sanborn hedged his advance on Boomer's movement is not certain, but Sanborn reported that "for some reason the troops on our right did not move, and I retained the same position with some loss." Lieutenant Colonel John E. Tourtellotte of the 4th Minnesota was in a similar quandary, writing that his unit was "ordered to charge upon one of the enemy's forts just in front as soon as I should see a charge made upon the fort next on my right." It never happened.[39]

Boomer did not like what he saw and refused to move forward, still some one hundred yards from the Confederate line. It saved lives, but "we had to keep close to the ground to hide from rebel bullets," H. M. Trimble wrote in his diary, adding that "it was very hot, and the hill layed toward the sun." In fact, one Iowan declared that much of the brigade never even went into line: "The ground was such that we could not form in line, we were to move forward in column of divisions until such time as we could find suitable ground to form line. As we did not move forward we did not form line." An Indianan noted that they merely lay on the sunny side of the ridge, barely under cover: "[We] placed the butts of our guns and our canteens of water, in front of our heads, as a shield from minnie balls." Boomer's lack of movement of course erased any chance of Sanborn moving forward or Holmes's troops to the rear moving up in support. That reserve brigade had merely moved across one of the elevated ridges "swept by the fire from the rebel forts and sharpshooters" and stood under orders to "repel any attack which the besieged might make, should the assault prove unsuccessful." Nothing of the sort occurred on either side, but casualties still mounted as the troops held the ridge under the heavy Confederate fire. As a result, Quinby's veteran division made no further advance that morning and well into the afternoon. One Indianan in Sanborn's brigade simply wrote home, "We were remarkably fortunate in the morning."[40]

Adam Badeau, one of Grant's earliest biographers, took a different slant. He wrote that "no great effort was made by them" and added "at this time, they were simply useful from the menacing attitude they held." It seems Quinby—oddly silent about his actions and whereabouts for these critical hours—had squandered an entire division's potential. One might also ask: Where was James B. McPherson?[41]

Although Ransom on the far right and Quinby's brigades on the far left of McPherson's corps took little part in the 10:00 A.M. assault, the same could not be said of John Logan's brigades. His was a fighting division of veterans, and it was led by this aggressive politician-general who made sure his brigades went forward at the right time much like Frank Blair, another politician-general who made the 10:00 A.M. start time. Maybe there was something to these politicians playing war.[42]

There was never any doubt whether John Logan was a fighter, either on the floor of Congress or on the battlefield. He had entered the army early and had been through some of the most horrific fighting of the war. Wounded terribly at Fort Donelson, he missed Shiloh but had been with the army throughout the following actions, including the heavy fighting at Port Gibson and Champion Hill. At one point on May 16, Grant had told a staff officer, "Go down to Logan and tell him he is making history to-day."[43]

Logan's brigade commanders were fighters too, including John E. Smith. His brigade was tapped to drive along the Jackson Road and assault to the north in the space between the road and Glass Bayou. Smith was a highly opinionated officer who was born in Switzerland, the son of one of Napoleon's officers who had fought at Waterloo. He had come to America as a child, and being from Galena, Illinois, actually played a role in bringing Grant back into the army. More significant, Smith was not always a Grant fan despite Grant being one of his. At one point, Smith labeled Grant a "Drunken Cuss"; yet Grant repeatedly requested (once to Lincoln himself) Smith's promotion to brigadier general for "worthiness on the *battle field* and in the *Camp of instruction.*" Charles Dana described him as having "a firmness of character, a steadiness of hand, and a freedom from personal irritability and jealousy."[44]

Smith had already reconnoitered the ground ahead of him since his arrival on May 19. When Logan sent Engineer Stewart R. Tresilian forward to look over the ground, he found Smith already there "taking a sketch of the enemy's position." In Smith's brigade were four Illinois regiments and one Indiana unit: the 20th, 31st, 45th, and 124th Illinois and 23rd Indiana. Smith had been the former colonel of the 45th Illinois, also known as the "Lead Mine Regiment" because of the lead-mining industry around its Galena area of origination. Division commander John Logan was the original commander of the 31st Illinois. All but the 124th Illinois were veterans of Shiloh and some were at Fort Donelson, the Indianans having been in Lew Wallace's division.[45]

Smith's force was ready at 10:00 A.M., unlike other units in his corps, and he moved his regiments forward precisely at a quarter past ten when, he said, "the batteries had ceased firing." He had moved forward to within three hundred yards of the enemy line and, with more reconnaissance from Engineer Tresilian, prepared his troops with orders "to move in quick time with fixed bayonets, and not to fire until the enemy's works were reached." In the 45th

Illinois, the brigade adjutant started a speech: "Now, boys, you must do your duty, just as you always," but he was cut short by a ball in the thigh. The major of the regiment finished: "Let every man stand to his post." Behind them was massed the pioneer corps "ready, in case we succeeded in the assault, to advance immediately and open a way for the artillery."[46]

Reaching those works, especially the redan occupied by the 3rd Louisiana, would be more problematic than even Smith realized after a thorough reconnaissance. According to orders from Grant himself, Smith ordered that the lead regiments—the 23rd Indiana followed by the 20th Illinois—should move by the right flank down the road itself toward the Confederate works before fanning out to the right and assaulting in linear formation when they were within a hundred yards of the enemy line: "I ordered the Twenty-third Indiana and Twentieth Illinois to move down," Smith reported, "under cover of the wood, by the flank, and, when the salient of Fort Hill was reached, to file to the right, under the dead space of the parapet, this seeming to be the most practicable way of reaching the rifle-pits." In the Indiana ranks, Lieutenant Colonel William P. Davis noted that his orders were to join "in a charge upon the enemy's works, which lay upon the Vicksburg road and about 300 yards from us."[47]

Dutifully, the Indianans surged forward in a long, snake-like line, ever closing on the Confederate position, which was now heavy with fire from the 3rd Louisiana and adjacent regiments. The Indianans had moved forward before, having acted as skirmishers, and Lieutenant Henry C. Foster fought with particular bravery and skill. Brigade commander Smith noted that "many of the rebels are indebted to him for their final account." The Indianans were covered for some of the way, but soon they broke into the open on the exposed ridgetop. They nevertheless reached their designated deployment area east of the redan and its works to the north, where Lieutenant Colonel Davis turned the head of the column to the right and moved it far enough for the entire regiment, upon facing to the left, to be deployed in a line. Davis marched his command into the ravines created by the branches of Glass Bayou "till my left was clear of the road." It was from here that the Indianans were to move forward.[48]

It was also here that the plan became unhinged. Instead of being at the very base of the Confederate works, the troops found that there was harsh terrain still to the front. Smith himself described how "a deep ravine was revealed in their front, covered with a heavy abatis." Davis gave more detail, writing that "filing to the right, we were obliged to pass over a ridge of ground which brought us in full view of the enemy's rifle-pits, from which a murderous fire was opened upon us." One of the casualties was the captain of the lead company, thus momentarily causing a loss of cohesion. The Indianans kept their line anyway but soon found this was a terrible decision. Smith reported that "they were exposed to a galling fire, which they were not permitted to return." Smith's troops were finding the ravines of the feeder branches of Glass Bayou just as problematic south of the stream as Ransom and Blair had found them north of it.[49]

Lieutenant Colonel Davis had to do something quickly, so he moved the regiment forward by the right flank, where he "obtained shelter from the enemy's fire in a shallow ravine, which ran parallel to the road." Davis moved the regiment forward under the cover, but the right soon became exposed to enemy fire as the ravine played out approaching the high ground on which the Confederate works sat: "Our right became again exposed to the fire from the rifle-pits, and also to a fire from a battery which was posted upon our right." Davis quickly halted the regiment and sent word to Smith of his predicament.[50]

The effect was instant: the Louisianans doubled down on their fire, and the steady cadence of the Mississippi, Alabama, and Arkansas gunners manning the cannons along the road and inside the redan created havoc in the Federal ranks. As the Indianans "sheltered themselves by the inequalities of the ground," Smith had to make some fast decisions. The stoppage, as bad as it was for the Indianans, also had an effect on other regiments of the brigade, namely the following 20th Illinois. Taking the same route in flank formation, the Illinoisans quickly realized that they would not be able to deploy with the Indianans, and even if they had it would have been useless because the terrain was just so formidable. Smith took decisive control and quickly ordered the Illinoisans back to the road and a few minutes of safety, although the head of the column soon plunged onward toward the redan with orders this time to file off to the left of the road. It was at this spot that a Union artillery round burst immediately upon exiting the breach, killing and wounding several Illinoisans in what they called a "rotten shell." Smith nevertheless told Major Daniel Bradley to "proceed on the road and gain the curtain of the left salient on our front."[51]

The 20th Illinois plunged ahead beneath the steady volleys of the Louisianans defending their redan. Ultimately, the Illinoisans made it to the parapet fronting the work, Smith noting that "this point was gained under a heavy fire from the enemy." Ira Blanchard of the Illinois regiment noted that the troops made "a rush for the base of the fort on a dead run amid a shower of lead that was hurled down upon us." The Illinoisans deployed in line but could go no farther. Smith explained that the "parapet was too high, and the effort was ineffectual."[52]

By this point—mere minutes into the fight—Smith knew that the attack had failed. He certainly was not going to send in the rest of the Illinois regiments; that would only add to the confusion and butchery. At least one regiment, the 124th Illinois, reported simply supporting the 12th Wisconsin Battery near a fine stand of pear and peach trees, from which position they could see all over the field, particularly all the way north to the Stockade Redan and Blair's division. Closer to the fighting, Smith took steps to aid his beleaguered regiments facing the Confederates. One Federal noted that although behind "a little ridge, . . . it was instant death to show even the top of the head above the intrenchments." Smith ordered his Illinoisans on the left to fall back to the cover of a ridge and to hold their position. At the same time, he sent word to the Indianans on the right to fall back in small groups. Davis was to recall his regiment "by company, it being extremely hazardous to return in regular order of regiment." Davis sent the companies to the rear one by one and soon had another line formed under cover, ready for action once more.[53]

As the 20th Illinois huddled beneath the fire from the Confederate fort, the famished troops were overjoyed to see their former slave camp follower, "Black Ben," struggling over the ridges toward them, laden with a camp kettle of coffee and bags of hardtack. But the delight only lasted so long as the full knowledge of what they had done and the fix they were in had sunk in. Smith summed up his decision to partially withdraw by stating that "the assault had failed, not for want of support but the impossibility of getting over the obstructions on the right of Fort Hill, and the ditch and parapet in front on the road being too high, which would have kept the men so long under fire that they would have inevitably been sacrificed without accomplishing the object."[54]

Smith's attempt had failed amazingly quickly; the fiery Logan could only hope that Stevenson's brigade to the left was doing better.

Logan's other brigade on the front line was just as veteran, led by a tough officer who took an odd a path to Vicksburg. John D. Stevenson was a native Virginian who had studied in South Carolina. He practiced law in Virginia before moving to Missouri, where he became involved in the Mexican War and then served in the legislature. When the Civil War erupted, he recruited a regiment and then became a brigadier general. Like Smith, for this assault Stevenson scouted ahead near a cotton gin, looking over the Confederate defenses. He probably did not like what he saw and no doubt made it known. Charles Dana described him as a "grumbler," but there was also some grumbling in his ranks; Stevenson "got lost for some time from us" at Raymond ten days previously, and word had slowly sifted down through the ranks. The response from Colonel James J. Dollins of the 81st Illinois had also filtered down. When Stevenson sent a staff officer to find the brigade, and the staffer told Colonel Dollins what had happened, Dollins replied, "Go back and tell Gen Stevenson that in battle if he wants to find the 81st to always go to the front."[55]

Stevenson's own 7th Missouri was the core of the brigade, being full of Irish immigrants in comparison to all the German regiments Missouri was producing. It soon became known as the "Irish Seventh" and carried a green flag adorned with golden harps and shamrocks. The three Illinois regiments of the brigade were also mostly veteran units of the western campaigns, the 8th, 17th, and 81st Illinois. The 32nd Ohio, for its part, had originally fought early in the war in western Virginia and then in the Valley Campaign before being one of the regiments surrendered at Harpers Ferry during the Antietam operation. Once exchanged and sent west, they were initially disliked and labeled "Harpers Ferry Cowards" by Grant's troops. The cajoling "caused many a fisticuff, and many an offender to wear a decorated eye or sore head," one of the Ohioans recalled.[56]

Stevenson's brigade was thus probably the most unique unit in the army: a southern commander with an Irish, an eastern, and an assortment of veteran and nonveteran Illinois regiments thrown in for good measure. But it was dependable, and Stevenson planned his attack well, intending to break the Confederate line south of the Jackson Road. Significantly, he faced the strongest Confederate fortifications at Vicksburg: the Great Redoubt. Fortunately for him, opposing it was Captain Samuel De Golyer's 8th Michigan Battery, one of the most powerful Union batteries in the army.[57]

Stevenson saw no use in attacking by the flank as Ewing had done on Sherman's front and as John E. Smith had done on the Jackson Road. Both of those attacks had been made on roads—the Graveyard Road and the Jackson Road, which separated the major watersheds in the area. Stevenson had no such roadways in his front and opted, therefore, to use different tactics. He formed his brigade into two columns of regiments, with orders to "have one days rations in our haversacks and our canteens filled."[58]

Stevenson took to heart his orders to "charge on the enemy's works . . . with loaded muskets and fixed bayonets, no shot to be fired until a foothold was obtained in the works of the enemy." He reconnoitered the front and realized he could move up under cover of the ravines to within about two hundred yards of the enemy works, but there he would have to cross a low valley that would be under fire the whole way. What was at the top of the opposite ridge was also worrisome, Stevenson calling it "Fort Hill," or what he described as "the strongest work of the enemy." Still, Stevenson was confident, and he distributed several scaling ladders the troops had built the night before to the heads of the columns for use when the brigade reached the top. Engineer Tresilian had fashioned the ladders from boards taken from a nearby cotton gin and "the Sherman Hospital," creating "forty scaling-ladders, varying in length from 16 to 22 feet, light enough for one man to carry, and strong enough to support two men, when used in a horizontal position, across a 10-foot ditch." The pioneer corps workers attached ropes to one end of each of the ladders to allow the troops to drag them so that "the enemy could not perceive them until the assault was made."[59]

First deployed was the 17th Illinois, which had just joined the division on May 18 while at the Big Black River. The regiment had first been assigned to John E. Smith's brigade. When the Illinoisans arrived, Smith told Major Frank F. Peats that "he had more men than he could use on his part of the line." The regiment then went the next day to Logan himself, who positioned it as skirmishers in front of the entire division. There, they stayed until the assaults on May 22.[60]

The Illinoisans took a position on the ridge east of the Great Redoubt, "as near the works of the enemy as possible" in order to cover the rest of the brigade as they advanced. Behind the ridge just two hundred yards from the Confederate line, but in total safety, Stevenson formed his two columns. On the right was his own 7th Missouri in front with the 81st Illinois in support. On the left was the 8th Illinois with the 32nd Ohio in support, they moving through a thick "cane brake." By 10:00 A.M. the brigade was drawn up in formation with orders "not to fire a shot until we reached the works." At that point the ladders were distributed, one 8th Illinoisan remembering that his regiment was given seventeen of them. Now, all that was needed was word from Stevenson to plunge ahead.[61]

Because Stevenson commanded the brigade and the regiment's other field officers were not present, command of the 7th Missouri fell to Captain Robert Buchannan. He marched the regiment nearly to the top of the hill from which they would begin the charge and ordered the men to load guns and fix bayonets. Then he called the company commanders together and told them what would happen. Gazing forward toward the Great Redoubt, also termed the "Black Fort" by the Federals, Buchannan "pointed out the place where the center of the regiment would rest when we reached the fort." After sending the captains back to their companies, Buchannan also personally briefed the color-bearer, telling him to plant the green flag at a specific angle of the fort "where the *big gun* was pointing toward us."[62]

Word came at 10:00 A.M. ("precisely," Stevenson noted), indicating perhaps he did not wait the few minutes for the artillery to cease firing as John E.

Smith did to the right on the Jackson Road. Rather, Stevenson quickly moved his troops forward over the top of the shielding ridge past the skirmish-deployed 17th Illinois and down into the valley between it and the steep hill on which the Great Redoubt sat. Both columns pushed off at the same time, but the Confederates were ready; Stevenson reported how very soon "volley after volley was poured upon them." Federals in George Boomer's stalled brigade to Stevenson's left were dumfounded as they watched: "Thus far we knew nothing of the meaning of our move," John Q. A. Campbell jotted in his diary, "but the riddle was soon solved by Stevenson's brigade of Logan's division coming up and passing us with twenty or thirty ladders. There was no mistaking this sign. The rebel works were to be stormed."[63]

One of Stevenson's Illinoisans described the pageantry:

> From the moment our company passed over the ridge immediately in front of the line of Confederate works, we advanced without cover, as all timber had been cut down and the face of the ridge and ravine at the foot and the ascending slope, thence to the Confederate works, was cleared of logs and brush, thus making us the fairest target possible for our Southern brothers to shoot at, and you can imagine that they made it so interesting for us that we had no time to look up the other Companies or regiments.

Indeed, the watching Confederates of the 21st Louisiana within the Great Redoubt, reinforced on their left by half of the 29th Louisiana, were amazed at the pageantry across the wide expanse. Confederate division commander John Forney was himself there, watching the show. He quickly picked up on the nationality of the troops leading Stevenson's attack, writing that "the troops making the assault were apparently of the Irish nation, as they carried the green flag, with golden harp and border, of that people." He also described how they "advanced in platoon front, with scaling ladders."[64]

Because of the lay of the land, the right column emerged first and took the brunt of the Louisianan's fire, including from the two still-firing cannons in the redoubts. A watching Federal described how "no rebels were to be seen until our force had approached close up to the rebel works, when their breastworks and forts swarmed with butternuts, who poured volley after volley into our advancing column." Captain Buchannan, leading the 7th Missouri, took so much heavy fire that the head of the column, the right wing, inadvertently veered to the left in natural response to the Confederate fire coming on the right. Buchannan wrote that "the firing was so severe that it cut my Regiment in two at the colors." The left wing sought shelter in a nearby ravine until Buchannan, who was with the right wing and ordered it to the ground, ran across the deadly slope and ordered it forward to the right. Once reunited, the

Missourians continued forward. Thus, a proud Stevenson noted that his old regiment pushed onward, "not stopping the steady advance, until the head of the column rested upon the ditch of the work." Somehow, the Missourians had made it up the hill amid the destructive fire, although they were yet to reach the ditch, much less the parapet itself. The 81st Illinois followed the Missourians, also under a heavy fire, Lieutenant Colonel Franklin Campbell recalling that they deployed and moved "in shot-range of the enemy's guns, and within full view of the enemy behind his intrenchments." One of his foot soldiers, Logan H. Roots, called the area the "slaughter pen."[65]

The conspicuous green flag of the 7th Missouri made a vivid showing during the assault, and numerous Louisianans used it as their target despite one of the Louisiana regiments defending the Great Redoubt being an Irish outfit itself from New Orleans that carried its own green flag. The result was a series of bearers shot down one after another, Captain Buchannan writing that "we lost seven color bearers before we reached the ditch." The original guard having been eradicated, at one point Private John B. Kelley of the intertwined 81st Illinois grabbed the flag and moved forward. Stevenson noted his bravery: "Seeing the flag go down, he instantly raised it to its place, to be himself instantly shot down." A couple of officers of the 7th Missouri then grabbed the standard. Lieutenant Robert Porter, "holding and waving the flag aloft," was shot down immediately upon grabbing it. Lieutenant Joshua W. Bourne ultimately carried it all the way to the face of the ditch.[66]

Despite the bravery of the Missourians, Stevenson had a problem on his hands. The 7th Missouri had veered to the left so far that it crossed in front of the path of the left column. That force, with Lieutenant Colonel Robert H. Sturgess leading his 8th Illinois, had not made as good time, and in fact the Illinoisans watched as the Missourians were "almost annihilated." In fact, the Illinoisans managed to reach only a small ridge by the time the Missourians had made it to the ditch, prompting Stevenson, in the middle of the chaos, to order the Missourians to form a line and the left column to halt and take cover, forming as a reserve for the veering right wing. George Durfee of the 8th Illinois remembered that his regiment stopped, but "the 81st Ills and 7th Mo went farther and suffered severely." To add more weight to the left wing, Stevenson ordered Colonel James J. Dollins to lead his 81st Illinois across the rear of the 7th Missouri and to take position in line on their left at the base of the parapet and ditch. The Illinoisans had followed "the gallant old Seventh Missouri," Lieutenant Colonel Campbell reported, and Dollins did so, bringing the two regiments, somewhat jumbled, to the face of the Great Redoubt. But it resulted in heavy casualties. Stevenson recounted that "this evolution we performed under a very destructive fire of both small-arms and field pieces, involving the loss of a large number of men." To cover them somewhat, he ordered the Missourians and Illinoisans up ahead to lie down and outwait the enemy fire, which soon slackened but did not stop. The fact that their own artillery in the rear soon opened up once more also helped the feelings of those sticking out before the parapet of the Great Redoubt.[67]

As might be expected, the destruction was awful, one 81st Illinoisan, Edwin Woolsey, writing his wife how "every man to my right for over 10 yards in both ranks was shot, leaving me almost alone there while thousands of rebels were pouring in deadly volleys in our ranks and batteries threw bushels of grape and canester shot and shells at us from each flank." Woolsey reported that two spent balls hit him but he was not hurt: "I expected to be shot every moment, but am not shot yet." He argued that the Illinois regiment "suffered a great deal more than any other regiment, and our company more than any other company." Although he was perhaps exaggerating, he did have numbers to prove the ordeal in his company: five killed, twenty-two wounded, and only thirteen unhurt. Captain John P. Reese of the 81st Illinois agreed, writing that the massacre was awful: "There was not a twig between us and the fort." He lamented how "if we had been allowed to fire we could of saved ourselves a little."[68]

As the Confederate fire slackened and the men caught their breaths, Stevenson ordered the final surge "up and forward" into the ditch and hopefully over the parapet and into Vicksburg's works. The Missourians and Illinoisans responded with "loud cheers and great vigor," Stevenson proudly related, but the Confederates responded as well. Artillery had been firing all along, but the cannoneers redoubled their efforts and "opened with grape and canister, literally sweeping down officers and men." The infantry behind the parapets also opened up once more, and scores if not hundreds of Federals began to fall. Still, the Missourians and Illinoisans in the first wave surged ahead. "They carried the ladders right to the walls and ditch," one Illinoisan farther down the hill wrote of the Missourians, "but there they laid them down or their carriers were shot." At the same time, Lieutenant Bourne managed to plant the emerald flag of the Irish 7th Missouri on the parapet of the Great Redoubt.[69]

Into the chaos also came the skirmishing 17th Illinois, portions of which crept forward after the columns passed and a few of whom entered the ditch as well. Sergeant Francis M. Smith remembered that "the place of greatest security was so close under the Confederate works that the charges of grape and cannister from the Confederate battery passed over us and tore the ground up behind or back of us." It was also the position, Smith asserted, from which "we were able to drive the artillery men from their guns, actually silencing this battery." In fact, the Illinoisans were so close that they captured three or four Confederates. Sergeant Smith, being alone with another sergeant in command of the company because the captain and a lieutenant had stayed back behind the first ridge, sent those captured to the rear with a private, Smith telling him to "cover himself with them."[70]

Yet at the Confederate parapet, like so many Federals before, Stevenson's men were forced to halt. The Louisiana infantry and Arkansas and Louisiana gunners laid down such a devastating fire that the Union column slowed because it was greatly thinned. The Missourians who were left poured into the ditch and began to plant their ladders, but Stevenson angrily noted that they "were found unserviceable." The Confederate brigade commander defending the redoubt went so far as to note that "at the redan of the Twenty-first Louisiana, a few scaling-ladders reached the outer ditch, but were not planted." The Illinoisans to the left were not even doing that well, taking awful numbers of casualties among both men and officers, including the regimental adjutant and Major Cornelius S. Ward. Most notably, Colonel Dollins himself was killed. One of his Illinoisans was not very talkative later when he recounted everything to his diary, including Dollins's death: "The charge was made but on nearing the fort we was obliged to fall back. The horrible seens our Regt. cut all to pieces. Our colonel killed. A great loss on our side. I was sunstruck." With Dollins's death—falling a mere rod or two from the earthworks—the Illinoisans could no longer stand the fire and melted rearward from the ditch "in much confusion," Stevenson explained. Lieutenant Colonel Campbell, who took command, reported that the regiment held "until the fire became too galling to bear."[71]

Because of such confusion, Stevenson's line began to break. Before his death, Colonel Dollins had given the command to "about-face and march around a point under the protection of the hill," but the regiment did not totally hold together. That left Stevenson's Missourians alone facing the parapet, and he knew by this point, like many others, that the assault had failed. "Finding the Seventh Missouri had sustained equally as heavy loss, and, from the strength of the work, that it was not possible to make a successful assault in the face of the work," Stevenson sadly related that he ordered his bloody regiments back from their precarious position. "I ordered the officers of the Seventh Missouri and Eighty-first Illinois to retire with the remnants of their commands to the rear and reform them," he explained, which they did, the Missourians behind the now reformed left wing that had taken position on the nearest ridge to the Confederate works and the Illinoisans all the way back at their camps. The 8th Illinois and 32nd Ohio covered their comrades as they fell back down the steep slope and through their ranks, as did the skirmishers of the 17th Illinois: "The Seventeenth Illinois Volunteers and their officers are entitled to special mention for the prompt manner in which they occupied the ground assigned to them, and the efficient services rendered in protecting their comrades in the advances and especially for the hot fire poured into the enemy as the column retired."[72]

Getting out was no easier than getting in, and although the brigade was under orders not to fire during the assault, Captain Buchannan of the 7th Missouri ordered his regiment to open fire once the order to retire came "in order to protect my men," he said. And they needed support to protect them, as the Union artillery had ceased firing because the troops were so near the Confederate line. In fact, Captain Buchannan reported that several shots fell short of the works while they were attacking and "tore up the ground in front of my line." With the artillery ceasing fire, Buchannan reported, "the enemy became emboldened and raised up in the forts, so that we could see their bodies to their waists." Buchannan thus had to combat the increasing fire, and while doing so he alternatingly withdrew a wing of his regiment while the other kept up a hot fire.[73]

Sergeant Smith of the 17th Illinois was still miffed at his captain during the retreat, he hearing the officer call from behind his ridge, "Company C. In retreat. March." Smith became so mad that he stood up amid the bullets and yelled, "If you are in command of this Company, come over here." Smith then ordered the men not to obey but rather to separate and get out "as best they could." Smith left with the last man and made it over the ridge "though shot fairly rained about us." Once safe, he went straight to his captain: "I went up to my Captain and called him a coward and said he was a disgrace to the uniform he wore." The captain threatened to court-martial him but instead resigned his commission. Smith later claimed to have had a general officer on his side. He related that Isaac Quinby heard the exchange and told Smith, "Sergeant, I cannot blame you, for your Company was in a terrible place, and I was waiting anxiously for the order to go forward to your support." Smith thought the lack of support for Stevenson created the defeat. If such were true, the failure lay higher up than just Quinby, perhaps on the shoulders of the corps commander, James B. McPherson.[74]

The common soldiers did their best amid the blunders of the officers. Captain John P. Reese wanted everyone to know about their bravery. He wrote his wife of a member of his company, Burt Morris, who found a log during the retreat and began to pepper the enemy with his fire. "He loaded and shot as deliberately as if he was shooting squirrels," Reese wrote home. "They were trying to hit his head all the time," the captain added, but "Burt said he could hit them at the waist every time he shot." Captain Reese concluded that "he is the most dauntless boy I ever saw," and admitted to his wife: "I should not of said so much for him but the papers will puff up the big officers and never say a word about the bravery of the privates."[75]

Other members of the 17th Illinois likewise had close calls. George Smith, writing of his experience as a skirmisher, told how friends fell to his left and right, many of whom experienced the premonition of death the night before when news of the assault filtered down. Smith himself had the same feeling but "prayed to God and promised him that if spared I would serve Him the rest of my life." Smith was spared, but not others. Of one in particular he fretted that "as far as I know he went unprepared." And Smith himself almost did not make it. He was skirmishing heavily, having just taken the place of one of his killed comrades when the order to move to the rear for replacement by a different company arrived. He was the only one who did not hear it, and the captain had to send a man to get him. The man "took hold of me and told me that the captain wanted to see me." Another man took his position and was almost instantaneously killed.[76]

John D. Stevenson had given it his best and expressed only praise for his men: "This assault, though unsuccessful, demonstrated that the command possessed the most reliable characteristics of soldiers, implicit obedience to orders, undaunted courage, and great endurance. Not a gun was fired during the entire assault, although the most earnest appeals were made to the commanding general to do so, and when at length the command was ordered to retire, the men did so under the control and direction of their officers." It just was not enough. This brigade lost 272 officers and men total, with 34 killed and 238 wounded. John Forney, watching from the Confederate works, knew it had been bloody, later writing that "the enemy's loss was very heavy, and ours also was quite severe, particularly among the cannoneers." The Great Redoubt had its name for a reason, and it stood defiantly against the assaults of one of the best brigades in the Army of the Tennessee.[77]

In the end, McPherson's attempts to breach the Confederate lines during the 10:00 A.M. assault had gone no better than Sherman's. Still, McPherson managed to get more troops engaged compared to his counterpart, although only two of his five frontline brigades—Smith's and Stevenson's—had in fact made an assault. McPherson was encountering the same problems as Sherman: the difficulty of even getting the brigades situated in the right places to assault and then for those who had managed to attack to overcome the terrain and the natural and artificial impediments. The heavy fire of the determined defenders had been a factor as well, these defenders along the Jackson Road having missed the mauling at Champion Hill and Big Black River Bridge.

Putting it all together, McPherson—like Sherman to his right—was hard-pressed to see how any assault would work. That left the chances of success in McClernand's hands. Not exactly the situation Grant had hoped for.

Ulysses S. Grant—Convinced that the Confederates would put up little resistance, Ulysses S. Grant assaulted Vicksburg twice. The smaller May 19 attack was rushed and isolated, while the May 22 assault was better-planned and -prepared. Both failed. Courtesy of Library of Congress.

John A. McClernand—As the ranking corps commander under Grant, John A. McClernand led the XIII Corps and voiced concerns over an assault. Nevertheless, his corps fought the hardest of any of the three. His claims of progress and calls for a renewed afternoon attack on May 22 were a major source of controversy leading to higher casualties and a fatal split with Grant. Courtesy of Library of Congress.

Eugene A. Carr—Division commander Eugene A. Carr led McClernand's attacks on the 2nd Texas Lunette and the Railroad Redoubt on May 22. His partial entrance into the Railroad Redoubt caused McClernand to call for renewed attacks by the other corps. Courtesy of Library of Congress.

William P. Benton—Brigade commander William P. Benton led his regiments against the 2nd Texas Lunette on the Baldwin's Ferry Road. Though bravely made, the assault failed. Courtesy of Francis Trevelyan Miller, *The Photographic History of the Civil War in Ten Volumes*, 1912.

Michael K. Lawler—Flush with victory at Big Black River Bridge on May 17, Michael K. Lawler's regiments tried to provide the same success on May 22. A few troops entered the tip of the Railroad Redoubt, but they could not make any more progress. Courtesy of Miller's *Photographic History*.

Peter J. Osterhaus—A German by birth, division commander Peter J. Osterhaus sent his two brigades against the Square Fort area of the Confederate lines on May 22. None of his troops had any success, and most huddled in front of the Confederate fortifications until nightfall. Courtesy of Library of Congress.

Albert L. Lee—Acting as John A. McClernand's chief of staff, Albert L. Lee took command of one of Peter Osterhaus's brigades on the morning of May 19. He was promptly wounded in the face and neck. Courtesy of Library of Congress.

Andrew Jackson Smith—A cantankerous regular army officer, Andrew Jackson Smith had trouble getting along with his subordinates. He nevertheless supported Carr's assaults on the 2nd Texas Lunette and the Railroad Redoubt. Courtesy of Library of Congress.

Stephen G. Burbridge—One of A. J. Smith's brigade commanders who had personal problems with his division commander, Stephen G. Burbridge supported William P. Benton's attack at the 2nd Texas Lunette. Courtesy of Miller's *Photographic History*.

William T. Sherman—Grant's friend William T. Sherman commanded the XV Corps and launched assaults on both May 19 and 22. It was his corps that sent forward the famous "forlorn hope" against the Stockade Redan. Courtesy of Library of Congress.

Francis P. Blair, Jr.—Politician-general Francis P. Blair commanded one of William T. Sherman's divisions. His was the only division to fully assault Vicksburg on both May 19 and 22, his attacks coming against the strong Stockade Redan. He later served as a United States senator. Courtesy of Library of Congress.

Giles A. Smith—Giles A. Smith commanded a brigade in Blair's division and assaulted through the steep ravines on both May 19 and 22. Both attacks near the Stockade Redan failed, although portions of his brigade made it to the ditches in front of the Confederate fortifications. Courtesy of Library of Congress.

Hugh Ewing—Sherman's brother-in-law, Hugh Ewing commanded a brigade of easterners in Blair's division. He attacked the north side of the Stockade Redan on May 19 and then supported the "forlorn hope" on May 22, only to be turned back by Confederate fire. Courtesy of Library of Congress.

Frederick Steele—Frederick Steele was Sherman's senior division commander and held the Federal line from the Mississippi River eastward. His troops managed to assault late on May 22, but they failed to break the Confederate line across Mint Spring Bayou. Courtesy of Library of Congress.

John M. Thayer—Nebraskan John M. Thayer commanded a brigade in Sherman's corps and led an assault over terrible terrain against Vicksburg's northern defenses. Although some in his regiments made it to the ditches fronting the Confederate works, the Confederate line held. Thayer later served as governor of Nebraska and as a United States senator. Courtesy of Library of Congress.

Joseph A. Mower—A brigade commander in James Tuttle's division, Joseph A. Mower led Sherman's renewed assault on the afternoon of May 22. He followed the exact path of the "forlorn hope," with the same results. Courtesy of Library of Congress.

James B. McPherson—Grant protégé James B. McPherson commanded the XVII Corps. His troops assaulted the 3rd Louisiana Redan and Great Redoubt along the Jackson Road. Courtesy of Library of Congress.

John McArthur—Detached to the south of Vicksburg, John McArthur had one brigade with him and likely could have punctured the Confederate lines had he not been called to the right by McClernand. Courtesy of Library of Congress.

Thomas E. G. Ransom—The only brigade of John McArthur's division on the front lines with McPherson's corps, Thomas E. G. Ransom was on his own. He showed aggressiveness in advancing on May 19 and 22. Courtesy of Library of Congress.

John A. Logan—Politician-general John A. Logan led one of McPherson's divisions. His troops assaulted the 3rd Louisiana Redan and Great Redoubt along the Jackson Road. He later served as a United States senator. Courtesy of Library of Congress.

John E. Smith—Brigade commander John E. Smith led one of Logan's brigades and twice assaulted the 3rd Louisiana Redan on May 22. Both advances failed, although Federal troops reached the base of the Confederate fortifications. Courtesy of Miller's *Photographic History*.

John D. Stevenson—A Southerner, John D. Stevenson made one of the most vicious assaults at Vicksburg. His brigade withstood heavy fire in an assault against the Great Redoubt. Although his troops reached the ditch in front of the fortifications, Stevenson could not break the Confederate lines. Courtesy of Miller's *Photographic History*.

John B. Sanborn—A cautious brigade commander in McPherson's corps, John B. Sanborn did not assault on the morning of May 22 and then reinforced McClernand's corps to the south that afternoon. His advance toward the 2nd Texas Lunette failed to break the Confederate line. Courtesy of Miller's *Photographic History*.

George B. Boomer—George B. Boomer commanded a brigade in McPherson's corps and refused to assault on the morning of May 22. He moved to the left with the rest of Isaac F. Quinby's division and advanced on the 2nd Texas Lunette. He was killed in the attack. Courtesy of Mary Amelia (Boomer) Stone, *Memoir of George Boardman Boomer*, 1864.

John C. Pemberton—Caught between orders from his theater commander and the Confederate president, John C. Pemberton chose to defend Vicksburg. Despite major defeats in the previous few days—causing him to wonder about how well his troops would fight—Vicksburg's defenders withstood two assaults on May 19 and 22. Courtesy of Library of Congress.

John H. Forney—Division commander John H. Forney held the most assailable portions of the Vicksburg defenses. His two brigades defended the Stockade Redan, 3rd Louisiana Redan, Great Redoubt, and 2nd Texas Lunette. Courtesy of Library of Congress.

Louis Hébert—Brigade commander Louis Hébert's Mississippians and Louisianans were in the thickest of the fighting on both May 19 and 22. His brigade defended the section of the line from the Stockade Redan to the Great Redoubt. Courtesy of Library of Congress.

John C. Moore—John C. Moore's brigade defended the critical Baldwin's Ferry Road entrance into Vicksburg. He withstood heavy attacks from brigades of two different corps on May 22. Courtesy of Library of Congress.

Martin L. Smith—Although blessed with the daunting Mint Spring Bayou to his front, division commander Martin L. Smith fought well with his two brigades on both May 19 and 22. He held the lines between the Stockade Redan and the Mississippi River. Courtesy of Library of Congress.

Francis A. Shoup—A Northerner by birth, Francis A. Shoup commanded one of Smith's brigades on the left of the Stockade Redan. His Louisianans repelled vicious attacks on both May 19 and 22. Courtesy of Miller's *Photographic History.*

John S. Bowen—Division commander John S. Bowen held the reserve with his two brigades. They provided much needed help at both the Stockade Redan and the 2nd Texas Lunette. Courtesy of Miller's *Photographic History.*

William D. Baldwin—Mississippian William D. Baldwin commanded one of Smith's brigades on the northern section of the Confederate lines facing Mint Spring Bayou. He was wounded in the defense of this line on May 22. Courtesy of Library of Congress.

Carter L. Stevenson—Division commander Carter L. Stevenson commanded the southernmost section of the Confederate lines. His forces confronted John McArthur's advance from the south and repelled the assault on the Railroad Redoubt and Square Fort. Courtesy of Library of Congress.

Stephen D. Lee—In some of the most historic fighting at Vicksburg, Stephen D. Lee and his brigade of Alabamians defended the Confederate line from the Railroad Redoubt to the Square Fort. Lee would later become one of the commissioners building the Vicksburg National Military Park. Courtesy of Miller's *Photographic History*.

Francis M. Cockrell—Commander of the famed Missouri brigade, Francis M. Cockrell and his Missourians fought at the Stockade Redan on both May 19 and 22. He later served as a United States senator. Courtesy of Library of Congress.

9

"They Seemed to Be Springing from the Bowels of the Earth"

"[I am] tired of furnishing brains for the Army of the Tennessee," John A. McClernand supposedly blurted out at one point in the contentious early months of the Vicksburg campaign. Such a statement carried the weight of insinuation: that Grant and company were not competent enough to command the army and that McClernand himself was the only one capable of doing so. McClernand obviously desired Grant's job and had gone to great lengths to get it. Consequently, the Grant-McClernand relationship was rocky and distant, and that was before the problems caused during the May 22 assaults.[1]

McClernand was a politician from Illinois who thought he was not getting his fair share of the glory. Worse, much of it was going to others a fraction of his age and, he thought, with much lesser talent. Although he was not a trained military officer, he was an avid politician. Both careers utilized many of the same principles of surprise, security, mass, and so on, and McClernand had learned his trade as a lawyer and then as a member of Congress. When McClernand was making his name in politics and serving in the national legislature, his now-current superiors and even peers were nobodies. The army commander Grant, whom he thought he should replace, was in his view none other than a drunk and a failure in life. Sherman was insane, and McPherson was seen as a mere boy, having been a lieutenant colonel at Shiloh while McClernand was the ranking division commander. Certainly, McClernand thought he was surrounded by incompetent upstarts who were wasting time and wrecking the army.[2]

McClernand thought he could do a much better job than Grant. Consequently, their run-ins had been numerous, as far back as McClernand's speech at Belmont, his taking of credit at Forts Henry and Donelson as well as Shiloh, and even after that. In fact, in endorsing McClernand's battle reports, Grant simply noted that his Fort Donelson account was "a little highly colored as to the conduct of the First Division," and he simply labeled McClernand's Shiloh report as "faulty."³

But as a politician McClernand had connections that Grant would never dream of having, even with President Lincoln himself. Although a Democrat, McClernand had usefulness to the Republican Lincoln, primarily early in the war when the president needed to shore up war support in the lower counties of Illinois, from which McClernand hailed. Lincoln appointed the politician a general and McClernand came through, keeping "little Egypt" in the Union and fostering massive recruitment in the area. McClernand then went to Washington, DC, in late 1862 to get his just due. He was with Lincoln on the famous visit captured by photographers at Antietam, meeting with George B. McClellan. McClernand wanted his own command in the Mississippi Valley and offered to raise it himself. Lincoln, wanting success, agreed, and he and Secretary of War Edwin Stanton gave McClernand the go-ahead without consulting military officials. It was a recipe for disaster.⁴

McClernand raised his troops and sent them southward, but Grant and Sherman hijacked them in the first efforts to get to Vicksburg, namely Sherman's Chickasaw Bayou effort. By the time McClernand realized what was happening it was too late, but he hurried southward, armed with Stanton's order and Lincoln's endorsement. To his friend Lincoln he wrote, "I believe I am superseded. Please advise me."⁵

Livid with the realization of what was happening, McClernand showed the letter with Lincoln's endorsement to everybody within sight and, upon catching up with Sherman's force, took over what he deemed as his command. Grant was aghast at McClernand's actions, but he had options. General in Chief Henry Halleck in Washington was not in on the political scheming and did everything he could to circumvent McClernand. He also gave Grant political cover, ordering that all that happened in Grant's department was his to oversee; McClernand's effort obviously came under his purview. Thus, Grant switched his movement from the dual Mississippi Central Railroad/Mississippi River lines of advance to a single one down the river itself, mainly so that Grant himself could command the whole, McClernand included. It did not come too soon, either; as soon as McClernand arrived near Vicksburg with Grant still in northern Mississippi, he took control of Sherman's troops and promptly led them off into Arkansas on what Grant termed a "wild-goose chase to the Post of Arkansas." Grant saw he had to hurry southward and rein in McClernand.⁶

McClernand continued to annoy Grant during the latter stages of the Vicksburg campaign. Once the army moved southward to cross the river below Vicksburg, McClernand even used some transports for his new wife and her baggage. The confrontations that occurred in the land campaign, and McClernand's perceived slowness in battles such as at Port Gibson and Champion Hill, only made the situation worse. In fact, Grant complained enough that while he was at Jackson he received permission from Halleck to relieve McClernand. Thinking it was not the correct time to do so in the face of the enemy, Grant stuck the note in his pocket for use on a later day. But he kept the possibility in the back of his mind.[7]

In reality, Grant did not want to change commanders of the XIII Corps right in the midst of battle. He needed McClernand to remain in command. In truth, although Grant would never have admitted it, he had depended on McClernand throughout the campaign. McClernand had led the dangerous march southward in Louisiana in April. McClernand had led the amphibious assault across the river and the advance inland in late April and early May. McClernand had held the critical and dangerous left flank of the army as it advanced northward toward the railroad in mid-May. Grant had depended heavily on McClernand, and he had performed fairly well, if not exactly matching his performance with his manners.[8]

On top of that, McClernand and his troops were fighters. He had proved that at Shiloh and elsewhere, and Grant needed a bold fighter to help break the Confederate lines at Vicksburg. Certainly, McClernand had good divisions to do it with, they fanning out south of McPherson's position, basically taking a front from the Baldwin's Ferry Road southward as far as the lines could extend, which was clearly not all the way to the river. Most of the division commanders were bold as well. The senior commander but oft-ill Eugene Carr was a West Point graduate, a wounded veteran of the Indian Wars in the 1850s, and a veteran of Wilson's Creek and Pea Ridge, for which he later earned the Medal of Honor. The War Department attaché Charles Dana considered him brave enough, "but [he] lacks energy and initiative." Andrew Jackson Smith was also a West Pointer and veteran of the Indian Wars, a bold and snappy fellow whom Dana described as "intrepid to recklessness, his head is clear though rather thick, his disposition honest and manly, though given to boasting and self exaggeration of a gentle and innocent kind." Perhaps because of Smith's West Point pedigree, Smith and McClernand were not the best of friends, and Smith had trouble getting along with his own subordinates as well. Alvin Hovey was considered by some as the best of McClernand's division commanders, the Indiana lawyer quickly learning his craft. He had made the dramatic initial charge at Champion Hill and was solid, as was perhaps the best division commander among them, the German-born Peter Osterhaus, whom his soldiers loved. One of his Ohioans kindly mocked him as saying, "He hash got te best division in te whole worlt tey gives te rebels te devel in battle." Yet Dana thought "on the battlefield he lacks energy and concentrativeness." Among the divisions' eight brigades, seven (the eighth, one of Hovey's, being left back at the Big Black River to guard the rear) were now on site and ready to advance toward the Confederate line while the artillery continued to pummel the Confederate works. McClernand reported his guns "breaching the enemy's works at several points, temporarily silencing his guns and exploding four rebel caissons."[9]

Still, McClernand was under a cloud here outside Vicksburg, rumors already circulating that the setback on May 19 was because McClernand "was not up, or at least failed to make an assault on the left." He was being watched this day, correspondent Sylvanus Cadwallader from Grant's headquarters taking a position "that promised reasonable protection, but was soon compelled to take refuge in a canyon, or gully, near by."[10]

McClernand was nevertheless anxious to get the real fighting started. "At five minutes before 10 o'clock, I ordered that the [bugler] sound the charge," he remembered. Hopefully, McClernand could break his way into Vicksburg and do something Grant's two protégés could not. Then, he could show the whole world that he alone was the real fighter in this army, essentially the brains of the operation.[11]

If McClernand had any advantages, it was that his front spanned the connection of two different Confederate divisions. The right of John Forney's division in the form of John C. Moore's brigade met the left of Carter Stevenson's division, Stephen D. Lee's brigade, at the railroad. Making the connection even less secure than normal was the fact that both the Baldwin's Ferry Road and the Southern Railroad of Mississippi ran roughly between the two brigades, and the fortifications at this point were not as strong or tidy as elsewhere. Still, there were three major Confederate bastions along this front of the two Confederate brigades, the other three brigades of Stevenson's division to the right not being confronted by any appreciable numbers of Federals as yet.[12]

On Moore's front and guarding the Baldwin's Ferry Road was the 2nd Texas Lunette tucked onto the high ground in a curve of the road. But there were problems. To take advantage of the terrain and to command the road, the fort had to be situated far out in front of the main line: "The rifle-pits connecting with the retired parts of the fort on the right receded very rapidly to take advantage of the ground," Colonel Ashbel Smith of the 2nd Texas explained. "For like reason, there was an interval of upward of 100 yards between the left of the fort and the continuation of the general line of defenses to the left."[13]

The 2nd Texas of Moore's brigade manned the fort, Colonel Smith describing it as "situated on a projecting swell or mamelon of ground well in advance of the general outline of the works." He went on to state:

> Our fort was an irregular lunette, with no flank on the left; or it may be considered a redan with a large *pan coupé,* having its left thrown forward and its right retired. Its left having no flank, its interior was exposed to an enfilading and reverse fire from the enemy approaching by the valley, which debouches on its left. Its parapet was about 4 1/4 feet high on the inside, its superior slope about 14 feet thick. It was surrounded by a ditch in front nearly 6 feet deep, with an irregular glacis made by the natural slope of the earth to the ferry road. There were two embrasures for cannon, with a traverse between them.

On the flanks of the 2nd Texas were other regiments of Moore's brigade, the 37th Alabama on the left and the 42nd Alabama on the right reaching down to the railroad. Inside the fortification were two cannons of Captain Thomas F. Tobin's Tennessee Battery.[14]

Guarding the other major thoroughfare through this section of the line, the railroad, was a redoubt on the south side of the line termed the "Railroad Redoubt." It too stuck out sharply from the main line of fortifications, almost like a crooked finger along a narrow sliver of high ground projecting off toward the upper reaches of Durden Creek. One Federal described it well: "In the shape of a horse shoe, open at the rear, with another smaller fort back commanding the entrance, so in case we get into the front fort we can be raked from the other."[15]

From the Railroad Redoubt, the line continued on southward toward the next major fortification, an enclosed bastion soon to be logically termed the "Square Fort." Beyond this point, Stevenson's division continued on southwestward, to the works along the Hall's Ferry Road on down to South Fort, but the three brigades there faced little opposition because McClernand's main line ended at the Square Fort. Only Colonel William Hall's brigade of McArthur's division was in that area. Thus, the only part of Stevenson's division in the crosshairs of McClernand's assaults was Lee's brigade, which ran from the railroad southward to Square Fort. A small portion of the 46th Alabama was under the command of Lieutenant Colonel Edmund W. Pettus of the 20th Alabama because their actual colonel, Michael Woods, had been captured at Champion Hill. These Alabamians held the Railroad Redoubt itself, although most of the regiment had marched away with Loring at Champion Hill. A few men of the 30th Alabama under Lieutenant James M. Pearson, recently having been placed in command of a consolidated company because of high casualties at Champion Hill, held the extension of the Railroad Redoubt. A 6-pound cannon from Waddell's Alabama Battery was perched inside the tip as well as two 12-pound howitzers of the Pettus Flying Artillery in the works closer to the main line. The rest of the brigade continued to the south with the 31st, 30th, 23rd, and 20th Alabama extending the line down to Square Fort, the 20th Alabama holding the fort itself. A 6-pound gun of Company L, 1st Mississippi Light Artillery and a 12-pound howitzer of Waddell's Alabama Battery studded the line. In reserve in the area was Waul's Texas Legion.[16]

The intense artillery bombardment of the morning began before daylight, Colonel Smith of the 2nd Texas describing it as "a most furious cannonade and fire of musketry, which were continued with occasionally varying intensity till 10 A.M." Such a bombardment kept most of the troops huddled behind their fortifications. That changed with the 10:00 A.M. hour, Smith later noting that "this was the hour designated in the enemy's orders, as afterward appeared, for a general assault on our lines throughout their entire length." It was not hard to figure it out quickly. Carter Stevenson noted that "a heavy force moved out to assault, making a gallant charge." Texan Thomas N. Waul in reserve behind the Railroad Redoubt described how "the enemy moved in distinct and separate columns against each of the salient points in General Lee's front, their forces massed in the rear. The advance and supporting columns started at a double-quick, with division front." Colonel Smith of the 2nd Texas, giving perhaps the most vivid picture, described "a sudden, sullen silence of the enemy's artillery," but something else is what really took his attention. "Hitherto the positions of the enemy were known only by the flash of their guns and the clouds of smoke which enveloped their heads. Instantaneously—the enemy springing up from the hollows and valley to our right and front—the earth was black with their close columns."[17]

It was all too evident to these Confederates what was happening: McClernand was on the attack. Grant staff officer James H. Wilson, who had ridden over to McClernand's front, wrote that "the assaulting columns began to move at the appointed hour and at twenty-one minutes past 10 the bugles sounded for the assault."[18]

If there would be any success on McClernand's line, it would not be because of his tactical prowess in organizing his assault forces. In fact, the way he deployed his corps's divisions was problematic in the extreme—and exactly opposite of what he had counseled Grant to do. McClernand had wanted to make a narrow assault with plenty of reserves to exploit the success. Grant overruled him and ordered all three corps to assault, leaving the minute tactical details of how they did it to the corps commanders. McClernand took Grant's larger operational mind-set to be his orders for the tactical effort as well, and, as historian Warren Grabau has observed, "he then tailored his tactical plan to conform to Grant's strategic [operational] one." Thus, McClernand planned to send in all of his divisions present at once across a wide front. Ironically, Sherman and McPherson both had done the opposite, attacking at specific points with many reserves behind ready to exploit a breakthrough.[19]

McClernand's mistakes did not end there. With two major forts around the Baldwin's Ferry Road and the Southern Railroad, McClernand placed Eugene Carr's two brigades on the front line, supported by Andrew Jackson Smith's two brigades. The result was that the two right brigades, one from Carr's division and one from Smith's, fronted the 2nd Texas Lunette on the road while the left two brigades faced the Railroad Redoubt. The result was that two different operations unfolded with brigades of different divisions acting in tandem. The confusion and chaos of coordinating movements among brigades of different divisions in the same assault quickly appeared, as did the overall coordination when division commanders found their attention split between two distinct and different assaults. Even one of Landram's Illinoisans voiced his confusion, writing his sister that "for some cause Carrs and Smiths divisions were split. Landrams Brigade in advance supported by a brigade from Carrs and on the right of us one of Carrs brigade supported by our first brigade." A much better choice would have been to allow Carr to concentrate on one fort and Smith the other. However, one historian has surmised that McClernand was reacting to Smith's lethargy at Champion Hill by placing Carr in tactical command.[20]

Accordingly, the two right brigades of the two divisions prepared to assault the 2nd Texas Lunette. In the front line was the Indiana lawyer and Mexican War veteran William P. Benton's brigade of Carr's division, made up of Illinois and Indiana troops, the 8th and 18th Indiana and 33rd and 99th Illinois, Benton himself being the colonel of the 8th Indiana. Unfortunately for them, the understrength 33rd Illinois had three companies on skirmish duty and one left back at the Big Black River guarding ammunition. Supporting Benton's brigade was Kentucky farmer Stephen G. Burbridge's brigade. Burbridge had attended the Kentucky Military Institute and was a veteran of Shiloh as colonel of the 26th Kentucky. He led four regiments from three different states, the 16th and 67th Indiana, both of which had been captured in the Kentucky campaign, and the 83rd Ohio and 23rd Wisconsin. Charles Dana considered

Burbridge "a mediocre officer, brave, rather pretentious, a good fellow, not destined to greatness."[21]

Coordination between the two brigades would be touchy as they hailed from two different divisions, and coordinating the assault with the other two brigades down on the railroad would be even more difficult, and that did not even take into account the Confederate resistance. It also did not take into account the hatred between Burbridge and his division commander A. J. Smith; in a couple of days Burbridge would actually write that "I am unwilling longer to be associated with him in a military capacity" because of "repeated instances" of "personal abuse."[22]

With all such issues, few liked the looks of things. One Ohioan in Burbridge's brigade lamented the possibilities, writing his sister that "they have selected the best places for their works of course but we have some as high positions as they." Charles Wilcox of the 33rd Illinois in Benton's brigade similarly wrote that "though not very confident of success we put on an air of confidence." An officer in the 33rd Illinois, Isaac H. Elliott, was out on skirmisher duty and came back to the regiment giving a similar foreboding opinion. He met Colonel David Shunk of the 8th Indiana sitting under a tent and drinking wine from his canteen. The colonel gave Elliott a swig, and Elliott later remembered it to be wine and not whiskey, but "I wished it had been." McClernand himself seemed to have fewer worries, he and Carr spying the Confederate line in front of the 8th Indiana, even amid bullets. "McClernand would dodge when a bullet would come close," wrote Amos York of the 8th Indiana, "and the boys was laughing at him; he sed he did not dodge it just dodged its selfe."[23]

Nevertheless, Benton led his Illinoisans and Indianans forward at about the same time the others jumped off, perhaps only a few minutes behind. The colonels had each wanted to lead the assault, so Benton had them draw lots to see who went first; the privates were obviously less enthused about leading, one Indianan telling his comrades: "Boys, you have just fifteen minutes to live." The orders soon came—"forward to battle and to victory" was the cry. Stacked in regiments in order by the flank, led by the 99th Illinois who won, or some might say lost, the lot, the brigade moved through a ravine and intersected another, up which they were to move. The troops were instructed to move up the draw and reach the level ground in front of the fort and deploy from their column of marching by the flank to a line of battle. Up out of the ravine the head of the column soon lunged but just as quickly caught the heavy Confederate fire in response. Because of the fire, the brigade angled slightly southward from the Baldwin's Ferry Road, approaching the eastern

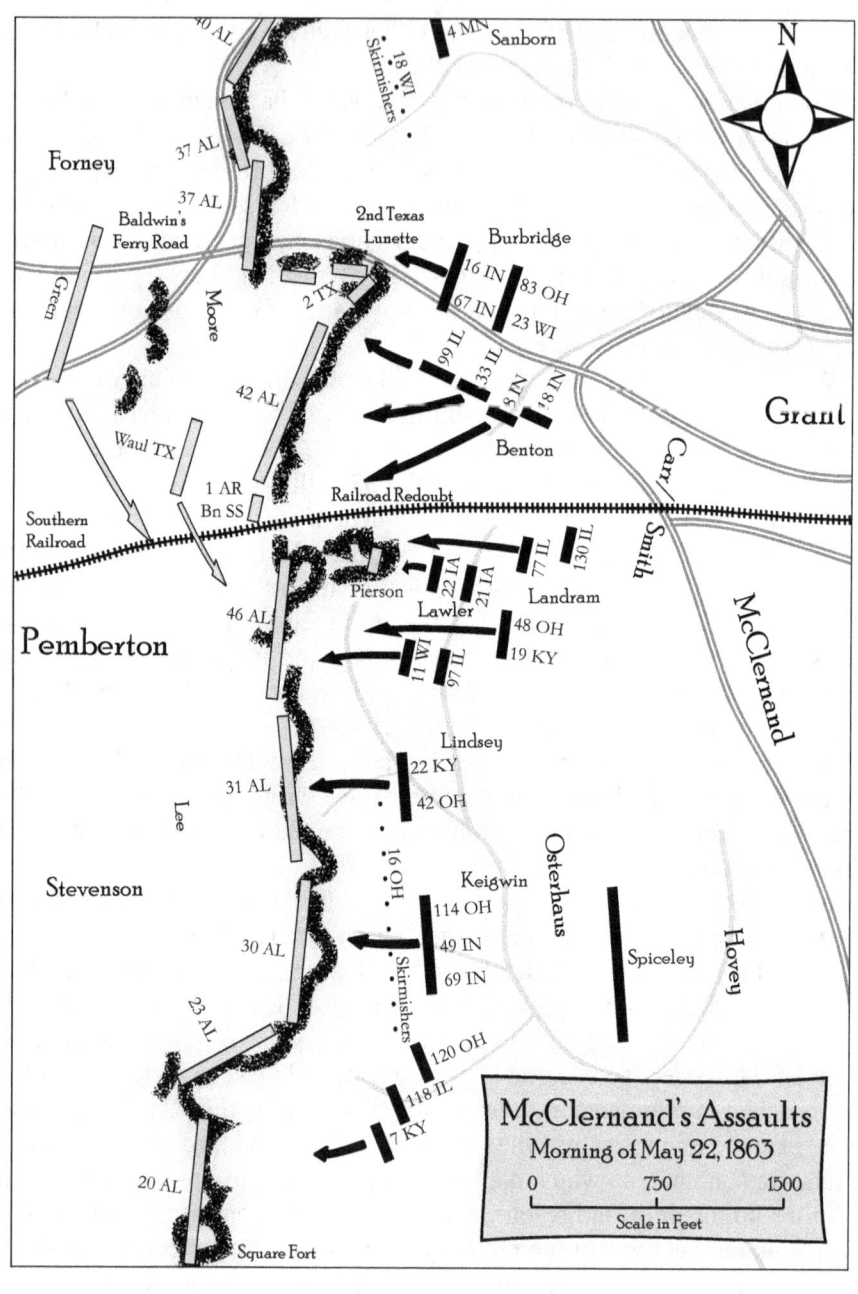

face of the 2nd Texas Lunette as well as the works defended by the 42nd Alabama farther to the south. Louis Knobe of the 18th Indiana recorded that "it was a bloody affair . . . the rebel forts were so constructed that they were impossible to charge into."[24]

The horror arrived quick and heavy. Colonel George W. Bailey in his "check shirt sleeves" led the 99th Illinois out of the ravine by companies; Bailey was soon wounded, as was the major, the command falling to Captain Asa C. Matthews. One of the 99th Illinois soldiers told of the destruction as they exited the ravine by company, writing, "I see our brave boys dropping around me, and how anyone could escape seems but a[n] interposition of providence." The lead company commander in the 33rd Illinois next in line told the same story: "When the companies of the 99th went out of the ravine, one by one, onto the open ground they were opened on by the fort and rifle pits and were practically torn to pieces." The wounded began to stumble back through that next regiment, but it moved on too, to a position above the head of the ravine and atop the Baldwin's Ferry Road, which was swept with bullets. The lead Illinoisans made a slight halt to await the rest of the regiment, but the forward companies found "it was too hot a place to wait for anybody or anything." They surged onward seeking cover, but all organization dissolved out in the open, especially when the rest of the regiments veered left into the expanse between the forts. Many of the Illinoisans sought any shelter they could, and one officer admitted that his regiment "was practically destroyed as a regimental organization, and was not brought together until after dark." Another member of the 33rd Illinois wrote that they "ran up near their fort and secreted ourselves in a little hollow. We dare not move for the enemy could fire on us from three directions." Indeed, all but one fell killed or wounded in a single company. The following Indianans also met the heavy fire and sought shelter, the 8th Indiana (minus one company sharpshooting to keep the Confederate artillerymen down) veering to the left with the 33rd Illinois, some all the way across the railroad. The 18th Indiana moved to the right with the 99th Illinois near the chimneys from the burned house. Yet it all seemed for naught, one Illinoisan writing that "it seems a useless contest." An Indianan simply noted the column was "destroyed four at a time, coming out of the hole in the ground."[25]

One trapped member of the 33rd Illinois, Charles Wilcox, described how "we lay there about eight minutes and yet it seemed an age to me, for showers of bullets and grape were passing over me and not a foot above me"; all he could think was "why don't they order us to charge." Then the thought occurred to him that perhaps all the officers were dead. Many were certainly wounded around him: "Some who were wounded groaned and shrieked, others were calm and resigned. Generally, those who were the slightest wounded shrieked the loudest, thinking they were wounded the worst." Eventually, Lieutenant Colonel Edward R. Roe ordered the Illinoisans forward, but it cost him a wound in the leg.[26]

Texan Colonel Smith in the lunette itself remembered that "ere Private Brooks could well exclaim, 'Here they come,' they were surging on within a few paces of the foot of our works." Benton's Indianans and Illinoisans braved the terrific fire from the Texans and Alabamians, Benton's troops, Smith reported, moving "in a column of five regiments, with a regiment front, and with stormers provided with tools and implements." He added that these Federals "hurled [themselves] against our works with the utmost fury and determination." But they were in a bad spot. Some of Benton's Federals were caught in an angle of the line where the lunette bent back to the west, one Illinoisan describing "our . . . left coming into a galling crossfire of musketry & artillery, which compelled them to fall back." The Federals were still able to push ahead on the right despite heavy casualties on the outer slopes of the lunette and the works on its right, McClernand reporting that they "rushed forward and carried the ditch and slope of another heavy earthwork, and planted their colors upon the latter." Confederate division commander John Forney agreed, writing that "the enemy succeeded in getting in the ditch of the work on the right of Baldwin's Ferry Road. Shell with five-second fuses were thrown over on them." He also noted that "the road in front of this position was left covered with the dead bodies of the enemy."[27]

In the assault, Colonel Charles E. Lippincott fell slightly wounded at the head of the 33rd Illinois, while the regiment's lieutenant colonel, E. R. Roe, fell more severely. As they lay dazed on the field, Lippincott jovially asked Roe if he was scared during the charge, to which Roe replied: "I do not think I was scared, but I certainly had an intellectual perception of danger." Knowing the Illinoisans were leaderless, Colonel David Shunk of the 8th Indiana, following along and taking the lead, yelled to the Illinoisans: "Fall in, my brave boys of the 33d, and I will lead you." The Illinoisans joined with their comrades of the 8th Indiana and moved on, some crossing the railroad and moving toward the entrenchments between the 2nd Texas Lunette and the Railroad Redoubt. Like everywhere else, however, it was not enough, and the Federal advance began to slow to a crawl at the base of the formidable Confederate earthworks.[28]

Flags were also lost. In the 99th Illinois, William Sitton rushed forward to the parapet with his banner, only to be cut down, his blood flowing on the flag itself. Tom Higgins grabbed the banner and moved on, actually entering the earthworks and being captured, along with his flag, the Confederates yelling "Don't shoot at that brave man again" and "Come on Yank, come on." Higgins topped the earthworks but faced a host of bayonets all centered on him. The Texans gave the credit of his surviving to a metal breastplate. Higgins denied the story, saying "if I had I would have put it on my rump." A Confederate officer felt for him and could only mutter in disbelief that "he never knew his men to fire at a man that close and miss him before." Higgins was a prisoner for the short term, but the flag remained in Confederate hands until 1873, at which time it was returned to Springfield, Illinois, one observer noting that "stains of blood can yet be seen on them, the patriot blood of the lamented Sitton."[29]

At the same time, upon the appearance of several staff officers sent from Benton to call up support, Stephen Burbridge's mixed brigade began to move forward as well behind Benton's troops. As the brigade stood in position in the rear, a short pause in the artillery bombardment informed all that it was 10:00 A.M. One Indianan wrote that "every experienced soldier knew what this calm portended, and with every nerve strung up to high tension, awaited the signal to do or die." Burbridge remembered that the brigade then went forward "with a yell and a rush, over the hill into the last ravine." One Wisconsin soldier merely told his parents they attacked the "walls of Vicks."[30]

Instead of putting more targets onto the high ground around the left side of the road in front of the lunette, Burbridge veered to the right when he approached the works, advancing on the lunette on its less-defensible northeastern face. Evidently, some Confederates were outside the works, possibly skirmishers, because Colonel Thomas J. Lucas of the 16th Indiana noted that they "drove the enemy inside the fort." Colonel Joshua J. Guppey of the 23rd Wisconsin also reported that the brigade "aided in shutting up a large number of the enemy in one of their forts." Burbridge brought his troops forward through an area of burned-out chimneys where a building had recently stood and moved on across the Baldwin's Ferry Road, with the 67th Indiana on the road itself. The brigade in two columns of regiments fanned out to the south, the 16th Indiana down the slope to the left of the ridge on which the road ran, with the 23rd Wisconsin directly in support of the 67th Indiana and the 83rd Ohio in support of the 16th Indiana.[31]

The Texans poured it into Burbridge's troops as well, Colonel Smith explaining that "the Second Texas was ready." He added a vivid description of the fighting inside the lunette: "Standing up boldly on the banquette, and exposing their persons to the fire of ten times our numbers, my men received the enemy with a most resolute and murderous fire; my cannon belched canister;

my men made the air reel with yells and shouts as they saw the earth strewn with the enemy's dead. One of the enemy's regiments staggered and was thrown into utter confusion."³²

As a result, just getting over the initial hill was problematic for Burbridge's men, illustrating the coming fury when actually approaching the Confederate works in the open. "It was the hottest place for men to be that I ever seen," Isaac Jackson of the 83rd Ohio wrote his brother. Colonel Frederick W. Moore of the 83rd Ohio reported that he took non–textbook measures to protect his men: "At the appointed time I detached the several companies of my command from each other as much as possible, to avoid drawing the enemy's fire while passing over the ridge between me and General Benton." Two companies also went around the head of the ridge.³³

Some minor corrections also took place as the brigade ascended the hill "upon which is the fort we were attacking," Burbridge remembered. The 67th and 16th Indiana veered away from each other, most likely because of the angles of the fortifications they were attacking, and the 83rd Ohio found the opening and moved up in between the Indianans to the front line. Burbridge also found what he described as "some symptoms of an attempt to turn our flanks," causing him to send four companies of the reserve 23rd Wisconsin to the right flank to aid the Indianans. Thinking there could also be a problem to the left, he sent the remaining six Wisconsin companies in that direction to shore up the 16th Indiana's flank, there being a gap developing between the brigade's left and Benton's troops.³⁴

Like Benton's troops on their left, Burbridge's brigade found the advance increasingly difficult, not only because of the heavy Confederate fire but also because of the steep terrain. Lieutenant Colonel Theodore E. Buehler of the 67th Indiana remembered that he led his men forward "with terrific cheering across the hill in front of me, and up to the brow of the next hill," but then became embroiled in a maze of ravines and all the while taking "a heavy fire of musketry." They managed to get to the top anyway after a short pause a mere twenty feet from the lunette, one Wisconsin soldier adding that "we fought our way right up to the fort." Soon, the flags of the various three forward regiments could be seen planted on the slopes of the Texas lunette, Burbridge describing them as "flying against the walls of the fort." Colonel Moore of the Ohio regiment declared that his troops "planted their colors on the glacis of the fort nearest them." A heavy fire unleashed by the Federals also kept the Confederates down. Lieutenant Colonel Buehler reported that "not a rebel would show the tip of his finger above the fort."³⁵

John Griffith Jones of the 23rd Wisconsin gave a detailed explanation of their arrival at the fort to his parents a few days later, writing that "we charged the forts with our bayonets, but when we reached the forts we found a ditch twelve feet wide and seven deep which we had to cross, as well as a wall 10 feet high. It was impossible to climb it." They were stuck, and it was miserable on the face of that fort; they could go no farther and could not retire without more heavy casualties. But they did not quit. Colonel Guppey of the 23rd Wisconsin reported that "our gallant soldiers seemed determined to get inside the fort by some means. Not being able to scale its walls, they tried to dig them down." Still, they were in comparable safety, Colonel Smith of the Texans writing that because of the lay of the land and the layout of the works, "my fort being thrown so far in advance of the general outline, and my rifle-pits on my right receding by so obtuse an angle . . . I had no flanking arrangements." He added that with the enemy "reaching the foot of our works, they were in security." Worse, Smith explained that the Federals "maintained an incessant and fierce storm of Minies, [and] under cover he made several very daring attempts to carry the fort, clambering up in force the external slope of the parapet." Smith's brigade commander John C. Moore described the enemy "coming up and even into the outer ditch of the Second Texas Redoubt," close enough that the Texans captured "a color-bearer and two stand[s] of colors."[36]

Colonel Smith was, not surprisingly, worried about the possibility of Federals topping the parapet. He wrote that "there were during this day three notable and most determined movements to sweep over the top of our works and dash with the bayonet into the fort." Accordingly, he took special care to compose a defense in depth. "As the enemy could not be seen until he should have mounted the superior slope and be ready to dash in," he had additional lines of Texans create a buffer zone inside the fort. He kept the front rank firing over the top while bringing the rear rank back a few paces, "on bended knees, with guns loaded and bayonets fixed and at a charge, ready to receive the enemy." Still farther back, Smith placed another line with bayonets, but they held a position thoroughly swept by enemy fire through the embrasures and had to lie down for protection. Smith alternated these three lines at times, especially the front one, "as their guns became heated."[37]

More than just heated guns soon became an issue for the Texans, especially those lying down to the rear. The embrasures of the lunette as well as the traverses inside had been made of cotton bales, and the artillery barrage that morning had "displaced and uncovered [these] of dirt." John Forney had recommended skinning dead horses and mules to cover them with their hides for precisely that reason, but little had been done in the bustle. Now, the Minié balls of the Federals tore into the cotton and "incessantly bowed out the cotton as if from the flue of a gin-stand, and scattered it all over the area of the fort." If the white fort was picturesque in any way, it soon became a major problem when all the firing ignited the cotton and produced a heavy smoke layer. Worse, the flames steadily crept toward the ammunition boxes in rear. Smith ordered the Texans lying down to "brush away with their hands the burning cotton," easing the danger. Other problems soon emerged, however. In particular, the Tennessee cannon crews at the embrasures were taking heavy casualties, weakening the defense. One of the two cannons, in fact, was put out of service, and the other's crew was so riddled that it "remained idle for several hours." Later, Smith ordered it "run up into battery and fired," but only one lone corporal still attended the gun, and as he raised up to aim a Minié ball killed him instantly. Smith noted it "passed through his heart and he rolled over dead." Both guns were ultimately disabled and had to be replaced with two 12-pound howitzers of Company A, 1st Mississippi Light Artillery.[38]

Thus the threat of a breach was very real, and Colonel Smith described one of his closest calls during the fighting. At one point several Federals surged toward the right embrasure, "amid the smoke of the burning cotton which enveloped and almost blinded the men in this angle of the fort." Smith believed they were "on the eve of dashing in." He shouted, "Volunteers to clear that embrasure!" and four men "sprang to the platform . . . and discharging their guns within 5 paces of the muzzles of the assailants, hurled them back headlong into the ditch outside." It cost dearly: Private T. E. Bagwell fell dead on the gun platform, and Sergeant William T. Spence took a bullet in the head, dying a little later. Privates A. S. Kittridge and J. A. Stewart survived. The Texans also tried to plug the embrasure with an entire cotton bale, but the wily Federals of the 18th Indiana set it afire with tow, a fiber used to clean the bores of their muskets.[39]

Consequently, Benton and Burbridge could not advance any farther. One reason was the heavy Confederate resistance the Texans were handing out, including what Smith described as "spherical case . . . used as handgrenades. . . . It is believed with good effect." Another reason was the high casualties, including officers. Colonel Thomas J. Lucas of the 16th Indiana was hit three times, but Burbridge reported "he continued to cheer on his men with unabated vigor." The Federals thus settled into a line on the outer slope of the ditch and fired as best they could, eventually fouling their muskets because of the heavy fire.[40]

Part of the blame for the assault's failure was also of McClernand's own making. His decision to send his brigades in tandem rather than as unified divisions caused a command issue when Smith sent Burbridge an order to send two of his regiments to the left to support Benton. Burbridge protested, arguing that "this would reduce my force one-half, and leave my front terribly exposed." Burbridge sent word back to Smith of this, to which the active Smith, positioning troops with his field glasses, replied that "it is an order from General Carr [who ranked Smith], and must be obeyed." Division commander Carr, who was operating with Benton's brigade of his own division, had given the order when Benton's troops ran into heavy trouble. Burbridge was not apt to obey so easily. He sent another aide to argue with Smith over the movement, and Smith relented, giving Burbridge "permission . . . to retain my position."[41]

That should have been the end of it, but Burbridge was not through suffering for McClernand's naïveté. Word quickly arrived from Carr inquiring "why the regiments were not forthcoming." Having had all he could take, Burbridge went to the rear and found McClernand himself, stating bluntly that to do so "would be the destruction not only of my regiments, but of the whole front." McClernand simply "referred" Burbridge to Carr, whom he then went to see, but Carr would not budge. "Notwithstanding my representations," Burbridge remembered, "General Carr renewed his order concerning the regiments." A flustered Burbridge simply responded in a heated manner, "telling him I obeyed his order under protest." He nevertheless went back to his brigade "with a heavy and foreboding heart" and prepared to send the 23rd Wisconsin and 67th Indiana to the left. He added that these regiments were forced to "withdraw from the ground which had been gained with so much labor and maintained with so much valor."[42]

Indeed, what Burbridge feared so much happened when the two units moved to the left. Lieutenant Colonel Buehler led his 67th Indiana out of line by the flank, and soon "a shower of balls hailed over our heads, sent after us from the forts we had silenced." Buehler was philosophical about it, however, writing that "yet we had our orders, and on we went." The 23rd Wisconsin moved as well. Burbridge's two remaining regiments were thus totally "unsupported," he said, and the Confederates realized what was happening. "As I had anticipated and feared, the rebels, finding the fire slackened and the line weakened in their front, opened a most destructive fire." His Indianans and Ohioans were taking increased casualties as a result, and Burbridge had all he could take. He moved over to talk with Benton himself, evidently finding the need was not so great as the division commander imagined, and there determined "to take the responsibility of replacing my regiments without delay." So, the Indiana and Wisconsin troops moved back to the right on Burbridge's orders, "but the work was now most difficult, as the rebels had the advantage and seemed determined to keep it." Lieutenant Colonel Buehler of the 67th Indiana agreed, writing that "my men went to work again with their old ardor, but the rebels had got bold, and not being supported on my left, as I should have been, we were exposed to a damaging cross-fire, losing several of our best men." Adding insult to injury, just as the regiments were returning under the heavy fire, Carr relented and sent word to Burbridge, "telling me to use my discretion about withdrawing my regiments." A sad Burbridge could not help but report that "such a message ten minutes before, or such consent when I pleaded for it, would have saved a hundred lives."[43]

Command chaos—laid mainly at the feet of McClernand himself—had caused many casualties. It had also caused the loss of any chance of forward progress against the 2nd Texas Lunette. About all Benton's and Burbridge's troops could do was to hug the parapets like so many other Federals were doing by this time all along the line. Still, one other action could be taken. Burbridge had some good reason left in him after all the mess, and he repeatedly asked permission to send a gun forward to aid his troops. "After repeated applications," he noted—again indicating a laggard command authority—some of the Wisconsin troops moved a single artillery piece from the Chicago Mercantile Battery forward to the position near the 16th Indiana. There, within "25 or 30 feet" of the Confederate line, the gun added a great deal of firepower for the Federals. McClernand himself noted that "Captain White, of the Chicago Mercantile Battery, carried forward one of his pieces by hand quite to the ditch, and, double-shotting it, fired into an embrasure, disabling a gun in it ready to be discharged, and scattering death among the rebel cannoneers."[44]

Even that feat had been problematic and chaos-stunted, however. Once the desire for a forward gun was known, division commander A. J. Smith became involved and asked numerous battery commanders to take their cannons forward. All protested, arguing "it was impossible to drag guns, by hand, down one slope and up another, under fire." Finally, Smith bellowed, "I know a battery that will go to _____ if you order it there," meaning Captain Patrick H. White's Chicago battery. When told what was desired, White enthusiastically responded, "Yes, sir, I will take my guns there." He started two to the front, and although one was hit and damaged during the move forward the other made it and gave good service. The cannoneers carried the ammunition in their haversacks to keep from hauling the limber up as well.[45]

Still, the cannon could only do so much, and the sad reality was that McClernand's assaults against the 2nd Texas Lunette had been stopped, just like all the rest of the Federals. Carr advised that although Smith's division had aided this advance and "did all that men could do to achieve success," they "were unable to make a lodgment inside the enemy's works." If McClernand was going to get his glory this day, it would have to come from elsewhere.[46]

Peter Osterhaus was quite the story. He was a full-blooded German by birth, having been born in what was then Prussia in 1823. He had come of age in the Prussian military, adept in stories of helping take down Napoleon himself. Osterhaus had an avid anti-imperial political outlook and became heavily involved in the democratic revolutions in the late 1840s in Germany. Like many others, including one of his Jewish colonels here at Vicksburg—Marcus Spiegel—Osterhaus had to flee his home country. He came to the United States, where he first settled in Illinois and then St. Louis. The looming Civil War allowed him the opportunity to resume his military career. Fighting at Wilson's Creek and Pea Ridge early in the war, eventually as colonel of the 12th Missouri, Osterhaus soon reached general officer rank and later took higher commands in Grant's army, although not always feeling deserving of his promotions. At one point when given a division under Grant, Osterhaus protested that he was not ready for such responsibility, but Grant wisely saw something in the transplanted German and insisted he take the command. Grant was right to do so.[47]

During the run-up to Vicksburg Osterhaus had fought his way northward with the rest of McClernand's corps, at one point being engaged at Port Gibson against these same Alabamians now across from him, as well as tangentially at Champion Hill. At Big Black River bridge, his troops had participated in the assault even though Osterhaus himself was slightly wounded. He was back now, if still limping somewhat, and held the extreme left of McClernand's line, facing the heavy defenses around the Square Fort on Confederate division commander Carter Stevenson's front.[48]

Osterhaus, like all of McClernand's divisions, had two brigades under his command. The first was under Colonel James Keigwin of the 49th Indiana. With a decidedly British surname instead of German, Keigwin was actually born in Indiana. Amazingly, Keigwin was the third commander of this unit in almost as many days. Theophilus T. Garrard had commanded the brigade at Champion Hill and Big Black River but had given over to Albert Lee while approaching Vicksburg because he had achieved a brigadier general's rank and was assigned to Benjamin Prentiss at Helena, Arkansas. Of course, Lee had been wounded on May 19, the command falling to Keigwin on that day. The disruption in the command seemingly had little effect on the solid regiments: the 118th Illinois, 120th Ohio, and the 49th and 69th Indiana, with the 7th Kentucky tagged on. Similarly, Osterhaus's second brigade was under a Frankfort, Kentucky, lawyer, Colonel Daniel W. Lindsey of the 22nd Kentucky. Lindsey had been trained at the Kentucky Military Institute and had served in the Kentucky State Guard, which he parlayed into a command when the war erupted. Lindsey's own 22nd Kentucky, with the 54th Indiana and 16th, 42nd, and 114th Ohio, made up the brigade.[49]

Perhaps because of the command turmoil in Keigwin's brigade, and because Osterhaus himself was still feeling the effects of his wound at Big Black River Bridge on May 17, Osterhaus chose to utilize his division basically without regard to brigade structure in the attack proposed for 10:00 A.M. Osterhaus wrote that "by 6 P.M. (May 21) an order from headquarters of the army corps advised me officially of a general assault, to be made on the next morning (May 22) at 10 o'clock by the whole line." Osterhaus immediately sent for Keigwin and Lindsey, as "I was hardly able to move about on horseback." He wanted "to come to a thorough understanding as to the anticipated attack."[50]

By the time Keigwin and Lindsey arrived, the limping Osterhaus had been out front to examine the ground once more to determine where to assault. It did not look good anywhere. He described the terrain in front of Vicksburg: "These hills and valleys are by no means regular, but, on the contrary, variously intersected by cross valleys and gorges, making a passage over them very difficult. To go straight forward over them with artillery is out of the question." He also was taken aback that the details of the attack were left up to him: "This very puzzling choice, according to the order, . . . [has] been left to every division commander." The ailing Osterhaus nevertheless examined the ground in "a very minute survey" and opted for a path in front of the Square Fort and against the works to its north, running up toward the Railroad Redoubt that Carr and Smith would be assailing; his attack here would be within supporting distance of those operations. Osterhaus admitted that this was a "very steep acclivity," but it did have its good points. There was a ridge near the works, or what Osterhaus described as "a well-covered approach," that could shield the forming troops. Likewise, there seemed to be less obstruction at this point, and there were also additional terrain features Osterhaus described: "The slope was here divided by spurs, running out and dividing the terrain into three sections, and thus affording some shelter to the troops while they made the escalade."[51]

Because of the spurs acting much like traverses dividing the approach into three sections, Osterhaus wanted three storming lines of regiments drawn up in "columns of divisions at half distance." Osterhaus explained that this would ensure "the necessary pressure and connections on the point of attack, without the danger of the lines being broken, which deployed lines in this terrain could not have avoided." On the right, Osterhaus placed the 22nd Kentucky and 42nd Ohio of Lindsey's brigade. The center force contained the 114th Ohio of Lindsey's unit as well as the 49th and 69th Indiana of

Keigwin's brigade. The left column consisted of Keigwin's 7th Kentucky and 118th Illinois. Across the entire front, the 16th Ohio deployed as skirmishers, and to the unguarded left Osterhaus deployed Colonel Spiegel's 120th Ohio "with orders to deploy, at the hour of attack, a very strong line of skirmishers on that wing, and open a heavy fire, and make all such demonstrations which could divert the enemy's attention from the point of our main attack." Casualties occurred even in the preparation, including the flag-bearer of the 16th Ohio, part of whose head was taken off by a shell while he still tightly gripped the shaft: "It could only be liberated after death had completely done its work."[52]

Interestingly, the only other regiment of the division not to be deployed was the 54th Indiana, but Osterhaus did not even know where it was. He had been ordered to leave the Indianans and the 120th Ohio at Raymond as the division moved forward to Champion Hill, and the Ohioans had later marched forward and rejoined the division. Nothing had been heard of the Indianans, however, Osterhaus writing as late as three days later that "I beg leave to inquire where the Fifty-fourth Indiana Infantry is stationed now. They were left at Raymond with the One hundred and twentieth Ohio. The latter regiment came up since, but the whereabouts of the former is not known to me. The regiment is not in Raymond anymore, but I would like very much to have it rejoin my command if such be possible." Thus, Lindsey would go into action one regiment short. In actuality, the Indianans were guarding prisoners.[53]

Despite the missing Indianans, Osterhaus had his division up and ready to move forward at the 10:00 A.M. signal, but his troops were not the only XIII Corps soldiers who were prepared on this front. Behind Osterhaus's three columns was the only brigade present from Alvin Hovey's division. Unlike Osterhaus's troops, who had not been heavily engaged at Champion Hill, Hovey's had made the dramatic initial assault up and over the hill to the crossroads before being driven back. The division had fought gallantly. Perhaps because of its firmness, one of the brigades under James Slack had been left at the Big Black River bridge to watch the rear while Grant went after Vicksburg. That left only George McGinnis's troops present with the corps now, and even McGinnis had left the command due to sickness. Colonel William T. Spiceley of the 24th Indiana was now in command. With only one brigade present, Hovey thus took a rearward position supporting Osterhaus, although his five regiments—the 11th, 24th, 34th, and 46th Indiana and 29th Wisconsin—deployed in line ready to advance and support any success Osterhaus's troops in front might gain. McClernand tasked Hovey himself with overseeing the artillery in this sector, Hovey having done good work with the artillery at Champion Hill, where he had congregated a mass of guns that helped turn back the vicious Confederate counterattack. "I was personally ordered to take charge of the batteries in front of Osterhaus' and my own command," he noted, and he gathered the guns of four batteries: Lieutenant Oscar F. Nutting's 1st Wisconsin, Captain Charles H. Lanphere's 7th Michigan, Lieutenant Augustus Beach's 2nd Ohio, and Lieutenant Russell P. Twist's 16th Ohio. The guns opened early that morning and continued toward the time Hovey described as the advance "simultaneous along the whole line."[54]

That time came—"precisely at 10 A.M.," Osterhaus wrote—when his three columns moved forward from their covered staging areas toward the Confederate lines. One Ohioan wrote how "there was a minute or two of ominous silence, broken only by cheers here and there, as the men climbed up out of the ravines and rushed across the exposed ground to the ditch. Then, all in a moment, the Rebels' parapet became a fringe of gray and steel, from which streamed a livid sheet of fire." The colonel of the 69th Indiana in the center hurried his men, yelling, "Hurry up, Boys, the firing has begun all along the line, and we will miss it if we do not get there soon!" His men did so, singing "We'll Rally 'Round the Flag, Boys." Colonel Keigwin noted the abundance of optimism: "At the signal the three columns moved, and, judging from their appearance, every officer and soldier seemed confident of success."[55]

The first task was to cross the ravines in front of the Confederate line, where many obstructions greeted them, including an abatis that Osterhaus described well: "All timber was cut down and converted into the most intricate abatis and extending almost all along my immediate front." The men, Osterhaus reported, "moved forward, breaking over all obstructions at the foot and in the slope of the hills, and against a terrible fire from all the rifle-pits and forts." The right and center columns had the luxury of moving up the feeder-branch ravines between the three spurs, but the left had no such aid and had to traverse the ridge of the left spur, which was raked with Confederate fire. Matters were difficult for the right and center columns too, as the ravines were likewise swept with fire, with the added problem of obstacles planted therein.[56]

The Alabamians of Stephen D. Lee's brigade were ready, Carter Stevenson noting that "they [the enemy] were allowed to approach unmolested to within good musket range, when every available gun was opened upon them with grape and canister." Lee himself was just as ready, perched in position to watch the assault all knew was coming and ready to control—or rally, if need be—his Alabamians.[57]

On the right, the 22nd Kentucky and 42nd Ohio advanced in the ravine between the right and center spur, moving along the natural line of the spurs, but these did not offer much safety from enfilade fire. One Ohioan described how the line in column pushed forward, "rounding the clump of willows at the bottom of the ravine" and taking a heavy fire. Colonel Lindsey, who led the column in person, wrote that "we crossed the abatis on the right, under fire from the right, left, and front." The Alabamians in the Square Fort and along the lines to the north were able to rake the Federal ranks, although little trouble came from the Railroad Redoubt to the right simply because other brigades of McClernand's corps were advancing on that work at the same time. The Mississippi and Alabama gunners manning the cannons inside the forts also let loose. Once the men arrived at a fairly sheltered locale, Lindsey ordered them to catch their breath while he scouted ahead. It had been rougher terrain than they had imagined, and he wanted to get a better look now that he was close. Lindsey realized that "on examining the ground, I found it utterly impossible to reach the enemy's works at the point I was ordered to." "And so reported to the general," he added.[58]

Stephen D. Lee's Alabamians were solid troops and easily held this portion of the line with the aid of the terrain and abatis. Major George W. Mathieson of the 31st Alabama, on Lindsey's front, described how "a heavy column of infantry appeared in front, and attempted to charge my position." He went on to describe the reaction from his Alabamians: "The men of my command poured a heavy fire into their ranks for about an hour. . . . His killed and wounded lay thick on the field, and he was evidently badly crippled." Apparently, a few of the Federals reached the fortifications, a lower-level soldier in the 31st Alabama giving more detail: "I'll tell you fighting hand to hand is not fun, we killed some with the breech of our guns."[59]

In the center, the 114th Ohio and 49th and 69th Indiana regiments likewise gained ground at terrible expense, the dead and wounded beginning to pile up as they moved forward up the ravine toward the Confederate line between the left and center spurs. Colonel Keigwin, who had been so optimistic moments before, suddenly changed his tune: "But as we neared the enemy we found obstacles which were more in our way than the balls of the enemy." He elaborated that the "abatis in the ravines between us and the enemy's works were almost impassable." Yet the Ohioans and Indianans stuck in the ravine could not remain where they were, and Keigwin motioned the 49th Indiana forward over the abatis; they succeeded in moving up toward the Confederate line a sufficient distance to find "cover behind a small hill under the works of the enemy." The fire of the 69th Indiana, which Keigwin had moved to the left and ordered to open up to cover the other Indiana regiment, materially aided the troops, although the 69th Indiana found the Confederates were "concentrating a fire on us from three different points." Still, the Indianans laid down such a heavy volume of fire that the 49th Indiana made it across the abatis.[60]

Yet they could go no farther. Oran Perry of the 69th Indiana noted how his regiment ascended the draw and topped the high ground: "We had all expected to find level ground in front of the works and how surprised we were to find it different." Confusion reigned, Perry adding that "everyone realized that we could go no further, consequently there was a hustling to get under cover." The Indianans simply "line[d] up on their bellies just under the brow of the hill, where the curiously inclined could peer over and see what was going on." There they stayed for hours, sending only details to the rear to make coffee, although the flag-bearer rushed up the hill and "screwed the flagstaff into the ground, which he did quickly and in very good time for himself, for immediately the dirt was knocked all around the flag by the bullets of the enemy." Casualties began to mount even there, including a future congressman, Colonel John Cradlebaugh of the 114th Ohio, who received a wound in the mouth.[61]

While the center and right columns bogged down, the left column actually suffered the most, it being closest to the major Confederate firepower in the Square Fort. There, the 7th Kentucky and 118th Illinois took major casualties, Osterhaus simply noting that "they suffered heavily." Colonel Keigwin went into more detail, writing that "the Seventh Kentucky suffered more severely than any of the rest of the regiments in the command. They were leading the charge on the left, and had to pass over a bare hill, when the enemy poured such a heavy and destructive fire into them that part were forced to retire, and those that did not get over the point were forced to remain there." He later joked that the troops "I suppose went upon the principle that good men were scarce, and they just went back under cover." Osterhaus similarly described how the Kentuckians "advanced to the top of the hill, and marched over the naked brow of it through murderous fire from the great redoubt on the left." There, the 20th Alabama of Stephen D. Lee's brigade, along with the artillery, poured heavy fire into the now-visible Federals.[62]

More Federal targets appeared for the Alabamians when the trailing 118th Illinois made it over the bare hill on the right of the Kentuckians. Colonel John G. Fonda remembered his orders were to "follow it over the hill." The Illinoisans watched in horror as the Kentuckians moved diagonally over the brow, Fonda reporting that "about two-thirds of it had reached the top of the hill when the enemy's fire became so severe that those who had not broke back and did not pass." Keigwin simply noted that they were also "forced to retire, as the fire of the enemy was too hot for them to remain, it also being evident that the abatis could not be passed." The Illinoisans managed to form a line at the top of the hill, from which they could pepper the Confederate lines, although one Ohioan declared that they "as usual, faltered." Another testified that the Illinoisans "fell back in utter confusion."[63]

Colonel Marcus Spiegel and the 120th Ohio followed, in large part to keep the 118th Illinois from "breaking" again as they had on May 19, one Ohioan declaring that "we were placed in their rear with orders, if needed, to drive them forward at the point of the bayonet." Colonel Keigwin was heard to say that "I have no fears of the 120th, I could give her any position." For his part, Spiegel reported: "When we arrived at the crest of the hill above the ravine, a terrible and withering fire from the enemy met us, from which the advance suffered greatly." Another noted that "they came back with such force that our (120th) could not advance, so we were all halted." Colonel Spiegel continued on as best he could, yelling "come on my bullies," but he found "that crossing the hill under such fire would be destructive, while even after crossing the hill an impassable ravine and abettis had to be confronted, and our forces would be at the mercy of the enemy, the column was halted and the charge abandoned." The Ohioans were soon sent to the left again to lengthen the line of skirmishers.[64]

Still, all three columns by this point had made some headway, despite struggling through the tangle of natural and man-made obstacles in the ravine in front of the Confederate works. In fact, all three columns had approached the Confederate fortifications, Osterhaus declaring that "all the columns reached the top of the hill, and came within so short a distance from the works that all orders and commands given on the enemy's side could be distinctly understood by our men." But there was more than shouted commands and orders emanating from the Confederate works. The heavy volume of infantry and artillery fire forced the Federals to face increasingly harsh circumstances as they held on to their tenuous position in front of the Confederate line.[65]

"The officers and men acted most courageously," Osterhaus said, "but, finding that new obstacles not seen before would impede their farther advance, the column halted to rest, availing themselves of the irregularities of the ground for shelter." The initial burst of Federal lead had been absorbed and contained, and the Confederate lines held. In fact, the Federals had not even made as much headway here as on other sections of the line where the actual ditches in front of the works were gained and where numerous flags were planted on the parapets.[66]

Confederate division commander Carter Stevenson described the successful fighting on his side: "The men, rising in the trenches, poured into their ranks volley after volley with so deadly an effect that, leaving the ground literally covered in some places with their dead and wounded, they precipitately retreated." Stephen D. Lee gave the same report, writing that "the assault upon my front was a determined one, but was handsomely repulsed, with a considerable loss to the enemy."[67]

Osterhaus's assault had been blunted, and Hovey had found no opportunity to throw in Spiceley's troops in reserve: he simply noted that Spiceley was "not seriously engaged." One 46th Indiana surgeon agreed, writing that the regiment spent the day in a ravine: "Bullets fell about us quite profusely, but [only] one of our regiment hurt however." That said, Hovey reported that the artillery under his command "did admirable execution, and fully sustained their part of the charge." One shot from the 1st Wisconsin Battery hit a Confederate caisson and blew it up, Lieutenant Oscar F. Nutting remarking that the explosion, "taking place within their fortifications, must have caused fearful havoc among their men." Then matters eased for a while as both sides caught their breaths in the intense heat. Yet just because the Federal advance had been blunted did not mean that Osterhaus withdrew his forces. There was the possibility of continuing the attack later, perhaps depending on what occurred elsewhere along the line, and Osterhaus wanted to be as close as possible if that happened. He simply kept the skirmishers and "leading divisions of the columns" active in keeping up a heavy fire; the division commander reported that it caused "their gunners to leave their guns, and prevent[ed] their infantry from showing themselves, except for moments."[68]

Nevertheless, Osterhaus's advance had ground to a halt on the nearest slopes abutting the Confederate works. If McClernand was going to provide the victory he so much desired, it would have to come somewhere else than here as well. Fortunately for him, McClernand had other assaults moving forward at the same time—and those would prove to be more successful.

If McClernand would enjoy personal victory this day, it would have to come from his center two brigades, the two left brigades of Carr's and Smith's divisions. They fronted the Confederate works south of the 2nd Texas Lunette that Benton and Burbridge were assaulting, but they were north of the Square Fort that Osterhaus was finding so difficult to reach. On this front, another fortification (the Railroad Redoubt, called "Fort Beauregard" by the Federals) loomed ahead of the Confederate line. It sat on a prominent point alongside the fort's namesake, the Southern Railroad of Mississippi, and was strong and foreboding, like all the rest. But McClernand deployed crack regiments from his division for the assault here. It had been Michael Lawler's Iowans who had done the almost unimaginable at Big Black River Bridge five days ago, and McClernand hoped the gargantuan Lawler could do it again. His troops certainly thought so, one who had fought with him at Big Black River simply jotting in his diary: "He will do."⁶⁹

Lawler, as the left brigade of Carr's division, held the front line of the Federal position, with William Landram's brigade of Smith's division in support. Lawler was no stranger to the fight, having led his men in the unlikely assault on the Confederate position at Big Black River. General Grant himself described that day, hearing "great cheering to the right of our line and, looking in that direction, saw Lawler in his shirt sleeves leading a charge upon the enemy." He was two hundred and fifty pounds of pure Irishman, having been born in County Kildare. A veteran of the Mexican War, Lawler became colonel of the 18th Illinois and was wounded at Fort Donelson. He ruled with an iron fist, although Charles Dana wrote that he "is as brave as a lion, and has about as much brains."⁷⁰

Equally brave were his men. The brigade normally contained four regiments: the 21st, 22nd, and 23rd Iowa and the 11th Wisconsin. The 23rd Iowa was detached from the brigade at this point to guard prisoners and "has since gone north with them," Lawler wrote, so he was left with only three regiments. To make up for it, the 97th Illinois of Landram's reserve brigade was temporarily transferred to Lawler for duty on the front line of the assault, one of the Illinoisans describing the preparations: "Everything was a hustle and bustle, officers hurrying to and fro, men falling in line and drums and bugles sounding."⁷¹

The Illinoisans were one of six regiments in Colonel William J. Landram's brigade, so it could spare one to operate with Lawler. Landram was a Kentucky lawyer and Mexican War veteran who became colonel of the 19th Kentucky, one of the regiments in his brigade. Three Illinois regiments (the 77th, 97th, and 130th) were also part of the brigade. Only the 48th Ohio under Lieutenant Colonel Job Parker was a truly veteran unit, having seen heavy action at Shiloh, holding Sherman's Shiloh Church line, as well as many of the actions between Shiloh and the Vicksburg campaign. Its normal commander, Peter J. Sullivan, had been dreadfully wounded at Shiloh and was still recovering on detached service in Memphis, thereby leaving Parker in command despite there being bad blood between the two.⁷²

Lawler was itching for a fight by the 10:00 A.M. time to move forward and had positioned his brigade in an advanced location actually under the cover of darkness, around 4:00 A.M. that morning. Colonel William M. Stone of the 22nd Iowa explained the nocturnal movement, writing that the regiment "moved over the brow of the hill and passed noiselessly down the ravine into which the enemy had felled trees in every conceivable manner, crawling cautiously on hands and knees for two or three hours we succeeded in reaching the desired position without drawing the attention of the enemy pickets which were posted about twenty yards distant." Once there, as the "day was dawning," one Iowan wrote that they then lay down to rest and "lay on our arms and patiently awaited the hour to come." Certainly, they had been through a lot already, one Iowan describing "it was almost an impossibility to get through the briars and branches. Faces were swollen, and masses of mosquito bites—with the vines and briars—left bleeding abrasions and scratches on their hands and faces." He described the brigade as "like caterpillars . . . crawling upon hands and knees through a veritable jungle of weeds and briar-bushes." By the time daylight shone, the troops had taken a covered position below the brow of the hill on which the Confederate line sat, within a hundred yards, Lawler explained, with some of the companies out as skirmishers to "stay on the hill and pick them off as they raised over the fort to fire." Here they were sheltered by the brow of the hill, "on the top and a little to the rear of which the enemy's works were constructed." Another Iowan declared "a heavy dew had fallen during the night, and a balmy freshness filled the air," making the ground soft and wet. One Iowan remembered "the hoof-marks of cattle could be seen in the mire."[73]

Even though the Confederates could not see the nearby enemy because of earlier darkness and the terrain, Stephen D. Lee knew an attack was coming. He and Colonel Charles M. Shelley of the 30th Alabama observed the lines and discussed their options. Lee told Shelley that he was afraid the main attack would come at the detached fortification and was "expecting the Yankees almost at any time, to make a dash on that work." Lee thought there were not enough men in the fort to hold it, and he cautioned Shelley to retake it in that event. Lee was correct in his concern, because inside the detached tip of the work were a mere fifteen or twenty men of Lieutenant James M. Pearson's Alabama company. And they had already endured casualties. One of Pearson's men learned he could stick his hat above the works with a ramrod and draw fire, whereupon he could lurch upward and fire at the sound and the smoke. He finally hit a Union sharpshooter "who raised and fell over backward," his friends catching him. This emboldened the Alabamian, who became reckless despite Pearson's admonition not to "needlessly expose himself." Pearson noted that he "lost all reserve and caution, and began to fire indiscriminately at the enemy." He also noted "it was not long before he was killed."[74]

As 10:00 A.M. approached, everybody could see that the fighting was about to begin. Colonel Shelley sent word for Pearson's men, who requested he withdraw them to a safer place, to "quit sharpshooting, keep in the trenches, stay where we were, and not fire except upon an advancing column." But the Union bombardment was getting quite severe; at one point three successive shells exploded in concert above the fort and its hapless defenders, "scattering dirt, trash, and debris in every direction that it seemed that the very elements were resolving themselves into chaos," Pearson remembered. He added that it seemed like "the very earth beneath us was as unstable as if an earthquake was in operation." Then the cannonading suddenly stopped. Lieutenant Pearson resolved to raise up quickly and look to see what was happening, and to his amazement the next issue on his list of worries became real: the Federals were advancing. "I sprang to my feet and looked in the direction of the enemy, when they seemed to be springing from the bowels of the earth a long line of indigo, a magnificent line in each direction, and they kept for a while the alignment as if on dress parade, but moving at double quick." Pearson was mad at himself: "I was greatly surprised to see him rise up out of the earth and in such close proximity to the fort." He thought he "would be able to see the enemy a quarter or half mile before he started." Only years later was it explained to him that Lawler had positioned his brigade under the hill very close to the fort under the cover of night.[75]

Providing that shock to the defenders of the Railroad Redoubt, Lawler had sent a staff officer to Colonel Stone with orders to move forward with the battle cry of "Remember the State you are from, and Col. Kinsman, of the 23rd Iowa, killed at Black river, and go in boys you shall have all the support you want." That staff officer, Bluford Wilson, ran into trouble, however. Leaving Lawler back at the main line, he approached the colonels as they were in deep discussion. They had examined the ground even more now that it was daylight and determined that, instead of a two-pronged attack as ordered, they should all concentrate on the Railroad Redoubt. Wilson told them that they were on the ground and knew best and to do as they desired, although they wanted Wilson to obtain permission, arguing that their "orders were specific, made on consultation with the General the evening before, [and] they did not feel at liberty to change them in any particular." Wilson even stated that he would take partial responsibility, but that did not satisfy them. Yet the decision was soon made as 10:00 A.M. quickly came and the troops, aligned as Lawler had dictated, had to move according to the original plan.[76]

Soon they were off, "promptly at that hour," Lawler reported as he watched from the main line with A. J. Smith. The brigade went forward in two columns, with the 22nd Iowa, minus a company serving as General Carr's provost guard, on the right directly in front of the Railroad Redoubt that stuck out like a finger. The 11th Wisconsin fronted the recessed Confederate works south of the fort. The 21st Iowa supported the 22nd Iowa, while the borrowed 97th Illinois supported the 11th Wisconsin. In such manner, the Federals moved forward "determined to dislodge the enemy or die in the attempt," one Iowan noted, until they topped the hill and gained the plateau before the fort, coming into full view of the waiting Confederates. There matters changed. "As soon as they reached the crest of the hill," Lawler described, "a terrible fire from the enemy in front and on both flanks swept the ground and did fearful execution. Officers and men fell on every side." Colonel Stone gave more detail, writing that "as our colours rose above the crest of the hill, a thousand bayonets glistened in the sunshine above the parapet." Also popping over was a Confederate officer, who one Iowan described as mounting "the parapet—waving a small flag with one hand—like the oriflamme of Navarre—and swinging his sword over his head—cried out at the top of his voice—'Come on ye damned yanks'—and almost instantly fell back into the fort—and into his long leaden sleep." Federal color-bearers were finding their own problems, in particular just getting the flags to the front as the "long silken-tassels" kept getting caught in the brush.[77]

They did not stop, despite one Federal describing how the "front [was] subject to an enfilading fire of musketry and artillery from almost every direction." Lawler said that the regiments bounded forward "with a courage that could not be daunted." But more unforeseen troubles loomed ahead. On the left, the Wisconsin troops topped the ridge and crossed it under heavy fire, thinking that they were right on the enemy. Instead, there was unbeknownst to them yet another one of those feeder branches that angled away from the Confederate line, making another ravine tucked in behind the main ridge they were crossing. As a result, the left of the brigade found it had to cross another ravine to get to the Confederates, and it was choked with abatis. Lawler explained that it was "a deep and hitherto concealed ravine, filled with abatis." Still, Colonel Charles L. Harris plunged his troops into the tangle toward the Confederate works held by the 46th Alabama.[78]

Many factors soon stopped this wing of the brigade. Lawler described how "owing partly to the difficulty of the ravine itself, partly to the concentrated fire of the enemy, and partly to a want of sufficient support, he found it impossible to advance." Indeed, Lawler was not impressed with his borrowed Illinoisans; while some of the Iowans to the right had become disconnected with their regiments and joined in the advance, Lawler noted that only "a portion of the Ninety-seventh Illinois" moved forward all the way. Colonel Harris could only "dispose ... of his men in the bottom and along the sides of the ravines as best he could, [but] he halted and bravely held his ground," Lawler noted. For his part, one Illinoisan wrote that "we all pushed forward and were met by a Rebel hurricane of shot and shell, grape, canister, shrapnel, solid shot, bomb shells, and tons of musket balls." Still, for whatever reason, the brigade's left column was stopped, just like all the other assaults thus far that morning.[79]

Miraculously, results were different on the right of the brigade, where a watching McClernand noted that "within fifteen minutes Lawler's and Landram's brigades had carried the ditch, slope, and bastion of the fort." Although some abatis were present on the right column's front as well, causing Colonel Stone to "reform the line, it having become very much scattered in crossing logs and obstructions which literally covered the ground," the Iowans still managed to move across and reach the fortifications despite the heavy Confederate fire that erupted just as the Federals topped the hill. The right of the leading 22nd Iowa continued on the farthest, directly toward the redoubt. Carter Stevenson described how "a party of about 60 of the enemy, under command of a lieutenant colonel, made a rush, and succeeded in effecting a lodgment in the ditch at the foot of the redoubt and planting two flags on the edge of the parapet." Most of the Federals stopped at the ditch, Lawler writing that "the width and depth of the ditch in front of the works, combined with the heavy fire poured into them by the rebels, checked the main advance." Captain Charles N. Lee of the 22nd Iowa gave more details about the Confederate works, describing the fort with a "ditch 10 feet deep, 6 feet wide, the walls being 20 feet high." Still, several men managed to reach the fort and plant the flag of the 22nd Iowa on the parapet.[80]

Major Joseph B. Atherton of the 22nd Iowa described the heavy fire they endured: "From our first appearance upon the hill we were exposed to a terrible fire from the enemy, concealed within their forts and rifle-pits." He proudly told how his men "maintained their line and advanced like veterans" even though "while here, we were exposed to a murderous fire from the front and an enfilading fire from the right and left, the enemy's works being so constructed as to effect this result." Still the Iowans pressed on. Their colonel, William M. Stone, was at the forefront but went down with "a ball through the arm" about the time the flag was planted. The following 21st Iowa, moving by the left flank despite what Major Salue G. Van Anda described as "the fire of the enemy from both flanks, as well as the front," also reached the fort, despite the loss of the regiment's lieutenant colonel, Cornelius W. Dunlap. He had remained in the rear initially because he was "quite lame" from a foot wound at Port Gibson, but he could not resist coming forward once the regiment reached the works. Lawler sadly noted that he "still managed to make his way to the advance of his regiment soon after the charge, where he was almost immediately killed by a shot through the head." Many others managed to reach the ditch as well and "sheltered themselves . . . in its front and the gullies washed on the sides of the hill," opening a heavy fire on the defending Confederates.[81]

The effect was not just in the Railroad Redoubt itself, at least according to several Federals. Some of the Confederates on either side of the redoubt also left the rifle pits, those on the north side evacuating the trenches all the way to the railroad. Colonel Stone of the 22nd Iowa also noted that some left the trenches on the south side of the redoubt and that "I stood with Lieutenant-Colonel Dunlap, of the 21st Iowa, on the highest and most exposed point near the fort. We saw them leave and conversed about it." Stone was evidently satisfied at the time. "I sent word back to General Carr to send me a brigade and I would hold the works," he noted, adding that "I then regarded the door to Vicksburg as opened, and so said to Colonel Dunlap." But the feeling of joy suddenly evaporated: "We were there looking over the ground, congratulating ourselves upon our success, when I was shot in the arm by a sharpshooter from the woods beyond their rifle-pits." Dunlap also went down.[82]

Unlike the situation elsewhere, however, that was not the extent of the surge. The Confederate ditches had been reached in several other points along the line, so this was nothing remarkable. Conversely, an actual breakthrough occurred at the Railroad Redoubt, at a place where the earlier artillery bombardment had breached the walls of the fort at the cannon embrasure. Engineer Peter Hains described how the fort had "been battered considerably by the fire from the 30-pounder battery, near the crossing of the wagon road over the railroad." Alabamian Edmund W. Pettus later explained that "it was battered down by the Federal Artillery to a level with the ground in the redoubt." Lawler described how "a few brave men, however, leaping into the ditch, clambered up the sides of the fort [and] rushed into it." Several Iowans, including the 22nd Iowa's lieutenant colonel, Harvey Graham, managed to move through the breach, where they met the defending Alabamians, at times the Iowans "raising one another up the wall." Hand-to-hand combat ensued. Of the thirteen Federals who actually entered the fortification, only Sergeant Joseph E. Griffith of the 22nd Iowa survived the ordeal long enough to get out after an hour inside the Confederate bastion; he was himself wounded. His counterpart, Sergeant Nicholas C. Messenger, who later testified that he and the others "[scaled] by redoubled energy the high walls of dirt," was wounded so badly he could not get out.[83]

Lieutenant Pearson was still in shock when the Federals began to breach the fortification, entering in mostly through the torn-out embrasure of the Alabama gun. Unfortunately, the cannoneers responded with little defense, never firing the cannon. When the Iowans began to pour through, the artillerymen left, Pearson calling out "Why don't you shoot your cannon, Lieutenant?" to which he replied "I have no lanyard." Pearson though for a moment that he did not even know what a lanyard was, but he watched nonetheless as the cannoneers "continued at a rapid gait to the rear." That left only the infantrymen, some of whom were down as well, one Alabamian dying when the first Federal through shot him as he was capping his musket. Pearson himself admitted that "I had a very strong inclination myself to retire at that time, but nothing but a fear of disastrous consequences resulting from such a course prevented me." Perhaps he should have, as more of the enemy were on the way. More Federals indeed followed, Pearson writing that "the enemy when they first began to enter came one behind the other, but soon came in numbers sufficient to begin a battle royal, by clubbing muskets, and a sort of knock down and drag out."[84]

Carter Stevenson knew full well what it meant and that it had to be contained. It was bad enough that the Federals had protection in that very area, but Stevenson wrote that "the work was constructed in such a manner that this ditch was commanded by no part of the line." At the breach itself a party of some sixty Federals appeared to be moving into the fortification. Stevenson had to think quickly, noting that "the only means by which they could be dislodged was to retake the angle by a desperate charge, and either kill or compel the surrender of the whole party by the use of hand-grenades." To reinforce the breach even more, Stevenson and Lee had already returned the 46th Alabama, which had been withdrawn for rest, to their former position "habitually held by the regiment." Stevenson also moved forward the actual reserve consisting of Waul's Texas Legion, two companies into the rear portion of the redoubt itself and the rest on the flanks. "We DOUBLE QUICKED it over the hill and into the Rifle Pits," remembered Albert C. Lenert of the Legion. "Here we scattered wherever we found room and commenced to shoot." Because this was a near crisis, Lee also called on reserves from elsewhere, including those behind Moore's line to his left. Martin Green's Arkansas and Missouri brigade quickly began moving toward the crisis point too, although it would take longer for them to arrive.[85]

Not all sixty Federals in the ditch entered the fort, but too many for comfort did. The small party of advancing Iowans found the cannon in the fortification, the Alabama crew having quickly scampered away without touching it off. Other Confederates soon appeared and rushed into the no-man's-land at the tip of the fort, however, firing as they advanced. Most of the Federals were down by this point, but Sergeant Griffith managed to recover from "the stunning effect of a shot" and grabbed a musket, with which he captured thirteen of the now unloaded Confederates who had just fired their muskets. The Confederate line had been breached, but it was tentative at best, actually held by one wounded Federal. Still, many rejoiced at the success. Lawler proclaimed that "a portion of their works were in our possession," and Major Van Anda of the 21st Iowa declared that "many of our officers and men fell on every side, but with a determination that knew no fear, the enemy's works were gained, and they were routed from their stronghold." Major Joseph Atherton of the 22nd Iowa similarly asserted that "the column pressed forward, stormed the fort, took possession of the same and its inmates, and held it until dark."[86]

That was technically true, but far from reality. The Railroad Redoubt had been constructed in a long, pointed fashion, much like an extended finger, and there were preformed traverses within the detached tip. When the Iowans managed to enter the tip of the fortification, the Confederate defenders mostly fell back to the next earthen wall that scaled it, a smaller version of Robert E. Lee's defense of the pierced Mule Shoe at Spotsylvania nearly a year later. John McClernand described it as "another defense commanding the interior." Thus, the few Federals who made it into the tip of the fort fought with only a few remaining Confederates under Pearson who did not get out. It was an isolated fight to be sure, but the Federals had indeed technically taken a portion of the Confederate defenses, and the flag of the 22nd Iowa waved over the Confederate works.[87]

Such success had not occurred anywhere else along the line as yet. And the assault was far from done. William Landram's support brigade was moving forward even then, and with more troops adding more pressure, this might actually have developed into a real breach leading to victory. Landram's troops had nervously awaited the time to advance, one Ohioan writing that it was "somewhat like that of the culprit awaiting the hour of his execution." Landram sent some of the regiments to the left to support the stalled 11th Wisconsin and 97th Illinois, Landram's own 19th Kentucky under Major Morgan V. Evans veering to the left and advancing "over the hill." It soon became embroiled in the same abatis in the ravine that stopped the others, and Major Evans himself went down in the fighting. The 48th Ohio under Lieutenant Colonel Job Parker also advanced on the left but soon had to take cover under the hill, one Ohioan recalling that "we all got under cover against the hill side and the work began in earnest." Parker himself was wounded, although his archenemy Colonel Peter Sullivan, who was on detached duty back at Memphis at the time, later related that he "received a very slight flesh wound on the cheek-bone, merely breaking the skin. He shortly after retired from the field." Making it worse for the regiment, Major Virgil H. Moats was mortally wounded, leaving the unit leaderless.[88]

Some of Landram's regiments also moved toward the redoubt itself, where the best chance of broadening the already-gained success existed. While the

130th Illinois remained in the ravine in reserve, Landram sent the 77th Illinois forward, one of its members recalling that it was "a beautiful, clear morning, and so calm that not a leaf moved upon the trees." There had been an officer's call at 9:00 A.M. in the regiment and preparation for the assault at ten o'clock. Now, the Illinoisans pressed toward the redoubt, "over & down & up two hills to the rebel fortifications," Colonel David Grier wrote home, "in plain view of them and exposed to a thunderous fire from their men." The fire was indeed heavy, one Illinoisan commenting that before the assault the Confederates did not respond "but were as still as though they were all dead." Now that the Federals had moved into the open, the Alabamians suddenly appeared, "which convinced us that instead of them all being dead they were entirely too much alive for any use," the same Union soldier remarked. The fire quickly told, the Illinoisans able only to keep "in tolerably fair line for about a hundred yards." Grier and his troops nevertheless managed to reach the ditch: "This they did in splendid style on the double quick with their bayonets fixed." Colonel Grier shouted to "plant our colors upon the ramparts," the bearer doing so beside those of the 22nd Iowa. The colonel later asserted that some of the Illinoisans also went over the top of the parapet and into the fort despite heavy fire coming on them, "most of it coming from the fort."[89]

The Illinoisans indeed planted their colors "after the excitement of tumbling into the ditch was over a little." The bearer was Bill Kerrick, who "carried the flag on the fort that day, and when he planted the flag on the fort his body was riddled with bullets and he lay dead under his flag." Other regiments soon did the same, although an Illinoisan later noted that if they did "it was not there long enough to be seen." McClernand later stated that the 48th Ohio's colors were also planted on the fortification, even though the regiment fought to the left, and even those of the 130th Illinois behind were brought forward and flew from "the counter-scarp of the ditch, while those of the Forty-eighth Ohio and Seventy-seventh Illinois waved over the bastion." Indeed, the 48th Ohio's color guard had become separated from the regiment, which was fighting to the left, and Lieutenant Joseph F. Parker of the 130th Illinois described how he planted the flag and positioned Ed Dunn to hold it in place. When the flag staff was shattered and Dunn wounded, the flag fell over into the Confederates, who grabbed it to haul it in. Parker shimmied up the parapet and grabbed the "slivered flag staff and snatched the flag from the hands of the Rebels and said to them 'Oh no I'll take care of this flag." He then shoved the "splintered" staff in the ground and cared for his wounded companion Dunn.[90]

Despite the bevy of Union flags on the parapet, Lawler and Landram had been stopped. Lawler sent a message back at 10:10 A.M. to division commander Smith, who sent it on to McClernand, stating that "the enemy are massing their forces in our front. No movements of our troops on our left. We ought to have re-enforcements." Unfortunately, McClernand had no reserves left to send in just then.[91]

Only on Lawler's front was there true success, if it could even be called that, as it was fleeting and limited. He ordered the exhausted troops to cover themselves as best they could and hang on: "As my men were already much exhausted, and as the reinforcements sent them were light, farther advance under the circumstances was deemed impracticable, and orders were accordingly issued directing the men of the two brigades to hold the ground already gained. This order went out with the hope that re-enforcements might soon be forwarded, with whose aid they might assault the rebel works with a certainty of success."[92]

That success had been only partially evident all along the lines, but the Confederates were realizing just how close it was here. John Forney noted that at all three roads to his front the enemy managed to get "a few men into our exterior ditches at each point of attack." Such concern can easily be seen in the messages racing between Confederate brigade and division commanders and on up to Pemberton himself. Moore sent a courier to Forney at 12:15 P.M.: "Enemy repulsed from my right. Attacking again or advancing. Captured one stand of colors." In detailing the worrisome action to his right on Lee's front, he added: "Seem to have been driven out by Lee, though colors were in his works." "Would like two regiments more." Forney sent Moore's critical message on to Pemberton, explaining the dire situation. "Enemy attack from time to time," he wrote, actually all the way up to the Jackson and even Graveyard roads. "I cannot, therefore, reinforce Moore from Hebert." Worse, he reminded Pemberton that Green had been sent down to support Lee: "We have now no reserve. Have sent to Generals Smith and Bowen for re-enforcements." He nevertheless ended by stating that "the men are standing to the work."[93]

Others were realizing the same thing, including correspondent Cadwallader, who was already formulating a story while he watched. He described how the Federal assault column "had been so mercilessly torn to pieces by Confederate shot and shell that it had lost nearly all resemblance to a line of battle, or the formation of a storming column. Officers and men were rushing ahead pell-mell without much attention to alignment." He added how "a straggling line, continually growing thinner and weaker, finally reached the summit."[94]

More important, at this time others were telling a similar story. Lawler sent such remarks up the chain of command, where they found willing listeners.

This partial success was something that had not occurred anywhere else along the lines of assault that morning, but it was such a development that it could be easily mistaken as a major success. And therein was the key. A jubilant John McClernand was ready to grasp at any straw he could to achieve the victory that the West Pointers could not provide and to obtain the glory due him. The Illinois politician was on the verge of victory, and he did not aim to let it slip through his grasp.[95]

10

"I Could Not Disregard His Reiterated Statements"

Ulysses S. Grant watched with great expectation as the Federal troops moved forward on a three-mile front. At times, he came under fire himself. Grant's twelve-year-old son Fred remembered that his father "and Logan had a narrow escape from a shell which was fired directly down a ravine which they had just entered." Even that did not lessen the general's enthusiasm. This was the day he had wanted so hard to see for almost seven months, and he expected great results. In fact, all the maneuvering, experiments, and battles had been for this sole reason: to position his army at a point where it could take Vicksburg. He had been successful, if through a lengthy process, in getting here, and now all he had to do was break through the dejected Confederates' lines and capture Vicksburg. The miniature effort on May 19 had indicated that it would not be as easy as previously thought, but Grant had no expectation that the Confederates could withstand a coordinated, heavy attack on many fronts this day.[1]

To watch the great victory unfold, Grant rode south from his headquarters area to a point on the Jackson Road to observe the climactic battle. He wanted a vantage point from which he could see all three corps in action if possible, although seeing the far extents of McClernand's and Sherman's corps in opposite directions at the same time would be tricky, especially any of Steele's efforts around the angle of the Stockade Redan. Nevertheless, Grant chose the highest ground along his lines, the ridge on which the Jackson Road entered the Confederate works: "I had taken a commanding position near McPherson's front, and from which I could see all the advancing columns from his corps, and a part of each of Sherman's and McClernand's." The ground was a bit higher at the enemy's redan north of the road, an obvious reason why Lockett chose to place the fortifications there, but the same ridge moving eastward was still high enough to allow Grant to see all the way down southward to McClernand's positions as well as northward to the Graveyard Road. Grant thus took station behind Logan's division of McPherson's corps in time to watch the great 10:00 A.M. assault that would hopefully end this campaign once and for all.[2]

Unfortunately for Grant, what he saw from his high-ground vantage point all morning was not anything like what he had desired or expected. He watched McPherson's troops bog down amid the terrain and Confederate fire in his front. He could see the debacle growing on the Graveyard Road to his north, as well as Blair's troops fanning out in the ravine just north of Glass Bayou. And he could see McClernand's troops push forward but then stop, like all the others, at the fortifications, although it was harder for him to see detail that far away, especially south of the railroad which was nearly a mile and a half away as compared to less than a mile to the Stockade Redan. Still, Grant could see enough to know the assault had not worked out as he had hoped.[3]

In an effort to find out as much as he could elsewhere than on McPherson's front, Grant decided to ride over to his most trusted corps commander, William T. Sherman, to discuss what should be the next move. Once he arrived, Hugh Ewing declared that Grant almost inadvertently rode into Confederate fire trying to get a better look and was turned away only when a staff officer "seized his horse's bridle and backed him out of danger." Thereafter, Grant left his horse well behind the lines and walked forward on foot. There, under as much cover as they could get, Sherman noted: "I pointed out to him the rebel works, admitting that my assault had failed." Grant responded that the same had occurred on both McPherson's and McClernand's fronts. The two then conferred about the difficulties that were growing.[4]

Then everything changed when Grant received a message from McClernand. He had been in touch with his commanders throughout the day, McClernand even telling him late that morning via signal that "I am hotly engaged with the enemy. He is massing on me from the right and left. A vigorous blow by McPherson would make a diversion in my favor." Grant received this note around noon while still on McPherson's lines and interpreted it that "he [McClernand] was hard pressed at several points." He simply told McClernand by return signal to use his reserves to plug any gaps or soft areas, and then, seemingly unconcerned, rode over to the right to see Sherman. It was there that a second, more definitive message from McClernand arrived: "We are hotly engaged with the enemy. We have part possession of two forts, and the Stars and Stripes are floating over them. A vigorous push ought to be made all along the line."[5]

Grant obviously had a decision to make. But could he trust McClernand, especially to the point of putting more lives at risk with additional assaults? Obviously, Grant had endured immense trouble with McClernand since their association began, the politicking general making speeches on battlefields and trying to usurp Grant's authority. Even in this most recent campaign, McClernand was standoffish and hardheaded, and Grant had real problems with his ranking corps commander even while giving him a choice piece of the work. In fact, Grant had in his pocket the permission from Halleck to remove McClernand at any time he wanted. He had received it while at Jackson on May 14 but had chosen not to use it. Now, Grant had to decide whether his senior general was trustworthy enough to restart the assaults that had obviously failed on most parts of the line he could plainly see.[6]

Given his history with McClernand, Grant had his doubts. He thought back to when he was at McPherson's line on the high ground and could detect no breakthrough. In fact, he reasoned that he could see McClernand's entire front from his vantage point back on the Jackson Road better than McClernand could up close. "The position occupied by me during most of the time of the assault," Grant reported, "gave me a better opportunity of seeing what was going on in front of the Thirteenth Army Corps than I believed it possible for the commander of it to have." He added, significantly, that "I could not see his possession of forts, nor necessity for re-enforcements, as represented in his dispatches, up to the time I left it." But if such was true, and he did not support McClernand, would Grant throw away a victory or even a chance for a victory? Ever trustful of Sherman, Grant showed him the letter.[7]

Grant argued that McClernand must be wrong: "I expressed doubts of it," he admitted. Sherman remembered it in a slightly more forceful way, writing that Grant blurted out, "I don't believe a word of it." Sherman counseled caution, however. He later wrote that "not dreaming that a major-general would at such a critical moment make a mere buncombe communication," it had to be acted on. "I reasoned with him," Sherman added. He argued that "this note was official, and must be credited." That pretty much turned Grant's mind.[8]

With Sherman's nudging, Grant decided to act: "At the time I could not disregard his reiterated statements, for they might possibly be true; and that no possible opportunity of carrying the enemy's stronghold should be allowed to escape through fault of mine." He thus ordered McClernand to call up McArthur's division of McPherson's corps, positioned down toward Warrenton to the south, to aid in his efforts. He also told Sherman that he would ride to McClernand to see for sure but that, if he had not been ordered any differently by 3:00 P.M., to restart the assaults. Grant then turned and rode southward to tell McPherson the same thing before moving on down to join McClernand to see exactly what was happening. While on the way, a third message arrived from McClernand, indicating that "we have gained the enemy's intrenchments at several points, but are brought to a stand." McClernand also noted he had ordered McArthur northward, as Grant ordered. Once he arrived at McPherson's headquarters, Grant showed him the dispatches as well and ordered him to restart his attacks too.[9]

In the largest bit of reshuffling, Grant also ordered Quinby's entire division of McPherson's corps to McClernand's aid. Grant reached McPherson and explained what was happening, demonstrating the need to send Quinby's brigades to McClernand. Apparently there was some hesitation on McPherson's part, Grant remembering that "I showed his dispatches to McPherson, as I had to Sherman, to satisfy him of the necessity of active diversion on their part to hold as much force in their fronts as possible." Then as Grant continued on, yet another messenger arrived from McClernand, who in the words of historian Michael Ballard "refused to be ignored." This fourth note stated that he "doubt[ed] not I will force my way through. I have lost no ground. My men are in two of the enemy's forts, but they are commanded by rifle pits in the rear. Several prisoners have been taken, who intimate that the rear is strong. At this moment I am hard pressed."[10]

Grant thus rekindled the attacks in the hope that McClernand was right. Certainly, the three messages indicated that McClernand had indeed done something, and Grant could with confidence think the right decision was to restart the assaults on Sherman's and McPherson's fronts. When the noise of battle began to be heard in those areas, he knew the optimum time for breaking the Confederate lines was at hand—if John A. McClernand could be trusted.

With the critical decision made to restart the assaults at 3:00 P.M. if he had heard nothing else from Grant, Sherman had to quickly plan his next move. He still had two of his three divisions fairly fresh, they having made no attacks at all, so his ability to spread around his weight and attack in multiple areas was still possible. In fact, Sherman at this point had overwhelming numerical odds in his favor. Three divisions of three brigades each surrounded the Stockade Redan area on three sides, Steele's concentrating division from the north, Blair's bloody division from the east, and Tuttle's entirely unengaged division along the Graveyard Road. With three brigades each, a total of nine brigades, more than fifteen thousand troops were concentrated on this one area of the Confederates lines less than a mile long. And parts of only four

Confederate brigades, actually only about eleven regiments in all, defended that small area. That was equivalent to about two of Sherman's brigades. Numbers were not the issue for the Federals.[11]

Obviously, the larger problems—which all from Sherman's position down to McClernand's lines were attuned to by this point—were the strong Confederate fortifications and the difficult terrain fronting them. All morning, Federals had hurled themselves across these ravines and toward the stiff defenses, mostly being driven back, with only partial lodgment on the sides of the fortifications themselves and only one or two debated breakthroughs. Terrain and cover had made up for the disproportionate numbers, as they normally do in warfare, and now Sherman had more decisions on his hands. If he was going to restart the advance, was it to be a repeat of May 19's style of attack across wide fronts in linear lines, or more pinprick-style assaults by the flank down the Graveyard Road? In actuality, and partially because Sherman had little control of his corps by this point, it would be both.[12]

Sherman remained at the Graveyard Road sector. From this high vantage point, where the Confederate line bent at a ninety-degree angle, he could see both directions where his troops were engaged, south and west. Had his line been straighter, more like McPherson's or McClernand's, he could have more than likely seen the entire length of his command from any point on the lines. But his corps wrapped around the Confederate lines, and the highest ground in the region was where the angle existed, which meant that Sherman could not see all his corps from one end or the other. Consequently, he had to stay in the center, from where he could see westward toward Steele's effort down the valley of Mint Spring Bayou as well as Blair's effort down the tributary than ran southward into Glass Bayou.[13]

Because Sherman was mostly tied to the high ground where he could command his entire corps, his personal control of the wings was less than firm. Accordingly, these divisions under Steele and Blair continued the fighting primarily under their division commanders. And by this time those commanders were not interested in trying any more of the assaults using flank attempts. In fact, Blair's brigades had spread out into a more linear formation, with Ewing's and Giles Smith's brigades side by side, although Kilby Smith's regiments were drawn up in reserve behind the other Smith's troops; they likely would have been posted on the main line as well had not Giles Smith's left rested on Ransom's brigade of McPherson's corps. There was not room for Kilby Smith to take a position in line, although one of his regiments had moved forward and supported some of Smith's Missourians at the front. Still, they took fire while getting into position, Cyrus Fisher of the 54th Ohio noting that they crossed a hill "over which a perfect storm of lead and iron was passing." Others remained on the safe side of a hill, although one 57th Ohio soldier declared that they had to "cling . . . to grape vines, stumps and roots to keep from slipping down."[14]

Similarly, Steele's stout brigades were massing for their attack. One Confederate remarked about the all-day gathering, describing the "enemy who had been collecting during the day at the foot of the hill opposite of the battery to the left of Co. K." Here too there was no effort to assault by the flank. In fact, the lead brigade under John Thayer was in linear formation with the next one under Charles Woods in column of regiments behind. Francis Manter's last brigade was farther back in reserve. So, while an assault in column was partially in the offing across Mint Spring Bayou, an assault by the flank was not considered.[15]

And so it happened that these two divisions moved forward in the afternoon largely without Sherman's direct guidance. Steele had been scheduled to make the attack with everyone else at 10:00 A.M., but the difficulties of getting the division in position had produced delay, and it was midafternoon before Steele was ready. One Iowan wrote that "we was ordered to march back about two miles round the hills." The suffering troops were getting annoyed in the meantime. One Iowan reflected the aggravation in his diary when he wrote that "at last Gen. Steele came and . . . examin[ed] the ground over which we must pass." Another soldier declared that Steele was slightly wounded in the head amid all the chaos. Once the brigades were in line, however, he motioned them forward without further input from Sherman, so in a sense the major assault on Steele's front was not necessarily in response to McClernand's request for renewed action but simply represented the first chance Steele had to actually advance under the 10:00 A.M. attack orders.[16]

Likewise, Blair's brigades were also operating on hours-old orders from Sherman, although there was some interaction as Blair was physically closer to his corps commander than Steele. The division had advanced by the flank but then spread out in linear formation, with orders to assault when all was ready. It took some time before Blair was in position and Giles Smith had coordinated with Thomas Ransom to his left. Sherman noted that around 2:00 P.M. "General Blair reported to me that none of his brigades could pass the point of the road swept by the terrific fire encountered by Ewing's, but that Giles Smith had a position to the left, in connection with General Ransom, of McPherson's corps, and was ready to assault." Thus, when Blair's brigades again moved forward, it was more a continuation of the morning's scramble to rectify the deteriorating situation than any orders from Sherman, although Sherman did arrange a renewed artillery bombardment and small arms fire "to be kept up to occupy the attention of the enemy in our front."[17]

Still, the timing was close enough that Sherman's extended brigades, as they marched forward yet again toward the Confederate lines on this midafternoon of May 22, provided what McClernand had asked for.

Frederick Steele had not had the best campaign, being sick for much of it, and had endured an even rougher morning, taking hours to move two-thirds of his division less than one air mile. War Department liaison Charles Dana described Steele as "a gentlemanly pleasant fellow" but reported that "his mind seems to work in a desultory way, like the mind of a captain of infantry long habituated to garrison duty at a frontier post. He takes things in bits, like a gossiping companion, and never comprehensively and strongly, like a man of clear brain and a ruling purpose." That was somewhat odd because, unlike the politician-turned-soldier Blair, who had handled his division deftly in terms of timing, Steele was a professional soldier. Originally from New York, he had graduated from West Point with Grant in 1843 and then served in the regular army in the antebellum years, and with distinction in the Mexican War. He had been mostly in the trans-Mississippi earlier in the conflict before being taken into Sherman's corps for the attack at Chickasaw Bayou. Steele was now the ranking general in the XV Corps behind Sherman, but his delay this day had cost Sherman a fully coordinated attack. His brigades were set now, however, by 4:00 P.M., and ready to advance.[18]

Steele's advance brigade under John Thayer was more than ready to move forward, they having been idle for hours waiting on the others to take their positions. It was an all-Iowa brigade, including the 4th and 9th Iowa, whose first colonels had been Grenville Dodge, a former railroader and now a Union general, and sitting congressman William Vandever, respectively. The 26th and 30th Iowa filled out the brigade. The 4th Iowa held the best spot, depending on how the soldiers viewed it, guarding a battery in the valley of the bayou. That left the 30th, 9th, and 26th Iowa in line left to right, ready to finally storm forward. Thayer himself was, according to Dana, "a fair but not first-rate officer."[19]

Directly behind the Iowans was Charles Woods's brigade, a mixture of Missourians and Iowans, with one Ohio regiment mixed in for good measure. The three Missouri regiments (the 3rd, 12th, and 17th) and two Iowa regiments (the 25th and 31st) joined Charles Woods's own 76th Ohio, which had been at Fort Donelson and Shiloh. The Ohioans had been left in their original position to cover the vacated areas of the division's line while the rest of the brigade waited to go forward in column of regiments behind Thayer's Iowans. Dana described Woods himself as "a Hercules in form, in energy,

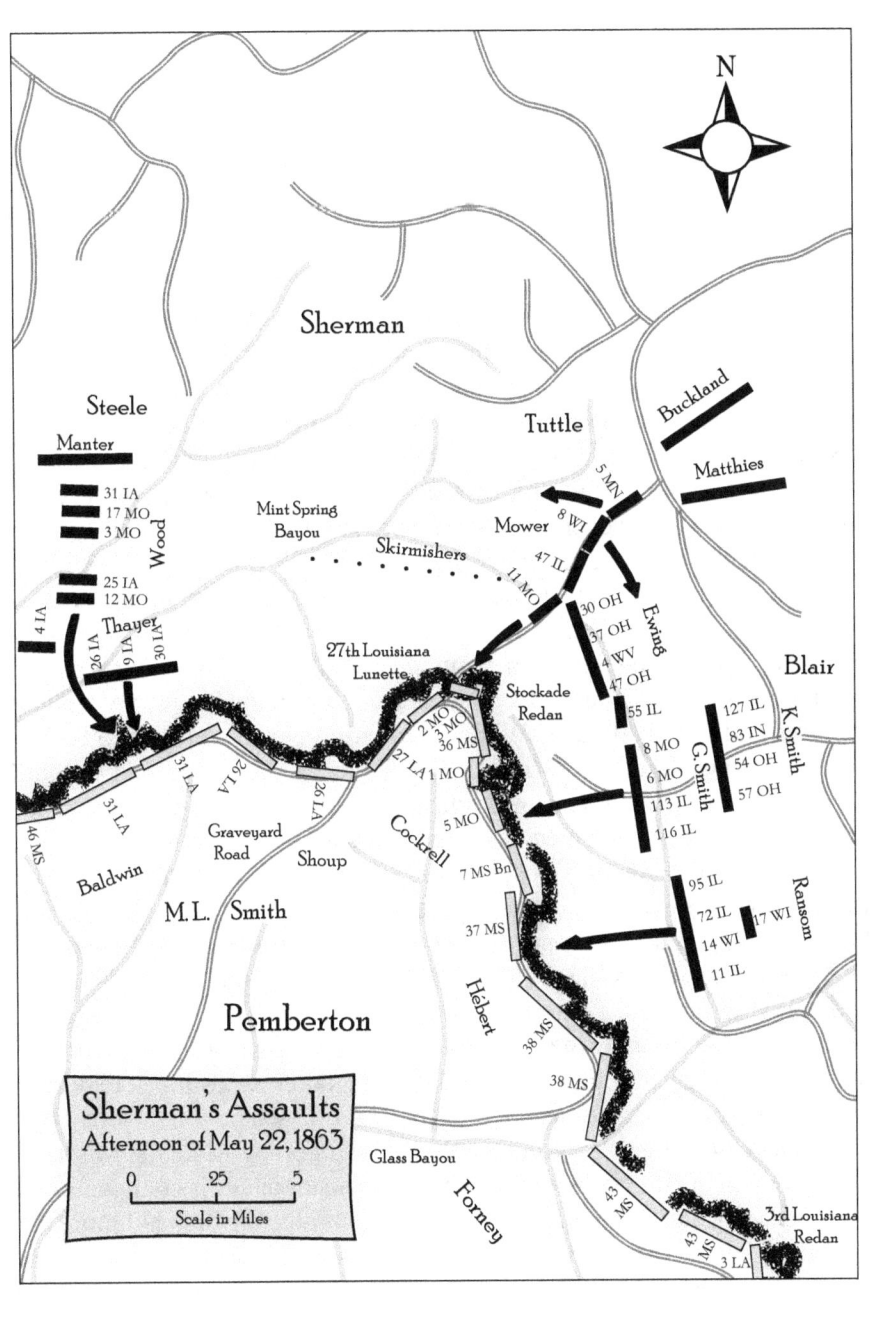

and in pertinacity, he is both safe and sure." Behind Woods's columns was Manter's brigade of five Missouri regiments, the 27th, 29th, 30th, 31st, and 32nd, plus the 13th Illinois.[20]

By 4:00 P.M., Steele ordered his troops forward, and the Iowans of Thayer's brigade began to move out. They had a rugged path across small ridges and ravines in the valley of Mint Spring Bayou, but the really hard part began once they reached the stream itself. The slope up to the Confederate works was almost vertical, prompting Sherman to describe the problems: "The ground over which he [Steele] passed was more open and exposed to the flank fire of the enemy's batteries in position, and was deeply cut up by gullies and washes." The Iowans soon found just keeping their footing among all the other issues was difficult at best, considering all the impediments they had to face. Obviously, the most notable problem was the Confederate fire coming from high atop the ridge south of Mint Spring Bayou, one of the Federals describing how "you never heard such a fire in your life[.] The rebels made a crossfire on our men and slaughter them awfully."[21]

Here, new Confederate troops joined the action. Most of the fighting heretofore on this northern flank had been done by Shoup's two Louisiana regiments. Confederate division commander Smith noted that "other parts of the line were free from assaults, but sustained a continuous fire from sharpshooters and light batteries." While the fighting would continue to be light westward toward the river, where the Mississippi State Troops and Vaughn's Tennessee brigade held the almost impossible terrain to traverse, action now quickly picked up in the area between Shoup and the river. Thayer's attack came just west of Shoup's position, only a half-mile west of the Stockade Redan, where Shoup's Louisianans gave way to new troops. The Confederate line here consisted of Colonel William E. Baldwin's brigade of Mississippians and Louisianans, the 17th and 31st Louisiana and 4th and 46th Mississippi, with the 29th Louisiana temporarily down to the south reinforcing Forney's division. Baldwin's right met Shoup's left just west of the fortifications held by the 26th Louisiana, and from that point westward were the men of the 17th Louisiana, although the larger 31st Louisiana soon took that post, the other regiment going in reserve also behind Forney while the Mississippians filled in the line farther west. The Louisianans and Mississippians were firmly ensconced behind the strong fortifications atop the high hill more than a hundred feet above the Iowans. Although the angle was far too steep for cannon fire from the attending artillery, the men could certainly make their small arms effective across the wide expanse that William Pitt Chambers of the 46th Mississippi described as a "deep valley, some two or three hundred yards in width, which was a cultivated field last year." The Louisianans did so, the main attack falling primarily on the 31st Louisiana.[22]

The recipients at the bottom of the hill were Thayer's Iowans, who began to go down quickly from impediments, exhaustion, and most of all Confederate fire. "We scaled the hill to a man," Alonzo Abernathy of the 9th Iowa recalled in his diary, "and on we went through the terrible hail, and fell down under the breastworks." In fact, Thayer's troops, only three regiments engaged, lost more men in this attack than any other brigade in Sherman's corps except the one following them into this heated fire. Charles Woods's brigade suffered more, but many of their casualties came while getting into position. Thayer's Iowans took the brunt of the Confederate fire now, but on they pressed, Sherman noting that "still, his column passed steadily through this fire and reached the parapet, which was also found to be well manned and defended by the enemy."[23]

Robert Hoadley of the 26th Iowa described the fearful time. "Oh what a fire they poured into us," he wrote, "we were swept down like grass before the Scythe.... [We] had to drop on the ground again & protect our selves the best we could from the bullets." Hoadley was hit by a spent ball himself "on the fore head," but those around him were much worse off. He described one Iowan who "went ahead of me stopped & looked around in less than a minute he was dead. As I lay I could just reach his feet." Hoadley described another friend to his right who was "shot through the head ball went in just above the right eye made a hole as large as my thumb he lived about 1 hour it was hard to see him lie there groaning but there was no help for him."[24]

As might be expected, the majority of the Iowans soon began to slow on the way up, only a few continuing on up the steep and rugged hill to the ditch in front of the Confederate fortifications. "Was as trying a time as it could be," wrote Uley Burk to his wife back home in Iowa, and he noted that the 30th Iowa's color-bearer was wounded dreadfully in the arm: "He will never do for a soldier again but he was a good one." The colonel, Charles H. Abbott, was killed outright. In fact, only a few Iowans reached the top, and that was miraculous in and of itself. One wrote that "our regiment had to take the heat and brunt of the battle, being in the front line and center." Colonel David Carskaddon of the 9th Iowa admitted that "our flag failed to waive from the enemy's fort only after the last one of the four color-guards had fallen, either killed or severely wounded, in the heroic attempt to plant and maintain it there." Another explained the reason, writing in his diary that "the secesh run out an English lance (pike poles we call them) and hooked fast the 9th flag staff and was in the act of drawing it within their works when the adjutant of the 9th grabbed the end of the staff and pulled it back but the colors were stripped from the staff by the 'pruning hook' on the end of the 'seceshers' lance."[25]

As in most all the other assaults on both days now, Federals found that getting to the parapets was the easy part, if such an effort could be called easy. Reaching those ramparts and then getting across or inside them were two completely different prospects, much like just getting to and then taking Vicksburg. Thayer's Iowans who managed to get to the Louisianans' fifteen-foot-high fortifications found it impossible to get across. Too few members had even made it to the ditch to create a surge, and going individually would be suicidal, especially with the soldiers of the various Louisiana regiments "mounting on top [of] the parapet to receive the enemy," as one Louisianan noted. The 26th Louisiana to the east watched to their left as the Federals "would run up until they were tired & then fall down, jumping up they would strive to reach our works but the fire was too severe for them." The same Louisianan also told of watching "one Yankee [who] came up with a pipe in his mouth. Very coolly he stooped behind a stump within 20 yards of us but there very soon ended his life of which he was so careless." Like in so many other places, the Iowans who managed to reach the ditches stayed there, clinging to any earth and protection they could find.[26]

Making matters worse for the Iowans, they were soon caught in a proverbial no-man's-land. Coming hard on the heels of the leading brigade were Charles Woods's Missourians and Iowans, but they immediately faced the same obstacles Thayer's troops had found, prompting one Iowan stuck on the parapet to declare that "it was very little support." Woods himself noted that "the ground being so broken and obstructed by ravines, brush, and logs, it was impossible to move forward with any regularity." The lead regiment was the 12th Missouri, which took an especially heavy fire once it popped over the covering ridge and into the valley of the bayou; Woods called the fire "withering." The Missourians rushed ahead right behind the Iowans of Thayer's brigade while Woods motioned the remainder of the brigade forward in the rear. The next regiment, the 25th Iowa, moved forward but was soon stopped by the withering fire. The following regiments halted before ever even starting to move very high up the bluff. In fact, the 25th Iowa deployed in a skirmish line to help keep down the Confederates, silhouetted against the sky, hoping to provide some cover for their comrades to the front. "From our position we could see it all," wrote Richard Burt of the 76th Ohio farther to the right, "and it beat any thing I ever witnessed."[27]

In the 12th Missouri, which went on alone, the regiment's major experienced a premonition of his death. Before the charge, Major Gustavus Lightfoot handed out cigars from his stash to all the officers of the brigade.

One of the officers cajoled, "Major, don't give them all away. You may need them yourself before we get back to camp." Lightfoot calmly replied, "Oh, take them; I will have no further use for cigars; this is my last smoke!" Sure enough, Major Lightfoot was killed in the assault, not thirty minutes after his declaration. The regiment's color-bearer had gone down and Lightfoot grabbed the colors and shouted "Forward, forward! Follow me, boys!" He was hit and killed at that exact point.[28]

The Missourians leading the brigade nevertheless raced up the hill, but just like Thayer's Iowans they found the going extremely difficult. Colonel Hugo Wangelin led his men forward despite the loss of Major Lightfoot, whom brigade commander Woods described as "a gentleman of high attainments, and a brave, gallant, and faithful officer." The heaviest fire came on the regiment's left, where Company F had all but nine men killed or wounded. The right fared better, four companies on that wing gaining some cover and being able to approach the base of the Confederate works. But there, the Missourians found that they could do no more than Thayer's Iowans, and they simply huddled for safety behind any obstruction they could find. "It was a slaughter," wrote John Buegel of the 3rd Missouri, "and it is a wonder that the whole division was not destroyed on the spot."[29]

An enthused William Baldwin inside those Confederate works described how the Federals made a "vigorous attack," but also that it was "gallantly repulsed with heavy loss to the enemy, who left the ground in our front covered with their dead." One of his Mississippians agreed, writing that "the ground in front of our lines [was] literally blue with the dead and wounded Federals." Shoup also described the effect from his vantage point to the east, writing that the force on his left "makes a dash at my line." He continued: "It is slaughtered, and flies in confusion. The [Confederate] troops behaved most admirably; mount the parapets with enthusiasm." A Louisianan put it even more bluntly: "They got in about 15 steps of our regiment when they charged it, but not one of them ever got away." There were Confederate casualties as well, of course, including brigade commander Baldwin a little earlier, his division commander Martin L. Smith describing him as being wounded "rather severely." He was disabled enough by the shoulder wound to turn over command of his brigade to Colonel Allen Thomas of the 29th Louisiana.[30]

To the Union rear, Frederick Steele watched in horror as his two brigades took fearful casualties, the most in Sherman's corps that day. He had to decide quickly what to do, although the decision was already being made on the ground. Plainly visible were the Federals in front of the Confederate earthworks, but they had been unable to penetrate, and the likelihood of that happening seemed remote. In particular, Steele had to decide whether to throw

Manter's Missourians into the attack. He quickly decided not to, mainly because it seemed the Confederate line was impossible to carry. Plus, there were full regiments of Woods's brigade in the bottom of the valley who had not pressed on, so moving Manter's men over the others would be problematic at best. Obviously, if most of Woods's brigade could not—or would not—move forward, then there was no use in sending in more troops. Steele accordingly called those who could to return, the others near the Confederate breastworks doomed to wait until nightfall and the cover of darkness to safely leave their predicament. One annoyed Iowan gave the view from the top, writing that "those who had not fallen before . . . then looked round for our support, for we were terribly thinned out, but to our disappointment and chagrin, none came, and there we lay hour after hour, and with Wellington saying: 'O that reinforcements or night would come. . . . '"[31]

Farther to the front, the same decision was already in process as well. As Manter's troops pushed forward over yet another ridge ("a task similar to the former, but more perilous," remembered Henry Seaman of the 13th Illinois), Colonel James A. Williamson of the 4th Iowa in reserve met the lead company and ordered the commander not to proceed farther lest he "lose the lives of half his men." Lieutenant Henry D. Dement replied that his orders were to move on and "go he would or die in the attempt." Colonel Williamson replied that he would take the responsibility of stopping the men until it could be referred to the brigade commander, which let the lieutenant off the hook. He stopped the forward movement, and soon Frederick Steele himself sent orders to hold the position and not move forward. Many a soldier was glad, Seaman describing the ridge about to be scaled as "the slope of a huge and precipitous hill."[32]

The watching Confederates were joyous. They had easily repelled this venture, probably still amazed that the attempt across such harsh terrain was even tried. Division commander Martin L. Smith, on whose brigades the assault fell, simply noted that "this was dispersed without great effort and with considerable [Federal] loss." William Pitt Chambers of the 46th Mississippi noted that "a line of the enemy advanced to the center of the valley in our front, but were compelled to retreat in utter confusion," but he also admitted that the major action was to the east: "Beyond them to our right, it appeared as though whole regiments went down at once, so terribly withering was the Confederate fire." Another Mississippian declared that "we gave them fits with buck and ball and canister. . . . That was a squally time."[33]

If there was any consolation for these Iowans and Missourians stuck on the Confederate outer works, however, it was that this assault had occurred so late in the day that nightfall was near. Whether the Iowans clinging to life atop the ridge and under the Confederate guns thought of their comrades of the forlorn hope to the left is not known, but they had been stuck in the same predicament in front of the Stockade Redan since ten o'clock that morning. It must have seemed like an eternity, but night soon neared. And with nightfall would come—hopefully—victory, if their renewal of the fighting had helped John McClernand's success in any way.

Just as Steele was late in launching his original attack west of the Graveyard Road and the Stockade Redan, Blair's division south of the road was likewise delayed in assaulting the Confederate lines. But unlike Steele, these three brigades had already had a taste of the fighting both on May 19 as well as earlier on this day, although none except the forlorn hope and the first two regiments of Ewing's brigade had actually managed an attack. Most of the intervening hours had been spent redeploying in the ravines south of the road, coordinating with nearby commands such as their own fellow brigades in the division as well as Ransom's brigade of McPherson's corps, as well as jockeying for a closer position from which to launch the attack. Sharpshooting thus became the main effort, with many casualties occurring on both sides. Within the Stockade Redan itself, Major Alexander Yates of the 36th Mississippi fell from a cannon shot, and Captain James S. Tatum of Company D also perished. Both, one member of the regiment declared, "were killed with muskets in their hands sharpshooting with the enemy."[34]

All the while, the Federals continued to hold their tenuous grip on the face of the Stockade Redan and revamped their lines, but it all took time. Getting reinforcements up was problematic for the survivors on the slopes. Frank Blair described the terrain: "So difficult and toilsome was the nature of the ground over which they moved, rendered still more so by the abatis and artificial entanglement thrown across it by the enemy." Casualties mounted in the process, including Sergeant James W. Larrabee of the 55th Illinois on the parapet of the Stockade Redan, who stuck his head up a little too high. The Confederate defenders had long since vacated the top of the parapet, they being under such heavy fire of the artillery and sharpshooters, but in just a fraction of a second's peek over the parapet Larrabee saw "a mass of men standing at a charge bayonet." He paid dearly for his momentary glimpse, being hit in the neck from a shot so close that powder was lodged in his neck and face and had to be dug out later.[35]

The division was consequently no stranger to action, but the effects of exhaustion and depression were taking their toll. Frank Blair seems to have been less of a force than he should have, as was Sherman, who was on the main Graveyard Road and not personally directing the action to the south. Perhaps both, and certainly Blair, could be exonerated for believing that it was hopeless to try any more assaults. It was, after all, his men who had tried the linear style of attack on May 19 and then the assault by the flank earlier this morning, both of which had failed. Now, it was back to linear formations and a continuation of the process, but Blair never sent his entire division ahead as one. Rather, he seemingly allowed the brigades to continue on their own with little more coordination than the original orders to fan out in line to the south and look for opportunities to attack any weak spots.[36]

Two of Blair's brigade commanders seemingly picked up on their commanders' waning interest in any more attacks. Kilby Smith was not necessarily in a position to do much, being in reserve behind Giles Smith's troops as he was. He simply sought cover for his regiments, although some casualties still occurred. Ultimately he drew his forces up in column of regiments behind the right wing of Giles Smith's Federals. Seeing an opening, Kilby Smith nevertheless sent one of his regiments, the 55th Illinois, forward and waited for any opportunity or call to aid those to the front.[37]

Just because Kilby Smith was in reserve did not mean there was no excitement in his lines. Nerves frayed and commanders argued. The brigade was told to move across a ridge and take position in the ravine in front, but when Lieutenant Colonel Cyrus Fisher of the 54th Ohio "ran to the top of the hill to see where we were going," he spied Union troops in the very ravine they were to occupy. Obviously, these were Giles Smith's Federals, of which Fisher informed Kilby Smith. The two argued once Kilby Smith, who was standing behind the ridge, declared that "I was mistaken; that there was not a man in the ravine below." Fisher returned to the top and clearly saw the Federals again and so informed Smith yet again. Kilby Smith said nothing except to order the brigade over the hill. Fisher was not enthused to say the least: "I did not desire to rush my men among them." He did, however, and even worse found that the Confederates were able to enfilade the ravine with an artillery battery. Fortunately, most of the small arms fire generally passed overhead, but the Ohioans only reached a point within fifty yards of the Confederate lines.[38]

Similarly, Hugh Ewing, who was closest to the Graveyard Road and the Stockade Redan itself, was in little mood to move forward. He simply kept up a heavy fire from his position in the ravine and the slight meandering ridges with it. Blair, in fact, recalled simply that "the sharpshooters from Ewing's brigade and our artillery opened upon the enemy at the same time with considerable effect."[39]

Giles Smith showed no such lethargy, perhaps because he had found in Thomas Ransom to his left a temporary soul mate, at least in terms of the need and desire to attack the Confederate lines again this afternoon. Whether Smith sought such cooperation from Ewing and Kilby Smith is not known, but Ransom is the one Giles Smith soon fashioned a plan with, and the two brigades ultimately conducted the second distinct assault of Sherman's corps on the Confederate works that afternoon.[40]

Problems nevertheless emerged even for these vigorous brigade commanders. One issue that faced Smith and Ransom was that their attack, having shuffled down the ravine through which the tributary of Glass Bayou ran, meant traversing tougher terrain than that closer to the Graveyard Road. Few if any Federal units had been in the area, Kilby Smith's three left regiments not having extended their lines this far south on May 19 and Ransom not extending this far north either day. Giles Smith's Illinoisans and Missourians were accordingly traversing new ground that was farther down the deepening watershed than the earlier attacks of Blair's troops. Because they were farther down the watershed to the south, this also meant that they were attacking fresh troops who had not been in heavy action as yet. They could bet that the Confederates behind those parapets were anxious and ready for a taste of the action.[41]

Those Confederates were still part of Louis Hébert's brigade, but they had not yet been heavily engaged in the fighting on either day. The Mississippians in the 37th and 38th Mississippi and 7th Mississippi Battalion had been present for all the earlier fighting but had not seen direct assaults on their positions, except for the slight advance by Ransom's troops on May 19. These were mostly veterans of Iuka and Corinth and thus were well aware of what battle looked like. Their army having attacked similar fortifications (particularly at Corinth on October 3 and 4, 1862), they also were fully aware of what regiments behind fortifications could do to troops advancing in the open. Unfortunately for some in the 38th Mississippi, there were sections of the line where the fortifications were not completed. The men simply laid down to get as much cover as possible.[42]

Accordingly, while Ewing provided cover and Kilby Smith waited for the call to support the assault, Giles Smith's Federals were the only ones of Blair's division to continue the attack on the afternoon of May 22. They did so, however, with Ransom's brigade firmly on their left. "Both brigades went forward with a cheer," Blair wrote, "when the signal was given to advance." But just like all the other attacks, whether by the flank or linearly, Giles Smith quickly found that the path was hard and difficult, especially due to logs and downed trees. Problems with officers, including heavy drinking in the long hours of waiting, did not help their plight.[43]

Smith nevertheless moved his Illinoisans and Missourians forward around 4:00 P.M., they beginning the move across the branch of Glass Bayou and up the steep slope toward the Confederate lines and the waiting Mississippians. The abatis that had become such a nuisance by this time was again a factor, as was the terrain itself. Several small rivulets, and one major feature, ran southeastward into this fork of Glass Bayou, and their attending ravines chopped up the area through which Smith and Ransom attacked so that formations were difficult to keep and steady progress was impossible. The troops were left to make their way as best they could through the maze of debris and the heavy Confederate fire. Sherman noted that the Federals "charged up against the parapet, but also met a staggering fire." Fortunately, the steep ground in some places also provided cover, Captain William L. Faulk of the 38th Mississippi writing that "fortune favored them in the way of a deep hollow that they would have had to cross and this hid them from our view."[44]

Despite the heavy resistance, Smith's regiments moved on toward the Confederate works, some as afraid of what was behind as what was in front. Captain John J. Kellogg described how, when he was out in front of the company, he gave a glance backward and saw the rows of bayonets behind him: "[It] made me realize that it only required a stumble of some lubber just behind me to launch his bayonet into the offside of my anatomy, somewhere in the neighborhood of my anterior suspender buttons." He admitted that "this knowledge so stimulated me that I feared the front far less than the rear, and forged ahead like an antelope." The resistance from the front was nothing to discount, however, Giles Smith explaining: "I again advanced, but met so severe a fire from my front and left by both musketry and artillery that I found it absolutely necessary to order the brigade to fall back behind the crest of the hill, which was done slowly and in good order." As in the other assaults, only a few reached and planted the colors on the parapets, especially on the small redan south of the main Stockade Redan.[45]

Aiding in this effort on the far right, between Giles Smith's troops and Ewing's covering brigade, was the 55th Illinois, the only regiment in Kilby Smith's reserve unit to take part in the advance. With barely enough room for a few troops, this regiment stormed ahead as well on the right of the 8th Missouri, Colonel Oscar Malmborg yelling to his men: "Boys, they'll give us one volley; before they can reload, we'll be inside their works. Forward, double-quick, march! And hurrah like _____!" It would not turn out so well for Malmborg, who had been wounded in the eye on May 19. He was now hit in the other eye, although both were slight wounds. More fatal was the wound suffered by his orderly David A. Sullivan, who was killed at Malmborg's side.[46]

James H. Jones of the 38th Mississippi described the vicious nature of the fighting south of the Stockade Redan: "They came on as rapidly as the fallen timber would permit, and in perfect order. We waited in silence until the first line had advanced within easy rifle range, when a murderous fire was opened from the breastworks." A continual process seemed to occur: "As they came down the hill one could see them plunging headlong to the front, and as they rushed up the slope to our works they invariably fell backwards, as the death shot greeted them." Jones admitted that "they came into the very jaws of death and died," and he marveled that "surely no more desperate courage than this could be displayed by mortal men." Another member of the Mississippi regiment, Eli Thornhill, described how "we were standing up taking deliberate aim" until a bullet hit the man next to him and he went down. "I began to think it was best to look out for number one," he declared, "so we all began to protect ourselves behind the breastworks." The fire did not slacken, however.[47]

Courage was abundant—but so was shock. In the ranks of the 113th Illinois, a cannonball exploded and dazed several men, including Captain Kellogg. When the dust settled, all saw that Private Louios Cazean had been dreadfully wounded. He held up his mangled and nearly severed right arm with his left, "his shattered right arm dangling from the white cords and tendons." Cazean calmly admitted: "Boys, I'd give five hundred dollars if that was my left arm instead of my right."[48]

It was soon clear that this effort was likewise doomed to fail. Blair recounted that "after reaching the face of the works of the enemy, they encountered a most fatal and deadly enfilading fire from the enemy's guns on the left, which came crashing through the ranks, while in front they were met by an obstinate resistance from an intrenched foe." Some troops had made it to the ditches and parapets fronting the Confederate works, but the Mississippi fire was so great that there they stopped and went to the ground. Others had to flee, Sherman noting that the brigades "recoiled under cover of the hillside." Little was accomplished besides planting the flags on the parapet, but by this time that was a common occurrence. The 10:00 A.M. assault earlier in the morning had done so, as had Thayer to the right; these very same Federals had done so at several locations on May 19. Now, Giles Smith's troops simply added more flags to denote their approach to the Confederate works, but a meaningful breakthrough, as elsewhere on the lines, seemed unlikely with the numbers at hand as the sun began to drift off to the west. One grateful Mississippian noted in his diary that "the enemy made tremendous exertions to force our lines, but with God's assistance, we have been able to hold it." Blair echoed this sentiment: "It was found impossible to advance," noting that "both brigades, however, maintained pertinaciously the ground they had won."[49]

Fortunately, as with Steele's troops, those trapped on the ramparts would have much less time to await nightfall than those poor souls who were still clinging to life on the ramparts of the Stockade Redan itself—and who had been doing so for some six or seven hours by this time in the fight.

While the majority of Sherman's corps was assaulting the Confederates' defensive works (essentially on its own accord that afternoon, operating on the original orders for the 10:00 A.M. attack that were only slightly updated since then), the corps commander, positioned on the Graveyard Road, also took matters into his own hands to renew the assaults. He had not had much effect on Steele's operations farther to the right, and only a little more so on Blair's to the left, but after his conference with Grant about McClernand's trio of requests for help Sherman threw in his last uncommitted division. He explained that "having heard General McClernand's report to General Grant read, that he had taken three [McClernand actually stated only two] of the enemy's forts, and that his flags floated on the stronghold of Vicksburg, I ordered General Tuttle to send directly to the assault one of his brigades." James Tuttle's division had been waiting patiently for hours: their moment for acting had come. At least one Federal declared that Tuttle himself offered up his division, stating how Tuttle confirmed that he "had a brigade that could successfully make the same assault." An incensed Ewing, nearby and having heard the conversation, piped up that "it could not be done, but that he might try."[50]

Steele's and Blair's divisions had by this point in the war seen their share of fighting, most notably as part of Sherman's operations at Chickasaw Bayou and Arkansas Post, as well as some in earlier actions at Pea Ridge. But Tuttle's division was arguably the most veteran of them all, even in light of Charles Dana's assertion that the commander's "bravery and zeal constitute his only qualifications for command." While there were some newer regiments sprinkled in, there were also plenty of high-profile units that had seen much action in the war to date. For instance, in Charles Matthies's brigade were the 8th and 12th Iowa, along with the newer 35th Iowa, the two former regiments having been at Shiloh (the 12th had also fought at Fort Donelson). Both regiments defended the famed Hornet's Nest at Shiloh, paying for it with months of captivity for most members. Similarly, Ralph Buckland's brigade contained veterans amid some newer regiments such as the 114th Illinois, 93rd Indiana, and 95th Ohio. The 72nd Ohio was with Sherman as far back as Shiloh and for hours staunchly defended the ridge on which Shiloh Church sat before they were outflanked and forced to withdraw. Their commander was also a veteran; Buckland commanded that very brigade at Shiloh.[51]

The last brigade of Tuttle's division was no slouch either, collectively seeing as much fighting as any brigade in the division. Commanded by Joseph "Fighting Joe" Mower (an accurate nickname), the brigade contained several regiments that had seen intense fighting, most notably at Corinth in October 1862. They were perhaps best known as the Eagle Brigade, after the famed mascot of the 8th Wisconsin, "Old Abe." In fact, Mower's troops (consisting of the 47th Illinois, 8th Wisconsin, 11th Missouri, and 5th Minnesota) wanted to fight to prove to their brand-new general what they could accomplish. As the brigade had marched toward Vicksburg on May 20, they were halted before crossing the Big Black River and formed into ranks for a ceremony. There, they were told that their colonel had received his brigadier's star, and his old regiment (the 11th Missouri) presented him with a new horse. One member of the 8th Wisconsin declared: "Then we gave cheer after cheer for the general is our idol." Charles Dana was less impressed, writing that Mower was "a brilliant officer, but not of large mental caliber."[52]

Knowing that he had a veteran division in the wings, Sherman chose to send them in, but he oddly reverted back to his original tactics of the morning: an assault by the flank up the Graveyard Road. He never stated why he did so, although Colonel Lucius Hubbard of the 5th Minnesota noted that "the broken nature of the country and inaccessible character of the position made it necessary that the storming column should move by the flank." There was certainly room to deploy Tuttle's entire division into linear line between Blair's right on the Graveyard Road and Steele's left to the west, but perhaps Sherman thought that wide-ranging frontal assaults like those on May 19 and again on this afternoon were doomed to fail. Perhaps also he thought he should continue the tactics dictated by Grant for the operations on this day. Most likely, the time of day, already nearing 3:00 P.M., was the major factor for his decision. It would take a while to redeploy Tuttle's three brigades into line formation amid all the ravines and ridges, as Steele's brigades had shown throughout the day. Rather, Sherman could make a quick stab at the Confederate defenses with the troops he now had in the positions they now occupied. Accordingly, he ordered Tuttle to send a brigade forward by the flank along the Graveyard Road, with the others to support the attack. "Have you a brigade that can carry that point," Sherman asked Tuttle, who responded: "I have one that can do it if it can be done." Sherman barked, "Then send them in."[53]

Tuttle chose his lead brigade under brand-new general Fighting Joe Mower, and he called Mower forward. "General Mower, can you carry those works," he asked. Mower shook his head "from side to side in his peculiar way" and answered, "I can try." Sherman jumped in and bellowed, "Then do it." Mower went back to his brigade, and Tuttle took a position with Sherman for a time in "the shelter of a little knoll." Wondering why they had been waiting all day (while "exposed to a musketry fire for several hours during the fore part of the day," according to Colonel Lucius F. Hubbard of the 5th Minnesota), Mower enthusiastically led his four regiments forward, his old 11th Missouri in the lead. He took a short stroll to look at the ground, one watching Ohioan observing that "General Mower, himself, in our full view, walked along the road its entire length, twice stopping to look back, with an air of perfect indifference, while scores of bullets whizzed around him." Mower was soon satisfied and brought up his brigade. They approached the ridge behind which they had been sheltered all day, and Sherman himself was there, ready to send them forward. Sherman remembered the drama of the moment: "While General Steele was hotly engaged on the right, and I could hear heavy firing all down the line to my left, I ordered their charge, covered in like manner by Blair's division, deployed on the hillside, and the artillery posted behind parapets within point-blank range."[54]

The Missourians moved forward "in most gallant style," Tuttle said, their arms at right shoulder shift. The Missourians surged ahead "punctually at 3 P.M.," Sherman noted, the other regiments right behind them and Matthies's brigade ready in rear to follow, although the advance caught the Union artillery off guard and they had to scramble to support the assault. Mower's troops took the exact same route that the forlorn hope and Ewing's brigade had taken five hours previously, while the remnants of that brigade, still lodged on the parapet of the Stockade Redan, watched as aid came to their side. Those near the road moved out of the way, one 30th Ohio soldier writing that "we got out of the road to let Mower's brigade try their luck." Some wondered about the idea of "a charge upon a strong point in the defenses, where a similar attempt had met with repulse in the morning," but they went anyway. And it was a beautiful advance. Sherman declared that "General Mower carried his brigade up bravely and well." Watching from the left, Blair called the effort "an impetuous assault" and declared that "the attack was made with the greatest bravery and impetuosity, and was covered by a tremendous fire from our batteries."[55]

The Confederates responded as soon as Mower's Federals topped the ridge, the Missourians in the lead. The 11th Missouri had made charges before, most notably at Corinth last October, but none like this. In October, they had met advancing Confederates with the bayonet at Battery Robinett, stopping the Confederate surge with cold steel as well as a well-timed volley. Here, however, there was no surging enemy to hit, only well-ensconced lines of Mississippians and fellow Missourians who had already repelled attack after attack and were confident they could repel this one as well.[56]

Also watching from the front were Lieutenant William C. Porter and the other survivors of the forlorn hope, who had been stranded on the parapets of the Stockade Redan since ten o'clock that morning. Porter later dejectedly wrote of craving any support during the interim, "which we did not succeed in getting." He was also livid at one lieutenant of the 127th Illinois who had faltered, "remaining about 4 rods from the fort, on the road, protected by its high banks, without attempting the march to the fort." Worse, he "kept back from the assaulting party 10 men, who remained where he did during the entire day on the road." More disconcerting, a flanking fire from the Confederate lines, as well as "a direct fire from the skirmishers of the First Brigade," continually tore at the survivors, but by 3:00 P.M. or so the Federals on the parapet could see a new wave coming toward them.[57]

The Missourians led the way but found the path well swept by Confederate fire, some of it from other Missourians of Cockrell's brigade, Sherman remarking that "again arose a fire more severe, if possible, than that of the first assault." The Missourians crossed through the very same cut in the ridge the forlorn hope had found so daunting, and like the others they took heavy fire. One of the Federals near the rear watched as the lead soldiers burst out into the open: "As the head of the column emerged from the cover of the timber and passed an open space leading to the work, it was met and literally melted down by a terrific fire of musketry and artillery, the latter double-shotted with canister and grape. From my position, within range, along the whole line of defenses a fire was concentrated upon this point, where the column must pass." Still, miraculously, the Missourians approached the ditch and the parapet of the Stockade Redan, Lieutenant Porter recalling that "about 30 of the Eleventh Missouri, with their colonel, major, and 2 lieutenants, succeeded in reaching us with their colors, which they planted alongside of ours."[58]

Colonel Andrew J. Weber reached the parapet along with the color-bearers, Lieutenant Porter writing of their bravery: "The bearing of the two color-bearers was all that bravery and true courage could do, waving their colors in defiance of enemies and traitors, marching straight and unwavering to the fort through the most murderous fire I ever experienced." Others testified to the remarkable scene as well: "The colors of the leading regiment, the Eleventh Missouri, were planted by the side of that of Blair's storming party," while one Wisconsin soldier farther back declared that "the color bearer of the 11th

Mo Regt a tall brave young fellow planted his flag on the rebel work, but he could not stay, with his flag, but jumped back into the ditch." [59]

But there the success stopped. Sherman explained that despite the pageantry this assault had "exactly a similar result." The Missourians were penned down before breaching the works, Colonel Weber himself losing the bill of his cap upon the explosion of a hand grenade nearby. Tuttle reported that "the ground being so uneven, and the fire of the enemy well concentrated, and heavy, they were compelled to fall back without being able to make a lodgment in his works."[60]

It had all taken only a short time: "Within probably the space of a minute," Colonel Hubbard of the 5th Minnesota in the rear declared, "the brigade lost upward of 200 men, principally sustained by the leading regiment." Confederate brigade commander Francis Shoup was just as astonished, writing that "many of the enemy are killed in the ditch of redan occupied by Third Missouri Volunteers. A terribly beautiful scene."[61]

By this time, Mower had seen enough, Hubbard writing that he "at once declared it futile to attempt to move the column on. The road had been blocked up with dead and wounded." One Illinoisan noted how "a perfect roar of musketry had commenced, above the noise of which the cheering would swell out distinctly at intervals." The Wisconsin and Minnesota troops caught in the roadway did not know what to do, especially with the chaos of an ammunition wagon going up in an explosion, so "the men began getting down, out of their places, wherever they could shelter themselves." With the head shattered and chaos brewing in the rear regiments, Mower motioned the three remaining regiments, which were also taking a heavy fire, to the ravines for cover, just as Ewing and Blair had done earlier. The Minnesotans, Illinoisans, and Wisconsinites soon dove for cover and reformed their lines behind any protecting ground they could find to the left or right. One 8th Wisconsin soldier declared that "it was terrible, the roar of cannon and the crash of musketry was something which cannot be described." He then tried to do so, writing of "the awful shrieks of the cannon balls and shells, and the hissing minnie balls."[62]

Despite the chaos, the 8th Wisconsin carried their famous eagle into the fray. One rearward surgeon described its advance, writing that "'Old Abe,' unconscious of danger, was flapping his wings and croaking, and appeared to be as lively as any of the soldiers." Two men carried the bird on a stand, but the regiment met a fearful fire as it advanced, even in the rear, and was soon stopped. Worse for the bird, its bearer tripped as he was moving forward, right about the same time a spent ball glanced off the eagle's breast, doing no damage but scaring man and beast. The eagle took flight and dragged his bearer a few feet. The Wisconsinites—both man and bird—soon had enough and withdrew into the ravines for protection.⁶³

Within the ranks of the 47th Illinois occurred a singularly impressive feat that caught the attention of both Tuttle and Sherman. One Illinoisan declared as they passed en route that "we charged in column, and as we swept up the hill from the shelter of the ravine, we passed a little group of great generals watching us 'go in'—Sherman, Tuttle and Mower. . . . Who wouldn't fight before such a 'cloud of witnesses'?" Unfortunately, some would not, and Company A's captain, John T. Bowen, as well as the second lieutenant both "deserted them." Sergeant John Watts took control and, according to Tuttle, "rallied the men as they hesitated under a terrific fire, and by waving his hat and cheering succeeded in moving them forward in gallant style, himself leading." Both Tuttle and later Sherman recommended that Captain Bowen and the second lieutenant be dismissed from service and that Sergeant Watts be commissioned and made captain of the company. Sherman eloquently added that "moments such as existed when General Mower's brigade charged in column across the exposed ridge develop the true soldierly qualities, which the sergeant is reported to have signally displayed at the expense of his captain."⁶⁴

Quite a different scene played out in the 8th Wisconsin as it regrouped in the ravine. The frightened eagle had calmed down by this point and was atop his perch again. Somehow, a member of the regiment caught a live rabbit that was scurrying in fright as well and immediately took him to Old Abe. "Here Abe," the proud soldier said, "you've earned this fellow." He threw it onto Abe's perch, and the eagle immediately caught it with his claws and began his work. "There, amidst the rage of battle," one Wisconsin soldier wrote, "he devoured his prey, heedless of noise and excitement. His self possessed demeanor pleased the boys."⁶⁵

Despite the bravery displayed in many instances, Sherman was no doubt chagrined to see the failure of this latest attempt; he loudly barked to Tuttle as he realized it was useless: "This is murder; order those troops back." Mower sent his chief of staff to carry the message, and he barely reached the 8th Wisconsin before they trudged up too far. Even there "the balls fell around him like hail." Ewing was also watching, admitting that the attempt was "bravely made, but the result was the same." He also claimed that Mower, contrary to other reports, later came to him and "apologized very earnestly for his part in it," stating that he had made the assault against his better judgment. A consoled Ewing recalled him saying that "he knew that where Ewing had failed it was useless to try." Sherman later simply noted that "it was a repetition of the first, equally unsuccessful and bloody." Indeed, Mower's brigade sustained nearly two hundred killed, wounded, and missing in the effort, most of the casualties being in the lead 11th Missouri. The following 47th Illinois and 8th Wisconsin accrued moderate casualties in the range that some of Blair's and Steele's less-exposed regiments were suffering, while the trailing 5th Minnesota accounted for only ten total, seven of them missing. Colonel Hubbard noted that the rear position saved his Minnesotans "from a fearful slaughter."[66]

The other brigades in line, Matthies's and Buckland's, had also suffered only slightly, as they had not advanced at all upon the quick realization of the failure of Mower's attack. The closest any of these brigades came to the worst of it was in forming a line to the right and left of the road to support the advances. In total, both brigades suffered a mere fourteen casualties, all wounded except one death. In reality, all this attempt did was to add more suffering Missourians to the collection of Federals huddled beneath the parapets from Steele's position on the right to Blair's on the left, all praying for nightfall. It could not come soon enough.[67]

William T. Sherman had begun the day with high hopes for success, but those hopes had been mercilessly dashed by a smaller number of defenders. He had expected to be in Vicksburg by this point as the sun started down on May 22, but nothing was farther from reality. But it was not because of a lack of effort on the part of his soldiers. Sherman's brigades had made a total of five assaults against the determined defenders but had only reached the ditches and parapets of Vicksburg's stout defenses. Each time, the attackers were stopped cold and forced to huddle for the rest of the day, awaiting nightfall and a safe return to their reconstructed lines. For some, that was a lengthy process, around eight or nine hours before they could safely move rearward, the Confederates continually calling "Surrender, Yanks!" and they responding "Come and get us." Theodore Hyatt of the 127th Illinois of the forlorn hope actually recalled that

> it may seem strange, but it is a fact nevertheless, that under these awful circumstances one of the things we had to battle against was sleepiness. It was all we could do to keep some of the men awake in spite of the peril of the situation.... It took a lot of pinching and thumping to keep some of the men awake, but we were determined that none of us would be taken prisoners, sleeping or alive.

Less dangerous but still miserable were the regiments confined to the deep ravines. Kilby Smith commented on the "horrible heat in the ravines and hillsides." A slight shower in the afternoon and gathering clouds helped alleviate the attackers' suffering somewhat.[68]

The fighting was not over, however, as the cannonading began again and the sharpshooting never really waned. One Mississippian described the results: "Irritated beyond degree by the failure of this second assault, the Federals at once opened on our lines with every battery that could be brought to bear, and it seemed that nothing living could escape certain destruction." The artillery was not all that kept up the fire; the sharpshooters also took aim, "and it became extremely dangerous for a man to raise his head above the works." The Mississippian even had sand knocked into his eyes by one certain Union sharpshooter behind a tree some two hundred yards out who was "making himself very conspicuous by this rapid firing." He and a comrade decided to shoot at him at the same time, whereupon "at the crack of our guns, he fell over on his back." The Mississippian admitted, "I do not know which of us hit him, or whether both, or whether the ball that killed him came from some other part of the line. I only know that when we fired, he fell and did not arise again." He added, "I am glad today that I do not know that I killed him."[69]

Worst of all, the massive failure had cost immensely. While the official numbers would not be calculated for some time, ultimately Sherman found that his corps of three divisions had sustained 858 casualties: 150 killed, 666 wounded, and forty-two missing. Sherman's only comment was that "our loss during the day was severe, and the proportion of dead to wounded exceeds the usual ratio." The heaviest losses fell on the six brigades that had seen the most action, Blair's three, Woods's and Thayer's of Steele's division, and Mower's of Tuttle's division. The losses were that much heavier when added to the 712 total casualties the corps had endured on May 19; the XV Corps had sustained a total of 1,570 casualties in trying to break Vicksburg's defenses.[70]

Sherman himself was convinced of several things. One was that these assaults by the flank would not work. He had tried with Ewing's and then Mower's brigades, and Woods to the right had gone forward in columns of regiments. It just simply could not be done. And assaulting in linear lines would not work either. He had tried it with all three of Blair's brigades on May 19, and then again with Giles Smith's and John Thayer's on May 22, all with the same result. Assaulting on a broad front was also out of the question.[71]

That realization led Sherman to his obvious conclusion: the Confederate lines could not be broken at this point by assault. He admitted to his wife, Ellen, that "the heads of columns are swept away as chaff thrown from the hand on a breezy day." As there was no other way to do it than by the flank or in line, Sherman was out of options, and he plainly said so later: "These several assaults, made simultaneously, demonstrated the strength of the natural and artificial defenses of Vicksburg, that they are garrisoned by a strong force, and that we must resort to regular approaches." Division commander Blair, who was very interested to see another brigade move "forward by the flank on the same road which had been attempted in the morning by the brigade of H. Ewing," agreed, writing that the "failure only served to prove that it is impossible to carry this position by storm." Hugh Ewing took a slightly different but eventually the same approach: "The troops bore themselves throughout with gallantry and spirit. Their general believes that nothing but the broken and entangled nature of the ground over which they charged, with a want of previous knowledge of its condition, prevented them from successfully entering the enemy's works." Yet Sherman had no complaints about Blair's troops, writing that "from my position on both days, I had this division in full view. If any troops could have carried and held the intrenchments of Vicksburg, these would."[72]

The fighting around the Stockade Redan also had larger ramifications than just the defeat. For one, it furthered the evidence that Sherman, in the words of historian Michael B. Ballard, "was not a master of offensive tactics." His efforts at other battles such as Kennesaw Mountain and Chattanooga, and even Chickasaw Bayou, were evidence enough, but the Vicksburg assaults added proof that Sherman's forte was not on the tactical level. In fact, no less an authority than Edwin C. Bearss has surmised that "Sherman had lost control of his corps."[73]

Yet Sherman still had hopes of success even in the midst of his isolated defeat. Perhaps the biggest effect Sherman hoped the renewed assaults had—and he was not immediately privy to this information—was to aid McClernand in whatever success he said he had to the south. Just because Sherman's assaults had failed did not mean the day was a total loss. McPherson and McClernand were still attacking to the south, and if he had been able to distract the Confederates enough to allow them success, then it would all have been worth it.

Accordingly, as Sherman prepared to disengage his troops because of the coming darkness, he could only hope that McPherson and McClernand had achieved more success than he had.

11

"The Assault Was Feeble Compared with the Fierce Onslaughts Earlier in the Day"

In a day filled with numerous crises, Confederate commanders parried most of the threats with the deft movement of reserves and a staunch defense by the troops themselves, aided obviously by the strong fortifications and the rugged terrain fronting them. "Enemy made several different charges to our right and left," one of John C. Moore's staff officers jotted in his diary that day, "*very* heavy on our front, but repulsed, great loss on both sides, much greater on enemy." That was certainly the case on John Forney's front, as McPherson's renewed assaults picked up once more in the afternoon. Hébert, along the Jackson and Graveyard Roads, had ample reserves, but the critical point soon became Moore's defense along the Baldwin's Ferry Road. He had some reserves as well, including two regiments that Martin L. Smith had sent southward, the 17th and 29th Louisiana, despite the action on his line being heavy and a 30-pounder Parrott bursting during the fighting, weakening the line west of the Stockade Redan.[1]

Also available initially was Green's brigade of Bowen's division, but the crisis on Lee's front to the south soon called them away. Green's brigade had been positioned to the right of Cockrell, in reserve behind Moore's troops on the front line. It was a hardy brigade, and a veteran one, having participated in Bowen's celebrated assault against the Union line at Champion Hill. But that battle had eaten up much of the brigade's effectiveness, and the debacle the next morning at Big Black River Bridge almost destroyed it. Colonel Thomas P. Dockery of the 19th Arkansas described what was left as "the remnant of the brigade . . . the most of it having been captured at Big Black Bridge."[2]

The brigade still had some power nonetheless and was held in reserve for several days, often being "marched to the support of different points on the line without doing but little or no fighting." That changed on May 22, when orders arrived to once again support Moore's brigade holding the line between the Jackson and Baldwin Ferry Roads. As the brigade moved forward, more orders arrived to head farther southward to support Lee's brigade of Stevenson's division. Lee himself had sent a courier to request reinforcements, telling Green that his "line had been broken by the enemy." The trans-Mississippians headed for the break at the double-quick. It seems that McClernand was not the only one who may have seen more to the breakthrough than really occurred.[3]

Once at the Railroad Redoubt, Green's troops found out that the crisis was over. If there had been one, it was contained now, Colonel Dockery writing that Lee's "men rallied and drove the enemy from their works; at least, when we arrived at the works, General Lee's line was complete and no enemy on his works, yet there was a considerable force in the ditch or ravine under General Lee's works." Green sent forward the 1st Arkansas Battalion Sharpshooters "to open on the enemy in the ditch."[4]

All the while, Green moved back northward to his original destination, behind Moore's brigade. Much like at the Stockade Redan, where Cockrell's reserve troops aided the defense, Green sent his regiments into the fortifications as well, the now-returned 19th and 20th Arkansas taking station within the large 2nd Texas Lunette along with their fellow westerners. Others went into the trenches to the left of the lunette. At the time, there were Federals just on the other side of the parapets, Dockery noting "the enemy occupying a position in the ditch and a ravine in front of the fort." The remainder of the brigade continued to form a reserve in case it was needed. And it soon would be, as the Federals quickly began to be active once more along both the Jackson and Baldwin's Ferry Roads.[5]

According to orders from Grant acting on word from McClernand, James B. McPherson was restarting his assaults on the XVII Corps's front.

If Sherman's renewed assaults were going nowhere fast at the Graveyard Road, perhaps McPherson could do better in the center along the Jackson and Baldwin's Ferry Roads. His advances during the 10:00 A.M. assault had netted little, if anything, with only two brigades of Logan's division on the Jackson Road actually advancing and assaulting at the appointed hour. One of those, John E. Smith's, did so with only a couple of regiments becoming involved before the realization set in that it was hopeless. That said, John Stevenson's brigade had mounted a full-blown assault against the Great Redoubt and suffered the results.[6]

The other five brigades present with the division had done little more than maneuver and position themselves for an assault. Over on the far right, north of Glass Bayou, the only brigade of McPherson's corps separated by the bayou, and the only brigade of McArthur's division present, had not actually made assaults but merely positioned itself to do so. When portions of Blair's division of Sherman's corps extended down toward Glass Bayou, Ransom met up with them and began to make preparations for an all-out assault. Still, despite one of his men describing Ransom as "bolder than a lion," the brigade had done little by early afternoon.[7]

Likewise, Quinby's division down on the Baldwin's Ferry Road had not assaulted as yet. Quinby had merely positioned it in the maze of ravines east of the Confederate line, with at least one of the brigade commanders balking at making a suicidal charge. As a result, just as elsewhere, John Sanborn's and George Boomer's brigades had yet to make an attack even though the afternoon was growing longer. And certainly the reserve brigades in Logan's and Quinby's divisions under Mortimer Leggett and Samuel Holmes had seen no action.[8]

Yet the day was not over, and neither were the assaults. With McClernand's prodding and Sherman's backing, Grant had commanded Sherman to keep moving, although Mower's brigade was stopped cold on the Graveyard Road just as all the other attacks had been. And the afternoon advance under Frederick Steele had netted nothing but more casualties. Once Grant left Sherman, however, he rode southward to McPherson and likewise ordered him to renew the assaults. Hopefully, the renewed advance would carry the works, if it were coordinated and made in total, but if nothing else it would take some pressure off McClernand to the south, still reporting he had been successful and he only needed the assaults elsewhere rejoined to allow him to capitalize on his success. With that in mind, McPherson, for better or worse, sent out orders for the renewal of the assaults.[9]

Unfortunately for him, at least some of McPherson's troops were out of his command control, much like Sherman's, as the corps had slipped from his direction all along. Most notably, Ransom's brigade detached north of Glass Bayou did not necessarily act on McPherson's orders but more so with the nearest troops, which happened to be of Sherman's corps on their right. In fact, as Giles A. Smith's troops bounded down into the valley of the northern branch of Glass Bayou and formed a line, Ransom went over and discussed with Smith the idea of an assault. Thus, terrain and position rather than orders from McPherson per se decided Ransom's actions. Significantly, Ransom never reported receiving any directions from McPherson during the assault. Still, Blair had plenty to say of Ransom's efforts: "The brigade was co-operating with one of my own, and was separated by the character of the ground from the corps to which it belonged. The officers and men of both brigades displayed a courage and coolness which could not have failed to win success in a less unequal struggle."[10]

Ransom the fighter wanted to move forward anyway and found the likeminded Giles Smith onboard with the idea. "Generals Giles A. Smith and Ransom and other officers got together in the ravine and arranged their watches and how they should start," recalled one Illinoisan in his diary. "After a long wait the word came to 'Forward,'" another Illinoisan wrote, and "every man raised to his feet and all moved forward." The two brigades began to move ahead, Ransom receiving some reinforcement from four companies (one of the 95th Illinois, one of the 17th Wisconsin, and two of the 11th Illinois, all under Captain George C. McKee of the 11th Illinois) that had been sent to the left across Glass Bayou as skirmishers toward Logan's division. They had held a position toward "the large white house to my left" since May 19 and had kept the Mississippians down along this section, but with Logan's full deployment they headed back to their parent brigade the morning of May 22 and arrived "just in time to participate in the charge of the 22d instant," Ransom explained.[11]

Unfortunately for Ransom's newly reinforced brigade, Smith's troops to the right were quickly halted; the Confederates of the 37th and 38th Mississippi and 7th Mississippi Battalion poured a heavy fire in on them, and they took cover. The ground on their front was not as good for cover as on Ransom's, and thus yet another of Sherman's assaults failed fairly quickly. It would be up to Ransom if the Confederate lines were broken in this vicinity between the Stockade Redan and the 3rd Louisiana Redan, and some of those defenses were weak in this area around Glass Bayou, one Confederate declaring they were "guarded only by a rude fence, with grapevines and briar entanglements."[12]

Ransom had painstakingly pushed his regiments forward to the cover of a ridge just sixty or so yards from the Confederate line and held there while he worked out the details of the assault. Behind the slight cover of the ridge, the regiments formed in columns of companies, the 11th Illinois on the left, the 95th Illinois next, with the 14th Wisconsin and 72nd Illinois to the right and the 17th Wisconsin still holding in reserve. In this second position, a lieutenant in one of the companies found he had left his sword in their previous position; Major Joseph Stockton climbed up and retrieved it, sending it to him "with my compliments." By midafternoon, however, the calm ended with Ransom shouting a fateful order: "Second Brigade, forward."[13]

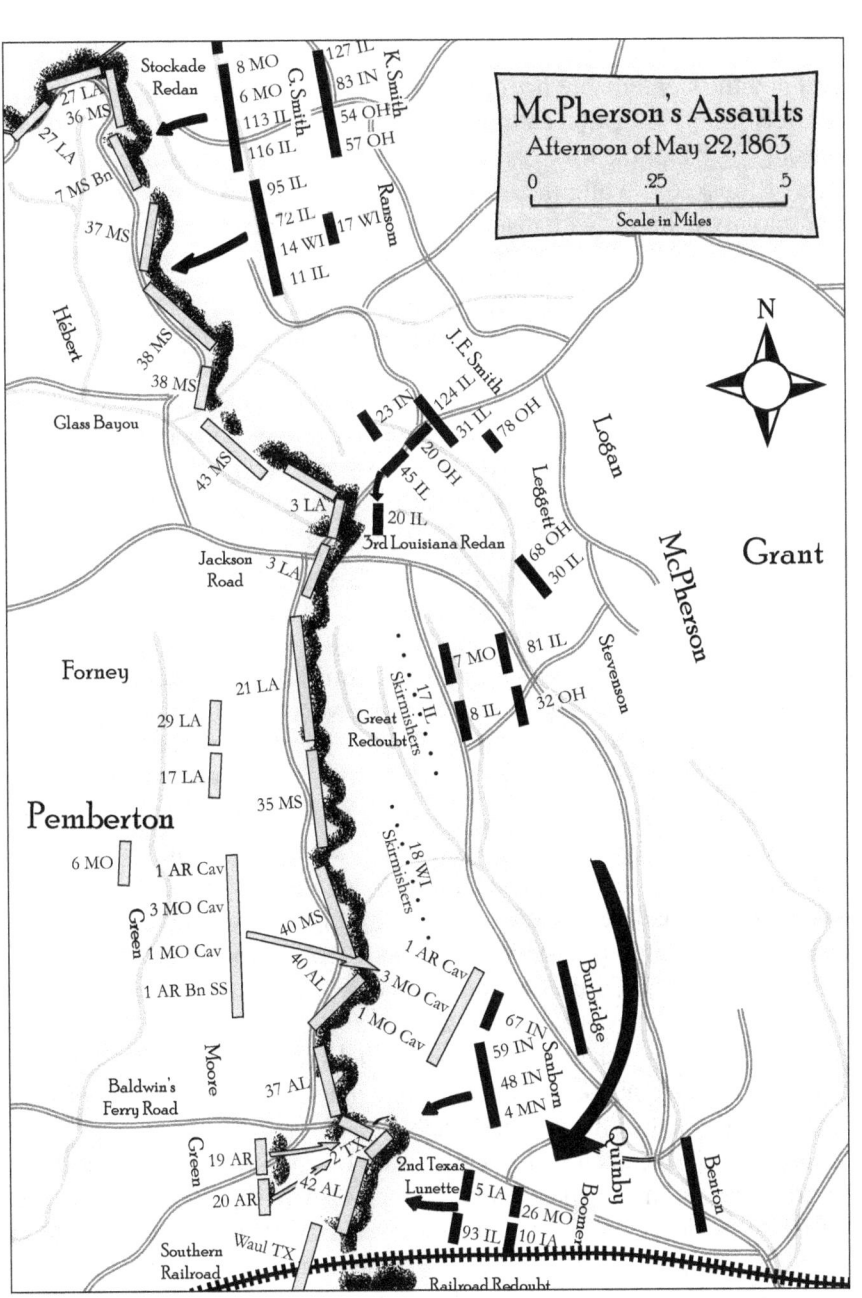

Once the advance began, the Illinois and Wisconsin troops had no more cover and the Confederate fire quickly swept through the ranks with disturbing effect, Major Stockton calling the initial burst "a most wondrous volley." Ransom noted that the Mississippians "poured into my ranks one continuous blaze of musketry, while the artillery on my left threw infilading shot and shell into my columns with deadly effect." The beloved Colonel Humphrey, leading the 95th Illinois (which had already lost a hundred men in these ravines on May 19), reported that "my command simultaneously advanced to the crest of the ridge, when they encountered the most sweeping and destructive fire to which troops were ever exposed. In vain did those brave men rally to the charge; to advance was but to meet certain death." The men had been partially shielded from this already heavy fire while in the ravine, but once they began the advance it quickly became very bloody. One Federal noted that "when one bullet was not sufficient, two, three, four, and even five did the work." Another testified that "the front companies advanced to the crest of the hill and were fairly swept off their feet by the most deadly, concentrated, cross and enfilading fire we were ever under."[14]

Most concerning for the 95th Illinois was the loss of their beloved colonel — or so they thought. "With the natural daring that characterized the man," one of his Illinoisans wrote, Colonel Humphrey dashed ahead of his regiment and over the hill, not to be seen again that day. "The regiment attempted to follow their leader," the Illinoisan continued, "and bravely rallied to the charge, but to advance was to meet certain death and it was plain that a farther prosecution of the undertaking would annihilate the regiment." The Illinoisans fell back to a covering ravine without their colonel, whom all gave up for dead: "Nothing had been seen or heard of him since he crossed the ridge." General Ransom even later had a coffin made "for the reception of the corpse, so certain was he of Colonel Humphrey's death."[15]

The 72nd Illinois was also having problems, in addition to the command falling to Major Joseph Stockton, the colonel being sick and the lieutenant colonel already having been wounded. One member of the 95th Illinois gave a different account of the colonel's sickness, describing him as "dead drunk and had to be carried from the field." The Illinoisans were moving to the left through a ravine, supposedly behind the 14th Wisconsin or 95th Illinois, when they suddenly popped out into the open to their surprise with no Union regiments in front of them. "When we came on the hill in charge," remembered one Illinoisan, "we were in the rear of nothing but Jonnies and them loaded with buckshot." Another noted that the "bullets came in in showers." The advance consequently became immediately problematic, and downed officers did not help. "Almost at the first fire two of my leading colonels fell," Ransom reported. Colonel Thomas Humphrey of the 95th Illinois was well out in front of his regiment and was quickly "stunned by the concussion of a shell." The regiment's major, William Avery, also went down, as did three company captains. Worse, Colonel Garrett Nevins of the 11th Illinois was instantly killed a mere "fifteen or twenty ft of the rebel works" when "a musket ball struck him about the center of the forehead from which the blood and brain was flowing." Nevins had been terribly wounded at Shiloh but had recovered to lead the regiment onward. His leadership only went as far as the ramparts of Vicksburg.[16]

Realizing what was happening and the effect the loss of these commanding officers would have, Ransom himself waded into the advance and urged the men on. "Fearing that the loss of their leaders might prove disastrous," he later explained, "I redoubled my efforts to press my column forward." One grateful Illinoisan noted that Ransom "had appeared on the side hill fully exposed to the fire." Another told more of the story, writing that he took a flag in hand and waved it over his head, shouting: "Forward, men! We must and will go into that fort. Who will follow me?" Ransom also utilized his staff well, sending them out to do the same in his name, and all did so despite the obvious danger. Ransom later specifically mentioned Captain Cyrus E. Dickey of his staff for special bravery.[17]

With the firm backing of the commander and his staff, the regiments surged ahead again through the heated fire, casualties growing by the step amid another valley filled with felled trees and brush. "No line could be maintained under such conditions," one Illinoisan admitted, but they somehow made it to the Confederate fortifications. Portions of many of the regiments approached within paces of the Confederate line, and in all some four flags soon waved from the parapets, much like those even then fluttering in the breeze on the slopes of the Stockade Redan and Great Redoubt. An excited Ransom declared how his troops "moved onward, and planted four stand of colors near the base of the earthworks."[18]

The Confederate fire was just too much and the earthworks too strong to permit going any farther, however. George Carrington of the 11th Illinois admitted that "the whole Regt' wilted and immediately fell back under cover." Most of the Illinoisans and the 17th Wisconsin were stopped below the earthworks, but the 14th Wisconsin had provided the most hope of breaking the enemy line. In fact, that regiment shoved on forward "with the greatest rapidity," Ransom explained, and was the first to plant their colors on the works. Their bravery won from Ransom the notation that they "approached nearest the works." Yet even they were soon halted, despite an attempt to continue on and break the enemy line. "The contest there was desperate for perhaps twenty minutes," he wrote, adding that they "held the position with a determination which entitles this little band and its gallant commander to a most prominent notice in the recorded history of this contest."[19]

The stories of the individual lives affected were most heartrending. Elliott Bush of the 95th Illinois could only think of his creator. He wore a sword, on the sheath of which was inscribed: "THE LORD IS ON MY SIDE; I WILL NOT FEAR. WHAT CAN MAN DO WITH ME." Bush repeated those words over and over before making the assault. One Wisconsin soldier, James K. Newton, wrote home of the fearful casualties in his company: "Our Co suffered pretty severely. Both Lieuts wounded. Our Capt hurt by a fall down hill. Every Sergt. Wounded and all but one Corporal wounded. The Corpl who is unhurt is Tom Stewart he was detailed as sharpshooter the day before and did not go into the charge." Newton added: "How I came off the field without being wounded with the rest I am sure I can't tell. The nearest that I came to being wounded was when a ball went through the rim of my hat brushing my forehead." In all, the company lost four killed and eighteen wounded.[20]

Despite the 14th Wisconsin's bravery, Ransom had a decision to make. Most of the rest of the brigade had not made it as far and evidently could not press ahead any farther. He had no troops to support the 14th Wisconsin and thus ordered a withdrawal, admitting that the assault had failed. He explained, "I was not sufficiently supported to enter the works under the raking fire of artillery and in the face of a superior force of the enemy, massed behind their works in my front." Indeed, Giles Smith's Federals to the right had not advanced this far and were turned back. Of course, when Ransom looked to his left, all he saw was the looming valley of Glass Bayou. The nearest troops in that direction were Logan's up on the Jackson Road. Ransom was indeed unsupported and had no choice but to admit defeat and withdraw.[21]

That was easier said that done, as many were finding out. The same ridge crossed while advancing would have to be crossed under fire in falling back, which would no doubt produce more casualties before reaching the relative cover from which the brigade had begun its advance, some sixty yards back. But staying here in the open would produce more casualties, and Ransom quickly ordered the men rearward to cover. To help take some heat off troops as they fell back, Ransom positioned the 17th Wisconsin on the ridge to "cover my movements, and removed my command in perfect order to the cover of the ravine about 40 yards to the rear." He shouted to the entire brigade: "Men of the second brigade! We cannot maintain this position. You must retire to the cover of that ravine, one regiment at a time." To make sure the retirement was orderly, he added that "the first man who runs or goes beyond that ravine, shall be shot. *I will stand here*, and see how you do it." Sure enough, Ransom mounted a stump in full view of the Confederates and, with arms folded, watched as the retreat began. A captain crawled up to him and begged him to take cover, which garnered only this response: "*Silence!*"[22]

Not all escaped or needed to. About six companies of the forward 14th Wisconsin had nudged up to the Confederate fortifications and found what Ransom described as "a position of comparable safety directly under the rebel works, and from which it was unsafe to move." Ransom left the troops there to await nightfall, like so many others huddled along the lines on the Confederate parapets. Darkness finally, mercifully, neared, as did Colonel Humphreys of the 95th Illinois. He had lain behind shelter under Confederate fire for hours, then sneaked back after dark to Ransom's headquarters—where his coffin awaited him. One of his soldiers noted he arrived "to the great delight and astonishment of all."[23]

Ransom's assault had failed, with 476 total casualties reported through the next day. Detached as he was north of Glass Bayou, Ransom had never actually acted under McPherson's direct command anyway, and in fact his movements and assault could just as well be properly described as a part of Sherman's attacks. Either way, Ransom was unable to provide the breakthrough needed, but McPherson still had the majority of his corps—two full divisions strong—farther to the south. His real afternoon assaults would take place there.[24]

John Logan's division, situated along the Jackson Road, packed far more punch than did Ransom's lone brigade of McArthur's division. As opposed to one single brigade, the hard-fighting Logan fielded three full brigades commanded by similarly hard fighters: John E. Smith, John D. Stevenson, and Mortimer D. Leggett. Not surprisingly, most had already been in action, Smith and Stevenson making dramatic assaults at the 10:00 A.M. advance time earlier this morning. Leggett had been held in reserve and saw no action.[25]

With McClernand's call for more help and Grant's agreement to support him, McPherson put Logan back in action. Yet for all the power available in this division, only one isolated attack would be forthcoming by one single regiment in Smith's brigade. It was certainly not an overwhelming attack, but then perhaps that was not what was needed. Maybe the thinking by McPherson and Logan was that McClernand needed only a slight diversion to allow him to complete his victory. Perhaps they thought, like Grant and Sherman to a lesser degree, that McClernand was overhyping his success and they did not want to waste any more lives in a response to a false claim. Maybe they thought it would not hurt to try one more time on an isolated front and, if it broke through, they could support the success with the rest of the brigades. Or maybe they had come to the conclusion that assaulting Vicksburg was a hopeless proposition and, although they were under positive orders to renew the assaults, they would do so with minimum force, thereby saving as many lives as possible.

For whatever reason, most of Logan's division stood idle when the renewal of the advance began. John Stevenson's brigade could be little faulted. It had made the boldest assault yet and paid dearly for it. This brigade was quite literally out of energy and was running out of men, and so it merely continued to hold the position it had taken after the repulse from the Great Redoubt.[26]

Similarly, Mortimer Leggett's brigade remained in the rear to support either frontline brigade in the division in case someone made a breakthrough; their orders were to "rush into the works if the assault should succeed, and, if it failed, to keep a firm front, and hold the enemy at bay." Neither had happened in the morning assault, but the brigade remained in the rear in case a breakthrough occurred that afternoon. To lend weight to Smith's renewed attack, however, Logan ordered the 20th Ohio of Leggett's brigade to move forward and attach itself to Smith's brigade in case more numbers were needed. These were good, sound troops, having seen action at Fort Donelson and Shiloh, as well as later battles such as Champion Hill.[27]

Consequently, the main attack that afternoon would be made by John E. Smith's troops, which still had units to the front. The 23rd Indiana had made the dramatic but futile advance north of the Jackson Road and was still deployed in the area even now, eventually making another run down the road before being called back. The following 20th Illinois had found the going so difficult that they veered off to the south side of the road and took cover behind a slight hill, but they nevertheless still fronted the 3rd Louisiana Redan. Now, Smith had to figure out his next move, and there were few options. Colonel Manning F. Force of the attached 20th Ohio admitted to his father that "no practical scaling point was found, and here we lie." He added that "the earthworks are so high and steep, and the ditches so wide, that it is difficult to do more."[28]

While there was second-guessing of the idea to launch another assault against what was looking increasingly like an impregnable Vicksburg, every commander in the army wanted to be the one who broke through if that were possible. Accordingly, when Smith received orders from Logan, who had just gotten them from McPherson, he decided to send his best regiment to make the attempt. "Although there is not a regiment in the brigade that I have not the fullest confidence in," Smith declared, "yet as the Forty-fifth Illinois had not been under fire, and knowing that they would go wherever I ordered and where it was possible to go . . . , I ordered them in advance." Of course, the 45th Illinois was Smith's old regiment that he had recruited and first commanded.[29]

Smith made his orders plain and simple. The "Illinois lead miners" were to move forward by the flank along the Jackson Road at the 3rd Louisiana Redan, followed by Colonel Force's 20th Ohio and others if they scored a breakthrough. They were still to operate "under the previous instructions, to move forward with fixed bayonets, and not fire until they had gained the enemy's works." Colonel Force gave specific directions to his Ohioans: "Upon entering the enemy's works a line of troops, or a second line of works, would be found close at hand, which must be promptly charged." Force was happy that his men "all earnestly promised to keep closed ranks and make the charge."[30]

The lead miners were soon in position, and Smith bellowed the command to move forward. The regiment lurched ahead in a long, snake-like line much as Ewing's and Mower's brigades had done before and still were doing on the Graveyard Road less than a mile to the north. The intention was to move to the left of the road, form their line, and advance up the hill toward the Confederate redan. But the same result happened here as on the Graveyard Road. Smith described how "the order was given to advance, and they were soon exposed to the fire of the whole of the rebel line, killing and wounding many at the head of the column." Among the killed was the commander of the 45th Illinois, Major Luther H. Cowan.[31]

The Confederate fire was devastating, one of the Illinoisans describing how it "was the hottest fire I ever had been under before (and I was at Shiloh)." Another Illinoisan described the results of Cowan's fall: "There was no one to give the command to halt, or right face and charge; the Major was killed and the ranking Captain didn't know it." The first sergeant of the lead company took it upon himself to stop the column after he thought enough room had been gained, and soon the ranking captain learned of the major's wounding and came forward to take command, ordering the regiment forward. By that time, however, matters were in such chaos that only a few reached the parapet of the Confederate works.[32]

John E. Smith himself was in the midst of the assault and heavy Confederate fire, and he knew immediately that this was only more of the same. In fact, he and his staff came under heavy fire, with his assistant adjutant general Captain Wimer Bedford being dangerously wounded directly by his side. As the minutes ticked by, matters became even worse. After the 3rd Louisiana's fire shattered the head of the 45th Illinois, the rest dove for cover, filing down the embankment of the road and toward the safety provided by the ridge where the 20th Illinois still retained its ground. No doubt the 20th Illinoisans were thankful for the break they received when the Confederate attention shifted to the lead miners, but they were then no doubt also chagrined when the others bolted for their very position, bringing another heavy wave of Confederate fire right onto them.[33]

Smith was convinced early on: "I became satisfied that the obstacles could not be overcome without sacrificing probably my whole command." He acted quickly to end this ludicrous attempt, ordering the following 20th Ohio to cease their advance and take cover along the road behind the ridge. There, they huddled "in front of the principal curtain of the fort," Smith reported, the Ohioans taking a place in a road cut where they were "sitting with our backs pressed against the side of the cut toward Vicksburg, the balls whistled by just outside of our knees." Force elaborated that the Ohio regiment simply "remained on Fort Hill, close to the parapets, partly in the road leading by the white house."[34]

Only a brave and fortunate few had actually made it to the base of the earthworks, the 3rd Louisiana Redan having no ditch like the others. Huddling pitifully under the fortifications, the cantankerousness of the soldiers soon became evident nonetheless and continued on for hours. One Illinoisan remembered how they could "pelt them [Confederates] with clods of dirt." Not to be outdone, one Confederate threw over an empty whiskey bottle, "to show us what they had to drink." The Federals responded by throwing over crackers, "to let them know what we had to eat."[35]

It had all happened so rapidly, and Smith had become so convinced of the futility of the effort so quickly, that the Ohioans had not even had time to make their full appearance on the scene. Still, the abortive attack had an influence on the higher command. Logan knew this assault could not be done now, and McPherson knew the same. But McPherson was not totally out of options, although storming the heights by the flank was obviously not working. There was still another full division to the left (Quinby's), although he was reluctant to send it forward to the same fate all the others had met. Instead, Grant began to think that if McClernand was having success on his front, maybe that is where Quinby should go. All eyes thus began to focus on the far left of the Union line, where McClernand's claims of a breakthrough dominated the day.[36]

If Grant was counting on Quinby's division to be the determining factor on McClernand's front, it would take a lot of work to get it done. For one thing, Quinby was far out of position by this point. Sidled up near Logan's division, Quinby simply fronted more of the same fortifications and steep ascents that

Logan had found impregnable. More assaults along these types of avenues would prove nothing except that the defending Confederates could kill any Yankee who foolishly surged against their fortifications. But there had, at least according to McClernand, apparently been some success farther to the south. If Quinby moved the brigades in that direction and joined in McClernand's success, then perhaps something truly profitable could be done. However, the division had to move to do so.[37]

Perhaps worse for the Federals, the command chaos in the division was already in place and was getting worse. Quinby had been in command only for a few days and was still adjusting, as were his subordinates. Those brigade commanders were mostly an opinionated set who seemed to know as much as their superiors. In fact, the entire morning assault against the Confederate line had come to nothing simply on the whim of Colonel George Boomer's doubts. He had stopped his brigade's advance because he had not liked the looks of things, causing Sanborn to also halt to keep from going in alone without support. Both Boomer and Sanborn had definite thoughts on the subject of attack, and its seems that their hearts were just not in it. The fact that the brigades had been moving nonstop for days was also a factor, Sanborn writing that "my command was exceedingly exhausted, having had no rest the night of the 19th, marching nearly 20 miles on the 20th, moving into camp the 21st, and having been under fire or marching all this day."[38]

Nevertheless, around 3:00 P.M. the order came to advance and assault once more. This was obviously a result of McClernand's initial desire for supporting action on Sherman's and McPherson's fronts. McClernand had also sent messages to McPherson for support, two messages arriving by the same staff officer at McPherson's headquarters within the span of thirty minutes. McClernand told McPherson in the first one that he needed support, but McPherson merely responded that McArthur was supposed to aid him. McClernand responded that McArthur was nowhere to be found and renewed the request for aid from the XVII Corps. McPherson relented and sent orders down to Logan and Quinby, and Quinby sent them further down the chain of command to his brigade commanders. Colonel Sanborn wrote that the orders were to "move at once and vigorously upon the works." Still wondering about the situation, Sanborn sent the orders to his regimental commanders through a staff officer.[39]

But there was no attack. General Grant was looking more into the situation and had quickly changed his mind about Quinby's advance. If Quinby's brigades were going in, and because his was the closest division of McPherson's or Sherman's corps to McClernand's breakthrough, why not send them a little farther south to exploit that very area? It was less than a mile, and more numbers there might turn the tide. McPherson soon received Grant's revised orders and fired off a note to Quinby: "By direction of Maj Genl Grant you will have your division to the support of Genl McClernand *immediately*[.] Send a messenger to report to Genl McClernand that you are coming[.] Move by the shortest line and keep out of sight of the enemy. Keep out a heavy line of skirmishers along your present front." McClernand soon received the note and sent a staff officer to lead the division into place.[40]

With these new orders, Quinby quickly countermanded the advance and took his division southward, although somewhat illogically not to the Railroad Redoubt but to the 2nd Texas Lunette. For some reason, McClernand directed the brigades to the more northern fort rather than the Railroad Redoubt where the only conceivable breakthrough had occurred. Perhaps it was because McClernand had also gotten word of partial success there, or maybe it was because the hour was getting late and this sector was much closer for the marching division. Perhaps it was both. There, Quinby was supposed to deploy in such a way that Boomer on the left would take the same front as Benton's brigade of Carr's division in their earlier assault on the fort while Sanborn would go in on the north side on Burbridge's (of A. J. Smith's division) front. This would place much more firepower in the area that had also been determined as a weak point.[41]

Sanborn and Boomer moved to the left quickly, Sanborn writing that his brigade moved "some 2 miles" altogether. To cover their original front, Sanborn left only the 18th Wisconsin, which was at the time deployed ahead as skirmishers. They would remain there actually until late the next day, a weak line amid Grant's assaulting columns. That thought crossed Sanborn's mind often.[42]

Sanborn's regiments filed to the left and eventually came up in the rear of Burbridge's troops, "then engaged in front of the enemy's works." A staff officer led them forward "up through a ravine that was raked . . . by musketry and artillery to a point a few yards in rear of the line of this [Burbridge's] brigade." Sanborn went forward and met Burbridge himself, who informed him that it was actually safer farther to the front: "The position close to the enemy's works was not so exposed as the ravine." Burbridge also recommended that Sanborn take the lead "nearer or in front of his line."[43]

Sanborn agreed and deployed his three remaining regiments right behind Burbridge's troops, the 59th Indiana on the right, 4th Minnesota on the left, and the 48th Indiana in the center. It did not take long for Sanborn to become even more concerned, however. Burbridge's troops soon thereafter "gave way," according to Sanborn, "and his troops left the ground." Lieutenant Colonel John E. Tourtellotte of the 4th Minnesota reported that "no sooner had we taken such position that General Burbridge withdrew his brigade from the action." Some of Burbridge's men corroborated it, a Wisconsin soldier writing that "we were relieved by a part of Quinby's division and most all of our regt. had left." Only one of Burbridge's regiments remained, the 67th Indiana on the far right supporting the 59th Indiana. Worse, the Confederate fire was increasing, and the shelter Burbridge described was nowhere to be found. Only a few sinkholes in the bottom of the ravine were available, and James Mahan of the 59th Indiana later described how he was glad to get into one: "I, for one, lost no time in tumbling into one of those sink holes, 'and lo and behold' I fell on top of Lieutenant Aiken of my company. Neither of us was ashamed of our act, for the next few minutes was no time to be out picking flowers around there." Sanborn mournfully said that "this position seemed very much exposed, and I lost several men during the formation." The temperature was also almost unbearable, one Indianan writing that "I am almost prostrated from the heat." Nevertheless, Sanborn pushed his men forward to relieve those "brave boys who had held their place till their cartridges were gone and more than half of their numbers were lost," one Indianan marveled.[44]

The Confederates had picked up on what was happening, and Colonel Ashbel Smith of the 2nd Texas faced his most dreaded fear. He had repelled the vicious morning attacks against his front and flanks. All the while, he had most worried about the approaches on the left, where a deep ravine, what he called a "debouche," led straight to his unprotected flank. That was exactly where Sanborn's troops were deploying, and after "an hour or more of great slackening of the enemy's fire," they were on the way again. Smith wrote that "he [the enemy] despaired, as it appeared, of being able to carry our works by an unsupported assault in front, and ordered an attack to be made on our left. Meanwhile, a heavy column came marching up the valley already described as debouching in the interval on our left."[45]

Unfortunately for him, Sanborn was not nearly as close to success as Colonel Smith feared. The Confederates were actually placing a good fire on Sanborn's troops, now in the front. A Mississippian described how "our men, as before, reserve their fire until they approach near, and then pour forth a perfect storm of Buck and Ball, so that the enemy fall by hundreds. They fill up the broken ranks and press on but they stagger before the deadly fire." Given the heavy volume of projectiles, Edward P. Stanfield of the 48th Indiana wrote his father that "we expected to die as sure as there was such a thing as death." Worse, it was about to get even hotter, because Confederate reinforcements were also on the way. Smith explained that Green's regiments had returned from Lee's crisis and entered the works on the left of the lunette, although it took some time to get them there. "Early in the day," Smith wrote, "I had observed our exposed condition on this side, and had asked for support from the reserves." Now was the critical time, Smith relating that "my numbers were so reduced by killed and wounded that I could ill spare any considerable body from my front." Fortunately, Green's trans-Mississippians arrived, but to Smith's horror they "hesitated for a moment, and allowed a most gallant lieutenant to get some 20 paces in advance of his company." An astonished Smith quickly ordered a company of his own regiment from the right to cross the "gorge" of the fort and take the position, but by the time they were on the move Green's troops had regained their edge and "dashed forward" into the fortifications. It was just in time, because Sanborn's Federals were even then approaching.[46]

The effect was not missed, despite the heavy supporting fire from the Union artillery that touched off a limber in nearby Battery G, 1st Mississippi Light Artillery. Sanborn noted that "the enemy was largely re-enforced, and fired rapid and destructive volleys into my command." Colonel Tourtellotte explained that his men were "under a direct fire from the fort in front, and a heavy cross-fire from a fort on our right." The Federals responded in kind, advancing farther to try to find the cover Burbridge had described to them. Tourtellotte noted that the three regiments "pressed forward up to and even on the enemy's works," but they were at a distinct disadvantage, having to fire uphill and against the formidable fortifications at the top. Sanborn admitted that the fire probably had little effect, "the enemy . . . having so high and strong works in front."[47]

Worse were the events happening to Sanborn's right, in the very expanse of ground the division had earlier left and now held by only a thin line of Wisconsin skirmishers. Sanborn reported that "once or twice the enemy came over his works in large numbers and formed on my right, with the evident design of turning my right flank." More to the point, Edward Wood of the 48th Indiana wrote his wife that the Confederates "sallied out from their fort on our right pouring in a terrible cross fire and threatening to outflank us and cut us off." Indeed, the reserve units of Green's brigade drawn up behind Moore's troops, those not deployed in the lunette itself, moved forward to outflank the enemy. Specifically, the 1st and 3rd Missouri Cavalry (dismounted) as well as the 1st Arkansas Cavalry (dismounted) moved across the fortifications, Colonel Dockery indicating that the regiments "sallied from the fort." Sanborn turned his attention in that direction and managed to keep a disaster from unfolding, arguing that the Confederates were "promptly driven back by my command with much slaughter." The Confederates countered that "after a short but desperate fight, [we] drove the enemy from the position with heavy loss." The truth was probably somewhere in the middle, but Sanborn went no farther and the Confederates eventually returned inside their fortifications. Members of the 48th Indiana indicated that they indeed withdrew, although having to run a gauntlet of Confederate fire to do so.[48]

With so much going on and none of it looking very positive, Sanborn decided to just hold what he had. He did so, he said, for the two or so hours left in the day, although Carr related that Sanborn's Federals "retreated in confusion as soon as it got under the enemy's fire." Either way, the Confederates inside the 2nd Texas Lunette had the upper hand, as Samuel Sneier of the 48th Indiana clearly understood: "The Rebels had the advantage of us they being inside of good fortifications, while we had but a low bank to protect us." Accordingly, taking over the front line from Burbridge was the extent of Sanborn's advance on the north side of the 2nd Texas Lunette, and the Confederates obviously easily contained the assault. Perhaps more could have been done, but Sanborn was clearly not in the mood and in fact later complained of the way things were being handled:

> The casualties in my command during this engagement, as the official lists will show, are greater than in all the balance of the campaign, and it seems to me all for no good. Success was no better than defeat, unless an assault was to be ordered, and I have not learned that such a thing was thought of, and, if thought of, would have been preposterous unless made by both brigades and in a most vigorous manner.

Obviously, there had been a disconnect between Sanborn and Quinby, and he apparently laid the fault at Quinby's feet. In truth, it went farther than that, McPherson also deserving some of the blame for the failure to make sure Quinby's division went in forcefully. Nevertheless, the opinionated Sanborn added: "I can but feel that there was official misrepresentation or misconduct that led to this matter which requires investigation."[49]

An obviously angry Sanborn thus did nothing for the rest of the day and around nightfall called his brigade back to a position of greater safety. Even in that he complained, however, writing that

> having no support, and seeing no reason why a position should be held at such sacrifice which, if lost, could be recovered at any time by a line of skirmishers, . . . and there being no general officer upon the ground, I ordered the position abandoned and my command to march back to the hill on the right of the railroad bridge, and there form and rest for the night.

On a positive note, the Minnesotans on the left succeeded in bringing out the Chicago cannon that Burbridge's brigade had pushed forward "to batter down the walls of the fort." The gun had been abandoned in the heavy fire, but Company C brought the cannon down the steep hill to safety.[50]

Sanborn was obviously not happy, even though he had only glowing remarks about his troops:

> The conduct of all the officers and men of my command . . . has been more than satisfactory—it has been most gallant and praiseworthy. There has been no shirking and no desire to shirk on the part of either officers or men, and I have not found or even heard of a man out of his position in battle or on the march. I know not how soldiers could do more.

That left the blame for the commanders, and his frequent cutting remarks of absent generals and what he considered stupid decisions were obviously aimed mostly at Quinby. "I am impelled to say this much in my report of this engagement," he wrote later, "by eloquent voices coming from the tombs of many of the most brave of my command, fallen in that fruitless struggle under the enemy's works."[51]

Still, as bad as it was in Sanborn's ranks that afternoon, he had no idea what was happening to his south on Boomer's front.

George Boomer was no more excited about the looks of things than was Sanborn. In fact, he had almost single-handedly paused the assault on Quinby's front earlier by stopping his brigade after its slight advance at 10:00 A.M. Because he did so, without orders from Quinby, Sanborn was not comfortable with going in alone and consequently halted his advance as well. Obviously, Holmes's troops in reserve did not move on either. Boomer's reluctance had thwarted the entire advance of a powerful, veteran division.[52]

Boomer was not that interested in restarting it either, although orders eventually came to do so. McClernand had called on McPherson to restart his advances, and McPherson sent the orders, which eventually filtered down through Logan and Quinby to the brigade commanders. Boomer could do little but obey, one of his colonels in the 93rd Illinois, Holden Putnam, writing that "preparations were immediately made and the charge ordered." As on Sanborn's front, the advance had not begun when more orders arrived changing the plan. Quinby was to move to the left to support McClernand himself. One Iowan mistakenly "supposed we were going back to camp, but we were only getting out of the frying pan into the fire."[53]

While moving in column on the rearward roadways about 3:30 P.M., the brigades changed deployment patterns, with Sanborn, who had been on the left, now going in on the right of the division in support of Burbridge's troops.

Boomer's Illinoisans, Iowans, and Missourians moved farther south and deployed south of the Baldwin's Ferry Road, intent on assaulting on the southeast side of the 2nd Texas Lunette while Sanborn hit it from the northeast. Boomer's men would take the place of Benton's brigade of Carr's division. Holmes moved even farther (one of his colonels reporting three miles) under orders to support Osterhaus's troops near the Railroad Redoubt. That was odd, considering Osterhaus already had an entire brigade of Hovey's division in reserve and not in use. The brigade marched but saw no action, Holmes writing that "upon my arrival I received orders to move to the attack of the enemy's works in his front, which order was almost immediately countermanded, owing to the lateness of the hour."[54]

Boomer arrived near his assigned position by around 4:00 P.M. and quickly met Carr himself. Carr had seen the trouble up front, particularly with Benton's earlier assault, and wanted these fresh troops to immediately go in to assault what he described as "the curtain between the salients [the 2nd Texas Lunette and the Railroad Redoubt] attacked by my two brigades, and thereby gaining a permanent lodgment." Colonel Putnam wrote that Carr only took time to call Boomer and his regimental commanders to the top of the ridge to point out the defenses and "immediately ordered the brigade to charge the enemy's intrenchments on the third range of hills in our front and about 120 rods distant," or nearly seven hundred yards to the front. The fact that Carr sent the brigade in instantly was significant, as he was desiring to keep the pressure on the enemy. His move had a drastic and unsurprising effect on the outcome. Most of the brigades, including Sanborn's, maneuvered among the ravines and hills to approach the Confederate line as close as possible without coming under heavy fire. That allowed them to make a shorter sprint during the attack. The fact that Carr sent Boomer in across seven hundred yards of ground and three successive ridges was a recipe for disaster, which Boomer plainly conceived. "No man can return from this charge alive," he lamented, handing his watch and money to a friend to keep in the rear.[55]

Although not liking what he was seeing, including the Federals of Benton's brigade huddled along the Confederate works to the front, Boomer nevertheless formed his brigade in two columns, much as John D. Stevenson had done in his assault on the Great Redoubt earlier that morning. One Illinoisan described the brigade taking position in "two lines parallel with each other and about fifty yards between," although numerous soldiers reported it was mere feet instead of yards. The 5th Iowa took the right front position, supported by the 26th Missouri, while the 93rd Illinois formed on the left front, with the 10th Iowa in their rear. Once formed, Boomer gave the word "right shoulder shift arms, forward, common time, march," and the brigade advanced. Like their commander, few of the troops liked the looks of things; one Illinoisan wrote that "if a soldier might at any time, or at all, weigh his life, in the scales, against his honor, that was a time to determine which he would lose." Worse, they quickly met a furious response: "As soon as we reached the top of the hill in our front, we came in plain view of the rebels, and they instantly opened fire on us with infantry and artillery, from our front and flanks." Another Illinoisan took exception, thinking they were there to support McClernand: "Instead of being a support simply we were ordered to charge the rebel rifle-pits between two forts, in which the guns had been silenced, as we were told. This was false."[56]

Although the ground was very broken and "tangled," as one Iowan described it, two distinct ridges or hills intervened between the brigade and the Confederate line. Matters went from bad to worse for Boomer as the brigade moved up and over the first ridge between them and the enemy fortifications. The brigade surged over the first ridge, the men moving down the hill into the cover of the ravine. "We were not under fire for more than a minute," J. Q. A. Campbell recalled, "but the balls flew about us like hail." An Illinoisan described it as "marching men to their graves in line of battle." Another said that all he could think of doing was "pulling my hat over my face, as if that would be any protection for me." The Confederate fire even this far out was indeed heavy, Colonel Putnam reporting that "the line moved steadily forward at common time, all the while exposed to a most deadly fire from the whole line of the enemy's works—right, left, and front." Lieutenant Colonel Ezekiel S. Sampson of the 5th Iowa also gave a splendid account of the movement, writing that

> in a few moments an advance was ordered, and in the most perfect order, at common time, and with arms at a right shoulder shift, and exposed to a most galling and deadly fire from the whole line of the enemy's works—right, left, and in front—we passed the first and principal range of hills, halted in the ravine beyond, under cover of the second range, dressed my lines, and were in readiness for a farther advance.[57]

That advance would have to wait. To make matters worse, the brigade had been aligned incorrectly and veered too far right, actually toward Sanborn's brigade, which at the time was fighting north of the Baldwin's Ferry Road. Once over the first ridge, Boomer ordered the brigade halted to dress ranks and rectify the situation: what Sampson called "a new disposition of the troops." Needing to put more men on the left, he opted to move the 5th Iowa on the right front by the left flank to a position on the left of the 93rd Illinois. That would extend the brigade's line at least a regiment's front to the south.[58]

The confusion mounted as the men stood in ranks slightly below the brink of the last hill, only partially covered from the Confederate fire coming from all directions. A watching Colonel Smith of the 2nd Texas noted that "this approach of the enemy's column on the left [Sanborn's] and the fighting was the signal for the renewal of his attack in front." Thus forewarned, the Texans were ready and poured fire into the oncoming Federals on the right too, causing most to realize what a mess they had gotten into. Sergeant Harvey M. Trimble of the 93rd Illinois admitted how "never have I felt less confident of accomplishing something than I did as we laid in line ready to advance." Numerous Federals went down during this lull while the Iowans moved their position, and the Iowans themselves found the new location much less covered than the former one. It was hot, and Boomer fretted that this was only going to be another disaster. If things were this bad two ridges out, what would they be like when the brigade finally approached the Confederate line?[59]

Boomer's fears were confirmed in a very ironic manner. He had told his men, "Boys, I shall be with you right between the lines." As he repositioned the brigade and dressed the ranks from his location between the troops on the second ridge out from the Confederates, Boomer was soon shot "through the head" by a Confederate sharpshooter, the bullet mortally wounding him and death coming quickly. One Iowan declared it came from "the rebel fort on our left flank." His fears had been realized, as had those of Sanborn to the right. Perhaps it was in "the gallant Boomer['s]" memory that Sanborn had written of the "eloquent voices coming from the tombs." The troops under fire simply placed a handkerchief over his face for now.[60]

Boomer's effect lived beyond his death, General Carr giving the ultimate epitaph, despite the horrific surroundings: "Boomer was perfectly cool and collected." Lieutenant Colonel Sampson of the 5th Iowa noted that "this circumstance caused a momentary delay," and indeed Colonel Smith of the Texas regiment noted that "the firing was very brisk, but the assault was feeble compared with the fierce onslaughts earlier in the day." Next in command of the brigade was Colonel Holden Putnam of the 93rd Illinois, and when he received word of Boomer's death and his new command, he immediately ordered the assault to be continued "as we had approached the works thus far." His command authority was clipped when Major Nathaniel McCalla of the 10th Iowa approached Putnam and in a loud voice, which the troops could hear, blurted that "Colonel Boomer's last words were to let the rifle-pits alone," while another declared he stated "tell Col. Putnam (of the 93rd Ills—our next senior Colonel) not to go over that hill." Colonel Putnam was certainly in a quandary, the brigade having heard the admonition. To continue would be going against Boomer's wishes; with doubt now firmly planted in the men's' minds, no assault could succeed.[61]

The chaos of the fog of war hit Colonel Putnam hard. He had just ascended to command of the brigade, which obviously caused commotion in the ranks of the 93rd Illinois as their command structure changed as well, each field officer moving up a notch. The movement of the 5th Iowa from one side of the brigade to the other also produced confusion. Worse, the Confederates, much like on Sanborn's right, had "advanced on my left and torn down a flag of ours, previously placed upon their works." His brigade was in chaos, the enemy was operating on his left, and Putnam was new to command. It was not the orderly advance and assault everyone had envisioned.[62]

Putnam waffled and rationalized that "as I was acting directly under orders from Colonel Boomer, and had received orders from no other commander, ... I deemed it advisable to, and did, send Lieutenant [Albert] Stoddard, aide-de-camp, to General Carr, to know if he wished me to move upon the works." By now, of course, the advance was stymied, as were the others, and Carr simply sent back word to forego any additional advance and remain in the position now held until dark, at which time the brigade could withdraw to the original position it had held earlier. One Iowan noted in his diary that they "were very glad to get out of it."[63]

Accordingly, this assault went no farther and was no more successful than was Sanborn's north of the road—or any other brigade's to the north for that matter. Conversely, at least one Illinoisan of Benton's brigade argued that Boomer's troops had to receive help in turn; while taking roll call back where they had left their knapsacks before charging, the 99th Illinois was called upon to move ahead again and shore up the line as Boomer's troops moved rearward, "probably saving the whole division from stampede," an immodest Illinoisan wrote. The results were the same, whatever the condition of Boomer's brigade. And it had cost more than normal, the eight killed and eighty-seven wounded being comparable to other brigades; but the loss of the brigade commander himself set this action apart.[64]

The tired Confederates realized as much, grateful simply to have survived another round of assaults. Colonel Smith of the 2nd Texas noted that "the day was now drawing to a close. As the shades of the night were setting in, the enemy's fire slowly and sullenly slackened. It ceased with the dark." The effect was evident nevertheless:

> The loss of the enemy, considering the numbers engaged on either side, was enormous. The ground in our front and along the road, and either side of the road for several hundred yards way to the right, was thickly strewn with their dead. In numbers of instances two and three dead bodies were piled on each other. Along the

road for more than 200 yards the bodies lay so thick that one might have walked the whole distance on them without touching the ground.

A Mississippi artilleryman put it much more succinctly in his diary: "We had a very hot time of it for a little while."[65]

Ultimately, it was all for naught, as both Sanborn and Boomer had realized. In that sense, the needless death of Boomer resounded far and wide, perhaps causing some of Sanborn's emotional outburst in his report. Yet Boomer had had an effect and, perhaps, saved lives with his caution: refusing to move forward the first time in what was obviously, to him, a suicidal situation. The second hesitation, when he counseled cover instead of assault, took effect only after his death. In that sense, Boomer saved more of his men from the fate he now endured.[66]

The dual effect of Boomer's mortal and posthumous influence, however, also took away any chance to break the Confederate lines along the Baldwin's Ferry Road, closing McPherson's attempts to score a breakthrough and perhaps a major victory with the assaults of the XVII Corps. Consequently, neither he nor Sherman had been able to break through all day, although especially in the afternoon's renewal of the advances it could be hoped that they had provided McClernand with whatever support or diversion he needed to capitalize on his loudly proclaimed morning success. Now, Sherman and McPherson were done, so whatever McClernand would do had to be on his own.

12

"It Is Absolutely Necessary That They Be Dislodged"

John A. McClernand had anxiously watched his corps's assaults from an area of high ground near Captain Maurice Maloney's battery of 30-pounder Parrotts. It was good, high ground from which McClernand could see nearly his entire line, the exception being part of the far right over near the 2nd Texas Lunette, hidden due to "the foliage of trees and the extreme unevenness of the ground." Here, throughout the morning and then as things stalled in the afternoon, many staff officers and others came and went as messages were delivered or sent out in a rush. "I could see, and did see, flags of my corps planted upon the enemy's works, and could see, and did see, officers and men of my command enter them and rebel captives brought out of them," McClernand reported. He could also see that progress was stopped fairly quickly. McClernand accordingly went to work to rectify the situation.[1]

It was a tense time—and also dangerous. One of McClernand's staff officers described how "this was the best point for observation along our entire line, and from the top of the battery, where you often went for observation, you could see perfectly everything in our front from right to left." Another staff officer with McClernand noted watching the trouble a flag-bearer across the valley on the Railroad Redoubt had: "The United States flag had been planted immediately outside the west of the parapet, barely low enough to secure protection to the color-bearer." McClernand was taking a chance as well, being within six hundred yards of the enemy line. Staff officer Captain F. H. Mason recalled to McClernand how "your post of observation owed its entire safety to the slight parapet in front, as many of the enemy's bullets went far beyond us into the woods, and men were continually being wounded all about you." In fact, another staff officer, Lieutenant Colonel Henry C. Warmoth, was wounded later in the day "by my side," as McClernand remembered. Fortunately surviving, Warmoth later wrote McClernand his reminiscences, including how "I was wounded and caught by you in your arms as I fell." The ball hit him in the shoulder, and "if it had not been so fully spent it would have cut my juggler vein and killed me."[2]

From this close but dangerous position, McClernand watched the events unfold and formed his initial conclusions as a result. Staff officer Mason noted how he and McClernand could initially see the men at the Railroad Redoubt that morning as they "continued to advance, leaped into the ditch, and began to climb the enemy's parapet. A moment afterward a flag was planted on the crest of the parapet and held there by two men, while a party of fifteen or twenty (as I should judge) sprang over into the fort." Significantly, the Confederates firing over the parapet disappeared at the same time. McClernand wanted more support for this obvious embryonic success and began to send the messages to Grant all while pushing others up as well, including Benton's brigade to the right of the railroad.[3]

Other information also began to arrive, causing an extremely fluid situation. Mason recalled that word came from the right that Andrew Jackson Smith had also had success in taking rifle pits near the 2nd Texas Lunette, although the staff officer later acknowledged that the messenger was less than specific and "whether the interior of the works had been reached, or merely the ditch, I did not understand." Similarly, word came from Landram's and Lawler's positions that the Railroad Redoubt was in Federals hands. They asked that fire be withheld from it.[4]

McClernand seemed bewildered at all the arriving information that was less than definitive. According to Mason, McClernand "seemed incredulous, and sent me to Colonel Landram, who was in a very advanced position, to ascertain as far as possible the exact state of the case." Mason returned with definite word from Landram that the fort was in Federal hands, also bringing a note from Lieutenant Colonel Harvey Graham of the 22nd Iowa that was described as being "written inside the fort," although an Iowan present stated later that it was "written on his knee in the ditch, and on paper torn from his diary." Graham was certainly there; he almost shot a prisoner who "attempted to obey the call of nature." But whether they were inside or outside made all the difference, and McClernand could not tell. There was also word of a possible breach in one of the smaller batteries to the left of the Railroad Redoubt.[5]

The intelligence also indicated that whatever success had occurred was now stalled. A message from the front arrived in which those in the ditches "sent back for spades and shovels with which to dig down the enemy's works." They were also needed to throw up a traverse of sorts to protect them from enfilading fire from down the Confederate lines. Few spades arrived, but brave runners did take in coffee, which was "boiled in the ditch, and gave men drink who were nearly famished with deadly-thirst." McClernand was almost as miserable back at his command post amid swirling rumors and reports. He could do little as he continued to watch, the minutes soon turning into hours as the troops held their precarious positions along the Confederate fortifications. "My men never fought more gallantly—nay, desperately," he asserted, before continuing with his penchant for the dramatic: "They maintained their ground with death-like tenacity. Neither a blazing sun nor the deadly fire of the enemy shook them."[6]

By this point McClernand had worked himself into a corner despite the apparent success. He had loudly recommended that the assault on May 22 not be across the board in wide linear fashion but rather in hefty pinpricks of weighty columns at certain points: a "concentration of our forces against one or two points, and not the dispersion of them into a multitude of columns." Yet when McClernand sent his divisions forward, he did so on that very linear fashion that he had recommended so loudly against the evening before. All three and a half divisions of his corps were arrayed in line and participated in the assault. That spread the attack over nearly a mile and a half, certainly not the pinpricks on one or two isolated positions. Even worse, all brigades were tasked with the assault. No reserves were kept for general use, having been doled out specifically to certain divisions. Hovey's one brigade, for instance, was to support Osterhaus's assault, while the two brigades of Smith's division acted as a tandem force for the two brigades of Carr's division. That choice was now haunting McClernand in that all brigades were allotted, although one Indianan of Hovey's unbloodied division griped: "Imagine our surprise a few days after the assault had been made when we learned that Gen. McClernand had asked for and received reinforcement from other corps of the army, while one of his divisions lay within a few hundred yards of his assaulting column, ready to render assistance at a moment's notice." In fact, Spiceley's troops could only laugh at one wounded Kentuckian who ambled back through their immobile lines and was despairing in response to questions of how it was going at the front: "My regiment have all been killed or captured but myself; I am the only survivor." Obviously, the idle Federals could see such was not the case, as shown by "the squads of wounded coming back." Still, with some success on Lawler's and Landram's front and in need of reinforcements to widen any breakthrough, McClernand believed he had no spare troops to send.[7]

McClernand consequently had to go outside his own corps for help, and thus he began to send the messages to Grant that he was in need of reinforcement. These requests were certainly based on hearsay, although Mason, the staff officer, declared that "the dispatches sent from time to time during the day to General Grant were less sanguine of success and less positive in regard to what had been already accomplished than my own opinion, and, as I believed, the opinion of the majority of your officers."[8]

Still, McClernand's requests did not sit well with the army commander, who was rightly interested in Sherman's and McPherson's success as well as McClernand's. In fact, Grant's return dispatches were not helpful at all. After McClernand's first message, Grant responded sharply: "If your advance is weak, strengthen it by drawing from your reserves or other parts of the lines." Thereafter, Grant advised the use of McArthur to the south, and "if one portion of your troops are pressed, re-enforce them from another." Ironically, perhaps showing some favoritism, two times Grant saw the need to tell McClernand that "Sherman has gained some successes" or "Sherman is getting on well." Whether intended to push the obviously unpopular corps commander to greater success or just to be informational, McClernand no doubt took the word with less satisfaction than Grant wrote it.[9]

Over the course of the afternoon and McClernand's messages, Grant showed a conflicting reaction. He knew McClernand and what the politician was capable of overstating, but at the same time he wanted to take advantage of any and all success. For that reason Grant erred on the side of potential victory and allowed McClernand to assume responsibility for McArthur's lone brigade down near Warrenton. He also sent the left division of McPherson's command to McClernand, who rejoiced at the "welcome intelligence" that Quinby would soon be coming.[10]

Unknown to McClernand, in the process he had also thrown down the gauntlet that he was on the brink of success. If it did not turn out that way, Grant would be calling soon wanting to know why all the success he had heard so much about had not led to ultimate victory. With all the problems McClernand had caused Grant thus far in the campaign, it was not out of the question that this might be his final chance. After all, Grant had in his hip pocket, figuratively if not literally, the War Department's permission to relieve McClernand at any time. The stakes were thus extremely high for all involved, from the ranking generals down to the privates in the trenches either defending or assaulting these works around Vicksburg.[11]

John McClernand's standing with Grant and the others was clearly at stake on the afternoon of May 22. For Confederate general John Pemberton, however, his entire fate hung in the balance. And Confederate nervousness about the events at the Railroad Redoubt grew as the minutes passed. Pemberton had watched as the Federals launched numerous assaults across a very wide front, and although his troops had parried each of them, the outcome was uncertain, especially at the Railroad Redoubt. Word soon filtered in that a portion of that fortification was in Union hands. Pemberton had been shuffling troops around for days now, nearly wearing out John Bowen's two brigades, but he had no other choice but to do the same again. Only by strengthening the areas he knew were under increasing pressure could he hope to hold everywhere. To make sure of the crisis point, Pemberton even made a "a change of base," moving his headquarters farther south to "Gen'l Lee's old quarters."[12]

Pemberton particularly worried about Lee and the Railroad Redoubt, the only confirmed Union breakthrough as yet. Obviously, Federals inside the Confederate works were a great cause of concern, and Pemberton acted to stem the crisis even if he had to take troops from elsewhere to do it. Even with his concern for the assaults on the Graveyard and Jackson Roads along Forney's front, Pemberton still ordered Forney to help Stevenson's left at the Railroad Redoubt: "It is absolutely necessary that they be dislodged. It may be done by throwing into them shrapnel with short fuses, say two seconds. If not, you must mass sufficient troops to accomplish this object."[13]

Forney complied, at the cost of sending his only reserve to the right: Green's brigade of Bowen's division. Upon Lee's call for help because his "line had been broken by the enemy," Green's brigade went to support Lee instead of Moore. "The brigade was moved at a double-quick," Colonel Thomas P. Dockery of the 19th Arkansas reported, but fortunately by the time the brigade crossed the railroad and arrived near the crisis, events seemed to be well in hand. Indeed, Lee's Alabamians had stopped the enemy even though the Federals punctured the redoubt itself. By now, it was evident they could go no farther and that Lee would be able to hold his new position even as the enemy held the tip of the fortification. Green consequently turned his brigade back to the north and Moore's position, leaving only an Arkansas Battalion in Lee's area to help sweep the parapets of Federals.[14]

Still, Forney was stretched just about as thin as he could be. He updated Pemberton around 2:45 P.M., alerting him that the Federals had been blunted on the Jackson Road but were "now [again] forming against General Hebert's left." He added: "I cannot, therefore, send any troops to Generals Moore or Lee," but he also noted that the situation looked better there and that Green had returned from Lee's position and was supporting Moore again. Matters seemed to ease even more for the Confederates as the afternoon wore on, mainly because of the lackadaisical attacks by Logan's troops and Quinby's shift to the left. Green's troops had determined the crisis was not that heavy at the Railroad Redoubt and returned to support Moore at the 2nd Texas Lunette, which allowed more troops to deploy outside the fortifications as

Pemberton had requested. Even if they did not succeed in flanking any of the Federals per se or scoring a huge success, they certainly took the attention of Eugene Carr, Andrew Jackson Smith, and John B. Sanborn, who had by this time moved forward in support of McClernand.[15]

As the afternoon passed, the shuffling of reserves seemed to be working. Another update from Forney informed Pemberton that Moore had repelled another assault around 5:00 P.M.: "This has been the most severe fighting," although Boomer's and Sanborn's assaults in no way matched the ferocity of Benton's and Burbridge's earlier in the day. Forney had maneuvered the reserve well, ultimately including the two Louisiana regiments sent down from Smith. The crisis had been so great in the center that Pemberton had ordered Smith on the far left to send a couple of regiments southward, "although the trenches in front of your position be temporarily thinned." Forney was grateful and informed Pemberton late in the afternoon that "we have also had hard fighting on my left, and on Jackson road. All quiet at these points now," although he added a postscript that simply said "General Moore is again hotly engaged."[16]

The center and left was not everything that Pemberton had to worry about, however. As the morning turned to afternoon, word came from the far right that trouble was also brewing there. There had always been some concern on that flank, certainly not helped by the fact that McClernand—perhaps remembering back to the turning movement against an uncovered flank at Fort Donelson—had sent cavalry "during the night of the 21st to build fires to my left in front of the enemy's works, and to push forward pickets close enough to them to excite the belief and apprehension that they were invested and threatened." More than just campfires and pickets soon emerged on that flank, however. By late morning, Federal troops of at least brigade size appeared on the Warrenton Road. Confederate brigade commander Seth Barton, holding the fortifications along that thoroughfare, sent word to Stevenson, who was away from his headquarters, that the enemy was approaching. Stevenson's staff sent the note on to Pemberton with the explanation that Stevenson "has gone on the right." Pemberton had no other troops to send, especially at such a distance, so he simply informed Barton: "I can only say to you to hold the place."[17]

Pemberton's lines were consequently getting stretched very thin, almost to the breaking point. Fortunately, he had been able to keep the lines intact by moving reserves here and there, but this new threat on the far right was most concerning. So was the continual Federal presence and renewed assaults on other portions of his lines. A worried Pemberton fully realized that if the Federals kept up their assaults and had more success breaking through, then the situation might turn fatal. The sun could not go down fast enough for the Confederate commander.

For all the hype of McClernand's breakthrough and his request for Sherman and McPherson to renew their assaults to aid his success, McClernand's own troops provided very little renewal themselves. In fact, all across his corps's front, the different brigades made only a slight show of renewing any attack and mostly held what they had already gained until dark. For instance, Colonel David P. Grier of the 77th Illinois wrote home two days later that the main fighting was of fairly short duration, and much of the afternoon was passed watching one another at close range. That short duration was nevertheless horrific: "For two hours [we] had one of the bloodiest times I ever witnessed or heard of." Exasperation built thereafter, as few did anything. William Landram, for instance, sent a message back to McClernand at 1:50 P.M., stating that "if General Osterhaus, on my left, will press forward, I think the works can soon be cleared."[18]

Such a case of lethargy was evident in front of the 2nd Texas Lunette, even with the Federal reinforcements that arrived late in the afternoon. Benton and Burbridge's brigades had made it to the ditches but no farther. The fighting had certainly not ended, however, the Federals keeping a heavy fire going throughout the long, hot afternoon. In fact, Burbridge reported that "by this time the guns of my command had become so foul by constant firing that I was compelled to use caliber .54 in place of .58, the caliber of the guns."[19]

Heavier fighting emerged later in the afternoon, around 5:00 P.M., when Quinby's division arrived to support the assaults on the 2nd Texas Lunette. McClernand's Federals were not impressed, one Ohioan writing that "the relief proved themselves but miserable soldiers as they all run before they had been there half an hour." Burbridge himself wrote that "owing to their incautious manner of approaching, [they] drew from the enemy a most galling fire of musketry and artillery, followed by an attempt of the enemy to charge." This, Colonel Thomas J. Lucas of the 16th Indiana related, "caused some little excitement." The fighting on the front was also heated, with Colonel Theodore E. Buehler of the 67th Indiana describing how "for about three hours the musketry fire, interspersed with grape, raged incessantly across the hill."[20]

Burbridge gave a little different account than did Sanborn, who stated that Burbridge asked him to relieve his brigade. Burbridge reported that Sanborn's troops went to the front and "broke and retired in great disorder," whereas his own brigade, "now greatly reduced in strength, manfully held its ground."

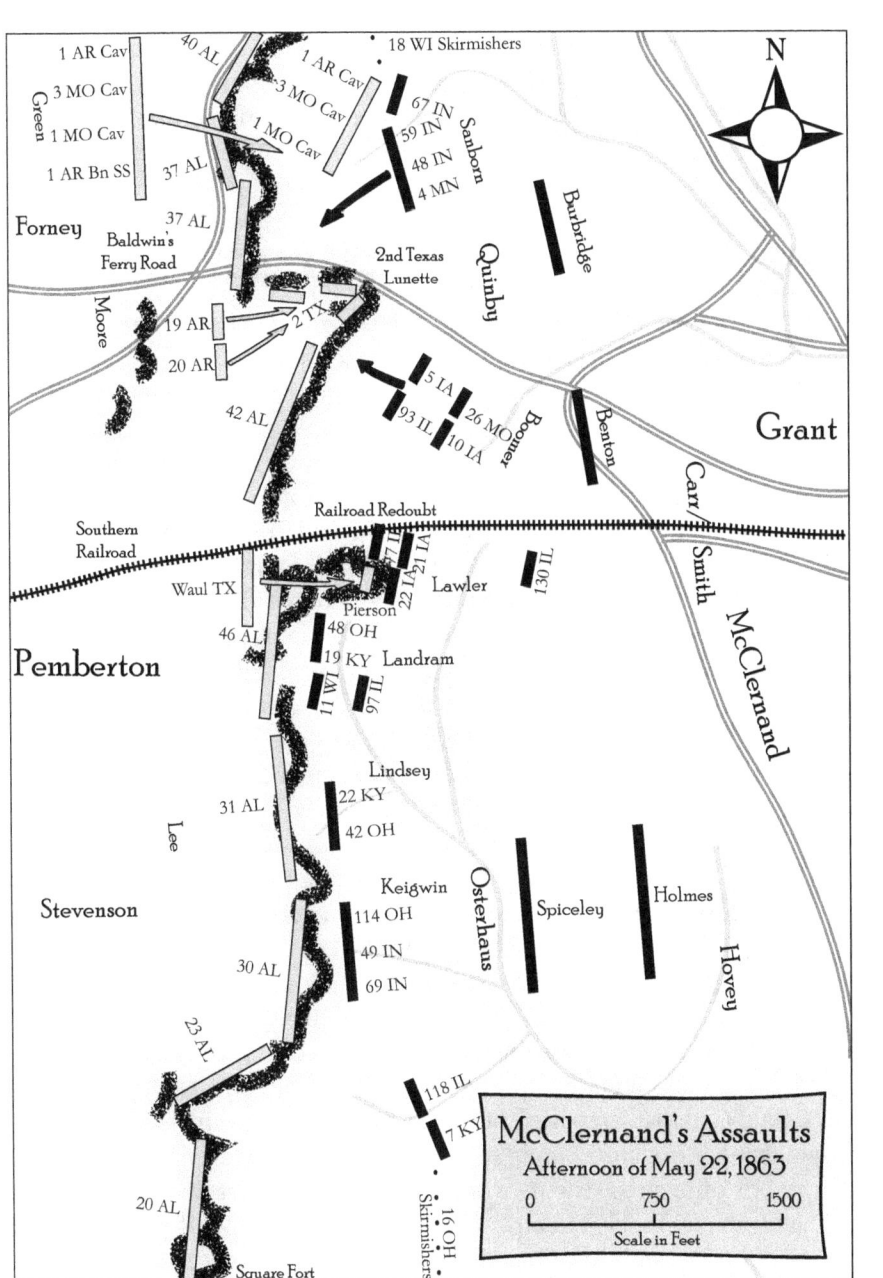

Nevertheless, some of Burbridge's troops admitted that they were glad to see Sanborn's Federals, even if they came in too fast and lost too many men "by exposing themselves too much." Colonel Buehler admitted that "I think it is to a great extent owing to their assistance and bravery that our retreat and that of other regiments on our left was not entirely cut off, for twice, once on our right and once on our left, carrying the Stars and Bars with them, the rebels attempted to charge." Buehler even requested some of the reinforcements to cover his regiment's withdrawal, as they were unable to fire after having shot some 200 rounds during the day. Perhaps part of the problem was a lack of communication, one of Burbridge's men describing "a brigade of Quinbys div. Came up to relieve us as it appears, though we did not understand it at the time that it was meant as a relief or receive any orders to that effect." Whoever was more truthful—and the differences can be chalked up to competition between not only differing brigades but also of differing divisions and corps—the fact of the matter was that the 2nd Texas Lunette was able to easily hold throughout the afternoon and toward nightfall against both Burbridge and Sanborn. At dark, Burbridge reported that "hostilities for the most part ceased." Nevertheless, it had been quite a day in front of the 2nd Texas Lunette, Colonel Buehler declaring that it was "the hardest day's work any of us have ever witnessed or been subjected to."[21]

Part of the reason the Texans were able to hold was because reinforcements arrived. The fact was not lost on the Federals either, Colonel Joshua J. Guppey of the 23rd Wisconsin writing that "heavy re-enforcements poured in to aid the enemy, and all that we could do was, with the aid of a covering brigade, to retire in good order." He nevertheless termed the "fire of musketry [as] the hottest that I have ever seen, and the bravery of our soldiers under it is beyond all praise." Still, Burbridge was miffed, writing: "I am of the opinion that, had we been re-enforced at 12 [noon], or the demonstration kept up along the line to our right, thus preventing the enemy from massing directly in our front, we could have gained a lodgment in the enemy's works."[22]

The exact same lethargy emerged in front of the Square Fort on Osterhaus's line. Osterhaus reported that his brigades, along with one of Hovey's division supporting him, simply held the ground they had gained while keeping up a brisk fire on the enemy works. It was done "under the most scorching sun," and several feeble attempts "to push farther on, and, if possible, reach the enemy's line, only developed more and more the exceedingly difficult task before us." Osterhaus came right out and declared that "the feasibility of taking the forts by assault was more than doubtful," committing the troops to hours of exposed danger. "How I wished for the sun to go down!" recalled one Ohioan.[23]

Osterhaus later elaborated on the condition of things, writing to McClernand that his brigade commanders had just left his headquarters and that the division was so much fatigued, due to low rations for several days and being constantly at the front under fire, that it could not be counted on to put many men in line. In fact, he desired to be relieved "for one day . . . if such an arrangement is compatible with the necessities and operations of to-morrow."[24]

All the while at the front casualties grew, including among officers. Sadly, the flag of the 69th Indiana began to tilt an hour or so after it went up, and Major John H. Finley jumped up and straightened it. His childhood and best friend described how then "he stiffened, turned deadly white, dropped on his right knee then on the left and tumbling down was caught by those of us below." A member of the 114th Ohio described the same event and that the colonel of the 69th Indiana was filled with indignation, calling to his regiment: "Men of the 69th: Major . . . [Finley] has been shot down like a dog; a braver man never lived; I want every man of the 69th to raise his hand and swear to avenge his death." The watching Ohioan declared how "every man, as far as I could observe, raised his hand." Ironically, Finley lived for another year before an accident reopened the wound and he bled to death.[25]

Others on the face of the Confederate works fought so hard that they almost ran out of energy and material. One Iowan described how "it was estimated that some of these guns had been fired three hundred times during the day. Hands and faces were black with powder stains, and often splotched with blood. Guns were discharged so rapidly that the barrels became so hot it would sear the hands to touch them. When too hot to use, they were exchanged for others in the ditch."[26]

Fire from the rear did not help either. As the various regiments of Osterhaus's division huddled near the crest of the ridges on which they were pinned, the Federal artillery in rear continually shelled the Confederate lines but at times came a little too close for comfort. At one point, artillery rounds fell close to the 114th Ohio in the center column, and Colonel Keigwin, who happened to be nearby, ordered Elbridge L. Hawk of that regiment "to go up the hill on the other side where this battery was, and notify the Commander that they were depressing their pieces too low, and to give them a greater elevation, as they were shooting into our men." Hawk scampered back and took the opportunity to view the panorama: "I recollect making that ascent, and of looking back and having an opportunity of seeing the enemy's work."[27]

Little could thus be done except, as brigade commander Colonel Lindsey described it, "frequently relieving the lines of skirmishers, who were actively engaged in keeping the enemy's artillery silent, until night." Colonel John G. Fonda of the 118th Illinois reported: "I remained at the top of the hill with my regiment during the day, skirmishing with the enemy all the time. Near night they opened a heavy fire upon us as though they intended to drive us from the hill."[28]

McClernand pushed anyway. He was not as lethargic, actually giving orders throughout the day to keep the pressure on. At one point around 1:30 P.M., he gave orders for Landram to position two of his regiments behind Lawler's right and for Burbridge to post two regiments behind Benton's left, "so as to fill up the space between Lawler's and Benton's brigades, and cover the space between the forts, and that the whole force move forward immediately and vigorously." Whether this was the impetus for Carr's order for Burbridge to move two regiments to the left is not known; certainly McClernand did not seem too knowledgeable when Burbridge appealed directly to him.[29]

At another point, McClernand informed Carr that he would send reinforcements if possible, and he sent Osterhaus a message: "You must advance and assault the enemy, and thereby make a diversion. If you can't do so, let me know it. In that case you can stand on the defensive, and I will apply General Hovey's brigade—at least a part—in support of Carr. One or other of these things must be done." To Hovey, he wrote: "If you believe nothing decisive will be accomplished on the left immediately, send a regiment or two to the right. By such reinforcement the lines in front of the right could be carried."[30]

Those Federals to the right at the Railroad Redoubt were just then waiting on those very reinforcements, although a look back toward Federal lines showed no sign of approaching support. Hours passed, and any hope for Union success at Vicksburg on this day was slowly slipping away.

Even if McClernand's divisions were making less of the show than they expected of Sherman's and McPherson's troops to their north, there were additional Federals who also became engaged as the afternoon wore on. On the extreme south end of the Confederate fortifications, new Federals soon arrived and made at least a demonstration of an attack, and even on the Mississippi River Admiral Porter's gunboats also became involved. It was a total effort, and ironically this was perhaps the best chance the Federals had of making a breakthrough.

John McArthur's division of McPherson's XVII Corps had been the most disrupted of all during the Federal advance and encirclement of Vicksburg. There was only one brigade of that division operating on the main line with the corps: Thomas Ransom's brigade, squeezed in between Sherman's left and Logan's division on the Jackson Road. John McArthur himself was not on site, at least not on the main line with the corps. And, at least according to the War Department liaison Charles Dana, he might not have made much of a difference, because Dana believed that McArthur was "a shrewd, steady Scotchman, trustworthy rather than brilliant, good at hard knocks, but not a great commander." He had two other brigades elsewhere, one of them under Hugh T. Reid, which had yet to cross the Mississippi River but were manning the Louisiana defenses continually. That left McArthur with only one other brigade: the Iowans and Illinoisans of Colonel William Hall's brigade. Commanding a large unit of six regiments, Hall had been moved about in the initial approach to Vicksburg, his mass thought to be needed at various points before the commanders realized that the places they were sent were no longer in jeopardy. For instance, the brigade had been initially stationed at Grand Gulf, "where it performed much efficient service in forwarding supplies to the army then investing Vicksburg," Hall noted. On May 19, the regiments boarded transports and moved northward to just below Vicksburg, where they disembarked and marched four miles overland to Young's Point and additional waiting transports. Then they steamed up the Yazoo River to Haynes' Bluff, where after only a few hours more orders came telling them to retrace their steps back south of Vicksburg to Warrenton. By the morning of May 22, they were camped on the Warrenton Road south of the city.[31]

When McClernand first informed Grant of his "breakthrough" and requested support, Grant told him to use what he had in reserve, which was nothing. Grant later told him to use McArthur's troops, and McClernand called them forward initially to shore up the gap between his corps and McPherson's. If that was not possible, they could add weight to his own assaults or even make new ones farther south. There, the remainder of Carter Stevenson's Confederate division manned the trenches south of the Square Fort and Lee's brigade. Alfred Cumming's Georgians, who had been handled so roughly at Champion Hill, held the lines on Lee's right, followed by Alexander W. Reynolds's Tennesseans, who had guarded the wagon train at the same battle and saw no action. Finally, Seth Barton's Georgians, who had also been handled roughly at Champion Hill, finished the line down to the river and the South Fort and then back to the city. The line crossed both the Hall's Ferry Road and Stout's Bayou.[32]

It was a thinly held line, these three brigades manning a stretch about as long as that held by the other three divisions to the north. As a result, Hall's six regiments had a good chance to score a breakthrough along the Warrenton Road, especially given their numbers. Also of importance was the veteran status of the brigade. The 11th and 13th Iowa had seen heavy action around the Crossroads at Shiloh, and the 15th and 16th Iowa had reinforced the line in Jones Field, also seeing heavy action. The brigade had also been engaged at Corinth in October. Only the 63rd and 87th Illinois were newer regiments, having mustered in after Shiloh.[33]

Hall marched forward midmorning and soon met Confederate skirmishers. He deployed five companies of Major William Purcell's 16th Iowa to drive them back to their fortifications, which was soon done. He then deployed the other Iowa companies as skirmishers for the brigade and continued onward. Hall noted that at "about 11 A.M. I took up my position within range of four rebel batteries on the right of the enemy's works." Those batteries shelled the Federals, although Alexander Downing of the 11th Iowa noted that "as their guns were aimed too high, our greatest danger was from the falling limbs of trees hit by their shells."[34]

But that is all McArthur did. Understandably out of position with the rest of the division and corps and getting orders from different corps commanders, he can hardly be faulted for caution. Hall merely noted that "here I remained during the day under fire from the batteries," Colonel William Belknap of the 15th Iowa writing that they were indeed "severely shelled by the enemy." Hall did send additional companies from the 11th, 13th, and 16th Iowa forward to test the enemy line, but they merely "engaged constantly along the lines with the enemy's sharpshooters." He gladly noted, however, that "I succeeded in driving them to the protection of their works, my skirmishers getting within 40 yards of the batteries."[35]

Hall's large brigade, with so much potential, thus played little role, except for giving John Pemberton more to think about. In truth, even that evaporated quickly, as around midday Hall received orders to break contact and march to the right: McClernand had made some sort of breakthrough and he needed support. Accordingly, the potential for a real breakthrough on the weaker southern end of the Confederate line was quashed inadvertently by McClernand's perceived success to the north.[36]

McArthur's was not the only Union force on the southern end of Vicksburg that was making noise, however. The United States Navy under Admiral Porter was also active and, actually, was working in tandem with McArthur prior to his disengagement and move northward. Grant had alerted Porter on May 21 that he would be assaulting the next morning and begged for his help: "I would request, and earnestly request it, that you send up the gunboats below the city and shell the rebel intrenchments." Grant desired a bombardment before the assault at 10:00 A.M. and for thirty minutes thereafter and, if possible, a shelling all night by the mortars. "I would like at least to have the enemy kept annoyed during the night," he related.[37]

Porter acquiesced to the letter of Grant's request, much as he had been doing throughout the entire campaign. Six mortars on the Mississippi River worked throughout the night, "playing rapidly on the works and town all night," Porter reported. He also used some of the ironclads to shell the lower batteries "and other places where troops might be resting during the night." But this fulfilled only half of the request, and Porter alerted his force that "the army attack the town at 10 o'clock to-morrow, and we must, with our small force, be heard from." They were. The next morning Porter sent four ironclads against the southern Confederate water batteries. The *Benton, Mound City, Carondelet*, and *Tuscumbia* all advanced at the appointed hour before the land assaults and pummeled the Confederate water batteries. It was, Porter said, "one of the best contested engagements of the kind during the war."[38]

Porter first advanced on the higher "hill batteries," silencing them enough to then proceed to the lower river batteries. He made the second move with the two City-class ironclad gunboats (also known as "Pook Turtles") and the *Benton*, leaving the *Tuscumbia* back at the hill fortifications to keep them smothered. The slow-moving ironclads breasting the strong current were almost stationary targets for the Confederate gunners who opened, Porter admitted, with a fire that was "very accurate and incessant." The firing lasted for two hours.[39]

Damage to both sides was significant. Colonel Edward Higgins, commanding the Confederate river batteries on the Mississippi, noted that two Confederate artillerymen were wounded and that two big guns were temporarily dismounted, while the Blakely gun "burst at the muzzle." Conversely, the Federals took the worse handling. Once he realized that the hill batteries were not reopening their fire, Admiral Porter ordered the *Tuscumbia* to catch up with the others. This vessel being of a different makeup, including a turret, could not stand the fire and in Porter's words was "soon disabled" and had to be sent back, having been hit three times. The ironclads were not doing much better. All three were hit, some dangerously near the waterline ("between wind and water"), so that after two hours (longer than Grant had in fact requested) Porter ordered them out of range. He admitted to Grant that "we had to haul out of action to repair damages." Indeed, the *Mound City* was hit sixteen times but sustained only slight casualties. The *Benton* fared slightly better, with thirteen hits, although only four were serious. Navy lieutenant commander James A. Greer reported that "at first the vessel leaked some, but we have it now completely under control." The *Carondelet* was in worse shape, but not just because of the two hits she received. The accumulating damage from all operations, including the Steele's Bayou debacle, had taken a toll on the vessel, and Lieutenant John M. Murphey reported that he had to replace one section of board "to keep the vessel afloat." Other problems mounted as well, Murphey explaining that "the boat [is] in such a leaky condition as to require the constant working of the pump." No wonder Porter pulled his vessels back, being sure to note how they fell back "in a cool, handsome, manner."[40]

The damage had been done, however. Porter admitted "this was the hottest fire the gunboats have ever been under," which was saying something given the thrashing they had endured at Fort Henry and Fort Donelson, and then elsewhere on the rivers, including (under his own command) at Grand Gulf. The iron plating had certainly helped, as did fighting bows forward, where the strongest iron plating was. Still, the navy retreated, but not without once more shelling the hill batteries as they passed; the Confederates were trying to remount some of their damaged guns, so Porter gave them another barrage as he steamed back southward.[41]

Admiral Porter hoped he had done Grant's assault some aid, although he admitted that "in the noise and smoke we could not see or hear it [the 10 A.M. assault]." He could see McArthur's advance, however, and even notified the land commander that he had silenced two batteries on his front. McArthur was well aware of the developments, later writing Porter: "I witnessed with intense satisfaction the firing on that day, being the finest I have seen yet." Still, McArthur was unable to take advantage because he was not around much longer, having been ordered to reposition elsewhere in support of McClernand. In fact, McArthur later wrote Porter explaining that "I would have taken advantage of the results then gained by your vessels, and had given the necessary orders to do so, when I received peremptory orders from Major-General McClernand to move my command around to the right of my position, to support a portion of his troops who had gained a lodgment in the enemy's works."[42]

Porter notified Grant of the navy's efforts, writing that the Confederate defenses were "a hard nut to crack." He concluded: "It is a pity that they [McArthur's troops] did not assault, for they would have taken the place without any trouble." Grant acknowledged the circumstances and sent McArthur back to the area, but by that time it was too late. McClernand—the politician-general who could at times be his own worst enemy—had thus inadvertently prevented perhaps the best chance the Federals had of breaking through the Confederate lines at Vicksburg.[43]

If McClernand was to receive glory this day, it would have to come at the Railroad Redoubt, where the only appreciable lodgment inside the Confederates works had occurred. There was little renewal of the assaults on McClernand's front elsewhere, even considering the arrival and advance of Quinby's two brigades at the 2nd Texas Lunette. It was logical that any major victory would be won only where success had already partially occurred.

Banking on Lawler and Landram to spread their achievements alone was unrealistic, however. They could go no farther, as illustrated by the message that came up the chain of command from Landram himself, written at 2:40 P.M.: "Our men are holding the flanks of the fort in our front. There is heavy crossfire upon us, and we have lost many killed and wounded. They are hurling hand-grenades upon us, and hurting us considerably in that way." The lighted shells thrown down on the Federals were particularly menacing. Some Iowans claimed to have caught them "on the fly" and thrown them back up, but it was still an uncomfortable few hours. Other dangers also existed. Merrick J. Wald of the 77th Illinois related that "they would run their bayonets over into our own who were lying in the ditch and could not get out."[44]

Everything hinged on receiving additional firepower, something Lawler plainly realized. He had ordered his brigade to "hold the ground already gained, and this with the hope that re-enforcements might soon be forwarded, with whose aid they might assault the rebel works with a certainly of success." The same feeling prevailed throughout the ranks, Captain Charles N. Lee of the 22nd Iowa writing: "Knowing unless we would be supported properly by re-enforcements we would have to fall back, we held our position." Unfortunately, none came. J. S. Miller recalled: "I prayed during those hours that some of those men would come to our relief and help us, but not a man came." Lawler similarly lamented that "no re-enforcements, however, could be spared us during the forenoon, and until late in the afternoon our position remained the same as in the morning." Obviously, the bulk of Quinby's brigades had gone to Carr while the reserve unit of that division moved on to aid Osterhaus in holding his position. McArthur was not called northward until too late as well, so it soon became clear that Lawler and Landram were on their own. They obviously had no fresh troops to send into the breach, so the likelihood of widening this success soon evaporated. With it also disappeared McClernand's chances for personal glory.[45]

Lawler by this time had turned his attention from broadening the success to holding what he had. He did so for several miserable hours as the hot sun beat down on the nearly defenseless Federals. Still, a heavy fire came crashing from the Iowans' ranks, Major Salue G. Van Anda reporting that his 21st Iowa "pour[ed] continually a destructive fire into their ranks." Major Joseph B. Atherton of the 22nd Iowa agreed, writing that "we maintained our position during the day, receiving and returning the fire, they concealed in their forts and other defenses, we in a great measure without any shelter."[46]

One soldier in the 21st Iowa gave a detailed account of the misery. He described lying in position "the rest of that dreadful day, beneath the fire of the sun and the fire of the foe." Fortunately,

> the rough and rounding contour of the hill, and the thickness of the rebel works protected us from the fire of the enemy, but almost any motion of the body was likely to be observed, and, bringing us within range, to bring us also the rebel compliments. The men around me frequently tested this by elevating caps on ramrods, and almost invariably with success, sometimes bringing the hissing messenger entirely too close for comfort.

The main problem by midafternoon was the heat: "It was a broiling hot day. The earth which we hugged so closely was like the floor of an oven. The water of the canteen was soon exhausted. My thirst became intolerable." That thirst made the Iowan consider things he would have labeled ludicrous just hours before: "About ten yards in front of me I noticed early a small wild plum-tree growing," he wrote.

> It was only a few feet in height and apparently bore but a single plum, which was only half grown and perfectly green. As my lips became hot and parched with thirst, and my throat struggled to relieve itself, this green plum hung temptingly before me and bade me risk my life for it. For a long time I resisted, but the long, weary hours prolonged themselves into eternities, the ground became hotter, and the sun's rays more scorching. At last I could resist no longer. By dint of digging fingers and toes into the hard ground, and pulling myself along by tufts of grass and twigs of shrubs, I reached the bush, and with a spring secured my prize. The few drops of juice more than repaid me for the risk, and the sweetest morsel of fruit ever tasted by man will live in my memory forever.[47]

As bad as it was on the Federal side, Confederate brigade commander Stephen D. Lee could do little better, and he became more and more perturbed that the enemy held a portion of his works. He reported to his division commander Stevenson that "the enemy have been repulsed along my front; they have made a lodgment in the ditch of the left work, and they have a stand of colors in the work. The work is full of our men. I can't reach them in the ditch. They made a gallant assault, and have lost a great many men." Later, he wrote that the enemy succeeded "in carrying an angle of the work immediately to the right of the railroad, and in planting two colors upon the parapet, which remained there for several hours."[48]

Lee tried in vain throughout the afternoon to organize a counterattack, calling on the Alabamians of his brigade to rush in and drive out the Federals. Few wanted any part of it. One Confederate wrote that "alive to the importance of the position, General Lee issued and reiterated orders to Colonel

[Charles M.] Shelley, commanding the Thirtieth Alabama, and Lieutenant Colonel [Edmund W.] Pettus of the Twentieth Alabama but now commanding the 46th Alabama, who occupied the fort, to retake it at all hazards." One attempt went ahead as Captain Henry Oden of the 30th Alabama dashed forward while whirling his sword in leading his company of Alabamians, but they met a devastating fire. Once near the tip of the fort, Oden encountered the sheltered Lieutenant Pearson and yelled "Why are you not fighting?" Having been caught between the combatants far too long, Pearson simply replied: "You will not be fighting long if you don't get in the trenches and you had better get there quick." As predicted, Oden was soon cut down, as were many of his men, leaving Pearson and his original defenders to huddle between the fighting. Lee made other attempts to raise relief as well, but the Alabamians, despite the powerful pushing of their leaders, would not budge, having seen what had happened to Oden's force. Lee even went so far as "offering the [Union] flags to the command capturing them." One watching Texan noted that "after several vain attempts, they refused to volunteer, nor could the most strenuous efforts of their chivalric commanders urge or incite them to the assault."[49]

Worse, the little Confederate force remaining inside the tip of the fort was soon neutralized. Pearson, with only eight other Alabamians, described the long hours of misery after the initial burst of Federals through the embrasure and, eventually, their withdrawal. The Alabamians were indeed miserable, huddled as they were between two larger forces, both of which were firing and tossing hand grenades. At one point, the Alabamians yelled at Confederates tossing grenades from the rear to "quit throwing those things you are killing Alabama troops." The reply came: "Damn Alabama troops from Ohio." Pearson was amazed: "My situation was such that it appeared that we had Scylla on the one side, Charibdis on the other. . . . It looked as if the sun were in the hands of Joshua of old and I thought of Wellington's prayer when he prayed that night or Blucher one would come."[50]

Soon, Pearson and his defenders began to wear down, Pearson himself huddling with a dead soldier on his leg "with his blood running over my pants and filling the leg of my boot so that afterwards as I walked it slushed in my boot just as water does when you step into it over your shoe tops." He could only see the Union flags floating over the parapet and decided to take a look when he was suddenly face-to-face with several muzzles. Pearson quickly surrendered, as did the rest of his command, the Federals marching them out the embrasure and to the rear. Sergeant Joseph E. Griffith of the 22nd Iowa, himself wounded and the only one of the breaching Federals still alive and fighting inside the fortifications by this time, brought the captured

Confederates out, telling them that "this place is too hot for any man to stay in. Come with me."[51]

Ultimately, Lee turned to his reserve of Texans to do the job of retaking the fort, and the result was not lost on the Federals. Lawler noted that "while my command was being strengthened . . . , the enemy were not idle. Heavy re-enforcements had been drawn from their right and massed in my front behind their works." Waul's Texas Legion had held various portions of the line throughout the day and was already heavily engaged, two companies manning the western parts of the Railroad Redoubt with the Alabamians while the Federals barely held on to the tip. Colonel Waul wrote that "unprotected by breastworks, they were subjected to the most galling fire, and well they sustained the noble cause for which they fought, never relaxing, but [fighting] with increased ardor." Chagrined at his Alabamians' refusal to lead the counterattack, Lee "then directed the colonel of the Legion to have the fort taken."[52]

Colonel Waul chose the two companies of his legion under Captain L. D. Bradley and Lieutenant James Hogue to make the attack. Bradley and Hogue "not only willingly agreed," Colonel Waul wrote, "but solicited the honor of leading their companies to the assault, not wishing to expose a larger force than necessary." Waul agreed, then directed them to choose fifteen or twenty men from their companies to take part in the assault, Bradley stipulating that only unmarried men should go. When Bradley began to lead them forward, his lieutenant told him, "Captain, you are a married man; let me lead the troops," to which Bradley answered: "No; where my troops go I lead them." While "the preparations were quietly and quickly made," division commander Stevenson noted, an embarrassed Lieutenant Colonel Pettus, brother of the Mississippi governor, "came, musket in hand," Waul wrote, "and most gallantly offered to guide and lead the party into the fort." One Confederate said the disgusted Alabamian shouted "he was going to show the Texans that an Alabamian would go as far as any of them." Pettus later remarked that Lee and Colonel Isham Garrott of the 20th Alabama had "taught him the duty of a soldier, more by example than precept," and he intended to act the part that day. Waul thought it a good idea, because Pettus's regiment had garrisoned the fort all along and he was "thoroughly acquainted with the locality and its approaches." In addition, three soldiers of the 30th Alabama also volunteered to go, and some of the 46th Alabama claimed to have done so as well. There was a little ruckus about Pettus leading the Texans, but he and Bradley agreed that "we will go together."[53]

The counterattack came near sundown, Pettus leading the way back into the fort. Lawler noted that "all the [afternoon] efforts of the enemy to dislodge or drive us back were unavailing." Then he admitted: "At sunset, however, a determined rush was made by the rebels to regain possession of their work, which, in consequence of the exhaustion of the men holding it, was successful." Confederate colonel Waul had a different take on the counterattack, writing that his men, "with promptness and alacrity . . . moved to the assault, retook the fort, drove the enemy through the breach they entered, tore down the stand of colors still floating over the parapet, and sent them to the colonel commanding the Legion, who immediately transmitted it, with a note, to General Lee."[54]

Carter Stevenson gave honest due to both sides, writing that "the enemy seemed at once to divine our intention, and opened upon the angle a terrible fire of shot, shell, and musketry." It did not stop the Confederate surge, however: "Undaunted, this little band, its chivalrous commander at its head, rushed upon the work, and in less time than it requires to describe it, it and the flags were in our possession." As for Pettus, he reportedly quipped that "he was an Alabamian by birth, but that he was going to be a Texan by adoption."[55]

Even though relatively small numbers of men were involved on each side, Colonel Waul was adamant that his brave Texans had performed the critical action of the day against long odds. "This feat," Waul wrote,

> considered with the accompanying circumstances — the narrow pass through which the party had to enter; the enfilading fire of musketry and artillery they had to encounter in approach; the unwillingness of the garrison, consisting of two regiments, to volunteer, and permitting the flags to float for three hours over their parapets; the coolness, courage, and intrepidity manifested — deserves the highest praise for every officer and man engaged in the hazardous enterprise.[56]

The fighting was swift, although larger numbers on both sides soon joined in. One Texan declared that the Federals gave up easily and "concluded to raise 'white rag'"; the hand grenades the Confederates had been throwing also took much of the resistance out of the Federals, who, the Texan declared, "said were a little too much for them." Not so for the Federals to the rear who poured in a massive volley, hitting both sides: "Several were killed of the Yankees after they had surrendered from their own men, for during the time of the charge and after, the Yankees poured in volleys of grape and canister but not a man of ours was killed in the charge but several were wounded."[57]

Once Pettus and the Texans cleared the fort, the fighting moved to the ditch and the parapets. Waul described how "the enemy, driven from the fort, ensconced themselves behind the parapet in the outer ditch." Waul quickly dispatched two more companies of Texans to enter the now secured fort in order to clear the ditch as well. "Many of the men mounted the parapet and fired," Waul explained, "into the ditch, subjecting themselves to the aim of its occupants and the concentrated fire from the enemy's lines." The Texans also tossed a few more shells across the parapet as hand grenades. One Texan described how the grenades "soon caused them to surrender, although so soon as we ceased casting missiles, under cover of the approaching darkness, more than half of the number escaped." Carter Stevenson even reported that merely informing the enemy in the opposite ditch that the Confederates were about to throw hand grenades caused some Federals to surrender.[58]

The Federals who had huddled on the outside of the Confederate works all day were no match for the comparatively fresh Texans, who surged back in to the tip of the redoubt and drove off those who had hung on, capturing many of the wounded, including Lieutenant Colonel Graham. "It was terrible when the Rebels charged on us with fixed Bayonets," remembered one Illinoisan, "but they had ten men to our one and they took the Fort in spite of us." Another related that "we were fished out of the ditch by the Confederates at the left end of the ditch facing the fortifications." Still, Lawler's Iowans were not totally beaten. The regiments took special care to take their flags with them; one officer of the 48th Ohio wrote, "perceiving his intention, we saved our flag before the charge was made." Although driven from the face of the redoubt, the Federals fell back eastward, but only to the lip of the ridge from which they had begun their short assault. There, protection offered them a chance to form a new line. "My men halted," Lawler reported, "and opened such a fire upon the enemy as effectually checked their advance and compelled them to remain close under the protection of their works." Only a few Confederates followed the fleeing Federals, including Lieutenant Colonel J. Wrigley, who captured another flag that had been "snatched by the enemy [Federals] from the parapet, but dropped in his flight." It was perhaps the national colors of the 77th Illinois; the color-bearer, James P. Black, noted how it had "faded to almost white and mistaken by some for a flag of truce, [and] it was ordered down." Another noted that the regimental banner "could not be brought away, and was covered with earth in the ditch," Illinoisan John P. Grier noting that it was the regimental flag "which Mrs. Coker presented us." Pemberton's astute engineer, Samuel Lockett, added that "the brave fellows paid for their success by being either killed or captured and having their colors fall into our hands."[59]

The two sides swapped fire during the rest of whatever daylight remained. Lawler explained how, at dark, "by mutual consent, it ceased." Major Atherton of the 22nd Iowa admitted that "a continuance of the contest was deemed unadvisable." Another Iowan declared that "there was no use in the 22nd Iowa trying to clean out the whole southern Confederacy all by its 'lonesome.'"

But everyone knew what all this fighting meant. Lee was excited, writing of "the intrepid Lieut. Col. E. W. Pettus" as well as the "gallant band of Waul's Texas Legion." Pettus certainly came in for praise, one Alabamian writing that the future US senator "greatly distinguished himself by his gallantry." Little excitement existed on the Union side as the refugees slinked back toward Federal lines once nightfall gave them the chance to recover in the darkness. As he and his comrades sullenly retreated, one Ohioan declared that "the town clock in Vicksburg struck the hour of 10 P. M."[60]

Perhaps Lee's greatest joy was when he gladly reported to Carter Stevenson that "the angle is carried and the enemy's colors taken. It was a gallant affair." In fact, Lee later declared that "a more daring feat has not been performed during the war, and too much praise cannot be awarded to every one engaged in it." Stevenson agreed, adding that "a more gallant feat than this charge has not illustrated our arms during the war."[61]

Consequently, McClernand's afternoon efforts were no more beneficial than those during the morning. And with the halting of any progress came the realization that the Confederates had indeed held Vicksburg's fortifications, even if only by the slimmest of margins. Put simply, McClernand had been unable to accomplish anything more than Sherman or McPherson during that afternoon. Neither the brigade of McArthur's division assigned to McClernand (which did not arrive in time to make any difference), nor Quinby's two brigades (which did in fact arrive in time to advance against the Confederates), made no difference. McClernand was no doubt disappointed at this failure. If he had been all-knowing, as he sometimes thought, he would have also realized that declaring himself to be on the brink of success—and then failing to break through—had put him in yet another fix. This time the extreme peril was not in the military realm but with his own army commander. Grant, after all, carried McClernand's future in his pocket.

13

"Five Days of Peril, Hardship, and Privation"

A slight rain began to fall on the evening of May 22 as the guns faded and darkness shrouded the Vicksburg battlefield. The coolness was welcome, as the heat of the day had been extreme. The little relief that emerged was especially welcomed by the wounded, who were now trapped in no-man's-land, and most of whom were immobile and could be saved only through the efforts of their comrades. Many Union soldiers—if they survived the fire—consequently remained where they lay throughout the night and for days after. The relief provided by any drizzle was indeed welcomed among the wounded.[1]

More welcome was a cessation of major fighting, John Forney reporting that night of the events on his lines during the day but that "all quiet at these points now." Most who survived the ordeal of May 22 were soon engulfed in concerns of their own rather than of the larger whole. Some were highly motivated to find friends or loved ones, either dead or alive. Some wanted sustenance and longed for the time they could return from their entrapment on the face of the Confederate works and eat and drink again. Others desired to sleep, exhausted from the day's activities. Still, for many, both North and South, there came an inherent wonder at what this all meant. "This day will be recorded in history," wrote Illinoisan George Lucas in his diary, "a memorable day it may be." Colonel Marcus Spiegel of the 120th Ohio remarked on "five days of peril, hardship, and privation," adding that "the fighting so far has been terrific and as yet we have not taken Vicksburg."[2]

Most realized they had been through something momentous. Frequent were the guesses of soldiers trying to make sense of what had just happened; they expressed the events as "the great charge on the works" or the "grand charge on the enemy's works." One soldier in the 93rd Illinois who was all too familiar with this sort of thing simply jotted in his diary: "Another fearful day for the 93rd." Anson Hemingway noted that "this has been the most terrible day that I have ever passed through. . . . It was terrible—terrible. It could hardly be called a fight. It was slaughter." Another Illinoisan could only try to make sense of it all by comparison to other action, writing that they "were under much the same fire as at Donelson, but Donelson was nothing to this. Nothing."[3]

Many Federals were in utter shock that they had been stopped. "We pride ourselves that we have performed the greatest campaign of the war," wrote John P. Jones, but he noted that once they reached Vicksburg "[we] have found our match at last." He labeled Vicksburg "the strongest natural position I ever saw," and he called the assault "the almost mad plan of storming the works." Certainly, after fighting the Confederate enemy five times in May and winning gloriously each time, for the Federals this sudden repulse was not expected. The orders from the generals had been so certain and confident. But the attacks were a failure—and a bloody one at that. One soldier described the assaults as "one of the bloodiest times I ever witnessed or heard of." Numerous Federals agreed. "I am at present helping to overthrow Vicksburg," wrote one Federal. "We have been besieging here for 7 days and I can't say but that we will for 7 more." Another echoed that he did not want any more fighting: "Well this was our last fight, and I hope it may be the last for some time."[4]

Rumors did not help, and they were already beginning to swell even as the rain began to fall in the night. "Most likely you will hear Some great Stories relative to our doings," Edward Chatfield wrote his parents, "but do not believe everything that you hear until it is confirmed for there is many rumors that go like the wind that has not the least particle of truth in them." All the soldiers knew was what they had seen, however, and it was shaping up in most accounts to have been a day of bravery but bloody failure for the Federals. Major Joseph B. Atherton reported as much: "All discharged their duty well and proved themselves worthy of being called defenders of our Union, and entitled to the gratitude of the country. Unsuccessful through no fault of theirs, they showed themselves patriots, obeyed orders with alacrity, and rushed into the storm of deadly missiles without faltering."[5]

Ulysses S. Grant agreed, writing that "the assault was gallant in the extreme on the part of all the troops, but the enemy's position was too strong, both naturally and artificially, to be taken in that way."[6]

Although night fell and provided relief to those involved, it did not mean that all fighting was finished. The Confederates were quick to fire at anything, Sergeant George Hyatt remembering that "the rebels followed us with bullets wherever they heard a noise." In other places, the Confederates did all they could to get the Federals to leave, even throwing cotton balls dipped in turpentine behind those who had not yet escaped at the Railroad Redoubt to illuminate them. That was certainly a motivator to get out of danger, but not all Federals left their hard-won gains, and others had to be ordered away. Some of Ransom's troops retained their forward positions, as did others along the lines. Most made sure everyone knew they fell back only because they were ordered: "The Forty-eighth [Ohio] was never driven back from its position near this fort until ordered to fall back" at 10 P.M., reported an officer of that unit.[7]

Under cover of darkness, many soldiers on both sides began to wander out into no-man's-land to look for wounded or retrieve equipment, and there was at least one reported instance of Federal black servants going in and carrying out wounded soldiers. Louis Hébert sent pickets in front of the Stockade Redan, one Mississippian declaring that "this was anything but a pleasant duty, as the dead bodies of the Federals, killed in battle, could be seen lying all around." One Louisianan described how some of the boys went out that night and "picked up 80 Hats every one with a Bullet hole in it." One captain in the 7th Missouri was interested in more than hats or even the wounded; he went back and retrieved the regiment's emerald Irish flag in front of the Great Redoubt.[8]

The wounded and dead were the chief concern, however, and many did what they could, even braving danger. Two 31st Alabama soldiers were tasked with taking their company's only casualty to the rear to bury him. They started after dark but "fell in a ravine with him on top of us[.] We had to go down it to the distance of 3 hundred yards before we could get him out." At times, the duty also stoked the hatred brewing over the tough day. A few Iowans went back to the Railroad Redoubt later in the night to gather wounded and heard the Confederates cursing the prisoners because they could not walk: "Oh, how our blood boiled for revenge at this inhuman treatment."[9]

The carnage was awful everywhere, but it fostered a novel experience in front of the 2nd Texas Lunette. Colonel Ashbel Smith described how "it was discovered on visiting our front after dark that the enemy had dug numerous holes in our glacis for protection against our fire. Major [George W. L.] Fly had these holes filled, and, to prevent their being opened again for a like purpose, he had buried in them 27 Yankee carcasses." His men also observed the Federals carrying off their wounded but nevertheless policed the field: "My men supplied themselves with Enfield rifles; we had upward of 200 surplus arms."[10]

As would be expected with such movement throughout the night, some fraternization took place. One Confederate was heard to call out to the Federals "lend us some coffee for supper, won't you, we will pay you when Johnston comes," to which a Federal replied "never mind the coffee, but Grant will take dinner in Vicksburg tomorrow."[11]

Most commanders took the opportunity during the night to explain what had happened. As a common example, Confederate Louis Hébert reported up the chain of command that "on my line his points of attack were the Jackson and Graveyard roads. He charged three times on the Graveyard road and twice on the Jackson road, but was as often repulsed with very heavy loss. A small number only succeeded in reaching our exterior ditch." The Federals were busy reporting as well. Sherman wrote Grant that "we have had a hard day's work, and all are exhausted." Realizing the situation they were now in and admitting that "the enemy and his works are stronger than we estimated," Sherman added that "I have ordered all to construct breastworks." McClernand informed Grant that his division commanders, including Quinby, reported "that their men are exhausted by fatigue and a want of sufficient food and rest. . . . I doubt if a considerable portion of their commands will be qualified for efficient action to-morrow." Apparently not coming to the same realization as Sherman, he repeated his previous recommendation: "I still think that to force the enemy's works we will have to mass a strong force upon some one or two points of his defenses."[12]

McClernand also took it upon himself to rectify any situations he deemed unacceptable. For instance, he advised McPherson that there was "a wide gap between our right and your left" and that he had moved one of Quinby's brigades in that direction but asked that "you would so extend your left by pickets as to close the gap." Later in the night he wrote: "Since my last dispatch, I have received corroborative evidence (doubted by me, however) that the enemy are trying to turn either your flank or mine. I have extended my right as much as possible. You will decide whether you will extend your line, infantry or pickets, so as to substantially connect with mine until morning."[13]

Contrary to Federal fears of a night assault, the main concern inside the Confederate fortifications were the works themselves, which had taken a pummeling throughout the day. John Forney described how "the fire of the enemy's artillery has damaged our works . . . considerably." The heavy artillery fire had also dismounted numerous guns, and at the 2nd Texas Lunette John C. Moore ordered the embrasures "filled up" because they were so damaged and there were no guns to use in them. "It is with great difficulty that we can procure spades and shovels to repair the damage done during the day," he reported. "New works will have to be constructed on the Baldwin's Ferry Road, and I earnestly request that spades and shovels be sent. The enemy remains in force opposite these three points."[14]

Samuel Lockett accordingly became the man on the spot once more. He had designed and supervised construction of the Confederate defensive works surrounding Vicksburg, and they had stood the test against two successive assaults. But damage was heavy, and now he was tasked with repairing them as soon as possible. Who knew what would unfold when daylight came the next morning? He sent out relief parties all night to repair what could be fixed and to rebuild what could not. "All damages were repaired, however, at night," he reported, "and the morning of [May] 23rd found our works in as good condition as at the beginning of the enemy's operations." Morale proportionately soared, especially with the confidence that numerous attacks had now been turned back. John Forney reported on the morning of May 23 that "the troops on the entire line are in fine spirits. Their work will be well done."[15]

That morning came all too soon, although by that time many who had welcomed the relief that night brought longed for sunrise and an ability to assess the damage and view the situation in the light of day. One Federal wrote that "it was a long night of dejection and weariness filled with the somber reflections of grief and death." The next morning brought only sporadic firing, however, as if all were still soaking in the events of the day before. "Everything is unusually quiet along the lines this morning," Forney wrote on May 23, "the enemy only firing occasionally with artillery and a few sharpshooters."[16]

All looked to the future nevertheless, the burning question being What would Grant do now on this "unusually quiet" May 23? He had many pushing him onward, Admiral Porter on the river writing on that day: "[I] hope you will soon finish up this Vicksburg business, or these people may get relief." For his part, McClernand was unsure of what Grant would do and simply gave orders to "during the night . . . make rifle-pits and intrench batteries in the most eligible positions." He admitted that "orders from the general commanding the department are awaited, and will probably control the operations of to-morrow." In the meantime, the Federals worked on supplying ammunition and food to the wearied commands.[17]

The light of day, with the obvious Confederate repairs undertaken during the night, illustrated even more the galling realization for the Federals that another assault would not work. One Union soldier wrote how the notion of "climbing their breastworks is played out. They are strongly fortified." Gould Molineaux added: "It is an almost if not entirely human impossibility to take this fort from this side. . . . It is a Gibraltar indeed." One especially irate Federal commented that the "enemy's odious defenses still block . . . access to Vicksburg. Treason still rules that rebellious city, and closes the Mississippi River against rightful use by the millions who inhabit its sources and the great Northwest."[18]

In the daylight of May 23, the repaired and still-looming fortifications—seemingly as strong and defiant as ever—no doubt convinced many Federals of the need for a siege. And the Confederate works quickly became the chief explanation for this surprising defeat. "The Rebels had the advantage of us," wrote one Indianan, "they being inside of good fortifications, while we had but a low bank to protect us." Charles A. Hobbs of the 99th Illinois added his opinion that "the movement intended for us, as we afterwards found out, could not have been accomplished by any human regiment on account of the rugged, obstructed country. . . . It was not want of courage that caused the failure." Samuel Lockett, now trapped inside the very works he had built, would have been proud if he had known that Kilby Smith, commanding one of the brigades that advanced on those works on two different days, termed them "masterpieces of skill in military engineering."[19]

William T. Sherman also gave his opinion of what caused the defeat, writing later that "the . . . several assaults made May 22d, on the lines of Vicksburg, had failed, by reason of the great strength of the position and the determined fighting of its garrison. I have since seen the position at Sevastopol (Crimea), and without hesitation I declare that at Vicksburg to have been the more difficult of the two."[20]

The idea of the enemy being trapped only added to the Federal explanation of the surprising Confederate resistance. "The Union troops had been chasing the Confederates ever since the first battle, and were not expecting a reception of this kind. . . . It was like a grizzly bear crawling into its hole," wrote one Iowan. Another described the Confederate garrison as "a rat in a hole with a dozen terriers scratching and barking around him." It was no wonder the Confederates put up such a stout defense.[21]

Yet for all the explanation and concern, there was never really any question about what Grant would do next. He had tried twice to assault Vicksburg: first, a quick shot attempting to take advantage of the chaos and low morale among the Confederate army reeling from major defeats, and then a second, larger, and more prepared effort. Neither worked, and one Federal correctly wrote that "the night of May 22, not only found us outside of Vicksburg, but well satisfied, officers and men, that a siege and not an assault must give us the city." One of Grant's engineers echoed his sentiments, writing that "the question as to the practicability of carrying the place by assault without previous preparation was now settled for men as well as for officers."[22]

Siege had indeed become the only option. James K. Newton of the 14th Wisconsin wrote home that "if we can't make them surrender any other way we can starve them out." Newton's commander agreed, Grant even beginning that very night of May 22 to suggest some siege-like activity; he wrote

Sherman: "Would it not be advisable to mine and blow up the salient near where you now have the flag planted on the enemy's parapet? I am sending after powder and expect to have it here sometime during the night." It was not long thereafter, as Grant stated in his memoirs, that he came to the full conclusion: "After the failure of the 22d, I determined upon a regular siege."[23]

Orders quickly went out that "any further assault on the enemy's works will for the present cease." Grant told his corps commanders to "hold all the ground you have acquired; get your batteries in position, and commence regular approaches toward the city." In order to make sure the entire line was covered as much as possible, Grant also tinkered with the positions of the troops, sending Quinby back to McPherson and McArthur back to the Warrenton Road. Supplying these troops was also most important. "Direct your commissary to get up full rations," he added. The orders quickly trickled down the chains of command, and Sherman informed his corps that "the works of the enemy being too strong to be carried by assault, [they] must be reduced by a system of regular approaches."[24]

The Confederates were in no way surprised by this decision, although they would like nothing better than for Grant to beat his head against the Confederate fortifications over and over and thus affect Union morale. Instead, they knew a siege was the obvious tactic—so obvious, in fact, that many Confederates commented in nearly identical terms. Louis Hébert wrote that "from that time [May 22] he seemed to abandon all hope of taking our works by assault, and applied himself assiduously to the reduction of our line by regular and systematic approach." Martin L. Smith similarly noted how "after the several decided repulses, the enemy seemed to have abandoned the idea of taking by assault, and went vigorously at work to thoroughly invest and attack by regular approaches." John C. Moore reported that "having failed to carry our works by assault, the enemy now appeared to determine not to attempt it again, but to take us by regular approaches, or by starving us out." Carter Stevenson echoed that sentiment: "The enemy relinquished all idea of assaulting us, and confined himself to the more cautious policy of a system of gradual approaches and mining."[25]

Even with the setback, most Federals were in no way turned from their ultimate goal. "To undertake to carry the place by assault cannot, in my opinion, be done," wrote W. B. Britton to his hometown newspaper, "for we have been up and had a look at the thing and are pretty well satisfied. We are not whipped, we hold all we have gained. . . . We have been successful in all the battles since we landed in Mississippi and will be successful here. We are in good spirits and will soon have the river open." A Wisconsin soldier echoed the same thought: "The result of the charge was as we all predicted before we went in[:] a repulse on our side. Although we fell back without accomplishing anything we are not at all disheartened or scared. Are ready to go in again any day."[26]

The Federal high command was just as upbeat. John E. Smith waxed eloquent in describing the Union soldiers' ability:

> The patient endurance of the men while on the march, their undaunted courage in battle, the unflinching steadiness and unwavering determination exhibited by them when under the fire of the enemy, cannot be too highly commended. The patriotic spirit evinced by them in all their actions clearly demonstrates their faith in the justice of their cause, and renders them fearless and invincible. The Federal Union should congratulate herself that she has in the field men who, in many hard-fought battles, have proved themselves as soldiers unsurpassed in intelligence and heroic bravery, men who hold their lives as nothing in comparison to the preservation of the Union and the maintenance of the supremacy of the American Constitution over the entire land. An army composed of such material, imbued with the spirit of justice and liberty, must and will be victorious.[27]

Although not in the thick of the fighting as he was at Champion Hill, Alvin Hovey similarly wrote to his wife on May 23 that "I have been in almost constant battle since the 1st of May—yesterday we fought all day and the cannon are now roaring around me. . . . We have been fighting at this point for three days and I think we will have to make a regular siege before we succeed. . . . We will have hot work here but Vicksburgh is surely ours." After Hovey had time to think it over, he later added to his thoughts and wrote incisively:

> After the bloody repulse of the 22nd, our feelings can [be] better imagined than described, for over one month we had been acting on the offensive and in every engagement so far we had been successful. . . . But now our further progress toward the grand goal of our labors was barricaded. We had attempted to carry their works by storm and had signally failed. This check upon us acted like a charm, for instead of discouraging us it only made us the more curious to see what the Rebs had inside, for well we knew that the eyes of the world were looking on us.[28]

Perhaps Sherman put it best: "Our position is now high, healthy and good," he informed Grant on May 24. "We are in direct and easy communication with our supplies, and the troops continue to manifest the same cheerful spirit which has characterized them throughout this whole movement." Despite the setbacks, it was only a matter of time.[29]

Even though the decision to lay siege to Vicksburg was universally understood and accepted, there were still rumblings of disgust within the Army of the Tennessee because of the failures on May 19 and 22 and the high casualties those assaults produced. Accordingly, morale became an instantly important barometer. Yet it seemed, despite the shellacking the army had taken over the last four days, spirits stood remarkably high. One Federal who channeled his inner Grant was not distraught at all, writing that "there is no escape but unconditional surrender, or utter annihilation."[30]

Many were the letters and diaries of Federals displaying a wishful future. "Boys all in good spirits," one Federal wrote home. Another contended that, despite the recent setbacks, "Old Grant has got them this time just where he wants them and I think they will either have to starve or surrender." An Indianan wrote to his wife that "Vicksburg is certainly a very strongly fortified place and cannot be taken only by the hardest fighting. Its defenders are obstinate and determined but no more so than our own men who are very sanguine of success. Give yourself no uneasiness on my account. We are annoying them from every side. The place must succumb, we are determined."[31]

Some even exhibited a willingness to assault again. Colonel Manning Force of the 20th Ohio wrote home with bluster that "if the 20th [Ohio] be ordered to charge, we will get in, or drop on the parapets. Once advanced, under an order to charge, there will be no return." He similarly wrote a friend: "The 20th will run against a brick wall, if ordered, and stand against it till shot down. If we should not be ordered to leave, we would find some way in." It is important to remember, of course, that Force's 20th Ohio had not endured the heavy fighting on either day, but the sentiment was plain. Indianan James C. Vanderbilt exhibited similar commitment when he wrote home that "we have been here seven days fighting at Vicksburg and we intend to stay seven years if they don't hoist the white flag in that time."[32]

Still, not all in the army were as eager and optimistic, and therein emerged some of the anonymous blame for such high casualties and the loss of momentum. "I am not given to exposing either myself or my men unnecessarily," wrote E. H. Twining, "& while I would not hesitate [to] do any duty which is ordered, I have no particular fondness for the sort of hailstorms I have seen in this country." James T. Buegel asked in his diary: "What had been accomplished? Nothing at all. However, something like a thousand men had fallen." He went on to muse that "the common soldier does not ascertain who was responsible for this murder. But it was rumored that it was again jealousy and betrayal that caused the death of so many. It was also asserted that a general attack was supposed to take place on the whole line, but was not carried out." Elliott Bush wrote his parents of the assaults "accomplishing nothing but a fearful loss on our side."[33]

Some of the blame was more direct. Sherman—perhaps the best-known face of the army aside from Grant—came in for ridicule himself because of how he had handled his corps. "Dissatisfaction exists beyond measure among certain regiments—relative to the fruitless assault of the 22nd," wrote Henry Seaman on the 13th Illinois of Sherman's own corps. "Sherman is generally blamed but I am impressed with the belief that Sherman acted strictly under the orders of his superior in rank. Sherman is an inferior officer although he might of exercised a powerful influence over the commanding general in having him order the charge." While he mitigated his complaint against Sherman, Seaman just could not understand why Sherman was so popular: "The rash move the boys all attribute to Sherman's 'hot headed' ambition. Notwithstanding the blunders and fruitless demonstrations Gen'l Sherman has made within the past six months he still retains an important command and received the eulogies and blessings of our people at home as being an able and efficient commander."[34]

Certainly, Grant came in for his share of the blame, although many defended him even while admitting a stumble. "Here the only mistake of the campaign was committed," Thomas B. White wrote his mother, "and that is a pardonable one." Edward Ingraham wrote his aunt that "the affair is now looked upon as a sad mistake but I do not blame Gen. Grant for at that time he expected a rebel army from the southeast and thought best to make a bold strike and get possession before rebel reinforcements came." Most viewed Grant not just in the context of the failed assaults but in light of the larger campaign, and not a few heaped praise on the general even after the May 22 debacle. "There were two words that Gen. Grant had no use for," wrote Daniel Buchwalter: "They were <u>fail</u> and <u>quit</u>." Others lofted the general to incredible heights: "Grant is one of the great military men of the present age," one wrote, while another took his praise almost to unbelievable levels: "Challenge this statement who may," one Illinoisan wrote, "we believe God Himself commanded the Federal army from the 14th to the 17th of May, 1863."[35]

Most of the blame Grant endured was a result of the high casualties, thereby perpetuating the idea of Grant-as-butcher, which has been roundly debunked. In speaking of his assault at Cold Harbor with the Army of the Potomac, which resulted in immense casualties later in the war, Grant told a newspaper correspondent: "I have always also regretted allowing McClernand to continue his attacks on the works at Vicksburg.... Such things are a part of the horrors of war. They belong to the category of mistakes which men necessarily see to have been mistakes after the event is over." Whether it was a true mistake or not is left to opinion, and historian Edwin C. Bearss, himself a wounded combat veteran, has argued that "at the end, only a general willing to spend the lives of his men can win a war; the key is to spend them at the proper time and place, so that each life buys the maximum increment of victory."[36]

That being said, there was still plenty of blame heaped on Grant and his commanders for the Union bloodshed suffered at Vicksburg. While Grant described the assaults as "gallant in the extreme," another Federal described them as "desperate and bloody in the extreme." The recriminations were quick and numerous: "The crudity of its preparations and the failure of proper support, necessarily resulted in a failure," wrote E. H. Twining. "It was one of the most fool hardy attempts that was ever ordered by any General," Ira W. Hunt jotted in his diary. "It was not well planned nor executed," explained George S. Durfee. "Our division made a charge but were driven back or rather by some terrible mismanagement were nearly sacrificed," W. L. Brown wrote to his father. "The officers was very foolish to make a charge where they ought to know it was impossible to be successful," opined James Thomas. But perhaps the Indianan Nicholas Miller put it best: "Here is where I first lost confidence in our Commander."[37]

Even if Grant received much criticism for the failed assaults, he had his own ideas on that notion and made sure the blame rested elsewhere: namely, corps commander John A. McClernand. Grant had questioned McClernand's messages earlier in the day, as he had during the entire campaign. But feeling the need to be supportive if there was any truth to the claim that McClernand's troops had broken the Confederate lines, Grant sent them in and renewed the assaults elsewhere. The picture was quickly emerging, however, that McClernand had overstated his case. Grant quickly pounced, assigning blame for the high casualty counts squarely on McClernand.[38]

Grant got a firsthand account when newspaperman Sylvanus Cadwallader returned to Grant's headquarters that night. Cadwallader reported that "the whole affair was miserable and inexcusable to a point past endurance." When he explained that "I was within plain view of the rebel earthworks—that McClernand never gained a footing inside them . . . I was questioned closely concerning it." He later noted: "[I] shall never forget the fearful burst of indignation from Rawlins, and the grim glowering look of disappointment and disgust which settled down on Grant's usually placid countenance, when he was convinced of McClernand's duplicity, and realized its cost in dead and wounded."[39]

Cadwallader's account started a free-for-all at headquarters, with McClernand becoming the main target. "Rawlins ordered Major Bower to open the record book and charge a thousand lives to that _____ McClernand," Grant staff officer James H. Wilson wrote. Engineer William L. B. Jenney reported that "Rawlins used strong language when the occasion required, and this was one of them."[40]

Grant soon reported his case against McClernand to Washington, although his initial dispatch to General in Chief Henry Halleck had stated that the assaults were "not entirely successful" but that "we hold possession however of some of the enemy's forts and have skirmishers close under all of them." However, Grant inaccurately reported that "our loss was not severe" while drily advising that "the nature of the ground about Vicksburg is such that it can only be taken by a siege." In Grant's defense, perhaps he wrote this dispatch before knowing the full story and was still acting on McClernand's suspect statements, but within two days Grant had changed his tune: "Our troops were not repulsed from any point, but simply failed to enter the works of the enemy." This in itself was a clear indictment of McClernand's perceived failure at a critical moment. But Grant went even further. Casualties, he explained to the Union high command, were "not very heavy at first, but receiving repeated dispatches from General McClernand" made them higher. Now fully realizing the selfish motives behind McClernand's missives, Grant averred that they had "caused us to double our losses for the day." Grant then directly implicated his corps commander for the ensuing bloodshed: "General McClernand's dispatches misled me as to the real state of facts, and caused much of this loss. He is entirely unfit for the position of corps commander, both on the march and on the battlefield. Looking after his corps gives me more labor and infinitely more uneasiness than all the remainder of my department." Nevertheless, Grant asserted reassuringly to Washington that "the enemy are now undoubtedly in our grasp. The fall of Vicksburg and the capture of most of the garrison can only be a question of time."[41]

But Grant's harsh assessment was not the only way by which Washington learned of McClernand's ineptness. The War Department's liaison on the ground, Charles Dana, wired similar indictments. Sent by Secretary of War Edwin Stanton to keep an eye on Grant and report back, Dana soon came under the general's wing and influence (an old adage is to keep friends close and enemies closer). And by this point in the campaign Dana had already come to strongly disfavor McClernand in his wires back to the high command. Writing in his memoirs decades after the events at Vicksburg, Dana's judgment on the politician-general was withering: McClernand "had not the qualities necessary for commander even of a regiment.... His judgment was not solid, and he looked after himself a good deal."[42]

Although Dana wrote that the Grant–Sherman–McPherson cabal was airtight—"the utmost cordiality and confidence existed between these three men"—McClernand was nothing less than an albatross around the Union army's neck; this defeat was all McClernand's fault. "The attempt failed, but without heavy loss," Dana informed Secretary of War Stanton. "McClernand's report was false, as he held not a single fort, and the result was disastrous." In terms of casualties, he added: "Though but for McClernand's mistake it would have been inconsiderable."[43]

Most of the other high-level commanders in the Army of the Tennessee followed suit and heaped the blame on McClernand. Sherman described the meeting that night at Grant's headquarters: "Most of the corps and division commanders were assembled. McClernand was spoken of in no complimentary terms." Sherman himself went so far as to describe McClernand as "a dirty dog." "McClernand's report of success must have been premature," he wrote, "for I subsequently learned that both his and McPherson's assaults had failed to break through the enemy's line of intrenchments, and were equally unsuccessful as my own." In reference to McClernand's giving his own corps the greatest credit, Sherman dismissed it as "such a catalogue of nonsense."[44]

Sherman later cooled somewhat in his assessment. In his memoirs he simply stated that "this affair caused great feeling with us, and severe criticisms on General McClernand." Another corps commander, McPherson, could always be counted on to take the high road and offer little fodder that might cause controversy. Though he condemned McClernand's claim to glory, McPherson also stated that "the assault failed, not, in my opinion, from any want of co-operation or bravery on the part of our troops, but from the strength of the works, the difficulty of getting close up to them under cover, and the determined character of the assailed."[45]

But McClernand could not help himself, and in letters to major politicians—including to Governor Richard Yates of Illinois, his home state—he claimed that his corps had done the most fighting and would have won if supported by the other commanders. He stated that the XIII Corps had the "first and largest success achieved anywhere along the whole line of our army." That mentality of pride seeped down into the ranks as well. Alvin Hovey wrote his wife that "my division alone has done more hard fighting than the balance of the army."[46]

Once Grant's accusations came to light, McClernand not surprisingly mounted a defense against "rumors which would fix upon me the responsibility of the failure of the assault." That defense unwisely reached the gamut of the Army of the Tennessee's command. He blamed reinforcements being too late and that "night cut short the engagement." In terms of people, he first heaped blame on McPherson: "On the 22d, I was the first to attack. I made the only lodgments; held them all day under a scorching sun and wasting fire, while the corps on my right, sustaining repulse, left the enemy to mass upon me." McClernand also blamed Sherman, alleging that he had not provided the support "Major–General Grant had specifically and peremptorily ordered, namely, simultaneous and persistent attack all along our lines."[47]

The most blame, according to McClernand, rested with Grant himself. He cited "orders which, under the circumstances, were incapable of execution." McClernand later asked in his defense that if Grant could go to Sherman and McPherson, "why could he not, why did he not, ride or send over to me?" In the end, McClernand seethed that the entire affair "makes General Grant responsible not only for the alleged increase of our mortality list, but for our whole loss."[48]

Yet there was some support for McClernand, not surprisingly from his own corps. David McKinney lamented the general's vilification and wrote that "McClernand was a good officer & performed his part admirably in the late battles." Others argued that victory was close, especially on McClernand's front. Lieutenant Colonel Harvey Graham of the 22nd Iowa, who had been captured when Pettus and the Texans retook the redoubt, later asserted to McClernand that "it is my firm conviction and belief that had the Thirteenth Army Corps been re-enforced by a few brigades, thus enabling you to send support to the front, the success of your command would have been complete. As it was, success was achieved, but was afterward lost. Victory was in your hands, but was wrested from you by superior numbers."[49]

In the final judgment, there seemed to be plenty of fault to go around. Grant was certainly open to blame. Sherman and McPherson achieved no stellar accomplishments on those days, and there has been some speculation that both saw that the assaults would not succeed and determined to lose as few of their troops as possible in as faint attacks as possible. Thus, each corps put in only a minuscule percentage of their numbers as opposed to the vast majority of McClernand's corps participating. Edwin C. Bearss, in fact, has surmised that Sherman's and McPherson's performance on May 22 was "an embarrassment," while he specifically labeled Sherman's attack as "pathetic."[50]

That being said, McClernand was also to blame, mainly for going against the exact recommendations he had made to assault on a few narrow fronts. Once Grant made McClernand the scapegoat, it was a done deal and historians have mainly taken Grant's side, Bruce Catton writing of McClernand's "excess of enthusiasm." The larger ramification, however, was the growing split between Grant and McClernand that widened dramatically on May 22.

Historian Terry Winschel has written that the affair "precipitated a command crisis within the Army of the Tennessee," and it would be stopped only when McClernand was gone. And that was not a long time in coming.[51]

Obviously, the most dire ramifications came in the casualty body count, and the numbers told the tale quite plainly. While the Confederates suffered around 500 casualties on May 22, there were obviously a lopsided number of Union losses, and everyone described it. "Poor fellows," one Confederate wrote, "they fell by hundreds in front of our lines and lay festering where they fell for two and a half days before they could be buried." Pemberton also noted in his diary how "they came up in good style but were repulsed with heavy loss." The Federals likewise knew it had been terrible, one writing that "if this is not a hot place, I hope I may never see one." David Grier similarly wrote his wife that "I never want to be engaged in anything of that kind again." Another soldier back in the rear and not even involved knew as much, writing: "From what we could see and what we hear, the result of the assault has been a terrible slaughter of our troops, and we are still outside of Vicksburg."[52]

The tally was indeed terrible. Added to the 157 killed, 777 wounded, and 8 missing from the May 19 assault, Grant reported 502 killed, 2,550 wounded, and 147 missing on May 22. The grand total in all the assaults amounted to a staggering 659 killed, 3,327 wounded, and 155 missing. More than four thousand total casualties had proved that Vicksburg was impregnable to frontal assault, one Alabamian claiming that "most of those that were killed or wounded were shot in the head." As would be expected, the "forlorn hope" at the Stockade Redan received much of the acclaim. Their casualties (more than one-third) ranged higher in percentage than that of the main army: of 150 volunteers, 19 were killed and 34 wounded. In some cases, oddities emerged amid the casualties, such as two different sets of brothers who died attacking the Railroad Redoubt: the Robbs and the Drummonds.[53]

Perhaps most sad was the fact that many of the dead and wounded lay on the field for days before being attended to. A slight spat erupted between Grant and Pemberton over humanity, Grant refusing to call for a truce to bury the dead and care for the wounded. In the meantime, the horror worsened. "The enemy's dead are becoming very offensive along portions of my front," Martin L. Smith reported. A Mississippian added that "the stench from the dead Federals is sufficient to warrant a flag of truce." The view was not any better: "The sight was horrible. The reeking bodies lay all blackened and swollen, and some with arms extended as if pleading to heaven for the burial that was denied them by man."[54]

Ultimately, Pemberton's commanders leaned on him enough that he called for a truce on May 25. "Hostilities will cease from 6 to 8:30 P.M., to enable the enemy to bury their dead," one grateful Confederate wrote. When it occurred, shock came to everyone involved. Part of the surprise came from the up-close look at the carnage. More shock came when the realization became evident that because of the delay few wounded were left; most had died within the span of three days. That being said, there were a few still found. "Yesterday afternoon when there was a cessation of hostilities to bury the dead," Carlos Colby wrote his sister, "one poor fellow from the [99?] Ills was found still alive shot through the legs. He had laid 76 hours without food . . . or water."[55]

Perhaps the biggest shock came when the two sides, working together to alleviate the horror, began to fraternize. While most of the dead and wounded were Federal, grateful Confederates lunged over the works and began to help, as much out of necessity as anything. "A flag of truce was granted to bury the enemy's dead which were almost stinking us out of the works," Missourian Theodore Fisher wrote. In doing so, the two sides acted as if nothing untoward had occurred and laughed and joked as friends. Some even found relatives in the opposite ranks. An amazed Indianan wrote home that "yesterday a flag of truce was sent out by the rebels and all firing ceased for the time and then to see both Armies meet and talk to each other as if they were on the very best of terms. A great many of the rebs stayed with us and would not go back."[56]

Saddest of all, the carnage and death seemed to produce no results in the larger scheme of Vicksburg operations, one Federal writing to his brother: "No evidence of much gain on either side." Obviously, the personal gain and loss was dramatic, as word of deaths and wounds began to spread across both the Union and the Confederacy. Some received good news, such as the wife of Edwin A. Loosley: "I have no time to write much, but be very thankful that I am able to write at all as it almost makes me shudder yet to think of the terrible ordeal of fire and blood through which I safely passed in the unsuccessful assault on the rebel fortifications." Others received worse news, as letter after letter emerged from Vicksburg explaining a loved one's death. For example, Colonel Benjamin Spooner of the 83rd Indiana wrote the wife of one of his captains about his death and last words: "<u>O, Col, I am killed</u>." At least in one case, the news was wrong. George D. Kellogg of the 23rd Wisconsin was reported dead but was not. Though news of his death was telegraphed back to Madison, he confessed how "that was a surprise to me."[57]

Perhaps most poignant was the diary of Israel M. Piper of the 99th Illinois.

He wrote in his journal the morning of May 22, scribbling: "A charge to be made on the entire line." It was the last entry. He was killed in front of the 2nd Texas Lunette.[58]

As in all wars, it was unfortunately not just the soldiers who suffered. Along with the armies, horrors attendant to the assaults quickly came to the civilians of Vicksburg and the surrounding area. In fact, chaos and confusion set in even before the assaults, as the armies fought closer and closer to the river city, the heavy cannonading being heard inside Vicksburg. One Texas soldier wrote of hearing the fighting on May 16 and 17: "One shot scarcely waited for another."[59]

Soon, word of the defeats at Champion Hill and Big Black River began to filter in. Worse, it seemed that the Federals were closely following the retreating Confederate masses. "They are upon us; the Yankees will be here by this evening," one Vicksburg woman reported, her informant exclaiming how the troops "are running back here as fast as they can come and the Yanks after them, in such numbers nothing can stop them." That was exactly what was happening, one Ohioan admitting it was like "driving the enemy into his hole round-a-bout Vicksburg."[60]

The outlying civilians were the first to meet the pressing throng of Federals, one nearby woman writing in her diary on May 18: "Yesterday was one of the saddest days it has ever been my fate to have experienced, our troops retreated from Big Black bridge to Vicksburg. . . . Oh! my heart ached, ached, as I hope it never will again." Soon, the Federals arrived, one of whom she asked "are there any Yankees about," and he replying "plenty, . . . for I am a Northern soldier, not a Yankee though." Making the situation worse for these Mississippians were the slaves who logically took this chance at freedom and ran away or followed the Union soldiers. One Mississippian had all he could stand, telling one freedman that "you think you are free, but you are in greater bondage than you were ever before." He also threatened to "blow his brains out" if he ever insulted a lady again. Emilie McKinley could only write, "Oh! how long how long will this last." Even though she wanted the misery to end, she still knew who was at fault and, later, admitted in reference to Federals who searched her home for the third or fourth time: "I could have killed them with real pleasure."[61]

Those inside Vicksburg had a little time to prepare, although some actually evacuated while they still could. Caroline Searles recalled that her family left the city "by the advice of the authorities, who thought it best that all women and children should seek a safer place." They moved about four miles out on the Benton Road but soon met stragglers from the Confederate army, one poor fellow wanting to stay at their house because of fatigue. The owner would not let him, considering the danger and what was coming behind the retreating Confederates, and "urged him to get inside the Vicksburg lines as soon a possible, as the Yankees would soon follow." Caroline commented to the soldier that she had never seen a Yankee, to which he replied: "Well, you will soon see them and you will never forget them." She noted that, "sure enough, the next morning they came in hordes."[62]

Some who tried to get out of Vicksburg could not. Jane Bitterman and her young son had left Vicksburg when it seemed the danger was real, traveling to Bovina to stay with her mother. Thereafter, she took every opportunity to return inside the city to see her husband, who was in the army. She returned in mid-May; not wanting to leave just yet, she "purposefully loitered until I missed the train on the appointed day." She did so again the next day but was determined to make it on the third: "My husband's anxiety for us was very evident." On the third day, news came that the Federals had blocked the route and that all trains were needed for military use. They were stuck, but her husband soon fashioned a nice cave in which they lived out the fighting.[63]

Others actually moved back into the city to be safer rather than being caught on the outlying plantations when the Federal army arrived. Lucy McRae remembered that Confederate officers quizzed some of them about what they had seen and how close the Federals were behind them. Similarly, young Lida Lord and her family had moved out of town to get away from the gunboat shelling, but upon word of the fall of Jackson and the approach of Grant's army they decided to go back to town for safety. They packed all night on May 17, with frequent updates from passing soldiers going to Vicksburg, most with the same refrain: "We are sold by General Pemberton." Lida remembered that "our hearts sank like lead." The next morning, the cooks were busy baking while the house servants manned the roadside giving out food "to the scores of dusty, ragged, and foot-sore men who pressed up to the front door." Lucy remembered "how they enjoyed their breakfast, poor fellows, thanking and blessing the ladies; and how they swore, within bounds, at Pemberton and the Yankees!"[64]

The Lord family—the father was the rector at Christ Episcopal Church in Vicksburg and was positioned at the rear as a guard—soon made their way toward the city, but the fear became even more harrowing as nightfall approached. One of the Lord children remembered: "At almost every turn we looked around in apprehension of the Yankee cavalry—when almost eight miles from town we were overtaken by a servant who said the Yankees were already at Parson Fox's." Fortunately, the family made it safely into Vicksburg.⁶⁵

Not all made it either in or out without mishap, including a group of some thirty women, mostly officers' wives, who were out for a picnic and trying to get back into the city. The blue flood caught them outside the fortifications. Not knowing what to do with the group, Grant had them quartered in an abandoned house behind his lines. "They plead and threatened, tearfully, scornfully, impertinently to effect their release," but Grant would not allow it. Fortunately, inside was an old piano, and one Federal noted the women "pounded the poor old thing until it would bellow like the bull of a Bashon."⁶⁶

As the dejected masses of both civilians and soldiers made their way mostly into Vicksburg, a decidedly harrowing sight met all eyes. Dora Miller described some of the soldiers taking a break sitting in her yard explaining, "ritreat, ritreat! They said, in broken English—they were Louisiana Acadians." She went on: "About three o'clock the rush began. I shall never forget that woeful sight of a beaten, demoralized army that came rushing back—humanity in the last throes of endurance. Wan, hollow-eyed, ragged, footsore, bloody, the men limped along unarmed, but followed by siege guns, ambulances, gun carriages, and wagons in aimless confusion." Still, there was some semblance of hope and cheer: "At twilight two or three bands on the court house hill and other points began playing Dixie, Bonnie Blue Flag, and so on, and drums began to beat all about; I suppose they were rallying the scattered army."⁶⁷

As the Confederate throngs returned to the city beaten and dejected, the scenes around Vicksburg itself soon gave off a certain melancholy, as all knew what it meant. One dentist noted on May 17 that "the hills ar[e] covered with men in every direction, and the day of our doom appears close at hand. Only God of heaven can save us an[d] in him I trust." A Vicksburg women commented on the feeling: "There seemed no life in the city; sullen and expectant were the men—tearful and hopeful the women."⁶⁸

Some of the citizens of Vicksburg had other troubles, which just happened to coincide with the gathering armies around the city. In addition to women and children, the horses and mules (and at least one camel) that had been in town or driven in suddenly became a problem. They would have to be fed, and they were present in such large numbers that they posed a real threat. "Human life will be endangered by the stampede amongst these creatures when terror seizes them," wrote Emma Balfour. "The only comfort is that we can live on them, for I fear we have not provender to feed them for long."⁶⁹

Some lost homes due to the military needs of clearing fields of fire. During the first night there occurred "a grand and awful spectacle," Emma Balfour wrote. "The darkness was lit up by the burning houses all along our lines. They were burnt that our firing would not be obstructed. It was sad to see. Many of them we knew to be handsome residences put up in the last few years as country residences—two of them very large and handsome houses, but the stern necessity of war has caused their destruction."[70]

Others were facing the most trying of all circumstances just as the armies engulfed Vicksburg. Mrs. Williamson, who lived near the Bowie family just outside the city, was very sick, and the fact that she was a widow with four small children only made the situation worse. After the Bowie house burned, the family went to a boardinghouse, where a large canvas tent was set up outside to care for the overflowing horde. There, the widow died that night. Four small orphans resulted, which the Bowie family took in and cared for.[71]

Making matters worse, the Federals soon arrived as well, as early as May 18 when many of those structures were burned. Balfour wrote on that day: "Still all seems confusion and we are cut off from all knowledge of the outside world." Later she commented that "the Yankees are at our intrenchments and we hear firing," noting that it "seems all along towards the Jackson road to the graveyard." She could only close with a foreboding entry: "A general battle is expected at daylight." As such, the citizens began to look toward their safety by seeking shelter in the many caves that had been dug into the hilly banks. In fact, Balfour met Stephen D. Lee in all the chaos, who recommended getting a cave to live in. Later Lee asked her "if we were provided with a rat-hole, [and] I told him it seemed to me that we were all caught in a rat hole."[72]

The initial burst of chaos and excitement, as bad as it seemed, was only the opening act of the terrible ordeal the civilians had to endure during the next few days. Soon, in coordination with the land army's efforts in rear of Vicksburg, the Union navy began to pummel Vicksburg with fire, particularly from the mortar boats in the river. Numerous people inside Vicksburg left their account of events. "Mortar boats and gunboats open on the city—fire scattered all over town—women & children pretty generally 'caved in,'" wrote one Confederate officer in his diary. A wounded Texan in a hospital described an artillery bombardment: "So as the day darkened, we sought a safer place in the cellar. The bombs, however, fell without ceasing all around our hospital. Pieces came flying into the house with a frightful howling. There was little rest to be thought of."[73]

Civilians who were not familiar with such military operations were dazed by the shock of it all. "A shell fell just back of the house and exploded which admonished us of the danger, when we took to the cave," wrote one citizen. He later elaborated in his diary that "we ware started by the report of big guns at one oclock this morning from the river." Later, he noted, the mortars across the river "opened on the town and kept up a constant fire all day with no affect only to scare the women and children." In the midst of one bombardment, one girl remembered a conversation between her mother and aunt when a shell exploded so near that it threw dirt on everyone. "Oh, sister, are you killed?" one asked, to which the other replied "No, are you?" She remembered that those listening, "realizing the absurdity of the conversation, were all laughing."[74]

This was no laughing matter, however—far from it—and the bombardment did "considerable injury to town," one Confederate wrote. Lida Lord gave a detailed synopsis, explaining that "our own trials began on Thursday, when the gunboats opened fire." A major had assured the Lords that they "need have no fear, as our home was out of range of the river." As the entire family waited in the study for the servant to call them for supper, the servant rang the bell and returned to the kitchen. Between the time the servant girl left the room and before the family could enter, a shell "burst in the very center of that pretty dining-room, blowing out the roof and one side, crushing the well-spread tea-table like an egg-shell, and making a great yawning hole in the floor, into which disappeared supper, china, furniture, and the safe containing our entire stock of butter and eggs." Lida noted that they were all frightened to know they had missed death by a mere moment; all realized that "one minute later we should have been seated about that table, now a mass of charred splinters at the bottom of that smoking gulf." Lida recalled that "we very soon decided to seek safety somewhere, and found it temporarily in the cave of a friend."[75]

Life in the Vicksburg caves was miserable, Lida counting as many as sixty-five people in hers alone. "The noise and concussion were deafening, the strain upon nerves and senses unrelaxed for hours. But our greatest misery was the suspense and inaction." The immediate horror was real too, including a shell that hit the side of the hill in which the cave was dug, collapsing one of the entrances "and causing a frightful panic." "A rush of hot smoke and a strong smell of powder filled the passages," and a general stampede began until a voice of authority calmed everyone.[76]

Young William Lord, son of the rector of Christ Church, also remembered the bombardment, including one time when the family had taken cover in the cellar of the church. He well remembered sitting atop a pile of coal with blankets thrown on top. He later described the scene when the shells flew thick and fast into town:

> My mother and sisters huddled around me upon the coal-heap, my father, in clerical coat, and a red smoking-cap on his head, seated on an empty cask and looking delightedly like a pirate (for I knew nothing of cardinals in those days), our negro servants crouching terror-stricken, moaning and praying in subdued tones in a neighboring coal-bin, and all lighted by the fitful glow of two or three tallow candles.

Lord admitted that "the war became to me for the first time a reality and not the fairy-tale it had hitherto seemed." Fortunately, the Lord family was able to escape soon thereafter to a plantation southward on the Big Black River.[77]

Just when it seemed that things could get no worse, the assaults began, causing a near panic among the people who knew that, if the Confederate defenses failed, then Vicksburg—and perhaps their lives and livelihoods—were gone. One Vicksburg citizen wrote in his diary on May 19: "Firing commenced early this morning and has continued ever since and at this time is brisk and we can heer the small arms distinctly." At "2 ¼ oclock . . . large guns and small arms are roaring with an awful sound. It produces a feeling of horror undiscribeable. The fireing continued until after 7 Oclock when it finally ceased and all was quiet." The residual effects were just as disturbing: "During the day it was lawghable to see the skulking of some cowardly men. They ware hideing in the hollows and behind trees. 7 or 8 cralled into our old cave and lay thair all day just like so many scared dogs."[78]

Emma Balfour described sewing in her room and "praying in my heart, oh so earnestly for our cause," when a servant girl came in with a pale expression and yelled, "Oh Mistress, the Yankees are pouring over the hill and our men are running." Balfour went to see but was amazed she was not more excited: "It brought before me forcibly what a state of excitement we were living in when I found that this coincidence did not startle me." Soon, she realized it was "not . . . so bad as she thought." Throughout the rest of the day her ears were well attuned to what was happening: "There is firing along the left wing toward the graveyard and toward the center, but not yet on the left."[79]

Mary Loughborough also described those wretched feelings of listening to the fighting but not immediately knowing what it meant. "Looking out from the back veranda," she wrote, "we could plainly see the smoke before the report of the guns reached us. Our anxiety was great, indeed, having been told by gentlemen the night before, that the works in the rear of Vicksburg were anything but of a superior kind." She went on to describe how

> the discharges of musketry were irregular. Yet, to us who were thinking of the dear ones exposed to this frequent firing, the restless forebodings and unhappiness caused by the distant din of battle pained us indeed. After listening for some time

to the reports, which sounded to us, in the distance, like the quick, successive droppings of balls on sheet iron, again and again sounded the cannon like thunderings near us. At every report our hearts beat quicker. The excitement was intense in the city. Groups of people stood on every available position where a view could be obtained of the distant hills, where the jets of white smoke constantly passed out from among the trees.[80]

The desire was to learn as much as they could, and so the idea of climbing up into the cupola of the Warren County Courthouse emerged, where a panoramic view presented itself:

In the centre and east of the river, the firing seemed more continuous, while to the left and running northly, the rattle and roar would be sudden, sharp, and vigorous, then ceasing for some time. The hills around near the city, and indeed every place that seemed commanding and secure, was covered with anxious spectators—many of them ladies—fearing the result of the afternoon's conflict. To the extreme left and north, near the river, the warfare became general, while toward the centre the firing became less rapid.[81]

Even those outside the fortifications reacted. Caroline Searles, who had left the city and was staying out near the fighting, recalled that "being only a short distance from the fortifications the first attack on our lines struck terror into our hearts. We walked the gallery all day, fearing to hear the result. We hardly dared to hope that any one was left alive in Vicksburg."[82]

When all was said and done, of course, the Confederate lines had held on May 19, and the civilians noticed the change it wrought. As Lida Lord remembered it: "All day the cannonading was terrific and the air was full of conflicting rumors, but toward evening the news was brought that in three tremendous charges the enemy had been repulsed with great slaughter." She was astute enough to realize what it meant and what effect it had: "Then began the moral reconstruction of our army. Men who had been gloomy, depressed, and distrustful now cheerfully and bravely looked the future in the face. After that day's victory but one spirit seemed to animate the whole army, the determination never to give up."[83]

But just holding out against what in reality was one small, isolated attack did not mean that Vicksburg was safe. In fact, the bombardment continued, and more assaults lay in the future. In the meantime, the Union navy relentlessly bombarded the town, and most residents headed to the caves. Emma Balfour noted this was the first time she had entered hers. With shells exploding on top and all around, she describing her situation as "between two fires," a momentary panic swept over her: "As all this rushed over me and the sense of suffocation from being underground, the certainty that there was no way to escape, that we were hemmed in, caged—for one moment my heart seemed to stand still—then my faith and courage rose to meet the emergency." Still, it was enough to cause her to spend most of her time outside: "I preferred to risk the danger in a house rather than in a cave with so many." Ironically, she was sitting on her gallery when a gunboat shell exploded in the shed out front, "making me involuntarily jump from my seat."[84]

The follow-on assaults started on May 22, and they produced quite the racket that all in the neighboring country heard, even Confederate prisoners in the river moving to prison camps in the North. The fighting began at daylight on May 22, as one civilian noted: "Shelling from the river was kept up all night, and at early dawn the firing commenced in front and at 5 oclock is quite rapid. The firing increased from the river and in front until 10 oclock when it became most tirific."[85]

At least one civilian was caught in the horror, Alice Shirley, and she remained in the "White House" on the Jackson Road. She had remained in place until the heavy fighting on May 22, guarding her house to keep soldiers from burning it down. Confederates had tried to do just that, and in fact burned the outbuildings, but advancing Federals shot the poor soldier detailed to burn the house itself. Mrs. Shirley and her slaves remained there for several days, but by the time of the major assaults on May 22, huddling in a chimney no longer seemed smart. McPherson himself went and talked her out of staying, ushering her to a cave in the rear, where she remained. Years later, her daughter described how the Federals in line of battle made "a narrow opening through their ranks for her to pass."[86]

Those inside the city proper were not immune from the fighting out on the lines either. Overshot shells and bullets hit amid the town, Dora Miller describing how "the half-spent balls coming all the way from those lines were flying so thick that they were obliged to dodge at every turn." Nevertheless, the Confederate lines held again, as they had on May 19, prompting Virginia Rockwood to declare that "our grand ole hills served as a strong bulwark against the foe, the Yanks."[87]

Although the major fighting ended with the repulse of the Union assaults on May 22, the civilians were still not in total safety and certainly were not relieved of the horrors of war. As more and more casualties mounted, the crowded buildings used as hospitals and the almost constant infusion of death taxed the citizens, as did the threat of disease and even the flies that attended so much destruction. Death was indeed rampant. It affected terribly those inside Vicksburg who had family on the front lines. One Louisianan told of explaining a loved one's death: "Last night went into town to see Mrs. Gibbs informed her of Felixs death," he wrote. "She & her daughter were very much affected his body was brought into town . . . he is to be buried today & I expect in Mrs Gibbs lot."[88]

The suffering was thus incredible among those civilians who remained inside Vicksburg, and at least one seemed to think it was more troublesome inside the city than on the front lines. "The worst sufferers during a battle are the non-combatants," Lida Lord related. "The victors and victims suffer afterward." One wonders whether the overheating Federals hugging the slopes of Vicksburg's ramparts for hours upon hours, or the hunkered down Confederates defending those fortifications, would have agreed.[89]

The Confederate repulse of the Federal assaults of May 19 and 22 did not, of course, mean the end of the Vicksburg campaign. Pemberton and his troops had held out in a brave and valiant attempt to hold at least part of the Mississippi Valley and its connection to the trans-Mississippi sector. Thus "Vicksburg" became synonymous with the ultimate defense, and some Confederates even began to refer to Vicksburg as the "Heroic City."[90]

And there was plenty of heroism, even in the wake of the successful defense against two major assaults. For example, Stephen D. Lee wrote his division commander Carter Stevenson shortly thereafter: "I send you the flag taken by Texans, under the lead of our gallant Lieutenant-Colonel [E. W.] Pettus, Twentieth Alabama Regiment. It was as gallant an act as I have ever seen during the war. I have pledged myself to give it to its captors. I beg that you and General Pemberton will bear me out." Stevenson endorsed giving it to the Texans. Other generals likewise sent colors up the chain of command, with John C. Moore sending the colors of the 99th Illinois as well as the color-bearer Higgins to Pemberton himself.[91]

Pemberton somewhat foolishly singled out Lee's brigade for praise in the defense and counterattack at the Railroad Redoubt, and it almost got him into even more trouble with his army. The soldiers had all but decided that Pemberton was a traitor after Big Black River, but the stout defense against the assaults had reformed some of their courage and morale—as well as their confidence in Pemberton. He had to be careful not to alienate anyone, however, and had to send out another memo stating that "it was not intended to compliment General Lee's brigade to any greater extent than any of the troops engaged in the trenches. No distinction can be drawn, all the troops having behaved with the greatest gallantry."[92]

Other misunderstandings also came about in the days and weeks following the assaults, even as Grant continued to constrict the enemy in the trap that was Vicksburg. Newspaper accounts were rife with rumors that Grant had taken the city, and one Federal even went so far as to caution that the episode "was not such a desperate thing as the papers made it out to be." That being said, others took a different view, one soldier writing: "Truly we are surrounded by a wall of fire."[93]

Still, the events of mid-May 1863 faded with the burning Mississippi sun as larger, more important victories and defeats followed. Still, many on both sides of the conflict remembered those early days at Vicksburg as horrific. "Their bones lay moldering around the Hill City of Mississippi[,] Vicksburg," one Federal wrote, and some marked the solemn dates later in the war. Others remembered the events in poetic prose. Federal brigade commander John B. Sanborn waxed eloquent in his report, recommending future memorialization on a grand scale:

> The living are rewarded by the consciousness of having done all that human nature is capable of to suppress a most wicked rebellion and to preserve order and good government for themselves and posterity. But alas, for the patriotic and gallant dead; no language of mine can do justice to their virtues. May some Macauley or Bancroft recite in interesting narration their hardships, endurance, patriotism, valor, and achievements, and some modern Homer or Virgil live to sing them in heroic verse.[94]

Most poignant, perhaps, Union bravery at Vicksburg was honored in medals that were awarded years later. In all, some 122 United States Medals of Honor were awarded for gallantry at Vicksburg; seventy-eight went to members of the forlorn hope. Blair himself was an important advocate, and his political clout went a long way: "I would recommend that the medal of honor voted by Congress be presented . . . to all the non-commissioned officers and privates composing the storming party on the 22d." Sherman agreed, writing that "if any troops could have carried and held the intrenchments of Vicksburg, these would."[95]

Hugh Ewing—no political slouch himself—also recommended that Captain John H. Groce and Lieutenant George O'Neal, who led the forlorn hope, be given "such high promotion as their gallantry merits." But he was not afraid to go the other way, writing at the same time: "I recommend that First Lieut. J. H. Talston, of the Fourth West Virginia Infantry, be reduced to the ranks, for absence without cause on the day of the battle, and that Corporals [Francis M.] Clendenin or [John W.] Boley, who saved their colors, be commissioned in his stead."[96]

Despite there being other, perhaps more decisive victories and defeats compared to the nondefinitive tactical outcome at Vicksburg between May

17 and 22, 1863, many still harkened back, years later, to those horrible hours below and above the fortifications of Vicksburg. They were, one Illinoisan wrote, "the most impressive events of my life." Another Illinoisan wrote decades afterward: "This memorable day I think will be as fresh to my memory forty years hence as it is at the present moment (Provided I attain that great age)." Yet another participant, an Iowan, simply reflected that "these [memories] were stamped so deeply in my very soul, that should I live a thousand years, I could not forget them."[97]

And those memories popped up in the oddest places. In the heavy fighting in front of the Stockade Redan, Robert J. Burdette of the 47th Illinois watched his second lieutenant, Christopher Gilbert, "stagger and fall crookedly forward." Burdette thought he was dead but then saw his compatriot attempt to rise, the lieutenant having been shot through the leg. Knowing Lieutenant Gilbert would not survive if he got up, Burdette and another soldier raced to him and carried him rearward, "away from the missiles that still pursued him spitefully as though they were bent on finishing the work they had begun."[98]

Lieutenant Gilbert recovered and went on to become a first lieutenant, but after the war Burdette lost track of Gilbert when Burdette went west and became pastor of the Temple Baptist Church in Los Angeles, California. It was there, through a curious set of circumstances, that Burdette experienced an astonishing meeting: "One day my lieutenant came before me, not to give orders, but to take them. He was a prisoner, and his fair captor stood beside him. She had done what Pemberton's sharpshooters in Vicksburg could not do. Love had won my lieutenant. I ordered him to accept the terms of the bride, to 'love her, comfort her, cherish her, honor and keep her, till death them did part.'" Burdette added simply of the groom: "And he obeyed willingly."[99]

As many things as go through the mind of a groom on his wedding day, Gilbert afterward piped up: "Bob, do you recall the hot afternoon on the slopes before the bastion at Vicksburg?" Reverend Burdette shot back "I was just thinking of it, Lieutenant," adding with a twinkle, "and I was wondering if now you might ever blame me for helping to drag you out of the range of Pemberton's sharpshooters?" Lieutenant Gilbert replied much more seriously: "Indeed no, I never will. I've often wondered why the dear Lord sent you back after me." He answered his own question as he looked about the wedding party: "But this is the 'Why.'"[100]

Epilogue

Word of the Union's repulse at Vicksburg slowly filtered out from the Mississippi Valley, eventually all the way to the capitals at Richmond and Washington. While Lincoln and the Army of the Potomac were on the defensive after the Union's trouncing at Chancellorsville and thus were not exactly bent on devising offensive plans, such was not the case in the Confederate capital at Richmond. Amply aware of the stakes in his native Mississippi Valley, President Jefferson Davis began to question the wisdom of his decision earlier that May to allow the Confederate invasion of the North. Especially with news of the dramatic defeats at Champion Hill and Big Black River Bridge, which arrived in the capital a few days afterward on May 19, Davis began to rethink his strategy. Falling into a major sickness again that precluded work in the office, Davis showed every sign of concern for the west. "No doubt he is also worried at the dark aspects in his own State—Mississippi," War Department clerk John B. Jones reflected.[1]

Jones elaborated on the Vicksburg problem—and the concerns Davis must have felt. "If Vicksburg falls," Jones noted in his diary, "and the Valley be held by the enemy, then the Confederacy will be curtailed of half its dimensions." Losing Vicksburg, he pointedly observed, would be "irremediably disastrous." With additional word of Pemberton falling back into the defenses and being bottled up against the Mississippi River, Jefferson Davis even more began to revisit the idea of turning Lee loose to gamble on the planned raid into Pennsylvania. Should the Confederacy's most potent army be gambled at a moment when so much potentially irreparable damage had been wrought elsewhere? Should troops be sent west instead?[2]

Even though heartening news soon arrived from Vicksburg, it did not totally assuage Davis's fears. On May 20, Pemberton informed Joseph E. Johnston of the Confederates' successful repulse of the Federals on May 19: "Enemy assaulted intrenchments yesterday on center and left; were repulsed with heavy loss; our loss small. Enemy's force at least 60,000." More news followed, especially after the Union's failed assault of May 22, but it took a while for that news to reach Johnston and then Richmond. In fact, the latest developments did not arrive at the Confederate capital until May 25. Yet even with cheering news that the lines outside Vicksburg were holding, Davis— spurred again by Postmaster General John H. Reagan—was at least open to changing the Confederacy's entire plan.[3]

Davis and his cabinet met "in council nearly all day" on May 26, Jones recorded, and he wondered: "Can they have intelligence from the West, not yet communicated to the public?" Throughout the day, Davis and his cabinet once more toiled over the question of Vicksburg and the wisdom of turning Robert E. Lee loose to invade the North again with his Army of Northern Virginia. Although Davis ultimately agreed to the movement—evidently based on the cheering news of Pemberton turning back the assaults at Vicksburg— the opposite news might have been enough to push Davis to cancel the risky plan.[4]

The failed Union assaults at Vicksburg thus came into play in a major strategic sense on both sides. If the Union's repulse at Vicksburg did not change the dynamics tactically or even operationally, the strategic implications remained enormous. The failure certainly affected Ulysses Grant, who harbored hopes of a quick end to the campaign in Mississippi. But now he had to plan for a lengthy siege. He wrote as much to his father shortly after the failed assaults:

> I do not look upon the fall of Vicksburg as in the least doubtful. If however I could have carried the place on the 22d of last month I could by this time have made a campaign that would have made the state of Mississippi almost safe for a solitary horseman to ride over. As it is the enemy have a large Army in it and the season has so far advanced that water will be difficult to find for an Army marching besides the dust and heat that must be encountered. The fall of Vicksburg now will only result in the opening of the Miss, river and demoralization of the enemy. I intended more from it. I did my best however and looking back can see no blunder committed.[5]

As for Jefferson Davis, news of the Union's repulse, and Pemberton's apparent ability to hold the defensive lines, changed minds yet again. Upon receiving the damaging news of Confederate defeats at Champion Hill and Big Black River Bridge in Mississippi a few days earlier, Davis had been at least open to canceling Lee's planned invasion, which in fact did not launch until June 3 and then begin in earnest until June 10. There was plenty of time to order Lee's army to remain in Virginia, to hold the defensive, and to keep intact the one Confederate force that had proved so capable of winning victories amid the gloom. Had those reports out of Vicksburg been followed up with word that the Federals had indeed captured the key to the Mississippi, one wonders if Davis would have been compelled to order Lee to stay home and defend Richmond—and the fate of the Confederacy—indefinitely. After all, following the Confederacy's disastrous defeat at Gettysburg in the summer of 1863, it did exactly that. Flying off into the North was an existential gamble to say the least.[6]

If Grant had succeeded in capturing Vicksburg on May 19 or 22, would that have altered the analysis to the point that Davis, who was already questioning the wisdom of an invasion of the North, would have changed his course? Would the Federal capture of Vicksburg have forced the Confederacy to hunker down and hold the defensive? Would the removal of the reason for the diversionary raid into the North have halted that diversion?

Put simply, had Grant captured Vicksburg on May 22, would there have even been a battle at Gettysburg?

Appendix A

Union Order of Battle at Vicksburg, May 17–22, 1863

Union Forces

ARMY OF THE TENNESSEE
  Major General Ulysses S. Grant
Escort
    4th Illinois Cavalry, Company A

Engineers
    1st Battalion Engineer Regiment of the West

XIII ARMY CORPS
  Major General John A. McClernand
Escort
    3rd Illinois Cavalry, Company L

Pioneers
    Kentucky Infantry (Independent Company)

Ninth Division
  Brigadier General Peter J. Osterhaus

First Brigade
  Brigadier General Albert L. Lee (w)
  Colonel James Keigwin
    118th Illinois
    49th Indiana
    69th Indiana

7th Kentucky
120th Ohio

Second Brigade
  Colonel Daniel W. Lindsey
    54th Indiana
    22nd Kentucky
    16th Ohio
    42nd Ohio
    114th Ohio

Cavalry
    2nd Illinois (five companies)
    3rd Illinois (three companies)
    6th Missouri (seven companies)

Artillery
  Captain Jacob T. Foster
    7th Battery Michigan Light Artillery
    1st Battery Wisconsin Light Artillery

Tenth Division
  Brigadier General Andrew J. Smith
Escort
    4th Indiana Cavalry, Company C

First Brigade
  Brigadier General Stephen G. Burbridge
    16th Indiana
    60th Indiana
    67th Indiana
    83rd Ohio
    96th Ohio
    23rd Wisconsin

Second Brigade
  Colonel William J. Landram
    77th Illinois
    97th Illinois

130th Illinois
19th Kentucky
48th Ohio

Artillery
    Chicago Mercantile Battery
    17th Battery Ohio Light Artillery

Twelfth Division
  Brigadier General Alvin P. Hovey
Escort
    1st Indiana Cavalry, Company C

First Brigade
  Brigadier General William T. Spiceley
    11th Indiana
    24th Indiana
    34th Indiana
    46th Indiana
    29th Wisconsin

Artillery
    1st Missouri Light Artillery, Battery A
    2nd Battery Ohio Light Artillery
    16th Battery Ohio Light Artillery

Fourteenth Division
  Brigadier General Eugene A. Carr
Escort
    3rd Illinois Cavalry, Company G

First Brigade
  Brigadier General William P. Benton
    33rd Illinois
    99th Illinois
    8th Indiana
    18th Indiana

Second Brigade
  Brigadier General Michael K. Lawler
    21st Iowa
    22nd Iowa
    11th Wisconsin

Artillery
  2nd Illinois Light Artillery, Battery A
  1st Battery Indiana Light Artillery

XV ARMY CORPS
  Major General William T. Sherman

First Division
  Major General Frederick Steele

First Brigade
  Colonel Francis H. Manter
    13th Illinois
    27th Missouri
    29th Missouri
    30th Missouri
    31st Missouri
    32nd Missouri

Second Brigade
  Colonel Charles R. Woods
    25th Iowa
    31st Iowa
    3rd Missouri
    12th Missouri
    17th Missouri
    76th Ohio

Third Brigade
  Brigadier General John M. Thayer
    4th Iowa
    9th Iowa
    26th Iowa
    30th Iowa

Artillery
    1st Battery Iowa Light Artillery
    2nd Missouri Light Artillery, Battery F
    4th Battery Ohio Light Artillery

Cavalry
    Kane Country (Illinois) Independent Company
    3rd Illinois, Company D

Second Division
    Major General Francis P. Blair

First Brigade
    Colonel Giles A. Smith
        113th Illinois
        116th Illinois
        6th Missouri
        8th Missouri
        13th United States 1st Battalion

Second Brigade
    Colonel Thomas Kilby Smith
        55th Illinois
        127th Illinois
        83rd Indiana
        54th Ohio
        57th Ohio

Third Brigade
    Brigadier General Hugh Ewing
        30th Ohio
        37th Ohio
        47th Ohio
        4th West Virginia

Artillery
    1st Illinois Light Artillery, Battery A
    1st Illinois Light Artillery, Battery B
    1st Illinois Light Artillery, Battery H
    8th Battery Ohio Light Artillery

Cavalry
    Thielemann's (Illinois) Battalion, Companies A and B
    10th Missouri, Company C

Third Division
    Brigadier General James M. Tuttle

First Brigade
    Brigadier General Ralph P. Buckland
        114th Illinois
        93rd Indiana
        72nd Ohio
        95th Ohio

Second Brigade
    Brigadier General Joseph A. Mower
        47th Illinois
        5th Minnesota
        11th Missouri
        8th Wisconsin

Third Brigade
    Brigadier General Charles L. Matthies
        8th Iowa
        12th Iowa
        35th Iowa

Artillery
    Captain Nelson T. Spoor
        1st Illinois Light Artillery, Battery E
        2nd Battery Iowa Light Artillery

Unattached Cavalry
    4th Iowa

XVII ARMY CORPS
    Major General James B. McPherson
Escort
    4th Company Ohio Cavalry, Captain John S. Foster

Third Division
  Major General John A. Logan
Escort
    2nd Illinois Cavalry, Company A

First Brigade
  Brigadier General John E. Smith
    20th Illinois
    31st Illinois
    45th Illinois
    124th Illinois
    23rd Indiana

Second Brigade
  Brigadier General Mortimer D. Leggett
    30th Illinois
    20th Ohio
    68th Ohio
    78th Ohio

Third Brigade
  Brigadier General John D. Stevenson
    8th Illinois
    17th Illinois
    81st Illinois
    7th Missouri
    32nd Ohio

Artillery
  Major Charles J. Stolbrand
    1st Illinois Light Artillery, Battery D
    2nd Illinois Light Artillery, Battery G
    2nd Illinois Light Artillery, Battery L
    8th Battery Michigan Light Artillery
    3rd Battery Ohio Light Artillery

Sixth Division
  Brigadier General John McArthur
Escort
    11th Illinois Cavalry, Company G

Second Brigade
  Brigadier General Thomas E. G. Ransom
    11th Illinois
    72nd Illinois
    95th Illinois
    14th Wisconsin
    17th Wisconsin

Third Brigade
  Colonel William Hall
    11th Iowa
    13th Iowa
    15th Iowa
    16th Iowa
    63rd Illinois
    87th Illinois

Artillery
  Major Thomas D. Maurice
    2nd Illinois Light Artillery, Battery F
    1st Battery Minnesota Light Artillery
    1st Missouri Light Artillery, Battery C
    10th Battery Ohio Light Artillery

Seventh Division
  Brigadier General Isaac F. Quinby
Escort
    4th Missouri Cavalry, Company F. Lieutenant Alexander Mueller

First Brigade
  Colonel John B. Sanborn
    48th Indiana
    59th Indiana
    4th Minnesota
    18th Wisconsin

Second Brigade
  Colonel Samuel A. Holmes
    56th Illinois
    17th Iowa

10th Missouri
24th Missouri
80th Ohio

Third Brigade
  Colonel George B. Boomer (k)
  Colonel Holden Putman
    93rd Illinois
    5th Iowa
    10th Iowa
    26th Missouri

Artillery
  Captain Frank C. Sands
  Captain Henry Dillon
    1st Missouri Light Artillery, Battery M
    11th Battery Ohio Light Artillery
    6th Battery Wisconsin Light Artillery
    12th Battery Wisconsin Light Artillery

Appendix B

CONFEDERATE ORDER OF BATTLE AT VICKSBURG, MAY 17–22, 1863

Confederate Forces

ARMY OF VICKSBURG
Lieutenant General John C. Pemberton

STEVENSON'S DIVISION
Major General Carter L. Stevenson

First Brigade
Brigadier General Seth M. Barton
40th Georgia
41st Georgia
42nd Georgia
43rd Georgia
52nd Georgia
Hudson's (Mississippi) Battery
Pointe Coupee (Louisiana) Artillery, Company A (section)
Pointe Coupee (Louisiana) Artillery, Company C

Second Brigade
Brigadier General Alfred Cumming
34th Georgia
36th Georgia
39th Georgia
56th Georgia
57th Georgia
Cherokee (Georgia) Artillery

Third Brigade
  Brigadier General Stephen D. Lee
    20th Alabama
    23rd Alabama
    30th Alabama
    31st Alabama
    46th Alabama
    Waddell's (Alabama) Battery

Fourth Brigade
  Colonel Alexander W. Reynolds
    3rd Tennessee (Provisional Army)
    39th Tennessee
    43rd Tennessee
    59th Tennessee
    3rd Maryland Battery

Attached
    Waul's Texas Legion
    1st Tennessee Cavalry (Carter's)
    Botetourt (Virginia) Artillery
    Signal Corps

FORNEY'S DIVISION
  Major General John H. Forney

Hébert's Brigade
  Brigadier General Louis Hébert
    3rd Louisiana
    21st Louisiana
    36th Mississippi
    37th Mississippi
    38th Mississippi
    43rd Mississippi
    7th Mississippi Battalion
    2nd Alabama Artillery Battalion, Company C
    Appeal (Arkansas) Battery

Moore's Brigade
  Brigadier General John C. Moore
    37th Alabama
    40th Alabama
    42nd Alabama
    35th Mississippi
    40th Mississippi
    2nd Texas
    Sengstak's (Alabama) Battery
    Pointe Coupe (Louisiana) Artillery, Company B

SMITH'S DIVISION
  Major General Martin L. Smith

Baldwin's Brigade
  Brigadier General William E. Baldwin (w)
  Colonel Allen Thomas
    17th Louisiana
    31st Louisiana
    4th Mississippi
    46th Mississippi
    Tobin's (Tennessee) Battery

Shoup's Brigade
  Brigadier General Francis A. Shoup
    26th Louisiana
    27th Louisiana
    28th [29th] Louisiana
    McNally's Battery

Mississippi State Troops
  Brigadier General Jeptha V. Harris
    5th Regiment
    3rd Battalion

Attached
    14th Mississippi Light Artillery Battery
    Mississippi Partisan Rangers
    Signal Corps

BOWEN'S DIVISION
Major General John S. Bowen

First Brigade
Colonel Francis M. Cockrell
1st Missouri
2nd Missouri
3rd Missouri
5th Missouri
6th Missouri
Guibor's (Missouri) Battery
Landis's (Missouri) Battery
Wade's (Missouri) Battery

Second Brigade
Brigadier General Martin E. Green
19th Arkansas
20th Arkansas
1st Arkansas Cavalry Battalion
12th Arkansas Battalion (Sharpshooters)
1st Missouri Cavalry
3rd Missouri Cavalry
3rd Missouri Battery
Lowe's (Missouri) Battery

RIVER BATTERIES
Colonel Edward Higgins
1st Louisiana Artillery
8th Louisiana Heavy Artillery Battalion
22nd Louisiana
1st Tennessee Heavy Artillery
Caruthers's (Tennessee) Battery
Johnston's (Tennessee) Battery
Lynch's (Tennessee) Battery
Vaiden (Mississippi) Battery

MISCELLANEOUS
54th Alabama (detachment)
City Guards
Signal Corps

NOTES

ABBREVIATIONS USED IN NOTES

AC	Augustana College, Rock Island, Illinois
ADAH	Alabama Department of Archives and History, Montgomery
AHC	Atlanta History Center, Atlanta, Georgia
ALPL	Abraham Lincoln Presidential Library, Springfield, Illinois
AU	Auburn University, Auburn, Alabama
BC	Bilby Collection
CHM	Chicago History Museum
CWD	Civil War Documents
CWTI	Civil War Times Illustrated Collection
DU	Duke University, Durham, North Carolina
EU	Emory University, Atlanta, Georgia
FHS	Filson Historical Society, Louisville, Kentucky
HCWRT	Harrisburg Civil War Round Table Collection
HL	Huntington Library, San Marino, California
IHS	Indiana Historical Society, Indianapolis
ISL	Indiana State Library, Indianapolis
ISU	Iowa State University, Ames
IU	Indiana University, Bloomington
KCPL	Kansas City Public Library, Kansas City, Missouri
LC	Library of Congress
LMU	Loyola Marymount University, Los Angeles
LOC	Library of Congress, Washington, DC
LSU	Louisiana State University, Baton Rouge
MDAH	Mississippi Department of Archives and History, Jackson
MHS	Missouri Historical Society, St. Louis
NC	Navarro College, Corsicana, Texas
NL	Newberry Library, Chicago
OCM	Old Courthouse Museum, Vicksburg, Mississippi
OHS	Ohio Historical Society, Columbus

OR	*War of the Rebellion: A Compilation of the Official Records of the Union and Confederate Armies* (Washington, DC: US Government Printing Office, 1880–1901)
ORN	*The Official Records of the Union and Confederate Navies in the War of the Rebellion*, 30 vols. (Washington, DC: Government Printing Office, 1894–1922)
PUSG	John Y. Simon and John F. Marszalek, eds., *The Papers of Ulysses S. Grant*. 32 vols. to date (Carbondale: Southern Illinois University Press, 1967–present)
SHSI	State Historical Society of Iowa, Iowa City
SHSM	State Historical Society of Missouri—St. Louis
SHSMC	State Historical Society of Missouri—Columbia
SIU	Southern Illinois University, Carbondale
SNMP	Shiloh National Military Park Regimental Files, Shiloh, Tennessee
SU	Stanford University, Stanford, California
TSLA	Tennessee State Library and Archives, Nashville
UA	University of Alabama, Tuscaloosa
UGA	University of Georgia, Athens
UI	University of Illinois, Urbana
UIA	University of Iowa, Iowa City
UMB	University of Michigan Bentley Library, Ann Arbor
UMC	University of Michigan Clements Library, Ann Arbor
UNC	University of North Carolina, Chapel Hill
UNT	University of North Texas, Denton
USAHEC	United States Army Historical Education Center, Carlisle, Pennsylvania
USGPL	Ulysses S. Grant Presidential Library, Starkville, Mississippi
UTA	University of Texas, Austin
UTK	University of Tennessee, Knoxville
UVA	University of Virginia, Charlottesville
UW	University of Washington, Seattle
VICK	Vicksburg National Military Park

Preface

1. E. B. Long, *The Civil War Day by Day: An Almanac, 1861–1865* (New York: Doubleday, 1971), 351–354; J. B. Jones, *A Rebel War Clerk's Diary: At the Confederate States Capital, Volume 1: April 1861–July 1863*, 2 vols., James I. Robertson, Jr., ed. (Lawrence: University Press of Kansas, 2015), 1:283, 285; Emory M. Thomas, *Robert E. Lee: A Biography* (New York: W. W. Norton & Company, 1995), 287.
2. Timothy B. Smith, *The Decision Was Always My Own: Ulysses S. Grant and the Vicksburg Campaign* (Carbondale: Southern Illinois University Press, 2018), 101–136.
3. C. S. Lewis, *The Screwtape Letters & Screwtape Proposes a Toast* (New York:

Macmillan, 1961), x; William C. Davis, *Jefferson Davis: The Man and His Hour: A Biography* (New York: HarperCollins, 1991), 504.
4. Jones, *A Rebel War Clerk's Diary*, 1:287.
5. *War of the Rebellion: A Compilation of the Official Records of the Union and Confederate Armies* (Washington, DC: US Government Printing Office, 1880–1901), 27(1):790, hereafter cited as *OR*; Jones, *A Rebel War Clerk's Diary*, 1:288; Steven E. Woodworth, *Jefferson Davis and His Generals: The Failure of Confederate Command in the West* (Lawrence: University Press of Kansas, 1990), 212; Thomas, *Robert E. Lee*, 288.
6. Jones, *A Rebel War Clerk's Diary*, 1:288–289; Noah Andre Trudeau, *Gettysburg: A Testing of Courage* (New York: HarperCollins, 2002), 5; Woodworth, *Jefferson Davis and His Generals*, 212–213, 230.
7. John H. Reagan, *Memoirs, With Special Reference to Secession and the Civil War*, Walter Flavius McCaleb, ed. (New York: Neale Publishing Company, 1906), 151–152; Jones, *A Rebel War Clerk's Diary*, 1:289.
8. *OR*, 25(2):790; Woodworth, *Jefferson Davis and His Generals*, 212–213.
9. Smith, *The Decision Was Always My Own*, 149–165.
10. James M. McPherson, *Battle Cry of Freedom: The Civil War Era* (New York: Oxford University Press, 1988), 631–633; Ronald C. White, *American Ulysses: A Life of Ulysses S. Grant* (New York: Random House, 2016), 279–282; Ron Chernow, *Grant* (New York: Penguin Press, 2017), 269–270; Herman Hattaway and Archer Jones, *How the North Won: A Military History of the Civil War* (Urbana: University of Illinois Press, 1983), 395.

Prologue

1. Bruce Catton, *U. S. Grant and the American Military Tradition* (Boston: Little, Brown, 1954), 104.
2. Arrell M. Gibson, "The Indians of Mississippi," in *A History of Mississippi*, Richard A. McLemore, ed., 2 vols. (Hattiesburg: University & College Press of Mississippi, 1973), 1:69–89; Dennis J. Mitchell, *Mississippi: A New History* (Jackson: University Press of Mississippi, 2014), 82.
3. Dunbar Rowland, *Mississippi; Comprising Sketches of Counties, Towns, Events, Institutions and Persons, Arranged in Cyclopedic Form*, 3 vols. (Atlanta: Southern Historical Printing Association, 1907), 2:858.
4. Rowland, *Mississippi*, 2:858.
5. Joseph C. G. Kennedy, *Population of the United States in 1860: Compiled From the Original Returns of the Eighth Census Under the Direction of the Secretary of the Interior* (Washington, DC: Government Printing Office, 1864), 271; Rowland, *Mississippi*, 2:858–859.
6. Rowland, *Mississippi*, 2:859–860; Richard Carwardine, *Lincoln: A Life of Purpose and Power* (New York: Knopf, 2003), 5; Richard Campanella, *Lincoln in New*

Orleans: The 1828–1831 Flatboat Voyages and Their Place in History (Lafayette: University of Louisiana at Lafayette Press, 2010).

7. Timothy B. Smith, *The Mississippi Secession Convention: Delegates and Deliberations in Politics and War, 1861–1865* (Jackson: University Press of Mississippi, 2014), 63–80; Dunbar Rowland and H. Grady Howell, Jr., *Military History of Mississippi: 1803–1898, Including a Listing of All Known Mississippi Confederate Military Units* (Madison, MS: Chickasaw Bayou Press, 2003), 662.
8. For Vicksburg's history, see Michael B. Ballard, *Vicksburg: The Campaign That Opened the Mississippi* (Chapel Hill: University of North Carolina Press, 2004), 1–8.
9. Arthell Kelley, "The Geography," in *A History of Mississippi*, Richard A. McLemore, ed., 2 vols. (Hattiesburg: University & College Press of Mississippi, 1973), 1:3–23.
10. Warren E. Grabau, *Ninety-Eight Days: A Geographer's View of the Vicksburg Campaign* (Knoxville: University of Tennessee Press, 2000), 14–28.
11. For an overview of this period, see Gordon S. Wood, *Empire of Liberty: A History of the Early Republic, 1789–1815* (New York: Oxford University Press, 2009).
12. McPherson, *Battle Cry of Freedom*, 234–275.
13. *OR*, 1, 10(2):340; *Journal of the State Convention and Ordinances and Resolutions Adopted in January, 1861, With an Appendix* (Jackson: E. Barksdale, 1861), 24–25; *Official Journal of the Proceedings of the Convention of the State of Louisiana* (New Orleans: J. O. Nixon, 1861), 235; Alex W. Randall to John J. Pettus, January 21, 1861, "Joint Resolutions of the General Assembly of the State of Ohio, January 12, 1861," Joint Resolutions on the State of the Union, February 2, 1861, Oliver P. Morton to John J. Pettus, unreadable date, and Unknown to John J. Pettus, February 2, 1861, all in Mississippi Governor, John J. Pettus, Correspondence and Papers, 1859–1863, Series 757, MDAH.
14. Ballard, *Vicksburg*, 9; Untitled Articles, Vicksburg *Evening Citizen*, January 14, 1861; "From the Seat of War," Vicksburg *Evening Citizen*, January 14, 1861. For Pettus, see Robert W. Dubay, *John Jones Pettus, Mississippi Fire-eater: His Life and Times, 1813–1867* (Jackson: University Press of Mississippi, 1975).
15. *OR*, 1, 10(2):340; *OR*, 1, 31(3):459.

Chapter 1. "I Will Fortify Vicksburg and Prevent Its Capture"

1. David Dixon Porter, *Incidents and Anecdotes of the Civil War* (New York: D. Appleton and Company, 1885), 95; Ballard, *Vicksburg*, 24.
2. Porter, *Incidents and Anecdotes of the Civil War*, 95–96.
3. Porter, 95–96.
4. Porter, 96.
5. John Y. Simon and John F. Marszalek, eds., *The Papers of Ulysses S. Grant*. 32 vols. to date (Carbondale: Southern Illinois University Press, 1967–present), 7:479–480, hereafter cited as *PUSG*.

6. Simon and Marszalek, eds., *PUSG*, 7:479–480; Daniel Roberts to mother and sister, July 6, 1863, Daniel Roberts Correspondence, ISL.
7. For Vicksburg's geography, see Grabau, *Ninety-Eight Days*, 39–50.
8. For the Delta's history, see James C. Cobb, *The Most Southern Place on Earth: The Mississippi Delta and the Roots of Regional Identity* (New York: Oxford University Press, 1994).
9. Kelley, "The Geography," 1:8–9; *OR*, 24(3):168; *OR*, 24(1):24; Simon and Marszalek, eds., *PUSG*, 7:489; Edwin C. Bearss, *The Vicksburg Campaign*, 3 vols. (Dayton: Morningside, 1985), 1:152–154.
10. Grabau, *Ninety-Eight Days*, 51–56.
11. *OR*, 24(1):83; Ulysses S. Grant, *Personal Memoirs of U. S. Grant*, 2 vols. (New York: Charles L. Webster & Co., 1892), 1:493, 495. For the best edited version of Grant's memoirs, see John F. Marszalek, David F. Nolen, and Louie P. Gallo, *The Personal Memoirs of Ulysses S. Grant: The Complete Annotated Edition* (Cambridge: Harvard University Press, 2017).
12. For the railroads, see Robert C. Black III, *The Railroads of the Confederacy* (Chapel Hill: University of North Carolina Press, 1952).
13. For naval operations, see Gary D. Joiner, *Mr. Lincoln's Brown Water Navy: The Mississippi Squadron* (New York: Rowman & Littlefield, 2007).
14. For the Pacific campaigns, see Ian W. Toll, *The Conquering Tide: War in the Pacific Islands, 1942–1944* (New York: W. W. Norton & Company, 2015).
15. Simon and Marszalek, eds., *PUSG*, 7:463, 480.
16. McPherson, *Battle Cry of Freedom*, 333–336.
17. Timothy B. Smith, *Mississippi in the Civil War: The Home Front* (Mississippi Heritage Series) (Jackson: University Press of Mississippi, 2010), 11–26.
18. Horace N. Fisher, "A Memory of Shiloh," undated, Horace N. Fisher File, SNMP. For early Tennessee operations, see Timothy B. Smith, *Grant Invades Tennessee: The 1862 Battles for Forts Henry and Donelson* (Lawrence: University Press of Kansas, 2016).
19. William Preston Johnston, *The Life of Gen. Albert Sidney Johnston: His Service in the Armies of the United States, The Republic of Texas, and the Confederate States* (New York: D. Appleton and Co., 1879), 569. For operations around Shiloh and Corinth, see Timothy B. Smith, *Shiloh: Conquer or Perish* (Lawrence: University Press of Kansas, 2014), and Timothy B. Smith, *Corinth 1862: Siege, Battle, Occupation* (Lawrence: University Press of Kansas, 2012). For Halleck, see John F. Marszalek, *Commander of All Lincoln's Armies: A Life of General Henry W. Halleck* (Cambridge, MA: Harvard University Press, 2004).
20. *The Official Records of the Union and Confederate Navies in the War of the Rebellion*, 30 vols. (Washington, DC: Government Printing Office, 1894–1922), 1, 18:492, hereafter cited as *ORN*.
21. For the Battle of New Orleans, see Robert V. Remini, *The Battle of New Orleans: Andrew Jackson and America's First Military Victory* (New York: Viking, 1999), and

Donald R. Hickey, *Glorious Victory: Andrew Jackson and the Battle of New Orleans* (Baltimore: Johns Hopkins University Press, 2015).
22. *ORN*, 18:152; *OR*, 6:504; Chester G. Hearn, *The Capture of New Orleans 1862* (Baton Rouge: Louisiana State University Press, 1995), 209–236.
23. *OR*, 6:513, 515–516; Hearn, *The Capture of New Orleans 1862*, 237–248; Charles P. Roland, *Albert Sidney Johnston: Soldier of Three Republics* (Austin: University of Texas Press, 1964), 352–353.
24. Timothy B. Smith, "A Frolic up the Tennessee," *America's Civil War* (March 2017): 44–49.
25. *OR*, 15:810–811; S. H. Lockett, "The Defense of Vicksburg," in *Battles and Leaders of the Civil War*, 4 vols. (New York: Century Company, 1884–1887), 3:482.
26. *OR*, 15:848–853.
27. *OR*, 6:783–784.
28. *OR*, 6:784.
29. *OR*, 6:783.
30. *OR*, 6:567, 877, 885.
31. *OR*, 6:624, 651.
32. *OR*, 6:515, 567, 570, 884; *OR*, 10(2):481.
33. *OR*, 15:810–811.
34. *OR*, 10(2):430; *OR*, 15:811.
35. *OR*, 10(2):430–431; *OR*, 15:811.
36. *OR*, 15:6–7, 811; Lockett, "The Defense of Vicksburg," 482.
37. *OR*, 15:6.
38. *ORN*, 18:159.
39. *ORN*, 1, 18:492, 610; *OR*, 15:13. For this first action around Vicksburg, see Edwin C. Bearss, *Rebel Victory at Vicksburg* (Vicksburg, MS: Vicksburg Centennial Commission, 1963).
40. Johnse to sister, July 7, 1862, 27th Louisiana File, VICK; Lockett, "The Defense of Vicksburg," 483.
41. *ORN*, 18:675, 682; *OR*, 15:9.
42. *OR*, 15:9.
43. *OR*, 15:11; Lockett, "The Defense of Vicksburg," 482; Bearss, *The Vicksburg Campaign*, 3:739; Samuel H. Lockett to wife, November 25, 1862, Samuel H. Lockett Papers, UNC.
44. *OR*, 15:849–853; Lockett, "The Defense of Vicksburg," 483–484; Samuel H. Lockett to wife, August 4, 1862, Samuel H. Lockett Papers, UNC.
45. *OR*, 15:920.
46. *OR*, 15:848, 852; Lockett, "The Defense of Vicksburg," 484; Samuel H. Lockett to wife, September 22, 1862, Samuel H. Lockett Papers, UNC.
47. Larry J. Daniel and Lynn N. Bock, *Island No. 10: Struggle for the Mississippi Valley* (Tuscaloosa: University of Alabama Press, 1996); Smith, *Grant Invades Tennessee*.
48. Lockett, "The Defense of Vicksburg," 484; John Kinsel to friend, June 28, 1863, Journals/Letters/Diaries, VICK; Allen C. Richard, Jr., and Mary Margaret Higginbotham

Richard, *The Defense of Vicksburg: A Louisiana Chronicle* (College Station, TX: Texas A&M University Press, 2004), 83.
49. Samuel H. Lockett to wife, September 17, 1862, Samuel H. Lockett Papers, UNC.
50. *OR*, 24(2):330; Lockett, "The Defense of Vicksburg," 484; *OR*, 24(1):273; Map of the Siege of Vicksburg, August 20, 1863, War of the Rebellion Collection, Baylor University.
51. *OR*, 24(1):273; *OR*, 24(2):330; Lockett, "The Defense of Vicksburg," 484.
52. *In Memoriam: Charles Ewing* (Philadelphia: J. B. Lippincott, 1888), 50–51. For topography and geography, as well as the siege lines, see George B. Davis, Leslie J. Perry, and Joseph W. Kirkley, *Atlas to Accompany the Official Records of the Union and Confederate Armies* (Washington, DC: Government Printing Office, 1891–1895), plates 36 and 37; Grabau, *Ninety-Eight Days*, map 8; Bearss, *The Vicksburg Campaign*, 3:738–742.
53. Davis, Perry, and Kirkley, *Atlas to Accompany the Official Records*, plates 36 and 37; Grabau, *Ninety-Eight Days*, 350.
54. Bearss, *The Vicksburg Campaign*, 3:740.
55. Davis, Perry, and Kirkley, *Atlas to Accompany the Official Records*, plates 36 and 37.
56. Davis, Perry, and Kirkley, *Atlas to Accompany the Official Records*, plates 36 and 37; S. N. Pickens to W. T. Rigby, April 16, 1902, 27th Louisiana File, VICK.
57. Davis, Perry, and Kirkley, *Atlas to Accompany the Official Records*, plates 36 and 37.
58. Bearss, *The Vicksburg Campaign*, 3:741.
59. Davis, Perry, and Kirkley, *Atlas to Accompany the Official Records*, plates 36 and 37; T. B. Marshall, *History of the Eighty-third Ohio Volunteer Infantry, The Greyhound Regiment* (Cincinnati: n.p., 1912), 84.
60. Davis, Perry, and Kirkley, *Atlas to Accompany the Official Records*, plates 36 and 37.
61. Davis, Perry, and Kirkley, plates 36 and 37.
62. Davis, Perry, and Kirkley, plates 36 and 37.
63. Lydia Minturn Post, ed., *Soldiers' Letters. From Camp, Battle-field and Prison* (New York: Bunce and Huntington, Publishers, 1865), 222; Richard and Richard, *The Defense of Vicksburg*, 91; Bearss, *The Vicksburg Campaign*, 3:739–742; *OR*, 24(2):169–170; Joel Strong Reminiscences, 1910, MHS, 14.
64. William P. Chambers, "My Journal," in *Publications of the Mississippi Historical Society, Centenary Series*, 5 vols. (Jackson, MS: Mississippi Historical Society, 1925), 5:252, Richard and Richard, *The Defense of Vicksburg*, 90–91.
65. George H. Chatfield to mother, April 15, 1863, George H. Chatfield Papers, CWD, USAHEC; H. T. Morgan to Ellen, April 4, 1863, Henry T. Morgan Papers, CWD, USAHEC.

Chapter 2. "The Accomplishment of This One Object"

1. *OR*, 24(1):63.
2. Timothy B. Smith, "'I am Thinking Seriously of Going Home': Mississippi's Role

in the Most Important Decision of Ulysses S. Grant's Life," *Journal of Mississippi History* 80, no. 1 and 2 (Spring/Summer 2018): 21–34.
3. *OR*, 17(2):101–102; Grant, *Personal Memoirs*, 1:393.
4. *OR*, 17(2):294, 296; Grant, *Personal Memoirs*, 1:421.
5. Smith, *The Decision Was Always My Own*, 6–79.
6. Bearss, *The Vicksburg Campaign*, 1:21–348.
7. *OR*, 17(2):315; *OR*, 17(1):467; Bearss, *The Vicksburg Campaign*, 1:21–112.
8. Grant, *Personal Memoirs*, 1:424, 435; Bearss, *The Vicksburg Campaign*, 1:231–348.
9. *OR*, 17(1):613; William T. Sherman, *Memoirs of General William T. Sherman: Written by Himself*, 2 vols. (New York: D. Appleton and Co., 1875), 1:295; Bearss, *The Vicksburg Campaign*, 1:113–230.
10. *OR*, 24(3):9, 12; *OR*, 24(1):10; Grant, *Personal Memoirs*, 1:446.
11. *OR*, 24(1):10; *OR*, 24(3):6; *OR*, 52(1):337.
12. *OR*, 24(3):9, 12, 38, 65, 126; *OR*, 24(1):10, 44; Simon and Marszalek, eds., *PUSG*, 7:311, 366, 383–384; Grant, *Personal Memoirs*, 1:446.
13. *OR*, 24(3):17.
14. *OR*, 24(3):18, 32.
15. *OR*, 24(3):33, 38, 131; Grant, *Personal Memoirs*, 1:449.
16. *OR*, 24(3):6; *OR*, 24(1):14, 45; Simon and Marszalek, eds., *PUSG*, 7:409, 463.
17. *OR*, 24(3):126. For the Yazoo Pass operation, see Timothy B. Smith, "Victory at Any Cost: The Yazoo Pass Expedition," *Journal of Mississippi History* 67, no. 2 (Summer 2007): 147–166.
18. *OR*, 24(3):112, 119; *OR*, 24(1):21; Grant, *Personal Memoirs*, 1:452.
19. *OR*, 24(3):112–113, 126; Simon and Marszalek, eds., *PUSG*, 7:423; Grant, *Personal Memoirs*, 1:453.
20. *OR*, 24(3):168; *OR*, 24(1):24; Simon and Marszalek, eds., *PUSG*, 7:489; *PUSG*, 8:110.
21. *OR*, 24(1):70; Simon and Marszalek, eds., *PUSG*, 7:471; Grant, *Personal Memoirs*, 1:460–461; Adam Badeau, *Military History of Ulysses S. Grant, From April, 1861, to April, 1865*, 2 vols. (New York: D. Appleton & Co., 1881), 1:182; Bruce Catton, *Grant Moves South* (Boston: Little, Brown, 1960), 407.
22. A. B. Balch Statement, undated, Joseph Forrest Papers, ALPL; James McLaughlin to father, May 11, 1863, James McLaughlin Papers, ISL; Catton, *U. S. Grant and the American Military Tradition*, 98.
23. Abraham Lincoln: "Proclamation 97—Appointing a Day of National Humiliation, Fasting, and Prayer," March 30, 1863. Online by Gerhard Peters and John T. Woolley, *The American Presidency Project*, www.presidency.ucsb.edu/documents/proclamation-97-appointing-day-national-humiliation-fasting-and-prayer; Grabau, *Ninety-Eight Days*, 143–149.
24. Timothy B. Smith, *The Real Horse Soldiers: Benjamin Grierson's Epic 1863 Civil War Raid through Mississippi* (New York: Savas Beatie, 2018), 300–301.
25. *OR*, 24(1):32–33, 48; Kenneth P. Williams, *Grant Rises in the West: From Iuka to Vicksburg, 1862–1863* (Lincoln: University of Nebraska Press, 1997), 344; Simon

and Marszalek, eds., *PUSG*, 7:491; Grant, *Personal Memoirs*, 1:480–481; George R. Buck to sister, June 9, 1863, OCM.
26. *OR*, 24(1):32.
27. Samuel Styre to parents, May 28, 1863, Samuel Styre Papers, DU.
28. Simon and Marszalek, eds., *PUSG*, 8:132.
29. *OR*, 24(3):288; Grant, *Personal Memoirs*, 1:492; John Russell Young, *Around the World With General Grant: A Narrative of the Visit of General U.S. Grant, Ex-President of the United States, to Various Countries in Europe, Asia, and Africa, in 1877, 1878, 1879. To which are Added Certain Conversations with General Grant on Questions Connected with American Politics and History* (New York: American News Company 1879), 2:621.
30. *OR*, 24(1):33, 35.
31. *OR*, 24(1):33, 35; Grant, *Personal Memoirs*, 1:493, 495.
32. *OR*, 24(3):273.
33. *OR*, 24(1):50, 84; *OR*, 24(3):285–286, 290; Grant, *Personal Memoirs*, 1:434–435; Samuel Styre to parents, May 28, 1863, Samuel Styre Papers, DU.
34. *OR*, 24(3):288, 299.
35. *OR*, 24(3):300; *OR*, 24(1):50.
36. *OR*, 24(1):50; *OR*, 24(3):282, 309–311; J. W. Greenman Diary, May 14, 1863, MDAH; Bennett Grigsby to family, May 18, 1863, Grigsby-McDonald Papers, IHS; James B. Owen to wife, May 26, 1863, James B. Owen Letters, TSLA.
37. Simon and Marszalek, eds., *PUSG*, 8:189.
38. *OR*, 24(3):313; Grant, *Personal Memoirs*, 1:503.
39. For background, see Timothy B. Smith, *Champion Hill: Decisive Battle for Vicksburg* (New York: Savas Beatie, 2004).
40. Smith, *Champion Hill*, 212.
41. Simon and Marszalek, eds., *PUSG*, 8:228; Samuel Styre to parents, May 28, 1863, Samuel Styre Papers, DU.
42. Simon and Marszalek, eds., *PUSG*, 8:228.
43. Smith, *The Real Horse Soldiers*, 231–232.
44. Grant, *Personal Memoirs*, 1:526; James Palmer Diary, undated, MDAH, 9. For detail on the battle at Big Black River, see Timothy B. Smith, "'A Victory Could Hardly Have Been More Complete': The Battle of Big Black River Bridge," in *The Vicksburg Campaign: March 29-May 18, 1863*, Steven E. Woodworth and Charles D. Grear, eds. (Carbondale: Southern Illinois University Press, 2013), 173–193; Leo M. Kaiser, ed., "The Civil War Diary of Florison D. Pitts," *Mid-America: An Historical Review* 40, no. 1 (January 1958): 39; James F. Elliott Diary, May 17, 1863, IHS.
45. Samuel Styre to parents, May 28, 1863, Samuel Styre Papers, DU; Richard Puffer to sister, May 28, 1863, William Puffer Papers, CHM; William T. Sherman to wife, May 25, 1863, William T. Sherman Papers, LC.
46. *OR*, 24(3):851–852.
47. *OR*, 24(1):256; Smith, *The Real Horse Soldiers*, 300–301.
48. *OR*, 24(1):257.

49. For Johnston, see Craig L. Symonds, *Joseph E. Johnston: A Civil War Biography* (New York: Norton, 1992).
50. *OR*, 24(3):814; *OR*, 24(3):842. For Davis, see Davis, *Jefferson Davis*.
51. *OR*, 24(1):257; *OR*, 24(3):805, 807.
52. *OR*, 24(1):259; *OR*, 24(3):815, 817.
53. *OR*, 24(1):258; *OR*, 24(3):816, 818, 821, 834, 842, 845, 850.
54. *OR*, 24(1):261; *OR*, 24(3):856, 859.
55. *OR*, 24(1):265.
56. *OR*, 24(1):266–267; John C. Taylor Diary, May 17, 1863, UVA; J. L. Power Diary, May 17, 1863, MDAH; Richard Blackstone Diary, May 17, 1863, LMU; Thomas Hogan to father, July 22, 1863, Thomas Hogan Letters, MHS.
57. James T. Kidd Memoir, undated, OCM, 15; "23rd Alabama Infantry," 23rd Alabama Infantry File, VICK; Emma Balfour Diary, May 21, 1863, MDAH.
58. *OR*, 24(3):851; A. R. Dyson to Louisa, June 8, 1863, Dyson-Bell-Sans Souci Papers, SHSM–St. Louis; Leonard Loomis to Elizabeth, May 24, 1863, Douwe B. Yntema Collection, Archives of Michigan; John Merrilees Diary, May 17, 1863, CHM, copy in OCM.
59. A. C. Lenert Diary, May 17, 1863, UNT, copy in OCM.

CHAPTER 3. "TUMBLING BACK INTO VICKSBURG IN UTTER CONFUSION"

1. Stephen D. Lee, "The Campaign of Vicksburg, Mississippi, in 1863—From April 15 to and Including the Battle of Champion Hills, or Baker's Creek, May 16, 1863," in *Publications of the Mississippi Historical Society*, 14 vols., Franklin L. Riley, ed. (Oxford, MS: Mississippi Historical Society, 1900), 3:51; John Sheriff to parents, May 17, 1863, John Sheriff Papers, ALPL; Osborn H. Oldroyd, *A Soldier's Story of the Siege of Vicksburg From the Diary of Osborn H. Oldroyd* (Springfield: published by the author, 1885), 25, copy in Osborn Oldroyd Diary, May 17, 1863, Journals/Letters/Diaries, VICK; *OR*, 24(1):63; Archer Jones, *Civil War Command and Strategy: The Process of Victory and Defeat* (New York: Free Press, 1992), 161.
2. Grant, *Personal Memoirs*, 1:250.
3. Simon and Marszalek, eds., *PUSG*, 7:331.
4. Grant, *Personal Memoirs*, 1:527–528.
5. *OR*, 24(3):321–322; *OR*, 24(1):54; Ballard, *Vicksburg*, 318; John F. Marszalek, "'A Full Share of All the Credit': Sherman and Grant to the Fall of Vicksburg," in *Grant's Lieutenants: From Cairo to Vicksburg*, Steven E. Woodworth, ed. (Lawrence: University Press of Kansas, 2001), 19; Simon and Marszalek, eds., *PUSG*, 8:231; Grant, *Personal Memoirs*, 1:526; J. H. Wilson, "A Staff Officer's Journal of the Vicksburg Campaign, April 30 to July 4, 1863," *Journal of the Military Service Institution of the United States* 43, no. 154 (July–August 1908): 109.
6. *OR*, 24(3):322; Sherman, *Memoirs*, 1:323–324; J. H. Wilson, "A Staff Officer's Journal of the Vicksburg Campaign, April 30 to July 4, 1863," *Journal of the Military*

Service Institution of the United States 43, no. 155 (September–October 1908): 261; Sylvanus Cadwallader, *Three Years with Grant*, Benjamin P. Thomas, ed. (Lincoln: University of Nebraska Press, 1996), 83.
7. Lockett, "The Defense of Vicksburg," 3:488.
8. J. L. Power Diary, May 17, 1863, MDAH; Lockett, "The Defense of Vicksburg," 3:488; *OR*, 24(1):269.
9. Theodore D. Fisher Diary, May 17 and 18, 1863, Civil War Collection, MHS, copy in 1st Missouri File, VICK.
10. Ballard, *Vicksburg*, 322; J. S. Wheeler Diary, May 19, 1863, OCM; William Brotherton to father, May 18, 1863, William Brotherton Papers, EU; William Roberts Diary, May 17, 1863, ADAH; C. S. O. Rice, "Incidents of the Vicksburg Siege," *Confederate Veteran* 12, no. 2 (February 1904): 77; C. S. O. Rice Memoir, undated, TSLA, 21–25.
11. Lockett, "The Defense of Vicksburg," 3:488.
12. *OR*, 24(1):267–268.
13. *OR*, 24(2):365–366; William Lovelace Foster to wife, June 20, 1863, William L. Foster Letter, UA, copy in Journals/Letters/Diaries, VICK.
14. *OR*, 24(2):343, 366, 397; *OR*, 24(1):268–269; George Powell Clarke, *Reminiscence and Anecdotes of the War for Southern Independence* (n.p.: n.p., n.d.), 99; Elbert Willett Diary, May 17, 1863, ADAH.
15. *OR*, 24(2):366; *OR*, 24(1):270–271; Eli W. Thornhill Memoir, undated, OCM, 9; Clarke, *Reminiscence and Anecdotes*, 99; Leonard B. Plummer, ed., "Excerpts from the Hander Diary," *Journal of Mississippi History* 26, no. 2 (May 1964): 142; Lynch Perry, "Vicksburg. Some New History in the Experience of Gen. Francis A. Shoup," *Confederate Veteran* 2, no. 6 (June 1894): 172 (172–174); W. H. Tunnard, *A Southern Record: The History of the Third Regiment Louisiana Infantry* (Baton Rouge, LA: n.p., 1866), 236; Edwin C. Bearss, ed., *A Southern Record: The History of the Third Regiment Louisiana Infantry* (Dayton, OH: Morningside, 1970), 236; Louis Hébert Autobiography, 1894, UNC, 13.
16. *OR*, 24(2):366; *OR*, 24(1):270–271; Plummer, ed., "Excerpts from the Hander Diary," 142; Claudius W. Sears Diary, May 1863, MDAH; "Facts About Company 'I' of the 46th Mississippi Infantry," 46th Mississippi File, VICK, 66; Elbert Willett Diary, May 17, 1863, ADAH; William Lovelace Foster to wife, June 20, 1863, William L. Foster Letter, UA.
17. *OR*, 24(2):343; Perry, "Vicksburg. Some New History in the Experience of Gen. Francis A. Shoup," 172.
18. Phillip Thomas Tucker, *Westerners in Gray: The Men of and Missions of the Elite Fifth Missouri Infantry Regiment* (Jefferson, NC: McFarland & Company, 1995), 215; Perry, "Vicksburg. Some New History in the Experience of Gen. Francis A. Shoup," 172; James Palmer Diary, undated, MDAH, 10; George Bradley Memoir, 1896, OCM, 9–10. For Bowen, see Philip Thomas Tucker, *The Forgotten Stonewall of the West: Major General John Stevens Bowen* (Macon, GA: Mercer University Press, 1997).

19. *OR*, 24(1):268, 272; Bearss, *The Vicksburg Campaign*, 3:737; John C. Taylor Diary, May 17, 1863, UVA; John S. Bell, "The Arkansas Sharp Shooters," undated, 12th Arkansas File, VICK; Perry, "Vicksburg. Some New History in the Experience of Gen. Francis A. Shoup," 172; Clarke, *Reminiscence and Anecdotes*, 99.
20. John S. Bell, "The Arkansas Sharp Shooters," undated, 12th Arkansas File, VICK; Emma Balfour Diary, May 17, 1863, MDAH.
21. Joseph Dill Alison Diary, May 17, 1863, UNC, copy in MDAH; Richard and Richard, *The Defense of Vicksburg*, 145–146, Sanders Diary in Jared Young Sanders II Diary, May 18, 1863, Journals/Letters/Diaries, VICK; also in OCM, and published as Mary Elizabeth Sanders, ed., *Diary in Gray: Civil War Journal of J. Y. Sanders* (Baton Rouge: Louisiana Genealogical & Historical Society, 1994); Douglas Maynard, ed., "Vicksburg Diary: The Journal of Gabriel M. Killgore," *Civil War History* 10, no. 1 (March 1964): 46–47 (33–53); John A. Leavy Diary, May 17, 1863, Journals/Letters/Diaries, VICK, copy in OCM; Louis Hébert Autobiography, 1894, UNC, 12.
22. *OR*, 24(3):890; Thomas Kirkpatrick Mitchell Diary, May 19, 1863, AU, 98; Richard and Richard, *The Defense of Vicksburg*, 145.
23. John M. Roberts Reminiscences, undated, IHS, 36; Cadwallader, *Three Years with Grant*, 85–86; John A. Ritter to Margarett, May 27, 1863, John Ritter Papers, NC.
24. *OR*, 24(3):322; Calvin Ainsworth Diary, May 18, 1863, UMB, copy in Journals/Letters/Diaries, VICK.
25. *OR*, 24(1):153, 755; *OR*, 24(2):16, 256; Charles E. Affeld Diary, May 17, 1863, Journals/Letters/Diaries, VICK.
26. *OR*, 24(3):321.
27. *OR*, 24(3):322; *OR*, 24(1):53, 755; Simon and Marszalek, eds., *PUSG*, 8:228–229; Sherman, *Memoirs*, 1:322–323; Grant, *Personal Memoirs*, 1:519.
28. *OR*, 24(1):755; Charles E. Affeld Diary, May 17, 1863, Journals/Letters/Diaries, VICK.
29. *OR*, 24(3):322; *OR*, 24(1):54, 755; *OR*, 24(2):276; Sherman, *Memoirs*, 1:323–324; Wilson, "A Staff Officer's Journal of the Vicksburg Campaign, April 30 to July 4, 1863," 261; Cadwallader, *Three Years with Grant*, 83; Charles E. Affeld Diary, May 17, 1863, Journals/Letters/Diaries, VICK.
30. For McPherson, see Elizabeth J. Whaley, *Forgotten Hero: General James B. McPherson* (New York: Exposition Press, 1955).
31. *OR*, 24(1):641; *OR*, 24(2):205; Anson Hemingway Diary, May 17, 1863, Journals/Letters/Diaries, VICK; George Carrington Diary, May 17–18, 1863, CHM.
32. *OR*, 24(1):641, 731; *OR*, 24(2):199, 205–206; Edward J. Wood to wife, May 25, 1863, Edward J. Wood Papers, IHS.
33. *OR*, 24(1):54, 641, 709; *OR*, 24(2):199.
34. Bearss, *The Vicksburg Campaign*, 2:681; *OR*, 24(1):153, 640.
35. *OR*, 24(1):640; Henry Cole Quinby, *Genealogical History of the Quinby (Quimby) Family in England and America* (Rutland, VT: Tuttle Company, 1915), 429; Oldroyd, *A Soldier's Story*, 26–27.
36. *OR*, 24(2):16–17; *Military History and Reminiscences of the Thirteenth Regiment of*

Illinois Volunteer Infantry in the Civil War in the United States 1861–1865 (Chicago: Women's Temperance Publishing Association, 1892), 316.
37. Gould D. Molineaux Diary, May 18, 1863, AC.
38. *OR*, 24(3):321–322, 324; Wilson, "A Staff Officer's Journal of the Vicksburg Campaign," 261, 263.
39. Gould D. Molineaux Diary, May 18, 1863, AC; Edward J. Wood to wife, May 25, 1863, Edward J. Wood Papers, IHS.
40. *OR*, 24(1):755.
41. *OR*, 24(1):755.
42. *OR*, 24(3):327; *OR*, 24(1):54, 755; *OR*, 24(2):249; Grant, *Personal Memoirs*, 1:527–528; Wilson, "A Staff Officer's Journal of the Vicksburg Campaign," 261.
43. *OR*, 24(2):250; Special Orders, May 20, 1863, Series 3, USGPL; Simon and Marszalek, eds., *PUSG*, 8:240–241; Grant, *Personal Memoirs*, 1:530; John Merrilees Diary, May 18, 1863, CHM.
44. *OR*, 24(3):328; Cadwallader, *Three Years with Grant*, 88; Fred Grant, "A Boy's Experience at Vicksburg," manuscript in Vicksburg files, USGPL, 29; Grant, *Personal Memoirs*, 1:528, 541–542; Anthony Burton Diary, May 20, 1863, ALPL; Don Pardee to wife, May 24, 1863, Don A. Pardee Papers, Tulane; Isaac T. Williams to brother, June 18, 1863, Isaac T. Williams Papers, Tim Brookes Collection, USAHEC.
45. OR, 24(1):755; Alonzo Abernathy Diary, May 18, 1863, 9th Iowa File, VICK.
46. *OR*, 24(1):641; *OR*, 24(2):199.
47. *OR*, 24(1):153; *OR*, 24(3):324; *OR*, 24(2):33; R. B. Scott, *The History of the 67th Regiment Indian Infantry Volunteers, War of the Rebellion* (Bedford, IN: Herald Book and Job Print, 1892), 34; Joseph Bowker Diary, May 18, 1863, 42nd Ohio File, VICK.
48. Don Pardee to wife, May 24, 1863, Don A. Pardee Papers, Tulane; Wilson, "A Staff Officer's Journal of the Vicksburg Campaign," 263; Thomas H. Barton, *Autobiography of Dr. Thomas H. Barton, The Self-made Physician of Syracuse, Ohio: Including a History of the Fourth Regt. West Va. Vol. Inf'y, with an Account of Col. Lightburn's Retreat Down the Kanawha Valley, Gen. Grant's Vicksburg and Chattanooga Campaigns, Together with the Several Battles in Which The Fourth Regiment Was Engaged, and Its Losses by Disease, Desertion and in Battle* (Charleston: West Virginia Printing Co., 1890), 152; William H. Jolly to Gus, June 12, 1863, William H. Jolly Letters, Keen Family Papers, SHSI.
49. Bearss, *The Vicksburg Campaign*, 3:746; Simeon R. Martin, "Facts About Company 'I' of the 46th Mississippi Infantry," undated, 46th Mississippi File, VICK, 64.
50. *OR*, 24(1):272, 274; *OR*, 24(3):892; Joseph Dill Alison Diary, May 18, 1863, UNC.
51. Clarke, *Reminiscence and Anecdotes*, 99; Joseph Dill Alison Diary, May 18, 1863, UNC; William R. Clack Diary, May 23, 1863, TSLA.
52. *OR*, 24(2):397, 402; *OR*, 24(1):272–273; *OR*, 24(3):890–891; Jeptha V. Harris, "The State Troops," undated, J. F. H. Claiborne Papers, UNC.
53. *OR*, 24(2):397.
54. *OR*, 24(2):366; Elbert Willett Diary, May 17, 1863, ADAH.

55. *OR*, 24(2):343–344; John S. Kountz, *Record of the Organizations Engaged in the Campaign, Siege, and Defense of Vicksburg* (Knoxville: University of Tennessee Press, 2011), 57.
56. *OR*, 24(2):343–344; Kountz, *Record of the Organizations Engaged in the Campaign, Siege, and Defense of Vicksburg*, 57; *OR*, 24(1):273.
57. William Lovelace Foster to wife, June 20, 1863, William L. Foster Letter, UA.
58. Lockett, "The Defense of Vicksburg," 3:488; *OR*, 24(2):330; William Lovelace Foster to wife, June 20, 1863, William L. Foster Letter, UA.
59. *OR*, 24(2):344, 488; Lockett, "The Defense of Vicksburg," 3:488; *OR*, 24(1):271.
60. Lockett, "The Defense of Vicksburg," 3:488.
61. *OR*, 24(1):272.
62. Richard and Richard, *The Defense of Vicksburg*, 145, 147; *OR*, 24(1):755; Sherman, *Memoirs*, 1:324; Perry, "Vicksburg. Some New History in the Experience of Gen. Francis A. Shoup," 172. Wigg's account can also be found in his March 24, 1902, letter to William T. Rigby found in the 27th Louisiana File, VICK; J. T. Hogane, "Reminiscences of the Siege of Vicksburg," *Southern Historical Society Papers* 11, no. 7 (July 1883): 294 (291–297); "Military History of Captain Thomas Sewell," 1889, DU.
63. *OR*, 24(1):274; *OR*, 24(2):344, 366, 397; Chambers, "My Journal," 270; Simeon R. Martin, "Facts About Company 'I' of the 46th Mississippi Infantry," undated, 46th Mississippi File, VICK, 63–64.
64. Simeon R. Martin, "Facts About Company 'I' of the 46th Mississippi Infantry," 46th Mississippi File, VICK, 63, copy in OCM.
65. *OR*, 24(1):272; *OR*, 24(3):892, 896. Johnston also advised Franklin Gardner at Port Hudson to evacuate.
66. *OR*, 24(1):272–273; Richard and Richard, *The Defense of Vicksburg*, 155; Clarke, *Reminiscence and Anecdotes*, 99; R. W. Memminger, "The Surrender of Vicksburg—A Defense of General Pemberton," *Southern Historical Society Papers* 12, no. 7–9 (July–September 1884): 355–356 (352–360).
67. *OR*, 24(1):273; Clarke, *Reminiscence and Anecdotes*, 100; Richard and Richard, *The Defense of Vicksburg*, 150; John C. Pemberton, *Pemberton: Defender of Vicksburg* (Chapel Hill: University of North Carolina Press, 1942), 180; Chambers, "My Journal," 274; J. L. Power Diary, May 20, 1863, MDAH.
68. *OR*, 24(1):273; Chambers, "My Journal," 274; Clarke, *Reminiscence and Anecdotes*, 100; Richard and Richard, *The Defense of Vicksburg*, 150; "War Diary of Brevet Brigadier General Joseph Stockton," Coco Collection, HCWRT, USAHEC, 15; J. L. Power Diary, May 20, 1863, MDAH.

CHAPTER 4. "WITHIN MUSKET-RANGE OF THE DEFENSES OF VICKSBURG"

1. Winchester Hall, *The Story of the 26th Louisiana Infantry, In the Service of the Confederate States* (n.p.: n.p., 1890), 67.

NOTES TO PAGES 76–82   401

2. Richard and Richard, *The Defense of Vicksburg*, 150–151, 153; William Lovelace Foster to wife, June 20, 1863, William L. Foster Letter, UA.
3. J. J. Kellogg, *The Vicksburg Campaign and Reminiscences, 'Milliken's Bend' to July 4, 1863* (Washington, IA: Evening Journal, 1913), 26–27, copy in Journals/Letters/Diaries, VICK.
4. Smith, *The Decision Was Always My Own*, 151–154.
5. *OR*, 24(3):329; *OR*, 24(1):55, 154; *OR*, 24(2):170; Grant, *Personal Memoirs*, 1:529; J. F. C. Fuller, *The Generalship of Ulysses S. Grant* (Bloomington: Indiana University Press, 1958), 154.
6. *OR*, 24(3):329; *OR*, 24(1):55, 154; *OR*, 24(2):170.
7. *OR*, 24(2):17; F. H. Mason, *The Forty-second Ohio Infantry: A History of the Organization and Services of That Regiment in the War of the Rebellion; With Biographical Sketches of Its Field Officers and a Full Roster of the Regiment* (Cleveland, OH: Cobb, Andrews and Co., Publishers, 1876), 218.
8. *OR*, 24(1):755.
9. John M. Roberts Reminiscences, undated, IHS, 36; *OR*, 24(1):755; Bearss, *The Vicksburg Campaign*, 3:768–769; Kountz, *Record of the Organizations Engaged in the Campaign, Siege, and Defense of Vicksburg*, 19–25; *OR*, 24(2):251; *OR*, 24(3):890–891; Chambers, "My Journal," 272; Lockett, "The Defense of Vicksburg," 489; Isaac O. Shelby Diary, May 20, 1863, UNC; Robert Hoadley to cousin, May 29, 1863, Robert B. Hoadley Papers, DU; James Thomas to Jones, May 26, 1863, Robert T. Jones Letters, UTK; Leo Rassieur to Robert Buchanan, October 12, 1901, 30th Missouri File, VICK.
10. *OR*, 24(1):755.
11. *OR*, 24(3):329.
12. Joseph Child Diary, May 19, 1863, UIA; Ephraim McD. Anderson, *Memoirs: Historical and Personal Including the Campaigns of the First Missouri Confederate Brigade* (St. Louis: Times Publishing Co., 1868), 327; Sherman, *Memoirs*, 1:324–325; R. S. Bevier, *History of the First and Second Missouri Confederate Brigades 1861–1865 and From Wakaruse to Appomattox, A Military Anagraph* (St. Louis: Bryan, Brand and Company, 1879), 202; *OR*, 24(2):251, 396, 414; Alonzo Abernathy Diary, May 18, 1863, 9th Iowa File, VICK. For Steele's maps of Vicksburg, see Frederick Steele Papers, Stanford University.
13. *OR*, 24(2):401; Perry, "Vicksburg. Some New History in the Experience of Gen. Francis A. Shoup," 172; "Joseph W. Westbrook's Story," 1903, Joseph W. Westbrook Papers, CWD, USAHEC.
14. *OR*, 24(2):406.
15. *OR*, 24(1):755. Kountz, *Record of the Organizations Engaged in the Campaign, Siege, and Defense of Vicksburg*, 19–25; Sherman, *Memoirs*, 1:324; *OR*, 24(2):266.
16. *OR*, 24(1):755. Kountz, *Record of the Organizations Engaged in the Campaign, Siege, and Defense of Vicksburg*, 19–25; Sherman, *Memoirs*, 1:324; *OR*, 24(2):266.
17. *OR*, 24(1):641, 709–710, 731; *OR*, 24(2):67; Ephraim Shay Diary, May 18, 1863, UMB.

18. *OR*, 24(1):641, 709–710, 731; *OR*, 24(2):67; Ephraim Shay Diary, May 18, 1863, UMB; Kountz, *Record of the Organizations Engaged in the Campaign, Siege, and Defense of Vicksburg*, 29–37; Charles R. Kock to W. T. Rigby, July 25, 1902, 11th Illinois File, VICK; John C. Swift Diary, May 19, 1863, IHS.
19. *OR*, 24(2):375–376, 387; Clarke, *Reminiscence and Anecdotes*,99–100; Elbert Willett Diary, May 17, 1863, ADAH.
20. *OR*, 24(2):367, 381, 387; W. O. Dodd, "Recollections of Vicksburg During the Siege," *The Southern Bivouac* 1, no. 1 (September 1882): 2; Emma Balfour Diary, May 19, 1863, MDAH.
21. *OR*, 24(1):153; Paul H. Hass, ed., "The Vicksburg Diary of Henry Clay Warmoth: Part II (April 28 1863—May 26, 1863)," *Journal of Mississippi History* 32, no. 1 (February 1970): 72; Edward J. Lewis Diary, May 18, 1863, 33rd Illinois File, VICK.
22. *OR*, 24(1):153; Charles A. Hobbs Letters, undated, 99th Illinois File, VICK, 18.
23. *OR*, 24(1):153; Kountz, *Record of the Organizations Engaged in the Campaign, Siege, and Defense of Vicksburg*, 6–17; Jean Powers Soman and Frank L. Byrne, eds., *A Jewish Colonel in the Civil War: Marcus M. Spiegel of the Ohio Volunteers* (Kent, OH: Kent State University Press, 1985), 281.
24. *OR*, 24(1):153–154; *OR*, 24(3):327; Samuel D. Pryce, *Vanishing Footprints: The Twenty-Second Iowa Volunteer Infantry in the Civil War*, Jeffry C. Burden, ed. (Iowa City: Camp Pope Bookshop, 2008), 109; Gould D. Molineaux Diary, May 19, 1863, AC; William Murray Diary, May 20, 1863, Journals/Letters/Diaries, VICK; Christian Wilhelm Hander Diary, May 18, 1863, UTA.
25. *OR*, 24(1):274; *OR*, 24(2):344, 366, 397; William Lovelace Foster to wife, June 20, 1863, William L. Foster Letter, UA.
26. Steven E. Woodworth, *Nothing but Victory: The Army of the Tennessee, 1861–1865* (New York: Knopf, 2005), 399; *OR*, 24(1):54; *OR*, 24(3):326, 329; *OR*, 24(2):169.
27. *OR*, 24(1):54; *OR*, 24(3):326, 329; *OR*, 24(2):169.
28. Brian Holden Reid, *America's Civil War: The Operational Battlefield, 1861–1863* (Amherst, NY: Prometheus Books, 2008), 147; Marszalek, ed, *Memoirs*, 366; James H. St. John Diary, May 19, 1863, ISL.
29. *OR*, 24(3):329; *OR*, 24(1):55, 154; *OR*, 24(2):170, 267; Simon and Marszalek, eds., *PUSG*, 8:237; Special Field Orders, May 19, 1863, John A. Rawlins Papers, CHM; George M. Rogers Diary, May 19, 1863, ISL; Calvin Ainsworth Diary, May 19, 1863, UMB.
30. Ballard, *Vicksburg*, 330; Fred Grant, "A Boy's Experience at Vicksburg," manuscript in Vicksburg files, USGPL, 29.
31. *OR*, 24(1):154; Bearss and Hills, *Receding Tide*, 237; Grabau, *Ninety-Eight Days*, 357; Mary Bobbitt Townsend, *Yankee Warhorse: A Biography of Major General Peter Osterhaus* (Columbia: University of Missouri Press, 2010), 106; Charles A. Hobbs Letters, undated, 99th Illinois File, VICK, 18; Soman and Byrne, eds., *A Jewish Colonel in the Civil War*, 278, 281; William Lowery Diary, May 19, 1863, ADAH; James B. Taylor Diary, May 19, 1863, 120th Ohio File, VICK.
32. *OR*, 24(1):154; Bearss, *The Vicksburg Campaign*, 3:774; *OR*, 24(2):17–18, 230–231;

Soman and Byrne, eds., *A Jewish Colonel in the Civil War*, 281; James Leeper to wife, May 23, 1863, James Leeper Papers, IHS.

33. *OR*, 24(1):154; Bearss, *The Vicksburg Campaign*, 3:774; *OR*, 24(2):17–18, 230–231; James Keigwin to W. T. Rigby, March 5, 1902, 49th Indiana File, VICK; Soman and Byrne, eds., *A Jewish Colonel in the Civil War*, 281; Mahlon Rouch Diary, May 19, 1863, 120th Ohio File, VICK; James B. Taylor Diary, May 19, 1863, 120th Ohio File, VICK; James Leeper to wife, May 23, 1863, James Leeper Papers, IHS.
34. *OR*, 24(1):596–597; James Leeper to wife, May 23, 1863, James Leeper Papers, IHS.
35. *OR*, 24(1):154; Bearss, *The Vicksburg Campaign*, 3:774; *OR*, 24(2):230–231; Christian Wilhelm Hander Diary, May 19, 1863, UTA.
36. Seth J. Wells, *The Siege of Vicksburg from the Diary of Seth J. Wells, Including Weeks of Preparation and of Occupation After the Surrender* (Detroit: William H. Rowe, Publisher, 1915), 65–66; Bearss, *The Vicksburg Campaign*, 3:777–778; *OR*, 24(2):292; Gould D. Molineaux Diary, May 19, 1863, AC; Edmund Newsome Diary, May 19, 1863, MDAH, copy in OCM; S. H. M. Byers, *With Fire and Sword* (New York: Neale Publishing Company, 1911), 88–89; H. M. Trimble Diary, May 19, 1863, 93rd Illinois File, VICK; Elbert Willett Diary, May 19, 1863, ADAH.
37. Gould D. Molineaux Diary, May 19, 1863, AC.
38. *OR*, 24(1):765; Joseph Stockton Diary, May 19, 1863, ALPL; "War Diary of Brevet Brigadier General Joseph Stockton," Coco Collection, HCWRT, USAHEC, 15.
39. A veteran newspaperman at Horace Greeley's *New York Tribune* before this period, Charles A. Dana was a civilian working on behalf of the War Department to report on events at Vicksburg and later in the east. Originally commissioned to be the "eyes and ears" of the Lincoln administration in rooting out corruption in the army bureaucracy in Cairo, Illinois, Dana would become one of Grant's most effective advocates back in Washington and a trusted colleague among the general's closest advisers. See Carl J. Guarneri, *Lincoln's Informer: Charles A. Dana and the Inside Story of the Union War* (Lawrence: University Press of Kansas, 2019).
40. Frederick H. Dyer, *A Compendium of the War of the Rebellion*, 3 vols. (Cedar Rapids, IA: Torch Press, 1908), 3:1048–1049, 1079, 1086–1087, 1679, 1680–1681; Ezra J. Warner, *Generals in Blue: Lives of the Union Commanders* (Baton Rouge: Louisiana State University Press, 1964), 389–390; *OR*, 24(2):299; Post, ed., *Soldiers' Letters*, 205; Charles A. Dana, *Recollections of the Civil War* (New York: D. Appleton and Co., 1898), 69; Grabau, *Ninety-Eight Days*, 355.
41. John Crane to Colonel Kirby, April 18, 1905, 17th Wisconsin File, VICK.
42. George Carrington Diary, May 19, 1863, CHM.
43. *OR*, 24(2):297, 299–300; Jeff T. Giambrone, *Beneath Torn and Tattered Flags: A History of the 38th Mississippi Infantry, C.S.A.* (Bolton, MS: Smokey Row Press, 1998), 71–72; Post, ed., *Soldiers' Letters*, 205; John Crane to Colonel Kirby, November 13, 1906, 72nd Illinois File, VICK; "War Diary of Brevet Brigadier General Joseph Stockton," Coco Collection, HCWRT, USAHEC, 15.
44. *OR*, 24(2):300; Bearss, *The Vicksburg Campaign*, 3:840; John Crane to Colonel Kirby, April 18, 1905, 17th Wisconsin File, VICK; Shelby Harriel, *Behind the Rifle:*

Women Soldiers in Civil War Mississippi (Jackson: University Press of Mississippi, 2019), 122–124.

45. *OR*, 24(2):297; Bearss, *The Vicksburg Campaign*, 3:778; Wales W. Wood, *A History of the Ninety-fifth Regiment Illinois Infantry Volunteers, From Its Organization in the Fall of 1862, Until Its Final Discharge from the United States Service, in 1865* (Chicago: Tribune Company's Book and Job Printing Office, 1865), 75; George Carrington Diary, May 19, 1863, CHM; Anson Hemingway Diary, May 19, 1863, Journals/Letters/Diaries, VICK.

46. Jim Huffstodt, *Hard Dying Men: The Story of General W. H. L. Wallace, General T. E. G. Ransom, and Their "Old Eleventh" Illinois Infantry in the American Civil War (1861–1865)* (Bowie, MD: Heritage Books, 1991), 142; John Crane to Colonel Kirby, November 13, 1906, 72nd Illinois File, VICK.

47. Marszalek, ed., *The Personal Memoirs of Ulysses S. Grant*, 366; Robert S. Martin Diary, May 19, 1863, SIU; Michael B. Ballard, *The Civil War in Mississippi: Major Campaigns and Battles* (Jackson: University Press of Mississippi, 2011), 165.

48. John F. Marszalek, *Sherman: A Soldier's Passion for Order* (New York: Free Press, 1993), 225; Calvin Ainsworth Diary, May 19, 1863, UMB.

49. Bearss, *The Vicksburg Campaign*, 3:775; Alonzo Abernathy Diary, May 19, 1863, 9th Iowa File, VICK; James Thomas to Jones, May 26, 1863, Robert T. Jones Letters, UTK; Uley Burk to family, June 8, 1863, 30th Iowa File, VICK.

50. Charles A. Willison, *Reminiscences of a Boy's Service with the 76th Ohio, In the Fifteenth Army Corps, Under General Sherman, During the Civil War, By That "Boy" at Three Score* (Menasha, WI: George Banta Publishing Company, 1908), 55; Stuart Bennett and Barbara Tillery, eds., *The Struggle for the Life of the Republic: A Civil War Narrative by Brevet Major Charles Dana Miller, 76th Ohio Volunteer Infantry* (Kent, OH: Kent State University Press, 2004), 96; Grabau, *Ninety-Eight Days*, 362–363.

51. *OR*, 24(3):892–893; Richard and Richard, *The Defense of Vicksburg*, 153; Martin, "Facts About Company 'I' of the 46th Mississippi Infantry," 46th Mississippi File, VICK, 65.

52. *OR*, 24(2):406.

53. Grabau, *Ninety-Eight Days*, 354–355.

54. *OR*, 24(3):892–893; Lockett, "The Defense of Vicksburg," 489.

55. Grabau, *Ninety-Eight Days*, 354–355.

56. *OR*, 24(2):406; Bearss, *The Vicksburg Campaign*, 3:753, 780; Terry G. Scriber, *Twenty-seventh Louisiana Volunteer Infantry* (Gretna, LA: Pelican Publishing Company, 2006), 135–136; Arthur W. Bergeron, *Guide to Louisiana Confederate Military Units, 1861–1865* (Baton Rouge: Louisiana State University Press, 1996), 135–137; Louis Guion Diary, May 19, 1863, LSU.

57. Rowland and Howell, *Military History of Mississippi*, 187–190, 319–334; Bearss, *The Vicksburg Campaign*, 3:783; G. P. Clark to friend, July 22, 1899, William M. Cleveland Papers, CWD, USAHEC.

58. Bearss, *The Vicksburg Campaign*, 3:780; John Bannon Diary, May 19, 1863, University of South Carolina.
59. Grabau, *Ninety-Eight Days*, 354–355.
60. Grabau, *Ninety-Eight Days*, 354–355.
61. Grabau, 354–355.
62. Grabau, 354–355.
63. William Lovelace Foster to wife, June 20, 1863, William L. Foster Letter, UA.
64. Clarke, *Reminiscence and Anecdotes*, 100.

Chapter 5. "My Whole Division Dashed Forward"

1. *OR*, 24(2):256. For a recent account of the May 19 assault, see J. Parker Hills, "Haste and Underestimation: May 19," in *The Vicksburg Assaults: May 19–22, 1863*, Steven E. Woodworth and Charles D. Grear, eds. (Carbondale: Southern Illinois University Press, 2019), 7–26.
2. William E. Parrish, *Frank Blair: Lincoln's Conservative* (Columbia: University of Missouri Press, 1998); Dana, *Recollections of the Civil War*, 66.
3. Parrish, *Frank Blair*, 15–78.
4. Simon and Marszalek, eds., *PUSG*, 8:164; Parrish, *Frank Blair*, 162, 164; Grant, *Personal Memoirs*, 1:573–574.
5. *OR*, 24(2):256–257, 263.
6. *OR*, 24(2):257, 281, 283.
7. *OR*, 24(2):263.
8. *OR*, 24(2):267.
9. *OR*, 24(2):257, 406; *OR*, 24(1):756, 763.
10. *OR*, 24(1):163, 756; *OR*, 24(2):257, 261; Badeau, *Military History of Ulysses S. Grant*, 1:672.
11. Clarke, *Reminiscence and Anecdotes*, 100; William Lovelace Foster to wife, June 20, 1863, William L. Foster Letter, UA.
12. Warner, *Generals in Blue*, 146; Kenneth J. Heinman, *Civil War Dynasty: The Ewing Family of Ohio* (New York: New York University Press, 2012), 76, 175.
13. Warner, *Generals in Blue*, 146.
14. *OR*, 24(2):281, 284; Edward Schweitzer Diary, May 17 (actually 18), 1863, CWTI, USAHEC.
15. Dyer, *A Compendium of the War of the Rebellion*, 3:1510–1511, 1513–1514, 1518–1519, 1657–1658; Edwin C. Bearss and J. Parker Hills, *Receding Tide: Vicksburg and Gettysburg, The Campaigns That Changed the Civil War* (Washington, DC: National Geographic, 2010), 236; Henry R. Brinkerhoff, *History of the Thirtieth Regiment Ohio Volunteer Infantry, From Its Organization, To the Fall of Vicksburg, Miss.* (Columbus, OH: James W. Osgood, Printer, 1863), 69; Thomas J. Taylor to W. T. Rigby, March 19, 1903, 47th Ohio File, VICK.

16. *OR*, 24(2):281–282; *History of the 37th Regiment, O. V. V. I., Furnished by Comrades at the Ninth Reunion Held at St. Mary's, Ohio, Tuesday and Wednesday, September 10 and 11, 1889* (Toledo, OH: Montgomery and Vrooman, 1890), 21; Henry Schmidt to wife, May 24, 1863, Schmidt Family Papers, FHS; Thomas J. Taylor to W. T. Rigby, March 19, 1903, 47th Ohio File, VICK.
17. *OR*, 24(2):281; Barton, *Autobiography of Dr. Thomas H. Barton*, 152; Anderson, *Memoirs*, 329; Joseph A. Saunier, *A History of the Forty-seventh Regiment Ohio Veteran Volunteer Infantry, Second Brigade, Second Division, Fifteenth Army Corps, Army of the Tennessee* (Hillsboro, OH: Lyle Printing Company, 1903), 144.
18. Bearss, *The Vicksburg Campaign*, 3:767; Barton, *Autobiography of Dr. Thomas H. Barton*, 152–153; Saunier, *A History of the Forty-seventh Regiment Ohio Veteran Volunteer Infantry*, 145.
19. *OR*, 24(2):281, 406, 414; Bearss, *The Vicksburg Campaign*, 3:767, 780, A. C. Riley Report, July 26, 1863, 1st Missouri File, VICK; *Supplement to the Official Records of the Union and Confederate Armies*, 100 vols. (Wilmington, NC: Broadfoot Publishing Company, 1994), 4:414; S. D. Lee to W. T. Rigby, January 26, 1903, 27th Louisiana File, VICK; Richard and Richard, *The Defense of Vicksburg*, 156; Louis Guion Diary, May 19, 1863, LSU.
20. Hogane, "Reminiscences of the Siege of Vicksburg," 293.
21. *OR*, 24(2):282; Richard and Richard, *The Defense of Vicksburg*, 156; Perry, "Vicksburg. Some New History in the Experience of Gen. Francis A. Shoup," 173.
22. *OR*, 24(2):282, 406.
23. Saunier, *A History of the Forty-seventh Regiment Ohio Veteran Volunteer Infantry*, 145.
24. *OR*, 24(2):282; Thomas J. Taylor to W. T. Rigby, March 19, 1903, 47th Ohio File, VICK; Unknown to Judy, May 24, 1863, John H. Wickizer Papers, ALPL.
25. *OR*, 24(2):397, 415.
26. *OR*, 24(2):263.
27. Warner, *Generals in Blue*, 456, 460.
28. Terrence J. Winschel, *Triumph and Defeat: The Vicksburg Campaign* (Mason City, IA: Savas Publishing Company, 1999), 113–114; Dyer, *A Compendium of the War of the Rebellion*, 3:1094–1096, 1325–1327; *OR*, 24(2):264; John Frist to W. T. Rigby, October 15, 1902, 113th Illinois File, VICK.
29. *OR*, 24(2):264; Charles E. Affeld Diary, May 19, 1863, Journals/Letters/Diaries, VICK.
30. *OR*, 24(2):264.
31. *OR*, 24(2):264, 406; Kellogg, *The Vicksburg Campaign and Reminiscences*, 28–29; Jim Russell to mother, May 27, 1863, Frederick W. Russell Letters, CHM.
32. *OR*, 24(2):257, 264, 406; *OR*, 24(1):756; Winschel, *Triumph and Defeat*, 119–120, 124; *In Memoriam*, 47–50; U. G. McAlexander, *History of the Thirteen Regiment United States Infantry, Compiled from Regimental Records and Other Sources* (n.p.: Regimental Press, Thirteenth Infantry, 1905), 39; Heinman, *Civil War Dynasty*,

182–183; John Frist to W. T. Rigby, October 15, 1902, 113th Illinois File, VICK; Ebenezer Werkheiser to sister, June 8, 1863, Journals/Letters/Diaries, VICK.
33. *OR*, 24(2):397–398, 402, 406, 414–415; Richard and Higginbotham, *The Defense of Vicksburg*, 154, 161; S. D. Lee to W. T. Rigby, January 26, 1903, 27th Louisiana File, VICK; William Lovelace Foster to wife, June 20, 1863, William L. Foster Letter, UA; Theodore D. Fisher Diary, May 23, 1863, Civil War Collection, MHS, copy in Journals/Letters/Diaries, VICK and OCM; Samuel Fowler Diary, May 19, 1863, SU; Louis Guion Diary, May 19, 1863, LSU.
34. *OR*, 24(2):397–398, 402, 406, 414–415; Richard and Higginbotham, *The Defense of Vicksburg*, 154, 161; Anderson, *Memoirs*, 329; S. D. Lee to W. T. Rigby, January 26, 1903, 27th Louisiana File, VICK; William Lovelace Foster to wife, June 20, 1863, William L. Foster Letter, UA; Theodore D. Fisher Diary, May 23, 1863, Civil War Collection, MHS, copy in Journals/Letters/Diaries, VICK and OCM; Samuel Fowler Diary, May 19, 1863, SU; Louis Guion Diary, May 19, 1863, LSU.
35. *OR*, 24(2):259, 398, 406; Jack D. Welsh, *Medical Histories of Union Generals* (Kent, OH: Kent State University Press, 1996), 309; Kilburn Knox to Eugene Carter, May 9, 1866, OCM.
36. Warner, *Generals in Blue*, 462; William Lovelace Foster to wife, June 20, 1863, William L. Foster Letter, UA.
37. *OR*, 24(2):267; Walter George Smith, *Life and Letters of Thomas Kilby Smith, Brevet Major-General United States Volunteers, 1820–1877* (New York: G. P. Putnam's Sons, 1898), 297.
38. Dyer, *A Compendium of the War of the Rebellion*, 3:1099–1100, 1148–1149; *OR*, 24(2):267; Will Jolly to parents, June 1, 1863, Journals/Letters/Diaries, VICK.
39. John M. Roberts Reminiscences, undated, IHS, 37.
40. Dyer, *A Compendium of the War of the Rebellion*, 3:1071, 1522–24; *OR*, 24(2):267, 270.
41. *OR*, 24(2):267.
42. Clarke, *Reminiscence and Anecdotes*, 100.
43. *OR*, 24(2):268, 277; Bearss, *The Vicksburg Campaign*, 3:783; John M. Roberts Reminiscences, undated, IHS, 37.
44. Clarke, *Reminiscence and Anecdotes*, 100.
45. Henry Johnson Reynolds Memoir, 1904, CWTI, USAHEC, 4–5.
46. Reynolds Memoir, 1904, CWTI, USAHEC, 5, 15.
47. James Carlisle Diary, May 19, 1863, Journals/Letters/Diaries, VICK.
48. *OR*, 24(2):414; Tucker, *Westerners in Gray*, 217, 220; Personal Memoirs of I. V. Smith, 1902, SHSMC, 30.
49. John B. Fletcher Diary, May 19, 1863, ALPL; *The Story of the Fifty-fifth Regiment Illinois Volunteer Infantry in the Civil War, 1861–1865* (Clinton, MA: W. J. Coulter, 1887), 234.
50. Smith, *Life and Letters of Thomas Kilby Smith*, 295; *OR*, 24(2):268, 376; Robert Oliver to W. T. Rigby, April 6, 1902, 55th Illinois File, VICK.

51. *OR*, 24(2):268, 376; Robert Oliver to W. T. Rigby, April 6, 1902, 55th Illinois File, VICK; Smith, *Life and Letters of Thomas Kilby Smith*, 295.
52. Clarke, *Reminiscence and Anecdotes*, 100; Smith, *Life and Letters of Thomas Kilby Smith*, 295–296; Tucker, *Westerners in Gray*, 220.
53. *OR*, 24(2):268, 277, 280; Sherman, *Memoirs*, 1:326; Owen Francis Diary, May 19, 1863, 57th Ohio File, VICK.
54. David W. Reed, *Campaigns and Battles of the Twelfth Regiment Iowa Veteran Volunteer Infantry From Its Organization, September, 1861, to Muster Out, January 20, 1866* (n.p.: n.p., 1903), 122; *The Story of the Fifty-fifth Regiment Illinois Volunteer Infantry in the Civil War*, 237–239.
55. *OR*, 24(2):274; Andrew McCormack to family, May 24, 1863, Andrew McCormack Papers, NC; John Carr Diary, May 19, 1863, HCWRT, USAHEC; "Military History of Captain Thomas Sewell," 1889, DU.
56. *OR*, 24(2):268–270, 274; J. Grecian, *History of the Eighty-third Regiment, Indiana Volunteer Infantry. For Three Years With Sherman* (Cincinnati: John F. Uhlhorn, printer, 1865), 30–31; J. R. Grassmeire to friend, May 27, 1863, Andrew McCormack Papers, Sword Collection, USAHEC; Benjamin Spooner to madam, June 7, 1863, Benjamin Spooner Letters, ISL. For casualties by name in the 83rd Indiana, see Benjamin Spooner to sir, May 24, 1863, Benjamin Spooner Letters, ISL.
57. John M. Roberts Reminiscences, undated, IHS, 37.
58. Roberts, 37.
59. Roberts, 37.
60. *OR*, 24(2):376; Andrew McCormack to family, May 24, 1863, Andrew McCormack Papers, NC.
61. *OR*, 24(2):268.
62. *OR*, 24(2):257.
63. *OR*, 24(2):269.
64. *OR*, 24(2):359, 398; Winschel, *Triumph and Defeat*, 126; Samuel Fowler Diary, May 19, 1863, SU; "Military History of Captain Thomas Sewell," 1889, DU; "Personal," *Chicago Tribune*, June 5, 1863, and "Personal," undated, *Utica* (New York) *Herald*, copies in "Military History of Captain Thomas Sewell," 1889, DU.
65. A. S. Abrams, *A Full and Detailed History of the Siege of Vicksburg* (Atlanta: Intelligencer Steam Power Presses, 1863), 31–32, copy in Journals/Letters/Diaries, VICK.
66. *OR*, 24(2):269; *The Story of the Fifty-fifth Regiment Illinois Volunteer Infantry in the Civil War*, 236; Henry Johnson Reynolds Memoir, 1904, CWTI, USAHEC, 5–6.
67. *OR*, 24(2):265, 268–269; William J. Pittenger Diary, May 19, 1863, VT.
68. Bearss, 3:775–776, 778; Richard and Richard, *The Defense of Vicksburg*, 161; Sherman, *Memoirs*, 1:325; Winschel, *Triumph and Defeat*, 127.
69. William Lovelace Foster to wife, June 20, 1863, William L. Foster Letter, UA.
70. John Merrilees Diary, May 19, 1863, CHM; Thomas J. Taylor to W. T. Rigby, March 19, 1903, 47th Ohio File, VICK; Civil War Memoir of C. S. O. Rice, undated, TSLA, 22; William Lovelace Foster to wife, June 20, 1863, William L. Foster Letter, UA.
71. *OR*, 24(1):163; Ephraim Shay Diary, May 19, 1863, UMB.

72. Smith, *Grant Invades Tennessee*, 215–216.
73. "Opening of the Mississippi," November 2, 1905, *National Tribune*.

CHAPTER 6. "THE ENEMY ARE EVIDENTLY PREPARING FOR AN ASSAULT"

1. Lockett, "The Defense of Vicksburg," 3:488; *OR*, 24(1):269.
2. William Drennan to wife, May 19, 1863, William A. Drennan Papers, MDAH; Joseph Dill Alison Diary, May 19, 1863, UNC; Samuel Fowler Diary, May 20, 1863, SU.
3. *OR*, 24(2):359.
4. A. C. Lenert Diary, May 19, 1863, UNT.
5. *OR*, 24(2):359; W. L. Faulk Diary, May 20, 1863, 38th Mississippi File, VICK; George S. Durfee to uncle, May 21, 1863, George S. Durfee Papers, UI.
6. *OR*, 24(2):359; William Clemans Narrative, undated, William Clemans Papers, UI.
7. Joiner, *Mr. Lincoln's Brown Water Navy*, 135–136; Barbara Brooks Tomblin, *The Civil War on the Mississippi: Union Sailors, Gunboat Captains, and the Campaign to Control the River* (Lexington: University Press of Kentucky, 2016), 262; George S. Durfee to uncle, May 21, 1863, George S. Durfee Papers, UI; Asa E. Sample Diary, May 22, 1863, ISL; Samuel Fowler Diary, May 21, 1863, SU; A. C. Lenert Diary, May 20, 1863, UNT; Civil War Memoir of C. S. O. Rice, undated, TSLA, 22; John A. Griffen Diary, May 20, 1863, ALPL.
8. *OR*, 24(2):360.
9. Clarke, *Reminiscence and Anecdotes*, 103; Richard and Richard, *The Defense of Vicksburg*, 156.
10. *OR*, 24(3):893–896; General Maury's Order Book, 1863, CHM, 271.
11. Louis W. Knobe Diary, May 19, 1863, ISL; Hass, ed., "The Vicksburg Diary of Henry Clay Warmoth," 72; William Lowery Diary, May 20, 1863, ADAH; John C. Pemberton Diary, May 1863, John C. Pemberton Papers, UNC.
12. William T. Sherman to wife, May 19, 1863, William T. Sherman Papers, LC.
13. William T. Sherman to wife, May 19, 1863, William T. Sherman Papers, LC.
14. *OR*, 24(3):899; Michael B. Ballard, *Pemberton: The General Who Lost Vicksburg* (Jackson: University Press of Mississippi, 1991), 170; John C. Taylor Diary, May 20, 1863, UVA; Joseph E. Johnston to Louis T. Wigfall, November 1, 1863, Louis T. Wigfall Papers, LC; Joseph Dill Alison Diary, May 20, 1863, UNC; William Lovelace Foster to wife, June 20, 1863, William L. Foster Letter, UA.
15. *OR*, 24(3):904.
16. *OR*, 24(3):899–901.
17. *OR*, 24(3):331–332; Richard L. Kiper, *Major General John A. McClernand: Politician in Uniform* (Kent, OH: Kent State University Press, 1999), 254, 256; Jeffrey L. Patrick, ed., *Three Years with Wallace's Zouaves: The Civil War Memoirs of Thomas Wise Durham* (Macon, GA: Mercer University Press, 2003), 144; Merrick J. Wald Diary, May 20, 1863, OCM.

18. *OR*, 24(3):331–332; Kiper, *Major General John A. McClernand*, 254, 256; Patrick, ed., *Three Years with Wallace's Zouaves*, 144; Merrick J. Wald Diary, May 20, 1863, OCM; Alvin P. Hovey to John A. McClernand, May 19, 1863, John A. McClernand Papers, ALPL.
19. *OR*, 24(3):332; Owen Francis Diary, May 20, 1863, 57th Ohio File, VICK.
20. *OR*, 24(3):332; Carlos Colby to sister, May 26, 1863, Carlos Colby Papers, NL.
21. *OR*, 24(1):719; *OR*, 24(2):140, 257, 262, 264; George S. Durfee to uncle, May 21, 1863, George S. Durfee Papers, UI; John Merrilees Diary, May 20–21, 1863, CHM; "Unidentified Soldier of the 31st Iowa Infantry Diary," May 20, 1863, MHS.
22. *OR*, 24(1):719; *OR*, 24(2):140, 257, 262, 264; John Merrilees Diary, May 20–21, 1863, CHM; "Unidentified Soldier of the 31st Iowa Infantry Diary," May 20, 1863, MHS; William Roberts Diary, May 21, 1863, ADAH.
23. Kellogg, *The Vicksburg Campaign and Reminiscences*, 36–37.
24. George M. Lucas Diary, May 21, 1863, ALPL; Nicholas Miller Memoir, undated, OCM, 11.
25. *OR*, 24(2):251; John T. Buegel Diary, May 19–21, 1863, SHSMC, copy in OCM, and published in William G. Bek, ed., "The Civil War Diary of John T. Buegel, Union Soldier," *Missouri Historical Review* 40, no. 4 (July 1946): 510.
26. *OR*, 24(2):376, 398, 402; *OR*, 24(3):903, 905; A. C. Lenert Diary, May 22, 1863, UNT.
27. *OR*, 24(2):367, 402, 407; Dodd, "Recollections of Vicksburg During the Siege," 3; General Maury's Order Book, 1863, CHM, 273–274, 276.
28. Soman and Byrne, eds., *A Jewish Colonel in the Civil War*, 279; *OR*, 24(2):387; Charles F. Smith Diary, May 21, 1863, NC.
29. *OR*, 24(1):597; General Maury's Order Book, 1863, CHM, 274; Joseph Bowker Diary, May 21, 1863, 42nd Ohio File, VICK.
30. Simon and Marszalek, eds., *PUSG*, 8:247; Tunnard, *A Southern Record*, 238; Saunier, *A History of the Forty-seventh Regiment Ohio Veteran Volunteer Infantry*, 146; Wells, *The Siege of Vicksburg from the Diary of Seth J. Wells*, 67.
31. Hass, ed., "The Vicksburg Diary of Henry Clay Warmoth," 72.
32. Manning F. Force, "Personal Recollections of the Vicksburg Campaign," in *Sketches of War History 1861–1865 Papers Read Before the Ohio Commandery of the Military Order of the Loyal Legion of the United States 1883–1886, Volume 1* (Cincinnati: Robert Clarke Company, 1888), 304; Anthony Burton Diary, May 17–22, 1863, Journals/Letters/Diaries, VICK; Charles F. Smith Diary, May 19, 1863, NC.
33. Charles Henry Snedeker Diary, May 29, 1863, AU; *OR*, 24(2):252.
34. Calvin Ainsworth Diary, May 18, 1863, UMB; George to sister, June 2, 1863, Safford Family Papers, ALPL; Thomas B. Beggs to aunt, June 19, 1863, Thomas B. Beggs Papers, ALPL.
35. George M. Rogers Diary, May 18 and 20, 1863, ISL; *OR*, 24(1):38, 54, 755–756; Grant, *Personal Memoirs*, 1:530, 535; *The Story of the Fifty-fifth Regiment Illinois Volunteer Infantry in the Civil War*, 234; Henry Clay Leeson to father, May 27, 1863, Leeson Family Papers, ISL.

36. Oldroyd, *A Soldier's Story*, 27.
37. *OR*, 24(1):38, 54, 755–756; Marshall, *History of the Eighty-third Ohio Volunteer Infantry*, 84–85; Grant, *Personal Memoirs*, 1:530, 535; George Carrington Diary, May 20, 1863, CHM; Jesse M. Lee Diary, May 20, 1863, 59th Indiana File, VICK.
38. *OR*, 24(3):327–328.
39. *OR*, 24(1):38, 54; Grant, *Personal Memoirs*, 1:530, 535; *OR*, 24(2):187–188; *OR*, 24(1):755–756.
40. *OR*, 24(1):38, 54; Grant, *Personal Memoirs*, 1:530, 535; *OR*, 24(2):187–188; *OR*, 24(1):755–756; Special Field Orders, May 20, 1863, John A. Rawlins Papers, CHM.
41. *OR*, 24(2):188; Wilson, "A Staff Officer's Journal of the Vicksburg Campaign," 264; Special Field Orders, May 20, 1863, John A. Rawlins Papers, CHM; James Dunlap to John A. McClernand, May 22, 1863, John A. McClernand Papers, ALPL.
42. *OR*, 24(1):38, 54; Parrish, *Frank Blair*, 169; Job H. Yaggy Diary, May 19, 1863, ALPL; Grecian, *History of the Eighty-third Regiment, Indiana Volunteer Infantry*, 31; Joseph Child Diary, May 22, 1863, UIA; Grant, *Personal Memoirs*, 1:530, 535; *OR*, 24(2):187–188; *OR*, 24(1):755–756; Henry Seaman Diary, May 21, 1863, 13th Illinois File, VICK; "83rd Indiana Volunteers Regimental History," 1963, ISL; James H. St. John Diary, May 20, 1863, ISL; John A. Griffen Diary, May 19, 1863, ALPL.
43. William L. B. Jenney, "Personal Recollections of Vicksburg," in *Military Essays and Recollections: Papers Read Before the Commandery of the State of Illinois, Military Order of the Loyal Legion of the United States, Volume III* (Chicago: Dial Press, 1899), 260–261.
44. William E. Lewis to wife, June 11, 1863, William E. Lewis Letters, SHSMC.
45. *OR*, 24(2):19; Grant, *Personal Memoirs*, 370.
46. *OR*, 24(1):38, 54; Grant, *Personal Memoirs*, 1:530, 535; John P. Jones to wife, May 27, 1863, John P. Jones Papers, FHS; Calvin Ainsworth Diary, May 19, 1863, UMB; George M. Rogers Diary, May 20, 1863, ISL; John T. Appler Diary, May 17 and 24, 1863, MHS.
47. James E. Payne, "Missouri Troops in the Vicksburg Campaign," *Confederate Veteran* 36, no. 10 (October 1928): 377.
48. *OR*, 24(2):19; *OR*, 24(1):54–55; Fuller, *The Generalship of Ulysses S. Grant*, 154.
49. Sherman, *Memoirs*, 1:325–326; *OR*, 24(1):55, 174–175; Badeau, *Military History of Ulysses S. Grant*, 1:311.
50. *OR*, 24(1):55, 174–175.
51. *OR*, 24(3):334.
52. *OR*, 24(3):334; J. Parker Hills, "Failure and Scapegoat: May 22," in *The Vicksburg Assaults: May 19–22, 1863*, Steven E. Woodworth and Charles D. Grear, eds. (Carbondale: Southern Illinois University Press, 2019), 34.
53. *OR*, 24(1):183.
54. *OR*, 24(3):334.
55. Henry Seaman Diary, May 21, 1863, 13th Illinois File, VICK, copy in CWTI, USAHEC; J. L. Power Diary, May 21, 1863, MDAH; J. H. Jones, "The Rank and File at Vicksburg," in *Publications of the Mississippi Historical Society*, 14 vols., Franklin

L. Riley, ed. (Oxford: Mississippi Historical Society, 1903), 7:20; Joseph Bowker Diary, May 21, 1863, 42nd Ohio File, VICK.
56. Brooks D. Simpson, *Ulysses S. Grant: Triumph over Adversity, 1822–1865* (Boston: Houghton Mifflin Company, 2000), 203; James R. Arnold, *Grant Wins the War: Decision at Vicksburg* (New York: John Wiley & Sons, 1997), 247; *OR*, 24(2):181; Isaac O. Shelby Diary, May 21, 1863, UNC; William Van Zandt Diary, May 21, 1863, ISU; Edward Ingraham to aunt, May 21, 1863, Edward F. Ingraham Papers, ALPL; Henry Schmidt to wife, May 24, 1863, Schmidt Family Papers, FHS.
57. George Carrington Diary, May 21, 1863, CHM; John Merrilees Diary, May 19, 1863, CHM; George S. Durfee to uncle, May 21, 1863, George S. Durfee Papers, UI; Gould D. Molineaux Diary, May 22, 1863, AC; Henry Schmidt to wife, May 24, 1863, Schmidt Family Papers, FHS; *The Story of the Fifty-fifth Regiment Illinois Volunteer Infantry in the Civil War*, 242.
58. Kiper, *Major General John A. McClernand*, 257; Thomas H. Johnson to Mary, 1863, Thomas H. Johnson Letter, Champan University.
59. Oldroyd, *A Soldier's Story*, 28–30.
60. Mason, *The Forty-second Ohio Infantry*, 223; *OR*, 24(1):178; William M. Stone Manuscript, undated, MDAH; John Cowan to W. T. Rigby, February 17, 1903, 19th Kentucky File, VICK; "War Diary of Brevet Brigadier General Joseph Stockton," Coco Collection, HCWRT, USAHEC, 15–16.
61. Pryce, *Vanishing Footprints*, 111; Oldroyd, *A Soldier's Story*, 32.
62. Bluford Wilson to J. C. Switzer, September 13, 1904, Bluford Wilson Papers, ALPL; Lyman Baker Memoirs, 1914, ALPL, 10–11.
63. Bluford Wilson to J. C. Switzer, September 13, 1904, Bluford Wilson Papers, ALPL; Walter B. Scates to John A. Rawlins, and Walter Scates to P. J. Osterhaus, May 22, 1863, John A. McClernand Papers, ALPL.
64. Hugh Ewing Statement, undated, Journals/Letters/Diaries, VICK.
65. Soman and Byrne, eds., *A Jewish Colonel in the Civil War*, 281; Charles A. Hobbs Letters, undated, 99th Illinois File, VICK, 20.
66. *OR*, 24(1):597.
67. Charles F. Smith Diary, May 22, 1863, NC.

Chapter 7. "Each Column Will Attack by the Watch"

1. *OR*, 24(3):179–180, 201; Smith, *The Decision Was Always My Own*, 84.
2. *OR*, 24(1):751–755; Smith, *The Decision Was Always My Own*, 154–159.
3. Alonzo Abernathy Diary, May 22, 1863, 9th Iowa File, VICK.
4. Sherman, *Memoirs*, 1:325–326.
5. W. T. Ratliff to J. L. Power, November 6, 1900, John P. Reese to wife, May 25, 1863, Journals/Letters/Diaries, VICK; Hugh Ewing Statement, undated, Journals/Letters/Diaries, VICK. For tactics, including columns and attacking by the flank, see Earl J. Hess, *Civil War Infantry Tactics: Training, Combat, and Small-Unit Effectiveness*

(Baton Rouge: Louisiana State University Press, 2015); Grady McWhiney and Perry D. Jamieson, *Attack and Die: Civil War Military Tactics and the Southern Heritage* (Tuscaloosa: University of Alabama Press, 1982); Paddy Griffith, *Battle Tactics of the Civil War* (New Haven: Yale University Press, 1987).
6. *OR*, 24(1):756.
7. *OR*, 24(2):257.
8. Sherman, *Memoirs*, 1:326.
9. *OR*, 24(1):756; John T. Buegel Diary, May 22, 1863, SHSMC; Henry J. Seaman Diary, May 19, 1863, CWTI, USAHEC; Isaac O. Shelby Diary, May 22, 1863, UNC.
10. *OR*, 24(1):756; *OR*, 24(3):334; *OR*, 24(2):264.
11. *OR*, 24(3):334–335.
12. *OR*, 24(1):756; *OR*, 24(3):334.
13. Grabau, *Ninety-Eight Days*, 354–355.
14. Grabau, *Ninety-Eight Days*, 354–355.
15. *OR*, 24(1):756; *OR*, 24(2):257, 269; *OR*, 24(3):334; James Lee McDonough, *William Tecumseh Sherman: In the Service of My Country: A Life* (New York: W. W. Norton & Company, 2016), 410; Sherman, *Memoirs*, 1:326; Benjamin Spooner to sir, May 24, 1863, Benjamin Spooner Letters, ISL.
16. *OR*, 24(3):334–335.
17. *OR*, 24(3):334–335.
18. *OR*, 24(2):269, 275, 277, 280; "George Theodore Hyatt," 1897, 127th Illinois File, VICK, original in Chicago *Times-Herald*, March 21, 1897. For a list of the volunteers, see *OR*, 52(1):62–64.
19. Andrew McCormack to family, May 24, 1863, Andrew McCormack Papers, NC.
20. John O'Dea, "A Forlorn Hope," Journals/Letters/Diaries, VICK, original in Chicago *Times Herald*, May 30, 1897, and reprinted in John O'Dea, "A Forlorn Hope," in *Transactions of the McLean County Historical Society*, vol. 1 (Bloomington, IL: McLean County Historical Society, 1899), 477–480.
21. *The Story of the Fifty-fifth Regiment Illinois Volunteer Infantry in the Civil War*, 245; Hugh Ewing Statement, undated, Journals/Letters/Diaries, VICK; Andrew McCormack to family, May 24, 1863, Andrew McCormack Papers, NC; "83rd Indiana Volunteers Regimental History," 1963, ISL.
22. *OR*, 24(3):335; Sherman, *Memoirs*, 1:326.
23. *OR*, 24(2):269, 275, 277, 280.
24. *OR*, 24(1):756.
25. *OR*, 24(2):367, 415; *OR*, 24(3):904, 907; Bearss, *The Vicksburg Campaign*, 3:780; Tucker, *Westerners in Gray*, 222; Payne, "Missouri Troops in the Vicksburg Campaign," 377; Lockett, "The Defense of Vicksburg," 489; John Bannon Diary, May 22, 1863, University of South Carolina; A. C. Riley Report, July 26, 1863, 1st Missouri File, VICK; William A. Ruyle Memoir, undated, HCWRT, USAHEC, 15.
26. *OR*, 24(2):415; S. D. Lee to W. T. Rigby, January 26, 1903, 27th Louisiana File, VICK.
27. *OR*, 24(2):361, 407, 415; Bevier, *History of the First and Second Missouri Confederate*

Brigades, 204; Fred Grant, "A Boy's Experience at Vicksburg," manuscript in Vicksburg files, USGPL, 30.
28. Jones, "The Rank and File at Vicksburg," 20–21; Payne, "Missouri Troops in the Vicksburg Campaign," 377.
29. Jones, "The Rank and File at Vicksburg," 21.
30. Clarke, *Reminiscence and Anecdotes*, 101.
31. Silas T. Trowbridge, *Autobiography of S. T. Trowbridge, M.D.* (n.p.: n.p., 1872), 143, reprinted as *Autobiography of Silas Thompson Trowbridge, M.D.* (Carbondale: Southern Illinois University Press, 2004); John O'Dea, "A Forlorn Hope," Journals/Letters/Diaries, VICK.
32. *OR*, 24(2):257, 376; Brinkerhoff, *History of the Thirtieth Regiment Ohio Volunteer Infantry*, 72; Clarke, *Reminiscence and Anecdotes*, 101; J. W. Larabee Statement, May 2, 1901, 55th Illinois File, VICK; Robert McRory to J. B. Allen, April 15, 1904, 30th Ohio File, VICK.
33. *OR*, 24(1):756; *OR*, 24(2):282; Heinman, *Civil War Dynasty*, 183–185; Badeau, *Military History of Ulysses S. Grant*, 1:674.
34. Andrew McCormack to family, May 24, 1863, Andrew McCormack Papers, NC; *OR*, 24(2):257, 376; Brinkerhoff, *History of the Thirtieth Regiment Ohio Volunteer Infantry*, 72; Clarke, *Reminiscence and Anecdotes*, 101; J. W. Larabee Statement, May 2, 1901, 55th Illinois File, VICK; Robert McRory to J. B. Allen, April 15, 1904, 30th Ohio File, VICK; Edward Schweitzer Diary, May 20, 1863, CWTI, USAHEC.
35. Clarke, *Reminiscence and Anecdotes*, 101.
36. *OR*, 24(1):756; *OR*, 24(2):262, 285, 361; Timothy C. Young Diary, May 22, 1863, Journals/Letters/Diaries, VICK; James C. Sinclair Diary, May 22, 1863, CHM.
37. Charles E. Affeld Diary, May 22, 1863, Journals/Letters/Diaries, VICK; Bjorn Skaptason, "The Chicago Light Artillery at Vicksburg," *Journal of the Illinois State Historical Society* 106, no. 3–4 (Fall/Winter 2013): 441–445.
38. *OR*, 24(1):757; *OR*, 24(2):361, 376; Sherman, *Memoirs*, 1:326; Heinman, *Civil War Dynasty*, 183–185.
39. "George Theodore Hyatt," 1897, 127th Illinois File, VICK.
40. John O'Dea, "A Forlorn Hope," Journals/Letters/Diaries, VICK.
41. *OR*, 24(2):414; Bearss, *The Vicksburg Campaign*, 3:7780, 783; Clarke, *Reminiscence and Anecdotes*, 101; Anderson, *Memoirs*, 331–332; Bevier, *History of the First and Second Missouri Confederate Brigades*, 204.
42. *OR*, 24(1):757; *OR*, 24(2):273, 282, 414; Clarke, *Reminiscence and Anecdotes*, 101–102; J. W. Larabee Statement, May 2, 1901, 55th Illinois File, VICK.
43. *OR*, 24(1):757; *OR*, 24(2):273, 282, 414; J. W. Larabee Statement, May 2, 1901, 55th Illinois File, VICK; Clarke, *Reminiscence and Anecdotes*, 101–102.
44. "George Theodore Hyatt," 1897, 127th Illinois File, VICK.
45. *OR*, 24(2):273, 367, 415; "George Theodore Hyatt," 1897, 127th Illinois File, VICK; Richard and Richard, *The Defense of Vicksburg*, 161; Robert McRory to J. B. Allen, April 15, 1904, 30th Ohio File, VICK.
46. *OR*, 24(2):273, 367, 415; Robert McRory to J. B. Allen, April 15, 1904, 30th Ohio

File, VICK; "George Theodore Hyatt," 1897, 127th Illinois File, VICK; Richard and Richard, *The Defense of Vicksburg*, 161.
47. *OR*, 24(2):273; Clarke, *Reminiscence and Anecdotes*, 102; Samuel Fowler Diary, May 22, 1863, SU.
48. *OR*, 24(1):757; *OR*, 24(2):282; "It Was the 30th Ohio," September 29, 1910, *National Tribune*; Brinkerhoff, *History of the Thirtieth Regiment Ohio Volunteer Infantry*, 72–73; *History of the 37th Regiment, O. V. V. I.*, 21–22; "83rd Indiana Volunteers Regimental History," 1963, ISL; J. B. Allen to W. T. Rigby, July 12, 1904, 30th Ohio File, VICK; Edward Schweitzer Diary, May 22, 1863, CWTI, USAHEC.
49. *OR*, 24(2):257; J. B. Allen to W. T. Rigby, July 12, 1904, 30th Ohio File, VICK; Robert McRory to J. B. Allen, April 15, 1904, 30th Ohio File, VICK; Isaac T. Williams to brother, June 18, 1863, Isaac T. Williams Papers, Tim Brookes Collection, USAHEC.
50. *OR*, 24(2):257–258, 282, 284; Brinkerhoff, *History of the Thirtieth Regiment Ohio Volunteer Infantry*, 74; W. Schalenburg to W. T. Rigby, March 12, 1901, 37th Ohio File, VICK.
51. Henry Schmidt to wife, May 24, 1863, Schmidt Family Papers, FHS; *OR*, 24(2):282.
52. *OR*, 24(2):257–258; Heinman, *Civil War Dynasty*, 183–185.
53. *OR*, 24(2):258, 398.
54. John O'Dea, "A Forlorn Hope," Journals/Letters/Diaries, VICK.
55. *OR*, 24(2):258; J. B. Allen to W. T. Rigby, July 12, 1904, 30th Ohio File, VICK.
56. Saunier, *A History of the Forty-seventh Regiment Ohio Veteran Volunteer Infantry*, 147–148.
57. *OR*, 24(2):258, 282, 284.
58. Clarke, *Reminiscence and Anecdotes*, 102.
59. *OR*, 24(2):258.
60. *OR*, 24(2):258, 282; Saunier, *A History of the Forty-seventh Regiment Ohio Veteran Volunteer Infantry*, 148; Barton, *Autobiography of Dr. Thomas H. Barton*, 154; Robert S. Martin Diary, May 22, 1863, SIU.
61. W. Grayum to Harriett, June 5 and 30, 1863, 4th West Virginia File, VICK.
62. Saunier, *A History of the Forty-seventh Regiment Ohio Veteran Volunteer Infantry*, 153.
63. *OR*, 24(2):258; Bearss, *The Vicksburg Campaign*, 3:818; *In Memoriam*, 50–52.
64. *OR*, 24(2):258, 264.
65. *OR*, 24(2):269.
66. *OR*, 24(2):269.
67. *OR*, 24(2):269.
68. *OR*, 24(2):258, 269–270, 281; Clarke, *Reminiscence and Anecdotes*, 102; Grecian, *History of the Eighty-third Regiment, Indiana Volunteer Infantry*, 31–32; George M. Rogers Diary, May 22, 1863, ISL; Owen Francis Diary, May 22, 1863, 57th Ohio File, VICK.
69. *OR*, 24(2):258.
70. *OR*, 24(1):757.
71. *OR*, 24(2):367, 415; Personal Memoirs of I. V. Smith, 1902, SHSMC, 30.

72. *OR*, 24(1):760.
73. Kountz, *Record of the Organizations Engaged in the Campaign, Siege, and Defense of Vicksburg*, 46; Hugh Ewing Statement, undated, Journals/Letters/Diaries, VICK. Lodi was a Napoleonic battle in 1796.
74. *OR*, 24(1):756.
75. *OR*, 24(3):335.
76. *OR*, 24(2):251.
77. *OR*, 24(2):251; Alonzo Abernathy Diary, May 22, 1863, 9th Iowa File, VICK.
78. *OR*, 24(2):251; Louis Guion Diary, May 22, 1863, LSU.
79. Willison, *Reminiscences of a Boy's Service*, 56; Bennett and Tillery, eds., *The Struggle for the Life of the Republic*, 96; Henry Seaman Diary, May 21, 1863, 13th Illinois File, VICK; James F. Mallinckrodt Diary, May 22, 1863, OCM; James Thomas to Jones, May 26, 1863, Robert T. Jones Letters, UTK.
80. Calvin Ainsworth Diary, May 22, 1863, UMB.
81. John T. Buegel Diary, May 22, 1863, SHSMC; *OR*, 24(2):407; Richard and Richard, *The Defense of Vicksburg*, 159.
82. Bearss, *The Vicksburg Campaign*, 3:842–843.
83. Sherman, *Memoirs*, 1:326.

Chapter 8. "There Was Not a Twig between Us and the Fort"

1. For the early years of the Army of the Tennessee, see Woodworth, *Nothing but Victory*.
2. Smith, *Shiloh*, 41–47.
3. Warner, *Generals in Blue*, 306–307.
4. Smith, *Shiloh*, 53.
5. Tamara A. Smith, "A Matter of Trust: Grant and James B. McPherson," in *Grant's Lieutenants: From Cairo to Vicksburg*, Steven E. Woodworth, ed. (Lawrence: University Press of Kansas, 2001), 151–167.
6. Simon and Marszalek, eds., *PUSG*, 5:103; John Y. Simon and Marszalek, eds., *The Personal Memoirs of Julia Dent Grant [Mrs. Ulysses S. Grant]* (New York: G. P. Putnam's Sons, 1975), 105.
7. J. Parker Hills, "Roads to Raymond," in *The Vicksburg Campaign*, Steven E. Woodworth and Charles D. Grear, eds. (Carbondale: Southern Illinois University Press, 2013), 65–95.
8. Kountz, *Record of the Organizations Engaged in the Campaign, Siege, and Defense of Vicksburg*, 29–40.
9. Kountz, *Record of the Organizations Engaged in the Campaign, Siege, and Defense of Vicksburg*, 35.
10. Warner, *Generals in Blue*, 387–388; Dana, *Recollections of the Civil War*, 69.
11. James Pickett Jones, *Black Jack: John A. Logan and Southern Illinois in the Civil War Era* (Carbondale: Southern Illinois University Press, 1995), 169; Dana, *Recollections of the Civil War*, 67–68.

12. Smith, "A Matter of Trust: Grant and James B. McPherson," 157.
13. *OR*, 24(1):709; *OR*, 24(2):199, 293, 295; Francis R. Baker Diary, May 22, 1863, ALPL; Wells W. Leggett to mother, June 6, 1863, Journals/Letters/Diaries, VICK, original in Lincoln Memorial Shrine. For Leggett, see the Mortimer Leggett Collection, University of California, Santa Barbara, and Mortimer D. Leggett Papers, Western Reserve Historical Society.
14. Bearss, *The Vicksburg Campaign*, 3:798.
15. *OR*, 24(2):367.
16. Lockett, "The Defense of Vicksburg," 3:488.
17. Ballard, *Vicksburg*, 323.
18. Bearss, *The Vicksburg Campaign*, 3:783, 821.
19. Ballard, *Vicksburg*, 323.
20. Bearss, *The Vicksburg Campaign*, 3:783, 821; John F. Hampton to J. O. Banks, June 22, 1903, 43rd Mississippi File, VICK; W. R. McCrary Diary, May 22, 1863, Journals/Letters/Diaries, VICK; J. N. and M. H. Ellis Diary, May 22, 1863, OCM; T. T. Smith Reminiscences, 1899, Columbus Sykes Papers, CWD, USAHEC, copy in MDAH. For the 43rd Mississippi, see W. Scott Bell, *The Camel Regiment: A History of the Bloody 43rd Mississippi Volunteer Infantry, CSA, 1862–1865* (Gretna, LA: Pelican Publishing Company, 2017).
21. Rowland and Howell, *Military History of Mississippi*, 319–334, 352; Bearss, *The Vicksburg Campaign*, 3:783; John F. Hampton to J. O. Banks, June 22, 1903, 43rd Mississippi File, VICK; W. R. McCrary Diary, May 22, 1863, Journals/Letters/Diaries, VICK; J. N. and M. H. Ellis Diary, May 22, 1863, OCM; T. T. Smith Reminiscences, 1899, Columbus Sykes Papers, CWD, USAHEC, copy in MDAH; Ezra J. Warner, *Generals in Gray: Lives of the Confederate Commanders* (Baton Rouge: Louisiana State University Press, 1959), 219.
22. *OR*, 24(2):382, 385; Robert H. Bunn to W. T. Rigby, July 4, 1904, 42nd Alabama File, VICK; Rex Miller, *Dowdell's Volunteers: 37th Alabama Infantry* (Depew, NY: Patrex Press, 1992), 12, copy in 37th Alabama File, VICK. See 37th and 42nd Alabama Regimental History Files, ADAH, for more on the 42nd Alabama. For more on Smith, see the Ashbel Smith Papers, University of Texas. For the 2nd Texas, see Joseph E. Chance, *The Second Texas Infantry: From Shiloh to Vicksburg* (Austin, TX: Eakin Press, 1984).
23. Smith, *The Mississippi Secession Convention*, 194–195, 200; Elbert Willett Diary, May 22, 1863, ADAH, copy in OCM, and *History of Company B (Originally Pickens Planters) 40th Alabama Regiment Confederate States Army 1862–1865* (Anniston, AL: Norwood, 1902), 35.
24. *OR*, 24(2):367, 420.
25. *OR*, 24(2):366–367.
26. Bearss and Hills, *Receding Tide*, 250; Hills, "Failure and Scapegoat: May 22," 50.
27. *OR*, 24(1):55.
28. *OR*, 24(2):297.
29. Dyer, *A Compendium of the War of the Rebellion*, 3:1048–1049, 1077, 1086–1087,

1679–1681. *OR*, 24(2):297; George Carrington Diary, May 22, 1863, CHM; "War Diary of Brevet Brigadier General Joseph Stockton," Coco Collection, HCWRT, USAHEC, 16. For the 11th Illinois, see Huffstodt, *Hard Dying Men*.
30. *OR*, 24(2):297–298, 300; George Carrington Diary, May 22, 1863, CHM; Elliott Bush to parents, May 29, 1863, Elliott N. and Henry M. Bush Papers, James S. Schoff Civil War Collection, UMC; Robert Ridge Diary, May 22, 1863, ALPL.
31. George Carrington Diary, May 22, 1863, CHM.
32. *OR*, 24(2):297–298.
33. Dyer, *A Compendium of the War of the Rebellion*, 3:1086, 1137–1138, 1166–1167, 1169, 1297–1298, 1332–1333, 1681; Dana, *Recollections of the Civil War*, 70; Smith, *Champion Hill*, 266–280.
34. *OR*, 24(2):67; *OR*, 24(1):732.
35. *OR*, 24(2):67, 316–317; H. M. Trimble Diary, May 22, 1863, 93rd Illinois File, VICK; Mahlon Head to W. T. Rigby, April 21, 1903, 5th Iowa File, VICK; J. Q. A. Campbell Diary, May 22, 1863, 5th Iowa File, VICK.
36. Byers, *With Fire and Sword*, 90–91.
37. Lyman Baker Memoirs, 1914, ALPL, 11–13.
38. *OR*, 24(1):732, 772.
39. *OR*, 24(1):732; *OR*, 24(2):62.
40. *OR*, 24(1):784; James C. Mahan, *Memoirs of James Curtis Mahan* (Lincoln, NE: Franklin Press, 1919), 124; Edward J. Wood to wife, May 25, 1863, Edward J. Wood Papers, IHS; H. M. Trimble Diary, May 22, 1863, 93rd Illinois File, VICK; E. B. Badcom to W. T. Rigby, March 27, 1903, 5th Iowa File, VICK.
41. Badeau, *Military History of Ulysses S. Grant*, 1:316.
42. For political generals, see David Work, *Lincoln's Political Generals* (Urbana: University of Illinois Press, 2009).
43. Smith, *Champion Hill*, 212.
44. Simon and Marszalek, eds., *PUSG*, 5:284; *PUSG*, 6:161, 318; Warner, *Generals in Blue*, 459; Dana, *Recollections of the Civil War*, 69; John E. Smith to S. Burbank, December 4, 1866, Isaac F. Quinby File, Journals/Letters/Diaries, VICK.
45. Dyer, *A Compendium of the War of the Rebellion*, 3:1053, 1058–1059, 1066, 1098–1099, 1128; *OR*, 24(2):206; P. C. Bonney to unknown, May 30, 1863, Philip C. Bonney Papers, ALPL, published in Winifred Keen Armstrong, ed., "The Civil War Letters of Pvt. P. C. Bonney," Lawrence [Illinois] County Historical Society, 1963; W. S. Morris, *History, 31st Regiment Illinois Volunteers: Organized by John A. Logan* (Herrin, IL: Crossfire Press, 1991); "Losses at Vicksburg," September 29, 1910, *National Tribune*; C. W. Randall to mother, May 25, 1863, Cyrus W. Randall Papers, ALPL; Stephen C. Beck, "A True Sketch of His Army Life," 1902, Journals/Letters/Diaries, VICK, copy in OCM.
46. *OR*, 24(1):710, 713; *OR*, 24(2):206–207; Post, ed., *Soldiers' Letters*, 269; G. W. Young to mother, May 28, 1863, Journals/Letters/Diaries, VICK.
47. *OR*, 24(1):710, 713; *OR*, 24(2):206–207; G. W. Young to mother, May 28, 1863, Journals/Letters/Diaries, VICK; Post, ed., *Soldiers' Letters*, 269.

48. *OR*, 24(1):710, 713; Tunnard, *A Southern Record*, 239.
49. *OR*, 24(1):710, 713; John E. Smith to Aimee, May 31, 1863, Kirby Smith Private Collection, Barrington, Illinois.
50. *OR*, 24(1):713.
51. *OR*, 24(1):710; Bearss, *The Vicksburg Campaign*, 3:783; Ira Blanchard, *I Marched With Sherman: Civil War Memoirs of the 20th Illinois Volunteer Infantry*, Nancy Ann Mattingly, ed. (New York: toExcel, 1992), 96.
52. *OR*, 24(1):710; Blanchard, *I Marched With Sherman*, 96.
53. *OR*, 24(1):710, 713; *OR*, 24(2):207; R. L. Howard, *History of the 124th Regiment Illinois Infantry Volunteers, Otherwise Known as the 'Hundred and Two Dozen,' From August, 1862, to August, 1865* (Springfield, IL: H. W. Rokker, 1880), 107; Lewis T. Hickok Diary, May 22, 1863, James S. Schoff Collection, UMC; Job H. Yaggy Diary, May 22, 1863, ALPL.
54. *OR*, 24(1):710; Blanchard, *I Marched With Sherman*, 96–97; James B. Owen to father, May 27, 1863, James B. Owen Letters, TSLA.
55. *OR*, 24(2):206; Warner, *Generals in Blue*, 476; Dana, *Recollections of the Civil War*, 68; Carroll Harriss to wife, June 13, 1863, Jordan C. Harriss Papers, NC.
56. Dyer, *A Compendium of the War of the Rebellion*, 3:1046–1047, 1052, 1081, 1325–1326, 1511–1512; Jerry Evan Crouch, *Silencing the Vicksburg Guns: The Story of the 7th Missouri Infantry Regiment As Experienced by John Davis Evans Union Private and Mormon Pioneer* (Victoria, BC: Trafford Publishing, 2005); E. Z. Hays, *History of the Thirty-second Regiment Ohio Veteran Volunteer Infantry* (Columbus, OH: Cott & Evans Printers, 1896), 44.
57. For the battery, see Martin N. Bertera, *De Golyer's 8th Michigan Black Horse Light Battery* (Wyandotte, MI: TillieAnn Press, 2015). For De Golyer himself, see Martin N. Bertera, *A Soldier at Dawn: A Remarkable and Heroic Exodus* (n.p.:n.p., n.d.).
58. *OR*, 24(1):719; George S. Durfee to uncle, May 21, 1863, George S. Durfee Papers, UI.
59. *OR*, 24(1):719; *OR*, 24(2):206–207; J. L. Power Diary, May 22, 1863, MDAH; George S. Durfee to uncle, May 21, 1863, George S. Durfee Papers, UI.
60. George O. Smith, "Brief History of the 17th Regiment of the Illinois Volunteer Infantry, U.S.A.," 1913, ALPL, 5.
61. *OR*, 24(1):718–719; Abram J. Vanauken Diary, May 22, 1863, ALPL; Richard Blackstone to W. T. Rigby, January 3, 1904, 32nd Ohio File, VICK; George S. Durfee to uncle, May 21, 1863, George S. Durfee Papers, UI; Richard Blackstone Diary, May 17, 1863, LMU.
62. Robert Buchanan to W. T. Rigby, February 21, 1905, 7th Missouri File, VICK.
63. *OR*, 24(1):719; William A. Lorimer to W. T. Rigby, December 22, 1904, 17th Illinois File, VICK; J. Q. A. Campbell Diary, May 22, 1863, 5th Iowa File, VICK, later published as Mark Grimsley and Todd D. Miller, eds., *The Union Must Stand: The Civil War Diary of John Quincy Adams Campbell, Fifth Iowa Volunteer Infantry* (Knoxville: University of Tennessee Press, 2000).
64. *OR*, 24(2):361, 376; *Supplement to the Official Records of the Union and Confederate*

Armies, 100 vols., 4:417; F. M. Smith to W. T. Rigby, January 9, 1905, 81st Illinois File, VICK.
65. *OR*, 24(1):719, 722; Bearss, *The Vicksburg Campaign*, 3:821; Logan H. Roots to sir, July 24, 1863, Edwin C. Hewett Correspondence, UI; J. Q. A. Campbell Diary, May 22, 1863, 5th Iowa File, VICK; Robert Buchanan to W. T. Rigby, February 21, 1905, 7th Missouri File, VICK.
66. *OR*, 24(1):720; William L. Shea and Terrence J. Winschel, *Vicksburg is the Key: The Struggle for the Mississippi River* (Lincoln: University of Nebraska Press, 2003), 150; Robert Buchanan to W. T. Rigby, February 21, 1905, 7th Missouri File, VICK.
67. *OR*, 24(1):719, 722; Edmund Newsome Diary, May 22, 1863, MDAH; George S. Durfee to W. T. Rigby, June 20, 1903, 8th Illinois File, VICK; George S. Durfee to uncle, May 21, 1863, George S. Durfee Papers, UI; Martin Whipkey to Cr. R. Koch, August 26, 1902, 81st Illinois File, VICK; Gould D. Mollneaux Diary, May 22, 1863, AC.
68. Edwin A. Loosley to wife, May 26, 1863, Edwin A. Loosley Papers, SIU; John P. Reese to wife, May 25, 1863, Journals/Letters/Diaries, VICK.
69. *OR*, 24(1):719–720; Gould D. Molineaux Diary, May 22, 1863, AC.
70. Wells, *The Siege of Vicksburg from the Diary of Seth J. Wells*, 68; F. M. Smith to W. T. Rigby, January 9, 1905, 81st Illinois File, VICK.
71. *OR*, 24(1):719–720, 722; *OR*, 24(2):376; Bearss, *The Vicksburg Campaign*, 3:783; George S. Durfee to W. T. Rigby, June 20, 1903, 8th Illinois File, VICK; J. L. Power Diary, May 22, 1863, MDAH; Thomas W. McCluer Diary, May 22, 1863, OCM; John A. Logan to wife, May 31, 1863, John A. Logan Papers, LC.
72. *OR*, 24(1):719–720, 722; *OR*, 24(2):376; George S. Durfee to W. T. Rigby, June 20, 1903, 8th Illinois File, VICK; John A. Logan to wife, May 31, 1863, John A. Logan Papers, LC; F. M. Smith to W. T. Rigby, January 9, 1905, 81st Illinois File, VICK.
73. Robert Buchanan to W. T. Rigby, February 21, 1905, 7th Missouri File, VICK.
74. F. M. Smith to W. T. Rigby, January 9, 1905, 81st Illinois File, VICK.
75. "Fighting For Vicksburg," August 23, 1894, *National Tribune*; John P. Reese to wife, May 25, 1863, Journals/Letters/Diaries, VICK.
76. George O. Smith, "Brief History of the 17th Regiment of the Illinois Volunteer Infantry, U.S.A.," 1913, ALPL, 5–6.
77. *OR*, 24(1):720; *OR*, 24(2):361.

Chapter 9. "They Seemed to Be Springing from the Bowels of the Earth"

1. Albert D. Richardson, *A Personal History of Ulysses S. Grant* (Hartford, CT: American Publishing Company, 1868), 284.
2. For McClernand, see Kiper, *Major General John Alexander McClernand*. For McClernand and Grant and the others, see Terrence J. Winschel, "Fighting Politician: John A. McClernand," in *Grant's Lieutenants: From Cairo to Vicksburg*, Steven E. Woodworth, ed. (Lawrence: University Press of Kansas, 2001), 129–150.

3. *OR*, 7:170; *OR*, 10(1):114.
4. Smith, *The Decision Was Always My Own*, 29–30.
5. *OR*, 17(2):420.
6. *OR*, 17(2):553.
7. *OR*, 24(1):84.
8. Winschel, "Fighting Politician: John A. McClernand," 137–139.
9. Warner, *Generals in Blue*, 70, 235, 352–353, 454; Dana, *Recollections of the Civil War*, 64–65; *OR*, 24(1):154, 624; *Supplement to the Official Records of the Union and Confederate Armies*, 4:393; John Merrilees Diary, May 19, 1863, CHM; Samuel Styre to parents, July 1, 1863, Samuel Styre Papers, DU.
10. Cadwallader, *Three Years with Grant*, 89.
11. *OR*, 24(1):154.
12. Grabau, *Ninety-Eight Days*, 379–382.
13. *OR*, 24(2):386.
14. *OR*, 24(2):385–386; Bearss, *The Vicksburg Campaign*, 3:782; Douglas Lee Broadaway, "A Texan Records the Civil War Siege of Vicksburg, Mississippi: The Journal of Maj. Maurice Kavanaugh Simons, 1863," *Southwestern Historical Quarterly* 105, no. 1 (July 2001): 108–109.
15. Carlos Colby to sister, May 26, 1863, Carlos Colby Papers, NL.
16. *OR*, 24(2):350, 355; Bearss, *The Vicksburg Campaign*, 3:, 785, 825; William T. Alexander to W. T. Rigby, September 24, 1904, 46th Alabama File, VICK; "Twenty Third Alabama Regiment," February 29, 1912, 23rd Alabama Regimental History Files, ADAH, 20–24; J. M. Pearson to S. D. Lee, May 17, 1902, 30th Alabama File, VICK.
17. *OR*, 24(2):344, 357, 387.
18. Wilson, "A Staff Officer's Journal of the Vicksburg Campaign," 264.
19. Grabau, *Ninety-Eight Days*, 376; Ballard, *Vicksburg*, 338; Kiper, *Major General John A. McClernand*, 266.
20. Grabau, *Ninety-Eight Days*, 376; Albert C. Boals Diary, May 22, 1863, ALPL; Carlos Colby to sister, May 26, 1863, Carlos Colby Papers, NL.
21. Dyer, *A Compendium of the War of the Rebellion*, 3:1060, 1089, 1120–1121, 1125–1126, 1143–1144, 1535, 1683; I. H. Elliott to Colonel Matthews, May 16, 1902, 33rd Illinois File, VICK; Dana, *Recollections of the Civil War*, 65.
22. S. G. Burbridge to John A. McClernand, May 25, 1863, John A. McClernand Papers, ALPL.
23. *OR*, 24(1):155; Henry Steele Commager, *The Blue and the Gray: The Story of the Civil War as Told By Participants, Revised and Abridged*, 2 vols. (New York: Meridian, 1994), 2:69; Edgar L. Erickson, ed., "With Grant at Vicksburg: From the Civil War Diary of Captain Charles E. Wilcox," *Journal of the Illinois State Historical Society* 30, no. 4 (January 1938), 441–503; I. H. Elliott to Colonel Matthews, May 16, 1902, 33rd Illinois File, VICK; Amos York to W. T. Rigby, January 6, 1904, 8th Indiana File, VICK; Nicholas Miller Memoir, undated, OCM, 11–12.
24. *OR*, 24(1):155; Bearss, *The Vicksburg Campaign*, 3:828; Commager, *The Blue and the Gray*, 2:69; Isaac H. Elliott, *History of the Thirty-third Regiment Illinois Veteran*

Volunteer Infantry in the Civil War, 22nd August 1861, to 7th December, 1865 (Gibson City, IL: The Association, 1902), 44; Louis W. Knobe Diary, May 22, 1863, ISL; Isaac Jackson to brother, May 30, 1863, Isaac Jackson Letters, James S. Schoff Civil War Collection, UMC; Charles A. Hobbs Letters, undated, 99th Illinois File, VICK, 21.

25. I. H. Elliott to Colonel Matthews, May 16, 1902, 33rd Illinois File, VICK; John H. Burnham, *The Thirty-third Regiment Illinois Infantry in the Civil War, 1861–1865; Prepared by Capt. J.H. Burnham at the Request of the Directors of the Illinois Historical Society for the 1912 Annual Meeting of that Society* (n.p.: n.p., 1912), no page; Elliott, *History of the Thirty-third Regiment Illinois Veteran Volunteer Infantry in the Civil War*, 43; *History of the 99th Illinois Vols. Containing Also the Names of Its Officers, Addresses of Survivors and Minutes of 1901 Meeting of Association*, 1901, George S. Marks Papers, CWD, USAHEC, 7; Commager, *The Blue and the Gray*, 2:69; J. M. Hobbs Diary, May 22, 1863, 33rd Illinois File, VICK; Edward J. Lewis Diary, May 22, 1863, 33rd Illinois File, VICK; Charles A. Hobbs Letters, undated, 99th Illinois File, VICK, 21; J. A. Nottingham to W. T. Rigby, December 1, 1901, 8th Indiana File, VICK; James R. Danby Diary, May 22, 1863, 8th Indiana File, VICK; James B. Black to W. T. Rigby, November 27, 1903, 18th Indiana File, VICK.
26. Commager, *The Blue and the Gray*, 2:69–70.
27. *OR*, 24(2):155, 361, 387; William Murray Diary, May 22, 1863, Journals/Letters/Diaries, VICK; E. H. Twining to Kate, June 9, 1863, Moody Family Papers, MHS.
28. James K. Bigelow, *Abridged History of the Eighth Indiana Volunteer Infantry, from Its Organization, April 21st, 1861, to the Date of Re-enlistment as Veterans, January 1, 1864* (Indianapolis: Ellis Barnes Book and Job Printer, 1864), 20; Elliott, *History of the Thirty-third Regiment Illinois Veteran Volunteer Infantry in the Civil War*, 9, 45, 84; Commager, *The Blue and the Gray*, 2:70.
29. Bearss, *The Vicksburg Campaign*, 3:829; Shea and Winschel, *Vicksburg Is the Key*, 150; Arnold, *Grant Wins the War*, 252; *History of the 99th Illinois Vols. Containing Also the Names of Its Officers, Addresses of Survivors and Minutes of 1901 Meeting of Association*, 1901, George S. Marks Papers, CWD, USAHEC, 8.
30. *OR*, 24(2):34, 37, 39, 236; Scott, *The History of the 67th Regiment Indian Infantry Volunteers*, 37; J. G. Jones to parents, May 29, 1863, John G. Jones Correspondence, LC.
31. *OR*, 24(2):34, 37, 39, 236; J. G. Jones to parents, May 29, 1863, John G. Jones Correspondence, LC; Scott, *The History of the 67th Regiment Indian Infantry Volunteers*, 37.
32. *OR*, 24(2):387–388.
33. *OR*, 24(2):37; Isaac Jackson to brother, May 30, 1863, Isaac Jackson Letters, James S. Schoff Civil War Collection, UMC.
34. *OR*, 24(2):33–34; Marshall, *History of the Eighty-third Ohio Volunteer Infantry*, 85–86; George Chittenden to wife, May 29, 1863, Chittenden Family Papers, ISL.
35. *OR*, 24(2):33–34, 37; *OR*, 24(1):598; T. Northrop to Ira, May 26, 1863, 23rd Wisconsin File, VICK; George D. Kellogg to parents, May 25, 1863, 23rd Wisconsin File, VICK.
36. *OR*, 24(2):39, 367, 382, 388; J. G. Jones to parents, May 29, 1863, John G. Jones Correspondence, LC.

37. *OR*, 24(2):388.
38. *OR*, 24(2):388; Bearss, *The Vicksburg Campaign*, 3:782; Ballard, *Vicksburg*, 334.
39. *OR*, 24(2):388–389; Bearss, *The Vicksburg Campaign*, 3:831.
40. *OR*, 24(2):34–35, 389; Bearss, *The Vicksburg Campaign*, 3:831; John B. Reid to W. T. Rigby, April 9, 1903, 130th Illinois File, VICK; George D. Kellogg to parents, May 25, 1863, 23rd Wisconsin File, VICK.
41. *OR*, 24(2):34–35, 389; Bearss, *The Vicksburg Campaign*, 3:831; John B. Reid to W. T. Rigby, April 9, 1903, 130th Illinois File, VICK; George D. Kellogg to parents, May 25, 1863, 23rd Wisconsin File, VICK.
42. *OR*, 24(2):34; Kiper, *Major General John A. McClernand*, 260.
43. *OR*, 24(2):34; *OR*, 24(1):598.
44. *OR*, 24(1):155; *OR*, 24(2):39.
45. Badeau, *Military History of Ulysses S. Grant*, 1:319–320.
46. *OR*, 24(1):617.
47. Warner, *Generals in Blue*, 352–353.
48. Original Osterhaus Report, May 26, 1863, James W. Thompson Papers, Folder 1, FHS.
49. *OR*, 24(2):17, 20; Warner, *Generals in Blue*, 168–169; Townsend, *Yankee Warhorse*, 109; Earl J. Hess, "Grant's Ethnic General: Peter J. Osterhaus," in *Grant's Lieutenants: From Cairo to Vicksburg*, Steven E. Woodworth, ed. (Lawrence: University Press of Kansas, 2001), 210; John A. McClernand Order, May 18, 1863, John A. McClernand Papers, ALPL; Dyer, *A Compendium of the War of the Rebellion*, 3:1096–1097, 1138, 1140, 1144–1145, 1200, 1503–1504, 1207, 1516, 1545–1547.
50. *OR*, 24(2):17, 20.
51. *OR*, 24(2):17, 20; George B. Marshall Reminiscences, 1912, ISL, 43–44.
52. *OR*, 24(2):20; Amos Pierson to W. P. Gault, February 5, 1904, 16th Ohio File, VICK; Enos Pierson, *Proceedings of Eleven Reunions Held by the 16th Regiment, O. V. I., Including Roll of Honor, Roster of the Survivors of the Regiment, Statistics, &c., &c.* (Millersburg, OH: Republican Steam Press, 1887), 59.
53. *OR*, 24(2):210; Adnah Eaton Diary, May 22, 1863, NC.
54. *OR*, 24(2):240; *History of the Forty-sixth Regiment Indiana Volunteer Infantry, September, 1861-September, 1865* (Logansport, IN: Press of Wilson, Humprheys and Co., 1888), 64; Alvin P. Hovey Memoir, undated, IU, 58; James R. Slack to Ann, May 24, 1863, James R. Slack Letters, ISL; William F. Hollingsworth Diary, May 22, 1863, OCM; Bernard Schermerhorn to wife, May 25, 1863, Bernard F. Schermerhorn Papers, IHS.
55. *OR*, 24(2):20, 232; Mason, *The Forty-second Ohio Infantry*, 221–222; E. L. Hawk to W. T. Rigby, April 21, 1914, 114th Ohio File, VICK.
56. *OR*, 24(2):20, 232; E. L. Hawk to W. T. Rigby, April 21, 1914, 114th Ohio File, VICK; Mason, *The Forty-second Ohio Infantry*, 221–222.
57. *OR*, 24(2):19–20, 344; Terrence J. Winschel, *Triumph and Defeat: The Vicksburg Campaign*, vol. 2 (New York: Savas Beatie, 2006), 159–160.
58. *OR*, 24(2):20, 27–28; Bearss, *The Vicksburg Campaign*, 3:785; Mason, *The Forty-second Ohio Infantry*, 223–224; Joseph Bowker Diary, May 22, 1863, 42nd Ohio File, VICK; William A. Sypher Diary, May 22, 1863, CHM.

59. *OR*, 24(2):354; Herman Hattaway, *General Stephen D. Lee* (Jackson: University Press of Mississippi, 1988), 93–94; William Roberts Diary, May 22, 1863, ADAH; "History of the Thirty-first Alabama," February 29, 1912, 31st Alabama Confederate Regimental History Files, ADAH 27–29.
60. *OR*, 24(2):20, 232; Oran Perry to H. C. Adams, February 11, 1909, 69th Indiana File, VICK.
61. Oran Perry to H. C. Adams, February 11, 1909, 69th Indiana File, VICK, copy in Carolyn S. Bridge, ed., *These Men Were Heroes Once: The Sixty-ninth Indiana Volunteer Infantry* (West Lafayette, IN: Twin Publications, 2005), 133–135; W. T. Rigby to Oran Perry, February 10, 1914, 69th Indiana File, VICK; Oran Perry, "Perry Tells Story of the Siege of Vicksburg," June 16, 1926, Vicksburg *Evening Post*, copy in 69th Indiana File, VICK; E. L. Hawk to W. T. Rigby, April 21, 1914, 114th Ohio File, VICK.
62. *OR*, 24(2):20, 232; Soman and Byrne, eds., *A Jewish Colonel in the Civil War*, 279; James Keigwin to W. T. Rigby, March 5, 1902, 49th Indiana File, VICK; James B. Taylor Diary, May 22, 1863, 120th Ohio File, VICK; W. L. Rand to family, May 25 and 26, 1863, Rand Family Papers, ALPL.
63. *OR*, 24(2):20, 232, 234; James Keigwin to W. T. Rigby, March 5, 1902, 49th Indiana File, VICK; James B. Taylor Diary, May 22, 1863, 120th Ohio File, VICK; W. L. Rand to family, May 25 and 26, 1863, Rand Family Papers, ALPL; Mahlon Rouch Diary, May 22, 1863, 120th Ohio File, VICK; Samuel Gordon to wife, May 25 and 29, 1863, Samuel Gordon Papers, ALPL.
64. *OR*, 24(2):20, 232, 234; Soman and Byrne, eds., *A Jewish Colonel in the Civil War*, 279–280; James Keigwin to W. T. Rigby, March 5, 1902, 49th Indiana File, VICK; James B. Taylor Diary, May 22, 1863, 120th Ohio File, VICK; W. L. Rand to family, May 25 and 26, 1863, Rand Family Papers, ALPL; Mahlon Rouch Diary, May 22, 1863, 120th Ohio File, VICK; Samuel Gordon to wife, May 25 and 29, 1863, Samuel Gordon Papers, ALPL.
65. *OR*, 24(2):20.
66. *OR*, 24(2):20.
67. *OR*, 24(2):344, 351.
68. *OR*, 24(2):20, 230, 240; Kiper, *Major General John A. McClernand*, 262; Joshua W. Underhill Diary, May 25, 1863, IHS.
69. J. M. Pearson to S. D. Lee, May 17, 1902, 30th Alabama File, VICK; George W. Gordon Diary, May 24, 1863, Gordon Collection, USAHEC; Steven E. Woodworth, "The Assault on the Railroad Redoubt," in *The Vicksburg Assaults: May 19–22, 1863*, Steven E. Woodworth and Charles D. Grear, eds. (Carbondale: Southern Illinois University Press, 2019), 57–71.
70. Warner, *Generals in Blue*, 276; Young, *Around the World With General Grant*, 2:623; Dana, *Recollections of the Civil War*, 65.
71. Dyer, *A Compendium of the War of the Rebellion*, 3:1173–1174; *OR*, 24(2):139–140; William R. Eddington Diary, May 22, 1863, ALPL, copy in 97th Illinois File, VICK; Carlos Colby to sister, May 26, 1863, Carlos Colby Papers, NL.
72. Dyer, *A Compendium of the War of the Rebellion*, 3:1079, 1088, 1100–1101, 1205–1206,

1519; *OR*, 24(2):236; Smith, *Shiloh*, 96; A. J. Smith et. al to Abraham Lincoln, June 1863, Journals/Letters/Diaries, VICK; William M. Stone Manuscript, undated, MDAH.
73. *OR*, 24(2):140, 242, 244; Pryce, *Vanishing Footprints*, 113; Myron Knight Diary, May 22, 1863, OCM.
74. J. M. Pearson to S. D. Lee, May 17, 1902, 30th Alabama File, VICK.
75. J. M. Pearson to S. D. Lee, May 17, 1902, 30th Alabama File, VICK.
76. *OR*, 24(2):140, 244; Bluford Wilson to J. C. Switzer, September 13, 1904, Bluford Wilson Papers, ALPL; Pryce, *Vanishing Footprints*, 115–116, 128; A. E. Cook Statement, undated, 21st Iowa File, VICK; Joseph R. Winslow Diary, May 22, 1863, John P. Reese to wife, May 25, 1863, Journals/Letters/Diaries, VICK; G. A. Remley to Howard, May 23, 1863, Remley Family Papers, NC; William M. Stone Manuscript, undated, MDAH.
77. *OR*, 24(2):140, 244; Pryce, *Vanishing Footprints*, 115–116, 128; A. E. Cook Statement, undated, 21st Iowa File, VICK; Joseph R. Winslow Diary, May 22, 1863, John P. Reese to wife, May 25, 1863, Journals/Letters/Diaries, VICK; G. A. Remley to Howard, May 23, 1863, Remley Family Papers, NC; William M. Stone Manuscript, undated, MDAH; Bluford Wilson to J. C. Switzer, September 13, 1904, Bluford Wilson Papers, ALPL.
78. *OR*, 24(2):140–141, 244; William R. Eddington Diary, May 22, 1863, 97th Illinois File, VICK; C. P. Alling, "Four Years With the Western Army," undated, 11th Wisconsin File, VICK; Ira W. Hunt Diary, May 22, 1863, 11th Wisconsin File, VICK.
79. *OR*, 24(2):140–141, 244; Ira W. Hunt Diary, May 22, 1863, 11th Wisconsin File, VICK; C. P. Alling, "Four Years With the Western Army," undated, 11th Wisconsin File, VICK; William R. Eddington Diary, May 22, 1863, 97th Illinois File, VICK.
80. *OR*, 24(2):140–142, 242–244, 344; *OR*, 24(1):154, 178; George Crooke, *The Twenty-first Regiment of Iowa Volunteer Infantry: A Narrative of Its Experience in Active Service, Including a Military Record of Each Officer, Non-Commissioned Officer, and Private Soldier of the Organization* (Milwaukee: King, Fowle & Co., 1891), 81, 83–84; S. C. Jones, *Reminiscences of the Twenty-second Iowa Volunteer Infantry, Giving Its Organization, Marches, Skirmishes, Battles, and Sieges, as Taken from the Diary of Lieutenant S. C. Jones of Company A* (Iowa City, IA: n.p., 1907), 38–39; William M. Stone Manuscript, undated, MDAH; Gilbert Gulbrandson to unknown, May 19, 1863, Gilbert Gulbrandson Papers, HCWRT, USAHEC.
81. *OR*, 24(2):140–142, 242–244, 344; *OR*, 24(1):154, 178; Crooke, *The Twenty-first Regiment of Iowa Volunteer Infantry*, 81, 83–84; Jones, *Reminiscences of the Twenty-second Iowa Volunteer Infantry*, 38–39; William M. Stone Manuscript, undated, MDAH; Gilbert Gulbrandson to unknown, May 19, 1863, Gilbert Gulbrandson Papers, HCWRT, USAHEC.
82. *OR*, 24(1):178; Pryce, *Vanishing Footprints*, 116.
83. OR, 24(2):140, 142, 181, 344; OR, 24(1):178–179; *Roster and Record of Iowa Soldiers in the War of the Rebellion, Together with Historical Sketches of Volunteer Organizations, 1861–1866*, 6 vols. (Des Moines, IA: Emory H. English, State Printer, 1910), 3:634; Richardson, *Personal History of Ulysses S. Grant*, 324; J. L. Power

Diary, May 22, 1863, MDAH; William M. Stone Manuscript, undated, MDAH; *Supplement to the Official Records of the Union and Confederate Armies*, 4:406; E. W. Pettus to W. T. Rigby, March 14, 1903, 30th Alabama File, VICK; Pryce, *Vanishing Footprints*, 118; E. J. C. Bealer to W. T. Rigby, April 21, 1903, 21st Iowa File, VICK.
84. J. M. Pearson to S. D. Lee, May 17, 1902, and J. M. Pearson to W. T. Rigby, September 10, 1902, both in 30th Alabama File, VICK.
85. *OR*, 24(2):344, 355, 357; A. C. Lenert Diary, May 22, 1863, UNT.
86. *OR*, 24(2):140, 142, 241–242; *OR*, 24(1):154; "An Incident of the Battle of Vicksburg," in *Military Order of the Loyal Legion of the United States, Commandery of the District of Columbia, War Papers 1* (n.p.: n.p., 1887), 63–72.
87. *OR*, 24(1):154.
88. *OR*, 24(2):141, 238; Bearss, *The Vicksburg Campaign*, 3:826; John A. Bering and Thomas Montgomery, *History of the Forty-Eighth Ohio Vet. Vol. Inf.* (Hillsboro, OH: Highland News Office, 1880), 86–87; S. H. Stevenson to parents, May 28, 1863, 48th Ohio File, VICK; John A. Bering to brother, May 28, 1863, 48th Ohio File, VICK; James J. Ray Diary, May 22, 1863, 19th Kentucky File, VICK.
89. *OR*, 24(2):141, 238; *OR*, 24(1):154–155; *Supplement to the Official Records of the Union and Confederate Armies*, 4:405; W. H. Bentley, *History of the 77th Illinois Volunteer Infantry, Sept. 2, 1862–July 10, 1865* (Peoria, IL: Edward Hine, Printer, 1883), 152; D. P. Grier to Anna, May 24, 1863, David P. Grier Papers, MHS; Jesse Sawyer to W. T. Rigby, February 14, 1903, 77th Illinois File, VICK; Merrick J. Wald Diary, May 22, 1863, OCM. For detail on the 77th Illinois, see Terrence J. Winschel, ed., *The Civil War Diary of a Common Soldier: William Wiley of the 77th Illinois Infantry* (Baton Rouge: Louisiana State University Press, 2001), xiii, although Wiley was not present for the assaults.
90. *OR*, 24(2):141, 238; *OR*, 24(1):154–155; *Supplement to the Official Records of the Union and Confederate Armies*, 4:405; Jesse Sawyer to W. T. Rigby, February 14, 1903, 77th Illinois File, VICK; John W. Carroll to comrades, October 28, 1902, 77th Illinois File, VICK; Joseph F. Parker to J. H. Robinson, June 24, 1902, 130th Illinois File, VICK.
91. *OR*, 24(1):177.
92. *OR*, 24(2):141, 367.
93. *OR*, 24(2):141, 360, 367; General Maury's Order Book, 1863, CHM, 278.
94. Cadwallader, *Three Years with Grant*, 90.
95. Kiper, *Major General John A. McClernand*, 262.

Chapter 10. "I Could Not Disregard His Reiterated Statements"

1. Fred Grant, "A Boy's Experience at Vicksburg," manuscript in Vicksburg files, USGPL, 30; Frederick D. Grant, "A Boy's Experience at Vicksburg," *Personal Recollections of the War of the Rebellion: Addresses Delivered before the Commandery of the*

NOTES TO PAGES 271–278 427

State of New York, Military Order of the Loyal Legion of the United States, A. Noel Blakeman, ed. (New York: G. P. Putnam's Sons, 1907), 86–100.
2. *OR*, 24(1):55–56.
3. *OR*, 24(1):55.
4. *OR*, 24(1):55; Sherman, *Memoirs*, 1:326–327; *In Memoriam*, 52–53; Hugh Ewing Statement, undated, Journals/Letters/Diaries, VICK.
5. *OR*, 24(1):55, 172–173; Simon and Marszalek, eds., *PUSG*, 8:253; Kiper, *Major General John A. McClernand*, 261; John A. McClernand to U. S. Grant, May 22, 1863, John A. McClernand Papers, ALPL; U. S. Grant to John A. McClernand, May 22, 1863, John A. McClernand Papers, ALPL.
6. Smith, *The Decision Was Always My Own*, 184–185.
7. *OR*, 24(1):56; Kiper, *Major General John A. McClernand*, 261.
8. *OR*, 24(1):55–56, 163; Sherman, *Memoirs*, 1:327; Kiper, *Major General John A. McClernand*, 261.
9. *OR*, 24(1):56; Sherman, *Memoirs*, 1:327; Signal Station Messages, May 19, 1863, John A. McClernand Papers, ALPL; John A. McClernand to U. S. Grant, May 22, 1863, John A. McClernand Papers, ALPL; John A. McClernand to John McArthur, May 22, 1863, John A. McClernand Papers, ALPL; U. S. Grant to John A. McClernand, May 22, 1863, John A. McClernand Papers, ALPL.
10. *OR*, 24(1):56, 172–173; Bearss, *The Vicksburg Campaign*, 3:837; Ballard, *Vicksburg*, 344; John A. McClernand to U. S. Grant, May 22, 1863, John A. McClernand Papers, ALPL.
11. *OR*, 24(1):757.
12. *OR*, 24(1):757.
13. *OR*, 24(1):757.
14. *OR*, 24(2):258–259, 278; Owen Francis Diary, May 22, 1863, 57th Ohio File, VICK; John D. Brownley, "History of John D. Brownley, Company D, 57th Ohio, Veteran Volunteer Infantry," undated, Anders Collection, USAHEC, 1.
15. *OR*, 24(2):251; Louis Guion Diary, May 22, 1863, LSU; W. H. Nugen to Mary, June 23, 1863, William H. Nugen Letters, DU.
16. *OR*, 24(1):757; Alonzo Abernathy Diary, May 22, 1863, 9th Iowa File, VICK; James Thomas to Jones, May 26, 1863, Robert T. Jones Letters, UTK; Richard and Richard, *The Defense of Vicksburg*, 159; Richard W. Burt to wife, May 23, 1863, Richard W. Burt Papers, SHSMC.
17. *OR*, 24(1):757.
18. Warner, *Generals in Blue*, 474; Dana, *Recollections of the Civil War*, 65–66.
19. Dyer, *A Compendium of the War of the Rebellion*, 3:1166, 1168–1169, 1175–1176, 1177; Dana, *Recollections of the Civil War*, 66; Unknown to W. T. Rigby, undated, 26th Iowa File, VICK.
20. Dyer, *A Compendium of the War of the Rebellion*, 3:1175, 1177–1178, 1323, 1328, 1329–1330, 1333–1135, 1532; Dana, *Recollections of the Civil War*, 66. For more on the 76th Ohio actions, see 76th Ohio Correspondence, 1863–1903, OHS.

21. *OR*, 24(2):252; *OR*, 24(1):757; James Thomas to Jones, May 26, 1863, Robert T. Jones Letters, UTK.
22. Bergeron, *Guide to Louisiana Confederate Military Units*, 116; Bearss, *The Vicksburg Campaign*, 3:843; *OR*, 24(2):394, 402; Chambers, "My Journal," 271. For the 17th Louisiana, see "17th Louisiana Volunteer Regiment," 17th Louisiana File, VICK; Samuel Addison Whyte Diary, May 25, 1863, UNC.
23. Bearrs, *The Vicksburg Campaign*, 3:865–866; *OR*, 24(1):757; Alonzo Abernathy Diary, May 22, 1863, 9th Iowa File, VICK; Unidentified 31st Iowa Diary, May 22, 1863, MHS; Joseph Child Diary, May 22, 1863, UI; Edwin C. Obriham to sister, May 22, 1863, Journals/Letters/Diaries, VICK.
24. UIA Robert Hoadley to cousin, May 29, 1863, Robert B. Hoadley Papers, DU.
25. *OR*, 24(2):254; Bearss, *The Vicksburg Campaign*, 3:844; James A. Fowler and Miles M. Miller, *History of the Thirtieth Iowa Infantry Volunteers. Giving a Complete Record of the Movements of the Regiment from Its Organization Until Muster Out* (Mediapolis, IA: T. A. Merrill, Printer, 1908), 29; Alonzo Abernathy Diary, May 22, 1863, 9th Iowa File, VICK; *Supplement to the Official Records of the Union and Confederate Armies*, 4:415; Uley Burk to family, June 8, 1863, 30th Iowa File, VICK; Henry Seaman Diary, May 21, 1863, 13th Illinois File, VICK; George D. Ward to brother, May 28, 1863, Ward Family Papers, UIA.
26. *OR*, 24(2):254; Bearss, *The Vicksburg Campaign*, 3:844; *Supplement to the Official Records of the Union and Confederate Armies*, 4:415; Richard and Richard, *The Defense of Vicksburg*, 159; George D. Ward to brother, May 28, 1863, Ward Family Papers, UIA; Louis Guion Diary, May 22, 1863, LSU.
27. *OR*, 24(2):252; Richard W. Burt to wife, May 23, 1863, Richard W. Burt Papers, SHSMC; Albert Hiffman Memoirs, undated, Hiffman Family Papers, MHS, 7; "A Narrative of the Services of Brevet Major Charles Dana Miller, 76th Ohio, in the War of the Great Rebellion, 1861–1865," undated, Journals/Letters/Diaries, VICK; Robert Hoadley to cousin, May 29, 1863, Robert B. Hoadley Papers, DU.
28. Bearss, *The Vicksburg Campaign*, 3:843–844.
29. *OR*, 24(2):252; Paul Dorweiler Diary, May 22, 1863, CWTI, USAHEC; John T. Buegel Diary, May 22, 1863, SHSMC; Joseph Kohout to family, May 25, 1863, Joseph Kohout Letters, UIA.
30. *OR*, 24(2):394, 402, 407; Chambers, "My Journal," 272; John Fuller Diary, May 22, 1863, 31st Louisiana File, VICK.
31. *OR*, 24(2):252; Alonzo Abernathy Diary, May 22, 1863, 9th Iowa File, VICK; Charles Willison to Ellie, May 26, 1863, 76th Ohio File, VICK.
32. Henry Seaman Diary, May 22, 1863, 13th Illinois File, VICK.
33. *OR*, 24(2):398; Chambers, "My Journal," 272; Abner J. Wilkes Memoir, undated, OCM, 5–6.
34. *OR*, 24(2):258, 361; Clarke, *Reminiscence and Anecdotes*, 103.
35. *OR*, 24(2):258; J. W. Larabee Statement, May 2, 1901, 55th Illinois File, VICK.
36. Parish, *Frank Blair*, 170.

37. *OR*, 24(2):269–270; W. J. Kennedy to wife, May 27, 1863, William J. Kennedy Letters, ALPL.
38. *OR*, 24(2):278; Samuel J. Oviatt to Libby, June 14, 1863, Samuel J. Oviatt Papers, NC.
39. *OR*, 24(2):258, 282.
40. *OR*, 24(2):264.
41. Grabau, *Ninety-Eight Days*, 369–373.
42. J. L. Jones to William T. Rigby, May 29, 1903, 38th Mississippi File, VICK; W. L. Faulk Diary, May 20, 1863, 38th Mississippi File, VICK, copy in OCM; Joseph B. Lightsey Memoir, 1908, OCM.
43. *OR*, 24(2):258; N. M. Baker to C. A. Noble, May 5, 1902, 116th Illinois File, VICK; Kellogg, *The Vicksburg Campaign and Reminiscences*, 42.
44. *OR*, 24(1):757; William L. Faulk to William T. Rigby, April 17, 1903, 3rd Louisiana File, VICK.
45. *OR*, 24(2):264; Kellogg, *The Vicksburg Campaign and Reminiscences*, 41; John Frist to W. T. Rigby, October 15, 1902, 113th Illinois File, VICK; Jim Russell to mother, May 27, 1863, Frederick W. Russell Letters, CHM.
46. *OR*, 24(2):270, 272; *The Story of the Fifty-fifth Regiment Illinois Volunteer Infantry in the Civil War*, 243; Ephraim Shay Diary, May 22, 1863, UMB; George Russell to friend, May 28, 1863, George W. Russell Papers, ALPL.
47. Jones, "The Rank and File at Vicksburg," 21; Eli W. Thornhill Memoir, undated, OCM, 10.
48. Kellogg, *The Vicksburg Campaign and Reminiscences*, 43.
49. *OR*, 24(2):258; *OR*, 24(1):757; W. L. Faulk Diary, May 22, 1863, 38th Mississippi File, VICK.
50. *OR*, 24(1):757; Hugh Ewing Statement, undated, Journals/Letters/Diaries, VICK.
51. Smith, *Shiloh*, 94–114, 197–216; Dana, *Recollections of the Civil War*, 66–67.
52. Dyer, *A Compendium of the War of the Rebellion*, 3:1067, 1298, 1327–1328, 1676–1677; Smith, *Corinth 1862*, 239–257; J. W. Greenman Diary, May 20, 1863, MDAH; Dana, *Recollections of the Civil War*, 67.
53. *OR*, 24(1):757, 768; Carey Campbell Wright, "The Civil War Letters of Carey Campbell Wright," undated, Wright Family Papers, AU, 135.
54. *OR*, 24(1):757, 768; Cloyd Bryner, *Bugle Echoes: The Story of the Illinois 47th* (Springfield, IL: Phillips Bros. Printers, 1905), 85–86; Brinkerhoff, *History of the Thirtieth Regiment Ohio Volunteer Infantry*, 75; Carey Campbell Wright, "The Civil War Letters of Carey Campbell Wright," undated, Wright Family Papers, AU, 135.
55. *OR*, 24(1):757, 768; *OR*, 24(2):259; Reed, *Campaigns and Battles of the Twelfth Regiment Iowa Veteran Volunteer Infantry*, 123; Brinkerhoff, *History of the Thirtieth Regiment Ohio Volunteer Infantry*, 75; Sherman, *Memoirs*, 1:327; John Merrilees Diary, May 2, 1863, CHM; Robert McRory to J. B. Allen, April 15, 1904, 30th Ohio File, VICK.
56. Smith, *Corinth 1862*, 246–248; "The Charge at Fort Hill," September 29, 1910, *National Tribune*.

57. *OR*, 24(2):273–274; John Carr Diary, May 22, 1863, Meadows Collection, HCWRT, USAHEC.
58. *OR*, 24(1):757, 760, 768; *OR*, 24(2):273; Dennis W. Belcher, *The 11th Missouri Volunteer Infantry in the Civil War: A History and Roster* (Jefferson, NC: McFarland & Company, 2011), 124; G. C. Adams to sister, May 25, 1863, John P. Reese to wife, May 25, 1863, Journals/Letters/Diaries, VICK; J. W. Greenman Diary, May 23, 1863, MDAH.
59. *OR*, 24(1):757, 760, 768; *OR*, 24(2):273; G. C. Adams to sister, May 25, 1863, John P. Reese to wife, May 25, 1863, Journals/Letters/Diaries, VICK; Belcher, *The 11th Missouri Volunteer Infantry in the Civil War*, 124; J. W. Greenman Diary, May 23, 1863, MDAH.
60. *OR*, 24(1):757, 760, 768; *OR*, 24(2):273; J. W. Greenman Diary, May 23, 1863, MDAH; Belcher, *The 11th Missouri Volunteer Infantry in the Civil War*, 124; G. C. Adams to sister, May 25, 1863, John P. Reese to wife, May 25, 1863, Journals/Letters/Diaries, VICK.
61. *OR*, 24(1):768; *OR*, 24(2):407.
62. *OR*, 24(1):768; *OR*, 24(2):407; "On Wrong Side of the Works," September 29, 1910, *National Tribune*; J. W. Greenman Diary, May 23, 1863, MDAH; John Merrilees Diary, May 22, 1863, CHM; S. D. Lee to W. T. Rigby, January 26, 1903, 27th Louisiana File, VICK; W. B. Britton to Editors Gazette, May 23, 1863, OCM.
63. Barton, *Autobiography of Dr. Thomas H. Barton*, 154; F. A. F., *Old Abe, The Eighth Wisconsin War Eagle. A Full Account of His Capture and Enlistment, Exploits in War and Honorable As Well As Useful Career in Peace* (Madison, WI: Curran and Bowen, 1885), 40; John Melvin Williams, "The Eagle Regiment," *8th Wis. Inf'ty Vols.: A Sketch of Its Marches, Battles and Campaigns From 1861–1865 With Complete Regimental and Company Roster, and a Few Portraits and Sketches of Its Officers and Commanders* (Belleville, WI: Recorder Print, 1890), 17, 61–63.
64. *OR*, 24(1):760–761; Robert J. Burdette, *The Drums of the 47th* (Urbana: University of Illinois Press, 2000), 80; Unknown to friend, June 2, 1863, Dixon and Jordan Family Papers, KCPL.
65. F. A. F., *Old Abe*, 41.
66. *OR*, 24(1):768; Bearss, *The Vicksburg Campaign*, 3:866; Bryner, *Bugle Echoes*, 85–86; Sherman, *Memoirs*, 1:327; Hugh Ewing Statement, undated, Journals/Letters/Diaries, VICK; *OR*, 24(2):398; Robert S. Martin Diary, May 22, 1863, SIU; Carey Campbell Wright, "The Civil War Letters of Carey Campbell Wright," undated, Wright Family Papers, AU, 136.
67. *OR*, 24(1):764, 770; Bearss, *The Vicksburg Campaign*, 3:866.
68. *OR*, 24(3):334–335; *OR*, 24(2):270; *The Story of the Fifty-fifth Regiment Illinois Volunteer Infantry in the Civil War*, 245; George M. Rogers Diary, May 22, 1863, ISL; "George Theodore Hyatt," 1897, 127th Illinois File, VICK.
69. Clarke, *Reminiscence and Anecdotes*, 103.
70. *OR*, 24(2):361; *OR*, 24(1):757–758; Bearss, *The Vicksburg Campaign*, 3:776, 864–866.

71. *OR*, 24(1):757.
72. *OR*, 24(1):757; *OR*, 24(2):259, 261, 283; William T. Sherman to wife, May 25, 1863, William T. Sherman Papers, LC.
73. Michael B. Ballard, *Grant at Vicksburg: The General and the Siege*, Steven E. Woodworth, ed. (Carbondale: Southern Illinois University Press, 2013), 20; Ballard, *Vicksburg*, 346; Bearss, *The Vicksburg Campaign*, 3:844.

CHAPTER 11. "THE ASSAULT WAS FEEBLE COMPARED WITH THE FIERCE ONSLAUGHTS EARLIER IN THE DAY"

1. J. H. Pepper Diary, May 22, 1863, MDAH; *OR*, 24(2):394.
2. *OR*, 24(2):420.
3. *OR*, 24(2):420.
4. *OR*, 24(2):420.
5. *OR*, 24(2):420.
6. *OR*, 24(1):719.
7. Post, ed., *Soldiers' Letters*, 214.
8. *OR*, 24(2):295.
9. *OR*, 24(1):56.
10. *OR*, 24(2):259; Charles R. Koch to W. T. Rigby, April 30, 1905, 95th Illinois File, VICK.
11. *OR*, 24(2):298; "War Diary of Brevet Brigadier General Joseph Stockton," Coco Collection, HCWRT, USAHEC, 16.
12. Payne, "Missouri Troops in the Vicksburg Campaign," 377; Giambrone, *Beneath Torn and Tattered Flags*, 73–74.
13. *OR*, 24(2):300; "War Diary of Brevet Brigadier General Joseph Stockton," Coco Collection, HCWRT, USAHEC, 16.
14. *OR*, 24(2):297–298, 300; George Carrington Diary, May 22, 1863, CHM; Elliott Bush to parents, May 29, 1863, Elliott N. and Henry M. Bush Papers, James S. Schoff Civil War Collection, UMC; "War Diary of Brevet Brigadier General Joseph Stockton," Coco Collection, HCWRT, USAHEC, 16.
15. Wood, *A History of the Ninety-fifth Regiment Illinois Infantry Volunteers*, 76–77; Post, ed., *Soldiers' Letters*, 213–214.
16. A. K. Heffelfinger to W. T. Rigby, August 27, 1905, 95th Illinois File, VICK; Charles R. Koch to W. T. Rigby, January 10, 1904, and April 30, 1905, 95th Illinois File, VICK; *OR*, 24(2):298, 300; Bearss, *The Vicksburg Campaign*, 3:840; George Carrington Diary, May 22, 1863, CHM; H. E. Harris to C. R. Kock, July 24, 1902, 11th Illinois File, VICK; Elliott Bush to parents, May 29, 1863, Elliott N. and Henry M. Bush Papers, James S. Schoff Civil War Collection, UMC; Anson Hemingway Diary, May 22, 1863, Journals/Letters/Diaries, VICK; "War Diary of Brevet Brigadier General Joseph Stockton," Coco Collection, HCWRT, USAHEC, 16.
17. *OR*, 24(2):298; L. P. Brockett, *The Camp, The Battle Field, and the Hospital; Or,*

Lights and Shadows of the Great Rebellion (Philadelphia: National Publishing Company, 1866), 511; George Carrington Diary, May 22, 1863, CHM.
18. *OR*, 24(2):298; Huffstodt, *Hard Dying Men*, 143–146; George Carrington Diary, May 22, 1863, CHM.
19. *OR*, 24(2):298; George Carrington Diary, May 22, 1863, CHM; "War Diary of Brevet Brigadier General Joseph Stockton," Coco Collection, HCWRT, USAHEC, 16.
20. Elliott Bush to parents, May 29, 1863, Elliott N. and Henry M. Bush Papers, James S. Schoff Civil War Collection, UMC; James K. Newton to parents, May 24, 1863, 14th Wisconsin File, VICK; Stephen E. Ambrose, ed., "A Wisconsin Boy at Vicksburg: The Letters of James K. Newton," *Journal of Mississippi History* 23, no. 1 (January 1961): 3–4. See also Stephen E. Ambrose, ed., *A Wisconsin Boy in Dixie: The Selected Letters of James K. Newton* (Madison: University of Wisconsin Press, 1961).
21. *OR*, 24(2):298; "War Diary of Brevet Brigadier General Joseph Stockton," Coco Collection, HCWRT, USAHEC, 16.
22. *OR*, 24(2):298; Brockett, *The Camp, The Battle Field, and the Hospital*, 511–512.
23. *OR*, 24(2):298; Wood, *A History of the Ninety-fifth Regiment Illinois Infantry Volunteers*, 77–78.
24. *OR*, 24(2):299.
25. *OR*, 24(1):710, 719.
26. *OR*, 24(1):719.
27. *OR*, 24(1):710; *OR*, 24(2):295. For the 20th Ohio, see D. W. Wood, *History of the 20th O. V. V. I. Regiment, and Proceedings of the First Reunion at Mt. Vernon, Ohio, April 6, 1876* (Columbus, OH: Paul and Thrall, Book and Job Printers, 1876).
28. *OR*, 24(1):713; Manning F. Force to father, May 23, 1863, Manning F. Force Papers, UW, copy in LC.
29. *OR*, 24(1):710.
30. *OR*, 24(1):710; *OR*, 24(2):295.
31. *OR*, 24(1):710.
32. Post, ed., *Soldiers' Letters*, 269; Wilbur F. Crummer, *With Grant at Fort Donelson, Shiloh and Vicksburg, and An Appreciation of General U.S. Grant* (Oak Park, IL: E. C. Crummer and Co., 1915), 110–113; George H. Woodruff, *Fifteen Years Ago, Or The Patriotism of Will County* (Joliet, IL: Joliet Republican Book and Job Steam Printing House, 1876), 126.
33. OR, 24(1):710; John M. Adair, *Historical Sketch of the Forty-fifth Illinois Regiment, With a Complete List of the Officers and Privates and an Individual Record of Each Man in the Regiment* (Lanark, IL: Carroll County Gazette Print, 1869), 11; "The 45th Ill. At Vicksburg," September 29, 1910, *National Tribune*.
34. *OR*, 24(1):710; *OR*, 24(2):295; Force, "Personal Recollections of the Vicksburg Campaign," 304.
35. Post, ed., *Soldiers' Letters*, 269.
36. Simon and Marszalek, eds., *PUSG*, 8:252.
37. *OR*, 24(1):56.
38. *OR*, 24(1):732.

39. *OR*, 24(1):732; Alonzo L. Brown, *History of the Fourth Regiment of Minnesota Infantry Volunteers During the Great Rebellion 1861–1865* (St. Paul, MN: Pioneer Press Company, 1892), 213; John Whitten Diary, May 22, 1863, LC.
40. James B. McPherson to I. F. Quinby and John A. McClernand to I. F. Quinby, May 22, 1863, John A. McClernand Papers, ALPL.
41. *OR*, 24(1):732.
42. *OR*, 24(1):732–733, 773.
43. *OR*, 24(1):732.
44. *OR*, 24(1):732; *OR*, 24(2):62; Mahan, *Memoirs of James Curtis Mahan*, 125; Isaac Vanderwarker Diary, May 22, 1863, 4th Minnesota File, VICK; John F. Lester Diary, May 22, 1863, IHS; Isaac Vanderwarker Diary, May 22, 1863, CWD, USAHEC; Edward J. Wood to wife, May 25, 1863, Edward J. Wood Papers, IHS; Jesse M. Lee Diary, May 22, 1863, 59th Indiana File, VICK; T. Northrop to Ira, May 26, 1863, 23rd Wisconsin File, VICK.
45. *OR*, 24(2):389.
46. *OR*, 24(2):389; William Lovelace Foster to wife, June 20, 1863, William L. Foster Letter, UA; Edward P. Stanfield to father, May 26, 1863, Edward P. Stanfield Papers, IHS.
47. *OR*, 24(1):732; *OR*, 24(2):62; Daniel P. Clore Diary, May 22, 1863, MDAH; J. H. Pepper Diary, May 22, 1863, MDAH.
48. *OR*, 24(1):732; *OR*, 24(2):62, 420; Bearss, *The Vicksburg Campaign*, 3:848; Edward J. Wood to wife, May 25, 1863, Edward J. Wood Papers, IHS.
49. *OR*, 24(1):617, 733; Edward P. Stanfield to father, May 26, 1863, Edward P. Stanfield Papers, IHS; Samuel E. Sneier to sir, June 21, 1863, Samuel E. Sneier Papers, IHS.
50. *OR*, 24(1):733; *OR*, 24(2):62.
51. *OR*, 24(1):733.
52. *OR*, 24(2):67.
53. *OR*, 24(2):67; J. Q. A. Campbell Diary, May 22, 1863, 5th Iowa File, VICK.
54. *OR*, 24(2):67, 312; *OR*, 24(1):776–777, 780, 784; H. M. Trimble Diary, May 22, 1863, 93rd Illinois File, VICK.
55. *OR*, 24(2):67; *OR*, 24(1):617; Cadwallader, *Three Years with Grant*, 91; Mary Amelia (Boomer) Stone, *Memoir of George Boardman Boomer* (Boston: Press of Geo. C. Rand & Avery, 1864), 256–257; Henry G. Hicks, "The Campaign and Capture of Vicksburg," in *Glimpses of the Nation's Struggle, Sixth Series: Papers Read Before the Minnesota Commandery of the Military Order of the Loyal Legion of the United States, January 1903–1908* (Minneapolis: Aug. Davis, 1909), 102–103.
56. *OR*, 24(2):67; Aaron Dunbar and Harvey M. Trimble, *History of the Ninety-third Regiment Volunteer Infantry From Organization to Muster Out* (Chicago: Blakely Printing Co., 1898), 36; H. M. Trimble to W. T. Rigby, March 5, 1903, 93rd Illinois File, VICK; H. M. Trimble Diary, May 22, 1863, 93rd Illinois File, VICK; Hicks, "The Campaign and Capture of Vicksburg," 102–103; Mahlon Head to W. T. Rigby, April 21, 1903, 5th Iowa File, VICK; J. Q. A. Campbell Diary, May 22, 1863, 5th Iowa File, VICK.

57. *OR*, 24(2):67, 316; H. M. Trimble to W. T. Rigby, March 5, 1903, 93rd Illinois File, VICK; H. M. Trimble Diary, May 22, 1863, 93rd Illinois File, VICK; Dunbar and Trimble, *History of the Ninety-third Regiment Volunteer Infantry*, 36; Lyman Baker Memoirs, 1914, ALPL, 13; E. B. Badcom to W. T. Rigby, February 25, 1907, 5th Iowa File, VICK; J. Q. A. Campbell Diary, May 22, 1863, 5th Iowa File, VICK, also in John Quincy Adams Campbell Diaries, Western Reserve Historical Society.
58. *OR*, 24(2):67, 316; J. Q. A. Campbell Diary, May 22, 1863, 5th Iowa File, VICK; E. B. Badcom to W. T. Rigby, February 25, 1907, 5th Iowa File, VICK; H. M. Trimble to W. T. Rigby, March 5, 1903, 93rd Illinois File, VICK; H. M. Trimble Diary, May 22, 1863, 93rd Illinois File, VICK; Dunbar and Trimble, *History of the Ninety-third Regiment Volunteer Infantry*, 36; Lyman Baker Memoirs, 1914, ALPL, 13.
59. *OR*, 24(2):67, 316, 389; H. M. Trimble Diary, May 22, 1863, 93rd Illinois File, VICK, Thomas Watson to parents, May 25, 1863, Thomas Watson Papers, ALPL.
60. *OR*, 24(2):67; *OR*, 24(1):617, 733; Stone, *Memoir of George Boardman Boomer*, 258; Byers, *With Fire and Sword*, 92; J. Q. A. Campbell Diary, May 22, 1863, 5th Iowa File, VICK.
61. *OR*, 24(2):67–68, 316, 389; J. Q. A. Campbell Diary, May 22, 1863, 5th Iowa File, VICK; Stone, *Memoir of George Boardman Boomer*, 257.
62. *OR*, 24(2):68.
63. *OR*, 24(2):68; James A. Woodson Diary, May 22, 1863, ALPL.
64. *OR*, 24(2):68; *History of the 99th Illinois Vols. Containing Also the Names of Its Officers, Addresses of Survivors and Minutes of 1901 Meeting of Association*, 1901, George S. Marks Papers, CWD, USAHEC, 7–8.
65. *OR*, 24(2):389; Daniel P. Clore Diary, May 22, 1863, MDAH. For casualties in the 2nd Texas, see "Report of the Killed, Wounded, Missing and Died of Disease or Privation *of the 2nd Regiment of the Texas Volunteer Infantry from the Siege of Vicksburg, Mississippi*," Texas Adjutant General's Department Papers, Texas State Library and Archives Commission.
66. *OR*, 24(1):733.

Chapter 12. "It Is Absolutely Necessary That They Be Dislodged"

1. *OR*, 24(1):176, 180–181.
2. *OR*, 24(1):157, 180–181; *Supplement to the Official Records of the Union and Confederate Armies*, 4:401; Hass, ed., "The Vicksburg Diary of Henry Clay Warmoth," 73.
3. *OR*, 24(1):180.
4. *OR*, 24(1):181; John A. McClernand Memo, May 22, 1863, John A. McClernand Papers, ALPL.
5. *OR*, 24(1):181; Pryce, *Vanishing Footprints*, 120–121; "Their Records," October 5, 1893, *National Tribune*.
6. *OR*, 24(1):155, 180; Pryce, *Vanishing Footprints*, 121.

7. Winschel, "Fighting Politician: John A. McClernand," 140, reprinted in Winschel, *Triumph and Defeat: The Vicksburg Campaign, Vol. 2*, 49–72; "Vicksburg Campaign," August 9, 1888, *National Tribune*.
8. *OR*, 24(1):174–175, 181.
9. *OR*, 24(1):172–173; Simon and Marszalek, eds., *PUSG*, 8:256.
10. *OR*, 24(1):155; "History of the Corps," February 16, 1893, *National Tribune*.
11. Smith, *The Decision Was Always My Own*, 185.
12. J. H. Pepper Diary, May 22, 1863, MDAH.
13. *OR*, 24(3):907.
14. *OR*, 24(2):420.
15. *OR*, 24(2):360.
16. *OR*, 24(3):908; *OR*, 24(2):360–361.
17. *OR*, 24(1):171; Kiper, *Major General John A. McClernand*, 258; *OR*, 24(3):908.
18. *OR*, 24(1):181; David P. Grier to wife, May 24, 1863, Grier Family Papers, MHS.
19. *OR*, 24(2):34.
20. *OR*, 24(2):34–35, 236; *OR*, 24(1):598; Charles F. Smith Diary, May 22, 1863, NC; Alex Frazier Diary, May 22, 1863, OCM.
21. *OR*, 24(2):34–35, 236; *OR*, 24(1):598–599; Charles F. Smith Diary, May 22, 1863, NC.
22. *OR*, 24(2):34–35, 39, 236.
23. *OR*, 24(2):20–21; John A. Bering to brother, May 28, 1863, 48th Ohio File, VICK.
24. P. J. Osterhaus to Walter Scates, May 22, 1863, John A. McClernand Papers, ALPL.
25. Oran Perry to H. C. Adams, February 11, 1909, 69th Indiana File, VICK; E. L. Hawk to W. T. Rigby, April 21, 1914, 114th Ohio File, VICK.
26. Pryce, *Vanishing Footprints*, 119.
27. E. L. Hawk to W. T. Rigby, April 21, 1914, 114th Ohio File, VICK.
28. *OR*, 24(2):28, 234.
29. *OR*, 24(3):340.
30. *OR*, 24(3):340; John A. McClernand to E. A. Carr, May 22, 1863, John A. McClernand Papers, ALPL; John A. McClernand to P. J. Osterhaus, May 22, 1863, John A. McClernand Papers, ALPL; John A. McClernand to Alvin Hovey, May 22, 1863, John A. McClernand Papers, ALPL.
31. Kountz, *Record of the Organizations Engaged in the Campaign, Siege, and Defense of Vicksburg*, 35; Bennett Grigsby to family, May 18, 1863, Grigsby-McDonald Papers, IHS; *OR*, 24(2):301; Dana, *Recollections of the Civil War*, 68; Anthony Burton Diary, May 22, 1863, ALPL, copy in Journals/Letters/Diaries, VICK.
32. Kountz, *Record of the Organizations Engaged in the Campaign, Siege, and Defense of Vicksburg*, 48; Simon and Marszalek, eds., *PUSG*, 8:256; John A. McClernand to John McArthur, May 22, 1863, John A. McClernand Papers, ALPL.
33. Dyer, *A Compendium of the War of the Rebellion*, 3:1074–1075, 1083, 1169–1172; Simon and Marszalek, eds., *PUSG*, 8:248.
34. *OR*, 24(2):301–302, 308; Olynthus B. Clark, ed., *Downing's Civil War Diary* (Des Moines: Historical Department of Iowa, 1916), 117.

35. *OR*, 24(2):302, 308–309; William W. Belknap, *History of the Fifteenth Regiment, Iowa Veteran Volunteer Infantry, from October, 1861, to August, 1865, When Disbanded at the End of the War* (Keokuk: R. B. Ogden and Son, Print., 1887), 256.
36. *OR*, 24(2):302; Clark, ed., *Downing's Civil War Diary*, 117.
37. *OR*, 24(3):333.
38. *ORN*, 25:21, 24, 278.
39. *ORN*, 25:22.
40. *OR*, 24(2):337; *ORN*, 25:22, 24–29, 32.
41. *ORN*, 25:22.
42. *ORN*, 25:23.
43. *ORN*, 25:30–32.
44. *OR*, 24(2):141, 244; *OR*, 24(1):177; Pryce, *Vanishing Footprints*, 123; *OR*, 24(3):341; J. S. Miller to W. T. Rigby, May 8, 1903, 22nd Iowa File, VICK; Merrick J. Wald Diary, May 22, 1863, OCM; W. J. Landram to A. J. Smith, May 22, 1863, John A. McClernand Papers, ALPL.
45. *OR*, 24(2):141, 244; *OR*, 24(1):177; W. J. Landram to A. J. Smith, May 22, 1863, John A. McClernand Papers, ALPL; Merrick J. Wald Diary, May 22, 1863, OCM; Pryce, *Vanishing Footprints*, 123; *OR*, 24(3):341; J. S. Miller to W. T. Rigby, May 8, 1903, 22nd Iowa File, VICK.
46. *OR*, 24(2):241–242; Crooke, *The Twenty-first Regiment of Iowa Volunteer Infantry*, 82, 84–85.
47. Crooke, *The Twenty-first Regiment of Iowa Volunteer Infantry*, 84–85; Jones, *Reminiscences of the Twenty-second Iowa Volunteer Infantry*, 39.
48. *OR*, 24(2):349, 351.
49. *OR*, 24(2):350, 357; Hattaway, *General Stephen D. Lee*, 93–94; William M. Kelly, "A History of the 30th Alabama Volunteers (Infantry), Confederate States Army," *Alabama Historical Quarterly* 9, no. 1 (Spring 1947): 141–142; "Reminiscences in the Life of Geo E. Brewer," undated, 46th Alabama Regimental History Files, ADAH, 68–69; J. M. Pearson to S. D. Lee, May 17, 1902, 30th Alabama File, VICK; C. M. Shelley to S. D. Lee, September 2, 1902, 30th Alabama File, VICK.
50. J. M. Pearson to S. D. Lee, May 17, 1902, 30th Alabama File, VICK.
51. J. M. Pearson to S. D. Lee, May 17, 1902, 30th Alabama File, VICK; *OR*, 24(2):140, 142, 181, 344; *OR*, 24(1):178–179; William M. Stone Manuscript, undated, MDAH; *Supplement to the Official Records of the Union and Confederate Armies*, 4:406; Pryce, *Vanishing Footprints*, 118; E. J. C. Bealer to W. T. Rigby, April 21, 1903, 21st Iowa File, VICK.
52. *OR*, 24(2):141, 357; A. C. Lenert Diary, May 22, 1863, UNT; Brandon Franke, "Texans in the Breach: Waul's Legion at Vicksburg," in *The Vicksburg Assaults: May 19–22, 1863*, Steven E. Woodworth and Charles D. Grear, eds. (Carbondale: Southern Illinois University Press, 2019), 72–90. For more on Waul's Legion, see Brandon Franke, "Waul's Texas Legion: Towards Vicksburg," *East Texas Historical Journal* 53, no. 1 (2015): 1–17.
53. *OR*, 24(2):357–358; Tom J. Foster, "Reminiscences of Vicksburg," *Confederate*

Veteran 2, no. 8 (August 1894): 244 ; Kelly, "A History of the 30th Alabama Volunteers (Infantry), Confederate States Army," 141–142; "Reminiscences in the Life of Geo E. Brewer," undated, 46th Alabama Regimental History Files, ADAH, 141; George E. Brewer to S. D. Lee, July 30 and August 20, 1902, 46th Alabama File, VICK; A. C. Lenert Diary, May 22, 1863, UNT; E. W. Pettus to W. T. Rigby, May 12, 1903, 20th Alabama File, VICK; "Eulogies of Senators Morgan and Pettus," 60th Cong., 1st sess., *Congressional Record* 42, pt. 6: 5258.

54. *OR*, 24(2):141, 358; William Lowery Diary, May 22, 1863, ADAH; C. M. Shelley to S. D. Lee, September 2, 1902, 30th Alabama File, VICK; A. E. Cook Statement, undated, 21st Iowa File, VICK; A. C. Lenert Diary, May 22, 1863, UNT.
55. *OR*, 24(2):344; Foster, "Reminiscences of Vicksburg," 244; "A History of the Twentieth Alabama Regiment," February 29, 1912, 20th Alabama Confederate Regimental History Files, ADAH, 40–43.
56. *OR*, 24(2):358.
57. A. C. Lenert Diary, May 22, 1863, UNT.
58. *OR*, 24(2):344, 358.
59. *OR*, 24(2):141, 238, 358; *OR*, 24(1):181; Lockett, "The Defense of Vicksburg," 489; *Supplement to the Official Records of the Union and Confederate Armies*, 4:403; Jesse Sawyer to W. T. Rigby, February 14, 1903, 77th Illinois File, VICK; D. P. Grier to Anna, May 24, 1863, David P. Grier Papers, MHS.
60. *OR*, 24(2):141, 242, 349, 351, 355; Pryce, *Vanishing Footprints*, 123–124; Bering and Montgomery, *History of the Forty-Eighth Ohio Vet. Vol. Inf.*, 88.
61. *OR*, 24(2):344, 349, 351.

CHAPTER 13. "FIVE DAYS OF PERIL, HARDSHIP, AND PRIVATION"

1. J. L. Power Diary, May 22, 1863, MDAH.
2. *OR*, 24(2):273, 361; George M. Lucas Diary, May 22, 1863, ALPL; Soman and Byrne, eds., *A Jewish Colonel in the Civil War*, 280.
3. J. H. Shackelford, "My Soldier Data," John H. Shackelford Papers, AU, 1; *OR*, 24(1):189; H. M. Trimble Diary, May 22, 1863, 93rd Illinois File, VICK; Anson Hemingway Diary, May 22, 1863, Journals/Letters/Diaries, VICK; Gould D. Molineaux Diary, May 22, 1863, AC.
4. John P. Jones to wife, May 27, 1863, John P. Jones Papers, FHS; D. P. Grier to Anna, May 24, 1863, David P. Grier Papers, MHS; Unknown to Robert Crouse, May 25, 1863, Robert Crouse Letters, UMB; Edward J. Wood to wife, May 25, 1863, Edward J. Wood Papers, IHS.
5. Edward L. Chatfield to parents, May 26, 1863, Edward L. Chatfield Papers, HL; *OR*, 24(2):243.
6. *OR*, 24(1):55.
7. William M. Stone Manuscript, undated, MDAH; *OR*, 24(2):238; "George Theodore Hyatt," 1897, 127th Illinois File, VICK.

8. J. W. Cook, "A Reminiscence of the Siege of Vicksburg," *Confederate Veteran* 14, no. 9 (September 1906): 408–409; Clarke, *Reminiscence and Anecdotes*, 103; Richard and Richard, *The Defense of Vicksburg*, 160; William A. Lorimer to W. T. Rigby, December 22, 1904, 17th Illinois File, VICK.
9. William Roberts Diary, May 22, 1863, ADAH; William M. Stone Manuscript, undated, MDAH.
10. *OR*, 24(2):389.
11. Emma Balfour Diary, May 22, 1863, MDAH.
12. *OR*, 24(2):376; *OR*, 24(3):339, 341; John A. McClernand to U. S. Grant, May 22, 1863, John A. McClernand Papers, ALPL.
13. *OR*, 24(3):339–340; John A. McClernand to James B. McPherson, May 22, 1863, John A. McClernand Papers, ALPL.
14. *OR*, 24(2):361.
15. *OR*, 24(2):330–331, 362.
16. Pryce, *Vanishing Footprints*, 128; *OR*, 24(2):362.
17. John C. Taylor Diary, May 23, 1863, UVA; Francis Bickett to wife, May 29, 1863, Francis Bickett Letters, UGA; *OR*, 24(3):340, 342.
18. W. L. Brown to father, May 25, 1863, William L. Brown Papers, CHM; Elihu P. Phillips to family, May 28, 1863, OCM; Gould D. Molineaux Diary, May 22, 1863, AC; *OR*, 24(1):161.
19. S. E. Snure to sir, June 21, 1863, S. E. Snure Letter, IHS; Charles A. Hobbs Letters, undated, 99th Illinois File, VICK, 23; Smith, *Life and Letters of Thomas Kilby Smith*, 296.
20. Sherman, *Memoirs*, 1:327.
21. Pryce, *Vanishing Footprints*, 109; Marion B. Richmond, "The Siege of Vicksburg," *Confederate Veteran* 37, no. 4 (April 1929): 139–141.
22. Richard L. Howard, "The Vicksburg Campaign," in *War Papers Read Before the Commandery of the State of Maine, Military Order of the Loyal Legion of the United States, Volume II* (Portland, ME: Lefavor-Tower Company, 1902), 34; *OR*, 24(2):170.
23. Ambrose, ed., "A Wisconsin Boy at Vicksburg: The Letters of James K. Newton," 4; Simon and Marszalek, eds., *PUSG*, 8:255; *OR*, 24(1):56; Donald Stoker, *The Grand Design: Strategy and the U.S. Civil War* (New York: Oxford University Press, 2010), 268; Catton, *U. S. Grant and the American Military Tradition*, 103.
24. *OR*, 24(3):343.
25. *OR*, 24(2):344, 376, 382, 398.
26. T. Northrop to Ira, May 26, 1863, 23rd Wisconsin File, VICK; W. B. Britton to Editors Gazette, May 23, 1863, OCM.
27. *OR*, 24(1):711.
28. Alvin Hovey to wife, May 23, 1863, Hovey Manuscript, IU; Hovey Memoir, undated, IU, 59.
29. *OR*, 24(1):758.
30. Joseph Bowker Diary, May 20, 1863, 42nd Ohio File, VICK; John Ruth to sister, June 11, 1863, OCM.

NOTES TO PAGES 350-355   439

31. Adoniram Judson Withrow to Lib, May 23, 1863, Adoniram Judson Withrow Papers, UNC; John Bowman to friends, May 27, 1863, OCM; James Leeper to wife, May 23, 1863, James Leeper Papers, IHS.
32. Manning F. Force to father, May 23, 1863, and Manning F. Force to Mr. Kebler, May 23, 1863, both in Manning F. Force Papers, UW, copy in LC; James C. Vanderbilt to Mary, May 25, 1863, James C. Vanderbilt Letters, ISL.
33. E. H. Twining to Kate, June 9, 1863, Moody Family Papers, MHS; John T. Buegel Diary, May 22, 1863, SHSMC; Elliott Bush to parents, May 29, 1863, Elliott N. and Henry M. Bush Papers, James S. Schoff Civil War Collection, UMC.
34. Henry Seaman Diary, May 21, 1863, 13th Illinois File, VICK.
35. Thomas B. White to mother, June 8, 1863, OCM; E. H. Ingraham to aunt, May 29, 1863, Edward F. Ingraham Papers, ALPL; Daniel Buchwalter Memoirs, undated, 120th Ohio File, VICK; John A. Ritter to Margarett, June 8, 1863, John Ritter Papers, NC; L. F. Phillips, "Some Things Our Boy Saw in the War," 1911, Lewis F. Phillips Papers, CWTI, USAHEC, 35.
36. Young, *Around the World With General Grant*, 2:304-305; Bearss, *The Vicksburg Campaign*, 3:788.
37. William E. Strong, "The Campaign Against Vicksburg," in *Military Essays and Recollections: Papers Read Before the Commandery of the State of Illinois, Military Order of the Loyal Legion of the United States, Volume II* (Chicago: A. C. McClurg and Company, 1894), 335; E. H. Twining to Kate, June 9, 1863, Moody Family Papers, MHS; Ira W. Hunt Diary, May 22, 1863, 11th Wisconsin File, VICK; George S. Durfee to uncle, May 21, 1863, George S. Durfee Papers, UI; W. L. Brown to father, May 25, 1863, William L. Brown Papers, CHM; James Thomas to Jones, May 26, 1863, Robert T. Jones Letters, UTK; Nicholas Miller Memoir, undated, OCM, 12.
38. *OR*, 24(1):56; Sherman, *Memoirs*, 1:327.
39. Cadwallader, *Three Years with Grant*, 91-92.
40. Jenney, "Personal Recollections of Vicksburg," 261-262; James Harrison Wilson, *Under the Old Flag: Recollections of Military Operations in the War for the Union, the Spanish War The Boxer Rebellion, Etc.*, 2 vols. (New York: D. Appleton and Co., 1912), 2:179-187, 216-217.
41. Simon and Marszalek, eds., *PUSG*, 8:249; *OR*, 24(1):37.
42. Dana, *Recollections of the Civil War*, 59.
43. Dana, 58; *OR*, 24(1):86-87.
44. Jenney, "Personal Recollections of Vicksburg," 261; Charles Bracelen Flood, *Grant and Sherman: The Friendship That Won the Civil War* (New York: Farrar, Straus and Giroux, 2005), 168; *OR*, 24(1):757; Badeau, *Military History of Ulysses S. Grant*, 1:671, 674.
45. Sherman, *Memoirs*, 1:327; Kiper, *Major General John A. McClernand*, 261; *OR*, 24(1):164.
46. John A. McClernand to Richard Yates, May 28, 1863, Jesse Jay Ricks Collection, ALPL; Alvin Hovey to wife, May 23, 1863, Hovey Manuscript, IU.
47. *Supplement to the Official Records of the Union and Confederate Armies*, 4:394; *OR*, 24(1):161, 167.

48. *OR*, 24(1):167, 176, 183; Hills, "Failure and Scapegoat: May 22," 48.
49. Jacob B. Wilkin, "Vicksburg," in *Military Essays and Recollections: Papers Read Before the Commandery of the State of Illinois, Military Order of the Loyal Legion of the United States, Volume IV* (Chicago: Cozzens and Beaton Company, 1907), 228–229; "Fighting Them Over," September 13, 1894, *National Tribune*; David McKinney to sister, June 21, 1863, David McKinney Papers, FHS; *OR*, 24(1):178.
50. Bearss, *The Vicksburg Campaign*, 3:859–860.
51. Bearss, 3:813; Smith, *The Decision Was Always My Own*, 162; Catton, *Grant Moves South*, 452; Williams, *Grant Rises in the West*, 391; Shea and Winschel, *Vicksburg Is the Key*, 152.
52. Clarke, *Reminiscence and Anecdotes*, 102; *Supplement to the Official Records of the Union and Confederate Armies*, 4:300; Joseph Dill Alison Diary, May 22, 1863, UNC; David P. Grier to wife, May 26, 1863, Grier Family Papers, MHS; J. W. Greenman Diary, May 23, 1863, MDAH; Bearss, *The Vicksburg Campaign*, 3:858.
53. William Lovelace Foster to wife, June 20, 1863, William L. Foster Letter, UA; Bearss, *The Vicksburg Campaign*, 3:816, 858; Pryce, *Vanishing Footprints*, 126–127.
54. *OR*, 24(3):914, 918; Thomas Smith Manuscript, MDAH, 5; Jones, "The Rank and File at Vicksburg," 22; Joshua W. Underhill Diary, May 25, 1863, IHS.
55. *OR*, 24(3):914, 918; Thomas Smith Manuscript, MDAH, 5; Carlos Colby to sister, May 26, 1863, Carlos Colby Papers, NL.
56. Theodore D. Fisher Diary, May 25, 1863, Civil War Collection, MHS; James C. Vanderbilt to Mary, May 26, 1863, James C. Vanderbilt Letters, ISL.
57. Simeon Wright to brother, June 22, 1863, Allen G. Wright Papers, UMB; Edwin A. Loosley to wife, May 26, 1863, Edwin A. Loosley Papers, SIU; F. McCullough to Sallie Drennen, undated, Drennen Family Papers, ALPL; Benjamin Spooner to madam, June 7, 1863, Benjamin Spooner Letters, ISL; Hugh McIntire to friend, June 4, 1863, Crosier Family Papers, IHS; Joseph Skipworth to wife, May 28, 1863, Joseph Skipworth Papers, SIU; John G. Sever to Mrs. Piper, July 5, 1863, 99th Illinois File, VICK; George D. Kellogg to parents, May 25, 1863, 23rd Wisconsin File, VICK. For more on reactions to the news, see Charles D. Grear, "'The North-West is Determined with the Sword': Midwesterners' Reactions to the Vicksburg Assaults," in *The Vicksburg Assaults: May 19–22, 1863*, Steven E. Woodworth and Charles D. Grear, eds. (Carbondale: Southern Illinois University Press, 2019), 97–111.
58. Israel M. Piper Diary, May 22, 1863, 99th Illinois File, VICK, copy in Israel M. Piper Diary, May 22, 1863, Journals/Letters/Diaries, VICK and OCM.
59. Christian Wilhelm Hander Diary, May 16 and 17, 1863, UTA.
60. Dora Richards Miller Diary, May 17, 1863, OCM, published as George W. Cable, ed., "A Woman's Diary of the Siege of Vicksburg," *Century Magazine* 30, no. 5 (September 1885): 767–775; James B. Taylor Diary, May 18, 1863, 120th Ohio File, VICK.
61. Emilie R. McKinley Diary, May 18–21, 1863, MHS.
62. Annie Laurie Broidrick, "A Recollection of Thirty Years Ago," 1893, UNC, 18; "Lady of 95 Years Tells of the War," Personal Accounts of the Siege of Vicksburg, Journals/Letters/Diaries, VICK.

63. Jane Bitterman—Cave Life, undated, Journals/Letters/Diaries, VICK, 1.
64. L. McRae Bell, "A Girl's Experience in the Siege of Vicksburg," *Harper's Weekly*, June 8, 1912, 12; Lida Lord Reed, "A Woman's Experiences During the Siege of Vicksburg," *Century Magazine* 61, no. 6 (April 1901): 922–923.
65. A. A. Hoehling, *Vicksburg: 47 Days of Siege* (Upper Saddle River, NJ: Prentice Hall, 1969), 19.
66. Kellogg, *The Vicksburg Campaign and Reminiscences*, Journals/Letters/Diaries, VICK, 35–36.
67. Dora Richards Miller Diary, May 17, 1863, OCM.
68. Rowland Chambers Diary, May 17, 1863, LSU; Mary Ann Loughborough, *My Cave Life in Vicksburg: With Letters of Trial and Travel* (New York: D. Appleton and Company, 1864), 42.
69. Emma Balfour Diary, May 17, 1863, Journals/Letters/Diaries, VICK.
70. Emma Balfour Diary, May 19, 1863, Journals/Letters/Diaries, VICK.
71. Aquilla Bowie Memoir, undated, OCM, 7; Elizabeth Bowie Reminiscences, undated, Journals/Letters/Diaries, VICK.
72. John A. McLaughlin to sister, June 15, 1863, McLaughlin-Jordan Family Papers, IHS; Emma Balfour Diary, May 18–19, 1863, Journals/Letters/Diaries, VICK.
73. John C. Taylor Diary, May 21, 1863, UVA; Theodosia McKinstry Memoirs, undated, Journals/Letters/Diaries, VICK; Christian Wilhelm Hander Diary, May 22, 1863, UTA.
74. Rowland Chambers Diary, May 20 and 22, 1863, LSU; Hoehling, *Vicksburg*, 38.
75. John C. Taylor Diary, May 22, 1863, UVA; Reed, "A Woman's Experiences During the Siege of Vicksburg," 923.
76. Reed, "A Woman's Experiences During the Siege of Vicksburg," 924.
77. "A Child at the Siege of Vicksburg," September 27, 1936, Vicksburg *Post Herald*.
78. Rowland Chambers Diary, May 19, 1863, LSU.
79. Emma Balfour Diary, May 19–20, 1863, Journals/Letters/Diaries, VICK.
80. Loughborough, *My Cave Life in Vicksburg*, 50–51.
81. Loughborough, *My Cave Life in Vicksburg*, 50–51.
82. "Lady of 95 Years Tells of the War," Personal Accounts of the Siege of Vicksburg, Journals/Letters/Diaries, VICK.
83. Reed, "A Woman's Experiences During the Siege of Vicksburg," 923.
84. Emma Balfour Diary, May 20 and 23, 1863, Journals/Letters/Diaries, VICK.
85. Rev. Ben E. Bounds Memoirs, 1911, Journals/Letters/Diaries, VICK, 6; Rowland Chambers Diary, May 22, 1863, LSU; Asa E. Sample Diary, May 22, 1863, ISL.
86. Ballard, *Vicksburg*, 333; Bearss, *The Vicksburg Campaign*, 3:795–796. See also Terrence J. Winschel, *Alice Shirley and the Story of Wexford Lodge* (Fort Washington, PA: Eastern National, 2003).
87. Dora Richards Miller Diary, May 28, 1863, OCM; Virginia Rockwood Memoir, undated, OCM, 1, copy in Journals/Letters/Diaries, VICK.
88. Winschel, *Triumph and Defeat*, 148; Richard and Higginbotham, *The Defense of Vicksburg*, 156.

89. Reed, "A Woman's Experiences During the Siege of Vicksburg," 924.
90. Unknown letter, July 28, 1863, Civil War Miscellany, IHS; J. B. Sanders to family, July 11, 1863, J. B. Sanders Papers, MDAH.
91. *OR*, 24(2):350; *OR*, 24(3):910.
92. *OR*, 24(3):909.
93. "Reports from Vicksburg" and "Latest from Vicksburg," May 26, 1863, Alexandria (Virginia) *Gazette*; "Most Important From Vicksburg," May 26, 1863, Washington, DC, *Evening Star*; Unknown to family, June 6, 1863, Civil War Vicksburg Letter, ISL; Unknown to unknown, June 8, 1863, Henry Ginder Papers, Tulane University.
94. *OR*, 24(1):734; George Boyd Smith Diary, 1863, LC, 8; Mark Anthony to Lizzie, May 22, 1864, Mark Anthony Civil War Letter, AHC; John A. Botts Poem, June 12, 1863, ISL.
95. Carlos W. Colby, "Memoirs of Military Service," undated, Bilby Collection, USA-HEC, 4; Shea and Winschel, *Vicksburg Is the Key*, 149; *OR*, 24(2):260–261.
96. *OR*, 24(2):282–283.
97. Jesse Sawyer to W. T. Rigby, February 14, 1903, 77th Illinois File, VICK; Henry Seaman Diary, May 22, 1863, 13th Illinois File, VICK; E. B. Badcom to W. T. Rigby, February 25, 1907, 5th Iowa File, VICK.
98. Burdette, *The Drums of the 47th*, 82–83.
99. Burdette, *The Drums of the 47th*, 82–83.
100. Burdette, *The Drums of the 47th*, 82–83.

Epilogue

1. Jones, *A Rebel War Clerk's Diary*, 1:291.
2. Jones, 1:291–292.
3. *OR*, 24(1):193; Jones, *A Rebel War Clerk's Diary*, 1:295–296.
4. Jones, *A Rebel War Clerk's Diary*, 1:295–296; Davis, *Jefferson Davis*, 505; Steven E. Woodworth, *Davis and Lee at War* (Lawrence: University Press of Kansas, 1995), 232–233.
5. Simon and Marszalek, eds., *PUSG*, 8:376.
6. *OR*, 27(2):305; Thomas, *Robert E. Lee*, 288; Stephen W. Sears, *Gettysburg* (Boston: Houghton Mifflin, 2003), 58.

BIBLIOGRAPHY

MANUSCRIPTS

Abraham Lincoln Presidential Library, Springfield, Illinois
 Francis R. Baker Diary
 Lyman Baker Memoirs
 Thomas B. Beggs Papers
 Albert C. Boals Diary
 Philip C. Bonney Papers
 Anthony Burton Diary
 Drennen Family Papers
 William R. Eddington Diary
 John B. Fletcher Diary
 Joseph Forrest Papers
 Samuel Gordon Papers
 John A. Griffen Diary
 Edward F. Ingraham Papers
 William J. Kennedy Letters
 George M. Lucas Diary
 John A. McClernand Papers
 Rand Family Papers
 Cyrus W. Randall Papers
 Jesse Jay Ricks Collection
 Robert Ridge Diary
 George W. Russell Papers
 Safford Family Papers
 John Sheriff Papers
 George O. Smith, "Brief History of the 17th Regiment of the Illinois Volunteer Infantry, U.S.A."
 Joseph Stockton Diary
 Abram J. Vanauken Diary
 Thomas Watson Papers
 John H. Wickizer Papers

Bluford Wilson Papers
James A. Woodson Diary
Job H. Yaggy Diary
Alabama Department of Archives and History, Montgomery
   20th Alabama Confederate Regimental History Files
   23rd Alabama Regimental History Files
   31st Alabama Regimental History Files
   37th Alabama Regimental History Files
   42nd Alabama Regimental History Files
   46th Alabama Regimental History Files
   William Lowery Diary
   William Roberts Diary
   Elbert Willett Diary
Archives of Michigan
   Douwe B. Yntema Collection
Atlanta History Center, Atlanta, Georgia
   Mark Anthony Civil War Letter
Auburn University, Auburn, Alabama
   Thomas Kirkpatrick Mitchell Diary
   John H. Shackelford Papers
   Charles Henry Snedeker Diary
   Wright Family Papers
Augustana College, Rock Island, Illinois
   Gould D. Molineaux Diary
Baylor University
   Map of the Siege of Vicksburg
   War of the Rebellion Collection
Chapman University, Orange, California
   Thomas H. Johnson Letter
Chicago History Museum, Chicago
   William L. Brown Papers
   George Carrington Diary
   General Maury's Order Book, 1863
   John Merrilees Diary
   William Puffer Papers
   John A. Rawlins Papers
   Frederick W. Russell Letters
   James C. Sinclair Diary
   William A. Sypher Diary
Duke University, Durham, North Carolina
   Robert B. Hoadley Papers
   "Military History of Captain Thomas Sewell"

William H. Nugen Letters
Samuel Styre Papers
Emory University, Atlanta, Georgia
William Brotherton Papers
Filson Historical Society, Louisville, Kentucky
John P. Jones Papers
David McKinney Papers
Schmidt Family Papers
James W. Thompson Papers
Huntington Library, San Marino, California
Edward L. Chatfield Papers
Indiana Historical Society, Indianapolis
Civil War Miscellany
Crosier Family Papers
James F. Elliott Diary
Grigsby-McDonald Papers
James Leeper Papers
John F. Lester Diary
McLaughlin-Jordan Family Papers
John M. Roberts Reminiscences
Bernard F. Schermerhorn Papers
Samuel E. Sneier Papers
S. E. Snure Letter
Edward P. Stanfield Papers
John C. Swift Diary
Joshua W. Underhill Diary
Edward J. Wood Papers
Indiana State Library, Indianapolis
"83rd Indiana Volunteers Regimental History"
John A. Botts Poem
Chittenden Family Papers
Civil War Vicksburg Letter
Louis W. Knobe Diary
Leeson Family Papers
George B. Marshall Reminiscences
James McLaughlin Papers
Daniel Roberts Correspondence
George M. Rogers Diary
Asa E. Sample Diary
James R. Slack Letters
Benjamin Spooner Letters
James H. St. John Diary
James C. Vanderbilt Letters

Indiana University, Bloomington
    Alvin P. Hovey Memoir
Iowa State University, Ames
    William Van Zandt Diary
Kansas City Public Library, Kansas City, Missouri
    Dixon and Jordan Family Papers
Kirby Smith Private Collection, Barrington, Illinois
    John E. Smith Letters
Library of Congress, Washington, DC
    Manning F. Force Papers
    John G. Jones Correspondence
    John A. Logan Papers
    William T. Sherman Papers
    George Boyd Smith Diary
    John Whitten Diary
    Louis T. Wigfall Papers
Lincoln Memorial Shrine, Redlands, California
    Wells W. Leggett Letter
Louisiana State University, Baton Rouge
    Rowland Chambers Diary
    Louis Guion Diary
Loyola Marymount University, Los Angeles
    Richard Blackstone Diary
Mississippi Department of Archives and History, Jackson
    Joseph Dill Alison Diary
    Emma Balfour Diary
    Daniel P. Clore Diary
    William A. Drennan Papers
    J. W. Greenman Diary
    Edmund Newsome Diary
    James Palmer Diary
    J. H. Pepper Diary
    Mississippi Governor, John J. Pettus, Correspondence and Papers, 1859–1863
    J. L. Power Diary
    J. B. Sanders Papers
    Claudius W. Sears Diary
    Thomas Smith Manuscript
    William M. Stone Manuscript
    Columbus Sykes Papers
Missouri Historical Society, St. Louis
    John T. Appler Diary
    Civil War Collection
        Theodore D. Fisher Diary

David P. Grier Papers
Hiffman Family Papers
Thomas Hogan Letters
Emilie R. McKinley Diary
Moody Family Papers
Joel Strong Reminiscences
Unidentified Soldier of the 31st Iowa Infantry Diary
Navarro College, Corsicana, Texas
   Adnah Eaton Diary
   Jordan C. Harris Papers
   Andrew McCormack Papers
   Samuel J. Oviatt Papers
   Remley Family Papers
   John Ritter Papers
   Charles F. Smith Diary
Newberry Library, Chicago
   Carlos Colby Papers
Ohio Historical Society, Columbus
   76th Ohio Correspondence, 1863–1903
Old Courthouse Museum, Vicksburg, Mississippi
   Stephen C. Beck, "A True Sketch of His Army Life"
   John Bowman Letter
   George Bradley Memoir
   W. B. Britton Letter
   George R. Buck Letter
   John T. Buegel Diary
   J. N. and M. H. Ellis Diary
   W. L. Faulk Diary
   Theodore D. Fisher Diary
   Alex Frazier Diary
   William F. Hollingsworth Diary
   James T. Kidd Memoir
   Myron Knight Diary
   Kilburn Knox Letter
   John A. Leavy Diary
   A. C. Lenert Diary
   Joseph B. Lightsey Memoir
   James F. Mallinckrodt Diary
   Simeon R. Martin, "Facts About Company 'I' of the 46th Mississippi Infantry"
   Thomas W. McCluer Diary
   John Merrilees Diary
   Dora Richards Miller Diary
   Nicholas Miller Memoir

    Edmund Newsome Diary
    Elihu P. Phillips Letter
    Israel M. Piper Diary
    Virginia Rockwood Memoir
    John Ruth Letter
    Jared Young Sanders II Diary
    Eli W. Thornhill Memoir
    Merrick J. Wald Diary
    J. S. Wheeler Diary
    Thomas B. White Letter
    Abner J. Wilkes Memoir
    Elbert Willett Diary
Shiloh National Military Park Regimental Files, Shiloh, Tennessee
    Horace N. Fisher File
Southern Illinois University, Carbondale
    Edwin A. Loosley Papers
    Robert S. Martin Diary
    Joseph Skipworth Papers
Stanford University, Stanford, California
    Samuel Fowler Diary
    Frederick Steele Papers
State Historical Society of Iowa, Iowa City
    William H. Jolly Letters
    Keen Family Papers
State Historical Society of Missouri—Columbia
    John T. Buegel Diary
    Richard W. Burt Papers
    William E. Lewis Letters
    Personal Memoirs of I. V. Smith
State Historical Society of Missouri—St. Louis
    William R. Clack Diary
    Dyson-Bell-Sans Souci Papers
    James B. Owen Letters
    C. S. O. Rice Memoir
    Tennessee State Library and Archives, Nashville
Texas State Library and Archives Commission, Austin
    "Report of the Killed, Wounded, Missing and Died of Disease or Privation of the 2nd Regiment of the Texas Volunteer Infantry from the Siege of Vicksburg, Mississippi"
    Texas Adjutant General's Department Papers
Tulane University, New Orleans, Louisiana
    Henry Ginder Papers
    Don A. Pardee Papers

Ulysses S. Grant Presidential Library, Starkville, Mississippi
  Fred Grant, "A Boy's Experience at Vicksburg"
  Series 3—Special Orders, May 20, 1863
United States Army Historical Education Center, Carlisle, Pennsylvania
  Anders Collection
    John D. Brownley, "History of John D. Brownley, Company D, 57th Ohio,
      Veteran Volunteer Infantry"
  Bilby Collection
    Carlos W. Colby, "Memoirs of Military Service"
  Tim Brookes Collection
    Isaac T. Williams Papers
  Civil War Documents
    George H. Chatfield Papers
    William M. Cleveland Papers
    George S. Marks Papers
    Henry T. Morgan Papers
    Columbus Sykes Papers
    Isaac Vanderwarker Diary
    Joseph W. Westbrook Papers
  Civil War Times Illustrated Collection
    Paul Dorweiler Diary
    Lewis F. Phillips Papers
    Henry Johnson Reynolds Memoir
    Edward Schweitzer Diary
    Henry Seaman Diary
  Coco Collection
  Gilbert Gulbrandson Papers
    "War Diary of Brevet Brigadier General Joseph Stockton"
  Gordon Collection
    George W. Gordon Diary
  Harrisburg Civil War Round Table Collection
    John Carr Diary
  Meadows Collection
    John Carr Diary
    William A. Ruyle Memoir
  Sword Collection
    Andrew McCornack Papers
University of Alabama, Tuscaloosa
  William L. Foster Letter
University of California, Santa Barbara
  Mortimer Leggett Collection
University of Georgia, Athens
  Francis Bickett Letters

University of Illinois, Urbana
   William Clemans Papers
   George S. Durfee Papers
University of Iowa, Iowa City
   Joseph Child Diary
   Edwin C. Hewett Correspondence
   Joseph Kohout Letters
   Ward Family Papers
University of Michigan, Ann Arbor
   Bentley Library
      Calvin Ainsworth Diary
      Robert Crouse Letters
      Ephraim Shay Diary
      Allen G. Wright Papers
   Clements Library
      Elliott N. and Henry M. Bush Papers
      Lewis T. Hickok Diary
      Isaac Jackson Letters
      James S. Schoff Civil War Collection
University of North Carolina, Chapel Hill
   Joseph Dill Alison Diary
   Annie Laurie Broidrick, "A Recollection of Thirty Years Ago"
   J. F. H. Claiborne Papers
   Louis Hébert Autobiography
   Samuel H. Lockett Papers
   John C. Pemberton Papers
   Isaac O. Shelby Diary
   Samuel Addison Whyte Diary
   Adoniram Judson Withrow Papers
University of North Texas, Denton
   A. C. Lenert Diary
University of South Carolina, Columbia
   John Bannon Diary
University of Tennessee, Knoxville
   Robert T. Jones Letters
University of Texas, Austin
   Christian Wilhelm Hander Diary
   Ashbel Smith Papers
University of Virginia, Charlottesville
   John C. Taylor Diary
University of Washington, Seattle
   Manning F. Force Papers

BIBLIOGRAPHY 451

Vicksburg National Military Park Journals/Letters/Diaries File, Vicksburg, Mississippi
  A. S. Abrams, *A Full and Detailed History of the Siege of Vicksburg*
  G. C. Adams Letter
  Charles E. Affeld Diary
  Calvin Ainsworth Diary
  Emma Balfour Diary
  Jane Bitterman—Cave Life
  Rev. Ben E. Bounds Memoirs
  Aquilla Bowie Memoir
  Elizabeth Bowie Reminiscences
  Anthony Burton Diary
  James Carlisle Diary
  Hugh Ewing Statement
  Theodore D. Fisher Diary
  William L. Foster Letter
  Anson Hemingway Diary
  Will Jolly Letter
  J. J. Kellogg Reminiscences
  John Kinsel Letters
  John A. Leavy Diary
  Wells W. Leggett Letter
  W. R. McCrary Diary
  Theodosia McKinstry Memoirs
  William Murray Diary
  "A Narrative of the Services of Brevet Major Charles Dana Miller, 76th Ohio, in the War of the Great Rebellion, 1861–1865"
  Edwin C. Obriham Letter
  John O'Dea, "A Forlorn Hope"
  Osborn Oldroyd Diary
  Personal Accounts of the Siege of Vicksburg
    "Lady of 95 Years Tells of the War"
  Israel M. Piper Diary
  Isaac F. Quinby File
  W. T. Ratliff Letter
  John P. Reese Letter
  Virginia Rockwood Memoir
  Jared Young Sanders II Diary
  A. J. Smith Letter
  Ebenezer Werkheiser Letter
  Joseph R. Winslow Diary
  G. W. Young Letter
  Timothy C. Young Diary

Vicksburg National Military Park Regimental Files, Vicksburg, Mississippi
   "17th Louisiana Volunteer Regiment," 17th Louisiana File
   "23rd Alabama Infantry," 23rd Alabama Infantry File
   Alonzo Abernathy Diary, 9th Iowa File
   William T. Alexander Letter, 46th Alabama File
   J. B. Allen Letter, 30th Ohio File
   C. P. Alling, "Four Years With the Western Army," 11th Wisconsin File
   E. B. Badcom Letter, 5th Iowa File
   N. M. Baker Letter, 116th Illinois File
   E. J. C. Bealer Letter, 21st Iowa File
   Stephen C. Beck, "A True Sketch of His Army Life"
   John S. Bell, "The Arkansas Sharp Shooters," 12th Arkansas File
   John A. Bering Letter, 48th Ohio File
   James B. Black Letter, 18th Indiana File
   Richard Blackstone Letter, 32nd Ohio File
   Joseph Bowker Diary, 42nd Ohio File
   George E. Brewer Letters, 46th Alabama File
   Robert Buchanan Letter, 7th Missouri File
   Daniel Buchwalter Memoirs, 120th Ohio File
   Robert H. Bunn Letter, 42nd Alabama File
   Uley Burk Letter, 30th Iowa File
   J. Q. A. Campbell Diary, 5th Iowa File
   John W. Carroll Letter, 77th Illinois File
   A. E. Cook Statement, 21st Iowa File
   John Cowan Letter, 19th Kentucky File
   John Crane Letter, 17th Wisconsin File
   James R. Danby Diary, 8th Indiana File
   George S. Durfee Letter, 8th Illinois File
   William R. Eddington Diary, 97th Illinois File
   I. H. Elliott Letter, 33rd Illinois File
   W. L. Faulk Diary, 38th Mississippi File
   William L. Faulk Letter, 3rd Louisiana File
   Theodore D. Fisher Diary, 1st Missouri File
   Owen Francis Diary, 57th Ohio File
   John Frist Letter, 113th Illinois File
   John Fuller Diary, 31st Louisiana File
   "George Theodore Hyatt," 127th Illinois File
   W. Grayum Letter, 4th West Virginia File
   John F. Hampton Letter, 43rd Mississippi File
   H. E. Harris Letter, 11th Illinois File
   E. L. Hawk Letter, 114th Ohio File
   Mahlon Head Letter, 5th Iowa File
   A. K. Heffelfinger Letter, 95th Illinois File

Charles A. Hobbs Letters, 99th Illinois File
Ira W. Hunt Diary, 11th Wisconsin File
Johnse Letter, 27th Louisiana File
J. L. Jones Letter, 38th Mississippi File
James Keigwin Letter, 49th Indiana File
George D. Kellogg Letter, 23rd Wisconsin File
Charles R. Koch Letter, 95th Illinois File
Charles R. Kock Letter, 11th Illinois File
J. W. Larrabee Statement, 55th Illinois File
Jesse M. Lee Diary, 59th Indiana File
S. D. Lee Letter, 27th Louisiana File
Edward J. Lewis Diary, 33rd Illinois File
William A. Lorimer Letter, 17th Illinois File
Simeon R. Martin, "Facts About Company 'I' of the 46th Mississippi Infantry," 46th Mississippi File
Robert McRory Letter, 30th Ohio File
J. S. Miller Letter, 22nd Iowa File
Rex Miller, *Dowdell's Volunteers: 37th Alabama Infantry*
James K. Newton Letter, 14th Wisconsin File
T. Northrop Letter, 23rd Wisconsin File
J. A. Nottingham Letter, 8th Indiana File
Robert Oliver Letter, 55th Illinois File
Joseph F. Parker Letter, 130th Illinois File
J. M. Pearson Letters, 30th Alabama File
Oran Perry Letter, 69th Indiana File
Oran Perry, "Perry Tells Story of the Siege of Vicksburg," 69th Indiana File
E. W. Pettus Letter, 30th Alabama File
S. N. Pickens Letter, 27th Louisiana File
Amos Pierson Letter, 16th Ohio File
Israel M. Piper Diary, 99th Illinois File
Leo Rassieur Letter, 30th Missouri File
James J. Ray Diary, 19th Kentucky File
John B. Reid Letter, 130th Illinois File
W. T. Rigby Letter, 69th Indiana File
A. C. Riley Report, 1st Missouri File
Mahlon Rouch Diary, 120th Ohio File
Jesse Sawyer Letter, 77th Illinois File
W. Schalenburg Letter, 37th Ohio File
Henry Seaman Diary, 13th Illinois File
John G. Sever Letter, 99th Illinois File
C. M. Shelley Letter, 30th Alabama File
F. M. Smith Letter, 81st Illinois File
S. H. Stevenson Letter, 48th Ohio File

James B. Taylor Diary, 120th Ohio File
Thomas J. Taylor Letter, 47th Ohio File
H. M. Trimble Diary, 93rd Illinois File
H. M. Trimble Letter, 93rd Illinois File
Unknown Letter, 26th Iowa File
Isaac Vanderwarker Diary, 4th Minnesota File
Martin Whipkey Letter, 81st Illinois File
James C. Wiggs Letter, 27th Louisiana File
Charles Willison Letter, 76th Ohio File
Amos York Letter, 8th Indiana File
Virginia Tech University, Blacksburg
William J. Pittenger Diary
Western Reserve Historical Society, Cleveland, Ohio
John Quincy Adams Campbell Diaries
Mortimer D. Leggett Papers

Newspapers

Alexandria (Virginia) *Gazette*
Chicago *Times-Herald*
Chicago Tribune
Harper's Weekly
Utica (New York) *Herald*
Vicksburg *Evening Citizen*
Vicksburg *Evening Post*
Vicksburg *Post Herald*
Washington, DC, *Evening Star*

Primary and Secondary Sources

Abrams, A. S. *A Full and Detailed History of the Siege of Vicksburg*. Atlanta: Intelligencer Steam Power Presses, 1863.
Adair, John M. *Historical Sketch of the Forty-fifth Illinois Regiment, With a Complete List of the Officers and Privates and an Individual Record of Each Man in the Regiment.* Lanark, IL: Carroll County Gazette Print, 1869.
Ambrose, Stephen E., ed. "A Wisconsin Boy at Vicksburg: The Letters of James K. Newton." *Journal of Mississippi History* 23, no. 1 (January 1961): 1–14.
———, ed. *A Wisconsin Boy in Dixie: The Selected Letters of James K. Newton*. Madison: University of Wisconsin Press, 1961.
Anderson, Ephraim McD. *Memoirs: Historical and Personal Including the Campaigns of the First Missouri Confederate Brigade*. St. Louis: Times Publishing Co., 1868.

Armstrong, Winifred Keen, ed. "The Civil War Letters of Pvt. P. C. Bonney." Lawrence County Historical Society, 1963.
Arnold, James R. *Grant Wins the War: Decision at Vicksburg.* New York: John Wiley & Sons, 1997.
Badeau, Adam. *Military History of Ulysses S. Grant, From April, 1861, to April, 1865.* 2 vols. New York: D. Appleton & Co., 1881.
Ballard, Michael B. *The Civil War in Mississippi: Major Campaigns and Battles.* Jackson: University Press of Mississippi, 2011.
———. *Grant at Vicksburg: The General and the Siege.* Carbondale: Southern Illinois University Press, 2013.
———. *Pemberton: The General Who Lost Vicksburg.* Jackson: University Press of Mississippi, 1991.
———. *Vicksburg: The Campaign That Opened the Mississippi.* Chapel Hill: University of North Carolina Press, 2004.
Barton, Thomas H. *Autobiography of Dr. Thomas H. Barton, The Self-made Physician of Syracuse, Ohio: Including a History of the Fourth Regt. West Va. Vol. Inf'y, with an Account of Col. Lightburn's Retreat Down the Kanawha Valley, Gen. Grant's Vicksburg and Chattanooga Campaigns, Together with the Several Battles in Which The Fourth Regiment Was Engaged, and Its Losses by Disease, Desertion and in Battle.* Charleston: West Virginia Printing Co., 1890.
Bearss, Edwin C. *Rebel Victory at Vicksburg.* Vicksburg: Vicksburg Centennial Commission, 1963.
———, ed. *A Southern Record: The History of the Third Regiment Louisiana Infantry.* Dayton, OH: Morningside, 1970.
———. *The Vicksburg Campaign,* 3 vols. Dayton, OH: Morningside, 1985.
Bearss, Edwin C., and J. Parker Hills. *Receding Tide: Vicksburg and Gettysburg, The Campaigns That Changed the Civil War.* Washington, DC: National Geographic, 2010.
Bek, William G., ed. "The Civil War Diary of John T. Buegel, Union Soldier," *Missouri Historical Review* 40, no. 4 (July 1946): 503–530.
Belcher, Dennis W. *The 11th Missouri Volunteer Infantry in the Civil War: A History and Roster.* Jefferson, NC: McFarland & Company, 2011.
Belknap, William W. *History of the Fifteenth Regiment, Iowa Veteran Volunteer Infantry, from October, 1861, to August, 1865, When Disbanded at the End of the War.* Keokuk: R. B. Ogden and Son, Print., 1887.
Bell, L. McRae. "A Girl's Experience in the Siege of Vicksburg." *Harper's Weekly* (June 8, 1912): 12–13.
Bell, W. Scott. *The Camel Regiment: A History of the Bloody 43rd Mississippi Volunteer Infantry, CSA, 1862–1865.* Gretna, LA: Pelican Publishing Company, 2017.
Bennett, Stuart, and Barbara Tillery, eds. *The Struggle for the Life of the Republic: A Civil War Narrative by Brevet Major Charles Dana Miller, 76th Ohio Volunteer Infantry.* Kent, OH: Kent State University Press, 2004.
Bentley, W. H. *History of the 77th Illinois Volunteer Infantry, Sept. 2, 1862–July 10, 1865.* Peoria, IL: Edward Hine, Printer, 1883.

Bergeron, Arthur W. *Guide to Louisiana Confederate Military Units, 1861–1865*. Baton Rouge: Louisiana State University Press, 1996.
Bering, John A., and Thomas Montgomery. *History of the Forty-Eighth Ohio Vet. Vol. Inf.* Hillsboro, OH: Highland News Office, 1880.
Bertera, Martin N. *De Golyer's 8th Michigan Black Horse Light Battery.* Wyandotte, MI: TillieAnn Press, 2015.
———. *A Soldier at Dawn: A Remarkable and Heroic Exodus.* N.p.: n.p., n.d.
Bevier, R. S. *History of the First and Second Missouri Confederate Brigades 1861–1865 and From Wakaruse to Appomattox, A Military Anagraph.* St. Louis: Bryan, Brand and Company, 1879.
Bigelow, James K. *Abridged History of the Eighth Indiana Volunteer Infantry, from Its Organization, April 21st, 1861, to the Date of Re-enlistment as Veterans, January 1, 1864.* Indianapolis: Ellis Barnes Book and Job Printer, 1864.
Black, Robert C. III. *The Railroads of the Confederacy.* Chapel Hill: University of North Carolina Press, 1952.
Blanchard, Ira. *I Marched with Sherman: Civil War Memoirs of the 20th Illinois Volunteer Infantry.* Ed. Nancy Ann Mattingly. New York: toExcel, 1992.
Bridge, Carolyn S., ed. *These Men Were Heroes Once: The Sixty-ninth Indiana Volunteer Infantry.* West Lafayette, IN: Twin Publications, 2005.
Brinkerhoff, Henry R. *History of the Thirtieth Regiment Ohio Volunteer Infantry, From Its Organization, To the Fall of Vicksburg, Miss.* Columbus, OH: James W. Osgood, Printer, 1863.
Broadaway, Douglas Lee. "A Texan Records the Civil War Siege of Vicksburg, Mississippi: The Journal of Maj. Maurice Kavanaugh Simons, 1863." *Southwestern Historical Quarterly* 105, no. 1 (July 2001): 93–131.
Brockett, L. P. *The Camp, The Battle Field, and the Hospital; Or, Lights and Shadows of the Great Rebellion.* Philadelphia: National Publishing Company, 1866.
Brown, Alonzo L. *History of the Fourth Regiment of Minnesota Infantry Volunteers During the Great Rebellion 1861–1865.* St. Paul, MN: Pioneer Press Company, 1892.
Bryner, Cloyd. *Bugle Echoes: The Story of the Illinois 47th.* Springfield, IL: Phillips Bros. Printers, 1905.
Burdette, Robert J. *The Drums of the 47th.* Urbana: University of Illinois Press, 2000.
Burnham, John H. *The Thirty-third Regiment Illinois Infantry in the Civil War, 1861–1865; Prepared by Capt. J.H. Burnham at the Request of the Directors of the Illinois Historical Society for the 1912 Annual Meeting of that Society.* N.p.: n.p., 1912.
Byers, S. H. M. *With Fire and Sword.* New York: Neale Publishing Company, 1911.
Cable, George W., ed. "A Woman's Diary of the Siege of Vicksburg." *Century Magazine* 30, no. 5 (September 1885): 767–775.
Cadwallader, Sylvanus. *Three Years with Grant.* Ed. Benjamin P. Thomas. Lincoln: University of Nebraska Press, 1996.
Campanella, Richard. *Lincoln in New Orleans: The 1828–1831 Flatboat Voyages and Their Place in History.* Lafayette: University of Louisiana at Lafayette Press, 2010.
Carwardine, Richard. *Lincoln: A Life of Purpose and Power.* New York: Knopf, 2003.

Catton, Bruce. *Grant Moves South*. Boston: Little, Brown, 1960.

———. *U. S. Grant and the American Military Tradition*. Boston: Little, Brown, 1954.

Chambers, William P. "My Journal." In *Publications of the Mississippi Historical Society, Centenary Series*. 5 vols. Jackson, MS: Mississippi Historical Society, 1925.

Chance, Joseph E. *The Second Texas Infantry: From Shiloh to Vicksburg*. Austin, TX: Eakin Press, 1984.

"The Charge at Fort Hill." September 29, 1910, *National Tribune*.

Chernow, Ron. *Grant*. New York: Penguin Press, 2017.

Clark, Olynthus B., ed. *Downing's Civil War Diary*. Des Moines: Historical Department of Iowa, 1916.

Clarke, George Powell. *Reminiscence and Anecdotes of the War for Southern Independence*. N.p.: n.p., n.d.

Cobb, James C. *The Most Southern Place on Earth: The Mississippi Delta and the Roots of Regional Identity*. New York: Oxford University Press, 1994.

Commager, Henry Steele. *The Blue and the Gray: The Story of the Civil War as Told by Participants, Revised and Abridged*. 2 vols. New York: Meridian, 1994.

Cook, J. W. "A Reminiscence of the Siege of Vicksburg." *Confederate Veteran* 14, no. 9 (September 1906): 408–409.

Crooke, George. *The Twenty-first Regiment of Iowa Volunteer Infantry: A Narrative of Its Experience in Active Service, Including a Military Record of Each Officer, Non-Commissioned Officer, and Private Soldier of the Organization*. Milwaukee: King, Fowle & Co., 1891.

Crouch, Jerry Evan. *Silencing the Vicksburg Guns: The Story of the 7th Missouri Infantry Regiment As Experienced by John Davis Evans Union Private and Mormon Pioneer*. Victoria, BC: Trafford Publishing, 2005.

Crummer, Wilbur F. *With Grant at Fort Donelson, Shiloh and Vicksburg, and An Appreciation of General U.S. Grant*. Oak Park, IL: E. C. Crummer and Co., 1915.

Dana, Charles A. *Recollections of the Civil War*. New York: D. Appleton and Co., 1898.

Daniel, Larry J., and Lynn N. Bock. *Island No. 10: Struggle for the Mississippi Valley*. Tuscaloosa: University of Alabama Press, 1996.

Davis, George B., Leslie J. Perry, and Joseph W. Kirkley. *Atlas to Accompany the Official Records of the Union and Confederate Armies*. Washington, DC: Government Printing Office, 1891–1895.

Davis, William C. *Jefferson Davis: The Man and His Hour: A Biography*. New York: HarperCollins, 1991.

Dodd, W. O. "Recollections of Vicksburg During the Siege." *The Southern Bivouac* 1, no. 1 (September 1882): 2–11.

Dubay, Robert W. *John Jones Pettus, Mississippi Fire-eater: His Life and Times, 1813–1867*. Jackson: University Press of Mississippi, 1975.

Dunbar, Aaron, and Harvey M. Trimble. *History of the Ninety-third Regiment Volunteer Infantry From Organization to Muster Out*. Chicago: Blakely Printing Co., 1898.

Dyer, Frederick H. *A Compendium of the War of the Rebellion*. 3 vols. Cedar Rapids, IA: Torch Press, 1908.

Elliott, Isaac H. *History of the Thirty-third Regiment Illinois Veteran Volunteer Infantry in the Civil War, 22nd August 1861, to 7th December, 1865*. Gibson City, IL: The Association, 1902.

Erickson, Edgar L., ed. "With Grant at Vicksburg: From the Civil War Diary of Captain Charles E. Wilcox." *Journal of the Illinois State Historical Society* 30, no. 4 (January 1938): 441–503.

"Eulogies of Senators Morgan and Pettus." 60th Cong., 1st sess., *Congressional Record* 42, pt. 6: 5247–5259.

F. A. F. (Anonymous). *Old Abe, The Eighth Wisconsin War Eagle. A Full Account of His Capture and Enlistment, Exploits in War and Honorable As Well As Useful Career in Peace*. Madison, WI: Curran and Bowen, 1885.

"Fighting For Vicksburg." August 23, 1894, *National Tribune*.

"Fighting Them Over." September 13, 1894, *National Tribune*.

Flood, Charles Bracelen. *Grant and Sherman: The Friendship That Won the Civil War*. New York: Farrar, Straus and Giroux, 2005.

Force, Manning F. "Personal Recollections of the Vicksburg Campaign." In *Sketches of War History 1861–1865 Papers Read Before the Ohio Commandery of the Military Order of the Loyal Legion of the United States 1883–1886, Volume 1*. Cincinnati: Robert Clarke Company, 1888, 293–309.

"The 45th Ill. At Vicksburg." September 29, 1910, *National Tribune*.

Foster, Tom J. "Reminiscences of Vicksburg." *Confederate Veteran* 2, no. 8 (August 1894): 244.

Fowler, James A., and Miles M. Miller. *History of the Thirtieth Iowa Infantry Volunteers. Giving a Complete Record of the Movements of the Regiment from Its Organization Until Muster Out*. Mediapolis, IA: T. A. Merrill, Printer, 1908.

Franke, Brandon. "Texans in the Breach: Waul's Legion at Vicksburg." In *The Vicksburg Assaults: May 19–22, 1863*. Ed. Steven E. Woodworth and Charles D. Grear. Carbondale: Southern Illinois University Press, 2019. 72–90.

———. "Waul's Texas Legion: Towards Vicksburg." *East Texas Historical Journal* 53, no. 1 (2015): 1–17.

Fuller, J. F. C. *The Generalship of Ulysses S. Grant*. Bloomington: Indiana University Press, 1958.

Giambrone, Jeff T. *Beneath Torn and Tattered Flags: A History of the 38th Mississippi Infantry, C.S.A*. Bolton, MS: Smokey Row Press, 1998.

Gibson, Arrell M. "The Indians of Mississippi." In *A History of Mississippi*. 2 vols. Ed. Richard A. McLemore. Hattiesburg: University & College Press of Mississippi, 1973, 1: 69–89.

Grabau, Warren E. *Ninety-Eight Days: A Geographer's View of the Vicksburg Campaign*. Knoxville: University of Tennessee Press, 2000.

Grant, Frederick D. "A Boy's Experience at Vicksburg." *Personal Recollections of the War of the Rebellion: Addresses Delivered before the Commandery of the State of New York, Military Order of the Loyal Legion of the United States*. Ed. A. Noel Blakeman. New York: G. P. Putnam's Sons, 1907: 86–100.

Grant, Ulysses S. *Personal Memoirs of U. S. Grant*. 2 vols. New York: Charles L. Webster & Co., 1892.

Grear, Charles D. "'The North-West is Determined with the Sword': Midwesterners' Reactions to the Vicksburg Assaults." In *The Vicksburg Assaults: May 19–22, 1863*. Ed. Steven E. Woodworth and Charles D. Grear. Carbondale: Southern Illinois University Press, 2019. 97–111.

Grecian, J. *History of the Eighty-third Regiment, Indiana Volunteer Infantry. For Three Years With Sherman*. Cincinnati: John F. Uhlhorn, printer, 1865.

Griffith, Paddy. *Battle Tactics of the Civil War*. New Haven, CT: Yale University Press, 1987.

Grimsley, Mark, and Todd D. Miller, eds. *The Union Must Stand: The Civil War Diary of John Quincy Adams Campbell, Fifth Iowa Volunteer Infantry*. Knoxville: University of Tennessee Press, 2000.

Guarneri, Carl J. *Lincoln's Informer: Charles A. Dana and the Inside Story of the Union War*. Lawrence: University Press of Kansas, 2019.

Hall, Winchester. *The Story of the 26th Louisiana Infantry, In the Service of the Confederate States*. N.p.: n.p., 1890.

Harriel, Shelby. *Behind the Rifle: Women Soldiers in Civil War Mississippi*. Jackson: University Press of Mississippi, 2019.

Hass, Paul H., ed. "The Vicksburg Diary of Henry Clay Warmoth: Part II (April 28 1863–May 26, 1863)." *Journal of Mississippi History* 32, no. 1 (February 1970): 60–74.

Hattaway, Herman. *General Stephen D. Lee*. Jackson: University Press of Mississippi, 1988.

Hattaway, Herman, and Archer Jones. *How the North Won: A Military History of the Civil War*. Urbana: University of Illinois Press, 1983.

Hays, E. Z. *History of the Thirty-second Regiment Ohio Veteran Volunteer Infantry*. Columbus, OH: Cott & Evans Printers, 1896.

Hearn, Chester G. *The Capture of New Orleans 1862*. Baton Rouge: Louisiana State University Press, 1995.

Heinman, Kenneth J. *Civil War Dynasty: The Ewing Family of Ohio*. New York: New York University Press, 2012.

Hess, Earl J. *Civil War Infantry Tactics: Training, Combat, and Small-Unit Effectiveness*. Baton Rouge: Louisiana State University Press, 2015.

———. "Grant's Ethnic General: Peter J. Osterhaus." In *Grant's Lieutenants: From Cairo to Vicksburg*. Ed. Steven E. Woodworth. Lawrence: University Press of Kansas, 2001. 199–216.

Hickey, Donald R. *Glorious Victory: Andrew Jackson and the Battle of New Orleans*. Baltimore: Johns Hopkins University Press, 2015.

Hicks, Henry G. "The Campaign and Capture of Vicksburg." In *Glimpses of the Nation's Struggle, Sixth Series: Papers Read Before the Minnesota Commandery of the Military Order of the Loyal Legion of the United States, January 1903–1908*. Minneapolis: Aug. Davis, 1909. 82–107.

Hills, J. Parker. "Failure and Scapegoat: May 22." In *The Vicksburg Assaults: May 19–22,*

1863. Ed. Steven E. Woodworth and Charles D. Grear. Carbondale: Southern Illinois University Press, 2019. 27–56.

———. "Haste and Underestimation: May 19." In *The Vicksburg Assaults: May 19–22, 1863*. Ed. Steven E. Woodworth and Charles D. Grear. Carbondale: Southern Illinois University Press, 2019. 7–26.

———. "Roads to Raymond." In *The Vicksburg Campaign*. Ed. Steven E. Woodworth and Charles D. Grear. Carbondale: Southern Illinois University Press, 2013. 65–95.

History of the 37th Regiment, O. V. V. I., Furnished by Comrades at the Ninth Reunion Held at St. Mary's, Ohio, Tuesday and Wednesday, September 10 and 11, 1889. Toledo, OH: Montgomery and Vrooman, 1890.

History of Company B (Originally Pickens Planters) 40th Alabama Regiment Confederate States Army 1862–1865. n.a. Anniston, AL: Norwood, 1902.

"History of the Corps." February 16, 1893, *National Tribune*.

History of the Forty-sixth Regiment Indiana Volunteer Infantry, September, 1861-September, 1865. Logansport, IN: Press of Wilson, Humphreys and Co., 1888.

Hoehling, A. A. *Vicksburg: 47 Days of Siege*. Upper Saddle River, NJ: Prentice Hall, 1969.

Hogane, J. T. "Reminiscences of the Siege of Vicksburg." *Southern Historical Society Papers* 11, no. 7 (July 1883): 291–297.

Howard, R. L. *History of the 124th Regiment Illinois Infantry Volunteers, Otherwise Known as the 'Hundred and Two Dozen,' From August, 1862, to August, 1865*. Springfield, IL: H. W. Rokker, 1880.

Howard, Richard L. "The Vicksburg Campaign." In *War Papers Read Before the Commandery of the State of Maine, Military Order of the Loyal Legion of the United States, Volume II*. Portland, ME: Lefavor-Tower Company, 1902. 28–40.

Huffstodt, Jim. *Hard Dying Men: The Story of General W. H. L. Wallace, General T. E. G. Ransom, and Their "Old Eleventh" Illinois Infantry in the American Civil War (1861–1865)*. Bowie, MD: Heritage Books, 1991.

"An Incident of the Battle of Vicksburg." In *Military Order of the Loyal Legion of the United States, Commandery of the District of Columbia, War Papers 1*. N.p.: 1887. 63–72.

In Memoriam: Charles Ewing. Philadelphia: J. B. Lippincott, 1888.

"It Was the 30th Ohio." September 29, 1910, *National Tribune*.

Jenney, William L. B. "Personal Recollections of Vicksburg." In *Military Essays and Recollections: Papers Read Before the Commandery of the State of Illinois, Military Order of the Loyal Legion of the United States, Volume III*. Chicago: Dial Press, 1899. 247–265.

Johnston, William Preston. *The Life of Gen. Albert Sidney Johnston: His Service in the Armies of the United States, The Republic of Texas, and the Confederate States*. New York: D. Appleton and Co., 1879.

Joiner, Gary D. *Mr. Lincoln's Brown Water Navy: The Mississippi Squadron*. New York: Rowman & Littlefield, 2007.

Jones, Archer. *Civil War Command and Strategy: The Process of Victory and Defeat*. New York: Free Press, 1992.

Jones, J. B. *A Rebel War Clerk's Diary: At the Confederate States Capital, Volume 1: April 1861–July 1863.* 2 vols. Ed. James I. Robertson, Jr. Lawrence: University Press of Kansas, 2015.
Jones, J. H. "The Rank and File at Vicksburg." In *Publications of the Mississippi Historical Society.* 14 vols. Ed. Franklin L. Riley. Oxford: Mississippi Historical Society, 1903. 7:17–31.
Jones, James Pickett. *Black Jack: John A. Logan and Southern Illinois in the Civil War Era.* Carbondale: Southern Illinois University Press, 1995.
Jones, S. C. *Reminiscences of the Twenty-second Iowa Volunteer Infantry, Giving Its Organization, Marches, Skirmishes, Battles, and Sieges, as Taken from the Diary of Lieutenant S. C. Jones of Company A.* Iowa City, IA: n.p., 1907.
Journal of the State Convention and Ordinances and Resolutions Adopted in January, 1861, With an Appendix. Jackson: E. Barksdale, 1861.
Kaiser, Leo M. ed. "The Civil War Diary of Florison D. Pitts." *Mid-America: An Historical Review* 40, no. 1 (January 1958): 22–63.
Kelley, Arthell. "The Geography." In *A History of Mississippi.* 2 vols. Ed. Richard A. McLemore. Hattiesburg: University & College Press of Mississippi, 1973. 1: 3–23.
Kelly, William M. "A History of the 30th Alabama Volunteers (Infantry), Confederate States Army." *Alabama Historical Quarterly* 9, no. 1 (Spring 1947): 115–167.
Kellogg, J. J. *The Vicksburg Campaign and Reminiscences, 'Milliken's Bend' to July 4, 1863.* Washington, IA: Evening Journal, 1913.
Kennedy, Joseph C. G. *Population of the United States in 1860: Compiled From the Original Returns of the Eighth Census Under the Direction of the Secretary of the Interior.* Washington, DC: Government Printing Office, 1864.
Kiper, Richard L. *Major General John A. McClernand: Politician in Uniform.* Kent, OH: Kent State University Press, 1999.
Kountz, John S. *Record of the Organizations Engaged in the Campaign, Siege, and Defense of Vicksburg.* Knoxville: University of Tennessee Press, 2011.
Lee, Stephen D. "The Campaign of Vicksburg, Mississippi, in 1863—From April 15 to and Including the Battle of Champion Hills, or Baker's Creek, May 16, 1863." In *Publications of the Mississippi Historical Society.* 14 vols. Ed. Franklin L. Riley. Oxford: Mississippi Historical Society, 1900. 3:21–53.
Lewis, C. S. *The Screwtape Letters & Screwtape Proposes a Toast.* New York: Macmillan, 1961.
Lockett, S. H. "The Defense of Vicksburg." In *Battles and Leaders of the Civil War.* 4 vols. New York: Century Company, 1884–1887. 3:482–492.
Long, E. B. *The Civil War Day by Day: An Almanac, 1861–1865.* New York: Doubleday, 1971.
"Losses at Vicksburg." September 29, 1910, *National Tribune.*
Loughborough, Mary Ann. *My Cave Life in Vicksburg: With Letters of Trial and Travel.* New York: D. Appleton and Company, 1864.
Mahan, James C. *Memoirs of James Curtis Mahan.* Lincoln, NE: Franklin Press, 1919.

Marshall, T. B. *History of the Eighty-third Ohio Volunteer Infantry, The Greyhound Regiment*. Cincinnati: n.p., 1912.
Marszalek, John F. *Commander of All Lincoln's Armies: A Life of General Henry W. Halleck*. Cambridge, MA: Harvard University Press, 2004.
———. "'A Full Share of All the Credit': Sherman and Grant to the Fall of Vicksburg." In *Grant's Lieutenants: From Cairo to Vicksburg*. Ed. Steven E. Woodworth. Lawrence: University Press of Kansas, 2001. 5–20.
———. *Sherman: A Soldier's Passion for Order*. New York: Free Press, 1993.
Marszalek, John F., David F. Nolen, and Louie P. Gallo. *The Personal Memoirs of Ulysses S. Grant: The Complete Annotated Edition*. Cambridge, MA: Harvard University Press, 2017.
Mason, F. H. *The Forty-second Ohio Infantry: A History of the Organization and Services of That Regiment in the War of the Rebellion; With Biographical Sketches of Its Field Officers and a Full Roster of the Regiment*. Cleveland, OH: Cobb, Andrews and Co., Publishers, 1876.
Maynard, Douglas, ed. "Vicksburg Diary: The Journal of Gabriel M. Killgore." *Civil War History* 10, no 1 (March 1964): 33–53.
McAlexander, U. G. *History of the Thirteen Regiment United States Infantry, Compiled from Regimental Records and Other Sources*. N.p.: Regimental Press, Thirteenth Infantry, 1905.
McDonough, James Lee. *William Tecumseh Sherman: In the Service of My Country: A Life*. New York: W. W. Norton & Company, 2016.
McPherson, James M. *Battle Cry of Freedom: The Civil War Era*. New York: Oxford University Press, 1988.
McWhiney, Grady, and Perry D. Jamieson. *Attack and Die: Civil War Military Tactics and the Southern Heritage*. Tuscaloosa: University of Alabama Press, 1982.
Memminger, R. W. "The Surrender of Vicksburg—A Defense of General Pemberton." *Southern Historical Society Papers* 12, no. 7–9 (July–September 1884): 352–360.
Military History and Reminiscences of the Thirteenth Regiment of Illinois Volunteer Infantry in the Civil War in the United States 1861–1865. Chicago: Women's Temperance Publishing Association, 1892.
Miller, Rex. *Dowdell's Volunteers: 37th Alabama Infantry*. Depew, NY: Patrex Press, 1992.
Mitchell, Dennis J. *Mississippi: A New History*. Jackson: University Press of Mississippi, 2014.
Miller, Francis Trevelyan. *The Photographic History of the Civil War in Ten Volumes*. 10 vols. New York: The Review of Reviews Co., 1912.
Morris, W. S. *History, 31st Regiment Illinois Volunteers: Organized by John A. Logan*. Herrin, IL: Crossfire Press, 1991.
O'Dea, John. "A Forlorn Hope." In *Transactions of the McLean County Historical Society*. Bloomington, IL: McLean County Historical Society, 1899. Vol. 1, 477–480.
Official Journal of the Proceedings of the Convention of the State of Louisiana. New Orleans: J. O. Nixon, 1861.

The Official Records of the Union and Confederate Navies in the War of the Rebellion. 30 vols. Washington, DC: Government Printing Office, 1894–1922.

Oldroyd, Osborn H. *A Soldier's Story of the Siege of Vicksburg From the Diary of Osborn H. Oldroyd*. Springfield, IL: published by the author, 1885.

"On Wrong Side of the Works." September 29, 1910, *National Tribune*.

"Opening of the Mississippi." November 2, 1905, *National Tribune*.

Parrish, William E. *Frank Blair: Lincoln's Conservative*. Columbia: University of Missouri Press, 1998.

Patrick, Jeffrey L., ed. *Three Years with Wallace's Zouaves: The Civil War Memoirs of Thomas Wise Durham*. Macon, GA: Mercer University Press, 2003.

Payne, James E. "Missouri Troops in the Vicksburg Campaign." *Confederate Veteran* 36, no. 10 (October 1928): 377–379.

Pemberton, John C. *Pemberton: Defender of Vicksburg*. Chapel Hill: University of North Carolina Press, 1942.

Perry, Lynch. "Vicksburg. Some New History in the Experience of Gen. Francis A. Shoup." *Confederate Veteran* 2, no. 6 (June 1894): 172–174.

Peters, Gerhard, and John T. Woolley. *The American Presidency Project*. www.presidency.ucsb.edu/documents/proclamation-97-appointing-day-national-humiliation-fasting-and-prayer.

Pierson, Enos. *Proceedings of Eleven Reunions Held by the 16th Regiment, O.V.I., Including Roll of Honor, Roster of the Survivors of the Regiment, Statistics, &c., &c.* Millersburg, OH: Republican Steam Press, 1887.

Plummer, Leonard B., ed. "Excerpts from the Hander Diary." *Journal of Mississippi History* 26, no. 2 (May 1964): 141–149.

Porter, David Dixon. *Incidents and Anecdotes of the Civil War*. New York: D. Appleton and Company, 1885.

Post, Lydia Minturn, ed. *Soldiers' Letters. From Camp, Battle-field and Prison*. New York: Bunce and Huntington, Publishers, 1865.

Pryce, Samuel D. *Vanishing Footprints: The Twenty-Second Iowa Volunteer Infantry in the Civil War*. Ed. Jeffry C. Burden. Iowa City, IA: Camp Pope Bookshop, 2008.

Quinby, Henry Cole. *Genealogical History of the Quinby (Quimby) Family in England and America*. Rutland, VT: Tuttle Company, 1915.

Reagan, John H. *Memoirs, With Special Reference to Secession and the Civil War*. Ed. Walter Flavius McCaleb. New York: Neale Publishing Company, 1906.

Reed, David W. *Campaigns and Battles of the Twelfth Regiment Iowa Veteran Volunteer Infantry From Its Organization, September, 1861, to Muster Out, January 20, 1866*. N.p.: n.p., 1903.

Reed, Lida Lord. "A Woman's Experiences During the Siege of Vicksburg." *Century Magazine* 61, no. 6 (April 1901): 922–928.

Reid, Brian Holden. *America's Civil War: The Operational Battlefield, 1861–1863*. Amherst, NY: Prometheus Books, 2008.

Remini, Robert V. *The Battle of New Orleans: Andrew Jackson and America's First Military Victory*. New York: Viking, 1999.

Rice, C. S. O. "Incidents of the Vicksburg Siege." *Confederate Veteran* 12, no. 2 (February 1904): 77–78.

Richard, Allen C., Jr., and Mary Margaret Higginbotham Richard. *The Defense of Vicksburg: A Louisiana Chronicle.* College Station, TX: Texas A&M University Press, 2004.

Richardson, Albert D. *A Personal History of Ulysses S. Grant.* Hartford, CT: American Publishing Company, 1868.

Richmond, Marion B. "The Siege of Vicksburg." *Confederate Veteran* 37, no. 4 (April 1929): 139–141.

Roland, Charles P. *Albert Sidney Johnston: Soldier of Three Republics.* Austin: University of Texas Press, 1964.

Roster and Record of Iowa Soldiers in the War of the Rebellion, Together with Historical Sketches of Volunteer Organizations, 1861–1866. 6 vols. Des Moines, IA: Emory H. English, State Printer, 1910.

Rowland, Dunbar. *Mississippi; Comprising Sketches of Counties, Towns, Events, Institutions and Persons, Arranged in Cyclopedic Form.* 3 vols. Atlanta: Southern Historical Printing Association, 1907.

Rowland, Dunbar, and H. Grady Howell, Jr. *Military History of Mississippi: 1803–1898, Including a Listing of All Known Mississippi Confederate Military Units.* Reprint with additional material. Madison, MS: Chickasaw Bayou Press, 2003.

Sanders, Mary Elizabeth, ed. *Diary in Gray: Civil War Journal of J. Y. Sanders.* Baton Rouge, LA: Louisiana Genealogical & Historical Society, 1994.

Saunier, Joseph A. *A History of the Forty-seventh Regiment Ohio Veteran Volunteer Infantry, Second Brigade, Second Division, Fifteenth Army Corps, Army of the Tennessee.* Hillsboro, OH: Lyle Printing Company, 1903.

Scott, R. B. *The History of the 67th Regiment Indian Infantry Volunteers, War of the Rebellion.* Bedford, IN: Herald Book and Job Print, 1892.

Scriber, Terry G. *Twenty-seventh Louisiana Volunteer Infantry.* Gretna, LA: Pelican Publishing Company, 2006.

Sears, Stephen W. *Gettysburg.* Boston: Houghton Mifflin, 2003.

Shea, William L., and Terrence J. Winschel, *Vicksburg Is the Key: The Struggle for the Mississippi River.* Lincoln: University of Nebraska Press, 2003.

Sherman, William T. *Memoirs of General William T. Sherman: Written by Himself.* 2 vols. New York: D. Appleton and Co., 1875.

Simon, John Y., ed. *The Personal Memoirs of Julia Dent Grant [Mrs. Ulysses S. Grant].* New York: G. P. Putnam's Sons, 1975.

Simon, John Y., and John F. Marszalek, eds. *The Papers of Ulysses S. Grant.* 32 vols. Carbondale: Southern Illinois University Press, 1967–2014.

Simpson, Brooks D. *Ulysses S. Grant: Triumph over Adversity, 1822–1865.* Boston: Houghton Mifflin Company, 2000.

Skaptason, Bjorn. "The Chicago Light Artillery at Vicksburg." *Journal of the Illinois State Historical Society* 106, no. 3–4 (Fall/Winter 2013): 422–462.

Smith, Tamara A. "A Matter of Trust: Grant and James B. McPherson." In *Grant's*

Lieutenants: From Cairo to Vicksburg. Ed. Steven E. Woodworth. Lawrence: University Press of Kansas, 2001. 151–167.

Smith, Timothy B. *Champion Hill: Decisive Battle for Vicksburg.* New York: Savas Beatie, 2004.

———. *Corinth 1862: Siege, Battle, Occupation.* Lawrence: University Press of Kansas, 2012.

———. *The Decision Was Always My Own: Ulysses S. Grant and the Vicksburg Campaign.* Carbondale: Southern Illinois University Press, 2018.

———. "A Frolic up the Tennessee." *America's Civil War* (March 2017): 44–49.

———. *Grant Invades Tennessee: The 1862 Battles for Forts Henry and Donelson.* Lawrence: University Press of Kansas, 2016.

———. "'I am Thinking Seriously of Going Home': Mississippi's Role in the Most Important Decision of Ulysses S. Grant's Life." *Journal of Mississippi History* 80, no. 1 and 2 (Spring/Summer 2018): 21–34.

———. *Mississippi in the Civil War: The Home Front.* Mississippi Heritage Series. Jackson: University Press of Mississippi, 2010.

———. *The Mississippi Secession Convention: Delegates and Deliberations in Politics and War, 1861–1865.* Jackson: University Press of Mississippi, 2014.

———. *The Real Horse Soldiers: Benjamin Grierson's Epic 1863 Civil War Raid through Mississippi.* New York: Savas Beatie, 2018.

———. *Shiloh: Conquer or Perish.* Lawrence: University Press of Kansas, 2014.

———. "Victory at Any Cost: The Yazoo Pass Expedition." *Journal of Mississippi History* 67, no. 2 (Summer 2007): 147–166.

———. "'A Victory Could Hardly Have Been More Complete': The Battle of Big Black River Bridge." In *The Vicksburg Campaign: March 29–May 18, 1863.* Ed. Steven E. Woodworth and Charles D. Grear. Carbondale: Southern Illinois University Press, 2013. 173–193.

Smith, Walter George. *Life and Letters of Thomas Kilby Smith, Brevet Major-General United States Volunteers, 1820–1877.* New York: G. P. Putnam's Sons, 1898.

Soman, Jean Powers, and Frank L. Byrne, eds., *A Jewish Colonel in the Civil War: Marcus M. Spiegel of the Ohio Volunteers.* Kent, OH: Kent State University Press, 1985.

Stoker, Donald. *The Grand Design: Strategy and the U.S. Civil War.* New York: Oxford University Press, 2010.

Stone, Mary Amelia (Boomer). *Memoir of George Boardman Boomer.* Boston: Press of Geo. C. Rand & Avery, 1864.

The Story of the Fifty-fifth Regiment Illinois Volunteer Infantry in the Civil War, 1861–1865. Clinton, MA: W. J. Coulter, 1887.

Strong, William E. "The Campaign Against Vicksburg." In *Military Essays and Recollections: Papers Read Before the Commandery of the State of Illinois, Military Order of the Loyal Legion of the United States, Volume II.* Chicago: A. C. McClurg and Company, 1894. 313–354.

Supplement to the Official Records of the Union and Confederate Armies. 100 vols. Wilmington, NC: Broadfoot Publishing Company, 1994.

Symonds, Craig L. *Joseph E. Johnston: A Civil War Biography*. New York: Norton, 1992.
"Their Records." October 5, 1893, *National Tribune*.
Thomas, Emory M. *Robert E. Lee: A Biography*. New York: W. W. Norton & Company, 1995.
Toll, Ian W. *The Conquering Tide: War in the Pacific Islands, 1942–1944*. New York: W. W. Norton & Company, 2015.
Tomblin, Barbara Brooks. *The Civil War on the Mississippi: Union Sailors, Gunboat Captains, and the Campaign to Control the River*. Lexington: University Press of Kentucky, 2016.
Townsend, Mary Bobbitt. *Yankee Warhorse: A Biography of Major General Peter Osterhaus*. Columbia: University of Missouri Press, 2010.
Trowbridge, Silas T. *Autobiography of S. T. Trowbridge, M.D.* N.p.: n.p., 1872.
———. *Autobiography of Silas Thompson Trowbridge, M.D.* Carbondale, IL: Southern Illinois University Press, 2004.
Trudeau, Noah Andre. *Gettysburg: A Testing of Courage*. New York: HarperCollins, 2002.
Tucker, Philip Thomas. *The Forgotten Stonewall of the West: Major General John Stevens Bowen*. Macon, GA: Mercer University Press, 1997.
———. *Westerners in Gray: The Men of and Missions of the Elite Fifth Missouri Infantry Regiment*. Jefferson, NC: McFarland & Company, 1995.
Tunnard, W. H. *A Southern Record: The History of the Third Regiment Louisiana Infantry*. Baton Rouge, LA: n.p., 1866.
"Vicksburg Campaign." August 9, 1888, *National Tribune*.
Warner, Ezra J. *Generals in Blue: Lives of the Union Commanders*. Baton Rouge: Louisiana State University Press, 1964.
———. *Generals in Gray: Lives of the Confederate Commanders*. Baton Rouge: Louisiana State University Press, 1959.
War of the Rebellion: A Compilation of the Official Records of the Union and Confederate Armies. Washington, DC: US Government Printing Office, 1880–1901.
Wells, Seth J. *The Siege of Vicksburg from the Diary of Seth J. Wells, Including Weeks of Preparation and of Occupation after the Surrender*. Detroit: William H. Rowe, Publisher, 1915.
Welsh, Jack D. *Medical Histories of Union Generals*. Kent, OH: Kent State University Press, 1996.
Whaley, Elizabeth J. *Forgotten Hero: General James B. McPherson*. New York: Exposition Press, 1955.
White, Ronald C. *American Ulysses: A Life of Ulysses S. Grant*. New York: Random House, 2016.
Wilkin, Jacob B. "Vicksburg." In *Military Essays and Recollections: Papers Read Before the Commandery of the State of Illinois, Military Order of the Loyal Legion of the United States, Volume IV*. Chicago: Cozzens and Beaton Company, 1907. 215–237.
Williams, John Melvin. "The Eagle Regiment," 8th Wis. Inf'ty Vols.: *A Sketch of Its Marches, Battles and Campaigns From 1861–1865 With Complete Regimental and*

Company Roster, and a Few Portraits and Sketches of Its Officers and Commanders. Belleville, WI: Recorder Print, 1890.

Williams, Kenneth P. *Grant Rises in the West: From Iuka to Vicksburg, 1862–1863*. Lincoln: University of Nebraska Press, 1997.

Willison, Charles A. *Reminiscences of a Boy's Service with the 76th Ohio, In the Fifteenth Army Corps, Under General Sherman, During the Civil War, By That "Boy" at Three Score*. Menasha, WI: George Banta Publishing Company, 1908.

Wilson, James Harrison. "A Staff Officer's Journal of the Vicksburg Campaign, April 30 to July 4, 1863." [First installment.] *Journal of the Military Service Institution of the United States* 43, no. 154 (July–August 1908): 93–109.

———. "A Staff Officer's Journal of the Vicksburg Campaign, April 30 to July 4, 1863." [Second installment.] *Journal of the Military Service Institution of the United States* 43, no. 155 (September–October 1908): 261–275.

———. *Under the Old Flag: Recollections of Military Operations in the War for the Union, the Spanish War The Boxer Rebellion, Etc.* 2 vols. New York: D. Appleton and Co., 1912.

Winschel, Terrence J. *Alice Shirley and the Story of Wexford Lodge*. Fort Washington, PA: Eastern National, 2003.

———, ed. *The Civil War Diary of a Common Soldier: William Wiley of the 77th Illinois Infantry*. Baton Rouge: Louisiana State University Press, 2001.

———. "Fighting Politician: John A. McClernand." In *Grant's Lieutenants: From Cairo to Vicksburg*. Ed. Steven E. Woodworth. Lawrence: University Press of Kansas, 2001. 129–150.

———. *Triumph and Defeat: The Vicksburg Campaign*. Mason City, IA: Savas Publishing Company, 1999.

———. *Triumph and Defeat: The Vicksburg Campaign*. Vol. 2. New York: Savas Beatie, 2006.

Wood, D. W. *History of the 20th O.V.V.I. Regiment, and Proceedings of the First Reunion at Mt. Vernon, Ohio, April 6, 1876*. Columbus, OH: Paul and Thrall, Book and Job Printers, 1876.

Wood, Gordon S. *Empire of Liberty: A History of the Early Republic, 1789–1815*. New York: Oxford University Press, 2009.

Wood, Wales W. *A History of the Ninety-fifth Regiment Illinois Infantry Volunteers, From its Organization in the Fall of 1862, Until Its Final Discharge from the United States Service, in 1865*. Chicago: Tribune Company's Book and Job Printing Office, 1865.

Woodruff, George H. *Fifteen Years Ago, Or The Patriotism of Will County*. Joliet, IL: Joliet Republican Book and Job Steam Printing House, 1876.

Woodworth, Steven E. "The Assault on the Railroad Redoubt." In *The Vicksburg Assaults: May 19–22, 1863*. Ed. Steven E. Woodworth and Charles D. Grear. Carbondale: Southern Illinois University Press, 2019, 57–71.

———. *Davis and Lee at War*. Lawrence: University Press of Kansas, 1995.

———. *Jefferson Davis and His Generals: The Failure of Confederate Command in the West*. Lawrence: University Press of Kansas, 1990.
———. *Nothing But Victory: The Army of the Tennessee, 1861–1865*. New York: Knopf, 2005.
Work, David. *Lincoln's Political Generals*. Urbana: University of Illinois Press, 2009.
Young, John Russell. *Around the World With General Grant: A Narrative of the Visit of General U.S. Grant, Ex-President of the United States, to Various Countries in Europe, Asia, and Africa, in 1877, 1878, 1879. To which are Added Certain Conversations with General Grant on Questions Connected with American Politics and History*. New York: American News Company, 1879.

INDEX

2nd Texas Lunette, 23, 136, 185, 208–209, 212–213, 226–227, 233, 237, 240, 243–244, 246–247, 250, 258, 298, 310, 313, 315, 320–321, 324, 326, 328, 335, 344–345, 358
3rd Louisiana Redan, 23, 91, 93, 184–185, 221, 224–225, 227–228, 300, 306–308
27th Louisiana Lunette, 99, 104, 108, 110–112, 160

Abbott, Charles H., 279
Abernathy, Alonzo, 279
Affeld, Charles, 165
Ainsworth, Calvin, 139, 144, 178–179
Alabama, 10, 16, 18, 195, 255, 264–265, 337
Alabama Troops
    2nd Artillery Battalion, 99, 384
    20th Infantry, 238–239, 256, 337–338, 366, 384
    23rd Infantry, 56, 239, 384
    30th Infantry, 239, 260, 337–338, 384
    31st Infantry, 239, 255, 344, 384
    37th Infantry, 185, 238, 385
    40th Infantry, 185, 385
    42nd Infantry, 185, 238, 243, 385
    46th Infantry, 238, 262, 265, 337–338, 384
    54th Infantry (detachment), 386
    Sengstak's Battery, 385
    Waddell's Battery, 185, 239, 384
Alison, Joseph Dill, 58, 69, 128
Amsterdam, Mississippi, 62
Anaconda Plan, 5
Anderson, Joseph W., 81
Antietam, Battle of, x, 106, 197, 235
A. O. Tyler, xvii, 11

Appalachian Mountains, xvi–xvii
Arkansas, xvi–xvii, 12, 90, 166, 195, 202, 235, 251, 265
Arkansas, CSS, 15
Arkansas Post, Battle of, 45, 111, 235, 288
Arkansas River, 1
Arkansas Troops
    1st Battalion Sharpshooters, 298, 324
    1st Cavalry (dismounted), 312
    1st Cavalry Battalion, 386
    12th Battalion Sharpshooters, 386
    19th Infantry, 297–298, 324, 386
    20th Infantry, 298, 386
    Appeal Battery, 99, 185, 384
    McNally's Battery, 99, 385
Army of Northern Virginia, 370
Army of Tennessee, 16
Army of the Potomac, x, 351, 369
Army of the Tennessee, 35, 41, 63, 140, 148, 180, 190, 204, 234, 350, 354, 356, 373–380
    XIII Corps, 143, 148, 207, 236, 253, 272, 354–355, 373
    XV Corps, 95, 141, 152, 214, 276, 295, 376
    XVII Corps, 62, 92, 150, 181–182, 221, 298, 309, 319, 330, 378
Atherton, Joseph B., 263, 266, 335, 340, 343
Autry, James L., 13–15
Avery, William, 303

Badeau, Adam, 192
Bagwell, T. E., 248
Bailey, George W., 243
Baker, Lyman, 191
Bakers Creek, 42, 141

Balaklava, Battle of, 119
Baldwin, William E., 55, 69, 73, 80–81, 98–99, 136–137, 177, 231, 278, 281, 385
Baldwin's Ferry, Mississippi, 54
Baldwin's Ferry Road, 21, 23–24, 55–56, 67, 70–71, 83–85, 97, 130, 183–185, 209, 229, 236–237, 240–241, 243–245, 297–299, 315–316, 319, 345
Balfour, Emma, 57, 83, 360–361, 363–364
Ballard, Michael B., xvii, 57, 273, 296
Banks, Nathaniel, 38, 77
Barber, Seth M., 149
Baron De Kalb, USS, 65
Barrett, Samuel, 135, 163
Barry, William S., 186
Barton, Seth M., 70, 325, 331, 383
Baton Rouge, Louisiana, 14–16
Bayou Pierre, 4, 36, 38–39
Beach, Augustus, 254
Bearss, Edwin C., 181, 183, 296, 352, 355
Beauregard, P. G. T., 9, 11–13, 15, 45
Bedford, Wimer, 307
Belknap, William, 332
Belmont, Battle of, 50, 234
Benton, USS, 333
Benton, William P., 85, 209, 213, 240–241, 244–246, 248–250, 258, 310, 315, 318, 321, 325–326, 330, 375
Benton Road, 65, 103, 359
Big Black River, 4, 21, 38–42, 44, 46–48, 50–52, 54–59, 65, 69–70, 73, 86, 113, 141, 198, 237, 240, 251, 259, 289, 297, 358, 363
Big Black River Bridge, Battle of, xi–xii, 43, 71–72, 85, 87, 97, 205, 209, 251–253, 258, 297, 358, 366, 369–370
Bitterman, Jane, 359
Black, James P., 340
Black Bayou, 33
Black River, 31
Blair, Francis P., 61–62, 65–66, 78, 81–82, 95, 102–106, 120, 124, 126–127, 131, 134, 136, 143, 148, 150, 153–155, 158–159, 162–163, 168, 170–176, 179, 182, 184, 186, 188–189, 193, 195–196, 215–217, 271, 273–276, 283–285, 287–292, 294–296, 299, 367, 377

Blair, Frank Sr., 102
Blair, Montgomery, 102
Blanchard, Ira, 195
Blessingh, Louis von, 106, 108, 169–170, 172
Boley, John W., 367
Bolton, Mississippi, 41
Bonaparte, Napoleon, 26, 54, 193, 251
Boomer, George B., 82–83, 150, 183, 190–192, 199, 226, 299, 309–310, 314–319, 325, 381
Bourne, Joshua W., 200–201
Boutell, Ira, 111
Bovina, Mississippi, 47, 52, 54, 359
Bowen, John S., 36, 42, 46–47, 52–54, 56–58, 69, 71, 80, 98, 131–132, 159–160, 186, 230, 268, 297, 324, 386
Bowen, John T., 293
Bowers, Theodore, 352
Bowie Family, 361
Bradley, Daniel, 195
Bradley, George, 57
Bradley, L. D., 338
Bragg, Braxton, xviii, 16
Breckinridge, John C., 16
Bridgeport, Mississippi, 51, 54, 59, 61–63, 65–66, 82, 102
Brierfield, xiv, 45
Britton, W. B., 348
Brown, W. L., 352
Bruinsburg, Mississippi, 34–36, 40, 45
Buchanan, James, xiv
Buchannan, Robert, 198–200, 203
Buchwalter, Daniel, 351
Buckland, Ralph P., 82, 105, 288–289, 294, 378
Buegel, John T., 136, 154, 281, 350
Buehler, Theodore E., 90, 137–138, 151, 246, 249, 326, 328
Buell, Don Carlos, 27
Buena Vista, Battle of, 115
Burbridge, Stephen G., 67, 85, 151, 213, 240–241, 245–246, 248–250, 258, 310–314, 325–326, 328, 330, 374
Burdette, Robert J., 368
Burk, Uley, 279
Burt, Richard, 280
Bush, Elliott, 304, 351

INDEX 471

Butler, Benjamin F., 8–9, 15
Byers, Samuel, 190–191

Cadwallader, Sylvanus, 58–59, 66, 237, 268, 352
Campbell, Franklin, 200, 202
Campbell, John Q. A., 199, 316
Carlisle, James, 118
Carolinas, xiv
Carondelet, USS, 333
Carr, Eugene A., 63, 85, 89, 149, 208, 212, 236, 240–241, 249–250, 252, 258–259, 261, 264, 310, 313, 315, 317–318, 322, 325, 330, 335, 375
Carrington, George, 93, 140, 148, 188–189, 303
Carskaddon, David, 279
Cashier, Albert, 94
Castens, John, 123
Catton, Bruce, xiii, 34, 355
Cazean, Louis, 287
Central America, 18
Chambers, William Pitt, 73, 278, 282
Champion Hill, Battle of, xi, xviii, 42–43, 47, 52, 61–63, 70–72, 82, 87, 97, 181–182, 190, 193, 205, 236, 238–240, 251, 253, 297, 306, 331, 349, 358, 369–370
Chancellorsville, Battle of, ix–x, 369
Chapultepec, Battle of, 92
Chatfield, Edward, 343
Chattanooga, Battle of, 26, 296
Chattanooga, Tennessee, ix, 8
Chickasaw Bayou, Battle of, 99, 111, 115, 152, 235, 276, 288, 296
Chickasaw Bayou, Mississippi, 17, 21, 38, 65–66, 141, 143
Christ Episcopal Church, 359, 362
Cincinnati, Ohio, xvii
City of Louisiana, xvii
Clarke, George, 55, 101, 117, 120, 161, 163, 168, 172, 174
Clendenin, Francis M., 367
Cockrell, Francis M., 71, 80, 98, 100, 109, 111, 114, 119, 132, 147, 159–160, 166–167, 175, 186, 233, 291, 297–298, 386
Coffeeville, Mississippi, 28
Coker, Mrs., 340

Colbert, Bruce, 186
Colby, Carlos, 357
Cold Harbor, Battle of, 351
Coldwater River, 32
Coleman, David C., 111–112, 158
Columbus, Kentucky, 6, 11–12, 18
Confederate States of America, ix
  Signal Corps, 384–386
  War Department, x, 369
Conway, J. J., 72
Cook Plantation, 68
Cooper, Samuel, 12
Corinth, Battle of, 8, 99, 185, 190, 285, 289–290, 332
Corinth, Mississippi, 6, 9, 12
Corinth, Siege of, 6, 10, 12–13, 26, 45, 115
County Kildare, Ireland, 259
Cowan, Luther H., 307
Cradlebaugh, John, 256
Crane, John, 93
Crocker, Marcellus M., 62, 182
Cumberland River, xvi, 11
Cumming, Alfred, 71, 331, 383

Dana, Charles, 92, 102, 182, 190, 193, 196, 236–237, 240, 259, 276, 288–289, 331, 353–354, 403n39
Davis, Charles H., 16
Davis, Jefferson, ix–xi, xiv, 17, 26, 44–46, 53, 69, 115–116, 369–371
Davis, William P., 194–196
Davis Bridge, Battle of, 185
Dayton, James H., 106, 108, 110, 172
Deer Creek, 33
De Golyer, Samuel, 82, 197
Delta, xiv, 3, 28, 30, 32
Dement, Henry D., 282
De Soto, Louisiana, 15
Dickey, Cyrus E., 303
Dillon, Henry, 381
Disharoon's Plantation, Louisiana, 34
Dix-Hill Cartel, 19
Dockery, Thomas P., 297–298, 312, 324
Dodge, Grenville, 276
Dollins, James J., 197, 200, 202
Downing, Alexander, 332
Drennan, William, 128

472   INDEX

Drummond Brothers, 356
Dunlap, Cornelius W., 263–264
Dunn, Ed, 267
Durden Creek, 22–24, 84–85, 89, 238
Durfee, George S., 129, 135, 148, 200, 352

Eastern Theater, x–xi, 106, 108, 197, 217
Edwards, Martha, 79
Edwards Station, Mississippi, 41, 86
Eldridge, Hamilton N., 115, 122, 157
Elliott, Isaac H., 241
Evans, Morgan V., 266
Evans Plantation, 64
Ewing, Charles, 113, 131
Ewing, Hugh, 81, 103–106, 108–114, 117, 122–123, 131, 150–151, 155–156, 158–159, 162, 167–175, 186, 189, 197, 217, 271, 274–275, 283–286, 288, 290, 292–293, 295–296, 307, 367, 377
Ewing, Thomas, 106

Farragut, David G., 8–10, 14–16
Faulk, William L., 129, 286
Ferguson House, 133
Finley, John H., 329
Fisher, Cyrus W., 116–117, 121, 274, 284
Fisher, Theodore, 357
Fisk, Archie C., 170
Fivemile Creek, 40
Florida, 4
Fly, George W. L., 344
Flynn, William O., 72
Fonda, John G., 256, 329
Fontaine, Edward, 11
Foote, Andrew H., 51
Force, Manning F., 149, 306–308, 350
Forlorn Hope, 156–159, 161–163, 165–166, 168–171, 214, 217, 220, 283, 290–291, 294, 356, 367
Forney, John H., 46, 53–58, 69–70, 72–73, 84, 97–98, 125, 128–130, 133, 136–138, 159–160, 165, 167, 175, 184–186, 199, 204, 227, 237, 244, 247, 268, 278, 297, 324–235, 342, 345–346, 384
Forrest, Nathan Bedford, 28
Fort Beauregard, 258

Fort Donelson, Battle of, 6, 10, 14, 18, 26, 45, 50, 92, 111, 127, 193, 234, 259, 276, 288, 306, 325, 334, 343
Fort Henry, Battle of, 6, 10, 14, 45, 234, 334
Fort Hill, 21, 23, 93, 183, 194, 196–197, 308
Fort Jackson, Battle of, 8–10, 12, 14
Fort McHenry, Battle of, 10
Fort Pemberton, Mississippi, 32, 46
Fort Pillow, Tennessee, 12–13
Fort Saint Philip, Battle of, 8, 10, 12, 14
Foster, Henry C., 194
Foster, Jacob T., 374
Foster, John S., 378
Foster, William L., 54, 56, 101, 126–127
Fourteenmile Creek, 40, 42
Fox, Gustavus, 1
Fox, Parson, 360
Frankfort, Kentucky, 251
Fredericksburg, Battle of, 30, 61–62
Fredericksburg, Virginia, xi
Freeman, Henry C., 61

Galena, Illinois, 180, 193
Garrard, Theophilus T., 90, 251
Garrott, Isham, 338
Gause, William R., 167–168
Georgia, 71, 331
Georgia Troops
    34th Infantry, 383
    36th Infantry, 383
    39th Infantry, 383
    40th Infantry, 383
    41st Infantry, 383
    42nd Infantry, 383
    43rd Infantry, 383
    52nd Infantry, 383
    56th Infantry, 383
    57th Infantry, 383
    Cherokee Artillery, 383
Germans, 89, 106, 197, 210, 236, 251
Gettysburg, Battle of, xi, xiii, 371
Gibbs, Mrs., 365–366
Gilbert, Christopher, 368
Gilmer, Jeremy F., 13
Glass Bayou, 22–23, 81–82, 92–93, 99–100, 104, 117, 126, 154, 172–173, 182–184,

186, 188–189, 193–195, 249, 271, 274, 285–286, 299–300, 304–305
Goodspeed, Arza M., 108
Grabau, Warren, 21, 240
Graham, Harvey, 264, 321, 340, 355
Grand Gulf, Mississippi, 18, 34–36, 38, 40, 46–47, 61–62, 66, 82, 104, 126, 140, 146, 162, 331, 334
Grant, Fred, 160, 270
Grant, Julia, 41, 51, 181
Grant, Ulysses S., ix–xi, xiv
 advance on Vicksburg, 50–52, 54, 58–59, 61, 64–68, 74
 afternoon May 22 assaults, 276, 288–289, 298–299, 305, 308–310, 321–323, 331–334, 341
 decision for more assaults, 270–273
 early Vicksburg operations, 2–6, 9, 14, 26–28, 30–36, 38–47
 interim between assaults, 131, 133–134, 138–141, 143–147, 150
 May 19 assaults, 77–78, 80, 85–87, 90, 95–97, 102–103, 105, 120, 124, 127–128
 morning May 22 assaults, 152–155, 160, 162, 170–172, 176, 180–182, 186, 192–194, 197, 205–207, 214, 221, 236–237, 239–240, 251, 253, 259
 results of assaults, 343, 345–357, 359–360, 366–367, 370–371, 373
Graveyard Road, 21–22, 65, 69–71, 73, 78, 80–81, 83, 92, 95–97, 99–100, 103–104, 113, 115–117, 119–121, 129, 154–156, 159, 161–163, 169, 171, 175–176, 183, 188–189, 197, 268, 271, 273–274, 283–285, 288–289, 297–299, 307, 324, 345, 361, 363
Gray, Andrew B., 13
Great Redoubt, 23, 91, 148, 184–185, 197–201, 204, 221, 224–225, 227, 298, 303, 306, 315, 344
Green, Martin E., 71, 99, 186, 265, 268, 297–298, 311–312, 324, 386
Green Bay, Wisconsin, 93
Green's Redan, 99
Greenville, Mississippi, xvi
Greenwood, Mississippi, 32, 46

Greer, James A., 333
Grenada, Mississippi, 28
Grier, David, 267, 326, 356
Grier, John P., 340
Grierson, Benjamin H., 35, 43–46, 152
Griffith, Joseph E., 264–265, 337
Groce, John H., 162, 167–168, 367
Gulf of Mexico, 3, 8, 16, 18
Guppey Joshua, J., 245, 247, 328

Hains, Peter C., 148, 264
Hall, William, 82, 238, 331–332, 380
Hall, Winchester, 58, 76, 99, 114
Halleck, Henry W., 8, 10, 13, 26–27, 30–31, 38, 181, 235–236, 272, 353
Hall's Ferry, Mississippi, 39
Hall's Ferry Road, 21, 23–24, 71, 97, 238, 331
Hankinson's Ferry, Mississippi, 39
Hard Times, Louisiana, 34
Harpers Ferry, Virginia, 197
Harris, Charles L., 150, 262
Harris, David B., 13–14
Harris, Jeptha V., 70, 385
Hatcher's Bayou, 23, 183–184
Hawk, Elbridge L., 329
Hayes, Thomas, 169
Haynes' Bluff, Mississippi, 3, 10, 17, 32–34, 51–52, 54–55, 59, 65, 67–68, 70, 74, 86, 139–141, 152, 331
Hebert, Louis, 55–58, 69–70, 81, 83, 91, 93, 97–100, 104, 109, 118, 123, 125, 129, 133–136, 154, 160, 162–163, 165, 184–186, 228, 268, 285, 297, 324, 344–345, 348, 384
Helena, Arkansas, xvi, 12, 90, 251
Hennessey's Bayou, 23–24
Hickenlooper, Andrew, 62
Higgins, Edward, 70, 333, 386
Higgins, Tom, 244–245, 366
Hildt, George A., 168
Hipp, Charles, 170, 172
Hoadley, Robert, 279
Hobbs, Charles A., 347
Hodgers, Jennie, 94
Hogane, James T., 109
Hoge, George B., 111

Hogue, James, 338
Holland, Orlando S., 99
Holly Springs, Mississippi, 28
Holmes, Samuel A., 82, 183, 190, 192, 299, 314–315, 380
Holt, Joseph, xiv
Hovey, Alvin P., 63, 86, 133, 236–237, 253–254, 258, 315, 322, 328, 330, 349, 354, 375
Howe, Orion P., 121
Hubbard, Lucius, 289–290, 292, 294
Hughes, Mrs., 98
Humphrey, Thomas W., 93–95, 189, 302–303, 305
Hunt, Ira W., 352
Hyatt, Theodore, 158, 165, 167–168, 294, 343

Illinois, xiv, 6, 64, 84–85, 92, 94, 112, 123, 127, 133–135, 139, 148, 151, 173, 180, 183, 189, 193, 199, 201–202, 234–235, 240, 244–245, 251, 269, 285–286, 292, 300, 302–303, 308, 315–316, 331, 340, 342–343, 351, 354, 368
Illinois Troops
  1st Artillery Battery A, 59, 92, 112, 163, 377
  1st Artillery Battery B, 135, 163, 165, 377
  1st Artillery Battery D, 379
  1st Artillery Battery E, 135, 163, 378
  1st Artillery Battery H, 163, 377
  2nd Artillery Battery A, 376
  2nd Artillery Battery G, 379
  2nd Artillery Battery F, 380
  2nd Artillery Battery L, 379
  2nd Cavalry, 374, 379
  3rd Cavalry, 373–375, 377
  4th Cavalry, 373
  8th Infantry, 135, 148, 197–198, 200, 203, 379
  11th Cavalry, 379
  11th Infantry, 92–95, 140, 188–189, 300, 303, 380
  13th Infantry, 278, 282, 351, 376
  17th Infantry, 197, 199, 201, 203–204, 379
  18th Infantry, 259
  20th Infantry, 193–196, 306–307, 379
  30th Infantry, 183, 379
  31st Infantry, 193, 379
  33rd Infantry, 240–241, 243–244, 375
  45th Infantry, 144, 193–194, 306–307, 379
  47th Infantry, 289, 293–294, 368, 378
  55th Infantry, 115–117, 119–122, 162, 168, 175, 283–284, 286, 377
  56th Infantry, 380
  63rd Infantry, 332, 380
  72nd Infantry, 75, 92, 94–95, 149, 188–189, 300, 302, 379
  77th Infantry, 259, 267, 326, 335, 340, 374
  81st Infantry, 92, 197–198, 200–202, 379
  87th Infantry, 332, 380
  93rd Infantry, 190–191, 314–318, 342, 381
  95th Infantry, 92–95, 188–189, 300, 302–305, 380
  97th Infantry, 259, 261, 266, 374
  99th Infantry, 89, 240–241, 243–244, 318, 347, 357, 366, 375
  113th Infantry, 76, 111–112, 172, 287, 377
  114th Infantry, 163, 289, 378
  116th Infantry, 112–114, 377
  118th Infantry, 251, 253, 256–257, 329, 373
  124th Infantry, 143, 193, 196, 379
  127th Infantry, 115, 122, 125, 157–158, 165, 291, 294, 377
  130th Infantry, 259, 267, 375
  Chicago Mercantile Battery, 250, 313, 375
  Kane County Independent Cavalry Company, 377
  Thielemann's Cavalry Battalion, 378
Indiana, 68, 79, 87, 115–117, 121–122, 131, 183, 192, 236, 240, 244–245, 251, 322, 347, 350, 352, 357
Indiana Troops
  1st Artillery, 376
  1st Cavalry, 375
  4th Cavalry, 374
  8th Infantry, 135, 240–241, 243–244, 375
  11th Infantry, 253, 375
  16th Infantry, 240, 245–246, 248, 250, 326, 374
  18th Infantry, 240, 243, 248, 375
  23rd Infantry, 193–196, 306, 379
  24th Infantry, 253, 375
  34th Infantry, 253, 375
  46th Infantry, 253, 258, 375
  48th Infantry, 63, 65, 310–313, 380
  49th Infantry, 90, 251–252, 255, 373

INDEX

54th Infantry, 252–253, 374
59th Infantry, 191, 310–311, 380
60th Infantry, 374
67th Infantry, 67, 90, 137, 157, 240, 245–246, 249, 311, 326, 374
69th Infantry, 251–252, 254–256, 329, 373
83rd Infantry, 59, 115, 122, 143, 174, 245, 357, 379
93rd Infantry, 92, 289, 378
Indians, 93, 96, 178
Indian Territory, xiii
Indian Wars, 236
Inghaham, Edward, 351
Iowa, 59, 66, 79, 85, 87, 91, 95–96, 104, 144, 148, 155, 177–179, 183, 191–192, 258, 260, 262, 265, 275–276, 278–282, 314–317, 329, 331, 335–336, 340, 344, 347, 368
Iowa Troops
    1st Artillery, 377
    2nd Artillery, 163, 378
    4th Cavalry, 65, 378
    4th Infantry, 179, 276, 282, 376
    5th Infantry, 190, 315–318, 380
    8th Infantry, 288, 378
    9th Infantry, 80, 96, 179, 276, 279, 376
    10th Infantry, 190, 315, 317, 380
    11th Infantry, 331–332, 380
    12th Infantry, 121, 288, 378
    13th Infantry, 331–332, 380
    15th Infantry, 331–332, 380
    16th Infantry, 331–332, 380
    17th Infantry, 380
    21st Infantry, 259, 261, 263–264, 266, 335, 376
    22nd Infantry, 149–150, 259, 261, 263–264, 266–267, 321, 335, 337, 340, 355, 376
    23rd Infantry, 259, 261
    25th Infantry, 79–80, 139, 177–178, 276, 280, 376
    26th Infantry, 143, 179, 276, 279, 376
    30th Infantry, 179, 276, 279, 376
    31st Infantry, 276, 376
    35th Infantry, 288, 378
Irish, 59, 154, 197, 199–201, 259, 344
Island, No. 10, Tennessee, 12, 18, 45
Iuka, Battle of, 99, 185, 190, 285

Jackson, Andrew, xvii, 8, 102, 106
Jackson, Battle of, 41
Jackson, Isaac, 246
Jackson, Mississippi, ix, xiv, 4–5, 11–12, 14, 28, 39–41, 44, 46–47, 95, 140, 236, 272, 359
Jackson, Stonewall, ix
Jackson Road, 21–23, 25, 41–42, 55, 62, 65, 70–71, 78, 82–83, 91–92, 94, 97–99, 103, 120, 129–130, 182–185, 189, 193, 197, 199, 205, 221, 224, 268, 270, 272, 297–298, 304–307, 324–325, 330, 345, 361, 365
Jefferson, Thomas, xvi
Jenney, William L. B., 141, 143, 353
Johnson, Thomas H., 148
Johnston, Albert Sidney, 6, 9, 11, 13, 16, 115
Johnston, Joseph E., 26, 40, 44–47, 52–53, 59, 69, 74–75, 77, 96, 132, 136, 145, 345, 369–370
Johnston Place Landing, 141
Jomini, Antoine-Henri, 26, 54
Jones, James H., 161, 287
Jones, John B., x, 369–370
Jones, John G., 246
Jones, John P., 144, 343
Jones, Theodore, 106
Jones, W. J., 96
Jones Field (Shiloh), 331

Kanawha Valley, Virginia, 106
Keigwin, James, 90, 251–257, 329, 373
Kelley, John B., 200
Kellogg, George D., 357
Kellogg, John J., 76–77, 112, 286–287
Kennesaw Mountain, Battle of, 296
Kentucky, 6, 10–12, 18, 27, 63, 240, 251, 259
Kentucky Military Institute, 240, 251
Kentucky State Guard, 251
Kentucky Troops (US)
    7th Infantry, 251, 253, 256, 374
    19th Infantry, 259, 266, 375
    22nd Infantry, 251–252, 254, 374
    26th Infantry, 240
    Infantry (Independent Company), 373
    Pioneer Corps, 63
Kerrick, Bill, 267

King Cotton Diplomacy, 45
Kinsman, William H., 261
Kittridge, A. S., 248
Klosterman, Herman, 143
Knobe, Louis, 131, 243

Lake Providence, Louisiana, 31–32
Lake's Landing, Mississippi, 65, 141
Landgraeber, Clemens, 96
Landram, William J., 85, 240, 259, 263, 266–267, 321–322, 326, 330, 335, 374
Lane, John, xiv
Lanphere, Charles, 254
Larrabee, James W., 162, 167, 283
Lawler, Michael K., 43, 85, 149–150, 209, 258–264, 266–268, 321–322, 330, 335, 338, 340, 376
Lee, Albert L., 85, 90, 211, 251, 373
Lee, Charles N., 263, 335
Lee, Robert E., ix–xiii, 48, 266, 369–371
Lee, S. Phillips, 14
Lee, Stephen D., 23, 48, 56, 71, 89, 91, 133, 135, 232, 237–239, 254–256, 258, 260, 265, 268, 297–298, 311, 324, 331, 336–339, 341, 361, 366, 384
Leeper, James, 90
Leggett, Mortimer D., 82, 140, 183, 299, 305–306, 379
Lenert, Albert C., 129, 265
Lewis, C. S., ix
Lewis, William E., 144
Lightfoot, Gustavus, 280–281
Lincoln, Abraham, xiv, 1–2, 5–6, 27, 30, 35, 68, 102, 193, 235, 369
Lindsey, Daniel W., 85, 251–253, 255, 329, 374
Lippincott, Charles E., 244
Little Egypt, 235
Lockett, Samuel H., 16–19, 21–25, 34–35, 38–39, 42, 44, 46–47, 49, 51–54, 56, 64, 71–72, 74, 79, 97, 101, 160, 184, 270, 340, 346–347
Lodi, Battle of, 176
Logan, John A., 42, 62–64, 67, 82, 91–92, 94, 182–183, 189–190, 193, 196, 198–200, 224–225, 270–271, 298–300, 304–306, 308–309, 314, 324, 330, 379

Loosley, Edwin A., 357
Lord, Lida, 359, 362, 364, 366
Lord, William, 359, 363
Loring, William W., 46–48, 52, 70, 238
Los Angeles, California, 368
Loughborough, Mary, 363–364
Louisiana, xvi–xvii, 11–12, 15, 18, 25, 30, 34, 45, 58, 73–75, 83, 97, 99, 108–113, 126–127, 130, 138, 177, 179–181, 184, 186, 195, 200, 202, 228, 230, 236, 278, 280, 325, 331, 344, 360, 365
Louisiana Purchase, xvi
Louisiana Troops
  1st Artillery, 386
  3rd Infantry, 99, 138, 185, 194, 307, 384
  4th Infantry, 14
  5th Infantry, 14
  8th Heavy Artillery Battalion, 386
  8th Infantry Battalion, 14
  17th Infantry, 99, 278, 297, 385
  20th Infantry, 14
  21st Infantry, 99, 185, 199, 202, 384
  22nd Infantry, 386
  26th Infantry, 58, 76, 98–99, 109, 114, 278, 280, 385
  27th Infantry, 14, 81, 98–99, 104, 109, 110, 114, 160, 167, 385
  28th Infantry, 14
  29th Infantry, 98, 199, 278, 281, 297, 385
  31st Infantry, 278–279, 385
  Pointe Coupee Artillery, 383, 385
Lovell, Mansfield, 9, 11–13, 16
Lucas, George, 342
Lucas, Thomas J., 245, 248, 326
Lynd, Adam, 108–109

Mahan, James, 311
Malmborg, Oscar, 116, 122, 286–287
Maloney, Maurice, 320
Manassas, Battle of, 1
Manter, Francis H., 79, 136, 154, 177, 179, 275, 278, 282, 376
Marks, Leon D., 81, 99, 114, 160
Maryland, 27
Maryland Troops, 3rd Artillery, 384
Mason, F. H., 320–322
Mathieson, George W., 255

Matthews, Asa C., 243
Matthies, Charles L., 82, 288, 290, 294, 378
Maurice, Thomas D., 380
McArthur, John, 62, 82, 92, 146, 182–183, 222–223, 232, 238, 272–273, 299, 305, 309, 323, 330–332, 334–335, 341, 348, 379
McClellan, George B., 1, 235
McClernand, John A.
  advance on Vicksburg, 59, 61, 63–64, 67
  afternoon May 22 assaults, 266–276, 283, 288, 296, 298–299, 305, 308–310, 314, 316, 319–323, 325–326, 329–332, 334–335, 341
  early Vicksburg operations, 31, 36, 41
  interim between assaults, 131, 133–134, 137, 143, 145–147, 150
  May 19 assaults, 78, 84–87, 89–91, 95, 103, 127
  morning May 22 assaults, 154, 159, 162, 180–182, 205, 207–208, 211, 222, 226, 234–241, 244, 248–251, 253, 255, 258, 263
  results of assaults, 345–346, 351–356, 373
McCormack, Andrew, 158
McFeeley, Robert, 143
McGinnis, George F., 253
McMahon, Thomas, 94
McPherson, James B.
  advance on Vicksburg, 61–65, 67
  afternoon May 22 assaults, 270–275, 283, 296–299, 305–306, 308–310, 313–314, 319, 323, 326, 330–331, 341
  early Vicksburg operations, 36, 38–41
  interim between assaults, 134, 145–146, 150
  May 19 assaults, 78, 82–83, 85–86, 91–92, 95, 104, 119–120, 127
  morning May 22 assaults, 154, 159, 162, 173, 175, 180–183, 186, 192, 203–205, 221, 223–224, 226, 234, 236, 240
  results of assaults, 345, 348, 353–355, 365, 378
McRae, Lucy, 359
McRory, Robert, 169
Memphis, Tennessee, 3, 8, 13, 16, 28, 66, 188, 259, 266
Meridian, Mississippi, 5, 46
Messenger, Nicholas C., 264
Methodists, xiii

Mexican War, 92, 102, 115, 196, 240, 259, 276
Mexico, 18
Michigan Troops
  7th Artillery, 254, 374
  8th Artillery, 197, 379
Middle Road, 42
Miller, Dora, 360, 365
Miller, J. S., 335
Miller, Nicholas, 135, 352
Milliken's Bend, Louisiana, 30, 34
Minnesota, xvii, 183, 292, 313
Minnesota Troops
  1st Artillery, 380
  4th Infantry, 192, 310, 313, 380
  5th Infantry, 289–290, 292, 294, 378
Mint Spring Bayou, 21–22, 69, 79–81, 86, 95–98, 100, 104, 108, 110, 112, 126, 153–154, 176–177, 218, 230–231, 274–275, 278
Mississippi, ix–xi, xiii–xiv, xvi, xviii, 3–4, 6, 8, 10–13, 15–16, 26, 28, 35, 40, 44–45, 52, 55, 57, 68–69, 72–77, 79–80, 83, 86, 97, 99, 104–105, 108, 113, 118–120, 126, 128, 130, 147, 163, 166, 169, 171, 173, 175, 195, 228, 231, 235, 255, 278, 281, 286–287, 291, 295, 300, 302, 311, 319, 338, 344, 348, 356, 358, 367, 369–371
  Secession Convention, xiv, 186
Mississippi Central Railroad, 28–29, 235
Mississippi River, ix–xi, xiii–xiv, xvi–xviii, 1–5, 8, 11, 19, 21, 24, 28, 30, 32, 34, 38–39, 44–45, 51, 54, 56, 61, 69, 78–79, 96, 104, 130, 136, 143–144, 152, 154, 176, 181–182, 185, 218, 230, 235, 330–332, 346, 369
Mississippi Troops
  1st Artillery Battery A, 185, 248
  1st Artillery Battery C, 160
  1st Artillery Battery G, 312
  1st Artillery Battery L, 239
  4th Infantry, 278, 385
  7th Infantry Battalion, 83, 99, 184, 285, 300, 384
  14th Battery, 385
  35th Infantry, 54, 185–186, 385
  36th Infantry, 55, 83, 99, 101, 104, 112, 116–117, 120, 125, 159–161, 163, 166–168, 172, 174, 184, 283, 384

Mississippi Troops (*continued*)
  37th Infantry, 99, 118, 184, 285, 300, 384
  38th Infantry, 55, 93, 99, 161, 184, 285–287, 300, 384
  40th Infantry, 185–186, 385
  43rd Infantry, 99, 184, 384
  46th Infantry, 56, 73–74, 278, 282, 385
  Cavalry Partisan Rangers, 385
  Hudson's Battery, 383
  Pettus Flying Artillery, 239
  State Troops, 15, 47, 70, 100, 278, 385
    3rd Infantry Battalion, 385
    5th Infantry, 385
    Vicksburg City Guards, 386
  Vaiden Battery, 386
Mississippi Valley, x, 8, 26, 36, 106, 235, 366, 369
Missouri, 6, 48, 53, 82, 102, 109, 114, 120, 124, 128, 130–131, 145, 147, 159–160, 166–169, 173, 175, 177, 183, 189, 196, 228, 265, 274, 280–282, 285–286, 315, 357
Missouri River, xvi
Missouri Troops (CS)
  1st Cavalry (dismounted), 312, 386
  1st Infantry, 100, 109, 114, 160, 386
  2nd Infantry, 100, 114, 160, 386
  3rd Artillery, 386
  3rd Cavalry (dismounted), 312, 386
  3rd Infantry, 100, 119, 159–160, 175, 292, 386
  5th Infantry, 57, 100, 119–120, 159, 386
  6th Infantry, 100, 114, 160, 386
  Guibor's Battery, 386
  Landis's Battery, 386
  Lowe's Battery, 386
  Wade's Battery, 386
Missouri Troops (US)
  1st Artillery Battery A, 375
  1st Artillery Battery C, 380
  1st Artillery Battery M, 381
  2nd Artillery Battery F, 96, 377
  3rd Infantry, 136, 154, 168, 276, 281, 376
  4th Cavalry, 380
  6th Cavalry, 374
  6th Infantry, 111–112, 122, 377
  7th Infantry, 197–203, 344, 379

8th Infantry, 78, 111–112, 114, 158, 162, 175, 286, 377
10th Cavalry, 378
10th Infantry, 381
11th Infantry, 289–292, 294, 378
12th Infantry, 136, 177, 251, 276, 280, 376
17th Infantry, 276, 376
24th Infantry, 381
26th Infantry, 144, 190, 315, 381
27th Infantry, 278, 376
29th Infantry, 278, 376
30th Infantry, 79, 278, 376
31st Infantry, 278, 376
32nd Infantry, 278, 376
Moats, Virgil H., 266
Mobile and Ohio Railroad, 28
Molineaux, Gould, 148, 346
Moltke, Helmuth von, 87
Moore, Frederick, W., 246
Moore, John C., 55, 70, 83, 91, 137, 160, 184–186, 228, 237–238, 247, 265, 268, 297–298, 312, 324–325, 345, 348, 366, 385
Moore, Thomas O., 11
Morris, Burt, 203
Mott, Samuel R., 174
Mound City, USS, 333
Mount Alban, Mississippi, 67
Mower, Joseph A., 82, 220, 289–290, 292–295, 299, 307, 378
Mudd, John J., 84
Mueller, Alexander, 380
Murphey, John M., 333

Nashville, Tennessee, 6
Natchez, Mississippi, xiii, xvi, 15
Nevins, Garrett, 303
New Mexico Territory, 102
New Orleans, Louisiana, xiv, xvi–xvii, 2, 8–14, 98, 200
  Battle of, xvii, 8
  French Quarter, 8
Newsome, Edmund, 92
Newton, James K., 304, 347
Newton Station, Mississippi, 44
New York, 276
Nutting, Oscar F., 254, 258

INDEX 479

Obion River, 28
O'Dea, John, 158, 161, 166, 170
Oden, Henry, 337
Ohio, 28, 44, 63, 67, 78, 89, 106, 108–110, 117, 127, 138, 140, 144, 151, 168, 172–173, 177, 183, 236, 341, 249, 254, 257, 266, 290, 326, 328, 337, 341, 358
Ohio River, xvi–xvii
Ohio Troops
  2nd Artillery, 254, 375
  3rd Artillery, 379
  4th Artillery, 377
  4th Cavalry Company, 378
  5th Artillery, 139
  8th Artillery, 377
  10th Artillery, 380
  11th Artillery, 381
  16th Artillery, 254, 375
  16th Infantry, 253, 374
  17th Artillery, 375
  20th Infantry, 140, 149, 183, 306–308, 350, 379
  30th Infantry, 66, 96, 106, 108, 110, 162, 168–169, 171–172, 290, 377
  32nd Infantry, 197–198, 203, 379
  37th Infantry, 106, 108, 110, 162, 169–172, 377
  42nd Infantry, 149, 252, 254, 374
  47th Infantry, 106, 108, 110, 138, 171–172, 377
  48th Infantry, 259, 266–267, 340, 344, 375
  54th Infantry, 115–117, 121, 274, 284, 377
  57th Infantry, 116, 121, 174, 275, 377
  68th Infantry, 183, 379
  72nd Infantry, 289, 378
  76th Infantry, 96, 136, 276, 280, 376
  78th Infantry, 183, 379
  80th Infantry, 381
  83rd Infantry, 137, 140, 240, 245–246, 374
  95th Infantry, 289, 378
  96th Infantry, 374
  114th Infantry, 252, 255–256, 329, 374
  120th Infantry, 85, 89–90, 137, 151, 251, 253, 257, 342, 374
Old Abe, 289, 292–293
Oldroyd, Osborn, 140, 149
O'Neal, George O., 162, 167–168, 367

Open Woods, xiii
Osterhaus, Peter J., 59, 63–64, 78, 85, 89–91, 145, 149–150, 210–211, 236, 251–254, 256–258, 315, 322, 326, 328–330, 335, 373
Overland Campaign, 26
Oxford, Mississippi, 28

Pardee, Don, 66
Parker, Job, 259, 266
Parker, Joseph F., 267
Parker's Crossroads, Battle of, 28
Parry, Augustus C., 106, 108–110, 171, 173
Patterson, William F., 63
Pea Ridge, Battle of, 185, 236, 251, 288
Pearson, James M., 239, 260–261, 264–266, 337
Peats, Frank F., 198
Pemberton, John C., x
  defense between assaults, 130–133, 136, 140–141, 144–145
  defense of afternoon May 22 assaults, 323–325, 332, 340
  defense of morning May 22 assaults, 185, 227, 268
  early defense of Vicksburg, 19, 26, 35, 39–49
  repelling May 19 assaults, 96, 98, 128
  results of assaults, 356–357, 359, 366, 368–370, 383
  withdrawal into Vicksburg, 51–55, 57–58, 64, 68–75
Perry, Oran, 256
Pettus, Edmund W., 238, 264, 337–339, 341, 355, 366
Pettus, John J., xvii, 11, 41, 47, 338
Pickett, George E., x–xi
Pittsburg Landing, Tennessee, 6
Pitzman, Julius, 80
Porter, David D., 1, 9, 33–34, 38, 65–66, 79, 86, 141, 146, 330, 332–334, 346
Porter, Robert, 200
Porter, William C., 167–168, 291
Port Gibson, Mississippi, ix, xi, 35–36, 38
  Battle of, xi, 36, 71, 190, 193, 236, 251, 263
Port Hudson, Louisiana, 12, 38, 45, 47
Power, James L., 48, 52

Prentiss, Benjamin M., 251
Prentiss Family, xiv
Prime, Frederick, 77
Prussia, 87, 251
Pryce, Samuel D., 149
Purcell, William, 332
Putnam, Holden, 190–191, 314–318

Quinby, Isaac F., 62–63, 67, 82–83, 91, 182–183, 189, 192, 203, 226, 273, 299, 308–311, 313–314, 323–324, 326, 328, 334–335, 341, 345, 348, 380

Railroad Redoubt, 24, 150, 208, 209, 212, 232, 238–240, 244, 252, 255, 258, 261, 264, 266, 298, 310, 315, 320–321, 323–324, 330, 334, 338, 344, 356, 366
Ransom, Thomas E. G., 62–63, 67, 82, 92–95, 99–100, 104, 119, 173–174, 182–184, 188–189, 192, 195, 223, 274–275, 283, 285–286, 299–300, 302–305, 330, 344, 380
Rawlins, John, 352–353
Raymond, Mississippi, 89, 182, 253
  Battle of, 40, 47, 181, 196
Raymond Road, 42
Reagan, John H., xi, 370
Red River, xvi, 1, 31
Reed, J. R., 163
Reese, John P., 201, 203–204
Reid, Hugh T., 82, 331
Reynolds, Alexander W., 71, 331, 384
Reynolds, Henry J., 117–118, 126
Rice, Americus V., 116, 122, 174
Richmond, Virginia, ix–xi, 12, 369–371
Riddle House, Green, 99
Riley, Amos C., 109
Robb Brothers, 356
Roberts, John, 123
Rockwood, Virginia, 365
Roe, Edward R., 244
Rolling Fork, 33
Roots, Logan H., 200
Rosecrans, William S., ix

Salient Work, 24
Sampson, Ezekiel S., 190, 316–317

Sanborn, John B., 63, 82–83, 183, 190–192, 226, 299, 309–319, 325–326, 328, 367, 380
Sands, Frank C., 381
Schweitzer, Edward, 106, 162
Scott, Winfield, 5
Screwtape Letters, The, ix
Seaman, Henry, 147, 177, 282, 351
Searles, Caroline, 358, 364
Sears, Claudius W., 56
Sebastian, Louis, 170
Seddon, James A., x
Sewell, Thomas, 122
Shalfer, A. K., 36
  Shaifer House, 36
Sharkey Family, xiv
Shelley, Charles M., 260, 337
Sherman, Ellen, 131, 295
Sherman, William T.
  advance on Vicksburg, 51–52, 54, 59, 61–67, 73
  afternoon May 22 assaults, 270–276, 278–279, 281, 283, 285–296, 298–300, 305, 309, 319, 323, 326, 330, 341
  early Vicksburg operations, 30–31, 34, 38–39, 41, 43–44, 46
  interim between assaults, 131–132, 134–136, 140–141, 143, 145–147, 150
  May 19 assaults, 78–82, 86–87, 92, 94–97, 102–106, 111, 113, 120–122, 126–128
  morning May 22 assaults, 152–160, 152–163, 165–167, 169, 175–176, 179–182, 186, 197–198, 204–205, 214–215, 217–220, 234–235, 240, 259
  results of assaults, 345, 347–349, 351, 353–355, 367, 376
Shiloh, Battle of, xviii, 6, 9–13, 16, 26, 51, 92, 111, 115–116, 153, 180–181, 185, 190, 193, 234–236, 240, 259, 276, 288–289, 303, 306–307, 331–332
Shiloh Church, 116, 259, 289
Shirley, Alice, 365
Shirley House, 78, 82, 183, 300–308, 365
Shoup, Francis A., 55–57, 69, 73, 76, 80–81, 97–100, 104, 109–114, 119, 133, 137, 154, 160, 177, 179, 230, 278, 281, 292, 385
Shunk, David, 241, 244

Silver Wave, xviii
Sitton, William, 244–245
Slack, James R., 253
Smedes Family, xiv
Smith, Andrew J., 63, 85, 89, 91, 133–134, 212–213, 236, 240–241, 248–250, 252, 258–259, 261, 268, 310, 321–322, 325, 374
Smith, Ashbel, 83, 137, 185, 237–239, 244–245, 247–248, 311–312, 317–318, 344
Smith, Charles, 137
Smith, Francis M., 201–203
Smith, George, 204
Smith, Giles A., 81, 103–104, 110–115, 117, 122–123, 134, 155–156, 173–175, 189, 216, 274–275, 284–287, 295, 299–300, 304, 377
Smith, I. V., 175
Smith, John E., 63, 82, 183, 193–199, 204, 225, 298, 305–308, 349, 379
Smith, Martin L., 12, 14, 17, 46, 53–57, 69–70, 72–73, 80, 83, 97–98, 111, 113–114, 125, 131, 136, 159–160, 170, 185–186, 229, 231, 268, 278, 281–282, 297, 325, 348, 356, 385
Smith, Morgan L., 111
Smith, Thomas Kilby, 81, 103–104, 114–126, 143, 154–158, 172–175, 189, 274, 284–286, 294, 347, 377
Snyder's Bluff, Mississippi, 10, 17–18, 32, 46, 51, 55–56, 65, 139, 141
Southern Railroad of Mississippi, 5, 12, 21, 39, 44, 150, 183, 237, 240, 258
South Fort, 24, 70, 238, 331
South Mountain, Battle of, 106
Spearman, James D., 178
Spiceley, William T., 253, 258, 322, 375
Spiegel, Marcus, 85, 89–90, 137, 151, 251, 253, 257, 342
Spooner, Benjamin J., 115–117, 120–123, 125, 357
Spoor, Nelson T., 163, 378
Spotsylvania, Battle of, 153, 266
  Mule Shoe, 266
Springfield, Illinois, 245
Square Fort, 24, 71, 89–90, 210, 232, 238–239, 251–252, 255–256, 258, 328, 331

Stanfield, Edward P., 311
Stanton, Edwin M., 235, 353–354
Steele, Frederick, 62, 78–81, 95–96, 104, 135, 141, 147–148, 154–155, 159, 175–177, 179, 186, 218, 270, 273–276, 278, 281–283, 288–290, 294–295, 299, 333, 376
Steele's Bayou Expedition, 32–33
Stevenson, Carter L., 46, 52–54, 56–57, 69–72, 86, 131, 232, 237–239, 251, 254, 257, 263, 265, 298, 324–325, 331, 338–341, 348, 366, 383
Stevenson, John D., 64, 82, 91, 134, 183, 196–204, 225, 298, 305–306, 315, 379
Stewart, J. A., 248
Stewart, Tom, 304
St. John, James H., 143
St. Louis, Missouri, xvi, 251
Stockade Redan, 22, 24, 55–56, 70–71, 73, 130, 132, 135–136, 147, 150, 344, 356, 368
  afternoon May 22 assaults, 270–271, 273, 278, 283–284, 286–288, 290–291, 296–298, 300, 303
  May 19 assaults, 82, 96–102, 104–105, 107, 111, 113–114
  morning May 22 assaults, 153–156, 159–162, 165–167, 169, 173, 175–176, 184, 186, 189, 196, 214–217, 227–228, 230, 233
Stockton, Joseph, 92, 149, 188, 300–302
Stoddard, Albert, 318
Stolbrand, Charles J., 91, 379
Stone, William M., 149–150, 259, 261–264
Stones River, Battle of, 30
Stout's Bayou, 23–24, 331
Sturgess, Robert H., 200
Sunflower River, 33
Sullivan, David A., 387
Sullivan, Peter J., 259, 266
Switzerland, 193

Tallahatchie River, 32
Talston, J. H., 367
Tangiapahoa, Louisiana, 12
Tatum, James S., 283
Taylor, Ezra, 163
Taylor, James B., 89

Taylor, John C., 57, 132
Temple Baptist Church, 368
Tennessee, ix–x, xvi–xvii, 3, 6, 10, 12, 25, 27–28, 130, 248, 278
Tennessee River, xvi, 6, 10–11, 28
Tennessee Troops
　1st Cavalry, 384
　1st Heavy Artillery, 386
　3rd Infantry, 384
　39th Infantry, 384
　43rd Infantry, 384
　59th Infantry, 384
　Caruthers' Battery, 386
　Johnston's Battery, 386
　Lynch's Battery, 386
　Tobin's Battery, 238, 385
Tensas Bayou, 31
Ternier, Pierre N., 114
Texas, xi, 49, 83, 85, 91, 130, 136–137, 185, 244–245, 247–248, 317, 328, 337–340, 355, 358, 361, 366
Texas Troops
　2nd Infantry, 83, 137, 185, 237–239, 245, 311, 317–318, 385
　Wall's Artillery, 100
　Waul's Legion, 71, 129, 131–132, 186, 239, 265, 338, 341, 384
Thayer, John M., 79–80, 96, 104, 106, 136, 154, 176–177, 179, 219, 275–276, 278–281, 287, 295, 376
Thomas, Allen, 281
Thomas, James, 352
Thornhill, Eli, 287
Tiffentown, Mississippi, 65
Tilghman, Lloyd, 45
Tishomingo County, Mississippi, 8
Tobin, Thomas F., 238, 385
Tombigbee River, 77
Tourtellotte, John E., 192, 310, 312
Trans-Mississippi, xi, 13, 16, 45, 276, 298, 312, 366
Tresilian, Stewart R., 62–63, 193, 198
Trimble, Harvey M., 190, 192, 317
Trogden, Howell, 158, 162, 167
Tunnard, William, 138
Tupper, Nathan W., 112

Tuscumbia, USS, 333
Tuttle, James M., 62, 78, 82, 95, 105, 121, 136, 155, 159, 175–176, 186, 220, 273, 288–290, 292–293, 295, 378
Twist, Russell P., 254

Ulm, Battle of, 26
United States, xiv, xvi–xviii, 1, 3, 8, 26, 78, 92, 103, 106, 111, 121, 123, 180, 215, 219, 224, 228, 320, 332, 367
　Congress, 77, 102–103, 180, 193, 234, 256, 276, 367
　Department of the Tennessee, 27
　House Committee on Military Affairs, 103
　Military Academy, 16, 53–54, 106, 121, 180, 182, 236, 269, 276
　Naval Academy, 121
　Navy, 1–2, 4, 8–10, 15–16, 32–35, 51, 66, 79, 141, 332–334, 361, 364
　War Department, 27, 102, 121, 182, 236, 276, 323, 331, 353, 403n39
United States Troops
　1st Engineers Battalion Regiment of the West, 373
　1st Infantry Siege Guns, 320
　13th Infantry, 78, 80, 103–104, 112–114, 122, 125–126, 173, 377
Upton, Emory, 153

Valley Campaign, 197
Valley Road, 19, 21–22, 69, 71, 79, 96
Van Anda, Salue G., 263, 266, 335
Vance, John L., 172
Vanderbilt, James C., 350
Van Dorn, Earl, 13, 16, 28
Vaughn, J. C., 55, 70, 114, 119, 278
Vick, Elizabeth, xiii–xiv
Vick, Newet, xiii–xiv
Vicksburg, Mississippi, ix–xiv, xvi–xviii
　afternoon May 22 assaults, 270, 280, 288–289, 294–196, 303, 306, 308, 323, 330–332, 334, 341–343
　early Vicksburg operations, 1–6, 8–19, 21–28, 30–36, 38–49
　interim between assaults, 127–131, 133, 136, 138–139, 141, 145–147, 149

May 19 assaults, 76–82, 84–87, 89, 92, 96–99, 102–103, 105–106, 111, 113, 120–121, 124
  morning May 22 assaults, 151–153, 155–159, 181, 183–184, 194, 196–197, 201, 206, 215, 219, 222, 225, 227, 229, 232, 234–237, 251–253, 259, 264
  results of assaults, 345–347, 349–353, 356–371
  Union advance on Vicksburg, 50–59, 63–75
Vicksburg *Evening Citizen*, xvii
Vicksburg National Military Park, xi–xii, 232
Virginia, ix–x, xiv, 106, 108, 196–197, 370
Virginia Troops, Botetourt Artillery, 384

Wald, Merrick J., 335
Wallace, Lew, 193
Walnut Hills, 10, 17
Wangelin, Hugo, 281
Ward, Cornelius S., 202
Warmoth, Henry C., 320
Warren County, Mississippi, xiv
  County Courthouse, 364
Warrenton, Mississippi, 18, 35, 39, 46–47, 54–55, 143, 182, 272, 323, 331
Warrenton Road, 21, 24, 146, 325, 331, 348
Washington, DC, 2, 27, 38, 102, 235, 353, 369
Washington, Edward C., 103, 111–112, 131
Washington, George, 111
Washita River, 31
Waterloo, Battle of, 193
Watts, John, 293
Waul, Thomas N., 71, 129, 131–132, 186, 239, 265, 338–341, 384
Weber, Andrew J., 291–292
Welles, Gideon, 1, 16
West Tennessee, 6, 12, 27–28
West Virginia, 106
West Virginia Troops, 4th Infantry, 68, 106, 108, 110, 171–173, 367, 377
White, Patrick H., 250
White, Thomas B., 351
White River, 1
Wiggs, James C., 73
Wilcox, Charles, 241, 243
Williams, Isaac, 66

Williams, Thomas, 15
Williamson, James A., 282
Williamson, Mrs., 361
Wilson, Bluford, 261
Wilson, James H., 64, 239, 353
Wilson's Creek, Battle of, 1, 185, 236, 251
Winschel, Terry, 356
Wintter, David, 72
Wisconsin, xvii, 93, 183, 245, 262, 291–293, 302, 304, 311–312, 318
Wisconsin Troops
  1st Battery, 254, 258, 374
  6th Battery, 92, 381
  8th Infantry, 289, 292–294, 378
  11th Infantry, 150, 259, 261, 266, 376
  12th Battery, 196, 381
  14th Infantry, 92, 94, 189, 300, 302–305, 347, 380
  17th Infantry, 92–94, 189, 300, 303–304, 380
  18th Infantry, 191, 310, 380
  23rd Infantry, 240, 245–247, 249–250, 328, 357, 374
  29th Infantry, 253, 375
Witherspoon, William W., 99, 117, 132–133
Wood, Edward, 63, 65, 312
Wood, Peter, 59
Woods, Charles R., 79–80, 95–96, 136, 154, 177–179, 275–276, 278–282, 295, 376
Woods, Michael, 238
Woolsey, Edwin, 201
World War II, 5
  Pacific Theater, 5
Wright, Joseph C., 188
Wrigley, J., 340

Yalobusha River, 28, 32
Yates, Alexander, 283
Yates, Richard, 354
Yazoo Pass Expedition, 32
Yazoo River, 1, 3, 10, 17–18, 21, 30, 32–34, 51, 54–56, 64–66, 71, 79, 132, 139, 141, 143, 331
Yerger Family, xiv
York, Amos, 241
Young's Point, Louisiana, 79, 331
Youst, Mr., 98